Dear Students and Families,

Welcome to *Into Algebra 2*! In this program, you will develop skills and make sense of mathematics by solving real-world problems, using tools and strategies, and collaborating with your classmates.

Every lesson includes Spark Your Learning, Build Understanding, and Step It Out tasks. A Spark Your Learning task provides an opportunity to make sense of the mathematics using concepts and procedures you know to try and solve it. The Build Understanding tasks guided by your teacher focus on understanding new concepts, and Step It Out tasks guided by your teacher focus on building efficient procedures and applying those procedures.

With the support of your teacher and by engaging with meaningful practice, you will learn to persevere when solving problems. *Into Algebra 2* will not only help you deepen your understanding of mathematics, but also build your confidence as a learner of mathematics.

We want you to be successful in learning math because it opens up a world of possibilities to you. By engaging and persevering in the learning tasks in *Into Algebra 2*, you will be well on the path to becoming college, career, and civic ready in mathematics. Enjoy your time with *Into Algebra 2*!

Sincerely,
The Authors

Authors

Edward B. Burger, PhD
President, Southwestern University
Georgetown, Texas

Robert Kaplinsky, MEd
Mathematics Educator
Long Beach, California

Juli K. Dixon, PhD
Professor, Mathematics Education
University of Central Florida
Orlando, Florida

Matthew R. Larson, PhD
Past-President, National Council
of Teachers of Mathematics
Lincoln Public Schools
Lincoln, Nebraska

Timothy D. Kanold, PhD
Mathematics Educator
Chicago, Illinois

Steven J. Leinwand
Principal Research Analyst
American Institutes for Research
Washington, DC

Consultants

English Language Development Consultant

Harold Asturias
Director, Center for Mathematics
Excellence and Equity
Lawrence Hall of Science, University of California
Berkeley, California

Program Consultant

David Dockterman, EdD
Lecturer, Harvard Graduate School of Education
Cambridge, Massachusetts

Blended Learning Consultant

Weston Kiercshneck
Senior Fellow
International Center for Leadership in Education
Littleton, Colorado

Open Middle™ Consultant

Nanette Johnson, MEd
Secondary Mathematics Educator
Downey, California

STEM Consultants

Michael A. DiSpezio
Global Educator
North Falmouth, Massachusetts

Marjorie Frank
Science Writer and
Content-Area Reading Specialist
Brooklyn, New York

Bernadine Okoro
Access and Equity and
STEM Learning Advocate and Consultant
Washington, DC

Cary I. Sneider, PhD
Associate Research Professor
Portland State University
Portland, Oregon

Unit 1

Functions and Equations

MODULE 1 Analyze Functions

(Top) ©SolStock/E+/Getty Images; (Bottom) ©Houghton Mifflin Harcourt

Build Conceptual Understanding   Connect Concepts and Skills   Apply and Practice

MODULE 2 Solve Quadratic Equations and Systems

©H.S. Photos/Alamy

Build Conceptual Understanding   Connect Concepts and Skills   Apply and Practice

MODULE 5 Polynomial Equations

Build Conceptual Understanding   Connect Concepts and Skills   Apply and Practice

Unit 4

Exponential and Logarithmic Functions and Equations

(Left) ©CNRI/Science Photo Library/Getty Images; (Right) ©Hero Images/Getty Images

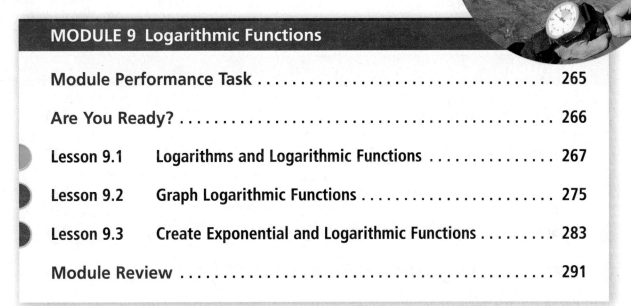

©Mauricio Graiki/Shutterstock

Build Conceptual Understanding   Connect Concepts and Skills   Apply and Practice

Rational Functions and Equations

MODULE 11 Rational Functions

MODULE 12 Rational Expressions and Equations

MODULE 13 Explicit Formulas for Sequences and Series

MODULE 14 Recursive Formulas for Sequences

Build Conceptual Understanding   Connect Concepts and Skills   Apply and Practice

Unit 7

Trigonometric Functions and Identities

MODULE 15 Unit-Circle Definition of Trigonometric Functions

MODULE 16 Graph Trigonometric Functions

Build Conceptual Understanding   Connect Concepts and Skills   Apply and Practice

Unit 8

Probability

(Top) ©Monkey Business Images/Shutterstock; (Bottom) ©Floortje/iStock/Getty Images

Unit 9 Statistics

MODULE 19 Data Distributions

MODULE 20 Make Inferences from Data

(Top) ©TokenPhoto/E+/Getty Images; (Bottom) ©Floortje/iStock/Getty Images

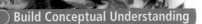

Build Conceptual Understanding   Connect Concepts and Skills   Apply and Practice

STUDENT RESOURCES

(Top) ©Warren Metcalf/Shutterstock; (Bottom) ©simonkr/iStock/Getty Images

Functions and Equations

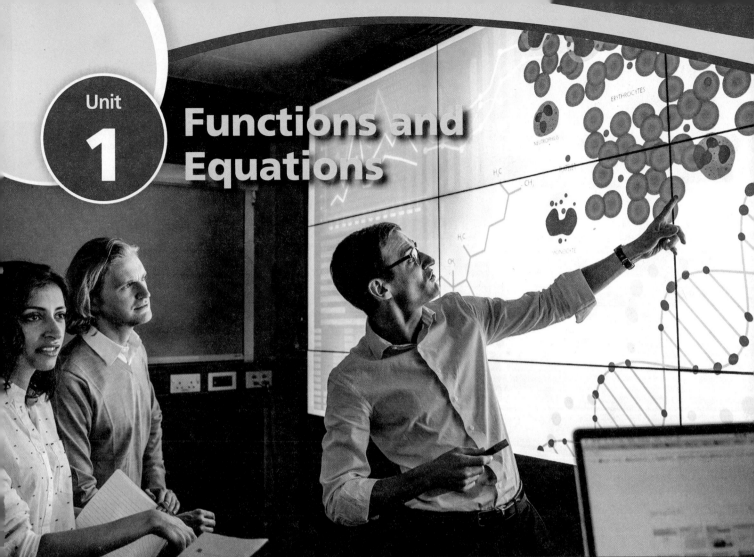

Medical Anthropologist

Medical anthropologists study the past and present health of the human species to promote future well-being. This requires the collection of vast amounts of data to be analyzed and described using functions, equations, and graphs. They correlate their analyses with social and cultural conditions to interpret and explain trends in different contexts.

STEM Task

Medical anthropologists use historical events to explain observed trends in context.

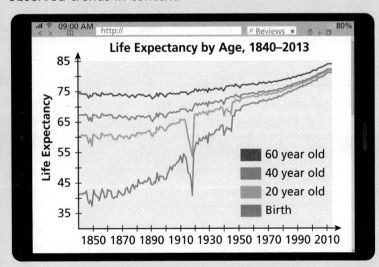

Life Expectancy by Age, 1840–2013

- 60 year old
- 40 year old
- 20 year old
- Birth

Use the graph and conduct research to explain how the life expectancy of each age group has changed over time.

Learning Mindset
Strategic Help-Seeking Identifies Sources of Help

Whenever you approach a new topic, it is important to recognize what you understand. It is just as important to know where you can get help on the things you don't understand or would like to understand better. Keeping track of the sources you have used to get to your current level of understanding can be useful when seeking sources of help. Here are some questions you can ask yourself to identify sources of help:

- What sources are available in my school or in my community that can help my understanding of the current task?

- Who is available to support me in my learning of this task? How can I reach out to them?

- How do I keep track of my sources? What methods of organizing the information I gather best helps me accomplish my goals?

- How do I use the sources I currently know about to help guide me to new resources?

- How can I be a source of help to someone in my learning community?

Reflect

Q What are the most common resources you use in your learning? Why are these resources helpful?

Q What are the most common resources a medical anthropologist would use? Are any of these resources the same as the most common resources you use in your learning?

1 Analyze Functions

Module Performance Task: Focus on STEM

Light Curves of Two Variable Star Systems

Variable stars are stars whose brightness appears to change periodically. The light curves of two variable stars, R Canis Majoris and Delta Cephei, are described by the measurements below.

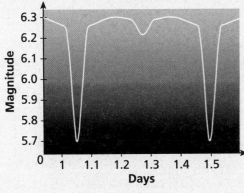

R Canis Majoris

Delta Cephei

Day	Magnitude	Day	Magnitude
0	3.48	6	3.65
1	3.76	7	3.92
2	4.01	8	4.14
3	4.22	9	4.35
4	4.37	10	4.07
5	3.71	11	3.48

A. Identify and compare coordinates of local maxima and local minima.

B. Identify and compare intervals of increasing, decreasing, and constant value.

C. Research the two stars. What information can you gather to help determine the reasons for their variability?

D. Conclude if the stars are variable for the same or different reasons. Explain how the data justifies your conclusion.

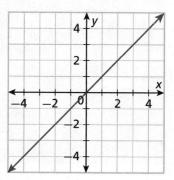

Are You Ready?

Complete these problems to review prior concepts and skills you will need for this module.

Graph Linear Equations in Slope-Intercept Form

Identify the slope, *m*, and *y*-intercept, *b*, of each equation. Then graph the line described by the equation.

1. $y = 2x + 1$

2. $y = x - 4$

3. $y = \frac{1}{4}x$

4. $y = -3x + 5$

Transform Linear Functions

The graph of the parent linear function $f(x) = x$ is shown on the coordinate grid.

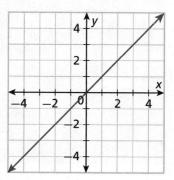

5. Describe the transformation used to map the graph of $f(x) = x$ onto the graph of $g(x) = 4x$.

6. Write the function that produces a graph of $f(x)$ translated 7 units down.

Graph Quadratic Functions in Standard Form

Graph each quadratic function.

7. $y = x^2 + 2x - 8$

8. $y = x^2 + 7x + 10$

9. $y = 2x^2 - 6x - 8$

10. $y = -x^2 + 4$

Connecting Past and Present Learning

Previously, you learned:

- to graph linear equations in slope-intercept form, $y = mx + b$,
- to identify and use transformations of linear functions, and
- to graph quadratic functions in standard form by rewriting in vertex form.

In this module, you will learn:

- to identify key characteristics of functions and graphs,
- to identify and apply transformations of functions, and
- to compare functions across different representations such as tables, graphs, equations, and verbal descriptions.

Domain, Range, and End Behavior

(I Can) relate the domain, range, and end behavior of a function to its graph.

Spark Your Learning

Pat and Sam are conducting an experiment involving a vertical spring with a weight attached to its end.

The weight is raised to a point above its resting point and then released.

A video camera recorded the experiment so the movement of the weight could be observed (and measured).

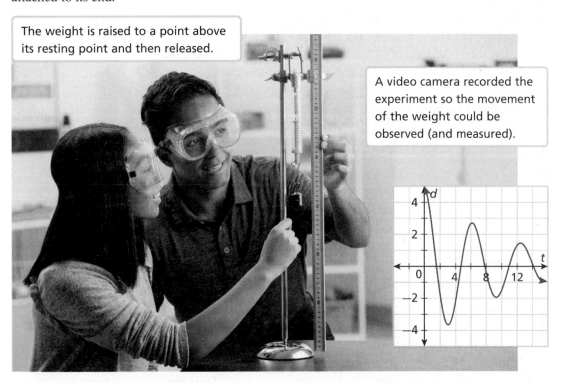

Complete Part A as a whole class. Then complete Parts B–D in small groups.

A. What is a mathematical question you can ask about this situation? What information would you need to know to answer your question?

B. Describe any patterns or trends in the graph. What would the graph look like if the domain is extended? Explain your reasoning.

C. To answer your question, what strategy and tool would you use along with all the information you have? What answer do you get?

D. Does your answer make sense in the context of the situation? How can you check your answer?

 Turn and Talk Predict how your answer would change for each of the following changes in the situation:
- The weight is raised to a higher point before being released.
- The weight is pulled down to a point below its resting point before being released.

Build Understanding

Represent an Interval on a Number line

In past courses, you graphed inequalities such as $x > 1$ by drawing a ray on the number line. Note that this describes an interval. A finite interval has two endpoints, which may or may not be included in the interval. An infinite interval is unbounded on at least one end.

> **Connect to Vocabulary**
>
> An **interval** is an unbroken portion of a number line.

You can represent an interval using an inequality, set notation, or interval notation. In set notation, $\{x \mid x > 1\}$ reads as "the set of all real numbers x such that x is greater than 1." Unless otherwise indicated, it is assumed that x is a real number. To specify a domain of all real numbers in set notation, write $\{x \mid x \in \mathbb{R}\}$. The symbol $\in$ means "is an element of" and the symbol $\mathbb{R}$ denotes the set of all real numbers. Interval notation encloses endpoints in parentheses or brackets. A parenthesis indicates that an endpoint is not included in the interval, and a bracket indicates that an endpoint is included. For infinite intervals, use the infinity symbols $+\infty$ and $-\infty$:

- An interval of the form $(a, +\infty)$ or $[a, +\infty)$ is unbounded in a positive direction.

- An interval of the form $(-\infty, a)$ or $(-\infty, a]$ is unbounded in a negative direction.

So, $x > 1$ written in interval notation is $(1, +\infty)$.

Type of Interval	Inequality	Graph	Set Notation	Interval Notation
Finite	$a < x \leq b$	a b	$\{x \mid a < x \leq b\}$	$(a, b]$
Infinite	$x < a$	a	$\{x \mid x < a\}$	$(-\infty, a)$
Infinite	$x \geq a$	a	$\{x \mid x \geq a\}$	$[a, +\infty)$

1   **A.** How can you verbally describe the finite interval shown first in the table above? How can you verbally describe the two infinite intervals shown?

B. An interval is modeled by the graph at the right. Use set notation and interval notation to write the interval represented.

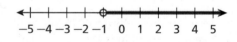

$-5\ -4\ -3\ -2\ -1\ \ 0\ \ 1\ \ 2\ \ 3\ \ 4\ \ 5$

Suppose the graph is changed so that the open circle at $x = -1$ becomes a solid circle. How do the set and interval notations change for the new interval?

C. How can you describe the set of all real numbers *not* shown in the graph in B? What would its graph look like? What are the set and interval notations for this set?

 Turn and Talk Suppose that you could "add" and "subtract" two sets of real numbers by combining the numbers in the sets ($+$), or removing numbers from a set ($-$). How would you express the result of "$(-\infty, -3) + [-3, 8]$" in interval notation? the result of the operation "$(-8, +\infty) - [4, +\infty)$"?

Determine Domain, Range, and End Behavior for a Function from Its Graph

Recall that the **domain** of a function $f(x)$ is the set of all x-values for which the function is defined (unless additional restrictions are added). The **range** is the set of all values $f(x)$ that are output for the input domain values. So, describing the domain and range of a function describes all possible input and output values.

The **end behavior** of a function describes what happens to the values of $f(x)$ as the x-values increase without bound ($x \to +\infty$), or as they decrease without bound ($x \to -\infty$).

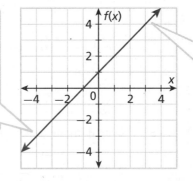

End Behavior

Words: As the value of x decreases without bound, the value of $f(x)$ decreases without bound.

Symbols:
As $x \to -\infty$, $f(x) \to -\infty$.

End Behavior

Words: As the value of x increases without bound, the value of $f(x)$ increases without bound.

Symbols:
As $x \to +\infty$, $f(x) \to +\infty$.

2   **A.** The graph of a quadratic function $f(x)$ is shown at the right. How can you verbally describe the domain of $f(x)$? How can you verbally describe the range of $f(x)$?

B. Suppose you could trace the curve of $f(x)$ left to right from its low point. Through what x- and y-values would you trace? How would this change if you could trace the curve right to left from the low point? What does this tell you about the end behavior of $f(x)$?

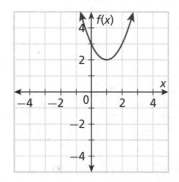

C. The graph of an exponential function $g(x)$ is shown at the right. How do the domain and range of $g(x)$ compare with the domain and range of $f(x)$?

D. Suppose you could trace the curve of $g(x)$ to the left and to the right from the y-axis. What would this tell you about the end behavior of $g(x)$? How does this compare with the end behavior of $f(x)$?

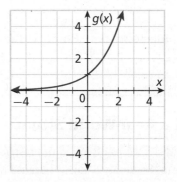

 Turn and Talk How do the possible end behaviors of linear, quadratic, and exponential functions compare? Use sketches to help you describe and compare the end behaviors.

Step It Out

Graph a Function Whose Domain is Restricted

The previous task dealt with functions with unrestricted domains. Sometimes, a function's domain values are restricted to a smaller set than all values for which the function is defined.

The graph of the function $f(x) = \frac{1}{2}x - 2$ is shown at the right for $x \geq 4$.

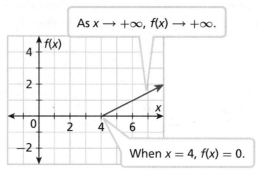

Restricting the domain to all real numbers greater than or equal to 4 changes the range from all real numbers to all nonnegative real numbers. While the end behavior as $x \to +\infty$ is not changed, the end behavior as $x \to -\infty$ can no longer be described.

3 ▶ Use the graph of the function with the given domain restriction to find the corresponding range.

A. $f(x) = x^2 - 2x + 2$ for $\{x \mid x \geq 0\}$

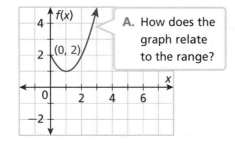

A. How does the graph relate to the range?

range: $\{f(x) \mid f(x) \geq 1\}$

B. $f(x) = 2^x$ for $\{x \mid x > 1\}$

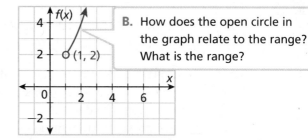

B. How does the open circle in the graph relate to the range? What is the range?

range: $\{f(x) \mid f(x) > 2\}$

 Turn and Talk How does the end behavior of the quadratic function given in Part A compare to that of the same function with no restrictions on its domain?

Model a Real-World Situation with a Function

Real-world situations often require restrictions on the domain of the functions that model them. Sometimes, this is because many real-world measurements, such as time or distance, must be nonnegative numbers. For example, the distance that a jogger travels at a constant speed of 6.5 miles per hour can be modeled by the linear function $f(x) = 6.5x$, where x is the time in hours the jogger runs. The domain in this context is then $\{x \mid x \geq 0\}$.

4 A home remodeling company is creating a kitchen "island" with a workspace countertop. The length of the countertop is to be 3 feet greater than the width. The width must be at least 20 inches to allow for sufficient workspace. Create and graph a model of the area given these restrictions. Is it possible for the countertop to have an area of 7 square feet? Explain why or why not.

Write a function to model the area.

Let l represent the length.
Let w represent the width.
The length is 3 feet greater than the width.
So, $l = w + 3$.
The area of a rectangle is given by lw. So, an equation for the area of the rectangle is $A(w) = $ ___?___

> **A.** What is the equation for the area in terms of the width only?

State the domain and range.

Domain: $\left\{ w \mid w > 1\frac{2}{3} \right\}$; Range: $\left\{ A(w) \mid A(w) > 7\frac{7}{9} \right\}$

Graph the function.

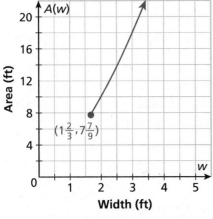

> **B.** How are these descriptions for the domain and range found?

> **C.** How do the domain and range affect the way you graph the function?

Find the possible areas.

The range of the function model is the real numbers greater than or equal to $7\frac{7}{9}$. So, the area of the countertop is at least $7\frac{7}{9}$ square feet, which means that it is not possible to create an island with a countertop of 7 square feet.

> **D.** How does the range of the function answer the question?

Turn and Talk The problem gave restrictions on both the width and length of the countertop. Do you think that there are other restrictions for this real-world scenario that were not described? Explain.

Check Understanding

1. 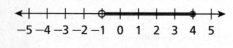 **Construct Arguments** Which two notations have identical graphs? What is different about the third graph?

    $(-\infty, 1)$ $\{x \mid x < 1\}$ $x > 1$

2. Write the solution of the inequality shown in the graph in set notation and interval notation.

    $-5\ -4\ -3\ -2\ -1\ \ 0\ \ 1\ \ 2\ \ 3\ \ 4\ \ 5$

For Problems 3 and 4, use set notation and interval notation to write the domain and range of the function shown in the graph. Describe the end behavior of the graph.

3.
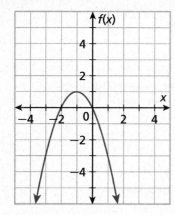

4.
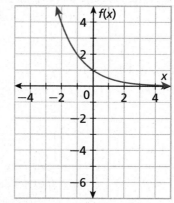

5. Graph $f(x) = x^2 + x + 4$ for $\{x \mid x \geq 0\}$. Define the corresponding range and describe the end behavior of the function.

6. An outfielder throws a baseball toward home plate. The height of the ball above the ground (in feet) until it hits the ground is modeled by the function $h(t) = -16t^2 + 30t + 5$ where t represents the time in seconds since the ball was thrown. Define and interpret the domain and range of the function.

On Your Own

7. **MP Use Structure** Write the set notation for the interval $[a, +\infty)$. How is the graph of this interval different from the graph of $[-a, +\infty)$? How are the graphs the same?

8. Write the inequality that describes all real numbers less than the square root of 2 in set notation and in interval notation.

For Problems 9–11, write the interval shown on the number line using set notation and using interval notation.

9. $-5\ -4\ -3\ -2\ -1\ \ 0\ \ 1\ \ 2\ \ 3\ \ 4\ \ 5$

10. $-5\ -4\ -3\ -2\ -1\ \ 0\ \ 1\ \ 2\ \ 3\ \ 4\ \ 5$

11. $-5\ -4\ -3\ -2\ -1\ \ 0\ \ 1\ \ 2\ \ 3\ \ 4\ \ 5$

Use Structure For Problems 12–14, match the description to the corresponding graph below.

A.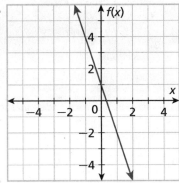

B.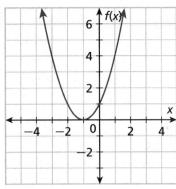

C.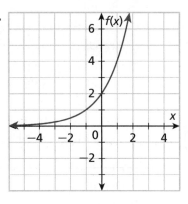

12. domain: $(-\infty, +\infty)$; range: $(0, +\infty)$
end behavior: As $x \to -\infty, f(x) \to 0$; as $x \to +\infty, f(x) \to +\infty$.

13. domain: $(-\infty, +\infty)$; range: $(-\infty, +\infty)$
end behavior: As $x \to -\infty, f(x) \to +\infty$; as $x \to +\infty, f(x) \to -\infty$.

14. domain: $(-\infty, +\infty)$; range: $[0, +\infty)$
end behavior: As $x \to -\infty, f(x) \to +\infty$; as $x \to +\infty, f(x) \to +\infty$.

15. Open Ended Graph a function with the following characteristics: domain $\{x \mid x > 0\}$, range: $\{y \mid y > 0\}$. Describe the end behavior of your function.

For Problems 16–19, write the domain and range of the function using set notation and interval notation. Then describe the end behavior of the function.

16.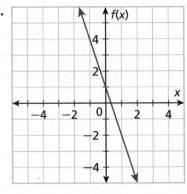

17.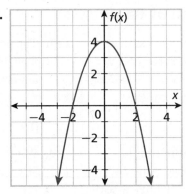

18.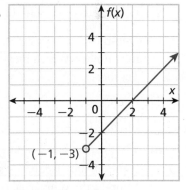

19.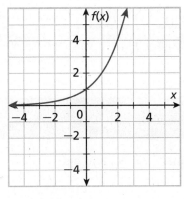

20. Kira's monthly gym bill is $50 plus $15 per class. She signs up for at least one class each month. Write a linear function to represent Kira's gym cost. What do the domain and range of the function represent?

GYM BILL

Monthly fee: $50
Fee per class: $15

Classes taken: 2

Total due: $80

21. Rachel drives at a constant speed of 70 miles per hour.

    A. Write a function model for Rachel's distance.

    B. Identify the domain and range.

    C. Graph the function and determine how far Rachel travels in 3 hours.

    D. Suppose Rachel travels 100 miles on the first day of a 2-day trip. On the second day, she drives at a constant speed of 70 miles per hour. How would the domain and range of the function representing Rachel's total distance on day 2 be affected? How would this change the graph?

22. The height of a triangle is 4 centimeters less than the base. Write a function that models the area of the triangle in terms of its base. Can the base of the triangle be 3 centimeters? Use the domain and range to explain why or why not.

23. Armando's vehicle averages 21 miles per gallon on the highway.

    A. Write a function that models the distance Armando can travel on g gallons of gasoline.

    B. Are any values excluded from the domain? Explain.

    C. Armando's vehicle has a 20-gallon gas tank. A low fuel light on the dash comes on when there is less than one-eighth tank of gas remaining. What is the greatest distance Armando can travel on the highway after the low fuel light comes on?

24. Regina claims that the end behavior of all linear functions is the same. Is Regina's claim correct? Why or why not?

$$\text{As } x \to -\infty, y \to -\infty, \text{ and as } x \to +\infty, y \to +\infty.$$

Spiral Review • Assessment Readiness

25. One-third a number is at least four less than the number. Which inequality represents the number?

    Ⓐ $n \le 6$ Ⓒ $n \le 3$

    Ⓑ $n \ge 6$ Ⓓ $n \ge 3$

26. A submarine is ascending upward from a depth of 6000 feet below sea level. After 150 seconds, the submarine is 4800 feet below sea level. What is the average rate of change that the submarine ascends during this interval?

    Ⓐ 0.8 ft/s   Ⓒ 40 ft/s

    Ⓑ 8 ft/s   Ⓓ 72 ft/s

27. The perimeter of a rectangular pen is less than 450 feet. Which inequality represents the amount of fencing that will enclose the pen?

    Ⓐ $2(x + y) \le 450$ Ⓒ $2(x + y) < 450$

    Ⓑ $2(x + y) \ge 450$ Ⓓ $2(x + y) > 450$

28. Which expressions are equivalent to $4x^2 - 4y^2$? Select all that apply.

    Ⓐ $2(x - y)(x + y)$ Ⓓ $(2x - 2y)(2x - 2y)$

    Ⓑ $4(x - y)(x - y)$ Ⓔ $(2x - 2y)(2x + 2y)$

    Ⓒ $(4x - 4y)(x + y)$ Ⓕ $4(x - y)(x + y)$

 I'm in a Learning Mindset!

How did I work together with classmates to find the domain, range, and end behavior of functions?

1.2

Characteristics of Functions and Graphs

(I Can) relate the characteristics of real-world phenomena to characteristics of its function graph.

Spark Your Learning

Brianna and Denver rode different roller coasters. They both claim that their coaster was more exciting.

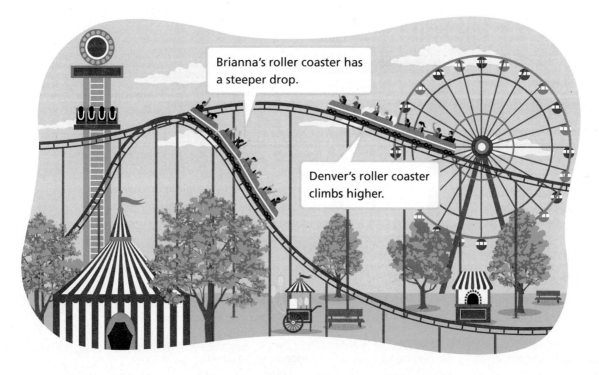

Brianna's roller coaster has a steeper drop.

Denver's roller coaster climbs higher.

Complete Part A as a whole class. Then complete Parts B–D in small groups.

A. What is a mathematical question you can ask about this situation? What information would you need to know to answer your question?

B. How would the maximum speed and average speed affect your answer? What unit of measurement would you use to compare them?

C. To answer your question, what strategy and tool would you use along with all the information you have? What answer do you get?

 Turn and Talk What additional information would help you to make more accurate comparisons about the two coasters?

Build Understanding

Sketch a Function Graph from a Verbal Description

You can sketch the graph of a function from a description of its key features.

Consider this situation: A dam controls a reservoir's water level. The level is currently steady and above normal. To prepare for coming rain, engineers will lower the water level at a constant rate until it is below normal. The water level is then expected to rise rapidly with the rains, and gradually level off well above the current level.

You can sketch a graph of the reservoir's water level as a function of time where the normal water level of the reservoir is represented by the horizontal axis.

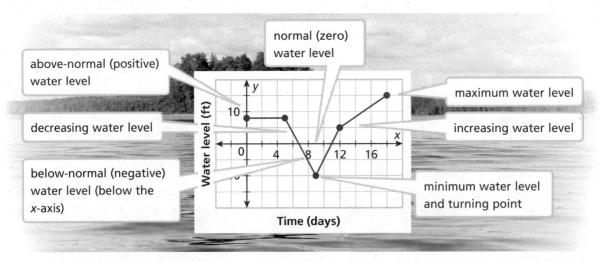

Refer to the sketch above. A function $f(x)$:

- is **increasing** on an interval if $f(b) \geq f(a)$ for any a and b in the interval such that $b > a$, and **decreasing** on an interval if $f(b) \leq f(a)$ for any a and b in the interval such that $b > a$.

- has a **turning point** where the function changes from increasing to decreasing or from decreasing to increasing.

- has a **maximum** value where $x = a$ if $f(a) > f(x)$ for all other values of x nearby, and a **minimum** value where $x = a$ if $f(a) < f(x)$ for all other values of x nearby. A maximum or minimum may occur at a turning point or at the endpoint of an interval

- has a **zero** at each value of x for which $f(x) = 0$.

1   **A.** Sketch a graph for this situation: The sun rises at 6 a.m., reaches its highest point above the horizon at 12 p.m., sets at 6 p.m, and reaches its lowest point below the horizon at 12 a.m.

     B. Compare and contrast your graph with the graph drawn by a partner. How are the graphs the same and how are they different?

     C. Analyze your graphs using the terms *positive, negative, increasing,* and *decreasing.* Are these characteristics exhibited in the same way on your graphs?

     D. Now analyze your graphs using the terms *zero, maximum,* and *minimum.* Where do these values occur on each graph?

Define Average Rate of Change in Context

You have found and interpreted the constant rate of change, or slope, for linear functions in many contexts. Nonlinear functions do not have a constant rate of change, but you can compare the average rate of change between pairs of points on a curve. The **average rate of change** of a function over an interval $[a, b]$ is the ratio of the change in the function values, $f(b) - f(a)$, to the corresponding change in the x-values, $b - a$. So, the average rate of change is positive on $[a, b]$ when $f(b) > f(a)$, and negative on $[a, b]$ when $f(b) < f(a)$.

2 The table models one day's predicted tide heights in relation to the "mean lower low water" level, or MLLW, at Weymouth Fore River Bridge, Massachusetts.

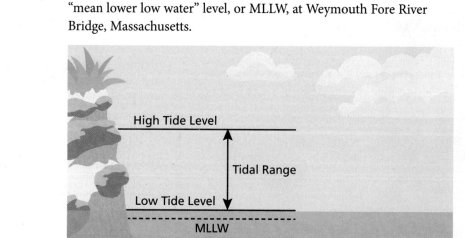

Tide Chart	
Time	**Height (ft)**
12 a.m.	1.19
2 a.m.	1.33
4 a.m.	5.05
6 a.m.	8.57
8 a.m.	8.66
10 a.m.	5.37
12 p.m.	1.92
2 p.m.	1.27
4 p.m.	5.09
6 p.m.	9.13
8 p.m.	10.25
10 p.m.	7.03

A. Plot the data on a graph, and sketch a smooth curve through the points.

B. The tidal range is the difference in height between consecutive high and low tide levels. What observations can you make about the tidal range at this site?

C. Compare the average rate of change between the first low tide and the high tide following it with the average rate of change for the second low tide and the high tide following it. How does this relate to the difference between each low tide level and the high tide level following it?

D. What is the average rate of change between 6 a.m. and 6 p.m.? What does this information tell you? What do you think will be the average rate of change over even longer periods? Explain.

E. What additional information would allow you to sketch a more accurate graph and compare average rates of change more precisely between high and low tides?

> **Turn and Talk** For a linear function, the average rate of change over any interval is the same, so you know the "shape" of the graph everywhere. For a nonlinear function, how does knowing the average rate of change over shorter and shorter intervals help you to sketch the curve?

Step It Out

Identify Key Characteristics in Context

Identifying key features of a graph in a real-world context gives you tools to interpret the function's behavior in its context, and may help you identify and interpret trends.

3 ▶ A car's suspension system connects the body of the car to its wheels. Springs are one component of the suspension system. The graph shows the vertical displacement of the spring in a car's suspension after the car hits a bump during a suspension test. Identify and interpret the key characteristics of the graph.

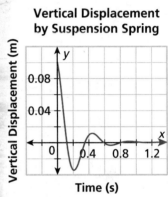

Vertical Displacement by Suspension Spring

Observations and Interpretations:

The greatest change in the spring's position occurred within the first 0.2 second of hitting the bump. The graph shows a maximum value at 0 and at about 0.45 second.

> **A.** How can the displacement value at 0 be a maximum value when it is not located at a turning point?

The lowest displacement, about −0.035 meter, occurred at about 0.2 second. The graph also shows a minimum value at about 0.65 second.

> **B.** What makes the displacement value at 0.65 second a minimum value when the displacement value at about 0.2 second was less?

The graph is increasing on [0.2, 0.45] and [0.65, 0.9]. The graph is decreasing on [0, 0.2], [0.45, 0.65], and [0.9, 1.2].

> **C.** How can 0.45 second be part of both an increasing interval and a decreasing interval?

The average rate of change from the first maximum to the first minimum is about $\frac{-0.35 - 0.1}{0.2 - 0} = -2.25$, or −2.25 m/s.

> **D.** Does this rate of change accurately represent the entire graph? Explain.

Turn and Talk How does the average rate of change from the second maximum to the second minimum compare to the average rate of change you found in Part D? Explain.

Apply Function Characteristics to a Real-World Context

A description of a real-world situation can be used to create a graph. Always pay careful attention when choosing the axes for a graph, since these determine what the values in the graph represent.

4 A roller coaster ride begins at ground level. The first 40 seconds of the ride includes only turns, with no changes in elevation. Next, the roller coaster rises steadily for 50 seconds to its maximum elevation, then plunges back to ground level in only 8 seconds. In the next 6 seconds, it rises to an elevation of 100 feet, then drops back down to ground level in the 6 seconds that follow. The remaining 90 seconds of the ride includes small inclines and drops before returning to the starting point.

Sketch a graph of this situation.

Maximum elevation: 205 feet

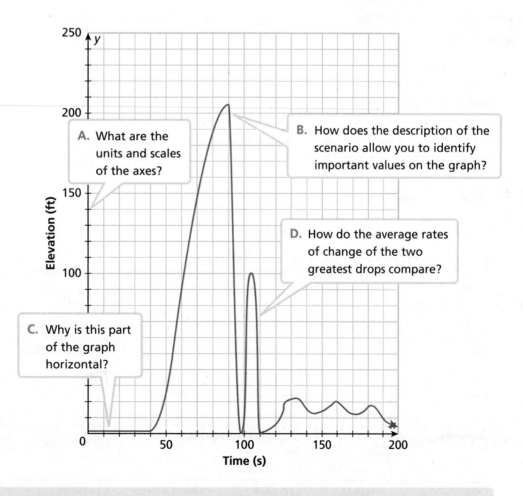

A. What are the units and scales of the axes?

B. How does the description of the scenario allow you to identify important values on the graph?

C. Why is this part of the graph horizontal?

D. How do the average rates of change of the two greatest drops compare?

Turn and Talk How might you change the axes to use your graph to give a different impression of the roller coaster?

©Armi Fello/EyeEm/Getty Images

Check Understanding

1. Sketch a graph that represents the following scenario. What should all graphs that represent this situation have in common?

   Maria runs laps around a track while her coach makes notes of her running form from the side of the track. What is Maria's distance from her coach as a function of time?

2. The table shows the air temperature in Death Valley over a 24-hour period. How does the average rate of change from 7 a.m. to 10 a.m. compare to the average rate of change from 7 p.m. to 10 p.m.? Explain what these average rates of change tell you about the situation.

Air Temperature								
Time	7 a.m.	10 a.m.	1 p.m.	4 p.m.	7 p.m.	10 p.m.	1 a.m.	4 a.m.
Temperature (°F)	57	70	74	72	64	56	53	49

3. Sketch a graph of the following scenario. Label the axes and identify any maximum or minimum values.

   A skydiver steps out of a plane. His speed increases due to gravity until he reaches terminal velocity of 40 meters per second after falling for about 25 seconds. His speed remains at terminal velocity for 5 seconds. Then he pulls the cord to release his parachute and his speed is rapidly reduced to about 12 meters per second. His speed then decreases to 5 meters per second and remains constant as he moves toward the ground. He reaches the ground about 55 seconds after he stepped out of the plane.

On Your Own

4. The graph shows the values of a stock for 5 days.

   A. What is the minimum value and what is the maximum value?

   B. What is the average rate of change for each day?

   C. How do the daily average rates of change compare to the 5-day average rate of change?

Use the labeled points to identify the location of key features on the graph of the height of a bouncing ball over time.

Height of Bouncing Ball

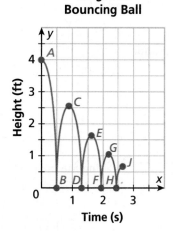

5. the maximum height

6. the minimum height

7. interval(s) when the height is increasing

8. interval(s) when the height is decreasing

9. interval of the greatest positive average rate of change

10. interval of the greatest negative average rate of change

For Problems 11 and 12, sketch a graph to represent the scenario. Label any maximum or minimum values. Identify intervals of increase and decrease.

11. The altitude of a hot air balloon increased at a steady rate after it left the ground. The balloon then maintained the same altitude for a while before it rapidly lowered to a new altitude, where it remained until making a slow descent to the ground.

12. Philip begins his workout with a slow walk to warm-up. Then he does intervals of jogging and running. At the end of his workout, he cools down with a slow walk.

13. The table shows data collected about the power output produced by a solar energy system over the course of 24 hours.

    A. Sketch a graph of the data and identify what scales to use on the axes. Identify any maximum or minimum values. On what intervals is the data increasing or decreasing? Describe the meaning of the characteristics in this context.

    B. (MP) **Use Structure** Based on the given data and your understanding of the context, what would a reasonable output in kW be for 4 p.m.? Explain your reasoning.

    C. The given data is for a sunny day. How do you think the graph of the kW of power produced would be different for a cloudy day?

Solar Energy Produced	
Time	**Output (kW)**
1 a.m.	0
5 a.m.	0.1
9 a.m.	1
1 p.m.	2.5
5 p.m.	0.5
9 p.m.	0

14. The graph shows the speed of a car over time.

    A. Identify and explain the behavior of the graph between any maximum and minimum values.

    B. (MP) **Attend to Precision** What is the average rate of change on the interval [6, 15]? Explain what it means in this context.

Speed of a Car

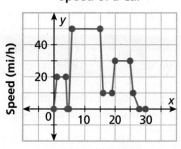

Time (min)

15. Open Ended

   A. Write a real-world scenario whose graph would have the following:

- maximum $= 30$

- minimum $= 10$

- increases on $(0, 15)$, $(45, 90)$

- decreases on $(15, 45)$

   B. Sketch the graph of the scenario. Label the axes.

   C. Find and interpret the average rate of change on the interval $[0, 45]$.

16. (Open Middle™) Using the integers -9 to 9, at most one time each, fill in the boxes to create a function with the corresponding range and zeros.

$$y = \boxed{} x^2 + \boxed{} x + \boxed{}$$

$$\text{range: } \left\{ y \mid y \; \boxed{} \right\}; \text{ zeros: } x = \boxed{} \text{ and } x = \boxed{}$$

Spiral Review • Assessment Readiness

17. What type of transformation does not produce a congruent figure?

   Ⓐ translation

   Ⓑ rotation

   Ⓒ dilation

   Ⓓ reflection

18. What is the end behavior of the graph of $h(t) = -16t^2 + 24t + 15$?

   Ⓐ As $x \to -\infty, y \to +\infty$; as $x \to +\infty, y \to +\infty$.

   Ⓑ As $x \to -\infty, y \to -\infty$; as $x \to +\infty, y \to -\infty$.

   Ⓒ As $x \to -\infty, y \to -\infty$; as $x \to +\infty, y \to +\infty$.

   Ⓓ As $x \to -\infty, y \to +\infty$; as $x \to +\infty, y \to -\infty$.

19. What is the interval notation of the solution shown in the graph?

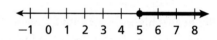

   Ⓐ $[5, +\infty)$ Ⓑ $(5, +\infty)$

   Ⓒ $(-\infty, 5)$ Ⓓ $(-\infty, 5]$

20. Which notation represents a domain that includes all nonnegative values of x? Select all that apply.

   Ⓐ $\{x \mid x > 0\}$

   Ⓑ $\{x \mid 0 < x < +\infty\}$

   Ⓒ $[0, +\infty)$

   Ⓓ $(-\infty, +\infty)$

   Ⓔ $x < +\infty$

   Ⓕ $x \geq 0$

I'm in a Learning Mindset!

Who can support me in my learning about key characteristics of functions and their graphs in a real-world context?

Transformations of Function Graphs

(I Can) relate a pre-image to its image through a transformation rule.

Spark Your Learning

Romanesco broccoli is an edible flower bud that grows in an outward spiral.

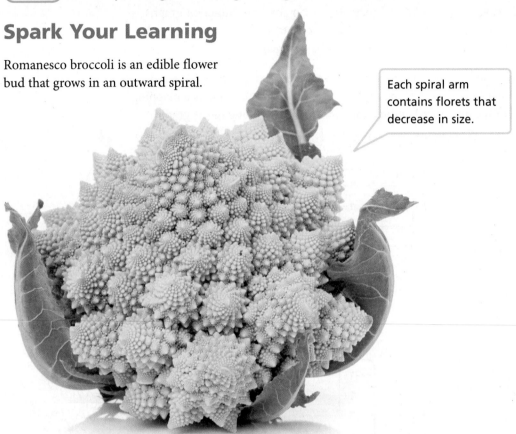

Each spiral arm contains florets that decrease in size.

Complete Part A as a whole class. Then complete Parts B–D in small groups.

A. What is a mathematical question you can ask about this situation? What information would you need to know to answer your question?

B. What is a reasonable size for the largest floret? What is a reasonable size for the smallest floret?

C. To answer your question, what strategy and tool would you use along with all the information you have? What answer do you get?

D. Does your answer make sense in the context of the situation? How do you know? Is it possible for the floret to contain infinitely many smaller florets? Explain your reasoning.

 Turn and Talk How might you use the photo of the Romanesco florets to create an image of a giant Romanesco?

Build Understanding

Translations of Function Graphs

In previous courses, you performed **transformations** of figures and function graphs. Different transformations are indicated in a function rule by different *parameters*. A **parameter** is a constant in a function rule that can be changed.

1 Each graph below shows a function $f(x)$ in blue, and a function $g(x)$ in red formed by translating the graph of $f(x)$. To the left of each graph is a mapping diagram of the inputs and outputs for f and g corresponding to the graph.

$g(x) = f(x) + 2$:

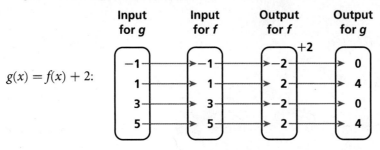
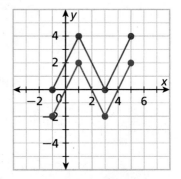

$g(x) = f(x - 2)$:

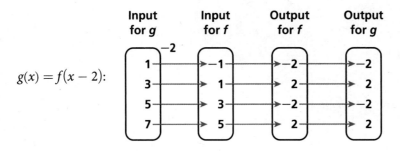
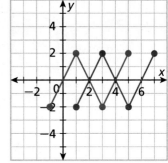

A. Compare the mapping diagram and graphs for f and g in the top row above. How do the inputs of f and g compare? How do the outputs compare? How does this relate to the parameter 2 in the rule $g(x) = f(x) + 2$? What is the effect of this parameter on the graph of f?

B. Compare the mapping diagram and graphs for f and g in the bottom row above. How do the inputs of f and g compare? How do the outputs compare? How does this relate to the parameter 2 in the rule $g(x) = f(x - 2)$? What is the effect of this parameter on the graph of f?

C. In Part A, *adding* 2 to the output value of f translates its graph in a positive (vertical) direction on the coordinate plane. In Part B, *subtracting* 2 from the input value of g to obtain the input value of f translates the graph of f in a positive (horizontal) direction on the coordinate plane. How does moving the parameter 2 from "outside" to "inside" the function result in this difference?

Turn and Talk In each of Parts A and B, how will the graph of g change if you replace the parameter 2 with -2? Explain your reasoning.

Stretches and Compressions of Function Graphs

While a translation of the graph of a function affects only its position on the coordinate plane, a vertical or horizontal stretch or compression affects the graph's appearance.

2 Each graph below shows a function $f(x)$ in blue, and a function $g(x)$ formed by stretching or compressing the graph of $f(x)$ in red. To the left of each graph is a mapping diagram of the inputs and outputs for f and g corresponding to the graph.

$g(x) = 2f(x)$:

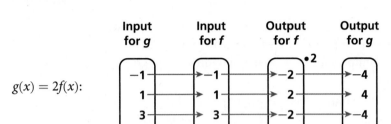

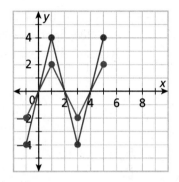

$g(x) = f\left(\dfrac{1}{2}x\right)$:

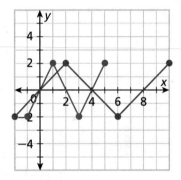

A. Compare the mapping diagram and graphs for f and g in the top row above. How do the inputs of f and g compare? How do the outputs compare? How does this relate to the parameter 2 in the rule $g(x) = 2f(x)$? What is the effect of this parameter on the graph of f?

B. Compare the mapping diagram and graphs for f and g in the bottom row above. How do the inputs of f and g compare? How do the outputs compare? How does this relate to the parameter 2 in the rule $g(x) = f\left(\frac{1}{2}x\right)$? What is the effect of this parameter on the graph of f?

C. In Part A, *multiplying* the output value of f by 2 stretches its graph vertically. In Part B, *dividing* the input value of g by 2 to obtain the input value of f stretches its graph horizontally. How does moving the parameter 2 from "outside" to "inside" the function result in this difference?

 Turn and Talk In each of Parts A and B, how will the graph of g change if you replace the parameter 2 with $\frac{1}{2}$? Explain your reasoning.

Reflections of Function Graphs

Besides the parameters in function rules that indicate translations and stretches or compressions, the parameter -1 (that is, a negative sign) can indicate a reflection across the x- or y-axis. Note that if a function is symmetric when its graph is reflected across the x-axis, it is an even function. An odd function also has a symmetric graph. Its graph, however, is not symmetric when it is reflected, but when it is rotated 180° about the origin.

3 Each graph below shows a function $f(x)$ in blue, and a function $g(x)$ formed by reflecting the graph of $f(x)$ in red. To the left of each graph is a mapping diagram of the inputs and outputs for f and g corresponding to the graph.

$g(x) = -f(x)$:

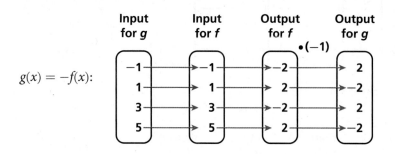

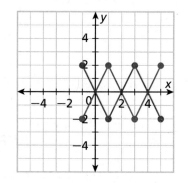

$g(x) = f(-x)$:

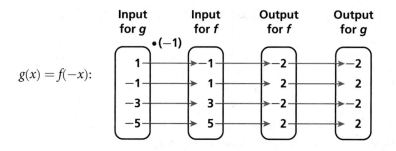

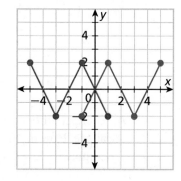

A. Compare the mapping diagram and graphs for f and g in the top row above. How do the inputs of f and g compare? How do the outputs compare? How does this relate to the parameter -1 (the negative sign) in the rule $g(x) = -f(x)$? What is the effect of this parameter on the graph of f?

B. Compare the mapping diagram and graphs for the functions f and g in the bottom row above. How do the inputs of f and g compare? How do the outputs compare? How does this relate to the parameter -1 in the rule $g(x) = f(-x)$? What is the effect of this parameter on the graph of f?

C. In Part A, the negative sign reflects the graph vertically, while in Part B, the negative sign reflects the graph horizontally. How does moving the negative sign from "outside" to "inside" the function result in this difference?

 Turn and Talk Is $f(x)$ an even function, an odd function, or neither? Can you translate $f(x)$ so that the image is an even or odd function? Explain.

Step It Out

Graph a Combined Transformation

A function rule may combine the transformation parameters you have seen in this lesson. The table below summarizes the effect of the parameters on a general function $f(x)$.

Graph of $g(x) = af\left(\frac{1}{b}(x - h)\right) + k$	
Parameter	**Transformation of the Graph of $f(x)$**
a	$a > 1$: vertical stretch by a factor of a $0 < a < 1$: vertical compression by a factor of a $-a$ where $a > 0$: adds a reflection across the x-axis
b	$b > 1$: horizontal stretch by a factor of b $0 < b < 1$: horizontal compression by a factor of b $-b$ where $b > 0$: adds a reflection across the y-axis
h	$h > 0$: horizontal translation right h units $h < 0$: horizontal translation left $|h|$ units
k	$k > 0$: vertical translation up k units $k < 0$: vertical translation down $|k|$ units

4 ▶ Describe how to transform the graph of $f(x)$ shown to obtain the graph of $g(x) = -f\big(2(x - 3)\big) - 1$, and show the graph.

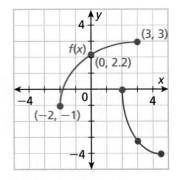

Identify the parameters and their effects:

$a = -1$: reflection across the x-axis

$b = \frac{1}{2}$: horizontal compression by a factor of $\frac{1}{2}$

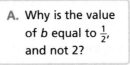
A. Why is the value of b equal to $\frac{1}{2}$, and not 2?

$h = 3$: horizontal translation right 3 units

$k = -1$: vertical translation down 1 unit

B. Why is h positive, but k negative, when the function has minus signs where both parameters appear?

Apply these transformations to a few reference points on the graph of $f(x)$. Remember: b and h affect the function's inputs, and a and k affect its outputs. For a point (x, y) on the graph of $f(x)$, the image on the graph of $g(x)$ is $(bx + h, ay + k) = \frac{1}{2}x + 3, -y - 1$.

C. Does the horizontal compression change all the reference points? Explain.

Reference and image points: $(-2, -1) \rightarrow (2, 0)$; $(0, 2.2) \rightarrow (3, -3.2)$; $(3, 3) \rightarrow (4.5, -4)$

The graph of $g(x)$ is shown in red.

 Turn and Talk How can you show the combined transformation from $f(x)$ to $g(x)$ above as a sequence of four transformations on the coordinate plane?

Model with Transformations

Recognizing that many real-world situations involve the transformation of a function and its graph gives you a greater ability to interpret the situation in its context.

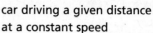

car driving a given distance at a constant speed

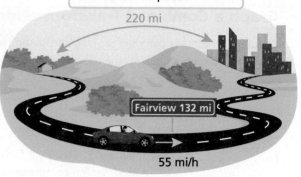

220 mi

Fairview 132 mi

55 mi/h

5 ▶ Matías is driving at a constant speed from his home to Fairview for the weekend, as shown. How can you use transformations of the graph of the distance Matías has driven from home as a function of time to obtain the graph of the distance that remains to Fairview?

Write and graph a model for the distance d Matías has driven from home as a function of time:

$d = 55t \ (0 \leq t \leq 4)$

A. Why is the domain restricted?

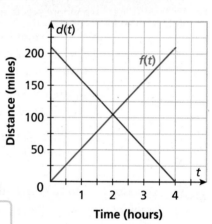

The graph is shown. Write a model for the distance d_r remaining to Junction City:

$d_r = 220 - 55t \ (0 \leq t \leq 4)$

B. How is this model found?

Let $d = f(t)$ and $d_r = g(t)$. Then $f(t) = 55t$ and $g(t) = 220 - 55t$, or $g(t) = -55t + 220$. Write $g(t)$ as a transformation of $f(t)$:

$g(t) = -f(t) + 220$

C. Which of the parameters a, b, h, and k apply? What are their values?

The graph of $g(t)$ is that of $f(t)$ reflected in the x-axis and translated up 220 units. It is shown in red.

6 ▶ Imagine that as Matías passes the sign in the diagram, he realizes he forgot his suitcase, and turns around to drive back home. How can you use transformations of the graph of the distance Matías has driven from home to the sign to obtain the graph of the distance remaining to drive back home?

Write and graph the model for the distance from home:

$d = 55t \ (0 \leq t \leq 1.6)$

A. Why has the domain changed?

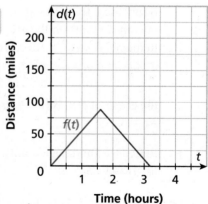

The graph is shown. Write a model for the distance home d_h remaining:

B. Why is 1.6 subtracted from t?

$d_h = 88 - 55(t - 1.6) \ (1.6 \leq t \leq 3.2)$

Let $d_r = g(t)$. Then $g(t) = 88 - 55(t - 1.6)$. Write $g(t)$ as a transformation of $f(t)$:

C. Which parameters apply? What are their values?

$g(t) = -f(t - 1.6) + 88$

The graph of $g(t)$ is that of $f(t)$ translated right 1.6 units, reflected in the x-axis, and translated up 88 units. It is shown in red.

D. Write a piecewise-defined function $h(t)$ to model Matías's distance from his home.

Check Understanding

Describe how the graph of $g(x)$ is related to the graph of the given function $f(x)$.

1. $g(x) = f(x + 7)$ **2.** $g(x) = f(4x)$ **3.** $g(x) = -f(x)$

4. Describe how to transform the graph of $f(x)$ shown to obtain the graph of $g(x) = f(-2x) - 4$, and show the graph. Include the effect of each parameter on the graph of the image. Also include the effects of each parameter on the coordinates of the reference points shown on the graph of $f(x)$.

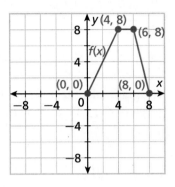

5. Francis takes an urban standing scooter on a 2-mile trip at a constant speed of 10 mi/h. If $f(t) = 10t$ represents the distance traveled as a function of time, what function represent the distance *remaining* on the trip? How can you write this as a transformation of $f(t)$? What is the relationship of the graphs?

On Your Own

 Use Structure The figure at the right shows the graph of a function $f(x)$. Match each transformation of $f(x)$ with the correct graph shown below.

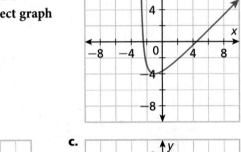

6. $f(x - 2)$ **7.** $f(x + 2)$ **8.** $f(x) - 2$

9. $f(2x)$ **10.** $\frac{1}{2}f(x)$ **11.** $-f(x)$

a.
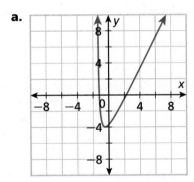

b.
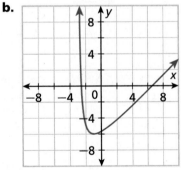

c.
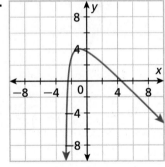

d.
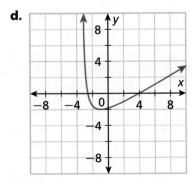

e.
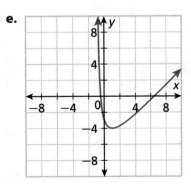

f.
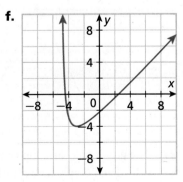

The graph of a function $f(x)$ is shown. Describe each transformation to the graph of $f(x)$ indicated by the function $g(x)$, and sketch the result.

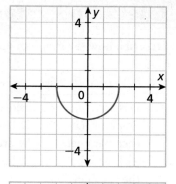

12. $g(x) = f(x) + 4$

13. $g(x) = f(-x)$

14. $g(x) = f(x + 3)$

15. $g(x) = 2.5f(x)$

16. $g(x) = f(2x)$

17. $g(x) = f\left(\frac{2}{5}x\right)$

18. Is the function $f(x)$ shown in the graph even, odd, or neither? Explain.

The graph of a function $f(x)$ is shown. Describe each transformation to the graph of $f(x)$ indicated by the function $g(x)$, and sketch the result.

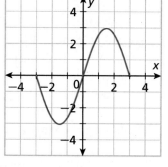

19. $g(x) = f(x - 2)$

20. $g(x) = \frac{4}{3}f(x)$

21. $g(x) = f\left(\frac{3}{2}x\right)$

22. $g(x) = f(x) - 1$

23. $g(x) = -f(x)$

24. $g(x) = f(-x)$

25. Is the function $f(x)$ shown in the graph even, odd, or neither? Explain.

26. Determine whether the function whose graph is shown is an even function, an odd function, or neither.

A.

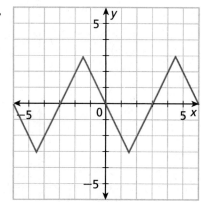

B.

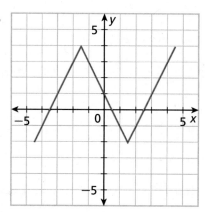

C.

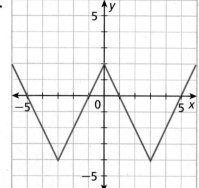

27. The graph of a function $f(x)$ is shown. Copy the graph on a coordinate grid. Then graph each transformation below on the same grid. What is the resulting figure?

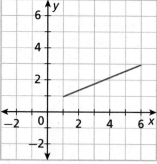

A. $-f(x) + 6$

B. $f\big(2(x + 2)\big) + 2$

C. $f\big(-2(x - 1.5)\big)$

Each function $g(x)$ is a transformation of a given function $f(x)$. Identify the parameters of the transformation, and describe how the graph of $f(x)$ can be transformed to obtain the graph of $g(x)$.

28. $g(x) = \frac{2}{3}f\left(-(x+4)\right)$ **29.** $g(x) = 3f(x+1) - 4$ **30.** $g(x) = -f\left(\frac{2}{5}(x+1)\right) + 8$

The graph of a function $f(x)$ is shown. Find the image of each labeled reference point after the indicated transformations, and use them to sketch a graph of $g(x)$.

31. $g(x) = \frac{3}{2}f(x) - 2$

32. $g(x) = -f(-x)$

33. $g(x) = -\frac{1}{2}f(x+1) + 1$

34. $g(x) = f\left(\frac{2}{3}(x+2)\right) - 3$

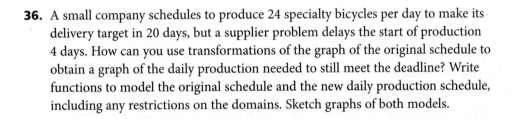

35. Until 1971, visitors at the Washington Monument in Washington, DC could climb the 897-step spiral staircase inside. Suppose Jackie climbed these stairs at a rate of 39 steps per minute. After she reached the top of the staircase, she immediately turned around and descended at a rate of 52 steps per minute. How can you use transformations of the graph of Jackie's climb to obtain a graph of Jackie's descent? Write functions to model the climb and descent, including any restrictions on the domains. Sketch graphs to model Jackie's climb and descent.

36. A small company schedules to produce 24 specialty bicycles per day to make its delivery target in 20 days, but a supplier problem delays the start of production 4 days. How can you use transformations of the graph of the original schedule to obtain a graph of the daily production needed to still meet the deadline? Write functions to model the original schedule and the new daily production schedule, including any restrictions on the domains. Sketch graphs of both models.

37. A jet makes daily deliveries of crucial supplies to a company. The 1200-mile trip is normally made at a constant speed of 400 mi/h, and leaves at noon. Today, the flight leaves 90 minutes late, but increases its speed 100 mi/h to help make up time. How can you use transformations of the graph of a normal flight to model and graph today's flight? How do the domain and range change? Explain.

38. The graphic shown will be part of a poster being created by a school's graphic design club. The base of each branch as you go upward is at the same height as the tip of the branch below it. Suppose the bottom right branch is represented by a function $f(x)$ with endpoints at $(0, 0)$ and $(16, 10)$.

Leafy logo diagram

A. What function represents the bottom left branch?

B. The function $g(x) = \frac{3}{4}f\left(\frac{4}{3}x\right) + 10$ represents the branch above $f(x)$. What transformations does this indicate? What are the coordinates of this branch's endpoints?

C. Does $j(x) = \frac{3}{4}g\left(\frac{4}{3}x\right) + 10$ represent the third branch up on the right? Justify your answer.

39. The graph shows a rounding function $f(x)$ that rounds a number to the nearest integer. For values such as $x = -3.5$ and $x = 1.5$ that are halfway between two integers, $f(x)$ rounds x up to the next integer.

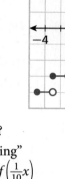

  A. How does the transformation $g(x) = 2f(x)$ affect the graph of $f(x)$? Graph the transformation. Does $g(x)$ have any meaning as a "rounding" function? Explain.

  B. How does the transformation $g(x) = f\left(\frac{1}{2}x\right)$ affect the graph of $f(x)$? Graph the transformation. Does $g(x)$ have any meaning as a "rounding" function? Explain.

  C. How does the transformation $g(x) = 2f\left(\frac{1}{2}x\right)$ affect the graph of $f(x)$? Graph the transformation. Does $g(x)$ have any meaning as a "rounding" function? Explain. What do you predict that the function $g(x) = 10f\left(\frac{1}{10}x\right)$ would do?

40. A carnival ride goes up and down twice from the ground. To graph the height in feet of the ride as it goes up and down the first time, graph the function $h(t) = -6t^2 + 48t$, where t is the time in seconds after the ride begins. The graph of the height in feet of the ride as it goes up and down a second time can be modeled by compressing the first graph three-fourths vertically and translating horizontally. Make a sketch of the graph of the height. Then write a piecewise-defined function to model the height.

41. (MP) **Reason** Is it possible for a function to be both even and odd? If so, under what circumstance(s). If not, explain why not.

Spiral Review • Assessment Readiness

42. For the given piecewise-defined linear function, what are the values for $f(-2)$ and $f(3)$? Select all that apply.

$$f(x) = \begin{cases} 2x & \text{if } x \geq 0 \\ -2x & \text{if } x < 0 \end{cases}$$

  (A) -4 (D) 2

  (B) -2 (E) 4

  (C) 1 (F) 6

43. What solution is shown in the graph?

  (A) $(a, +\infty)$ (C) $(-\infty, a)$

  (B) $[a, +\infty)$ (D) $(-\infty, a]$

Use the graph below for Problems 44 and 45.

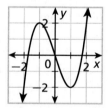

44. On what interval(s) is the function decreasing?

  (A) $(-1, 1)$ (C) $(-\infty, -1)$

  (B) $(-\infty, -1), (1, +\infty)$ (D) $(-\infty, +\infty)$

45. What is the maximum value of the function on $[-2, 2]$?

  (A) -1 (C) 1

  (B) 0 (D) 2

 I'm in a Learning Mindset!

What questions can I ask to encourage my classmates to share their knowledge about combined transformations of functions?

Transformations of Absolute Value and Quadratic Functions

(I Can) use parameters to identify changes in the key characteristics of a function.

Spark Your Learning

A professional stunt rider performs a jump between two ramps. The jump follows a parabolic path as the force of gravity pulls the rider back down to Earth. The ramp is at a 45° angle, so it does not factor into determining the range.

The two ramps are *d* meters apart.

Complete Part A as a whole class. Then complete Parts B–D in small groups.

A. What is a mathematical question you can ask about this situation? What information would you need to know to answer your question?

B. What variable(s) are involved in this situation? What unit of measurement would you use for each variable?

C. To answer your question, what strategy and tool would you use along with all the information you have? What answer do you get?

D. Does your answer make sense in the context of the situation? How do you know?

 Turn and Talk Predict how your answer would change for each of the following changes in the situation:
- The distance doubled.
- The angle of the ramp is increased.

Build Understanding

Analyze Absolute Value and Quadratic Parent Functions

You can graph different types of functions using transformations of **parent functions**, which are the most basic form of each type of function. Recall that the absolute value of a number is its distance from 0 on the number line. The parent **absolute value function**

is $f(x) = |x| = \begin{cases} x & \text{if } x \geq 0 \\ -x & \text{if } x < 0 \end{cases}$. Recall that this is an example of a **piecewise-defined function**.

A **quadratic function** is a function defined by a quadratic expression of the form $ax^2 + bx + c$ and has the parent function $g(x) = x^2$. The graph of a quadratic function is a curve called a parabola. The point at which the graph of an absolute value function or a quadratic function changes directions is called the **vertex**.

1 ▶ **A.** The graphs of $f(x) = |x|$ and $g(x) = x^2$ are shown. Compare the domain and range of f to those of g.

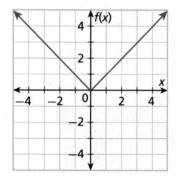 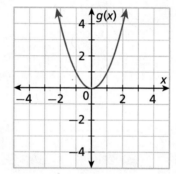

B. The two graphs have some features that are the same and others that are similar. Compare and contrast the graphs with respect to their vertices, intervals where they are increasing or decreasing, and their end behavior.

C. Describe the symmetry of both of the graphs. Are the functions even, odd, or neither?

D. How do the end behaviors of the parent absolute value function and parent quadratic function compare to that of linear functions you have analyzed?

E. How does the value of the parent absolute value function change between $x = 0$ and $x = 1$? between $x = 1$ and $x = 2$? between $x = 2$ and $x = 3$? How does the value of the parent quadratic function change between these same pairs of x-values? Contrast the rate of change between consecutive nonnegative integer values of x for the two functions.

 Turn and Talk How are the intervals where the parent absolute value function is increasing and decreasing linked to the piecewise definition of the function? What connection is there between the piecewise definition and the point where its graph changes from decreasing to increasing?

Step It Out

Transform Absolute Value and Quadratic Functions

Multiple transformations of an absolute value function or quadratic function occur when at least two of the parameters of the function change. Identifying the effect of changing each individual parameter helps to describe a combination of transformations.

2 Describe how to transform the graph of the parent absolute value function $f(x) = |x|$ to obtain the graph of the function $g(x) = -2f\left|\frac{1}{4}(x+1)\right| - 3$. Then draw the graph of the function g.

Identify the parameters and their effect on the parent graph.

Parameter	Effect on the Graph of the Parent Function f
$a = -2$	vertical stretch by a factor of 2 and reflection across the x-axis
$b = 4$	horizontal stretch by a factor of 4
$h = -1$	horizontal translation left 1 unit
$k = -3$	vertical translation down 3 units

A. Which transformations occur inside the function f and which occur outside of f?

So the combined transformation of the graph of f to draw the graph of g involves a reflection, both a vertical and a horizontal stretch, and a translation both horizontally and vertically.

Create a mapping rule for the combined transformation.

Applying the transformations to any point (x, y) on the graph of f results in the point $(4x - 1, -2y - 3)$ on the graph of g.

B. Which parameters impact the x-coordinate and which impact the y-coordinate? How is this connected to your answer to Part A?

Use the mapping rule to transform the reference points on f to those on g.

Point on the Graph of f	Corresponding Point on the Graph of g
$(-1, 1)$	$\left(4(-1) - 1, -2(1) - 3\right) = (-5, -5)$
$(0, 0)$	$\left(4(0) - 1, -2(0) - 3\right) = (-1, -3)$
$(1, 1)$	$\left(4(1) - 1, -2(1) - 3\right) = (3, -5)$

C. How can you use the mapping rule to quickly verify that the ordered pairs of g were calculated correctly?

Use the transformed reference points to graph the function g.

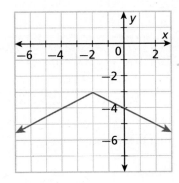

D. Analyze the graph of g. Are the expected transformations exhibited by the graph? Explain your reasoning.

3 ▶ Describe how to transform the graph of the parent quadratic function $f(x) = x^2$ to obtain the graph of the function $g(x) = f\left(4(x - 2)^2\right) + 1$. Then draw the graph of g.

Identify the parameters and their effect on the parent graph.

Parameter	Effect on the Graph of the Parent Function f
$a = 1$	no vertical stretch
$b = \frac{1}{4}$	horizontal compression by a factor of $\frac{1}{4}$
$h = 2$	horizontal translation right 2 units
$k = 1$	vertical translation up 1 unit

A. Which transformations occur inside the function f? which occur outside of f?

The combined transformation needed to draw the graph of g involves a horizontal compression and a translation both horizontally and vertically.

Create a mapping rule.

Applying these transformations to any point (x, y) on the parent graph of f results in the point $\left(\frac{1}{4}x + 2, y + 1\right)$ on the graph of g.

B. Which parameters impact the x-coordinate and which impact the y-coordinate? Explain the connection to your answer to Part **A**?

Use the mapping rule to transform the reference points on f to those on g.

Point on the Graph of f	Corresponding Point on the Graph of g
$(-1, 1)$	$\left(\frac{1}{4}(-1) + 2,\ 1 + 1\right) = \left(\frac{7}{4}, 2\right)$
$(0, 0)$	$\left(\frac{1}{4}(0) + 2,\ 0 + 1\right) = (2, 1)$
$(1, 1)$	$\left(\frac{1}{4}(1) + 2,\ 1 + 1\right) = \left(\frac{9}{4}, 2\right)$

C. How can you use the mapping rule to quickly verify that the ordered pairs of g were calculated correctly?

Use the transformed reference points to graph the function g.

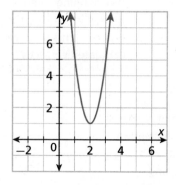

D. Are the expected transformations exhibited by the graph? Explain your reasoning.

 Turn and Talk Why are three reference points used for graphing these transformations? Why not more or less?

Model with Absolute Value and Quadratic Functions

Transformations of absolute value and quadratic functions can be used to model many real-world situations. For example, engineers use mathematical models as they design structures. These models facilitate the use of virtual testing before construction begins.

4 ▶ **STEM** Engineers working on a bridge project are considering two different designs. One design has a single tower supporting the roadway and the other design uses two towers.

The engineers need to determine a mathematical model for the cable in each design. The figures below show drawings of the cables with a coordinate grid used to identify key points on each cable.

One-Tower Design

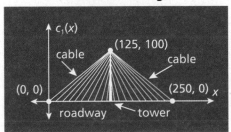

Two-Tower Design

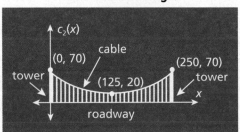

The model for the outermost cable of the one-tower design has the form $c_1(x) = a|x - h| + k$, where x is the horizontal distance (in feet) from the left end of the roadway and $c_1(x)$ is the cable's height (in feet) above the roadway.

The model for the cable of the two-tower design has the form $c_2(x) = a(x - h)^2 + k$, where x is the horizontal distance (in feet) from the left end of the roadway and $c_2(x)$ is the cable's height (in feet) above the roadway.

One-Tower Design

$c_1(x) = a|x - h| + k$

$0 = a|0 - 125| + 100$

$0 = a|-125| + 100$

$-100 = 125a$

$-0.8 = a$

> **A.** What points on each graph were used for the substitutions?

> **B.** Why is a negative used for the absolute value model but not for the quadratic model?

Two-Tower Design

$c_2(x) = a(x - h)^2 + k$

$70 = a(0 - 125)^2 + 20$

$70 = a(-125)^2 + 20$

$50 = 15{,}625a$

$\dfrac{2}{625} = a$

So the model for the cable in the one-tower design is $c_1(x) = -0.8|x - 125| + 100$ and the model for the cable in the two-tower design is $c_2(x) = \frac{2}{625}(x - 125)^2 + 20$.

 Turn and Talk How would the work change if the points $(250, 0)$ and $(250, 70)$ are used in their respective models, rather than $(0, 0)$ and $(0, 70)$?

Check Understanding

1. Which of the following characteristics of the parent absolute value function and the parent quadratic function will allow you to distinguish between the two functions without drawing their graphs? Explain.

    - vertex
    - average rate of change
    - intervals where they are increasing and decreasing
    - end behavior
    - symmetry
    - reference points

2. Write the transformed function for $h_2(x)$ using a vertical stretch that produces the same graph as $h_1(x) = k\left|\frac{1}{6}x\right|$.

3. The graphs of f and g are shown at the right. Write the function $g(x)$ as a transformation of $f(x)$.

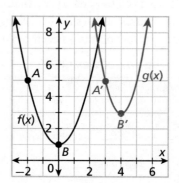

4. Sam is using a laser pointer to measure the height h of a building. The laser pointer is aimed at a mirror placed on the ground so that the light beam reflects off the mirror up to the top edge of the building's exterior wall. The beam can be model by an absolute value function where x is the distance from the exterior wall of the building.

    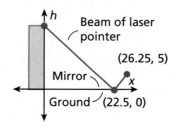

    A. Write the function that models the path of the beam from the laser pointer.

    B. The units on the axes are in feet. How tall is the building?

On Your Own

5. Compare the key characteristics of the parent absolute value function to those of the parent linear function, $f(x) = x$.

Describe how to transform the graph of $f(x) = |x|$ to obtain the graph of the related function $g(x)$. Then draw the graph of g.

6. $g(x) = f(x + 1)$

7. $g(x) = f(x) + 4$

8. $g(x) = 2f(x)$

9. $g(x) = 3f(x - 2)$

10. $g(x) = -f(x) + 1$

11. $g(x) = f\left(\frac{1}{2}(x - 8)\right)$

12. $g(x) = \frac{2}{3}f(x) - \frac{1}{2}$

13. $g(x) = -f\left(x - \frac{1}{4}\right) + \frac{1}{4}$

14. $g(x) = -3f(x - 2) + 6$

Describe how to transform the graph of $f(x) = x^2$ to obtain the graph of the related function $g(x)$. Then draw the graph of g.

15. $g(x) = f(x) - 5$

16. $g(x) = f(x + 1) + 3.5$

17. $g(x) = f\left(\frac{1}{2}x\right)$

18. $g(x) = -f(x + 1)$

19. $g(x) = \frac{3}{4}f(x) + 1$

20. $g(x) = -2f(x + 1) + 1$

21. $g(x) = 4f(x) - 2$

22. $g(x) = \frac{1}{5}f(x + 5) - 3$

23. $g(x) = f(x + 2) - 2$

24. **STEM** In the Atlantic Basin (Atlantic Ocean, Gulf of Mexico, and Caribbean Sea), the official hurricane season extends from June 1 to November 30. The peak number of hurricanes occurs between mid-August and the end of October. During the last 100 years, a high of 55 hurricanes have been recorded on September 10, while only 5 were recorded on November 10. A model of the number of hurricanes over the last 100 years has the form shown on the photo, where x is the number of days since the beginning of the hurricane season and $f(x)$ is the number of recorded hurricanes on that day.

Model of number of hurricanes:
$f(x) = -a|x - h| + k$

A. Write the rule for f.

B. State the domain and range of f.

C. About how many hurricanes would you estimate to have occurred over the last 100 years on October 1?

D. Sketch a graph of the function. Describe how the parent absolute value function is transformed to obtain the graph.

25. (MP) **Construct Arguments** The angle that a ball bounces off the side of a pool table is equal to the angle at which it hits the pool table. So the path of a ball bouncing off the side of a pool table can be modeled with an absolute value function. Anna is using this knowledge in a game with her friends. She claims that she can shoot the seven ball, located at (7, 4.25), with the cue ball, at (9, 2.75), into the corner pocket as shown in the diagram. Anna plans to bank the ball off the side of the pool table at (6, 5).

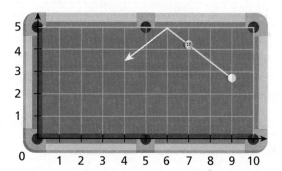

A. Write an equation to model the path of the ball.

B. Is Anna's claim correct? Explain your answer.

26. (MP) **Model with Mathematics** One fireworks shell is launched and then an identical shell is set off 2 seconds later with the same launch velocity and launch angle. The shells are designed to explode at their maximum height. The height (in feet) of the shells t seconds after the first shell was launched are given by the functions $h_1(t) = -16t^2 + 64t$ and $h_2(t)$.

A. Use transformations to write a rule for $h_2(t)$ in terms of $h_1(t)$.

B. Use your rule for $h_2(t)$ to write a quadratic function that models the height of the second fireworks shell t seconds after the first shell was launched?

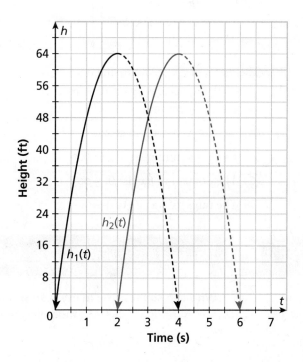

©lavizzara/Shutterstock

27. A photographer uses a mirror placed on the ground to create an under-lighting effect by shining a strong light at the mirror which bounces the light up and under the subject of the photograph as shown in the image. The base of the subject of the photo is 4 meters above the floor. At what height should the light source be placed?

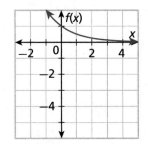

28. A hammock hangs between two trees and forms a curve that can be approximated by a parabola. The two trees are 8 meters apart. One end of the hammock is 1 meter to the right of the one tree and 3 meters above the ground. The other end of the hammock is 1 meter to the left of the second tree and 3 meters above the ground. The center of the hammock is halfway between the two trees and is 2.635 meters above the ground.

   A. Make a sketch of a graph representing the hammock. Label the ends and the center.

   B. Write a function that models the hammock, using transformations of the parent quadratic function. Include the domain and range of the function.

Spiral Review • Assessment Readiness

29. What is the domain of the function?

   (A) $(0, +\infty)$

   (B) $[0, +\infty)$

   (C) $(-\infty, +\infty)$

   (D) $(-\infty, 0)$

30. The graph of $f(x)$ is increasing on $(-\infty, 0)$ and decreasing on $(0, +\infty)$. Which statement must be true?

   (A) $f(x)$ has a maximum at $x = 0$.

   (B) $f(x)$ has a minimum at $x = 0$.

   (C) The domain of $f(x)$ is $(0, +\infty)$.

   (D) The range of $f(x)$ is $(0, +\infty)$.

31. Which transformation represents a vertical stretch by a factor of 5 of the graph of the function $f(x)$?

   (A) $g(x) = f\left(\frac{1}{5}x\right)$ (C) $g(x) = \frac{1}{5}f(x)$

   (B) $g(x) = f(5x)$ (D) $g(x) = 5f(x)$

32. The graph of $f(x)$ is shown and $g(x) = 4|x - 2| - 3$. Which function has a vertex at $(2, -3)$?

   (A) $f(x)$

   (B) $g(x)$

   (C) Neither

   (D) Both

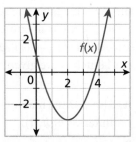

I'm in a Learning Mindset!

Who can support me in my learning about writing transformed absolute value and quadratic functions modeling real-world situations?

Compare Functions Across Representations

(**I Can**) compare the properties of two or more functions when they are represented in different ways.

Spark Your Learning

Bryan and Felix are football players practicing their punting skills. They agree that their practice goal for the day will be to improve the maximum height of their punts. At the end of practice, they compare their work.

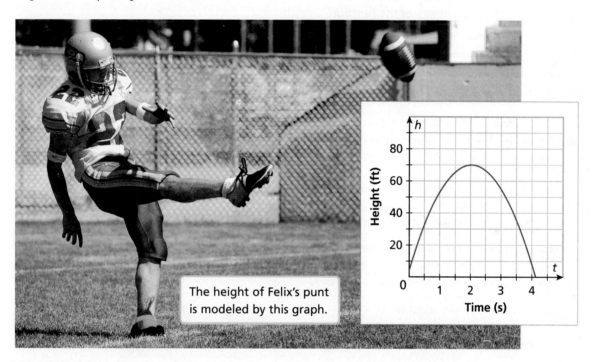

The height of Felix's punt is modeled by this graph.

Complete Part A as a whole class. Then complete Parts B and C in small groups.

A. What is a mathematical question you can ask about this situation? What information would you need to know to answer your question?

B. Why would the players represent their best punt in a different way? How can you compare properties of two functions each represented in a different way?

C. To answer your question, what strategy and tool would you use along with all the information you have? What answer do you get?

Turn and Talk Felix says that a greater maximum height always implies a longer hang time (the time from being kicked until the ball reaches the ground). Is that correct? Explain why or why not.

Build Understanding

Investigate Properties Revealed by Different Function Representations

You can represent a function using a verbal description, a table, a graph, or an algebraic equation. The representations are each good for revealing different properties of the function they represent.

Representation	Strengths of Representation
Verbal Description	useful for aiding in visualization and interpretation, particularly when compared to the parent function
Table	can help identify/approximate intercepts and key values, as well as reveal any symmetry of the function
Graph	provides a quick visual for the approximate maximum/minimum values, intervals of increasing/deceasing behavior, x- and y-intercepts, symmetry, and key values
Equation	can be used to find any value given one of the variable values

The key to comparing different representations of functions is to recognize if the given forms already allow for the comparison to be made. If not, you will need to alter one or both of the given representations to make the comparison possible.

1 Four different representations of a function are shown below.

Verbal Description	Equation
The function is a vertical compression of the parent quadratic function by a factor of $\frac{1}{2}$, its vertex is $(-1, -2)$, and its end behavior is $y \to +\infty$ as $x \to \pm\infty$.	$f(x) = \frac{1}{2}x^2 + x - \frac{3}{2}$

Graph	Table

Graph:

x	$f(x)$
-5	6
-3	0
-1	-2
1	0
3	6

A. What are $f(-1)$, $f(0)$, and $f(2)$? Explain how you determined each value.

B. How would you find the vertex, maximum/minimum values, intervals of increasing or decreasing, and intercepts given each representation by itself?

C. For each representation shown above, if that is the only information you have, can it be used to describe the symmetry of the function? Explain your answers.

 Turn and Talk How might you determine a feature of a function that is not easily identifiable by the representation you are given? Give an example.

Step It Out

Compare Functions Given Using Different Representations

If two functions are presented using different representations, you may need to convert one or both of the functions to another representation before comparing key features.

2 The function g is a horizontal stretch by a factor of 2 of the parent absolute value function, followed by a translation of 2 units left and 3 units up. The function f is an absolute value function represented by the table of values shown at the right. Which function has the greater minimum value?

x	$f(x)$
−2	7
−1	6
0	5
2	5
3	6

Method 1 – Use the Given Representations

The parent absolute value function has vertex $(0, 0)$.

Only the translation affects the vertex for g.

> **A.** Why is the vertex of g not affected by the compression?

Translating $(0, 0)$ left 2 units and up 3 units gives g a vertex at $(-2, 3)$.

So the minimum value of g is 3.

Look at the pattern of values in the table for f. Due to the symmetry of an absolute value function, the vertex of f must have x-coordinate 1.

> **B.** Why must the x-coordinate be 1? And why is $f(1) = 4$?

Using the pattern in the table, the vertex of f is $(1, 4)$.

So the minimum value of f is 4.

Comparing the two minimum values, the function f has the greater minimum.

Method 2 – Use a Common Representation

Since f is represented by a table, the given ordered pairs $(x, f(x))$ can be plotted and used to draw its graph.

To graph the function g, first create an equation using the verbal description. The function has the form $g(x) = a|x - h| + k$.

$$g(x) = 2|x - (-2)| + 3 \qquad a = 2, h = -2, \text{ and } k = 3$$
$$= 2|x + 2| + 3 \qquad \text{Simplify.}$$

> **C.** How are the values of a, h, and k determined?

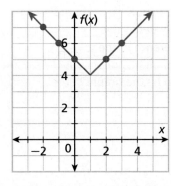
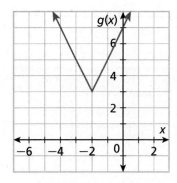

From the graphs, the minimum value of f is 4 and the minimum value of g is 3. So the function f has the greater minimum value.

The ability to compare functions given different representations is helpful for comparing a variety of key features of real-world situations.

3 Two teams are launching pumpkins. The height h_A (in feet) of Team A's pumpkin is given by the equation shown, where t is the time (in seconds) since launch. The height of Team B's pumpkin is shown by the graph. How do the maximum height and time in air of the two teams' pumpkins compare?

Team A

$$h_A(t) = -16t^2 + 56t + 18$$

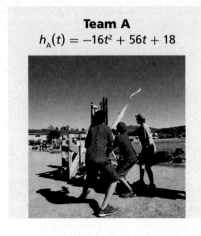

Team B

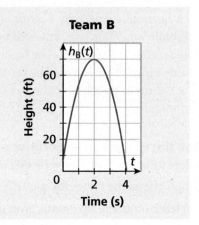

Method 1 – Use the Given Representations

Team A: The function is quadratic. The maximum height occurs at its vertex. The vertex of a quadratic function $f(x) = ax^2 + bx + c$ occurs at $x = -\frac{b}{2a}$. For $h_A(t)$, $-\frac{b}{2a} = \frac{7}{4}$.

A. How was this value calculated?

$$h_A\left(\frac{7}{4}\right) = -16\left(\frac{7}{4}\right)^2 + 56\left(\frac{7}{4}\right) + 18 = -49 + 98 + 18 = 67$$

The maximum height reached by Team A's pumpkin is 67 feet.

Team B: Only an approximation of the maximum height can be made from the graph. The graph shows that the maximum height is approximately 70 feet.

Team B's pumpkin reaches a greater maximum height.

Method 2 – Use a Common Representation

The graph of function h_A can be created using its equation.

Team A

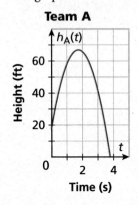

Team B

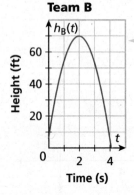

B. How can you visually determine a difference in the maximum heights shown by the graphs?

 Turn and Talk If the pumpkins are launched at the same time, how can you determine when the pumpkins reach the same height?

Check Understanding

1. In a homework problem, the table at the right is given as the representation for a quadratic function f. The equation for a function g is also given. The problem asks to compare the values of the two functions when $x = 2$. Lisa determined that $g(2) = 4$ but she says it is not possible to determine $f(2)$ since $x = 2$ is not given in the table. Do you agree or disagree? Explain your answer.

x	$f(x)$
−1	4
0	6
1	4

2. The graph of the function f is shown at the right. The graph of an absolute value function g has a slope of 2 where $x < 0$ and a slope of −2 where $x > 0$. The graph of g passes through the point $(1, -1)$. Compare the values of the two functions when $x = 0$.

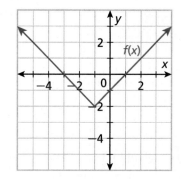

3. Jim is taking batting practice. The height of his first hit, as a function of time after the ball was hit, is represented by the table below. The height of his second hit is represented by the graph at the right. Compare the maximum heights of each hit.

Second Hit

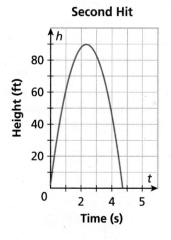

First Hit					
Time (s)	1	0.5	1	1.5	2
Height (ft)	0	20.5	32	35.5	31

On Your Own

4. **(MP)** **Use Repeated Reasoning** The graph of an exponential function f is shown at the right. The function g is a vertical compression by a factor of $\frac{1}{2}$ of the function f, followed by a horizontal translation 1 unit to the right.

   A. How is the average rate of change of f between $x = 0$ and $x = 4$ related to the average rate of change of g between these two x-values?

   B. How do the values $f(0)$ and $g(0)$ compare?

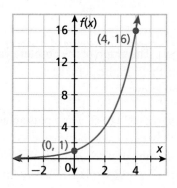

5. Teams A and B of the pumpkin launching competition in Task 3 are comparing the maximum height and distance of their launched pumpkins. The trajectory of each team's pumpkin is the relationship between the horizontal and vertical distances of the pumpkin from the point at which it was launched. The trajectory function f represents the vertical distance (in feet) for Team A's pumpkin, where x is its horizontal distance (in feet). The trajectory function g for Team B's pumpkin is represented by the data shown in the table.

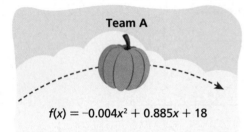

Team A

$f(x) = -0.004x^2 + 0.885x + 18$

Team B	
Horizontal distance, x (ft)	Vertical distance, $g(x)$ (ft)
0	6
50	45
100	66
150	69
200	54
250	21

A. Which team's pumpkin traveled the highest? How high did it travel? How does this value compare to the value found in Task 3?

B. Which team's pumpkin traveled the farthest? How much farther did it travel compared to the other team's pumpkin?

6. The costs for two different parking options near a civic center are shown. A cost function can be written for each option. Which option would you choose if you were parking for 20 minutes? Which option would you choose if you were parking for 150 minutes? Explain your answers.

Option 1

PARKING RATES

First half hour:
free

Each additional half hour:
$2.00

Option 2

Ⓟ RATES

up to 1 h	$1.25
up to 2 h	$2.50
up to 3 h	$3.75
up to 4 h	$5.00
up to 5 h	$6.25
up to 6 h	$7.50
up to 7 h	$8.75
up to 8 h	$10.00

7. Let $f(x) = |2 - x|$. The graph of the absolute value function g has a maximum at $(0, 2)$ and passes through the point $(2, 0)$. For what values of x is $f(x) > g(x)$? Explain how you know.

8. One plumber charges $80 to show up plus an additional $40 per hour of work. A second plumber changes customers based on the function $C(t) = 50t + 40$, where t is the number of hours of work and C is the cost in dollars. Which plumber charges more for 3 hours or work? Explain how you know.

9. Suppose the vertical height (in meters) of the support arch of the Gateshead Millennium Bridge is given by the function shown, where x is the horizontal distance (in meters) from the left bank of the river. The vertical height (in meters) of the support arch of the Sydney Harbour Bridge is shown in the graph. How do the maximum heights of the support arches for the two bridges compare?

Gateshead Millennium Bridge

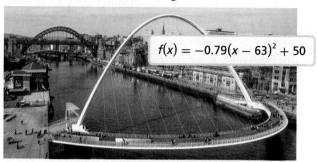

$$f(x) = -0.79(x - 63)^2 + 50$$

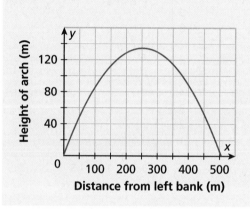

Sydney Harbour Bridge

10. The revenues of zip line companies increase to their maximums near the middle of the summer season and then decreases. The daily revenues R (in dollars), where d is the number of the day with $1 =$ January 1, of three different zip line companies are represented below. Compare the maximum daily revenue of the three companies.

   A. Which company experienced the greatest daily revenue? Which company reached its revenue peak earliest in the year?

   B. How can you determine if there is a day when two of the companies have the same daily revenue?

Company A

$R(d) = -0.067d^2 + 24.12d - 1670.8$

Company B

d (day)	$R(d)$ ($)
50	250
100	400
150	450
200	400

Company C

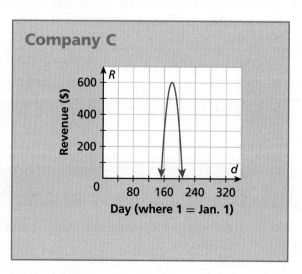

11. Trevor is comparing two containers that both have square bases. The volume of Container A is represented by the function $V_A(x) = 8x^2$, where x is the length (in centimeters) of the side of its square base. The volume of Container B is modeled by the quadratic function represented by the table. What is the difference in volume of the containers when x and s are both 2.5. Explain how you know.

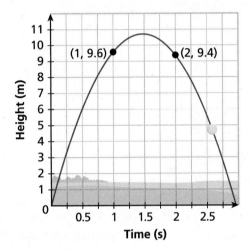

Container B	
Base side length, s (cm)	Volume, $V_B(s)$ (cm³)
2	28
4	112
6	252
8	448

12. Ann and Brian are playing golf. Their golf balls are close together near the green but there is a 10-meter tall tree between their balls and the hole. Suppose the height h (in meters) of Ann's golf ball after she hits it is modeled by $h(t) = -4.9t^2 + 13t$, where t is time in seconds. Suppose the height h of Brian's golf ball is modeled by the quadratic function shown in the graph. Will either player's golf ball go high enough to clear the tree? Why or why not?

Spiral Review • Assessment Readiness

13. Which function has the same end behavior as $f(x) = x^2 - 5$?

Ⓐ $g(x) = x - 3$

Ⓑ $g(x) = -|2x| + 1$

Ⓒ $g(x) = x^3 + 2$

Ⓓ $g(x) = 3|x + 1|$

14. The length of a rectangle is 7 inches more than its width w. If the area of the rectangle is less than or equal to 44 square inches, what is the domain of the function describing the area as a function of the width w?

Ⓐ $w \leq 4$　　　　Ⓒ $w \leq 11$

Ⓑ $w \leq 7$　　　　Ⓓ $w \leq 44$

15. The parent graph $f(x) = |x|$ is transformed to obtain the graph of $g(x)$. Match each transformation equation on the left with the description of the transformation on the right.

A. $g(x) = 2f(x)$　　　　**1.** translation 2 units right

B. $g(x) = f(x - 2)$　　　　**2.** translation 2 units down

C. $g(x) = f(x) - 2$　　　　**3.** vertical stretch by a factor of 2

D. $g(x) = f(2x)$　　　　**4.** horizontal compression by a factor of 2

 I'm in a Learning Mindset!

Who can support me while I learn about different representations of functions?

Review

Domain, Range, and End Behavior

The graph of a function is shown. You can use the graph to identify its domain, range, and end behavior.

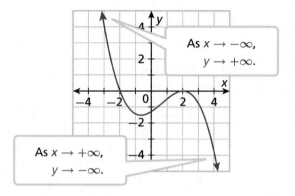

As $x \rightarrow -\infty$, $y \rightarrow +\infty$.

As $x \rightarrow +\infty$, $y \rightarrow -\infty$.

Domain: $\{x \mid x \in \mathbb{R}\}$; Range: $\{x \mid x \in \mathbb{R}\}$

Characteristics of Functions

The graph of the height of a kicked ball over time reveals key characteristics of the function.

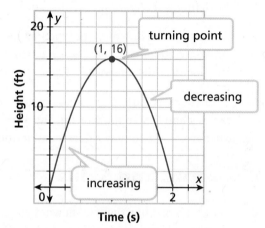

turning point

(1, 16)

decreasing

increasing

The graph has zeros at $x = 0$ and $x = 2$. It has a maximum value of 16 when $x = 1$.

Transformations

The function $g(x) = -16(x - 1)^2 + 16$ models the kicked ball's height. You can identify how $g(x)$ transforms the parent function $f(x) = x^2$ by using the transformation model $g(x) = af(x - h) + k$.

$a = -16$: vertical stretch by a factor of 16 and a reflection across the x-axis

$h = 1$: horizontal translation 1 unit right

$k = 16$: vertical translation 16 units up

You can also identify how $g(x)$ maps the reference points $(-1, 1)$, $(0, 0)$, and $(1, 1)$ on the graph of $f(x) = x^2$ to the graph of the ball's height:

$(-1, 1) \rightarrow (-1 + 1, -16(1) + 16) = (0, 0)$
$(0, 0) \rightarrow (0 + 1, -16(0) + 16) = (1, 16)$
$(1, 1) \rightarrow (1 + 1, -16(1) + 16) = (2, 0)$

Different Representations

A basketball is shot at the same time the ball above is kicked. Its height is given in the table.

Time (s)	0	0.75	1.5	1.75
Height (ft)	8	17	8	1

You can compare the heights of the balls by graphing the data. By symmetry, you can see that it gives the basketball's maximum height, which is 1 foot higher than the other ball's.

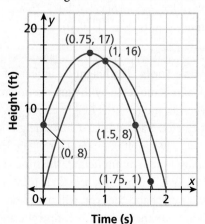

(0.75, 17)

(1, 16)

(1.5, 8)

(0, 8)

(1.75, 1)

Vocabulary

Choose the correct term from the box to complete each sentence.

1. A(n) ___?___ is a constant in a function or equation that may be changed.

2. A function f is a(n) ___?___ if $f(-x) = -f(x)$ for all x in the domain of f, and a(n) ___?___ if $f(-x) = f(x)$ for all x in the domain of f.

3. A(n) ___?___ is the simplest example of a family of functions that has the defining characteristics of the family.

4. The ratio of the difference of function values $f(b) - f(a)$ to the corresponding difference of domain values $b - a$ on an interval $[a, b]$ is the ___?___ of the function over the interval.

5. A function f is a(n) ___?___ on an interval if $f(a) < f(b)$ whenever $a < b$ for any values a and b from the interval, and a(n) ___?___ on an interval if $f(a) > f(b)$ whenever $a < b$ for any values a and b from the interval.

Concepts and Skills

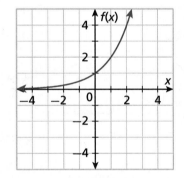

6. The graph of a function f is shown. Use set notation and interval notation to write the domain and range of the function, and describe the end behavior of the graph.

7. Julieta walks at a steady rate straight from her house to the park, where she sits on a bench and watches the birds and squirrels for a while. Afterward, Julieta jogs at a steady rate straight home. What would a sketch of a graph showing Julieta's distance from home as a function of time look like? Include a description of some of the characteristics of the graph.

8. The graph of a function for the distance y, in feet, an object falls in x seconds passes through $(0, 0)$, $(1, 16)$, $(2, 64)$, $(3, 144)$, $(4, 256)$, and $(5, 400)$. What is the average rate of change over the first two seconds? the last two seconds? the entire time?

9. A transformation of the graph of a function $f(x)$ has equation $g(x) = f\big(3(x + 2)\big) - 1$. How can the graph of $f(x)$ be transformed to obtain the graph of $g(x)$?

10. Describe how to transform the graph of $f(x) = |x|$ to obtain the graph of $f(x) = \big|-0.5(x + 4)\big| + 7$. What are the images of the reference points $(-1, 1)$, $(0, 0)$, and $(1, 1)$ on the transformed graph?

11. **(MP) Use Tools** The height h_1, in feet, of a rock ejected from a volcano is modeled by the graph shown, where t is measured in seconds and h_1 is the height above the volcano. Another rock ejected 5 seconds later has a height h_2 modeled by $h_2(t) = -16t^2 + 400t - 1600$ for $t \geq 5$. How do the rocks compare in maximum height, the time at which they return to their original heights, and their total time of flight? State what strategy and tool you will use to answer the question, explain your choice, and then find the answer.

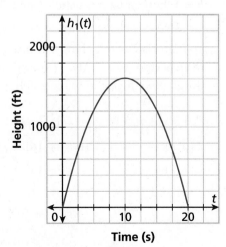

2 Solve Quadratic Equations and Systems

Module Performance Task: Focus on STEM

Engineering Structural Resilience

A tuned mass damper (TMD) is a device mounted in structures to reduce the maximum extent of a vibration. In some ways, a TMD is like a shock absorber in a car—it absorbs mechanical kinetic energy. As wind, earthquakes, and other events perturb the building, the resulting vibrations can be intense, causing the occupants to become ill and even threatening the structural integrity of the building. The John Hancock Tower needed to be retrofitted with a TMD for this reason.

Engineers use the equation $mx^2 + bx + k = 0$ to determine whether a TMD is underdamped, critically damped, or overdamped by analyzing the number of real solutions (2, 1, or 0) in the system.

The number of solutions is determined by the three parameters, k, a spring constant $\left(\text{kg/s}^2\right)$, b, a constant that describes the damping force (kg/s), and m, a mass (kg).

A. Graph the equation with a variety of values for the parameters and categorize different combinations as underdamped, critically damped, or overdamped.

B. Describe what it means to be underdamped, critically damped, and overdamped.

C. Write an algebraic condition that ensures a given combination of parameters will define a critically damped system.

D. Research the three parameters and summarize your findings by describing the relationship between them. Use your research as evidence when explaining your reasoning.

Are You Ready?

Complete these problems to review prior concepts and skills you will need for this module.

Simplify Square Roots

Simplify each square root completely.

1. $\sqrt{48}$

2. $\sqrt{72}$

3. $\sqrt{343}$

4. $6\sqrt{45}$

5. $8\sqrt{112}$

6. $5\sqrt{200}$

Multiply Binomials

Find each product. Simplify your result.

7. $(4x - 1)(x + 7)$

8. $(x - 2)(x - 9)$

9. $(2x + 3)(6x - 5)$

10. $(x^2 - 3x - 1)(x^2 + 1)$

Solve Quadratic Equations Using the Quadratic Formula

Solve each equation using the Quadratic Formula. Simplify your result.

11. $x^2 - 2x - 15 = 0$

12. $9x^2 - 5 = 12x - 5$

13. $-4x^2 + 6x = 1$

14. $2x^2 + 11x + 6 = 0$

Connecting Past and Present Learning

Previously, you learned:

- to simplify square roots by factoring out any perfect squares,
- to multiply polynomials using the Distributive Property, and
- to solve quadratic equations using square roots, completing the square, and the Quadratic Formula.

In this module, you will learn:

- to find imaginary and complex solutions to quadratic equations by taking the square root, completing the square, or by using the Quadratic Formula,
- to operate with imaginary and complex numbers, and
- to solve systems of nonlinear functions graphically and algebraically.

Use Square Roots to Solve Quadratic Equations

(I Can) use equations to model and solve real-world problems.

Spark Your Learning

A bungee jumper, wearing safety equipment, falls backward from a platform. They claim that they were in a free fall for 5 seconds before the bungee cord recoiled.

Acceleration due to gravity is 9.8 m/s².

Complete Part A as a whole class. Then complete Parts B–D in small groups.

A. What is a mathematical question you can ask about this situation? What information would you need to know to answer your question?

B. What do the input and output of the function represent? What unit of measurement is used for each?

C. To answer your question, what strategy and tool would you use along with all the information you have? What answer do you get?

D. Does your answer make sense in the context of the situation? How do you know?

Turn and Talk Predict how your answer would change for each of the following changes in the situation:
- a taller platform
- a longer bungee cord
- stronger or weaker gravity

Build Understanding

Investigate Solutions of Simple Quadratic Equations

Recall that the number x is a square root of a real number a provided $x^2 = a$. To solve for the square root of a graphically, plot $f(x) = x^2$ and $g(x) = a$ on the same coordinate grid. The square roots of a, if any exist, are represented by the x-values of the intersection points of the graphs of $f(x) = x^2$ and $g(x) = a$.

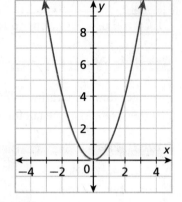

1 ▶ For Parts A–E, use a graph to consider how many real solutions exist for any simple quadratic equation.

    A. Consider the equation $x^2 = 9$. What are the solution(s) to the equation? How does the graph represent the solution(s)?

    B. Consider the equation $x^2 = 12$. What are the solution(s) to the equation? Does the graph allow you do determine an exact solution? Explain why or why not.

    C. Consider the equation $x^2 = 0$. What are the solution(s) to the equation? What characteristics of 0 distinguish it from other numbers? How does this change the number of potential solutions?

    D. Consider the equation $x^2 = -1$. What are the solution(s) to the equation? Explain your reasoning.

    E. Consider the equation $x^2 = a$. What can you conclude about the number of solutions? Explain your reasoning.

    F. Ariana is looking to purchase a square painting that will fill 10 square feet of wall space. Write and solve a simple quadratic equation to find the side length of the square painting, x. Explain your reasoning.

 Turn and Talk What can you conclude about the number of solutions for the equation $bx^2 = a$? Explain your reasoning.

Investigate Non-Real Solutions of Simple Quadratic Equations

You saw that $x^2 = -1$ had no real-number solutions. When a number system does not meet your needs as a mathematician, you can develop a new extension. Define a number i such that $i^2 = -1$. Then i is a solution to the equation, and thus i is a square root of -1. When you take the square root of a negative number, the result is called an **imaginary number**. The equation $x^2 = -1$ now has two imaginary solutions, $x = \pm i$.

Imaginary Unit
$i = \sqrt{-1}$

Imaginary numbers have the form ri, where r is a nonzero real number and i is the **imaginary unit**.

2 Consider the equation $x^2 = -4$. The solutions steps are shown.

$$x^2 = -4$$
$$x = \pm\sqrt{-4}$$
$$= \pm\sqrt{4 \cdot -1}$$
$$= \pm\sqrt{4} \cdot \sqrt{-1}$$
$$= \pm 2i$$

A. How are the solutions of $x^2 = -4$ related to the solutions of $x^2 = 4$?

B. What are the solution(s) of $x^2 = -9$? How can you demonstrate that your answer is truly a solution?

C. How are the solutions of $x^2 = -a$ related to the solutions of $x^2 = a$?

 Turn and Talk Are the solutions of $x^2 = -a$ always imaginary? Explain your reasoning.

3 To determine the type of solution(s) a given equation will have, rewrite the equation into the form $(x - k)^2 = a$. Some equations are categorized in a table below.

A. How can you classify the solutions of $(x + 2)^2 = 2$? the solutions of $-2(x + 5)^2 = 8$?

B. How can you tell if the solutions are real? Explain your reasoning.

C. Give a value of a that ensures the equation $2(x - 8)^2 = a$ has exactly one real solution. Explain your reasoning.

D. Is it possible to have only one imaginary solution? Explain your reasoning.

E. What can you conclude about the number of solutions for the equation $b(x - k)^2 + c = a$? Explain your reasoning.

Two real solutions	$-3x^2 = -2$ $(x - 3)^2 = 1$
One real solution	$3x^2 = 0$
Two imaginary solutions	$x^2 = -5$ $-2x^2 = 1$ $(x - 3)^2 = -1$

 Turn and Talk How can you use a graph to determine the type of solution(s) a given equation will have?

Step It Out

Find Real Solutions of Simple Quadratic Equations

When communicating solutions, it is helpful to reduce solutions to the simplest form possible. When solving quadratic equations, you will often need to simplify a square root. You may need to use the following properties to simplify your solution.

Property Name	Words	Symbols	Numbers
Product Property of Square Roots	The square root of a product equals the product of the square roots of the factors.	$\sqrt{cd} = \sqrt{c} \cdot \sqrt{d}$ where $c \geq 0$ and $d \geq 0$	$\sqrt{20} = \sqrt{4 \cdot 5}$ $= \sqrt{4} \cdot \sqrt{5}$ $= 2\sqrt{5}$
Quotient Property of Square Roots	The square root of a fraction equals the quotient of the square roots of the numerator and the denominator.	$\sqrt{\frac{c}{d}} = \frac{\sqrt{c}}{\sqrt{d}}$ where $c \geq 0$ and $d > 0$	$\sqrt{\frac{7}{16}} = \frac{\sqrt{7}}{\sqrt{16}}$ $= \frac{\sqrt{7}}{4}$

Additionally, when the denominator contains an irrational number, you must rationalize the denominator.

Step 1: Multiply by 1, written as an equivalent fraction with the same square root as the denominator.

Step 2: Then, simplify.

$$\frac{2}{\sqrt{10}} = \frac{2}{\sqrt{10}} \cdot \frac{\sqrt{10}}{\sqrt{10}} = \frac{2\sqrt{10}}{\sqrt{100}} = \frac{2\sqrt{10}}{10} = \frac{\sqrt{10}}{5}$$

4 ▶ Determine the solution(s) of the equation $3x^2 - 8 = 0$.

$3x^2 - 8 = 0$

$3x^2 = 8$

$x^2 = \frac{8}{3}$

$x = \pm\sqrt{\frac{8}{3}}$

A. Why is there a $\pm$ in this step?

$x = \pm\frac{\sqrt{8}}{\sqrt{3}}$

B. Why should the answer continue to be rewritten?

$x = \pm\frac{\sqrt{8}}{\sqrt{3}} \cdot \frac{\sqrt{3}}{\sqrt{3}}$

C. Why can you multiply by $\frac{\sqrt{3}}{\sqrt{3}}$?

$x = \pm\frac{\sqrt{24}}{3}$

D. What property is being applied in this step?

$x = \pm\frac{\sqrt{4} \cdot \sqrt{6}}{3}$

E. How can you verify that both of these values are solutions?

$x = \pm\frac{2\sqrt{6}}{3}$

Find Imaginary Solutions of Simple Quadratic Equations

You can solve simple quadratic equations that do not have real solutions by using imaginary numbers.

5 ▶ The steps for solving the equation $9x^2 + 15 = 8$ and checking the solution are shown below, but the steps have been scrambled.

A. Write the solutions steps in the correct order.

$$9x^2 = -7$$

$$x = \pm \frac{\sqrt{7}}{3} i$$

$$x = \pm \sqrt{\frac{-7}{9}}$$

$$x^2 = -\frac{7}{9}$$

$$9x^2 + 15 = 8$$

B. Write the check steps in the correct order.

$$8 = 8$$

$$9 \left(\frac{7}{9}\right) i^2 + 15 \overset{?}{=} 8$$

$$7i^2 + 15 \overset{?}{=} 8$$

$$9 \left(\pm \frac{\sqrt{7}}{3} i\right)^2 + 15 \overset{?}{=} 8$$

$$-7 + 15 \overset{?}{=} 8$$

Solve a Real-World Problem Using a Quadratic Model

Quadratic equations can be used to model real-world situations. It is often the case that only one solution will be viable in the context of the situation.

A projectile near Earth's surface follows a quadratic trajectory as gravity, $g = 32$ ft/s^2, pulls it down to Earth. The height, $h(t)$, at time t seconds, is then dependent on its initial height, h_0.

6 ▶ A person drops an orange from a window that is 30 feet above the ground. After how long will the orange land on the ground?

$$h(t) = h_0 - \frac{1}{2}gt^2$$

$$0 = 30 - \frac{1}{2}(32)t^2$$

$$-30 = -16t^2$$

$$\frac{-30}{-16} = t^2$$

$$\pm \sqrt{\frac{30}{16}} = t$$

$$\pm \sqrt{\frac{30}{4}} = t$$

A. What are the units of each variable?

B. What do the values 0, 30, and 32 represent?

C. Why isn't the negative solution viable in the context of this situation?

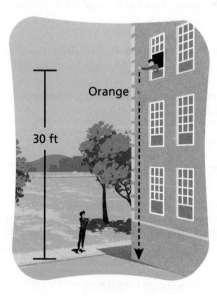

Orange

30 ft

The orange lands on the ground after $t = \frac{\sqrt{30}}{4}$ seconds.

 Turn and Talk In what other contexts would a negative solution not be viable?

Check Understanding

1. How can you use a graph to determine the number of real solutions to the equation $x^2 = a$?

2. If the solutions to $x^2 = a$ are given by $x = \pm\sqrt{a}$, what are the solutions to $x^2 = -a$? Explain your reasoning.

Determine if the following equations have two real solutions, one real solution, or two imaginary solutions.

3. $-3x^2 = -3$

4. $x^2 + 5 = 1$

Solve the following equations and write your solution in simplest form.

5. $2x^2 - 45 = 0$

6. $8x^2 + 30 = 4$

7. A patio is composed of two parts, a square and a rectangle. The rectangular part has an area of 120 square feet and the total area is 376 square feet.

   A. Write and solve an equation to find the side length of the square part of the patio.

   B. Explain whether or not all solutions are viable.

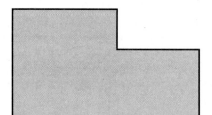

On Your Own

8. How can you use a graph to determine the type of solutions a quadratic equation will have?

9. How can you use algebra to determine the type of solutions a simple quadratic equation will have?

10. (MP) **Critique Reasoning** Penelope solved the equation $x^2 + 25 = 0$ to get $x = 5$ or $x = -5$. Did Penelope solve the equation correctly? Explain why or why not.

Determine if the following equations have two real solutions, one real solution, or two imaginary solutions.

11. $3x^2 - 240 = 0$

12. $-5x^2 = 60$

13. $\frac{x^2}{4} + 9 = 0$

14. $7(x + 1)^2 - 24 = 0$

15. $2(3x^2 + 16) = 32$

16. $-\frac{x^2}{2} + 12 = 0$

Open Ended Write a simple quadratic equation of the form $ax^2 + b = c$, where $a \neq 0$, $b \neq 0$, and $c \neq 0$, with the following types of solutions.

17. real, integer solutions

18. real, irrational solutions

19. imaginary solutions

20. Given a simple quadratic equation of the form $ax^2 + b = c$, what can you conclude if the equation has only one solution? Explain your reasoning.

Solve the following equations. Show the check steps for your solutions.

21. $x^2 = -25$

22. $(x + 2)^2 - 3 = 1$

23. $3(x - 1)^2 = -27$

24. $4x^2 - 25 = 0$

Solve the following equations. Write your solution in simplest form.

25. $5x^2 + 84 = -36$

26. $18x^2 - 1 = 0$

27. $4(x - 2)^2 = 9$

28. $4x^2 + 24 = 9$

29. The area of a square is 400 square inches.

    A. Write and solve an equation to find the side length of the square.

    B. Are all solutions viable? Explain your reasoning.

30. A batter hits a baseball into the air to a maximum height of h feet. It descends until the outfielder catches the ball y feet above the ground. The height in feet of the ball after it descends for t seconds is modeled by the equation $y = h - 16t^2$. Solve this equation for t, the time the ball has been descending.

31. (MP) **Model with Mathematics** Carlos drops a rock from a platform that is 50 feet tall. The equation $h = -16t^2 + 50$ models the height of the rock as it falls, where h is the height in feet and t is the time in seconds.

    A. After how long will the rock land on the ground?

    B. Are all solutions viable? Explain your reasoning.

    C. Jeanine sees the rock when it is about half way to the floor. If s is the number of seconds she has been watching the rock, what would the negative values of s represent?

32. Kiaya leans a 10-foot ladder against the house she is painting. The ladder forms a right triangle with the house. How high can the ladder reach on the house?

    A. How can you use the Pythagorean Theorem to find how high the ladder can reach on the house?

    B. Write and solve an equation you can solve in order to find how high the ladder can reach on the house. Round your answer to the nearest tenth of a foot.

    C. How far above the top of the ladder in feet must Kiaya be able to reach in order to paint a spot 12 feet above the ground?

3 ft

33. (MP) **Use Structure** A water balloon is shot straight into the air, and its height h in meters above its release point after t seconds is modeled by a quadratic equation. After how many seconds will the water balloon return to its release height?

$$h = 20t - 5t^2$$

A. What are the values of t and h when the water balloon is at its release point?

B. Can you take a square root to solve this equation? Explain why or why not.

C. Are all solutions viable? Explain your reasoning.

Spiral Review • Assessment Readiness

34. How do you transform the graph of $f(x) = |x|$ to obtain the related function $g(x) = -f(x)$?

Ⓐ translation 1 unit down

Ⓑ reflection over the x-axis

Ⓒ reflection over the y-axis

Ⓓ vertical compression; factor of -1

35. Which expression is equivalent to $7y - 3(2y + 4) + 2$?

Ⓐ $13y - 14$

Ⓑ $13y - 10$

Ⓒ $y - 14$

Ⓓ $y - 10$

36. Match the type of representation of a function on the left with its strength on the right.

A. Graph

B. Equation

C. Verbal Description

D. Table

1. useful for aiding in visualization and interpretation, particularly when compared to the parent function

2. can help identify/approximate intercepts and key values, as well as reveal any symmetry of the function

3. provides a quick visual for the approximate maximum/minimum values, intervals of increasing/deceasing behavior, x- and y-intercepts, symmetry, and key values

4. can be used to find any value given one of the variable values

 I'm in a Learning Mindset!

What can I contribute to my learning community regarding quadratic equations or projectile motion?

Operations with Complex Numbers

(I Can) identify, add, subtract, and multiply complex numbers.

Spark Your Learning

Whenever something is flowing, there is opposition to that flow, whether from friction or other obstacles. In an electric circuit, there are three components that produce an opposition, or impedance, which are represented by real or imaginary numbers depending on how it relates to the phase of the flow.

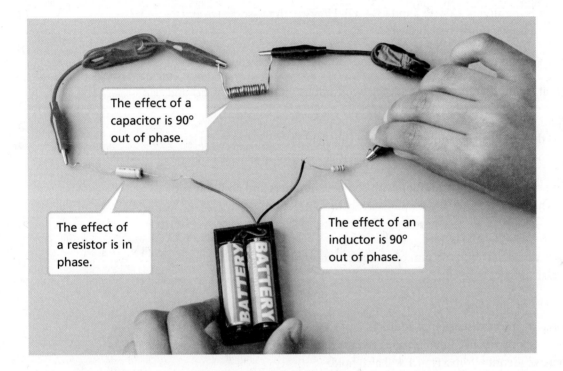

The effect of a capacitor is 90° out of phase.

The effect of a resistor is in phase.

The effect of an inductor is 90° out of phase.

Complete Part A as a whole class. Then complete Parts B–D in small groups.

A. What is a mathematical question you can ask about the current flowing through the circuit? What information would you need to know to answer your question?

B. What does the word impede mean? Why would impedance be used to describe this phenomenon?

C. Why is the impedance represented by two different types of numbers? How do the different components of opposition interact?

D. To answer your question, what strategy and tool would you use along with all the information you have? What answer do you get?

 Turn and Talk Assume that the electric circuit has a current of $24 + 12i$. Multiply the current by the total opposition you found. What do you notice about the product?

Build Understanding

Explore Operations Involving Complex Numbers

In this lesson, you'll perform operations with complex numbers. A **complex number** is any number that can be written in the form $a + bi$, where a and b are real numbers and i is the imaginary unit. You will be working with the same operations as with real numbers, and so, their properties will also hold. The Associative and Commutative Properties of Addition apply to the complex number system. The Additive Identity Property of 0 will also hold. The system of polynomials is directly analogous to the system of complex numbers through the substitution $x = i$.

  A. What is the sum of $(2 + 6x)$ and $(3 - x)$? How are the Associative and Commutative Properties applied?

    B. What would be the sum of $(2 + 6i)$ and $(3 - i)$? What do you observe?

    C. What would be a formula for adding two complex numbers, $(a + bi)$ and $(c + di)$?

    D. Use the formula you wrote in Part C to calculate $(4 - i) + (-7 + 3i)$. Do you get the same sum when using the Associative and Commutative Properties?

    E. Compare and contrast addition with complex numbers and addition with polynomials. Do your observations apply to subtraction?

 Turn and Talk Will the sum of two complex numbers always be complex? Explain why or why not.

Multiplication is a natural extension of addition, and so, the Associative, Commutative and Distributive Properties of Multiplication also apply to the complex number system. The Multiplicative Identity Property of 1 will also hold.

  A. What is the product of $(2 + 6x)$ and $(3 - x)$? How are the Associative, Commutative and Distributive Properties applied?

    B. What would be the product of $(2 + 6i)$ and $(3 - i)$? What do you observe?

    C. What would be a formula for multiplying two complex numbers, $(a + bi)$ and $(c + di)$?

    D. Use the formula you wrote in Part C to multiply $(5 - 3i)$ by $(-1 + 4i)$. Do you get the same product when using the Associative, Commutative, and Distributive Properties?

    E. Compare and contrast multiplication with complex numbers and multiplication with polynomials. Do your observations apply to division?

 Turn and Talk Will the product of two complex numbers always be complex? Explain why or why not.

Step It Out

Define Complex Numbers

In a complex number, $a + bi$, a is called the real part and b is called the imaginary part. (Note that the imaginary part refers to the real multiplier of i; it does not refer to the imaginary number bi.) The Venn diagram shows some examples of complex numbers.

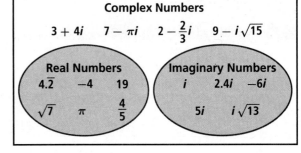

Complex Numbers

$3 + 4i$ $7 - \pi i$ $2 - \frac{2}{3}i$ $9 - i\sqrt{15}$

Real Numbers
$4.\overline{2}$ -4 19
$\sqrt{7}$ π $\frac{4}{5}$

Imaginary Numbers
i $2.4i$ $-6i$
$5i$ $i\sqrt{13}$

3 ▸ Match the expression on the left with the type of number on the right. Each expression may have more than one correct type.

A. $-6i$

B. $-5 + 2i$

C. 14.6

D. 0

E. i^2

1. Real Number

2. Imaginary Number

3. Complex Number

Turn and Talk Is an imaginary number always complex? Is a complex number always imaginary? Explain your reasoning.

Add and Subtract Complex Numbers

The properties of addition and multiplication (Associative Property, Commutative Property, Identity Property, and Distributive Property) also apply to complex numbers. You can use these properties to operate with complex numbers and simplify the result.

When adding and subtracting complex numbers, group like terms to add or subtract the real and imaginary parts separately.

$$(a + bi) + (c + di) = (a + c) + (b + d)i$$

4 ▸ Subtract $(3 + 2i) - (-4 + 7i)$.

$(3 + 2i) - (-4 + 7i) = 3 + 2i + 4 + (-7i)$ Distributive Property

$= 3 + 4 + 2i + (-7i)$

    A. What property allows these terms to change places?

$= (3 + 4) + (2 - 7)i$

    B. What property allows i to be factored out?

$= 7 - 5i$

Turn and Talk Can the sum or difference of two complex numbers be a purely real number? Can the sum or difference be purely imaginary? Explain why or why not.

Multiply Complex Numbers

The Distributive Property holds when multiplying complex numbers, just like when multiplying real numbers.

5   Multiply $(-4 + 7i)(2 + 3i)$.

$$(-4 + 7i)(2 + 3i) = (-4)(2 + 3i) + (7i)(2 + 3i)$$

$$= -8 - 12i + 14i + 21i^2$$ **A. What property justifies this step?**

$$= -8 - 12i + 14i + 21(-1)$$

$$= (-8 - 21) + (-12 + 14)i$$ **B. What definition justifies this step?**

$$= -29 + 2i$$

 Turn and Talk Can the product of two complex numbers be a purely real number? Can the product be purely imaginary? Explain why or why not.

Divide Complex Numbers

When dividing complex numbers, you need to ensure that the denominator is a real, rational number, just like when you rationalize the denominator. In order to do so, you need will need to multiply by a fraction, equivalent to 1, with a denominator referred to as the *complex conjugate*. The product of a complex number and its complex conjugate is always a real number.

Complex Number	Complex Conjugate
$a + bi$	$a - bi$

6   Simplify the expression $\dfrac{3 - 2i}{4 + i}$.

$$\frac{3 - 4i}{5 + 2i} = \frac{3 - 4i}{5 + 2i} \cdot \frac{5 - 2i}{5 - 2i}$$ **A. Why can you multiply by $\dfrac{5 - 2i}{5 - 2i}$?**

$$= \frac{15 - 6i - 20i + 8i^2}{25 - 10i + 10i - 4i^2}$$

$$= \frac{15 - 26i - 8}{25 + 4}$$ **B. Why is $-4i^2 = 4$?**

$$= \frac{7 - 26i}{29}$$

$$= \frac{7}{29} - \frac{26}{29}i$$

 Turn and Talk How can you express the product of a complex number and its complex conjugate in a general form? Justify your reasoning.

Solve a Real-World Problem Using Complex Numbers

Electrical engineers analyze electric circuits by using complex numbers. In an electric circuit, there are three kinds of components. The table shows each component and its symbol as well as the complex number that represents it.

Circuit Component	Resistor	Inductor	Capacitor
Symbol in a circuit diagram			
Representation as a complex number	A real number a	An imaginary number bi, where $b > 0$	An imaginary number bi, where $b < 0$

An alternating current (AC) electric circuit diagram shows a power source on the left side of the diagram, labeled 120 V (for volts). The power source causes electrons to flow through the circuit. The *impedance*, or opposition to the flow of the electrons, of each component of the circuit is also shown using complex numbers.

7 ▶ **Use the diagram of the electric circuit to answer the following questions.**

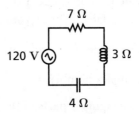

The total impedance in the circuit is the sum of the impedances for the individual components. What is the total impedance for the given circuit?

Write the impedance for each individual component as a complex number.

Resistor: 7 Inductor: $3i$ Capacitor: $-4i$

Total impedance: $7 - i$

> **A.** Why is the total impedance a complex number?

Ohm's Law states that the voltage is the product of the current and the impedance. If the current for this circuit is $16.8 + 2.4i$ amps, what is the voltage, V, for each component in the circuit?

$V_{resistor} = (16.8 + 2.4i)(7) = 117.6 + 16.8i$

$V_{inductor} = (16.8 + 2.4i)(3i) = -7.2 + 50.4i$

> **B.** Will the voltage always have a real and an imaginary part?

$V_{capacitor} = (16.8 + 2.4i)(-4i) = 9.6 - 67.2i$

 Turn and Talk Find the sum of the voltages for the three components. What do you notice?

Check Understanding

What properties apply to the following operations with complex numbers?

1. Addition

2. Multiplication

3. Identify the real and imaginary parts of the complex number $-12i$.

Perform the following operations.

4. $(-4 - 9i) + (15 - 3i)$ **5.** $(5 - 6i)(-2 - 10i)$ **6.** $4 \div (1 + i)$

7. A circuit shows that the impedance of a component is $-56i$. Is the component a resistor, a capacitor, or an inductor?

On Your Own

8. Find the sum of the binomials $4 + 3x$ and $5 - 2x$. Explain how you can use the result to find the sum of the complex numbers $4 + 3i$ and $5 - 2i$.

9. Find the product of the binomials $2 - x$ and $1 + 3x$. Explain how you can use the result to find the product of the complex numbers $2 - i$ and $1 + 3i$.

Tell whether each statement about the properties of complex numbers is True or False. If the statement is false, explain your answer.

10. The Commutative Property of Addition states that $a + bi = b + ai$.

11. Subtraction of complex numbers is commutative.

Identify the real and imaginary parts of the given complex numbers. Then classify the number as real, imaginary, or complex.

12. $6 + i$ **13.** $i\sqrt{17}$ **14.** $8 - 2i$

15. $\sqrt{43}$ **16.** 13 **17.** $20i$

Tell whether each statement about the types of numbers is True or False. If the statement is false, explain your answer.

18. All complex numbers are imaginary numbers.

19. The sum of two complex numbers is always a complex number.

20. Every real number is a complex number.

21. The product of two imaginary numbers is a real number.

Add.

22. $(4 + 6i) + (7 + 3i)$ **23.** $(5 - 2i) + (2 - i)$

24. $(-2 + 3i) + (5 - 4i)$ **25.** $(7 - 4i) + (-1 - 9i)$

Subtract.

26. $(2 + 3i) - (5 + 4i)$ **27.** $(6 - i) - (8 - 2i)$

28. $(-7 - 4i) - (-9 - 3i)$ **29.** $(10 - i) - (3 - 5i)$

Multiply.

30. $(1 + 2i)(4 + 3i)$

31. $(-5 - i)(-3 - 2i)$

32. $(-4 - 7i)(2 + 5i)$

33. $(3 + 9i)(-6 - 4i)$

Divide.

34. $\dfrac{5i}{3 - i}$

35. $\dfrac{2 + i}{1 + i}$

36. $\dfrac{7}{1 - 2i}$

37. $\dfrac{17}{4 - i}$

Elaborate, self-similar figures, called *fractals*, can be plotted on the complex plane using a recursive rule.

38. Just as real numbers can be graphed on a real number line, complex numbers can be graphed on a complex plane, which has a horizontal real axis and a vertical imaginary axis.

Consider Julia sets having the recursive quadratic rule $f(n + 1) = \big(f(n)\big)^2 + c$ for some complex constant c. A complex number $f(0)$ belongs to the "filled-in" Julia set if the magnitude of the numbers in the sequence remains bounded.

A. Letting $c = i$ and $f(0) = 1$, generate the first few numbers in the sequence. Copy and complete the table.

n	$f(n)$	$f(n + 1) = \big(f(n)\big)^2 + i$
0	$f(0) = 1$	$f(1) = \big(f(0)\big)^2 + i = (1)^2 + i = 1 + i$
1	$f(1) = 1 + i$	$f(2) = \big(f(1)\big)^2 + i = (1 + i)^2 + i = \underline{\ ?\ }$
2	$f(2) = \underline{\ ?\ }$	$f(3) = \big(f(2)\big)^2 + i = \big(\underline{\ ?\ }\big)^2 + i = \underline{\ ?\ }$
3	$f(3) = \underline{\ ?\ }$	$f(4) = \big(f(3)\big)^2 + i = \big(\underline{\ ?\ }\big)^2 + i = \underline{\ ?\ }$

B. The *magnitude* of a complex number $a + bi$ is the real number $\sqrt{a^2 + b^2}$. What does this quantity represent in the complex plane?

C. Based on your table, does $f(0) = 1$ belong to the "filled-in" Julia set corresponding to $c = i$? Explain.

D. Does $f(0) = i$ belong to the "filled-in" Julia set corresponding to $c = i$? Explain.

Use the diagram of the electric circuit and the given current to find the total impedance for the circuit and the voltage for each component.

39.

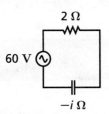

The current for this circuit is $24 + 12i$ amps

40.

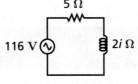

The current for this circuit is $20 - 8i$ amps.

41. (MP) **Attend to Precision** Kailey multiplied $(3 - 4i)(4 + 3i)$. Did Kailey multiply correctly? Explain why or why not.

$$(3 - 4i)(4 + 3i) = 12 + 9i - 16i - 12i^2$$

$$= 12 + 9i - 16i - 12(1)$$

$$= 12 + 9i - 16i - 12$$

$$= -7i$$

42. (MP) **Reason** Show that $\sqrt{5} + i\sqrt{5}$ and $-\sqrt{5} - i\sqrt{5}$ are the square roots of $10i$.

43. (Open Middle™) Using the integers -9 to 9, at most one time each, fill in the boxes to make a real-number product with the least possible value.

$$\left(\boxed{} + \boxed{}\, i \right)\left(\boxed{} + \boxed{}\, i \right)$$

Spiral Review • Assessment Readiness

44. What is the solution to the equation $3(x + 4)^2 = 27$? Select all that apply.

    Ⓐ $x = -7$ Ⓓ $x = 1$

    Ⓑ $x = -3$ Ⓔ $x = 3$

    Ⓒ $x = -1$ Ⓕ $x = 7$

45. Laura completes 5 pages in 2 hours and then 5 pages in the next hour. Jason's page count is given by $p(t) = 3t$. When does Laura surpass Jason's page count?

    Ⓐ 2 h   Ⓒ 3 h

    Ⓑ 2.5 h   Ⓓ 3.5 h

46. Determine if the following equations have two real solutions, one real solution, or two imaginary solutions.

Equation	Two Reals	One Real	Two Imaginary
A. $2 = 4.5x - 7x^2$	?	?	?
B. $-6 = -1.5 + 3.2x$	?	?	?
C. $2 = |3x + 4|$	?	?	?

 I'm in a Learning Mindset!

Who can support me in my learning about complex numbers?

Derive and Apply the Quadratic Formula

(I Can) **find the solutions of any quadratic equation.**

Spark Your Learning

Jesse is practicing shooting free throws.

10 ft

15 ft

Complete Part A as a whole class. Then complete Parts B–D in small groups.

   A. What is a mathematical question you can ask about this situation? What
      information would you need to know to answer your question?

   B. What variable(s) are involved in this situation? Are there any reasonable
      assumptions that should be made? Explain your reasoning.

   C. To answer your question, what strategy and tool would you use along with
      all the information you have? What answer do you get?

   D. Does your answer make sense in the context of the situation? How do you
      know?

 Turn and Talk How many times does the function reach the height of the
basketball hoop? Is it possible for the ball to go in at more than one point? How
does the slope affect your conclusion? Explain your reasoning.

Build Understanding

Investigate Non-Real Solutions of Quadratic Equations

Recall from Lesson 2.1 that you found that there are no real solutions for the equation $ax^2 = c$ when $c < 0$. However, you learned to find the imaginary solutions by taking square roots.

1 A softball player hits a softball into the air. The path of the softball is given by the function $y = -0.14(x - 10)^2 + 15$, where x is the horizontal distance (in meters) the ball has traveled and y is the vertical distance (in meters) the ball is above the ground.

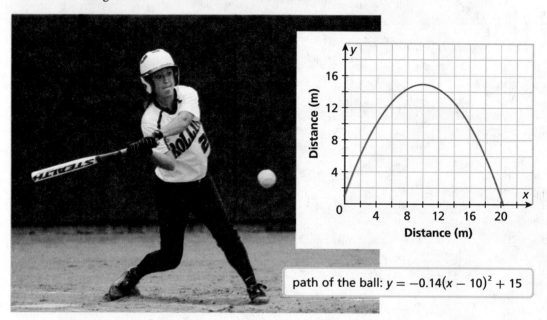

path of the ball: $y = -0.14(x - 10)^2 + 15$

Use the graph of the function to answer Parts A–C.

A. For what approximate value(s) of x will the ball be 10 meters above the ground?

B. For what value(s) of x will the ball be 15 meters above the ground?

C. For what value(s) of x will the ball be 16 meters above the ground?

D. Substitute 16 for y in the equation $y = -0.14(x - 10)^2 + 15$ to represent when the ball is 16 meters above the ground. Then isolate the constant and take square roots to begin solving the equation. What type of number do you think the solution(s) will be?

E. The solutions of the equation $16 = -0.14(x - 10)^2 + 15$ are $x = \frac{70 + 5i\sqrt{14}}{7}$ and $x = \frac{70 + 5i\sqrt{14}}{7}$. Does this make sense with respect to the situation? Explain.

 Turn and Talk When does a quadratic equation of the form $d = ax^2 + bx + c$ have just one real solution? Explain.

Step It Out

Find Complex Solutions by Completing the Square

In a previous course, you used **completing the square** to solve quadratic equations when you could not use factoring. This method allowed you to find irrational solutions. The same method will now allow you to find complex solutions of quadratic equations.

To make the expression $x^2 + bx$ a perfect square trinomial, add the term $\left(\frac{b}{2}\right)^2$ to get $x^2 + bx + \left(\frac{b}{2}\right)^2 = \left(x + \frac{b}{2}\right)^2$. When completing the square to solve quadratic equations, make sure to add the same number to both sides of the equation.

2 ▶ Solve $x^2 - 3x + 2 = -3$ by completing the square.

$x^2 - 3x + 2 = -3$	Original equation
$x^2 - 3x = -5$	Rewrite to isolate the constant term.
$b = -3$ and $\left(\frac{b}{2}\right)^2 = \left(\frac{-3}{2}\right)^2 = \frac{9}{4}$	Identify b and find $\left(\frac{b}{2}\right)^2$.
$x^2 - 3x + \frac{9}{4} = -5 + \frac{9}{4}$	**A.** What property justifies adding $\frac{9}{4}$ to each side of the equation?
$\left(x - \frac{3}{2}\right)^2 = -\frac{11}{4}$	Factor.
$\sqrt{\left(x - \frac{3}{2}\right)^2} = \pm\sqrt{-\frac{11}{4}}$	Take square roots of each side.
$x - \frac{3}{2} = \pm\sqrt{-\frac{11}{4}}$	
$x = \frac{3}{2} \pm \sqrt{-\frac{11}{4}}$	Add $\frac{3}{2}$ to each side.
$x = \frac{3 + i\sqrt{11}}{2}$ or $x = \frac{3 - i\sqrt{11}}{2}$	**B.** Why is there an i in the solution?

Check the solutions using substitution.

$$\left(\frac{3 + i\sqrt{11}}{2}\right)^2 - 3\left(\frac{3 + i\sqrt{11}}{2}\right) + 2 = -3 \qquad \left(\frac{3 - i\sqrt{11}}{2}\right)^2 - 3\left(\frac{3 - i\sqrt{11}}{2}\right) + 2 = -3$$

$$\frac{9 + 6i\sqrt{11} - 11}{4} + \frac{-9 - 3i\sqrt{11}}{2} + 2 = -3 \qquad \frac{9 - 6i\sqrt{11} - 11}{4} + \frac{-9 + 3i\sqrt{11}}{2} + 2 = -3$$

$$\frac{-12}{4} = -3 \qquad\qquad \frac{-12}{4} = -3$$

$$-3 = -3 \qquad\qquad -3 = -3$$

 Turn and Talk In the equation above, if x^2 were changed to $2x^2$, how would the process of completing the square change?

Find Complex Solutions Using the Quadratic Formula

You can use completing the square to derive the **Quadratic Formula**. Rewrite the quadratic equation $ax^2 + bx + c = 0$ as $ax^2 + bx = -c$ and then divide both sides by a to get $x^2 + \frac{b}{a}x = -\frac{c}{a}$. From there, you can complete the square.

$$x^2 + \frac{b}{a}x = -\frac{c}{a}$$

$$x^2 + \frac{b}{a}x + \left(\frac{b}{2a}\right)^2 = \left(\frac{b}{2a}\right)^2 - \frac{c}{a}$$

$$\left(x + \frac{b}{2a}\right)^2 = \frac{b^2}{4a^2} - \frac{c}{a}$$

$$\left(x + \frac{b}{2a}\right)^2 = \frac{b^2}{4a^2} - \frac{4ac}{4a^2}$$

$$\left(x + \frac{b}{2a}\right)^2 = \frac{b^2 - 4ac}{4a^2}$$

$$\sqrt{\left(x + \frac{b}{2a}\right)^2} = \pm\sqrt{\frac{b^2 - 4ac}{4a^2}}$$

$$\left(x + \frac{b}{2a}\right) = \pm\frac{\sqrt{b^2 - 4ac}}{2a}$$

$$x = \frac{-b \pm \sqrt{b^2 - 4ac}}{2a} \quad \longleftarrow \quad \text{Quadratic Formula}$$

3 When using the Quadratic Formula, put the equation you are solving in standard form. Then substitute values and solve.

$$x^2 + 10 = 2x$$

$$x^2 - 2x + 10 = 0 \qquad \text{Write the equation in standard form.}$$

$$x = \frac{2 \pm \sqrt{(-2)^2 - 4(1)(10)}}{2(1)} \qquad \text{Use the Quadratic Formula:}$$
$$a = 1, b = -2, c = 10.$$

> How do you know which values to use for a, b, and c?

$$x = \frac{2 \pm \sqrt{-36}}{2} \qquad \text{Simplify.}$$

$$x = \frac{2 \pm 6i}{2} \qquad \text{Rewrite using } i.$$

$$x = 1 \pm 3i \qquad \text{Simplify.}$$

Check one solution. Use $x = 1 + 3i$.

$$(1 + 3i)^2 + 10 \overset{?}{=} 2(1 + 3i)$$

$$1 + 6i - 9 + 10 \overset{?}{=} 2 + 6i$$

$$2 + 6i = 2 + 6i \checkmark$$

 Turn and Talk When you check a non-real solution, and it works, why do you not need to check the other non-real solution?

70

Identify Whether or Not Solutions are Real

The part of the Quadratic Formula inside the radical, $b^2 - 4ac$, is called the **discriminant**. You can use the discriminant to determine how many solutions a quadratic equation has.

Using the Discriminant of $ax^2 + bx + c = 0$		
$$x = \dfrac{-b \pm \sqrt{b^2 - 4ac}}{2a}$$		
$b^2 - 4ac > 0$ 2 real solutions	$b^2 - 4ac = 0$ 1 real solution	$b^2 - 4ac < 0$ 0 real solutions; 2 non-real solutions

4   A sock manufacturing company's profits can be modeled by the function $p(x) = -0.05x^2 + 125x - 3600$, where x is the number of pairs of socks sold. Can the sock company's profits ever reach $90,000?

> x = number of t-shirts sold

You can use the discriminant to analyze the sock company's profits by finding whether there are any real solutions of the equation for a given profit.

Write an equation to represent the situation.

To determine whether the company's profits can ever reach $90,000, substitute 90,000 for $p(x)$ in the function. Then write the resulting equation in standard form.

$$90,000 = -0.05x^2 + 125x - 3600$$

$$0 = -0.05x^2 + 125x - 93,600$$

> **A.** Why should you write the equation in standard form?

Find the discriminant.

Use $a = -0.05$, $b = 125$, $c = -93,600$.

$$b^2 - 4ac = 125^2 - 4(-0.05)(-93,600)$$

$$= -3095$$

Answer the question.

The discriminant is negative, so the equation when the profit is $90,000 has no real solutions and 2 non-real solutions. This means that the sock company cannot make a profit of $90,000 given the profit function $p(x) = -0.05x^2 + 125x - 3600$.

> **B.** What would a positive discriminant tell you about whether the company could make a given profit?

Turn and Talk When might analyzing the discriminant be better than computing the actual solutions?

Check Understanding

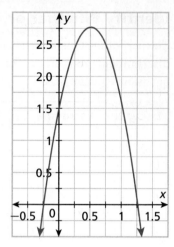

1. A T-shirt leaves a launcher 1.5 meters off the ground with an initial vertical velocity of 5 m/s. The function $h = -4.9t^2 + 5t + 1.5$ gives the height h of the T-shirt in meters after t seconds. Use the graph of the function to determine whether the T-shirt ever reaches a height of 3 meters. Explain what this can tell you about the solutions to the equation $3 = -4.9t^2 + 5t + 1.5$.

2. Solve $2x^2 + 8x + 30 = 5$ by completing the square.

3. Use the Quadratic Formula to solve the equation $8 = -12x - 12x^2$. Show your work and justify each step.

Find the value of the discriminant. Then tell the number and type of solutions.

4. $-2p^2 + 4p - 8 = -6$ 5. $-8n^2 - 10n - 5 = 2$ 6. $-3m^2 - 4m + 17 = 10$

7. Carl wants to hang a rope swing from a 20-foot tall branch on a tree. He ties a weight to the end of the rope and tries to throw it over the branch. The motion of the weight can be modeled by the equation $h = -16t^2 + 32t + 5$, where t is the time since he threw the weight and h is the height of the weight. Will the weight reach the height of the branch? Use the discriminant to justify your answer.

On Your Own

8. **(MP) Reason** A person kicks a soccer ball from the ground into the air. The soccer ball's initial upward velocity is 5 m/s. The function $h = -4.9t^2 + 5t$ approximates the height h in meters of the ball at time t in seconds. Are there values of h for which there is one real solution of the equation, no real solutions of the equation, two real solutions of the equation? Explain.

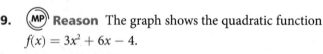

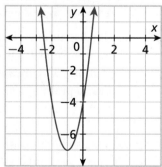

5 m/s

9. **(MP) Reason** The graph shows the quadratic function $f(x) = 3x^2 + 6x - 4$.

   A. For what value(s) of $f(x)$ will there be just one solution of the related equation? Justify your answer.

   B. For what value(s) of $f(x)$ will there be no solution of the related equation? Justify your answer.

   C. For what value(s) of $f(x)$ will there be two solutions of the related equation? Justify your answer.

10. **(MP) Use Repeated Reasoning** A girl tosses a coin into a wishing well. The graph shows its height h in meters t seconds after she tosses the coin.

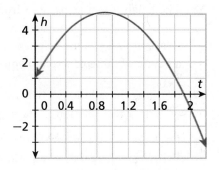

   A. Give an example of a height that the coin will be at exactly once.

   B. Give an example of a height that the coin will never reach.

   C. Give an example of a height that the coin will be at twice.

   D. If the well is 10 meters deep, after approximately how long will the coin land on the bottom?

Solve each equation by completing the square.

11. $n^2 - 14n + 85 = 0$ 12. $x^2 + 16x + 106 = 6$

13. $k^2 - 18k + 93 = -3$ 14. $z^2 + 4z + 65 = 6$

15. $8v^2 - 16v + 82 = -2$ 16. $8m^2 + 16m + 88 = -10$

17. $-2x^2 + 4x - 7 = 0$ 18. $-3t^2 + 12t = 2$

Solve each equation by using the Quadratic Formula.

19. $9x^2 + 7x + 3 = 0$ 20. $6n^2 - 10n - 6 = 0$

21. $6 = -11a^2 - 5a$ 22. $-4r = -3 - 9r^2$

23. $3p^2 + 8 = 0$ 24. $4r = 3 + 9r^2$

25. $-4t^2 + t = 2$ 26. $-2x^2 = 3x - 1$

For each equation, find the value of the discriminant. Then tell the number and the type of solutions the equation has.

27. $6p^2 + 8p + 6 = 0$ 28. $7k^2 + 2k - 5 = 0$

29. $-9n^2 - 6n - 1 = 0$ 30. $3x^2 + 8x + 4 = 0$

31. $-6p^2 - 7p - 13 = -3$ 32. $4b^2 + 6b - 8 = -10$

33. $5x^2 - 3x - 10 = -2$ 34. $3x^2 + 6x + 1 = -2$

35. To fight a fire inside a building, a firefighter stands on the ground and aims water at a window where the flames are visible. The path of the water can be modeled by the function $v = -0.02h^2 + 1.05h + 3.5$, where v is the vertical distance and h is the horizontal distance of the water. Can the firefighter find a distance from the building so that the water reaches the window? Justify your answer by using the discriminant.

The firefighter holds a hose 3.5 feet above the ground, spraying water at a window 32 feet above the ground.

36. The height of an arrow shot from a bow is modeled by the function $y = -16x^2 + 21x + 4$, where x is the number of seconds since the arrow was shot and y is the height of the arrow in feet. Will the arrow ever reach a height of 10 feet? Explain your reasoning.

37. Consider the solutions to a quadratic equation. You know that there are three options: 1 real solution, 2 real solutions, or 2 non-real solutions.

  A. When are the real solutions integers? Explain your reasoning.

  B. Why is there only one solution when the discriminant equals 0?

  C. If you know that one of the non-real solutions is $-4 + 2i\sqrt{3}$, what is the other solution? Explain your reasoning.

38. (Open Middle™) Using the digits 0 to 9, at most one time each, fill in the boxes to create two quadratic equations, one with real solutions and the other with complex solutions.

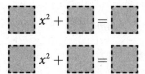

Spiral Review • Assessment Readiness

39. Which of the following expressions are equivalent to $14 + 5i$? Select all that apply.

  Ⓐ $2(7 + 2.5i)$

  Ⓑ $(4 + i)(2 - 6i)$

  Ⓒ $(3 + 2i)(4 - i)$

  Ⓓ $(2 + i) + (12 + 4i)$

  Ⓔ $(17 + 5i) - (3 - i)$

  Ⓕ $(8 + 4i) - (6 - i)$

40. Solve $49 - 4x^2 = 625$.

  Ⓐ $x = -12$

  Ⓑ $x = 12$

  Ⓒ $x = \pm12i$

  Ⓓ $x = 12i$

41. What is the solution of the system?

$$\begin{cases} 4x + y = 4 \\ 2x + y = 8 \end{cases}$$

  Ⓐ $x = -2, y = 12$

  Ⓑ $x = \dfrac{2}{3}, y = \dfrac{20}{3}$

  Ⓒ $x = 2, y = 4$

  Ⓓ $x = -\dfrac{2}{3}, y = \dfrac{20}{3}$

42. During a rainstorm, the data shows the amount of rain (mm) that falls within two-hour time intervals.

Time	12 p.m.	2 p.m.	4 p.m.	6 p.m.
Amount (mm)	0	5.1	6.6	10.9

What is the average rate of change between 2 p.m. and 6 p.m.?

  Ⓐ 0.69 mm/h   Ⓒ 2.9 mm/h

  Ⓑ 1.45 mm/h   Ⓓ 5.8 mm/h

 I'm in a Learning Mindset!

How could I think about finding complex solutions using the Quadratic Formula differently?

Solve Linear-Quadratic Systems

(I Can) use different methods to solve and graph nonlinear systems.

Spark Your Learning

Jean is practicing ski jumping. The length of the jump from the end of the ramp to the landing point is measured to the nearest half-meter.

The jump is recorded so the length can be measured later.

Complete Part A as a whole class. Then complete Parts B–D in small groups.

A. What is a mathematical question you can ask about this situation? What assumptions can you make?

B. What do the input and output of each function represent? What unit of measurement is used for each?

C. To answer your question, what strategy and tool would you use along with all the information you have? What answer do you get?

D. Does your answer make sense in the context of the situation? How do you know?

 Turn and Talk Predict how your answer would change for each of the following changes in the situation:
- The slope of the mountain is steeper.
- Jean's jump is further up the mountain.

Build Understanding

Investigate Intersections of Lines and Graphs of Quadratic Equations

Previously, you have solved linear systems, which are formed by linear equations. Now you will work with linear-quadratic systems, which are formed by a linear equation and a quadratic equation. Recall that the graphs of quadratic equations can be parabolas or, as you have seen in previous courses, circles.

A real world example of a linear-quadratic system is shown at the right. The coverage area of a cell phone tower can be represented using a circle with the cell phone tower at the center. The line represents a road that passes through the area. The road intersects the edge of the cell phone tower's coverage area at two points.

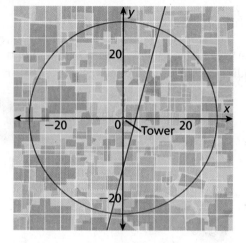

1 ▶ A. The graph at the right shows a linear-quadratic system composed of a parabola and a line, which is represented by the equation $y = 2$. How many points of intersection does this system have?

B. Vertically translate the line up by 3 units. How many points of intersection does this new system have? Use a sketch to justify your answer.

C. Vertically translate the original line $y = 2$ down by 4 units. How many points of intersection do the parabola and this translated line have? Use a sketch to justify your answer.

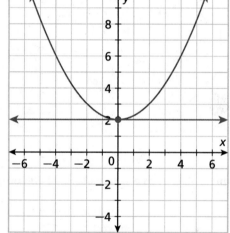

D. What do you recall about a line that is tangent to a circle? How many solutions are possible in a system where a line is tangent to a circle? Explain your answer.

E. How many ways can the graph of a linear function intersect the graph of a circle? Can the system have no solutions? one solution? two solutions? three solutions? more than three solutions? Use sketches of the system to justify your answer.

F. How does the possible number of solutions for a system with a linear equation and a circle compare to a system with a linear equation and a parabola?

G. Is it possible for a linear-quadratic system to have infinitely many solutions? Explain your answer.

  Turn and Talk How does the number of solutions in a linear system compare to a system with a linear and a quadratic equation?

Step It Out

Solve a Linear-Quadratic System by Graphing

In an earlier course, you solved systems of two linear equations by graphing. You can use the same strategy to find the solutions to a system of a linear equation and a quadratic equation.

2 Solve the system of equations by graphing.

$$\begin{cases} 3x + 4y = 25 \\ x^2 + y^2 = 25 \end{cases}$$

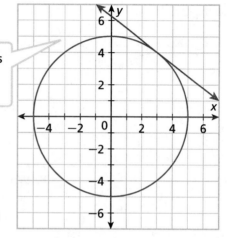

Rewrite the linear equation to be in slope-intercept form.

> **A.** How many solutions will this system have? Explain.

$$y = -\frac{3}{4}x + \frac{25}{4}$$

Then graph both equations on the same coordinate plane using a graphing calculator.

Find the solution by identifying the point of intersection: $(3, 4)$.

Check the solution by substituting values into the equations.

$$3(3) + 4(4) = 25 \qquad 3^2 + 4^2 = 25$$

$$25 = 25 \qquad 25 = 25$$

> **B.** Why must the solution satisfy both equations?

The substituted values $x = 3$ and $y = 4$ satisfy both of the equations in the system, so the solution $(3, 4)$ is confirmed.

 Turn and Talk Many solutions to equations found graphically are approximations rather than exact solutions. Is this solution an approximation or an exact solution?

Solve a Linear-Quadratic System by Elimination

You can solve a nonlinear system of equations algebraically using elimination as a solution strategy. Add or subtract the two equations to eliminate one of the variables. If necessary, multiply one or both of the equations so that coefficients of one of the variables will have a sum or difference of zero.

3 Solve the following system algebraically:

$$\begin{cases} y + 9 = 2x \\ y + 1 = 3(x + 4)^2 \end{cases}$$

Eliminate the variable that is the same in both equations, y.

$$y + 9 = 2x$$
$$\underline{y + 1 = 3(x + 4)^2}$$
$$8 = 2x - 3(x + 4)^2$$

> **A.** Should you add or subtract to eliminate y? Explain.

Solve the new equation for x.

$8 = 2x - 3(x + 4)^2$

$8 = 2x - 3(x^2 + 8x + 16)$ Square $(x + 4)$.

$8 = 2x - 3x^2 - 24x - 48$ Distributive Property

$0 = -3x^2 - 22x - 56$ Combine like terms.

Use the Quadratic Formula.

$$x = \frac{-(-22) \pm \sqrt{(-22)^2 - 4(-3)(-56)}}{2(-3)}$$ Use $a = -3, b = -22, c = -56$.

$$x = \frac{22 \pm \sqrt{484 - 672}}{-6}$$ Simplify.

$$x = \frac{22 \pm \sqrt{-188}}{-6}$$ Simplify.

B. What does this value tell you about the solutions to the system?

Graph the equations in the system to check the solutions.

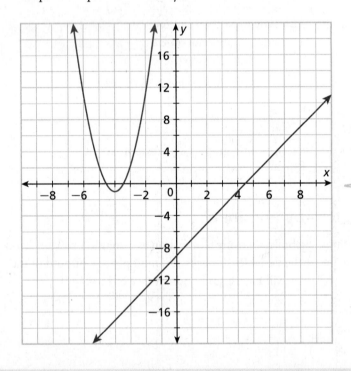

C. Does the graph verify your results? Explain.

 Turn and Talk Explain how there can be many different ways to arrive at the same solution. What are the advantages and disadvantages for each of these three methods?
- graphing
- elimination
- substitution

Solve Real-World Problems

 4 A router broadcasts a wifi signal an equal distance in every direction. The range of the broadcast of a router that can reach up to 50 ft can be modeled with the equation $x^2 + y^2 = 2500$. Carl walks across the yard on a path modeled by the equation $y = 2x + 35$. At what points will Carl enter and leave the broadcast signal?

This situation can be modeled by the system:

$$\begin{cases} x^2 + y^2 = 2500 \\ y = 2x + 35 \end{cases}$$

Solve the system of equations using substitution. Substitute $y = 2x + 35$ into $x^2 + y^2 = 2500$ and solve for x.

$$x^2 + (2x + 35)^2 = 2500$$

$$x^2 + 4x^2 + 140x + 1225 = 2500$$

$$5x^2 + 140x - 1275 = 0$$

> **A.** Why do you write the equation in standard form?

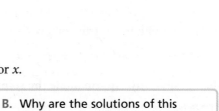

Use the Quadratic Formula.

$$x = \frac{-140 \pm \sqrt{(140)^2 - 4(5)(-1275)}}{2(5)}$$

$$x = \frac{-140 \pm \sqrt{45{,}100}}{10}$$

$$x = \frac{-140 \pm 10\sqrt{451}}{10}$$

$x \approx 7.24$ and $x \approx -35.24$

Use x to find the corresponding y-values.

$y = 2x + 35$

$y \approx 2(7.24) + 35$ Substitute 7.24 for x.

$y \approx 49.48$

$y = 2x + 35$

$y \approx 2(-35.24) + 35$ Substitute -35.24 for x.

$y \approx -35.48$

The solutions are approximately

$(7.24, 49.48)$ and $(-35.24, -35.48)$.

> **B.** Why are the solutions of this system approximate? Can the exact solutions be given? Explain.

 Turn and Talk What is a different scenario that could be modeled with the same system? What would the solution mean in this context?

Check Understanding

1. Which of the systems shown below could have two solutions? Explain your reasoning.

$$\begin{cases} y = x^2 - 6x + 3 \\ y = 2x - 11 \end{cases} \quad \begin{cases} 3x^2 + 3y^2 = 8 \\ y = x + 1 \end{cases} \quad \begin{cases} y = -x + 7 \\ y = 2x + 1 \end{cases}$$

Solve each system graphically. Approximate the solution to the nearest tenth, if necessary.

2. $\begin{cases} y = 2x^2 + 6x - 2 \\ y - 1.5x + 12 = -8 \end{cases}$

3. $\begin{cases} y = -2x^2 - 12x - 17 \\ y = 2x - 7 \end{cases}$

Solve each system by substitution.

4. $\begin{cases} y = x^2 - 5x + 7 \\ y = 2x + 1 \end{cases}$

5. $\begin{cases} y^2 = -x^2 + 25 \\ 4y = 3x \end{cases}$

Solve each system by elimination.

6. $\begin{cases} y = x^2 - 2x + 2 \\ y = 2x + -2 \end{cases}$

7. $\begin{cases} y = x^2 + 1 \\ y = x - 5 \end{cases}$

8. The trajectory of an apple shot by a cannon can be modeled by the quadratic function $y = 22 + 0.16x - 0.004x^2$, where x is the horizontal distance in feet the apple has traveled and y is its height in feet. The ground slope can be modeled by a linear function $y = -0.1x + 20$. Where will the apple land? Interpret the solution in terms of the context.

On Your Own

9. (MP) **Critique Reasoning** Matthew graphs a linear-quadratic system of equations. His results are shown. He concludes that there are no solutions to this system. Is Matthew correct? Explain why or why not.

10. (MP) **Reason** Why does a point of intersection of the graphs of two equations represent the solution of the system formed by those two equations? Do you think this is true for any two types of equations? Explain.

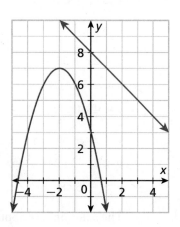

Solve each system graphically. Approximate the solution to the nearest tenth, if necessary.

11. $y = x^2 + 3x - 5$
    $y = x + 3$

12. $y = x^2 + 7x - 5$
    $y = 2x + 9$

13. $y = x^2 - 6x + 3$
    $y = -2x - 10$

14. $y = x^2 - 6x + 3$
    $y = 2x - 13$

15. $6 - y = x^2 + x$
    $y - 1 = 0.5x$

16. $y = x^2 - 4x - 2$
    $y = x - 8$

Solve each system by substitution.

17. $y = x^2 - 9$

$y = 2x + 6$

18. $y = x^2 + 8x + 11$

$y = x + 1$

19. $y = x^2 + 2x + 1$

$y = x + 0.75$

20. $-y^2 = x^2 - 49$

$y = -x - 10$

21. $y = 2x^2 - 5$

$y = -4x + 1$

22. $36 = x^2 + y^2$

$6 = x + y$

Solve each system by elimination.

23. $y = x^2 + 8x + 16$

$y = x + 6$

24. $y = x^2 - 6x - 20$

$y = -x - 6$

25. $y = x^2 + 1$

$y = x - 5$

26. $y = x^2 + 2x$

$y = 2x + 4$

27. $y - x^2 = 7 - 5x$

$8y - 16x = -42$

28. $y = 3x^2 - 2x$

$y = 2x - 2$

29. (MP) **Attend to Precision** At the varsity girls' volleyball game, the cheerleaders launch free school spirit T-shirts into the stand along a path modeled by $y = -0.08x^2 + 2.4x + 3$, where x is a T-shirt's horizontal distance in feet and y is a T-shirt's vertical distance in feet. The cheerleaders stand 24 feet from the bleachers, which have a slope of $\frac{3}{4}$.

   A. What is the equation that models the edge of the bleachers?

   B. What are the solutions to the system?

   C. Shaundra's little sister desperately wants a T-shirt. Where should Shaundra tell her to sit to be sure to get a T-shirt?

   D. How can you use graphing to solve the problem?

30. **STEM** A sea lion dives into the ocean. Its path can be modeled by a quadratic equation where x is its horizontal distance in feet and y is its vertical distance in feet. At the same time, a fish is swimming towards the surface on a path modeled by $y = 4x - 30$. Where will the sea lion and fish meet? Justify your answer.

The sea lion's path: $y = -0.5x^2 - x + 6$

31. The broadcast range of a cell tower is bounded by a circle that can be modeled by the equation $x^2 + y^2 = 1225$. A road that passes through the area near the tower can be modeled by the equation $y = 0.3x - 40$. At which points, if any, does a car on the highway enter and exit the broadcast range of the cell tower? Justify your answer.

32. Caleb and a friend are throwing snowballs at a red bucket on a hill. The flight of a snowball can be modeled by the equation $y = -0.02x^2 + x + 4$, where x is the horizontal distance and y is the height of the snowball in feet. The hill's slope can be modeled by the equation $y = 0.3x - 7.2$. What is the approximate location where the red bucket should be placed? Justify your answer.

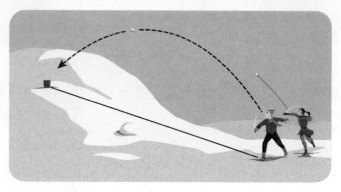

33. (Open Middle™) Using the digits 0 to 9, at most one time each, fill in the boxes to create a line and circle that intersect at exactly one point.

$$y = \boxed{} x + \boxed{}$$

$$\left(x - \boxed{}\right)^2 + \left(y - \boxed{}\right)^2 = \boxed{}^2$$

Spiral Review • Assessment Readiness

34. A circuit has a current of $12 + 16i$ amps.

Add the impedance of each element to find the total impedance. Then multiply by the current to find the voltage. What is the voltage for this circuit?

- (A) 110 V
- (B) 120 V
- (C) 200 V
- (D) 240 V

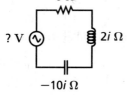

35. What is the maximum number of turning points of the graph of a polynomial function $f(x)$ with degree 5? If $a > 0$, what is the end behavior of $f(x)$ as $x \to -\infty$?

- (A) $5; f(x) \to -\infty$
- (B) $5; f(x) \to +\infty$
- (C) $4; f(x) \to -\infty$
- (D) $4; f(x) \to +\infty$

36. Match each equation on the left with its discriminant and description of its solutions on the right.

- **A.** $x^2 - 3x + 6 = 0$
- **B.** $8x^2 -+ 4x - 8 = 0$
- **C.** $6x^2 -+ 12x + 2 = -4$
- **D.** $7x^2 -+ 2x - 5 = -10.$

- **1.** 272; two real solutions
- **2.** −136; two imaginary solutions
- **3.** −15; two imaginary solutions
- **4.** 0; one real solution

 I'm in a Learning Mindset!

What can I contribute to my learning community regarding solving and graphing nonlinear systems?

Quadratic Equations and Square Roots

Solve $3x^2 + 54 = 0$ by taking square roots.

$$3x^2 + 54 = 0$$
$$3x^2 = -54$$
$$x^2 = -18$$

The non-real quantity $i = \sqrt{-1}$ allows you to find the square roots of a negative number.

$$x^2 = -18$$
$$x = \pm\sqrt{-18}$$
$$x = \pm\sqrt{18} \cdot \sqrt{-1}$$
$$x = \pm\sqrt{9 \cdot 2} \cdot i$$
$$x = \pm 3i\sqrt{2}$$

The solutions are $x = 3i\sqrt{2}$ and $x = -3i\sqrt{2}$.

Operations with Complex Numbers

Operations with complex numbers work like operations with binomials, but you must remember that i^2 simplifies as -1.

Addition and subtraction: Combine the real parts and the imaginary parts.

$$(3 + 4i) + (2 - 7i)$$
$$= (3 + 2) + (4 - 7)i$$
$$= 5 - 3i$$

Multiplication: Use the Distributive Property.

$$(6 - 3i)(-1 + 8i)$$
$$= 6(-1) + 6(8i) + (-3i)(-1) + (-3i)(8i)$$
$$= -6 + 48i + 3i + (-24i^2)$$
$$= -6 + 51i + 24$$
$$= 18 + 51i$$

Using the Quadratic Formula

Solve $2x^2 = -3x - 5$.

Write in standard form, $ax^2 + bx + c = 0$. Then apply the Quadratic Formula,

$$x = \frac{-b \pm \sqrt{b^2 - 4ac}}{2a}.$$

$$2x^2 + 3x + 5 = 0$$

> $a = 2, b = 3, c = 5$

$$x = \frac{-3 \pm \sqrt{3^2 - 4(2)(5)}}{2(2)}$$

$$x = \frac{-3 \pm \sqrt{-31}}{4}$$

$$x = \frac{-3 \pm i\sqrt{31}}{4}$$

The solutions are $x = \dfrac{-3 + i\sqrt{31}}{4}$ and $x = \dfrac{-3 - i\sqrt{31}}{4}$.

Nonlinear Systems

To prevent large avalanches of snow in mountainous areas, explosive shells can be launched to trigger carefully-placed smaller avalanches. A shell is launched on a path modeled by $y = -0.16x^2 + x$, where the distances are in kilometers. The mountainside can be modeled by $y = 0.75x - 2$. Where does the shell hit?

Graph to find an approximate solution.

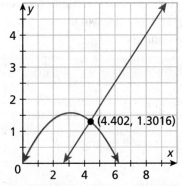

The shell hits about 1.3 kilometers high on the mountainside at a horizontal distance away of about 4.4 kilometers.

Vocabulary

Choose the correct term from the box to complete each sentence.

1. A(n) ___?___ is the square root of a negative number, and can be written in the form bi, where b is a real number and i is the ___?___, which is $\sqrt{-1}$.

2. A(n) ___?___ can be written in the form $a + bi$ where a and b are real numbers and $i = \sqrt{-1}$.

3. The ___?___ states that the solutions of the equation $ax^2 + bx + c = 0$, where $a \neq 0$, are given by $x = \dfrac{-b \pm \sqrt{b^2 - 4ac}}{2a}$. The radicand, $b^2 - 4ac$, is called the ___?___, and indicates the number of real solutions.

Concepts and Skills

4. Anchara drops a penny from a height of 60 feet above the ground. The equation $h = -16t^2 + 60$ models the penny's height h in feet as a function of time t in seconds.
   A. What are all solutions of $0 = -16t^2 + 60$?
   B. Do the solutions to Part A describe when the penny hits the ground? Explain.

Perform the indicated operation.

5. $(4 - i) + (9 - 3i)$

6. $(-8 - 2i) - (-10 - 6i)$

7. $(1 + 6i)(-2 - 5i)$

8. $(2 + 4i)^2$

9. Without solving, can you tell how many and what type of solution(s) the equation $0 = x^2 - 8x + 17$ has? Explain your answer.

10. The graph of $f(x) = x^2 - 2x + 2$ is shown. For what value(s) of $f(x)$ does the related equation have two real solutions? one real solution? two non-real solutions?

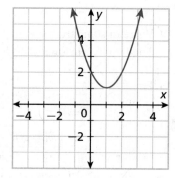

11. **(MP) Use Tools** For a water balloon launched from a 49-meter overlook with an initial vertical velocity of 24.5 meters per second, the height h in meters as a function of time t in seconds is $h = -4.9t^2 + 24.5t + 49$. When will the balloon land and burst? Use completing the square. State what strategy and tool you will use to answer the question, explain your choice, and then find the answer.

12. Solve $2x^2 + x + 10 = -x^2 + 6$ using the Quadratic Formula.

13. Use substitution to solve the system $\begin{cases} x + y = 30 \\ 2y = -x^2 + 16x - 12 \end{cases}$.
    Verify your result by graphing.

14. Use elimination to solve the system $\begin{cases} y = x^2 - 4x - 2 \\ -x + y = -2 \end{cases}$.

Polynomial Functions and Equations

Telecommunications Engineer

Telecommunications engineers manage communications data such as voice, video, calls, and text. They use their expertise to design, install, and manage systems to perform reliable, high-speed data transmissions. Telecommunications engineers ensure that messages are being transmitted securely.

STEM Task

To encrypt the message, add the original to the cipher. Coefficients that are even change to 0. Coefficients that are odd change to 1.

Cipher polynomial:
$C(x) = x^5 + x^2 + x$

Original message	Encrypted message
$x^5 + x^4 + x^2 + 1$	$x^4 + x + 1$
$x^4 + x^3 + x$	___?___
___?___	$x^5 + x^3 + x + 1$

Why does adding the cipher both encrypt and decrypt the message? Explain your reasoning.

Learning Mindset

Resilience Monitors Emotions

While engaging in the learning process, it is important to monitor your emotions and stress levels. Checking in with yourself and pausing to reflect about your current mindset can help you relieve stress and develop an effective plan for positive growth. Here are some questions you can ask yourself to help monitor your emotions:

- What kind of emotions detract from my progress? What kind of emotions can help me accomplish my goals?

- What makes me feel stressed? How can I focus on a growth mindset to develop positive emotions?

- Am I feeling overwhelmed? What stress-management skills can I use to help me overcome the situation?

- Who can offer me positive reinforcement? Who can help me develop a plan to move towards my goal?

- How can I assess my level of stress while working to master polynomials? How can I pace myself to accomplish the task?

Reflect

Q What are the most helpful methods that you use to identify and monitor your emotions? Why do these methods work well for you? How do you benefit from this practice?

Q Imagine you are a telecommunications engineer. What sort of emotions would you encounter throughout the trajectory of a project? How would you monitor your emotions while working on the job?

Module

3 Polynomial Functions

Module Performance Task: Focus on STEM

Gravitational Potential Energy of Water

When designing a hydroelectric dam, the potential energy of a layer of water is dependent on how far the water falls. Engineers balance the energy needs of the community with the available potential energy by selectively releasing water.

Known information about the dam	Gravitational potential energy, U
• The efficiency of the hydroelectric dam, η, is 90%. • The density of water, ρ, is 1000 kg/m³. • The gravitational constant, g, is 9.8 m/s². • The volume, V (in cubic meters), of a particular layer of water is given by $0.001(2h + 10)(10h + 20)$, where h is the height.	$U = \eta\rho gV(h - 10)$

A. Describe what happens to the width $(2h + 10)$ and the length $(10h + 20)$ of the reservoir as the height of the water rises.

B. Write a function for the gravitational potential energy in terms of the height. Analyze the equation to determine the units of energy.

C. Identify when the gravitational potential energy is 0. Explain how these points appear on a graph of the function.

D. Identify at what height the dam would begin to produce energy for the community. Is the dam producing energy whenever the graph is positive? Explain your reasoning.

Are You Ready?

Complete these problems to review prior concepts and skills you will need for this module.

Graph Linear Equations in Standard Form

Graph each linear equation.

1. $2x - y = 4$

2. $2x + y = -1$

3. $x + 2y = 6$

4. $6x - y = 0$

Graph Quadratic Functions in Vertex Form

Graph each quadratic function.

5. $y = (x + 1)^2 - 2$

6. $y = (x - 1)^2$

7. $y = (x + 2)^2 + 1$

8. $y = x^2 - 4$

9. $y = \frac{1}{2}(x - 2)^2 - 3$

10. $y = -(x + 3)^2 + 2$

Graph Quadratic Functions in Intercept Form

Graph each quadratic function.

11. $y = x(x - 2)$

12. $y = (x + 1)(x - 2)$

13. $y = -(x - 3)^2$

14. $y = (x - 1)(x + 1)$

15. $y = (x + 5)(x + 2)$

16. $y = -(x - 4)(x - 6)$

Connecting Past and Present Learning

Previously, you learned:

- to graph linear equations in standard form by rewriting in slope-intercept form,

- to graph quadratic functions in vertex form using the values of the vertex (h, k) and the value of a to determine the direction the parabola will open as well as the horizontal stretch or compression, and

- to graph quadratic functions in intercept form using the factors to identify the x-intercept(s).

In this module, you will learn:

- to use key features, such as intercepts, maxima, minima, intervals of increasing or decreasing behavior, intervals where the function is positive or negative, and end behavior, to graph polynomial functions, and

- to analyze graphs of polynomial functions and interpret the key features in the context of a given real-world situation.

Graph Polynomial Functions

(I Can) use the degree of a polynomial function to determine the shape and characteristics of its graph.

Spark Your Learning

Emmett wants to put a fish tank in the middle of the science classroom. To maximize viewing potential, he's looking for an aquarium with a 360° viewing area.

The pet store carries four sizes of cylindrical fish tanks, each having an inside height that is twice the inside diameter.

Emmett plans to place the aquarium on top of a cabinet.

Complete Part A as a whole class. Then complete Parts B–D in small groups.

A. What is a mathematical question you can ask about this situation? What information would you need to know to answer your question?

B. What formula(s) will be needed to answer your question?

C. To answer your question, what strategy and tool would you use along with all the information you have? What answer do you get?

D. Does your answer make sense in the context of the situation? How close to the maximum weight supported by the cabinet should the tank choice be?

 Turn and Talk Predict how your answers would change if the height of the aquarium were equal to the diameter.

Build Understanding

Investigate the Graph of the Parent Cubic Function

You previously worked with linear functions $f(x) = ax + b$, where a and b are real numbers and $a \neq 0$, and quadratic functions $f(x) = ax^2 + bx + c$, where a, b, and c are real numbers and $a \neq 0$. Now you will work with **cubic functions**, which are a type of polynomial function that have the standard form $f(x) = ax^3 + bx^2 + cx + d$, where a, b, c, and d are real numbers and $a \neq 0$. First you will investigate the parent cubic function $f(x) = x^3$ by analyzing its graph.

 The graph of the parent cubic function $f(x) = x^3$ is shown. The curve passes through the ordered pairs given in the table below the graph.

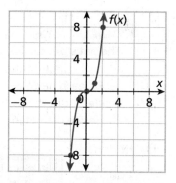

A. Sketch a graph of $y = x$ and $y = x^2$. Notice that the domain of all three parent functions $\left(y = x, y = x^2, \text{ and } y = x^3\right)$ is the set of all real numbers. How do the ranges and end behavior of the three parent functions compare?

B. Use the graph of $f(x) = x^3$ to identify the following information about the parent cubic function.

- any zeros of the function
- the interval on which the function is positive
- the interval on which the function is negative
- the interval on which the function is increasing
- the interval on which the function is decreasing

How do these features compare to the same features on the parent linear and quadratic functions? With which function does the graph of $f(x) = x^3$ have the most in common? How would you describe the differences?

x	$f(x) = x^3$
−2	−8
−1	−1
0	0
1	1
2	8

C. Recall that an even function is a function in which $f(-x) = f(x)$, and an odd function is a function in which $f(-x) = -f(x)$. Is $f(x) = x^3$ an even function, an odd function, or neither? How does this classification compare to the parent linear and quadratic functions?

 Turn and Talk How is the graph of the parent cubic function similar to the graph of the parent quadratic function, and how is it different?

Investigate the Graphs of Parent Polynomial Functions

A **polynomial function of degree** n has the standard form $p(x) = a_n x^n + a_{n-1} x^{n-1} + \ldots + a_2 x^2 + a_1 x + a_0$, where $a_n, a_{n-1}, \ldots, a_2, a_1$, and, a_0 are real numbers and $a_n \neq 0$. The values $a_n, a_{n-1}, \ldots, a_2, a_1$, and a_0 are the coefficients of the expressions $a_n x^n, a_{n-1} x^{n-1}, \ldots, a_2 x^2, a_1 x$, and a_0, which are the terms of $p(x)$. Note that the constant term a_0 appears to have no power of x associated with it. The term is actually $a_0 x^0$, but since $x^0 = 1$, you can write $a_0 x^0$ as a_0.

Polynomial functions of degree 4 are called *quartic* functions, and polynomial functions of degree 5 are called *quintic* functions. Polynomial functions of degree greater than 5 are generally referred to using their degree, as in "a sixth-degree polynomial function."

2 ▶ Graph A shows the graphs of $f(x) = x$, $f(x) = x^3$, $f(x) = x^5$. Graph B shows the graphs of $f(x) = x^2$, $f(x) = x^4$, and $f(x) = x^6$.

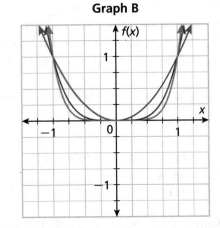

Graph A

Graph B

A. Identify the domain, range, and end behavior of the functions in Graph A. What do you notice?

B. Identify the domain, range, and end behavior of the functions in Graph B. What do you notice?

C. Determine whether $f(x) = x$, $f(x) = x^3$, and $f(x) = x^5$ are even, odd, or neither. Explain how you know.

D. Determine whether $f(x) = x^2$, $f(x) = x^4$, and $f(x) = x^6$ are even, odd, or neither. Explain how you know.

E. How can you use the graph of the parent functions to determine whether it is even, odd, or neither? How can you use the equation of the parent function to determine whether it is even, odd, or neither?

Turn and Talk How would you expect the key features to change for the functions $f(x) = -x$, $f(x) = -x^2$, $f(x) = -x^3$, ... , and $f(x) = -x^6$? Explain your reasoning and use a graphing calculator to check your predictions.

Step It Out

Graph Transformations of Parent Polynomial Functions

In Lesson 1.3, you examined transformations of the graphs of functions. Writing equations of transformed functions were limited to absolute value and quadratic functions. Now you will use similar techniques to examine transformations of polynomial functions. As with absolute value and quadratic functions, it is helpful to understand the effect of the transformation on the three

$f(x) = x^n$		$f(x) = a\left(\frac{1}{b}(x - h)\right)^n + k$	
x	**y**	**x**	**y**
-1	$(-1)^n$	$(-1)b + h$	$(-1)^n a + k$
0	0	h	k
1	1	$b + h$	$a + k$

reference points $\left(-1, f(-1)\right)$, $\left(0, f(0)\right)$, and $\left(1, f(1)\right)$ found on the graph of the parent function $f(x)$. The table lists these three points for the parent function $f(x) = x^n$ and the corresponding points on the graph of $f(x) = a\left(\frac{1}{b}(x - h)\right)^n + k$

3 Identify the transformations of the graph of $f(x) = x^3$ that produce the graph of $g(x) = \frac{1}{3}(x + 1)^3 - 2$. Then graph $g(x)$ on the same coordinate grid as the graph of $f(x)$.

Identify the values of the parameters a, b, h, and k.

$a = \frac{1}{3}, b = 1, h = -1, k = -2$

> **A.** In general, what do the parameter values a, b, h, and k tell you about the how the parent function is transformed?

Describe how the graph of g(x) is related to the graph of f(x).

- a vertical compression by a factor of $\frac{1}{3}$
- a translation of 1 unit left and 2 units down

> **B.** What values would result in a vertical *stretch* of the parent function?

Create a transformation table and graph the functions.

$f(x) = x^3$		$g(x) = \frac{1}{3}(x + 1)^3 - 2$	
x	**y**	**x**	**y**
-1	-1	$(-1)(1) + (-1) = -2$	$(-1)^3\left(\frac{1}{3}\right) + (-2) = -2\frac{1}{3}$
0	0	-1	-2
1	1	$(1) + (-1) = 0$	$\frac{1}{3} + (-2) = -1\frac{2}{3}$

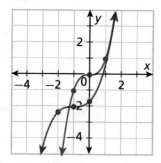

C. Why are these three reference points used to graph the transformation? Could you use any three points? Explain why or why not.

4 ⟩ Identify the transformations of the graph of $f(x) = x^4$ that produce the graph of $g(x) = \left(\frac{1}{2}(x - 3)\right)^4 + 1$. Then graph $g(x)$ on the same coordinate grid as the graph of $f(x)$.

Identify the values of the parameters a, b, h, and k.

$a = 1, b = 2, h = 3, k = 1$

Describe how the graph of g(x) is related to the graph of f(x).
- a horizontal stretch by a factor of 2
- a translation of 3 units right and 1 unit up

Create a transformation table and graph the functions.

$f(x) = x^4$		$g(x) = \left(\frac{1}{2}(x - 3)\right)^4 + 1$	
x	**y**	**x**	**y**
-1	1	$(-1)(2) + 3 = 1$	$1 + 1 = 2$
0	0	3	1
1	1	$2 + 3 = 5$	$1 + 1 = 2$

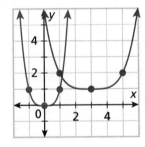

A. Could you rewrite the equation for $g(x)$ so that there was a vertical compression, but no horizontal stretch? Explain.

B. Why are there no calculations associated with the transformation of the point $(0, 0)$?

C. Does the graph of $g(x)$ appear to match the description based on the analysis of the parameter values? Explain.

Turn and Talk Suppose the same transformations are performed on the parent functions below:
- $f(x) = x^2$
- $f(x) = x^6$

How would this affect the corresponding reference points? How are the transformed functions similar? How are they different?

Write Equations for Transformations of Parent Polynomial Functions

Given the graph of the transformed function $g(x) = a\left(\frac{1}{b}(x - h)\right)^n + k$, you can write the equation for $g(x)$ by determining the values of the parameters using the same reference points examined in Tasks 3 and 4.

5 ▶ The general equation for the function shown in the graph is $h(x) = a(x - h)^4 + k$. Write a specific equation for the function.

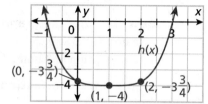

Identify the values of the parameters.
Create a table using the given points on the graph. Then solve for the parameter values.

$f(x) = x^4$		$h(x) = a(x - h)^4 + k$	
x	y	x	y
-1	1	$-1 + h = 0$	$(1)a + k = -3\frac{3}{4}$
0	0	$0 + h = 1$	$(0)a + k = -4$
1	1	$1 + h = 2$	$(1)a + k = -3\frac{3}{4}$

You can solve $0 + h = 1$ to find $h = 1$.
You can solve $(0)a + k = -4$ to find $k = -4$.

To solve for a, substitute -4 for k in $(1)a + k = -3\frac{3}{4}$. Then simplify to $a = \frac{1}{4}$.

Write the equation for the transformed function.

$h(x) = a(x - h)^4 + k$

$h(x) = \frac{1}{4}(x - 1)^4 - 4$

A. How is the process for writing the equation of the transformed function similar to graphing the transformed function?

6 ▶ The general equation for the function shown in the graph is $h(x) = \left(\frac{1}{b}(x - h)\right)^3 + k$. Write a specific equation for the function.

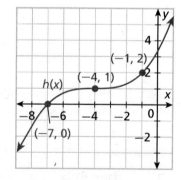

Identify the values of the parameters.
Create a table using the given points on the graph. Then solve for the parameter values.

$f(x) = x^3$		$h(x) = \left(\frac{1}{b}(x - h)\right)^3 + k$	
x	y	x	y
-1	-1	$(-1)b + h = -7$	$-1 + k = 0$
0	0	$(0)b + h = -4$	$0 + k = 1$
1	1	$(1)b + h = -1$	$1 + k = 2$

A. How do you use the entries in the table to find the values of b, h, and k?

The parameter values are: $h = -4$, $k = 1$, and $b = 3$.

Write the equation for the transformed function.

$h(x) = \left(\frac{1}{b}(x - h)\right)^3 + k$

$h(x) = \left(\frac{1}{3}(x + 4)\right)^3 + 1$

B. How can you use the given general equation to write the specific equation for the function?

Model with a Transformation of a Polynomial Function

Many real-world situations can be modeled with polynomial functions. Situations involving volume may be modeled using a cubic function. Mass and volume are related through density, which is defined as the ratio of the object's mass to the object's volume. The density of an object with mass m and volume V is given by the equation $d = \frac{m}{V}$. The mass of the object is then $m = dV$, and the volume is $V = \frac{m}{d}$.

 In a development that could reduce the consumption of plastic bottles, scientists have created an edible water sphere. The capsule that encases it is made using a calcium chloride solution and brown algae extract. What is the approximate radius of an edible water sphere with a mass of 116 grams and a density of 1.04 g/cm³?

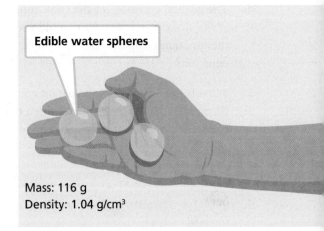

Edible water spheres

Mass: 116 g
Density: 1.04 g/cm³

Write a polynomial function to model the situation.

Let r represent the radius (in centimeters) of the sphere. The volume V (in cubic centimeters) of the sphere is $V(r) = \frac{4}{3}\pi r^3$. The mass m (in grams) of the sphere is $m(r) = 1.04 \cdot V(r) \approx 4.36r^3$.

Make a table of values for the function $m(r)$. Then use a graph to answer the question.

Radius (cm)	0	1	2	3
Mass (g)	0	4.36	34.88	117.72

The graph of the mass function is a vertical stretch of the parent cubic function by a factor of about 4.36.

The intersection of the graph of the mass function and the horizontal line $m = 116$ gives the estimated value of $r \approx 2.99$. So the radius of an edible water sphere with a mass of 116 grams is about 3 cm.

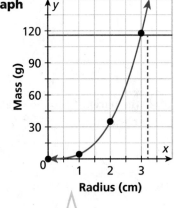

B. How is this answer indicated in the table?

A. How do you know the graph is a vertical stretch of the parent function? Explain.

 Turn and Talk Is a mass of 30 grams reasonable if the radius is 1.5 cm? Explain your answer using the table or the graph.

Check Understanding

1. Describe the end behavior of the cubic parent function.

2. How is the graph of an even function different from the graph of an odd function?

3. Describe how the graph of $g(x) = 3(x - 1)^5 + 4$ is related to the graph of $f(x) = x^5$.

4. The general equation for the cubic function shown in the graph is $g(x) = \left(\frac{1}{b}(x - h)\right)^3 + k$. How could you write a specific equation for the function using the reference points shown in the graph? What is the equation?

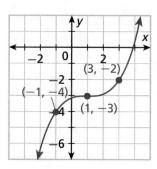

5. What transformation of the parent cubic function can you use to estimate the radius of a concrete sphere with a mass of 1400 kilograms and a density of 2400 kg/m³? What is the estimate of the radius?

On Your Own

6. (MP) **Use Structure** Compare the graphs of $f(x) = x^3$ and $g(x) = x^2$ on the interval $[-1, 1]$.

7. (MP) **Critique Reasoning** Amber evaluates a function with the following behavior:
   - $f(b) > f(a)$ for all intervals (a, b) on the domain of the function.
   Amber states that the function must be an even function since $f(2) > f(1)$ for $f(x) = x^2, f(x) = x^4, f(x) = x^6$, and so on. Is Amber correct? Explain why or why not.

State the parent function of $g(x)$ and describe how the graph of $g(x)$ is related to its parent graph.

8. $g(x) = (x + 2)^3$

9. $g(x) = x^4 - 3$

10. $g(x) = \left(\frac{1}{2}(x + 2)\right)^3 + \frac{1}{3}$

11. $g(x) = \frac{1}{2}(x - 1)^2 - 4$

12. $g(x) = \frac{1}{5}x^2$

13. $g(x) = (x - 6)^3$

14. $g(x) = \left(\frac{2}{3}x\right)^4 + 2$

15. $g(x) = 3(x - 1)^3$

16. $g(x) = 2x^5 - 4$

17. $g(x) = (2x - 6)^3$

Identify the transformations of the graph of the parent function $f(x) = x^n$ that produce the graph of the given function $g(x)$. Then graph $g(x)$ on the same coordinate plane as the graph of $f(x)$ by applying the transformations to the reference points $\left(-1, f(-1)\right)$, $\left(0, f(0)\right)$, and $\left(1, f(1)\right)$.

18. $g(x) = 2x^3$

19. $g(x) = (x - 1)^6$

20. $g(x) = \frac{1}{2}x^4$

21. $g(x) = (x + 4)^5 - 1$

22. $g(x) = \left(\frac{1}{2}x\right)^3 + 1$

23. $g(x) = 4(x + 1)^4 - \frac{1}{2}$

A general equation for each polynomial function $g(x)$ is given along with the function's graph. Use the reference points shown on each graph to identify values of the parameters and write a specific equation for the graphed function.

24. $g(x) = \left(\frac{1}{b}(x - h)\right)^3 + k$

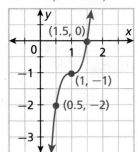

25. $g(x) = a(x - h)^4 + k$

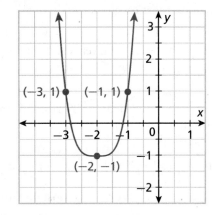

26. $g(x) = a(x - h)^3 + k$

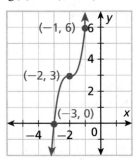

27. $g(x) = \left(\frac{1}{b}(x - h)\right)^4 + k$

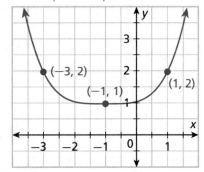

28. (MP) **Model with Mathematics** A cylindrical concrete pier used in house construction is shown. The mass is 837 kilograms and the density of the concrete is 2400 kilograms per cubic meter.

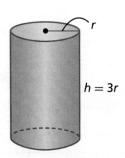

A. Write a polynomial function to model the mass of the cylinder in terms of r.

B. Graph the relationship between the mass and the radius of the cylinder.

C. Based on the graph, for a mass of 400 kilograms, is an estimate of 0.15 m for the radius reasonable? Explain.

29. A hemisphere design is proposed to create a cover for picnic food. Estimate the radius of the food cover if it is to have an interior volume of 1525 cubic centimeters.

30. Magnetic spheres are arranged in the shape of a rectangular prism to fit inside a box as shown in the image. Use a cubic function to model the volume of a rectangular prism shaped box. Then graph the function using calculated values of the function. Use the graph to estimate the dimensions of the prism if each sphere has a mass of 8 grams and the density of the magnet is 6.9 g/cm³.

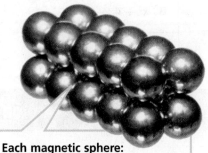

Each magnetic sphere:
mass: 8 grams
density of the magnet: 6.9 g/cm³

31. A cylindrical length of 14k gold wire is used in jewelry making. Estimate the diameter of the wire if a jeweler uses 2.380 grams of gold wire and the length is 50 times the width.

Density of gold wire: 14 g/cm³

32. (MP) **Use Structure** Consider the parent function $f(x) = x^n$ and the related transformation function $g(x) = a\left(\frac{1}{b}(x - h)\right)^n + k$.

A. For what values of a and b ($a \neq 1$ and $b \neq 1$) would a horizontal stretch be equivalent to a vertical compression? Explain your reasoning.

B. For what values of a and h ($a \neq 1$ and $h \neq 1$) would a horizontal translation be equivalent to a horizontal stretch? Explain your reasoning.

C. For what values of b and k ($b \neq 1$ and $k \neq 1$) would a vertical translation be equivalent to a vertical stretch? Explain your reasoning.

33. (Open Middle™) Using the digits 0 to 9, at most one time each, fill in the boxes to create a cubic function with its x-intercept.

$$y = \boxed{}\left(x - \boxed{}\right)^3 + \boxed{} \text{ with } x\text{-intercept } x = \boxed{}$$

Spiral Review • Assessment Readiness

34. Which ordered pair is a solution of the system $\begin{cases} y = -x^2 - 2x + 8 \\ y = 2 \end{cases}$?

Ⓐ $(2, 0)$ 　　　Ⓒ $(-4, 0)$

Ⓑ $\left(1 + \sqrt{7}, 2\right)$ 　　Ⓓ $(2, 2)$

35. For a given quadratic function, $f(x) \rightarrow +\infty$ as $x \rightarrow -\infty$. Which of the following statements must be true?

Ⓐ As $x \rightarrow +\infty, f(x) \rightarrow 0$.

Ⓑ As $x \rightarrow 0, f(x) \rightarrow 0$.

Ⓒ As $x \rightarrow +\infty, f(x) \rightarrow +\infty$.

Ⓓ As $x \rightarrow +\infty, f(x) \rightarrow -\infty$.

36. For each quadratic equation, identify the number and type of solution(s).

Equation	One real solution	Two real solutions	Two non-real solutions
A. $x^2 + 6x + 12 = 0$	?	?	?
B. $x^2 + 4x + 2 = -1$	?	?	?
C. $x^2 + 4x + 4 = 0$	?	?	?

 I'm in a Learning Mindset!

How does my stress level affect my learning outcome?

3.2

Analyze Graphs of Polynomial Functions

(I Can) use intercept form to graph and analyze polynomial functions.

Spark Your Learning

A woodworker is crafting an open-top box from a rectangular piece of wood. The woodworker will make the cuts marked, then place the sides on top of the edges of the base. The corner cut-outs will be discarded.

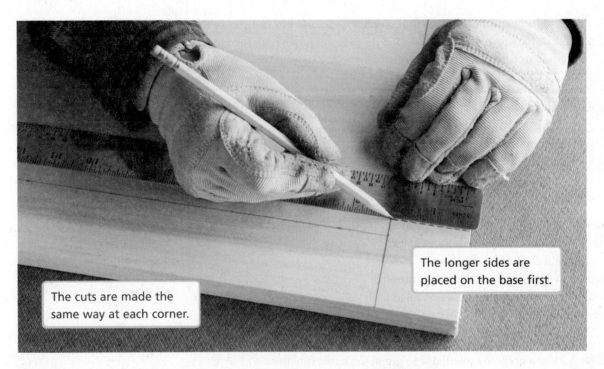

The cuts are made the same way at each corner.

The longer sides are placed on the base first.

Complete Part A as a whole class. Then complete Parts B–D in small groups.

A. What is a mathematical question you can ask about this situation? What information would you need to know to answer your question?

B. How are the dimensions of the corner cut-outs related to your question?

C. To answer your question, what strategy and tool would you use along with all the information you have? What answer do you get?

D. Are there any limits to the possible dimensions of the corner cut-outs? Explain your reasoning.

Turn and Talk Suppose a piece of wood with a 0.25-inch thickness is used to create the same box. How would this affect your answers?

©Houghton Mifflin Harcourt

Build Understanding

Identify Key Features of Graphs of Polynomial Functions

The cubic function $f(x) = x^3$ has three factors: x, x, and x. Replacing one or more of these factors with other linear factors in x, such as $x - 1$, still results in a cubic function.

Polynomial Functions

A polynomial function with n variable factors can be written in *intercept form* $p(x) = a(x - x_1)(x - x_2)\dots(x - x_n)$, where a, x_1, x_2,..., x_n are real numbers.

The x-intercepts of the graph of a polynomial function are x_1, x_2,..., and x_n.

The intercept form of a polynomial function helps identify key features of its graph. For example, examine the graph of $p(x) = (x + 1)^2(x - 1)$ shown here for $-2 \leq x \leq 1.75$.

The graph of $p(x)$ intersects the x-axis at its x-intercepts. Between two intercepts, the graph must move away from and return to the x-axis. This means the graph must have a **turning point** between the x-intercepts. The graph of $p(x)$ also has a turning point *on* the x-axis where it is tangent to the x-axis at the turning point.

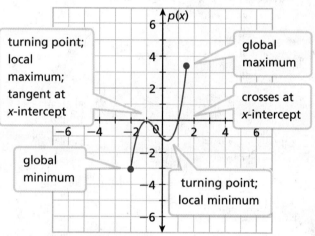

The y-values of the coordinates of turning points are maximum or minimum values, or *extrema*. A function value is an **absolute (or global) maximum or minimum** if that value is the greatest or least value for all domain values, and is a **local (or relative) maximum or minimum** at all other turning points of the graph.

1 ▶ **A.** Use a graphing calculator to graph the cubic functions $f(x) = x^3$, $f(x) = x^2(x - 1)$, and $f(x) = x(x - 1)(x + 1)$. Then copy and complete the table below.

Function	$f(x) = x^3$	$f(x) = x^2(x - 1)$	$f(x) = x(x - 1)(x + 1)$
Number of distinct factors	1	?	?
x-intercept(s)	$x = 0$	?	?
Tangent to or crosses the x-axis at each x-intercept?	crosses	?	?
Number of turning points	1	?	?
Number of turning points at a global maximum; at a local (non-global) maximum	0; 0	?	?
Number of turning points at a global minimum; at a local (non-global) minimum	0; 0	?	?

B. Use a graphing calculator to graph the quartic functions $f(x) = x^4$, $f(x) = x^3(x - 1)$, and $f(x) = x^2(x - 1)(x + 1)$. Then copy and complete the table below.

Function	$f(x) = x^4$	$f(x) = x^3(x - 1)$	$f(x) = x^2(x - 1)(x + 1)$
Number of distinct factors	1	?	?
x-intercept(s)	$x = 0$	?	?
Tangent to or crosses the x-axis at each x-intercept?	tangent	?	?
Number of turning points	1	?	?
Number of turning points at a global maximum; at a local (non-global) maximum	0; 0	?	?
Number of turning points at a global minimum; at a local (non-global) minimum	1; 0	?	?

C. Examine your tables from Parts A and B. What seems to determine the number of x-intercepts the graph of a polynomial function has? What observation(s) can you make about the degree of a polynomial function and the number of x-intercepts its graph can have?

D. What observation(s) can you make about the degree of a polynomial function and the number of turning points its graph can have? How is this related to the total number of extrema indicated by the graph? Graph $f(x) = x(x - 0.5)(x - 1)(x + 1)$. Do your observations here and in Part C hold for this function?

E. What observation(s) can you make about the degree of a linear factor of a polynomial function and whether its graph crosses the x-axis at the indicated x-intercept or is tangent to the x-axis at that point?

F. How would a leading coefficient of -1 for each polynomial affect the graphs and the answers in your tables for Parts A and B? Explain.

G. For polynomial functions for which the domain is all real numbers, will the graphs of cubic functions have a global maximum or minimum? Will the graphs of quartic functions have a global maximum or minimum? Explain. Can you extend your reasoning for these functions to polynomial functions of greater degree?

 Turn and Talk Look back at the graph of the cubic function on the previous page. Why does this graph indicate a global maximum and a global minimum when none of the graphs of the cubic functions you graphed for Part A do?

Step It Out

Sketch the Graph of a Polynomial Function in Intercept Form

A polynomial function's value is zero at each x-intercept. Over the interval between two consecutive x-intercepts or beyond any x-intercepts, the function values can be only positive or only negative. Otherwise, the graph would cross (or touch) the x-axis again. Because intercept form is a product of factors, the sign of the function for any value of x is found by multiplying the signs of the factors for that value of x.

The end behavior of a polynomial function $p(x) = a(x - x_1)(x - x_2)...(x - x_n)$ is determined by the degree of n and the sign of a. Using this and the intercept form as described above lets you sketch polynomial function graphs.

2 Sketch a graph of $f(x) = x(x + 4)(x - 2)$.

Identify the end behavior of the graph.
The degree of $f(x)$ is 3 and $a = 1$ is positive. So, $f(x)$ has the following end behavior:

As $x \rightarrow -\infty$, $f(x) \rightarrow -\infty$.

As $x \rightarrow +\infty$, $f(x) \rightarrow +\infty$.

> **A.** What does the end behavior tell you about the graph?

Identify the graph's x-intercepts, use them to define intervals, and create a table to find the sign of the function over each interval.
The x-intercepts are $x = -4$, $x = 0$, and $x = 2$. They divide the x-axis into four intervals: $x < -4$, $-4 < x < 0$, $0 < x < 2$, and $x > 2$. Test a value of x in each interval to determine the sign of $f(x)$ on the interval, then plot the signs above a number line.

Interval	$x < -4$	$-4 < x < 0$	$0 < x < 2$	$x > 2$
Sign of constant factor	+	+	+	+
Sign of x	−	−	+	+
Sign of $x + 4$	−	+	+	+
Sign of $x - 2$	−	−	−	+
Sign of $f(x)$	$(+)(-)(-)(-)$ $= -$	$(+)(-)(+)(-)$ $= +$	$(+)(+)(+)(-)$ $= -$	$(+)(+)(+)(+)$ $= +$

> **B.** How can you verify the results of this column?

> **C.** How does the number line relate to the graph of $f(x)$?

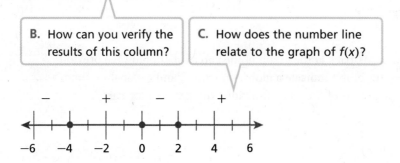

Sketch a graph.

Plot the intercepts. Use the sign table and the number line to help sketch a rough curve. For this purpose, you do not need to be precise about the y-coordinates of the points on the graph. Even a rough sketch reveals many key features, including increasing or decreasing behavior, intervals over which there is a local maximum or a local minimum, and the presence or absence of a global maximum or a global minimum.

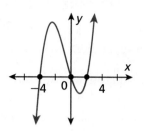

 Turn and Talk Can you think of situations for which you would need your graph to be more precise? Explain.

 Sketch a graph of $f(x) = -(x + 2)(x + 1)^2(x - 1)$.

Identify the end behavior of the graph.

The degree of $f(x)$ is 3 and $a = 1$ is positive, so $f(x)$ has the following end behavior:

As $x \to -\infty$, $f(x) \to -\infty$.

As $x \to +\infty$, $f(x) \to -\infty$.

A. How does the negative leading coefficient of $f(x)$ affect its end behavior?

Identify the graph's x-intercepts, use them to define intervals, and create a table to find the sign of the function over each interval.

The x-intercepts are $x = -2$, $x = -1$, and $x = 1$.

B. How do you identify the x-intercepts?

Interval	$x < -2$	$-2 < x < -1$	$-1 < x < 1$	$x > 1$
Sign of constant factor	−	−	−	−
Sign of $x + 2$	−	+	+	+
Sign of $(x + 1)^2$	+	+	+	+
Sign of $x - 1$	−	−	−	+
Sign of $f(x)$	$(-)(-)(+)(-)$ $= -$	$(-)(+)(+)(-)$ $= +$	$(-)(+)(+)(-)$ $= +$	$(-)(+)(+)(+)$ $= -$

Sketch the graph.

Plot the intercepts. Use the sign table to help sketch a rough curve.

C. Is the graph of $f(x)$ positive on $(-2, 1)$? Explain.

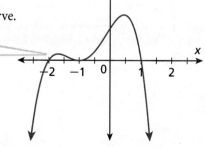

 Turn and Talk How will replacing the factor $(x + 1)^2$ in $f(x)$ in Task 3 by $(x + 1.1)(x + 0.9)$ change the key features of this graph? Explain.

Model Using a Polynomial Function

Polynomial functions model many real-world situations. Cubic polynomial function models often arise in applications about volume.

4 Sheena is creating an open-top box from a piece of cardboard. She forms a square flap of side length x at each corner by making a single cut (solid line) and then folding (dashed line) to form the flap. She then folds up the four sides of the box, and glues each flap to the side it overlaps. What value of x, to the nearest tenth, maximizes the box's volume?

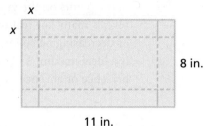

Use a verbal model.

Notice that folding up the sides shortens the length and width of the box as a function of the value x of a side length of the corners.

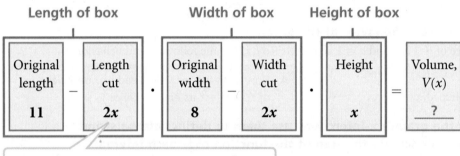

Length of box   Width of box   Height of box

Original length	Length cut		Original width	Width cut		Height		Volume, $V(x)$
11	2x	•	8	2x	•	x	=	?

A. Why are expressions in x subtracted for the length and width, but not for the height?

Write the function.
$$V(x) = (11 - 2x)(8 - 2x)(x)$$

B. What assumption is the volume model making about the thickness of the cardboard?

The box's dimensions must all be positive, which gives these domain restrictions:
$11 - 2x > 0$, or $x < 5.5$; $8 - 2x > 0$, or $x < 4$; and $x > 0$.
So, the domain is $0 < x < 4$.

Find the maximum of the function.
Use a graphing calculator to graph the volume function on its domain, and zoom in to find the maximum. The maximum value of about 60.0 occurs when $x \approx 1.53$.

Interpret the results.
The box has a maximum volume of about 60 in³ when square flaps with a side length of about 1.5 in. are made at the corners of the cardboard before folding the box.

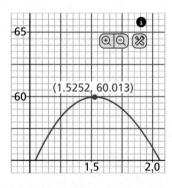

Turn and Talk What would the graph of the cubic function that provides the model look like over its unrestricted domain?

Check Understanding

1. Is it possible for a point on the graph of a polynomial function to represent a turning point, a local maximum, and a zero? Use a graph to justify your answer.

For Problems 2 and 3, use a graphing calculator to graph the polynomial function. Determine the x-intercepts, whether the graph crosses or is tangent to the x-axis at the x-intercept, the number of turning points, and the number and type (global, or local but not global) of any maximum or minimum values.

2. $f(x) = x(x - 1)(x + 2)$

3. $f(x) = -(x + 5)(x + 1)^2(x - 2)$

4. Sketch a graph of $f(x) = x(x - 2)(x + 1)$.

5. Ricardo is creating an open-top box from a piece of cardboard. He forms a square flap of side length x at each corner by making a single cut (solid line) and then folding (dashed line) to form the flap. He then folds up the four sides of the box, and glues each flap to the side it overlaps. What value of x, to the nearest tenth, maximizes the box's volume?

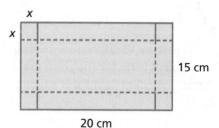

15 cm

20 cm

On Your Own

6. Is it possible for the graph of a quartic function to have exactly two turning points? Explain why or why not.

7. (MP) **Use Structure** Match each graph with its polynomial function in intercept form.

a. $y = \left(x - 2\frac{3}{4}\right)\left(x + 2\frac{3}{4}\right)^2\left(x + \frac{1}{4}\right)\left(x - \frac{1}{4}\right)$

b. $y = \left(x - 2\frac{3}{4}\right)\left(x + 2\frac{3}{4}\right)^2\left(x - 1\frac{3}{4}\right)$

c. $y = \left(x - 2\frac{3}{4}\right)\left(x + 2\frac{3}{4}\right)\left(x + 1\frac{3}{4}\right)\left(x^2 + \frac{1}{4}\right)$

d. $y = \left(x - 2\frac{3}{4}\right)\left(x + 2\frac{3}{4}\right)\left(x - 1\frac{3}{4}\right)\left(x + \frac{1}{2}\right)^2$

A.

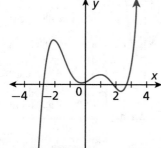

B.

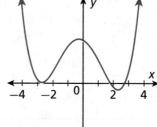

C.

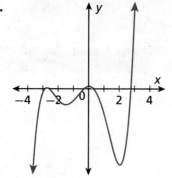

D.

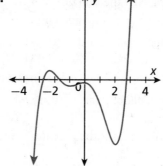

For Problems 8–13, use a graphing calculator to graph the polynomial function. Determine the x-intercepts, whether the graph crosses or is tangent to the x-axis at the x-intercept, the number of turning points, and the number and type (global, or local but not global) of any maximum or minimum values.

8. $f(x) = x(x - 2)(x - 3)$

9. $f(x) = (x + 1)(x - 1)(x - 2)$

10. $f(x) = -x(x - 1)^2$

11. $f(x) = (x - 2)^2(x - 3)^2$

12. $f(x) = -x(x + 2)^2(x - 5)$

13. $f(x) = x(x + 2)(x - 2)(x - 4)$

For Problems 14–17, sketch the graph of the polynomial function.

14. $f(x) = x(x + 2)^2(x - 2)$

15. $f(x) = -x(x + 3)^2(x - 1)$

16. $f(x) = x^2(x - 5)$

17. $f(x) = (x + 2)(x - 1)(x - 3)$

For Problems 18–21, write a cubic or quartic function with the least degree possible in intercept form for the given graph. Assume that all x-intercepts are integers, and that the constant factor *a* is either 1 or −1.

18.

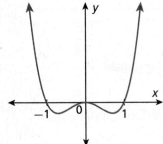

19.

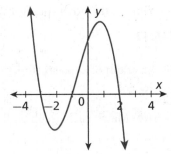

20.

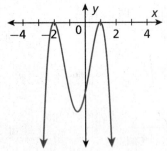

21.

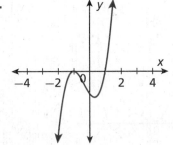

22. A company's profit P (in hundreds of thousands of dollars) from sales as one product cycle is replaced by a new one are modeled by the function shown, where $t = 0$ represents the just-concluded month.

$P(t) = 1.4(t + 1.5)(t - 8.8)(t - 17.4)$

  A. Sketch a rough graph of $P(t)$ for $0 \leq t \leq 20$ (do not include a vertical scale). How did you make your sketch? What do the x-intercepts represent?

  B. Using a graphing calculator's Table feature for whole-number values of t, what values are given for the initial and final profit? the maximum and minimum profit?

23. Tri forms a box from the poster board pattern shown by cutting along the solid segments and folding along the dashed segments. He glues the square corner flaps of side length x to the sides they overlap when they are folded. He then folds the left side of the pattern over the right side. The narrow rectangle in the pattern's center forms a side of the box. To close the lid, Tri tucks the sides of the lid inside the sides of the bottom. Find a polynomial function model $V(x)$ for the volume. What is the maximum volume to the nearest cubic inch?

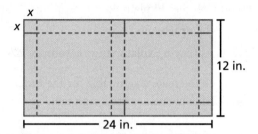

24. (MP) **Model with Mathematics** A rectangular piece of carton stock is rolled to form a cylindrical oatmeal container. The stock's perimeter is 96 cm. If x represents its length, then the cylinder has circumference $C = x - 1$, since a 1-centimeter overlap is glued to the other edge when the carton is formed. The top and bottom 1 centimeter are also folded or turned before the top and bottom are added. Find an expression for the interior height of the carton, then write a function that models the volume. What are the diameter and height (to the nearest tenth) that maximize the container's volume?

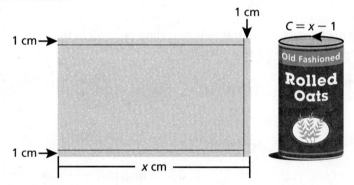

25. A company compares the profit/loss of two new products (in thousands of dollars) over a period of 4 years. The function $f(x) = x^2(x - 3.2)$ models the profit/loss for Product A, where x represents the number of years. The function $g(x) = x^2(x - 2.5)(x - 4.7)^2$ models the profit/loss for Product B, where x represents the number of years.

A. Estimate the maximum profit for the two products during the 4 years.

B. Estimate when the two products have the same value. What is that value? Explain how you determined your answer.

26. (MP) **Use Structure** Use your knowledge of sketching cubic and quartic polynomial functions to sketch a graph of the quintic polynomial function $f(x) = x(x + 2)^3(x - 1)$. Use a graphic calculator to check your sketch. Describe the behavior of the graph at the x-intercept -2.

27. Consider the polynomial function $f(x) = x(x - b)(x + b)$ where $b \neq 0$. Identify the domain and range of the function. Determine the x-intercepts and the number of turning points, then sketch a graph of the function. Is the function even, odd, or neither?

28. The graph of the polynomial function $f(x)$ has two x-intercepts, $x = -4$ and $x = 2$, and three turning points. The graph also shows a global maximum.

    A. Does $f(x)$ have an even degree or an odd degree? Explain your reasoning.

    B. Can you determine the degree of $f(x)$? Why or why not?

    C. What is the sign of the leading coefficient of $f(x)$? Explain your reasoning.

29. (MP) **Construct Arguments** Tory was asked to create a sign table for the function $f(x) = x(x - 2)(x + 3)$. Describe her error. Then create a correct sign table and sketch a graph of $f(x)$.

Interval	$x < -2$	$-2 < x < 0$	$0 < x < 3$	$x > 3$
Sign of constant factor	+	+	+	+
Sign of x	−	−	+	+
Sign of $x - 2$	−	−	−	+
Sign of $x + 3$	+	+	+	+
Sign of $f(x)$	$(+)(-)(-)(+)$ $= +$	$(+)(-)(-)(+)$ $= +$	$(+)(+)(-)(+)$ $= -$	$(+)(+)(+)(+)$ $= +$

30. (Open Middle™) Using the integers -9 to 9, at most one time each, fill in the boxes to create a polynomial function with matching roots.

$y = \boxed{}x^3 + \boxed{}x^2 + \boxed{}x + \boxed{}$ with roots of $x = \boxed{}$, $x = \boxed{}$, and $x = \boxed{}$

Spiral Review • Assessment Readiness

31. Which equation has one real solution?

    (A) $2x^2 + 4x = 14$ (C) $x^2 + 2 = 16x$

    (B) $-9 - x^2 + 3x = -3x$ (D) $x^2 + 3 = x - 12$

32. What is the solution to the system
$$\begin{cases} y = x^2 + 3x - 4 \\ y = -2x + 2 \end{cases}?$$

    (A) $(1, 0)$ and $(-6, 14)$ (C) $(0, 1)$ only

    (B) $(2, 6)$ and $(-2, -6)$ (D) no real solution

33. A magnetic sphere has a mass of 22 grams and a density of 0.36 g/cm³. What is the approximate radius of the sphere?

    (A) 1.44 cm   (C) 7.61 cm

    (B) 2.44 cm   (D) 9.13 cm

34. What is the sum of $(a + b)$ and $(a - b)$?

    (A) $a^2 - b^2$ (C) $2a - 2b$

    (B) $2a + 2b$ (D) $2a$

 I'm in a Learning Mindset!

What stress-management skills can I use to complete tasks involving polynomial functions?

Review

Transformations of Polynomial Functions

Identify the transformations of the graph of $f(x) = x^3$ that produce the graph of $g(x) = -2(x - 1)^3 + 3$. Then graph $g(x)$ on the same coordinate grid as the graph of $f(x)$.

Identify the parameters for $g(x)$.

$a = -2, b = 1, h = 1, k = 3$

> These values indicate that the graph of $g(x)$ is a reflection of the graph of $f(x)$ over the x-axis, a vertical stretch by a factor of 2, and a translation 1 unit right and 3 units up.

Use the three reference points on $f(x)$ to find the corresponding points for $g(x)$.

$f(x) = x^3$		$g(x) = -2(x - 1)^3 + 3$	
x	**y**	**x**	**y**
−1	−1	0	5
0	0	1	3
1	1	2	1

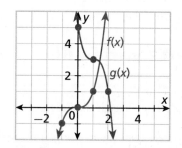

Graph Polynomial Functions in Intercept Form

Use a sign table to sketch a graph of $f(x) = x(x - 1)^2$.

The x-intercepts are $x = 0$ and $x = 1$.

> Use the x-intercepts to determine the intervals.

Interval	$x < 0$	$0 < x < 1$	$x > 1$
Constant	+	+	+
x	−	+	+
$(x - 1)^2$	+	+	+
Sign of $f(x)$	$(+)(-)(+)$ $= -$	$(+)(+)(+)$ $= +$	$(+)(+)(+)$ $= +$

> Use the x-intercepts and the positive and negative intervals from the sign table to sketch the graph.

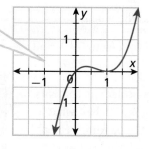

Model with Polynomial Functions

What is the maximum volume of a box created by folding up the sides of the sheet of cardboard modeled below?

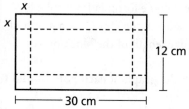

> The domain of $V(x)$ is restricted to values of x that give positive dimensions for the box.

Write an equation for the volume of the box.

$V(x) = (30 - 2x)(12 - 2x)(x)$

Find the maximum value of the function.

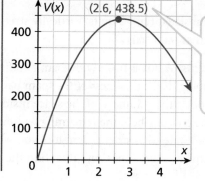

> The maximum volume of the box is about 438.5 cm³ when x is 2.6 cm.

Vocabulary

Choose the correct term from the box to complete each sentence.

Vocabulary

cubic function
global maximum
local minimum
polynomial function

1. A __?__ is a function that has the standard form $f(x) = ax^3 + bx^2 + cx + d$, where a, b, c, and d are real numbers and $a \neq 0$.

2. A __?__ is a function that has the standard form $p(x) = a_n x^n + a_{n-1} x^{n-1} + \ldots + a_2 x^2 + a_1 x + a_0$, where $a_n, a_{n-1}, \ldots, a_2, a_1,$ and a_0 are real numbers and $a \neq 0$.

3. A function f has a __?__ at $x = a$ if $f(x) < f(a)$ for all values of $x \neq a$ in its domain.

4. A function f has a __?__ at $x = a$ if $f(x) > f(a)$ for all values of $x \neq a$ in an interval around a.

Concepts and Skills

5. Describe how the graph of $g(x) = 2(x - 1)^4 - 3$ is related to the graph of $f(x) = x^4$. Then sketch the graph of f and g on the same coordinate grid.

6. The general equation for the graph shown at the right is $g(x) = a(x - h)^3 + k$. Use the reference points given on the graph to identify the values of a, h, and k. Then use the values to write an equation for $g(x)$.

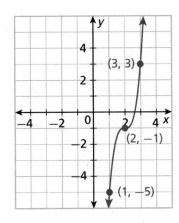

7. A cube-shaped block of ice has a mass of 59 kilograms. The density of ice is 917 kilograms per cubic meter. The mass of an object is the product of its density and its volume. Write a cubic function to model the mass of a block of ice in terms of its edge length x (in meters).

   Recall that the volume formula for a cube is $V = s^3$, where s is the length of each edge of the cube. Use a graph of the mass function to estimate the edge length of the block of ice.

For 8 and 9, sketch the graph of each polynomial function.

8. $f(x) = x(x + 2)(x + 4)$

9. $f(x) = x^2(x - 3)(x + 3)$

For 10 and 11, write an equation for $g(x)$ given the description of how the graph of $f(x)$ is transformed to obtain the graph of $g(x)$.

10. $f(x) = x^3$; translated down 3 units and reflected across the y-axis

11. $f(x) = x^5$; translated right 2 units, vertically stretched by a factor of 3, and reflected across the x-axis

12. (MP) **Use Tools** A box is lined with foam padding to protect its contents during shipping. If the thickness of the foam padding is x inches, what function models the volume V of the space inside of the padding? How thick can the padding be if the remaining volume is to be at least 891 cubic inches? State what strategy and tool you will use to answer the question, explain your choice, and then find the answer.

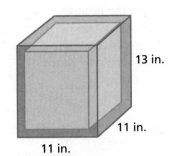

13 in.

11 in.

11 in.

Module 4

Function Operations and Polynomials

Module Performance Task: Focus on STEM

Secret-Sharing Schemes

A secret-sharing scheme is a way to make sure that only a specific group of authorized individuals can reconstruct coded information. Secret-sharing schemes are important tools in cryptography, and they are used as a key building block for digital security.

One secret-sharing scheme uses Lagrange polynomials to reconstruct the protected secret. If the available information is given as $(1, 4)$, $(2, 16)$, $(3, 36)$ and (m, n), then one piece of the Lagrange polynomial is found with the equation below.

$$L_1(x) = 4 \cdot \frac{(x - 2)(x - 3)(x - m)}{(1 - 2)(1 - 3)(1 - m)}$$

A. Identify what happens when the function is evaluated at the x-coordinate of each of the construction points. Explain how the form of the expression guarantees this.

B. Write the corresponding Lagrange polynomials L_2, L_3, and L_m. Describe what pattern you used.

C. Explain why the sum $L(x) = L_1(x) + L_2(x) + L_3(x) + L_m(x)$ is guaranteed to pass through each of the construction points. Use a graph to support your reasoning.

D. Choose values for m and n and simplify the expression. Show a partner your simplified expression and have them guess what values you chose.

Are You Ready?

Complete these problems to review prior concepts and skills you will need for this module.

Simplify Algebraic Expressions

Simplify each expression.

1. $\frac{1}{2}(6x + 5) - x + \frac{7}{2}$

2. $5x - 9 + 3(x - 4)$

3. $27x + 7x(6 - 2x) - 4(-3x + 2)$

4. $0.76 + 0.25(8x - 2) - 0.56x + 2.82$

5. $\frac{2}{3}(6x - 1) - \frac{1}{3}(12x + 4)$

6. $1.54x - 4(2.5x + 3) + 8.2x$

Multiply Binomials

Simplify each expression.

7. $(4x + 1)(3x - 2)$

8. $(3x - 7)^2$

9. $(x - 5)(x + 5)$

10. $(2x - 9)(3x - 4)$

11. $(2x - 5)(2x + 3)$

12. $(5x - 6)(5x + 6)$

Factor Quadratic Expressions

Factor each quadratic expression.

13. $x^2 + 6x + 9$

14. $x^2 - 64$

15. $x^2 + 2x - 24$

16. $3x^2 + x - 10$

17. $2x^2 + 5x - 12$

18. $4x^2 - 8x - 5$

Connecting Past and Present Learning

Previously, you learned:

- to use properties of operations to write equivalent expressions,
- to use properties of operations to add, subtract, factor, and expand linear expressions with rational coefficients, and
- to add, subtract, and multiply polynomials.

In this module, you will learn:

- to explain why the set of polynomials is closed under addition, subtraction, and multiplication, and perform these operations along with division,
- to combine functions using arithmetic operations, and
- to factor polynomials completely and identify zeros.

Function Operations

(I Can) create a new function by adding, subtracting, multiplying, or dividing two two existing functions.

Spark Your Learning

As part of a report she was writing, María researched data about the fuel consumption of cars in the United States.

From 2006 to 2016, the average total fuel consumption per U.S. passenger vehicle decreased, while the average vehicle fuel economy increased.

Complete Part A as a whole class. Then complete Parts B–D in small groups.

A. What is a mathematical question can you ask about this situation? What information would you need to know to answer your question?

B. How could you find a linear model for the average fuel consumption per vehicle over this time period? How could you find a linear model for the average fuel efficiency over the same period?

C. To answer your question, what strategy and tool would you use along with all the information you have? What answer do you get?

D. Does your answer make sense in the context of the situation? Can you use your answer to predict the average number of miles driven in 2026? Explain.

Turn and Talk How would the model change if instead of combining linear models, you instead found the average total number of vehicle miles driven in 2006 and 2016 and used these values to find a linear model? Do you think one model is better than another? Explain.

Build Understanding

Investigate Combining Functions

You have combined algebraic expressions using all of the basic arithmetic operations $(+, -, \times, \div)$ before. Similarly, you can use these operations to combine the expressions that represent two functions so that you can write a new function.

1 How can you create a new function by using arithmetic operations to combine two functions?

A. Let $f(x) = 2x^2$ and $g(x) = x + 5$. Evaluate $f(x)$ and $g(x)$ for $x = -1, 2,$ and 5. Then use the values of $f(x)$ and $g(x)$ to evaluate $f(x) + g(x)$, $f(x) - g(x)$, $f(x) \cdot g(x)$, and $\frac{f(x)}{g(x)}$. Organize your answers in a table like the one shown below.

x	f(x)	g(x)	f(x) + g(x)	f(x) − g(x)	f(x) · g(x)	$\frac{f(x)}{g(x)}$
−1	?	?	?	?	?	?
2	?	?	?	?	?	?
3	?	?	?	?	?	?

B. Now combine the expressions in x that define $f(x)$ and $g(x)$ by using the four arithmetic operations to obtain algebraic expressions for the combined functions below.

$$f(x) + g(x) = \underline{\quad ? \quad} \qquad f(x) - g(x) = \underline{\quad ? \quad}$$

$$f(x) \cdot g(x) = \underline{\quad ? \quad} \qquad \frac{f(x)}{g(x)} = \underline{\quad ? \quad}$$

Simplify the resulting expressions.

C. Create a new table similar to the one in Part A, but without the columns for $f(x)$ and $g(x)$. Write the simplified expressions that you found in Part B as the column heads of Columns 2–5. Then, in Rows 2–4, evaluate each of these expressions for $x = -1$, $x = 2$, and $x = 5$.

D. Compare the table from Part A with the table you created for Part C. What do you observe about the values?

E. What can you conclude from your answer to Part D?

F. When combining functions, how does division differ from addition, subtraction, and multiplication? Explain.

 Turn and Talk How do you know that each arithmetic operation with two function expressions creates a new function?

Step It Out

Operate with Functions

In the Build Understanding, you saw functions combined using arithmetic operations to produce a new function. The table below summarizes the four basic function operations.

Arithmetic Operations with Functions $f(x)$ and $g(x)$	
Operation	**New function $h(x)$**
Addition	$h(x) = (f + g)(x) = f(x) + g(x)$
Subtraction	$h(x) = (f - g)(x) = f(x) - g(x)$
Multiplication	$h(x) = (fg)(x) = f(x) \cdot g(x)$
Division	$h(x) = \left(\dfrac{f}{g}\right)(x) = \dfrac{f(x)}{g(x)}$, where $g(x) \neq 0$

2 ▸ Let $f(x) = x^2 - 3x - 15$ and $g(x) = x^2 + 7x + 8$.

Find $(f + g)(x)$ and $(f - g)(x)$. Simplify your results.

$$(f + g)(x) = f(x) + g(x)$$

$$(f - g)(x) = f(x) - g(x)$$

A. What properties justify proceeding from this step to the conclusion?

$$= (x^2 - 3x - 15) + (x^2 + 7x + 8)$$

$$= x^2 - 3x - 15 + x^2 + 7x + 8$$

$$= 2x^2 + 4x - 7$$

$$= (x^2 - 3x - 15) - (x^2 + 7x + 8)$$

$$= x^2 - 3x - 15 - x^2 - 7x - 8$$

$$= -10x - 23$$

B. How can you justify this result from the subtraction expression in the step above?

3 ▸ Let $f(x) = 3x^2$ and $g(x) = 4x - 5$.

Find $(fg)(x)$ and $\left(\dfrac{g}{f}\right)(x)$. Simplify your results.

$$(fg)(x) = f(x) \cdot g(x)$$

$$\left(\dfrac{g}{f}\right)(x) = \dfrac{g(x)}{f(x)}$$

$$= (3x^2) \cdot (4x - 5)$$

$$= \dfrac{4x - 5}{3x^2}$$

$$= 12x^3 - 15x^2$$

A. How can you justify the values of the exponents of x in this step?

B. Are there any values of x for which $\left(\dfrac{g}{f}\right)(x)$ is undefined?

Turn and Talk How do the domains of the new functions compare to the domains of the original functions?

Model with Function Operations

4 Reynaldo self-publishes a travel book. His revenue r in dollars from selling x books is modeled by $r(x) = 15x$. The function $c(x) = 6x + 7250$ models the cost c to print x copies of the book. Write a function that models Reynaldo's profit P from selling x books. What is his profit from printing and selling 3500 books?

Remember that profit is the difference of revenue and cost. So, Reynaldo's profit is modeled by the function $P(x) = (r - c)(x)$.

$$P(x) = (r - c)(x) = r(x) - c(x)$$

A. What does it mean if the value of $P(x)$ is negative?

$$= 15x - (6x + 7250)$$

$$= 9x - 7250$$

B. For this expression to give the true profit, what must be true about x in $r(x)$ and $c(x)$? Explain.

So, $P(3500) = 9(3500) - 7250 = 24{,}250$.

Reynaldo's total profit is $24{,}250.

5 A coffee shop chain is growing both in its number of locations and its revenue per location. The projected number of shops f and the annual revenue r per shop (in thousands of dollars) x years from now are shown at the right. Find a function that models the total projected annual revenue for the chain x years from now. What is the total projected revenue 4 years from now?

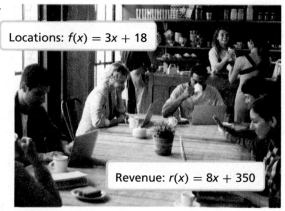

Locations: $f(x) = 3x + 18$

Revenue: $r(x) = 8x + 350$

The total revenue T from all the shops is the product of the number of shops and the revenue per shop, or the product of $r(x)$ and $f(x)$.

$$T(x) = (rf)(x) = r(x) \cdot f(x)$$

$$= (8x + 350)(3x + 18)$$

A. How can you verify that this function expression gives the correct units?

$$= 24x^2 + 1194x + 6300$$

So, $T(4) = 24(4)^2 + 1194(4) + 6300 = 11{,}460$.

Because $T(x)$ is in thousands of dollars, 11,460 represents $11,460,000.

The total projected revenue in 4 years is $11,460,000.

B. Does this result seem reasonable? Explain.

 Turn and Talk Are there any algebraic or real-world limitations on the models for Tasks 4 and 5? Explain your reasoning.

Check Understanding

1. **(MP) Use Structure** Evaluate $f(x) = 3x - 2$ and $g(x) = 4 + x$ at $x = -1, 2,$ and 5. Use these values of $f(x)$ and $g(x)$ to evaluate $f(x) + g(x)$, $f(x) - g(x)$, $f(x) \cdot g(x)$, and $\frac{f(x)}{g(x)}$ for these values of x. Next, combine the function expressions to form four new functions, and evaluate each at $x = -1, 2,$ and 5 to verify that the results are the same.

For Problems 2 and 3, use $f(x) = 2x^2 - 3x + 7$ and $g(x) = -x^2$.

2. Find $(f + g)(x)$ and $(f - g)(x)$.

3. Find $(fg)(x)$ and $\left(\frac{f}{g}\right)(x)$.

4. **(MP) Model with Mathematics** Sri turns on the bathtub spout to warm up the water already in the tub. The amount of water (in gallons) in the tub x minutes after turning on the spout if no other water leaves or enters is modeled by $f(x) = 2.4x + 15$. When Sri turns on the spout, however, he accidentally opens the drain, which drains 3.1 gallons per minute from the tub. Use a function operation to write a model for the amount of water in the tub x minutes after the spout is turned on and the drain is opened. If Sri leaves when he turns on the water and returns 10 minutes later, how much water is in the tub?

5. **(MP) Model with Mathematics** The function model $p(x) = 5 + 2x$ represents the number of employees p of a small company where x is the number of years after 2018. The average employee salary s in thousands of dollars for this period can be modeled by $s(x) = 1.05x + 46$. Use a function operation to write a model for the total salary T for the staff at the company after x years. If these models hold until 2030, what is the approximate total staff salary in 2030?

On Your Own

6. **(MP) Reason** Consider the functions $f(x) = 8 - 5x$ and $g(x) = -3x^2$. Write a new function $h(x) = \frac{g(x)}{f(x)}$. What is the domain of the new function? Explain.

7. **(MP) Communicate with Mathematics** How can some transformations of functions be represented by arithmetic combinations of functions?

Find an expression for the indicated function if $f(x) = 5x - 3$, $g(x) = 4x^2$, and $h(x) = 9 - x^2$.

8. $(f + h)(x)$

9. $(f - h)(x)$

10. $(g - f)(x)$

11. $(gh)(x)$

12. $(h - g)(x)$

13. $(fh)(x)$

14. $\left(\frac{f}{g}\right)(x)$

15. $\left(\frac{g}{h}\right)(x)$

16. **(MP) Use Structure** Andrei earns money mowing lawns, but must pay for gas and upkeep of his equipment. The models shown are in dollars, and x represents the number of lawns mowed.

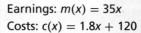

Earnings: $m(x) = 35x$
Costs: $c(x) = 1.8x + 120$

   A. Write a model that represents Andrei's profit p.

   B. How much profit will Andrei make for mowing 75 lawns?

17. Let $f(x) = 2x^2 + 3x$. Given that $(f \cdot g)(x) = 2x^3 - 3x^2 - 9x$, what is $g(x)$? What operation did you use to find $g(x)$?

18. A specialty bicycle shop plans to produce $P(m) = 120 + 20m$ bicycles each month this year, where m is the month number (January $= 1$). As they gain efficiencies with growing production, they expect the cost C of producing each bicycle to decrease according to the model $C(m) = 680 - 10m$.

　A. What is the predicted cost to produce a bicycle in January? In December?

　B. Find a model for the total cost T of production in month m. What is $T(12)$? What is the meaning of $T(12)$?

19. (MP) **Model with Mathematics** A family is 500 feet above the ground in the basket of a hot air balloon and ascending at the constant rate shown. At that height, someone accidentally drops a penny out of the balloon.

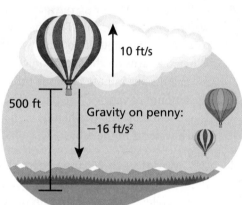

10 ft/s

500 ft

Gravity on penny: -16 ft/s²

　A. Write models for the height b (in feet) of the balloon and the height h of the penny x seconds after the penny is dropped.

　B. Write a model for the distance between the balloon and the penny? What is the approximate domain of the model? Explain.

　C. Can you find the distance between the balloon and penny 10 seconds after the penny is dropped? Explain.

Spiral Review • Assessment Readiness

20. The graph of which equation has a vertex at $(2, -5)$?

　Ⓐ $y - 5 = 2(x - 2)^2$

　Ⓑ $y - 5 = -2(x + 2)^2$

　Ⓒ $y + 5 = -3(x - 2)^2$

　Ⓓ $y + 5 = 3(x + 2)^2$

21. Which are zeros of the function $f(x) = 2x^2 + x - 28$? Select all that apply.

　Ⓐ -7　　　　　Ⓓ $\frac{7}{2}$

　Ⓑ -4　　　　　Ⓔ 7

　Ⓒ $-\frac{7}{2}$　　　　Ⓕ 8

22. How many x-intercepts does the graph of $y = (x - 5)(x - 3)(x + 1)$ have?

　Ⓐ 1　　　　　Ⓒ 3

　Ⓑ 2　　　　　Ⓓ 4

23. What is the result of the operation $(x^3 - 2x + 7) - (2x^2 - 5x + 11)$?

　Ⓐ $-x^3 + 3x + 15$

　Ⓑ $x^3 + 2x^2 - 7x + 15$

　Ⓒ $x^3 - 2x^2 - 7x - 4$

　Ⓓ $x^3 - 2x^2 + 3x - 4$

I'm in a Learning Mindset!

What stress-management skills can I use to help me as I combine functions in this lesson?

Add and Subtract Polynomials

(I Can) add and subtract polynomial expressions, including those representing real-world situations.

Spark Your Learning

Latisha researched the participation of men and women in sports at NCAA colleges. She gathered data on the total participation from Divisions I, II, and III for men and women over the school years 1989–1990 to 2015–2016 and plotted the data. Then she calculated and graphed polynomial functions that modeled the data.

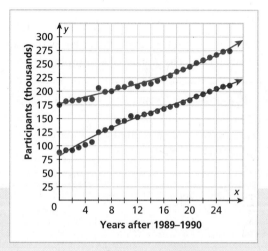

Complete Part A as a whole class. Then complete Parts B–D in small groups.

A. What is a mathematical question you can ask about this situation? What information would you need to know to answer your question?

B. How can you compare the growth of women's participation versus men's participation in college sports?

C. To answer your question, what strategy and tool would you use along with all the information you have? What answer do you get?

D. Are you able to calculate the difference in the number of participants in the school year 2020–2021? Show how or explain why not.

Turn and Talk Predict how your answer would change if the number of women's sports opportunities increased significantly.

Build Understanding

Identify and Analyze Monomials and Polynomials

A **monomial** is a number or a product of a number and variables with whole number exponents. A **polynomial** is a monomial or sum of monomials.

Monomials	Polynomials
-10	$x + 2$
x^4	$1 + 4x - x^2$
$3xy^5$	$x^2y + xy^3 + 2x - 23$

Monomials and polynomials can be classified by the exponents of their variable terms. The **degree of a monomial** is the sum of the exponents of the variables in the monomial, and the **degree of a polynomial** is the greatest degree of its monomial terms. Polynomials are often written in standard form, in which the terms of the polynomial are ordered from greatest degree to least degree. When written in standard form, the coefficient of the first term is called the **leading coefficient**.

Polynomial	Standard Form	Degree	Leading Coefficient
$4 - 3x$	$-3x + 4$	1	-3
$18x + 6 - 2x^2$	$-2x^2 + 18x + 6$	2	-2
$4x^7 - 2x^3 + x^4 + 16x^5$	$4x^7 + 16x^5 + x^4 - 2x^3$	7	4

1 **A.** Give two examples of expressions that are not polynomials for different reasons. Explain why each expression is not a polynomial.

B. Write the polynomial $9x + 4x^4 - 2x^2 + 16x^3 - x^5$ in standard form. Then identify the degree and leading coefficient.

C. If k is a real number, then k is a polynomial expression. What is the degree of the polynomial k? Explain your reasoning.

D. Give an example of a polynomial that has three terms, a leading coefficient of -4, and a degree of 5.

 Turn and Talk Is $(2x)(4x)$ a polynomial? Explain your reasoning.

2 **A.** Use the Distributive Property to add the monomials $-3x^2y$ and $9x^2y$.

B. Can the Distributive Property be used to add the monomials $8x^3y^2$ and $2x^2y^3$? Explain your reasoning.

C. Given that a and b are real numbers, and n is a whole number, write $ax^n + bx^n$ as a monomial. Use the result to find $-3x^4 + x^4$.

D. When the polynomials $3x^2 + 7x^5 - 24$ and $2 - 4x^3 + x^5$ are added, which pairs of monomial terms can be added? Why might it be helpful to write the polynomials in standard form before performing the addition?

 Turn and Talk What conditions must be met in order to be able to write the sum of two monomials as a monomial?

120

Step It Out

Add Polynomials

To add two polynomial, add the like terms of the two polynomials. When working with polynomials in one variable, like terms are monomials that have the same variable and exponent.

3   Two methods for adding $2x^3 - 9 - 7x + 3x^2$ and $6x^2 - 8x - x^3 + 12$ are shown.

Method 1: Vertically

$$
\begin{array}{rcrcrcr}
2x^3 & + & 3x^2 & - & 7x & - & 9 \\
+ \quad -x^3 & + & 6x^2 & - & 8x & + & 12 \\
\hline
(2-1)x^3 & + & (3+6)x^2 & + & (-7-8)x & + & (-9+12) \\
x^3 & + & 9x^2 & - & 15x & + & 3
\end{array}
$$

First polynomial in standard form
Second polynomial in standard form
Add terms vertically by adding coefficients.
Simplify.

Method 2: Horizontally

$$
\left(2x^3 - 9 - 7x + 3x^2\right) + \left(6x^2 - 8x - x^3 + 12\right)
$$
$$
= \left(2x^3 - x^3\right) + \left(3x^2 + 6x^2\right) + \left(-7x - 8x\right) + \left(-9 + 12\right)
$$
$$
= (2-1)x^3 + (3+6)x^2 + (-7-8)x + (-9+12)
$$
$$
= x^3 + 9x^2 - 15x + 3
$$

A. Describe how the methods are similar and how they are different.

B. Which method do you prefer? Why?

Subtract Polynomials

To subtract two polynomials, add the opposite of the subtracted polynomial.

4   Two methods for subtracting $-9y - 2y^3 + 6 + 12y^2$ from $8y^3 - 3y^2 + 5$ are shown.

Method 1: Vertically

$$
\begin{array}{rcrcrcr}
8y^3 & - & 3y^2 & + & 0y & + & 5 \\
+ \quad 2y^3 & - & 12y^2 & + & 9y & - & 6 \\
\hline
(8+2)y^3 & + & (-3-12)y^2 & + & (0+9)y & + & (5-6) \\
10y^3 & - & 15y^2 & + & 9y & - & 1
\end{array}
$$

First polynomial in standard form
Opposite of second polynomial in standard form
Add terms vertically by adding coefficients.
Simplify.

Method 2: Horizontally

$$
\left(8y^3 - 3y^2 + 5\right) - \left(-2y^3 + 12y^2 - 9y + 6\right) = \left(8y^3 - 3y^2 + 5\right) + \left(2y^3 - 12y^2 + 9y - 6\right)
$$
$$
= (8+2)y^3 + (-3-12)y^2 + (0+9)y + (5-6)
$$
$$
= 10y^3 - 15y^2 + 9y - 1
$$

A. Describe how the methods are similar and how they are different.

B. Which method do you prefer? Why?

 Turn and Talk Is the sum or difference of two polynomials always another polynomial? How do you know?

Model Using Polynomial Addition or Subtraction

5 A fitness supply company manufactures stretching rollers. The functions $O(x) = 0.25x^3 - 1.8x^2 + 32.4x + 30$ and $R(x) = 0.04x^3 - 3.04x^2 + 57.76x$ give the number of online sales and retail sales, in thousands, during the xth month after being placed on the market, respectively. Estimate the total number of sales during the fourth month.

> **A.** How can you decide which pairs of terms to add in this step?

The function $T(x) = O(x) + R(x)$ models the total number of sales.

$$O(x) + R(x) = \left(0.25x^3 - 1.8x^2 + 32.4x + 30\right) + \left(0.04x^3 - 3.04x^2 + 57.76x\right)$$

$$= \left(0.25x^3 + 0.04x^3\right) + \left(-1.8x^2 - 3.04x^2\right) + \left(32.4x + 57.76x\right) + (30)$$

$$= (0.25 + 0.04)x^3 + (-1.8 - 3.04)x^2 + (32.4 + 57.76)x + 30$$

$$= 0.29x^3 - 4.84x^2 + 90.16x + 30$$

Substitute 4 for x to find the total number of sales during the fourth month.

$$0.29(4)^3 - 4.84(4)^2 + 90.16(4) + 30 \approx 332$$

> **B.** Which property allows you to write the sum in this way from the previous step?

About 332,000 stretching rollers were sold online and in retail stores during the fourth month.

6 According to data from 2010 to 2018, the monthly value of U.S. exports can be modeled by the function $E(x) = 0.0103x^4 - 1.603x^3 + 55.7x^2 + 944.44x + 144{,}000$, where x is the number of months since the beginning of 2010 and $E(x)$ is the value of exports in millions of dollars. Similarly, the monthly value of U.S. imports can be modeled by the function $I(x) = 0.0073x^4 - 0.8319x^3 - 5.93x^2 + 2562.5x + 181{,}000$. Estimate how much more the value of imports was in January, 2014 than the value of exports.

Value of exports:
$E(x) = 0.0103x^4 - 1.603x^3 + 55.7x^2 + 944.44x + 144{,}000$

Value of imports:
$I(x) = 0.0073x^4 - 0.8319x^3 - 5.93x^2 + 2562.5x + 181{,}000$

The function $D(x) = I(x) - E(x)$ models the difference in imports and exports. Subtract the polynomial functions that model imports and exports.

> **A.** Why is this addition instead of subtraction?

$$\begin{array}{r} 0.0073x^4 - 0.8319x^3 - 5.93x^2 + 2562.5x + 181{,}000 \\ + -0.0103x^4 + 1.603x^3 - 55.7x^2 - 944.44x - 144{,}000 \\ \hline -0.003x^4 + 0.7711x^3 - 61.63x^2 + 1618.06x + 37{,}000 \end{array}$$

> **B.** How do the coefficients in the difference relate to the coefficients in the polynomial functions?

Substitute 48 months for x to find how much greater the value of imports were in January, 2014.

$$-0.003(48)^4 + 0.7711(48)^3 - 61.63(48)^2 + 1618.06(48) + 37{,}000 \approx 42{,}000$$

The value of imports was about $42 billion more than exports.

Check Understanding

1. Write the polynomial $2y - 6y^2 + 7 - 8y^3 + 3y$ in standard form. Then determine its degree and leading coefficient.

2. Add the monomials $8x^4y$ and $-7x^4y$ using the Distributive Property.

Perform the indicated operation. Write the result in standard form.

3. $\left(2x^2 - 3 + 4x\right) + \left(9 - 5x^2 - x^3\right)$

4. $\left(5 + z^3 - 3z^2\right) - \left(4z^2 - 2z + 7z^3 - 5\right)$

5. Water is being pumped into two tanks at variable rates. The volume of water in Tank A is modeled by $V_A(t) = -0.067t^3 + t^2$, and the volume of water in Tank B is modeled by $V_B(t) = -0.083t^3 + 1.125t^2 + 2.5t$, where t is the time in minutes since the tanks started to be filled. The volume is measured in gallons.

   A. Write an expression to model the total amount of water in tanks A and B. How much water is in both tanks after 3 minutes?

   B. Write an expression to model how much more water Tank B has than Tank A. How much more water is in Tank B after 4 minutes?

On Your Own

Write the polynomial in standard form. Find the degree and leading coefficient.

6. $-2x + 7x^3 - 9 + 4x^5$

7. $3y - 7y^2 + 4y^3 + 5y^4$

Perform the indicated operation. Write the result in standard form.

8. $\left(2x + 3x^2 - 5 + x^3\right) + \left(8x^2 - 6x - x^3\right)$

9. $\left(8x^2 - 4x + 12\right) - \left(5x^2 + x - 3\right)$

10. $\left(6x - 2x^3 + 1\right) - \left(7x^2 - 5 - 4x^3\right)$

11. $\left(4 - 3x + 2x^2\right) + \left(x^3 - 7x + 5\right)$

12. $\left(x^3 + 3x^2 - 4x + 1\right) + \left(2 - x^3 + x^2\right)$

13. $\left(5x^4 - x^2 + x\right) - \left(-2x^2 + 7x^4 - x\right)$

14. $\left(0.5x^2 - 0.1x + 2\right) - \left(5x - 1.6x^2\right)$

15. $\left(-9 + 2x^7 - x\right) + \left(9 + x - 2x^7\right)$

16. The population, in thousands, of a city is $58 + x - 0.05x^2$. The population of the rest of the towns in the county is $24 + 3x$. The number of years since 2010 is represented by x in both populations.

    A. Write an expression to represent the population of the entire county x years after 2010.

    B. What is the predicted population of the entire county in the year 2024?

17. According to data from 2008–2016, the number of full-time students enrolled in a degree-granting institution can be modeled by the function $F(x) = -2.634x^4 + 57.36x^3 - 444.5x^2 + 1258x + 10{,}236$, where $F(x)$ is the number of students in thousands and x is the number of years since 2008. Similarly, the number of part-time students can be modeled by the function $P(x) = 6.34x^3 - 99.5x^2 + 432.7x + 6105$. Estimate how many more students were full time than part time in 2012.

Part-time students:
$P(x) = 6.34x^3 - 99.5x^2 + 432.7x + 6105$

18. Charisse is volunteering at a local park where they are fencing in a rectangular area with several basketball courts. The length of the area to be fenced is 5 meters less than twice the width.

   A. Write an expression for the perimeter of the area if the width of the area is w meters.

   B. If the area is 18 meters wide, what is the total amount of fencing needed?

19. (MP) **Construct Arguments** Present a formal argument for why the set of polynomials is closed under addition and subtraction. Use the polynomials $ax^m + bx^m$ and $ax^m - bx^m$ for real numbers a, b, and whole number m to explain your reasoning.

20. (Open Middle™) Using the integers -9 to 9, at most one time each, fill in the boxes to make a true statement.

$$\left(\boxed{}x^3 + \boxed{}x + \boxed{}\right) - \left(\boxed{}x^3 + \boxed{}x^2 + \boxed{}x - \boxed{}\right)$$

$$= \left(\boxed{}x^3 + \boxed{}x^2 + \boxed{}x + \boxed{}\right)$$

Spiral Review • Assessment Readiness

21. Which describes the transformation of the graph of $f(x) = x^2$ to obtain the graph of $g(x) = (x - 3)^2$?

   (A) a translation 3 units right

   (B) a translation 3 units left

   (C) a translation 3 units down

   (D) a translation 3 units up

22. Use the the table to calculate $(fg)(2)$.

x	0	1	2	3
f(x)	0	2	3	10
g(x)	1	6	-2	-4

   (A) -12 (C) -4

   (B) -6 (D) 1

23. A box assembled from a sheet of cardboard has a height of x inches. The volume of the box is modeled by $V(x) = 4x^3 - 60x^2 + 200x$. What is the approximate maximum volume of the box?

   (A) 200 in^3 (C) 15 in^3

   (B) 192 in^3 (D) 7.5 in^3

24. Let $f(x) = x^2 - 10x + 8$ and $g(x) = 3x^3$. What is the value of $\left(\frac{f}{g}\right)(-2)$?

   (A) $-\frac{4}{3}$ (C) $\frac{3}{4}$

   (B) $-\frac{3}{4}$ (D) $\frac{4}{3}$

♦ **I'm in a Learning Mindset!**

How does my stress level affect my learning outcome?

Multiply Polynomials

(I Can) multiply polynomials and use products of polynomials to model real-world quantities.

Spark Your Learning

Every day all over the state of Texas, oil wells are producing crude oil.

For 2010–2017, the number of active oil wells (in thousands) can be modeled by $W(t) = -0.253t^3 + 1.60t^2 + 4.88t + 157$, where t is the number of years since 2010.

Complete Part A as a whole class. Then complete Parts B–D in small groups.

A. What is a mathematical question you can ask about this situation? What information would you need to know to answer your question?

B. To answer your question, what strategy and tool would you use along with all the information you have? What answer do you get?

C. How can you use your function from Part B to predict the total number of barrels of oil produced per day in Texas during 2018? What is your prediction?

D. How can you use the Distributive Property to simplify your function from Part B? What is the simplified function?

Turn and Talk Use your simplified function to make the prediction asked for in Part C. How can your answer help you determine whether you simplified the function correctly?

Build Understanding

Analyze a Visual Model for Polynomial Multiplication

A **binomial** is a polynomial with two terms. You can represent a product of two binomials as the area A of a rectangle with the binomials as side lengths. You can then find the product by breaking the rectangle into smaller rectangles. The area models below show that $(x + 4)(x + 2) = x^2 + 6x + 8$.

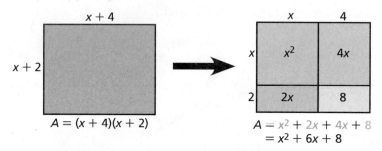

To find the product of three expressions that are binomials or monomials, you can use a volume model instead of an area model.

1 The first diagram below represents the product $(x + 3)(x + 2)x$ as the volume of a rectangular prism with dimensions $x + 3$, $x + 2$, and x. The second diagram shows this prism subdivided into four smaller prisms.

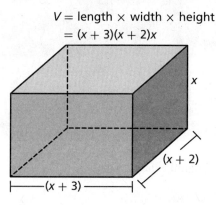

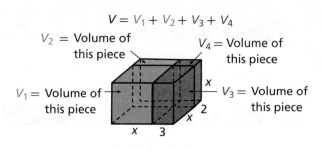

A. What is the volume V_1 of the blue prism in the second diagram? Explain.

B. What is the volume V_2 of the green prism in the second diagram? Explain.

C. What is the volume V_3 of the red prism in the second diagram? Explain.

D. What is the volume V_4 of the purple prism in the second diagram? Explain.

E. How can you represent the volume of the original prism in the first diagram, $(x + 3)(x + 2)x$, as a polynomial in standard form? Use your results from Parts A–D to justify your answer.

F. Find the product $(x + 3)(x + 2)x$ by repeatedly applying the Distributive Property. Compare your result with your answer to Part E.

 Turn and Talk In Task 1, suppose all three dimensions of the prism are binomials. Into how many smaller prisms would you divide the prism in order to represent its volume as a polynomial in standard form?

Step It Out

Multiply Polynomials

You can use the Product of Powers Property and the Distributive Property to multiply polynomials. The table shows how to find several types of polynomial products.

Multiplying Polynomials		
Product	**Example**	**Method**
Two monomials with a single variable	$5x^3(-6x^2) = [5(-6)]x^{3+2} = -30x^5$	Multiply coefficients and add exponents of the variable.
Two monomials with multiple variables	$2a^3b^4(4a^6b^2) = (2 \cdot 4)a^{3+6}b^{4+2}$ $= 8a^9b^6$	Multiply coefficients and add exponents of like variables.
Two binomials	$(x + 3)(2x - 1) = x(2x - 1) + 3(2x - 1)$ $= 2x^{1+1} - x + 6x - 3$ $= 2x^2 + 5x - 3$	Use the Distributive Property to multiply each term in the second binomial by each term in the first binomial.

You can extend the techniques described above to find products involving *trinomials*. A **trinomial** is a polynomial with three terms.

2 ▶ Cam and Jacob used two different methods to find the product $(7 + x)(x + 2x^2 - 4)$.

Cam's method (vertical method):

$$
\begin{array}{r}
2x^2 + x - 4 \\
\times \quad\quad x + 7 \\
\hline
14x^2 + 7x - 28 \\
2x^3 + \quad x^2 - 4x \\
\hline
2x^3 + 15x^2 + 3x - 28
\end{array}
$$

Write each polynomial in standard form and align the polynomials on the right.

Multiply 7 and $2x^2 + x - 4$.

Multiply x and $2x^2 + x - 4$.

Combine like terms.

Jacob's method (horizontal method):

$(7 + x)(x + 2x^2 - 4)$ Given product

$= (x + 7)(2x^2 + x - 4)$ Write the polynomials in standard form.

$= x(2x^2 + x - 4) + 7(2x^2 + x - 4)$ Distributive Property

$= 2x^3 + x^2 - 4x + 14x^2 + 7x - 28$ Distributive Property

$= 2x^3 + 15x^2 + 3x - 28$ Combine like terms.

A. How is Cam's method similar to the vertical method for multiplying whole numbers?

B. Which method do you prefer? Why?

 Turn and Talk If a polynomial $p(x)$ has degree m and a second polynomial $q(x)$ has degree n, what is the degree of $p(x) \cdot q(x)$? Explain.

Model with Polynomial Multiplication

3 Amber opened a cell phone repair company in 2000. From 2000 to 2020, the function $N(t)$ that models the annual number of cell phone repairs (in thousands) and the function $C(t)$ that models the average cost of a repair (in dollars) are as shown in the photo, where t is the number of years since 2000. Find a function $R(t)$ that models Amber's total annual revenue from cell phone repairs. Then use the function to estimate Amber's total revenue in 2015.

Annual number of repairs: $N(t) = 0.03t^2 - 0.4t + 2.1$
Average cost per repair: $C(t) = 0.12t^2 + 1.1t + 23$

Find the function $R(t)$.

Since annual revenue equals the annual number of repairs times the average cost per repair, a function for annual revenue is $R(t) = N(t) \cdot C(t)$. Use polynomial multiplication to find the product of $N(t)$ and $C(t)$.

$$
\begin{array}{r}
0.03t^2 - 0.4t + 2.1 \\
\times\ 0.12t^2 + 1.1t + 23 \\
\hline
0.69t^2 - 9.2t + 48.3 \\
0.033t^3 - 0.44t^2 + 2.31t \\
0.0036t^4 - 0.048t^3 + 0.252t^2 \\
\hline
0.0036t^4 - 0.015t^3 + 0.502t^2 - 6.89t + 48.3
\end{array}
$$

So the annual revenue function is $R(t) = 0.0036t^4 - 0.015t^3 + 0.502t^2 - 6.89t + 48.3$. Note that since $N(t)$ is measured in thousands of repairs and $C(t)$ is measured in dollars per repair, their product $R(t)$ gives revenue in thousands of dollars.

Estimate the total revenue in 2015.

Since 2015 is 15 years after 2000, substitute 15 for t in the equation for $R(t)$.

$R(t) = 0.0036t^4 - 0.015t^3 + 0.502t^2 - 6.89t + 48.3$

$R(15) = 0.0036(15)^4 - 0.015(15)^3 + 0.502(15)^2 - 6.89(15) + 48.3$
$ = 189.525$

Amber's total revenue in 2015 was about $190,000.

A. Finn says that since $R(15) = 189.525$, Amber's total revenue in 2015 was about $190, not $190,000. Why is Finn incorrect?

B. In what year did Amber's total revenue first exceed $300,000? How did you find your answer?

 Turn and Talk How can you approximate Amber's total revenue in the year 2000 without doing any calculations?

Verify and Use Polynomial Identities

A **polynomial identity** is an equation stating that two polynomials are equivalent. For example, the equation $(a + b)^2 = a^2 + 2ab + b^2$ showing how to square the sum of two terms is a polynomial identity. One way to verify an identity is to start with one side of the equation and rewrite it until it matches the other side. Another way is to show that both sides of the equation equal a third expression and are therefore equal to each other.

4 Verify the polynomial identity $(a - b)(a^2 + ab + b^2) = a^3 - b^3$.

Since the right side of the equation is simplified, simplify the left side.

$(a - b)(a^2 + ab + b^2)$ Left side of equation

$= a(a^2 + ab + b^2) - b(a^2 + ab + b^2)$ ____?____

$= a^3 + a^2b + ab^2 - a^2b - ab^2 - b^3$ Distributive Property

$= a^3 + \overline{a^2b} - a^2b + \overline{ab^2} - ab^2 - b^3$ Rearrange terms.

$= a^3 - b^3$ Simplify.

> **A.** What property justifies this step?

> **B.** What property justifies rearranging the terms of the expression?

Therefore, $(a - b)(a^2 + ab + b^2) = a^3 - b^3$.

5 The polynomial identity $(x^2 + y^2)^2 = (x^2 - y^2)^2 + (2xy)^2$ can be used to find Pythagorean triples. Verify the identity. Then find a Pythagorean triple using $x = 5$ and $y = 4$.

To verify the identity, show that each side simplifies to the same expression.

$(x^2 + y^2)^2 = (x^2)^2 + 2x^2y^2 + (y^2)^2$

$\qquad\qquad = x^4 + 2x^2y^2 + y^4$

> **A.** How is the known identity $(a + b)^2 = a^2 + 2ab + b^2$ used in this step?

$(x^2 - y^2)^2 + (2xy)^2 = \left[(x^2)^2 - 2x^2y^2 + (y^2)^2\right] + 4x^2y^2$

$\qquad\qquad\qquad\quad = (x^4 - 2x^2y^2 + y^4) + 4x^2y^2$

$\qquad\qquad\qquad\quad = x^4 + 2x^2y^2 + y^4$

Both sides of the equation simplify to $x^4 + 2x^2y^2 + y^4$. So, the equation is an identity.

To find a Pythagorean triple using $x = 5$ and $y = 4$, note that the identity $(x^2 + y^2)^2 = (x^2 - y^2)^2 + (2xy)^2$ has the form $c^2 = a^2 + b^2$ where $a = x^2 - y^2$, $b = 2xy$, and $c = x^2 + y^2$. Find the values of a, b, and c when $x = 5$ and $y = 4$.

$a = x^2 - y^2 = 5^2 - 4^2 = 9$

$b = 2xy = 2(5)(4) = 40$

$c = x^2 + y^2 = 5^2 + 4^2 = 41$

So, the Pythagorean triple is 9, 40, 41.

> **B.** How can you check that 9, 40, 41 is a Pythagorean triple?

Check Understanding

1. Write a polynomial in standard form that represents the volume of the rectangular prism shown.

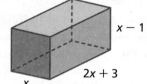

2. Find the product $(3 - x^2 + 2x)(5 - x)$.

3. Jason owns a small bookstore. For the period 2010–2016, he models the annual number of books (in thousands) that his store sold using the function $N(t) = -0.1t^3 + t^2 - 3t + 4$. He models the average selling price per book (in dollars) using the function $P(t) = 12 + 0.5t$. For both functions, t represents the number of years since 2010.

   A. Write a polynomial function $R(t)$ in standard form that models the bookstore's annual revenue (in thousands of dollars) for the period 2010–2016.

   B. Estimate the bookstore's revenue in 2012.

   C. Is the function $R(t)$ you wrote an appropriate model for the bookstore's annual revenue for years after 2016? Explain.

4. Verify the polynomial identity $(a + b)(a^2 - ab + b^2) = a^3 + b^3$.

5. Use the polynomial identity $(a + b)^2 = a^2 + 2ab + b^2$ to find the square of 52 mentally. Explain the steps you used.

On Your Own

6. (MP) **Use Structure** The edge lengths of a cube are increased from x feet to $(x + 2)$ feet. The resulting cube is shown.

   A. What is the volume of the original cube?

   B. What is the volume of the new cube?

   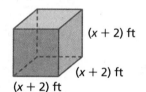

   C. What polynomial represents the increase in the cube's volume?

Multiply the polynomials.

7. $(x + 2)(x^2 + 3)$

8. $(x^3 + 2x)(x - 1)$

9. $(7 - x)(x^2 + 1)$

10. $(2 + x^3)(4 - x^2)$

11. $(4 - 3x)(2x + x^2 - 9)$

12. $(-2x^2 - 5x + 1)(4 - x)$

13. $(-3x^2 - x + 6)(2 - 5x)$

14. $(4x + 8)(x^2 + x - 1)$

15. $(x^2 + 4x - 8)(x^2 - x - 2)$

16. $(x^2 - 2x - 1)(x^2 - 2x - 1)$

17. $(x^2 + 2 - 2x)(2x^2 + x - 3)$

18. $(2x^3 + x - 4)(x^2 - x - 6)$

19. $(x^3 + x^2 + x)(3x^2 + 2x - 4)$

20. $(x - 3x^2 - 5)(7x^2 - 2 + x)$

21. $(2x + 2y)(3x^2 - xy + y^2)$

22. $(x - 3y)(x^2 + 2xy + y^2)$

23. $(x + 3y)(-2x^2 + 4xy + y^2)$

24. $(3x - 2y)(-3x^2 - 5xy - 2y^2)$

25. The number of students enrolled at a college is modeled by $S(t) = 40t + 2000$, and the average tuition paid per student (in thousands of dollars) is modeled by $T(t) = 0.05t^2 + 0.7t + 15$. In both models, t represents the number of years since 2010. Write a function $R(t)$ to model the annual revenue that the college receives from tuition payments. Then predict the revenue received in 2020.

26. (MP) **Critique Reasoning** Gael found the product $(x - 4)(x^2 + 2x - 3)$ in two ways as shown below, but got different results. Explain and correct Gael's error.

Vertical Method

$$x^2 + 2x - 3$$
$$\times \qquad x - 4$$
$$\overline{4x^2 + 8x - 12}$$
$$\underline{x^3 + 2x^2 - 3x}$$
$$x^3 + 6x^2 + 5x - 12$$

Horizontal Method

$(x - 4)(x^2 + 2x - 3)$
$= x(x^2 + 2x - 3) - 4(x^2 + 2x - 3)$
$= x^3 + 2x^2 - 3x - 4x^2 - 8x + 12$
$= x^3 - 2x^2 - 11x + 12$

27. (MP) **Model with Mathematics** A beachside resort has a "low season" with fewer guests and lower prices, and a "high season" with more guests and higher prices. The occupancy function $O(m)$ shown models the average percent of rooms filled at the resort (expressed as a decimal) in month m of the year, where $m = 1$ is January, $m = 2$ is February, and so on. The function $R(m)$ shown models the resort's maximum possible revenue (in thousands of dollars) in month m if all of its rooms are filled, based on the room prices the resort charges during that month.

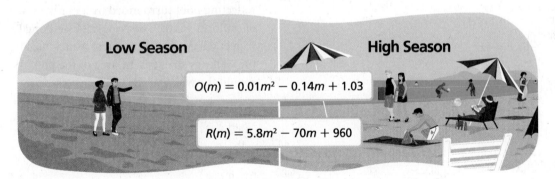

Low Season

High Season

$O(m) = 0.01m^2 - 0.14m + 1.03$

$R(m) = 5.8m^2 - 70m + 960$

A. Write a function $A(m)$ that models the resort's actual revenue in month m.

B. Use a spreadsheet or graphing calculator to make a table of values for $A(m)$ for $m = 1, 2, 3, \ldots, 12$. During what month is the resort's actual revenue highest? What is the actual revenue for that month?

28. **Open Ended** Write a problem that can be solved using the product of two polynomial functions. Find the product of the functions, and use the product to solve the problem.

29. (MP) **Reason** For what value of b is the following equation true? Explain your reasoning.

$$(x^2 + bx + 2)(2x^2 + bx + 5) = 2x^4 + 9x^3 + 18x^2 + 21x + 10$$

Verify the polynomial identity.

30. $(a^2 + b^2)(a + b)(a - b) = a^4 - b^4$

31. $(x^2 + y^2)(x^4 - x^2y^2 + y^4) = x^6 + y^6$

32. $(z - 1)(z^3 + z^2 + z + 1) = z^4 - 1$

33. $(a^2 + b^2)(x^2 + y^2) = (ax - by)^2 + (bx + ay)^2$

Use the given polynomial identity to find the indicated value.

34. $(a + b)^2 = a^2 + 2ab + b^2; 32^2$

35. $(a - b)^2 = a^2 - 2ab + b^2; 98^2$

36. $(a + b)(a - b) = a^2 - b^2; 51 \cdot 49$

37. $(a + b)(a - b) = a^2 - b^2; 48 \cdot 32$

38. Consider the polynomials $2x^2 + 3x - 4$ and $-3x^3 - 8x + 10$.

A. Multiply the polynomials using the vertical method.

B. Multiply the polynomials using the horizontal method.

C. What challenges did you experience while using the vertical method that you did not experience while using the horizontal method?

D. What challenges did you experience while using the horizontal method that you did not experience while using the vertical method?

39. (Open Middle™) Using the whole numbers 1 through 9, at most one time each, fill in the boxes to make a true statement.

$$\left(\boxed{}x - 5\right)\left(2x^2 + \boxed{}x + \boxed{}\right) = \boxed{}x^3 + \boxed{}x^2 - 11x - \boxed{}$$

Spiral Review • Assessment Readiness

40. If $f(x) = 12x^8$ and $g(x) = 3x^2$, what is an equation for $\left(\dfrac{f}{g}\right)(x)$?

Ⓐ $\left(\dfrac{f}{g}\right)(x) = 4x^4$

Ⓑ $\left(\dfrac{f}{g}\right)(x) = 4x^6$

Ⓒ $\left(\dfrac{f}{g}\right)(x) = 9x^4$

Ⓓ $\left(\dfrac{f}{g}\right)(x) = 9x^6$

41. An architect is designing a rectangular reflecting pool surrounded by a marble walkway of uniform width. The pool is 24 feet long by 16 feet wide, and the architect wants the area of the walkway to equal the area of the pool. What should the width of the walkway be?

Ⓐ 1 foot

Ⓑ 2 feet

Ⓒ 4 feet

Ⓓ 8 feet

42. Match each sum or difference on the left with the equivalent expression on the right.

A. $(-2x^2 + x + 9) + (3x^2 - 4x + 6)$

B. $(5x - 9x^2 + x^3) + (x^3 + 3 + 9x^2)$

C. $(x^2 - 6x + 5) - (x^2 + x - 2)$

D. $(7x^3 + 1) - (-3x^2 - x^3 + 8 + 2x)$

1. $8x^3 + 3x^2 - 2x - 7$

2. $x^2 - 3x + 15$

3. $-7x + 7$

4. $2x^3 + 5x + 3$

 I'm in a Learning Mindset!

What about multiplying polynomials triggers a fixed-mindset voice in my head or makes me feel stressed?

Factor Polynomials

(I Can) use factoring to write a polynomial as the product of polynomials of lesser degree.

Spark Your Learning

A cube has a smaller cube cut out of it as shown in Figure 1. Eli and Julia consider how to find the volume of this figure.

Julia wants to subtract the smaller cube's volume from the larger cube's volume.

Figure 1

Figure 2

Eli wants to break the figure into three prisms and add the prisms' volumes.

Complete Part A as a whole class. Then complete Parts B–D in small groups.

A. What is a mathematical question you can ask about this situation? What information would you need to know to answer your question?

B. To answer your question, what strategy and tool would you use along with all the information you have? What answer do you get?

C. How can you write the sum of the volumes of the three prisms in Figure 2 as the product of $a - b$ and another polynomial?

D. What equation can you write to show how to factor $a^3 - b^3$?

 Turn and Talk How can you use the equation you wrote in Part D to factor the polynomial $8x^3 - 27$?

Build Understanding

Analyze a Visual Model for Polynomial Factorization

Factoring a polynomial involves finding factors of lesser degree that can be multiplied together to produce the polynomial. You have already factored polynomials of degree 2, as in the example below.

$$x^2 + 5x + 6 = (x + 2)(x + 3)$$

When a polynomial has degree 3, you can think of it as the volume of a rectangular prism whose dimensions you need to determine. The dimensions are the factors of the polynomial.

 A rectangular prism is subdivided into four smaller rectangular prisms as shown. The volumes of the smaller prisms are given below.

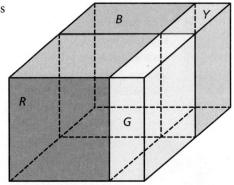

Red (R): $V = x^3$

Green (G): $V = 2x^2$

Yellow (Y): $V = 8x$

Blue (B): $V = 4x^2$

Total volume: $V = x^3 + 6x^2 + 8x$

A. The volume of the red prism is found by cubing the length of one edge. This edge is the height of the large prism. What is the height of the large prism?

B. The volume of the green prism is found by multiplying two of its dimensions shared with the red prism and one other dimension. What are the dimensions of the green prism?

C. The combined width of the red and green prisms makes up the width of the large prism. What is the width of the large prism? Explain how you knew which dimension of the green prism to add to the red prism's width.

D. The yellow prism shares two dimensions with the green prism. Using the volume of the yellow prism and the two shared dimensions, find the third dimension of the yellow prism. What does this make the length of the large prism?

E. Use the fact that the volume of a prism is $\ell \times w \times h$ to write an expression for the volume of the large prism. Do not simplify the expression.

F. Simplify the expression you found in Part E. What do you notice? What is the factored form of $x^3 + 6x^2 + 8x$?

G. Can you factor any cubic polynomial of the form $x^3 + bx^2 + cx$ by modeling the polynomial with a rectangular prism and finding the prism's dimensions? Explain.

 Turn and Talk Notice that the polynomial $x^3 + 6x^2 + 8x$ that represents the volume of the large prism in Task 1 can be written as $x(x^2 + 6x + 8)$. How does writing the polynomial in this form help you factor it completely?

Step It Out

Factor Out the Greatest Common Factor First

Not all polynomials can be *factored over the integers*. That is, they cannot be rewritten using only factors with integer coefficients and constants. When a polynomial is factored, the degree of each factor is less than the degree of the polynomial. While the goal is to rewrite the polynomial as a product of linear factors, this is not always possible. A factor of degree 2 or greater that cannot be factored further is an **irreducible factor**.

The first step for factoring a polynomial is to factor out the greatest common factor (GCF) of the terms, assuming it is not 1.

 Below are two examples of factoring a polynomial over the integers.

Example 1:

$$8x^3 - 4x^2 - 12x = 4x(2x^2 - x - 3)$$
$$= 4x(2x - 3)(x + 1)$$

> **A.** How do you know that the GCF is $4x$?

Example 2:

$$3x^3 - 21x = 3x(x^2 - 7)$$

> **B.** Why can't you factor $x^2 - 7$ over the integers, but you could factor $x^2 - 9$?

Recognize Special Factoring Patterns

You have previously seen the factoring patterns for the difference of two squares and for perfect square trinomials. The patterns for the sum or difference of two cubes are also helpful for factoring polynomials.

Special Factoring Patterns	
Pattern name	**Factoring pattern**
Difference of two squares	$a^2 - b^2 = (a + b)(a - b)$
Perfect square trinomials	$a^2 + 2ab + b^2 = (a + b)^2$ $a^2 - 2ab + b^2 = (a - b)^2$
Sum of two cubes	$a^3 + b^3 = (a + b)(a^2 - ab + b^2)$
Difference of two cubes	$a^3 - b^3 = (a - b)(a^2 + ab + b^2)$

3 Factor $8x^3 + 125$.

$$8x^3 + 125 = (2x)^3 + 5^3$$
$$= (2x + 5)\left[(2x)^2 - (2x)(5) + 5^2\right]$$
$$= (2x + 5)(4x^2 - 10x + 25)$$

> **A.** Which factoring pattern is used here?

> **B.** How can you check that this factorization is correct?

 Turn and Talk What is the factored form of $27x^3 - 1$?

Factor by Grouping

If you can group together pairs of terms of a polynomial that have a common factor, you may be able to use a method called *factoring by grouping* to factor the polynomial. The pattern for this method is shown below.

$$ra + rb + sa + sb = r(a + b) + s(a + b)$$
$$= (r + s)(a + b)$$

4 Factor $x^4 - x^3 - 8x + 8$ by grouping.

$x^4 - x^3 - 8x + 8 = (x^4 - x^3) + (-8x + 8)$ Group terms with a common factor.

$= x^3(x - 1) - 8(x - 1)$ Factor out each group's common factor.

$= (x^3 - 8)(x - 1)$ Factor out the common binomial factor.

$= (x - 2)(x^2 + 2x + 4)(x - 1)$ Factor the difference of cubes.

$= (x - 1)(x - 2)(x^2 + 2x + 4)$ Write linear factors first.

A. What property justifies rewriting $x^3(x - 1) - 8(x - 1)$ as $(x^3 - 8)(x - 1)$?

B. How do you know that the polynomial $x^2 + 2x + 4$ is irreducible?

 Turn and Talk What is the factored form of $x^4 + x^3 + x + 1$?

5 The steps and their justifications for factoring the polynomial $4x^3 + 8x^2 - 9x - 18$ by grouping are shown.

A. Write the factoring steps in the correct order.

$4x^2(x + 2) - 9(x + 2)$

$(2x + 3)(2x - 3)(x + 2)$

$(4x^3 + 8x^2) + (-9x - 18)$

$4x^3 + 8x^2 - 9x - 18$

$(4x^2 - 9)(x + 2)$

B. Write the justifications in the correct order.

Factor the difference of squares.

Factor out each group's common factor.

Group terms with a common factor.

Given polynomial

Factor out the common binomial factor.

 Turn and Talk Can you factor the polynomial in Task 5 by grouping the terms as $(4x^3 - 9x) + (8x^2 - 18)$? Explain.

Factor a Polynomial to Solve a Real-World Problem

Previously you have used the Zero-Product Property to solve factorable quadratic equations. You can also use this property to solve equations involving higher-degree polynomials that can be factored.

6 A landscape architect is designing a marble flower planter for an outdoor mall. The planter should hold 4 cubic feet of soil. The architect wants the length of the planter to be 6 times the height and the width of the planter to be 3 times the height. The sides of the planter should be 1 foot thick. Because the planter will be on a sidewalk, it does not need a bottom. What should the outer dimensions of the planter be?

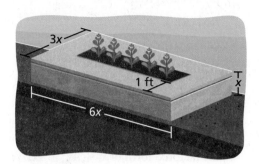

Use a verbal model.

Length of inside of planter (ft) $6x - 2$	·	Width of inside of planter (ft) $3x - 2$	·	Height of planter (ft) x	=	Volume of inside of planter 4 ft^3

Write an equation.

$(6x - 2)(3x - 2)x = 4$

Solve the equation.

$(6x - 2)(3x - 2)x = 4$

$(18x^2 - 18x + 4)x = 4$

$18x^3 - 18x^2 + 4x = 4$

$18x^3 - 18x^2 + 4x - 4 = 0$

$18x^2(x - 1) + 4(x - 1) = 0$

$(18x^2 + 4)(x - 1) = 0$

$18x^2 + 4 = 0 \ \text{ or } \ x - 1 = 0$

$x = \pm\sqrt{-\frac{2}{9}} \ \text{ or } \ x = 1$

A. Which factoring technique is used to solve the equation?

B. Which property justifies this step?

C. Why do the solutions $x = \pm\sqrt{-\frac{2}{9}}$ not make sense in this situation?

Answer the question.

Since x is the planter's height, the only solution that makes sense is $x = 1$. The planter's outer length is $6x = 6$ feet, its outer width is $3x = 3$ feet, and its height is $x = 1$ foot.

 Turn and Talk Look at the equation $18x^2 + 4 = 0$ in Task 6. Without solving the equation, how can you tell that it has no real-number solutions?

Check Understanding

1. A rectangular prism is subdivided into four smaller prisms as shown. The volumes of the smaller prisms are given below.

   Red (R): $V = x^3$

   Green (G): $V = 2x^2$

   Yellow (Y): $V = 4x$

   Blue (B): $V = 2x^2$

   Total volume: $V = x^3 + 4x^2 + 4x$

   How can you use the given information to determine the factored form of $x^3 + 4x^2 + 4x$? What is the factored form?

2. Factor $6x^3 - 21x^2 - 12x$ over the integers.

3. Factor $2x^3 - 54$ using a factoring pattern.

4. Factor $x^3 - 2x^2 + 5x - 10$ by grouping.

5. A fish tank is being designed in the shape of a rectangular prism. The sides and bottom of the tank will be made with glass that is 3 centimeters thick. The outer length of the tank should be twice the outer width. The outer height should be the same as the outer width. What should the outer dimensions of the tank be if it is to hold 972 cubic centimeters of water?

On Your Own

6. (MP) **Use Structure** The volume of a rectangular prism is given by $V = x^3 + 7x^2 + 10x$ where x is the height of the prism. Find linear factors with integer coefficients that could represent the prism's length and width.

For Problems 7–14, factor the polynomial over the integers or identify it as irreducible.

7. $45x^3 + 15x$

8. $3x^3 + 6x^2 - 24x$

9. $-2x^4 + 12x^3 - 10x^2$

10. $x^3 - 4x^2 + 4x$

11. $64x^3 + 125$

12. $x^3 + 16$

13. $125x^3 - 1$

14. $x^4 - 8x^3 + 12x^2$

For Problems 15–24, factor the polynomial by grouping.

15. $x^3 - 7x^2 - x + 7$

16. $10x^3 - 8x^2 + 25x - 20$

17. $2x^3 + 6x^2 - x - 3$

18. $8x^3 - x^2 - 8x + 1$

19. $3x^4 - x^3 + 3x - 1$

20. $2x^9 - 2x^6 - x^3 + 1$

21. $x^4 - 2x^3 + 2x - 4$

22. $x^7 + 8x^4 - 2x^3 - 16$

23. $3x^4 + 15x^3 - 4x - 20$

24. $2x^6 - 14x^4 + x^2 - 7$

25. (MP) **Use Structure** A cylinder with base radius x is subdivided into two smaller cylinders as shown. The volumes of the smaller cylinders are given below.

Red (R): $V = 8\pi x^3$

Green (G): $V = 24\pi x^2$

Total volume: $V = 8\pi x^3 + 24\pi x^2$

What is the area of the base of each smaller cylinder? What are the heights of the smaller cylinders? Explain how you know.

26. **Art** An ice sculpture has a base that is a rectangular prism. The length of the base is 8 inches less than 7 times the height. The width of the base is 20 inches less than 7 times the height.

A. Write an equation for the volume of the base of the ice sculpture without multiplying or simplifying. Identify the real-world meaning of each factor.

B. Rewrite the equation in Part A as a polynomial expression in standard form set equal to zero. Then factor the polynomial expression. What does the linear factor tell you? Explain.

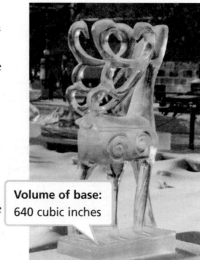

Volume of base: 640 cubic inches

27. Mr. Murphy is designing a concrete fire pit. The concrete sides and bottom will be 5 inches thick. The interior length will be 3 times the interior height, and the interior width will be 2 times the interior height. What should the outer dimensions of the fire pit be if the inner volume is to be 6000 cubic inches?

28. A block of marble is being cut for a statue podium. The length of the podium is to be 4 times the height, and the width of the podium is to be twice the height. What should the dimensions of the podium be if its volume is to be 512 cubic feet?

Find the real-number solutions of the equation.

29. $x^3 - 4x^2 = 0$

30. $3x^3 + 4x^2 - 5x = 0$

31. $8x^3 - 1 = 0$

32. $4x^3 - 9x = 0$

33. $3x^3 - 2x^2 - 9x + 6 = 0$

34. $x^3 - 7x^2 = 7 - x$

35. $5x^4 - 8 = -48$

36. $x^4 - 13x^2 = -36$

37. (MP) **Construct Arguments** Is it possible to factor any polynomial with four terms using factoring by grouping? Explain why or why not.

38. Sabrina is building a rectangular flower bed using four boards to form the bed's sides. The boards on the two shorter sides are 6 inches thick, and the boards on the two longer sides are 4 inches thick. Sabrina wants the outer length of her flower bed to be 4 times its height and the outer width to be 2 times its height. She also wants the boards to rise 4 inches above the level of the soil in the bed. What should the outer dimensions of the flower bed be if it is to hold 3136 cubic inches of soil?

©Sublimage/Alamy

39. The manufacturer of a hefty wooden feeding trough for farm animals makes the sides and bottom of the trough be 1 foot thick. The outer height and outer width of the trough are the same, and the outer length is twice the outer height and outer width. What should the outer dimensions of the trough be if the trough is to hold 36 cubic feet of feed?

40. (MP) **Critique Reasoning** Amber incorrectly factored the polynomial $2x^3 + 3x^2 - 2x - 3$ as shown below.

> $2x^3 + 3x^2 - 2x - 3$
>
> $= (2x^3 - 2x) + (3x^2 - 3)$ Group terms with a common factor.
>
> $= 2x(x^2 - 1) + 3(x^2 - 1)$ Factor out each group's common factor.
>
> $= 5x(x^2 - 1)$ Factor out the common binomial factor.
>
> $= 5x(x + 1)(x - 1)$ Factor the difference of squares.

Explain and correct Amber's error.

Spiral Review • Assessment Readiness

41. Which expression is equivalent to $(11 - 2x)(x^2 + x - 1)$?

(A) $-2x^3 + 9x^2 + 13x - 11$

(B) $-2x^3 + 13x^2 + 9x - 11$

(C) $2x^3 - 9x^2 - 13x + 11$

(D) $2x^3 - 13x^2 - 9x + 11$

42. If $f(x) = x^2 + 7x$ and $g(x) = 4x - 5$, what is $(f + g)(-1)$?

(A) -15

(B) -3

(C) 3

(D) 15

43. The sum of $2x^2 + 4$ and another polynomial is $3x^2 - 3x - 1$. What is the other polynomial?

(A) $-x^2 - 3x + 5$

(B) $x^2 - 3x - 5$

(C) $5x^2 - x + 3$

(D) $x^2 - 5x + 5$

44. What is the remainder when 4805 is divided by 124?

(A) 0.75

(B) 38

(C) 93

(D) 4712

 I'm in a Learning Mindset!

What stress-management skills can I use to complete my assignments that involve factoring polynomials?

Divide Polynomials

(I Can) divide polynomials using both long division and synthetic division.

Spark Your Learning

Sam is experiencing the effects of a current produced by a Van de Graaf generator.

The Van de Graaf generator has a current *I* and a power *P*.

The voltage *V* of the system is found using the current and the power.

Complete Part A as a whole class. Then complete Parts B–D in small groups.

  A. What is a mathematical question you can ask about this situation? What information would you need to answer your question?

  B. What would need to be true about the variables in the functions modeling the power, the current, and the voltage?

  C. To answer your question, what strategy and tool would you use along with all the information you have? What answer do you get?

  D. Are there any restrictions for the values in this situation? If so, explain what the restrictions are.

 Turn and Talk What is the advantage of writing the expression for the voltage of the system as simply as possible?

Build Understanding

Evaluate a Polynomial Function Using Synthetic Substitution

You have used the order of operations to evaluate polynomials written in standard form for a given value of the variable. Polynomials can also be written in *nested form* using layers of parentheses. For polynomials written in nested form, the order of operations calls for evaluating the expression from the innermost parentheses outward. The steps to evaluate the polynomial $p(x)$ below alternate between multiplication and addition.

	Algebra	Numbers
Polynomial	$p(x) = ax^4 + bx^3 + cx^2 + dx + e$	$p(x) = 5x^4 + 3x^3 + x^2 + 2x + 7$
Nested form	$p(x) = x\Big(x\big(x(ax + b) + c\big) + d\Big) + e$	$p(x) = x\Big(x\big(x(5x + 3) + 1\big) + 2\Big) + 7$
Evaluation steps	For a given value of x: *multiply a* by x, add b, *multiply* by x, add c, *multiply* by x, add d, *multiply* by x, add e.	For a given value of x: *multiply 5* by x, add 3, *multiply* by x, add 1, *multiply* by x, add 2, *multiply* by x, add 7.

Evaluating a polynomial function $p(x)$ for a specific value of x can also be accomplished using a technique called **synthetic substitution**. This technique parallels the sequence of steps for evaluating a nested polynomial. Synthetic substitution uses an array to model the sequence of steps needed to find the value of a polynomial function $p(x)$ for any value of x.

1 ▶ The nested form of the $p(x) = 2x^4 + 5x^3 - 2x^2 - 8$ is

$p(x) = x\Big(x\big(x(2x + 5) - 2\big) + 0\Big) - 8$. Notice that $p(x)$ lacks a linear term, which must still be accounted for in the nested form.

A. List the order of operations performed when evaluating the nested form of the polynomial $p(x) = 2x^4 + 5x^3 - 2x^2 - 8$ for $p(-3)$. What is $p(-3)$?

B. The synthetic substitution array for finding $p(-3)$ for $p(x) = 2x^4 + 5x^3 - 2x^2 - 8$ is shown below. How are the numbers in the top row of the array related to $p(x)$?

$$
\begin{array}{r|rrrrr}
-3 & 2 & 5 & -2 & 0 & -8 \\
   &   & -6 & 3 & -3 & 9 \\
\hline
   & 2 & -1 & 1 & -3 & 1
\end{array}
$$

C. What number in the array tells you the value of $p(-3)$?

D. How does the framework in the synthetic substitution array show the sequence of multiplications and additions used to evaluate the nested polynomial?

E. Why might you choose to use synthetic substitution to evaluate a polynomial instead of regular substitution?

 Turn and Talk Write the synthetic substitution array you would use to evaluate the polynomial $p(x) = 4x^4 - 8x^2 + x + 3$ for $x = -1$.

Step It Out

Divide Polynomials Using Long Division

Recall that arithmetic long division involves a sequence of multiplications and subtractions. The result of the long division is $\frac{dividend}{divisor} = quotient + \frac{remainder}{divisor}$. In the example shown, the result is $\frac{225}{14} = 16 + \frac{1}{14}$.

$$
\begin{array}{r}
16 \leftarrow \text{Quotient} \\
\text{Divisor} \rightarrow 14\overline{)225} \leftarrow \text{Dividend} \\
\underline{14} \\
85 \\
\underline{84} \\
1 \leftarrow \text{Remainder}
\end{array}
$$

Multiplying each term by the divisor yields dividend = (divisor)(quotient) + remainder. You can use this fact to check your work.

2 Use long division to find the quotient and remainder of $(2x^3 + 4x^2 - 2) \div (x^2 + 5x + 1)$.

Write the problem the same way you would when dividing numbers. Write the dividend and divisor in standard form and include a coefficient of 0 for any missing consecutive terms.

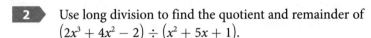

$x^2 + 5x + 1\overline{)2x^3 + 4x^2 + 0x - 2}$

> **A.** Why is the term $0x$ in the dividend?

Determine the monomial expression you need to multiply the divisor by in order to produce the first term of the dividend.

$$
\begin{array}{r}
2x \\
x^2 + 5x + 1\overline{)2x^3 + 4x^2 + 0x - 2}
\end{array}
$$

> **B.** Why is this not $2x^2$?

Multiply each term in the divisor by the term of the quotient you just found. Subtract the expression that results from the dividend. Repeat these steps using the difference as the new dividend.

$$
\begin{array}{r}
2x - 6 \\
x^2 + 5x + 1\overline{)2x^3 + 4x^2 + 0x - 2} \\
\underline{-(2x^3 + 10x^2 + 2x)} \\
-6x^2 - 2x - 2 \\
\underline{-(-6x^2 - 30x - 6)} \\
28x + 4
\end{array}
$$

> **C.** How do you determine the values in this line and the line that follows?

> **D.** How do you when to stop dividing?

The quotient is $2x - 6$ and the remainder is $28x + 4$.

Write the result in the form dividend = (divisor)(quotient) + remainder.

$$2x^3 + 4x^2 - 2 = (x^2 + 5x + 1)(2x - 6) + (28x + 4)$$

Verify the result.

$$2x^3 + 4x^2 - 2 \stackrel{?}{=} (x^2 + 5x + 1)(2x - 6) + (28x + 4)$$

$$\stackrel{?}{=} 2x^3 - 6x^2 + 10x^2 - 30x + 2x - 6 + 28x + 4$$

$$= 2x^3 + 4x^2 - 2$$

Divide $p(x)$ by $x - a$ Using Synthetic Division

The last row of the synthetic substitution array gives the coefficients of the quotient and the remainder. The remainder is the value of the polynomial for the value of a in $x - a$.

> **Remainder Theorem**
>
> When $p(x)$ is divided by $x - a$, the remainder is $p(a)$.

This means that synthetic substitution can be used to perform division of polynomials. For this reason, another name for synthetic substitution is *synthetic division*.

Long Division

$$\begin{array}{r} 2x^2 - 6x + 22 \\ x + 3 \overline{) 2x^3 + 0x^2 + 4x + 5} \\ -(2x^3 + 6x^2) \\ \hline -6x^2 + 4x \\ -(-6x^2 - 18x) \\ \hline 22x + 5 \\ -(22x + 66) \\ \hline -61 \end{array}$$

Synthetic Division

The divisor is $x + 3 = x - (-3)$, so -3 is used in the synthetic division array.

$$\begin{array}{r|rrrr} -3 & 2 & 0 & 4 & 5 \\ & & -6 & 18 & -66 \\ \hline & 2 & -6 & 22 & \boxed{-61} \end{array} \leftarrow p(a)$$

The final row gives the coefficients of the quotient and the value of $p(a)$.

3 ▶ Use synthetic division to write $(2x^4 + x^3 - 35x^2 - 7) \div (x - 4)$ in the form $p(x) = (x - a)(\text{quotient}) + p(a)$. Then check your work.

Use the coefficients of $p(x)$ and the value of a to set up the synthetic division array. Complete the array following the same process as for synthetic substitution.

$$\begin{array}{r|rrrrr} 4 & 2 & 1 & -35 & 0 & -7 \\ & & 8 & 36 & 4 & 16 \\ \hline & 2 & 9 & 1 & 4 & \boxed{9} \end{array}$$

> **A.** How do the values in the synthetic division show the quotient and $p(a)$?

Using the results of the synthetic division, $p(x) = (x - 4)(2x^3 + 9x^2 + x + 4) + 9$.

Multiply and then combine like terms to check your work.

$$p(x) = (x - 4)(2x^3 + 9x^2 + x + 4) + 9$$

$$= 2x^4 + 9x^3 + x^2 + 4x - 8x^3 - 36x^2 - 4x - 16 + 9$$

$$= 2x^4 + x^3 - 35x^2 - 7$$

> **B.** Why is the degree of the quotient 3 and not 4?

C. Why does the check step confirm that the work is correct?

D. Does long division produce the same results? Show the work to justify your answer.

 Turn and Talk Is it possible to use synthetic division to divide a polynomial by a nonlinear binomial? Explain why or why not.

Use Synthetic Division to Find Factors of a Polynomial

You can use synthetic division to determine whether $x - a$ is a factor of $p(x)$.

Factor Theorem
If the remainder is 0 when $p(x)$ is divided by $x - a$, then $x - a$ is a factor of $p(x)$.

4 Determine whether the binomial $x + 7$ is a factor of $p(x) = x^3 + 8x^2 + 5x - 14$. If it is, identify any other binomial factors of $p(x)$.

Use synthetic division, with $a = -7$:

$$\begin{array}{r|rrrr} -7 & 1 & 8 & 5 & -14 \\ & & -7 & -7 & 14 \\ \hline & 1 & 1 & -2 & \underline{|0} \end{array}$$

A. Why is -7 used as the value of a and not 7?

Since the remainder is 0, $x + 7$ is a factor of $p(x)$.

B. What is the justification for this statement?

So, $p(x)$ can be written as $p(x) = (x + 7)(x^2 + x - 2)$. Factor the trinomial.

$$p(x) = (x + 7)(x^2 + x - 2)$$
$$= (x + 7)(x - 1)(x + 2)$$

C. If $x^2 + x - 2$ had not been factorable, would that mean $x + 7$ was the only factor of $p(x)$? Explain.

Therefore, the factors of $p(x)$ are $x + 7$, $x - 1$, and $x + 2$.

 Turn and Talk How does determining one factor of a polynomial lead to determining the other factors of that polynomial?

Polynomials and Closure

A set of numbers is said to have **closure** under a given operation if the result of the operation on any two numbers in the set is also in the set. You can extend this definition of closure to determine under which operations, if any, the set of polynomials is closed.

5 Determine if the set of polynomials is closed under addition.

The polynomial $p(x)$ consists of a sum of monomial terms of the form ax^m where a is a real number and m is a whole number. If ax^m is a term in the polynomial $p(x)$ and bx^m is a term in the polynomial $q(x)$, then:

$$p(x) + q(x) = \cdots + (ax^m + bx^m) + \cdots$$
$$= \cdots + (\underline{})x^m + \cdots$$

A. What is the missing entry for this step?

B. The set of real numbers is closed under addition. What does this mean for the coefficient of the x^m-term above? Is the x^m-term a monomial then? Explain.

C. Is every term of the sum $p(x) + q(x)$ a monomial? Is the sum a polynomial? Explain.

D. If the sum of the polynomials is itself a polynomial, what does this mean for the set of polynomials? Justify your answer.

Check Understanding

1. Explain how to use synthetic substitution to find $p(-3)$ given $p(x) = x^4 - x^3 - x^2 - 2$.

2. Use long division to find the quotient and remainder of $(3x^3 - x^2 + 5) \div (x^2 - 4x + 1)$. Write the result in the form dividend = (divisor)(quotient) + remainder. Then, check your work.

3. Use synthetic division to write $(3x^4 + x^3 - 22x^2 + x - 8) \div (x + 2)$ in the form $p(x) = (x - a)(\text{quotient}) + p(a)$. Then check your work.

4. Determine whether $x + 1$ is a factor of $p(x) = x^3 + x^2 + 2x - 4$. If it is a factor, find the remaining factors of $p(x)$.

5. Show that the set of polynomials is closed under subtraction sum.

On Your Own

6. Explain how synthetic substitution and long division of polynomials are related. Use each method to find $p(-1)$ given $p(x) = 6x^4 - 2x^3 - x - 2$ and point out the similarities and differences of the two methods.

Use synthetic substitution to find $p(-2)$ for each polynomial.

7. $p(x) = 2x^3 - 4x^2 - 15$

8. $p(x) = -x^3 + 11x^2 - 4$

9. $p(x) = x^4 - x^3 + 2x^2 + x - 3$

10. $p(x) = -x^4 + 2x^3 - 3x^2 + 4$

11. $p(x) = 3x^4 - 4x^2 + 5x - 20$

12. $p(x) = 5x^4 - x^2 - 15$

13. $p(x) = x^4 - 3x^2 + 7x$

14. $p(x) = 5x^3 - 3x^2 - 10x + 1$

For Problems 15–20, use long division to find the quotient and the remainder. Write the result in the form dividend = (divisor)(quotient) + remainder.

15. $(-8x^3 + 40x^2 - 37x + 30) \div (x - 4)$

16. $(6x^3 + 42x^2 - 50x - 20) \div (x + 8)$

17. $(4x^3 - 9x^2 + 9x + 3) \div (x - 1)$

18. $(x^4 - 8x^3 - x^2 + 62x - 34) \div (x - 7)$

19. $(x^4 + 11x^3 + 33x^2 + 24x + 32) \div (x + 6)$

20. $(x^4 - 2x^3 - 16x^2 + 28x + 9) \div (x - 4)$

21. **(MP) Model with Mathematics** The volume (in cubic inches) of a cardboard box is modeled by the function $V(t) = 2t^3 + 47t^2 + 338t + 693$, where t is twice the thickness of the cardboard. Given that the dimensions are binomials with integer coefficients and the width of the box is modeled by $w(t) = t + 9$, what are the other two dimensions of the cardboard box in terms of t?

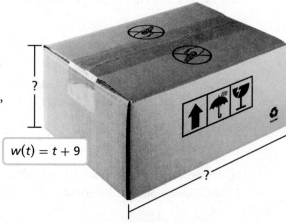

$w(t) = t + 9$

For Problems 22–27, use synthetic division to determine the quotient and the remainder. Write the result in the form $p(x) = (x - a)(\text{quotient}) + p(a)$.

22. $(2x^3 + 10x^2 - 12x + 5) \div (x - 3)$

23. $(-4x^3 + 12x^2 - 25x - 20) \div (x - 1)$

24. $(8x^3 - 5x^2 + 15) \div (x + 2)$

25. $(x^4 - 10x^3 + 44x - 34) \div (x - 5)$

26. $(2x^4 - 30x^2 + 6x - 25) \div (x - 6)$

27. $(6x^4 - 2x^3 + 40) \div (x - 3)$

28. (MP) **Critique Reasoning** Greg used synthetic division to determine if $x + 2$ is a factor of the polynomial $p(x) = 2x^4 + 7x^3 + 5x - 2$. His work is shown below.

$$
\begin{array}{r|rrrr}
-2 & 2 & 7 & 5 & -2 \\
 & & -4 & -6 & 2 \\
\hline
 & 2 & 3 & -1 & 0 \\
\end{array}
$$

Based on his work, he claims that $x + 2$ is a factor, but his teacher says that he is incorrect. What mistake(s) did Greg make? Show the correct synthetic division.

For Problems 29–34, determine whether the given polynomial is a factor of the polynomial $p(x)$. If so, find the remaining factors of $p(x)$.

29. $(x - 2)$; $p(x) = x^3 - 4x^2 + 5x - 2$

30. $(x + 2)$; $p(x) = x^3 - 2x^2 - x + 2$

31. $(x - 3)$; $p(x) = 2x^3 - 5x^2 - 4x + 3$

32. $(x - 2)$; $p(x) = x^4 - 4x^3 + 2x^2 + 4x - 3$

33. $(x + 1)$; $p(x) = 3x^3 - 2x^2 - 7x - 2$

34. $(x + 1)$; $p(x) = 9x^4 + 12x^3 - 2x^2 - 4x + 1$

35. The volume of a pyramid with a regular hexagonal base is modeled by the function $V(x) = \frac{1}{3}x^3 + \frac{4}{3}x^2 + \frac{2}{3}x - \frac{1}{3}$. Use polynomial division to determine an expression for the area of its base. Recall that for a pyramid, $V = \frac{1}{3}Bh$.

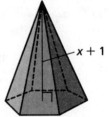
$x + 1$

36. **STEM** The voltage V of an experimental electrical system can be modeled by the function $V(t) = 0.5t^3 + 4.5t^2 + 4t$, where t represents time in seconds. The resistance R in the system is modeled by $R(t) = t + 1$. The current I is related to voltage and resistance by the equation $I = \frac{V}{R}$. Write a function that models the current.

37. (MP) **Model with Mathematics** A company sells build-your-own robot kits. The profit (in thousands of dollars) for the first 500 kits sold can be modeled by the function $P(x)$, where x is the number of kits sold (in hundreds). Use synthetic substitution to determine the total profit from the sale of 120 robot kits.

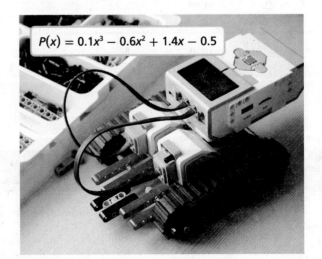
$P(x) = 0.1x^3 - 0.6x^2 + 1.4x - 0.5$

38. (MP) **Reason** Consider the set of polynomials of the form
$p(x) = a_n x^n + a_{n-1} x^{n-1} + \cdots + a_1 x + a_0$.

A. Determine whether the set of polynomials is closed under multiplication. If so, justify your reasoning. If not, give a counterexample.

B. Determine whether the set of polynomials is closed under division. If so, justify your reasoning. If not, give a counterexample.

C. (MP) **Construct Arguments** Use the table to tell whether the set of whole numbers, the set of integers, the set of rational numbers, and the set of polynomials are closed under each of the four basic operations. Then explain whether polynomials are like whole numbers, integers, or rational numbers with respect to closure.

	Whole numbers	Integers	Rational numbers	Polynomials
Addition	?	?	?	?
Subtraction	?	?	?	?
Multiplication	?	?	?	?
Division (nonzero)	?	?	?	?

Spiral Review • Assessment Readiness

39. Which expressions are factors of $x^4 + 2x^3 - 21x^2 - 62x - 40$? Select all that apply.

Ⓐ $(x + 5)$ Ⓓ $(x + 1)$

Ⓑ $(x + 4)$ Ⓔ $(x - 4)$

Ⓒ $(x + 2)$ Ⓕ $(x - 5)$

40. Which expression is equivalent to $(x^2 + x^3 - 1)(5 - x)$?

Ⓐ $-x^4 + 4x^3 + 5x^2 + x - 5$

Ⓑ $x^4 - 4x^3 - 5x^2 - x + 5$

Ⓒ $-x^3 + 5x^2 + x - 5$

Ⓓ $x^3 - 5x^2 - x + 5$

41. The sum of two polynomials is $5x^2 - 2x + 3$. One of the polynomials is $3x^2 + 3$. What is the other polynomial?

Ⓐ $2x^2 - 2x$

Ⓑ $-2x^2 + 2x$

Ⓒ $8x^2 - 2x + 6$

Ⓓ $-2x^2 - 2x + 6$

42. What is the zero of the polynomial function $f(x) = \dfrac{2}{5}x + 9$?

Ⓐ $x = -\dfrac{45}{2}$ Ⓒ $x = 9$

Ⓑ $x = -9$ Ⓓ $x = 45$

 I'm in a Learning Mindset!

What about dividing polynomials gives me stress?

Function Operations

What function gives Jin and Caleb's total combined earnings for a week in which they each give lessons the same number h of hours if their total weekly earnings are modeled by the functions below? What is their combined income when $h = 10$?

$J(h) = 42h + 500$

$C(h) = 48h + 750$

> Jin and Caleb each earned a fixed income and an hourly income.

You can add the function expressions to find a new total function $T(h)$.

> Their combined income when they each work 10 hours is $2150.

$T(h) = J(h) + C(h)$

$\quad = (42h + 500) + (48h + 750)$

$\quad = 90h + 1250$

$T(10) = 90(10) + 1250 = 2150$

Add and Subtract Polynomials

What is the difference in Jin's and Caleb's income in a week if each work the same number h of hours?

Find an expression for the difference $D(h)$ of the two functions.

$D(h) = C(h) - J(h)$

$\quad = (48h + 750) - (42h + 500)$

$\quad = 48h + 750 - 42h - 500$

$\quad = 6h + 250$

> This model assumes they each work the same number of hours. If h is 10 hours, the difference is $6(10) + 250 = \$310$.

Multiply Polynomials

What function models Jin's earnings per month if 4 weeks is counted as a month?

Note that the number of weeks counted as a month, 4, is constant, so multiply the function for Jin's weekly earnings by the constant function 4 to find the monthly earnings M per month.

$M(h) = 4 \cdot J(h)$

$\quad = 4(42h + 500)$

$\quad = 168h + 2000$

> If Jin gives lessons 10 hours per week, her monthly earnings are $3680.

Factor Polynomials

How can you factor the polynomial

$3x^4 - 2x^3 + 24x - 16$?

> Notice the common ratio between pairs of terms. Factor by grouping.

$3x^4 - 2x^3 + 24x - 16 = (3x^4 - 2x^3) + (24x - 16)$

$\quad = x^3(3x - 2) + 8(3x - 2)$

$\quad = (x^3 + 8)(3x - 2)$

$\quad = (x + 2)(x^2 - 2x + 4)(3x - 2)$

> Factor the sum of cubes. The quadratic term is irreducible.

Divide Polynomials

Use synthetic division to divide $x^3 - 2x^2 - 5x + 6$ by $x - 3$.

$$\underline{3|}\ \begin{array}{rrrr} 1 & -2 & -5 & 6 \\ & 3 & 3 & -6 \\ \hline 1 & 1 & -2 & \underline{|0} \end{array}$$

The remainder is 0, so

$(x^3 - 2x^2 - 5x + 6) \div (x - 3)$

$= x^2 + x - 2$.

Vocabulary

Choose the correct term from the box to complete each sentence.

1. The ___?___ states that if the polynomial function $P(x)$ is divided by $x - a$, then the remainder r is $P(a)$.

2. An operation on the set of polynomials has ___?___ when performing that operation on polynomials always results in another polynomial.

3. The ___?___ states for any polynomial $P(x)$, $x - a$ is a factor of $P(x)$ if and only if $P(a) = 0$.

4. Instead of using long division to divide a polynomial by a factor in the form $x - a$, you can use ___?___.

Concepts and Skills

Perform the operation. Then simplify.

5. $\left(3x^3 + x - 12\right) + \left(x^3 - 5x + 6\right)$

6. $\left(4x^2 - 6x + 2\right) + \left(3x^3 - 4x + 7\right)$

7. $\left(3x^3 + 2x - 8\right) - \left(2x^2 - 3x + 5\right)$

8. $\left(6x^2 - 6x + 20\right) - \left(7x^2 + 5x - 9\right)$

9. $\left(3x - 2\right)\left(5x + 1\right)$

10. $\left(6x - 5\right)\left(6x + 5\right)$

Factor each polynomial.

11. $x^3 - 64$

12. $6x^2 + 14x - 15x - 35$

13. $x^3 + 8$

14. $12x^2 + x - 20$

15. $8x^3 - 27$

16. $18x^2 + 45x - 8$

Divide and simplify.

17. $\left(3x^3 + 4x^2 - 2x + 1\right) \div (x - 4)$

18. $\left(x^4 - 2x^3 + 3x^2 + 54x + 1\right) \div (x + 3)$

Write the new function and answer the problem.

19. Jeanie's flower shop's weekly sales (in dollars) for the first half of the year can be modeled by the function $S(w) = 0.25w^2 + 5.5w + 894$, where w is the number of weeks. Her weekly costs for the same period can be modeled by the function $C(w) = 0.1w^2 + 2w + 128$, where w is the number of weeks. What function $P(w)$ models Jeanie's weekly profits? What was Jeanie's profit in the fourth week?

20. (MP) **Use Tools** Roberto makes skateboards. From 2010 to 2020, the number of skateboards Roberto produced can be modeled by the function $S(x) = 0.42x^2 - 1.8x + 280$, and the average cost to make each skateboard can be modeled by the function $C(x) = -0.001x^2 - 0.52x + 12$, where x is the number of years since 2010. What was Roberto's total cost to produce his skateboards in 2018? State what strategy and tool you will use to answer the question, explain your choice, and then find the answer.

Polynomial Equations

Module Performance Task: Focus on STEM

Deflection of a Beam

Horizontal beams are used to provide support to other features when they cannot be directly supported by the ground. Ideally, these support beams would be perfectly rigid, but they bend, or deflect from their ideal position, when under a force.

Given information	Deflection function, $d(x)$
$w = 1 \times 10^5$ N/m $EI = 6 \times 10^7$ N/m^2 $\ell = 5$ m	The function $d(x)$ (in meters) outputs the deflection of a beam that supports a uniformly distributed load in terms of a percent. $$d(x) = \frac{100wx}{24EI}(\ell^3 - 2\ell x^2 + x^3)$$ x (in m) is the horizontal position on the beam. w (in N/m) is the linear load density. E (in N/m^2) is the modulus of elasticity. I (in m^4) is the area moment of inertia. ℓ (in m) is the beam length.

A. Determine all zeros of the function $d(x)$. Explain what a zero of the function means in the context of deflection.

B. Identify which zeros make sense in the context of the problem. Explain your reasoning.

C. Graph the function $d(x)$ and identify when the maximum deflection occurs, and what percentage of the beam length does it deflect. Why does this x-location make sense in terms of this situation?

D. The maximum allowable deflection for the construction project is 2%. What is the maximum load density that this beam is permitted to hold?

Are You Ready?

Complete these problems to review prior concepts and skills you will need for this module.

Solve Multi-Step Equations

Solve each equation.

1. $\frac{1}{3}(8x - 3) = \frac{2}{3}x + 7$

2. $-2(x - 5) + 3x = 7 - 4(x - 9)$

3. $6(x - 1) + 5 = 3x - 2(x + 4)$

4. $-3(0.25x - 0.5) = 0.75x - 0.5(4x + 6)$

Solve Quadratic Equations by Factoring

Solve each equation.

5. $x^2 - 12x = 0$

6. $x^2 + x - 30 = 0$

7. $x^2 = 7x - 12$

8. $9x^2 = 36$

9. $56 = 2x^2 + 9x$

10. $-10x^2 - 40x = -600$

Solve Nonlinear Systems

Solve.

11. $\begin{cases} y = 2x - 2 \\ y = -x^2 - 2x + 3 \end{cases}$

12. $\begin{cases} y = 6x + 17 \\ y = 4x^2 + 2x - 31 \end{cases}$

Connecting Past and Present Learning

Previously, you learned:

- to solve linear equations and inequalities with rational number coefficients in one variable,

- to solve quadratic equations by recognizing the most appropriate method: taking the square root, completing the square, using the quadratic formula, or by factoring, and

- to explain why the x-coordinates of the points of intersection of the graphs of two functions $f(x)$ and $g(x)$ are the solutions of the equation $f(x) = g(x)$.

In this module, you will learn:

- to find the zeros of polynomial functions using the Rational Zero Theorem,

- to apply the Fundamental Theorem of Algebra to determine the zeros of polynomial functions, and

- to write a polynomial function given its zeros, using the Irrational Root Theorem and the Complex Conjugate Root Theorem.

Solve Polynomial Equations

(I Can) use the Rational Roots Theorem to determine the roots of polynomials and to find solutions to polynomial equations.

Spark Your Learning

The county commissioners are discussing the attendance at past county fairs. They are not quite sure which year it was that the fair attendance reached 100,000. All they have is a clipping of a newspaper article without a date.

Taped to the newspaper article was a note showing a polynomial function given as a model for the fair attendance each year from 2005 to 2014.

Complete Part A as a whole class. Then complete Parts B–D in small groups.

A. What is a mathematical question you can ask about this situation? What information would you need to know to answer your question?

B. What variables are involved in this situation? What is the relationship between the variables? How can you rewrite the model to better represent the variables involved?

C. To answer your question, what strategy and tool would you use along with all the information you have? What answer do you get?

D. Does the answer make sense in the context of the situation? How do you know?

Turn and Talk How would your answer change for each change in situation:
- The commissioners want to know what year(s) the attendance was over 99,000.
- The commissioners want to know what year(s) the attendance was below 97,000.

Build Understanding

Relate Zeros and Coefficients of Polynomial Functions

A **root** is a solution of the polynomial equation $f(x) = 0$. A zero of a function $f(x)$ is any value of x for which $f(x) = 0$. Thus, the term *root* is used when referring to an equation and the term *zero* is used when referring to a function. The zeros and coefficients of any polynomial function $p(x)$ are related in a specific way. Any constant c can be rewritten as cx^0. For example, the constant 4 can be rewritten as $4x^0$. So the constant of a polynomial function is also a coefficient of the function.

 The function $f(x) = (x + 4)(x + 1)(x - 1)(x - 4)$ is a polynomial function written in factored form.

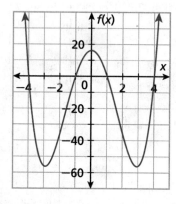

A. What are the zeros of f?

B. How does the function f appear when written in standard form?

C. What are the coefficients of f?

D. How are the zeros of the function f related to the standard form of the function?

 Turn and Talk Look at the zeros of the function. Are any of them factors of the leading coefficient? Support your answer.

 Now consider the polynomial function $g(x) = (4x + 3)(2x + 1)(2x - 1)$.

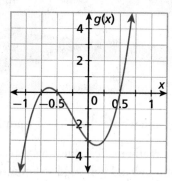

A. What are the zeros of g?

B. How does the function g appear when written in standard form?

C. What are the coefficients of g?

D. How are the zeros of the function g related to the standard form of the function?

 Turn and Talk
- How are the numerators of the zeros in a polynomial related to the coefficients of the polynomial in standard form?
- How are the denominators of the zeros in a polynomial related to the coefficients of the polynomial in standard form?

Step It Out

Find Zeros Using the Rational Zero Theorem

The Rational Zero Theorem can be used to determine the rational zeros of a polynomial function. The theorem is based on the observations you made in Tasks 1 and 2. The zeros of a polynomial function are related to the coefficients when the function is written in standard form.

> **Rational Zero Theorem**
>
> If $p(x)$ is a polynomial function with integer coefficients, and if $\frac{m}{n}$ is a zero of $p(x)$, that is $p\left(\frac{m}{n}\right) = 0$, then m is a factor of the constant term of $p(x)$ and n is a factor of the leading coefficient of $p(x)$.

3 Use the Rational Zero Theorem to determine the rational zeros of the polynomial function $p(x) = x^3 - 8x^2 + x + 42$.

Since the leading coefficient is 1, all possible rational zeros will be factors of 42.

> **A.** How does the Rational Zero Theorem support this statement?

The factors of 42 are:

$\pm 1, \pm 2, \pm 3, \pm 6, \pm 7, \pm 14, \pm 21, \pm 42$.

Use a synthetic division table to test each factor.

Possible zeros	1	−8	1	42
1	1	−7	−6	36
2	1	−6	−11	20
3	1	−5	−14	0

> **B.** Can you use the Rational Zero Theorem to factor the quadratic?

The table shows that 3 is a zero, so the binomial $x - 3$ is a factor of $p(x)$. Therefore, $p(x) = (x - 3)(x^2 - 5x - 14)$.

Factoring the trinomial, the factored form of the polynomial function p is

$$p(x) = (x - 3)(x - 7)(x + 2).$$

The zeros of the function are $x = -2$, $x = 3$, or $x = 7$.

 Turn and Talk How would the possible rational zeros differ if the polynomial function had a factor of $2x - 3$ instead of $x - 3$?

4 Use the Rational Zero Theorem to determine the rational zeros of the polynomial function $p(x) = x^4 + 5x^3 - 21x^2 - 125x - 100$.

Since the leading coefficient is 1, all possible rational zeros will be factors of -100.

The factors of -100 are:

> **A.** Does the fact that the constant term is negative affect the possible rational zeros?

$\pm 1, \pm 2, \pm 4, \pm 5, \pm 10, \pm 20, \pm 25, \pm 50, \pm 100.$

Use a synthetic division table to test each factor.

Possible zeros	1	5	−21	−125	−100
1	1	6	−15	−140	−240
2	1	7	−7	−139	−378
4	1	9	15	−65	−360
5	1	10	29	20	0

The table shows that 5 is a zero, so the binomial $x - 5$ is a factor. Therefore, $p(x) = (x - 5)(x^3 + 10x^2 + 29x + 20)$.

Apply the Rational Zero Theorem again. Since the leading coefficient of the cubic polynomial is 1, all possible rational zeros will be factors of 20. The factors of 20: $-1, -2, -4, -5, \pm 10, \pm 20.$

> **B.** Why are some factors of 20 missing from the list?

Possible zeros	1	10	29	20
−1	1	9	20	0

According to the table, -1 is a factor such that $p(x) = (x - 5)(x + 1)(x^2 + 9x + 20)$. The polynomial function $p(x)$ in factored form is

$$p(x) = (x - 5)(x + 1)(x + 4)(x + 5).$$

The zeros are $x = -5$, $x = -4$, $x = -1$, or $x = 5$.

 Turn and Talk Would the Rational Zero Theorem work on any quadratic function? Why or why not?

Solve a Real-World Problem Using the Rational Root Theorem

Rational Root Theorem
If the polynomial $p(x)$ has integer coefficients, then every rational root of the polynomial equation $p(x) = 0$ can be written in the form $\frac{m}{n}$, where m is a factor of the constant term of $p(x)$ and n is a factor of the leading coefficient of $p(x)$.

5 A resort rents beach cabanas that are shaped like rectangular prisms. Each cabana has a length 4 feet less than twice its width and a height 1 foot less than its width. The least expensive cabana for rent is shown in the photo. What are the dimensions of this cabana?

> The space enclosed by the cabana has a volume of 420 cubic feet.

In order to find the dimensions using the given volume, write expressions for the length, width, and height of the cabana.

Let w be the width of the cabana. Then its length (in feet) is $2w - 4$ and its height (in feet) is $w - 1$.

> **A.** Why are the expressions in terms of width?

$$420 = w(2w - 4)(w - 1)$$
$$0 = w^3 - 3w + 2w - 210$$

> **B.** What formula was used to create the equation?

Since the leading coefficient is 1, the possible rational roots will be factors of 210. The factors of 210 are ± 1, ± 2, ± 3, ± 5, ± 6, ± 7, ± 10, ± 14, ± 15, ± 21, ± 30, ± 35, ± 42, ± 70, ± 105, and ± 210.

> **C.** Why was the equation $420 = w(2w - 4)(w - 1)$ rewritten as the equation $0 = w^3 - 3w + 2w - 210$?

Test the possible roots one at a time. Since 7 is a root of the equation, $w = 7$ and the width of the cabana is 7 feet. Therefore, its length is 10 feet and its height is 6 feet.

This result makes sense since $7 \times 10 \times 6 = 420$ cubic feet.

Find Irrational Zeros Using Successive Approximations

The Rational Zero Theorem only works if at least one of the zeros is rational. When a zero or zeros are irrational, you can use successive approximations to estimate the value of the zero. **Successive approximations** are closer and closer estimates for a zero of a polynomial function found by systematically decreasing the interval that contains the zero until a desired place value is achieved.

6 The function $V(r) = \frac{10}{9}\pi r^3 - 2\pi r + 5$ represents the volume of a snow globe, where r is the radius, in centimeters. Use successive approximations to determine the radius to three decimal places when the volume is 1900 cm³. Use a spreadsheet to perform the calculations, beginning with the interval [8, 9].

> **A.** Why was the interval [8, 9] selected for the first approximation?

> **B.** How is the spreadsheet used to calculate the radius to three decimal places?

B2	▲▼	✕ ✓	fx	= (10/9)*PI()*C3^3−2*PI()*C3+5−1900							
	C	D	E	F	G	H	I	J	K	L	M
	r	V		r	V		r	V		r	V
1	8	−158.048		8.2	−21.8847		8.23	−0.87177		8.231	−0.16867
2	9	593.1414		8.21	−14.8976		8.231	−0.16867		8.2311	−0.09835
3	8.1	−90.8148		8.22	−7.8933		8.232	0.534602		8.2312	−0.02803
4	8.2	−21.8847		8.23	−0.87177		8.233	1.238047		8.2313	0.042293
5	8.3	48.76272		8.24	6.166992		8.234	1.941665		8.2314	0.112618
6	8.4	121.1485		8.25	13.22301		8.235	2.645455		8.2315	0.182944
7	8.5	195.2936		8.26	20.29631		8.236	3.349417		8.2316	0.253273
8	8.6	271.2189		8.27	27.38691		8.237	4.053552		8.2317	0.323602
	8.7	348.9454		8.28	34.49483		8.238	4.75786		8.2318	0.393934
	8.8	428.494		8.29	41.62009		8.239	5.46234		8.2319	0.464267
	8.9	509.8857		8.3	48.76272		8.24	6.166992		8.232	0.534602

Check Understanding

1. How are the zeros of the polynomial function $p(x) = (2x - 1)(5x + 7)(8x + 9)$ related to the coefficients when written in standard form?

2. Use the Rational Zero Theorem to determine the rational zeros of the polynomial function $f(x) = 6x^3 + 19x^2 + 9x - 10$.

3. Use the Rational Zero Theorem to determine the rational zeros of the polynomial function $g(x) = x^4 + 6x^3 + 7x^2 - 6x - 8$.

4. Tara had a sale and tracked her profits for 6 consecutive weeks. Her total profits for each week of the sale can be represented by the polynomial function $P(w) = 20w^4 - 300w^3 + 1060w^2 + 300w + 3920$ where w is the whole number of weeks after Tara started the sale. How many weeks after the sale started did Tara have $8000 in profits?

5. Jason makes different sized apple cinnamon pastries that are in the shape of a cone. The function $V(r) = \frac{7}{3}\pi r^2$ represents the volume (in cubic inches) of the pastry where r is the radius (in inches) of the base of the pastry. Use successive approximations to determine the radius of the pastry to three decimal places when the volume is 32 in^3. Start with the interval $[2, 3]$.

On Your Own

6. **(MP) Use Structure** Chris stated that $\frac{3}{2}$ is a zero of the function $f(x) = 9x^3 + 18x^2 - 4x - 8$. Is he correct? Why or why not?

7. **(MP) Reason** Derek thinks 5 is a zero of the function $p(x) = 25x^4 - 226x^2 + 9$, but John does not agree. John thinks 3 is a zero of $p(x)$. One of these students is correct. Which student is correct and why?

8. What is the missing binomial factor for the function $g(x) = (4x - 1)(x + 2)(?)$ if $g(x) = 20x^3 + 63x^2 + 39x - 14$ when written in standard form?

9. What is the missing binomial factor for the function $h(x) = (2x - 1)(x + 3)(?)$ if $h(x) = 2x^3 + 21x^2 + 37x - 24$ when written in standard form?

10. What is the missing binomial factor for the function $j(x) = (x + 8)(x + 3)(?)$ if $j(x) = 3x^3 + 32x^2 + 61x - 24$ when written in standard form?

11. What is the missing binomial factor for the function $k(x) = (x - 4)(4x + 3)(?)$ if $k(x) = 8x^3 - 14x^2 - 63x - 36$ when written in standard form?

Use the Rational Zero Theorem to determine the rational zeros of the polynomial functions.

12. $p(x) = 25x^3 - 55x^2 + 28x$

13. $p(x) = 15x^3 + 2x^2 - 13x - 4$

14. $p(x) = 4x^3 + 12x^2 - 100x - 300$

15. $p(x) = 6x^3 + 29x^2 - 6x - 5$

16. $p(x) = 98x^3 + 245x^2 - 32x - 80$

17. $p(x) = 12x^3 + 2x^2 - 34x + 20$

For Problems 18-28, use the Rational Zero Theorem to determine the rational zeros of the polynomial functions.

18. $p(x) = 16x^3 + 74x^2 - 31x - 5$

19. $p(x) = 8x^3 + 2x^2 - 15x - 9$

20. $p(x) = 18x^3 + 24x^2 - 88x - 64$

21. $p(x) = 2x^3 + 2x^2 - 18x - 18$

22. $p(x) = 6x^4 + 7x^3 - 8x^2 - 5x$

23. $p(x) = 36x^4 + 19x^3 - 34x^2 - 21x$

24. $p(x) = 3x^4 + 5x^3 - 190x^2 - 320x - 128$

25. $p(x) = 4x^4 - 28x^3 + 15x^2 + 63x - 54$

26. $p(x) = 49x^4 - 147x^3 + 97x^2 + 3x - 2$

27. $p(x) = x^4 + 2x^3 - 45x^2 + 34x + 80$

28. $p(x) = 36x^4 + 36x^3 - 153x^2 - 81x + 162$

29. The function $M(y) = -y^3 + 19y^2 - 94y + 420$ represents the number of members that belong to a community center where y is the whole number of years after it was founded. How many years after the community center was founded was the number of members 350?

30. The function $S(m) = m^3 - 18m^2 + 72m + 100$ represents the number of skateboards sold each month at a store where m is the whole number of months after releasing a new model. How many months after the model was released were 181 skateboards sold?

31. The function $S(y) = 5y^3 - 45y^2 - 70y + 5000$ represents the yearly sales for Bonnie's company where y is the whole number of years after 2000. In what year did Bonnie's company have $4800 in sales?

The number of skateboards sold each month is modeled by the function:
$S(m) = m^3 - 18m^3 + 72m + 100$

32. The function $L(d) = 2d^4 - 21d^3 + 38d^2 + 21d + 6160$ represents the total number of likes Simon's video had received d days after he posted it online. After what whole number of days did his video get 12,320 likes?

33. The surface area of a globe is a function of its radius. Use successive approximations to determine the radius to three decimal places when the surface area of the globe is 500 in². Start with the interval [6, 7].

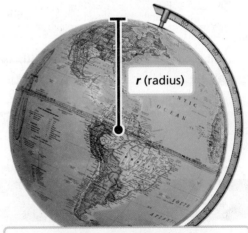

r (radius)

34. The function $V(r) = 2\pi r^3$ models the volume V of a plastic container, where r (in inches) is the radius. Use successive approximations to determine the radius to three decimal places when the volume of the container is 250 in³. Start with the interval [3, 4].

The surface area S of a sphere is modeled by $S(r) = 4\pi r^2$, where r is the radius.

35. The function $V(r) = \frac{2}{3}\pi r^3$ represents the volume of a hemispherical dome, where r (in feet) is the radius. Use successive approximations to determine the radius to three decimal places when the volume of the dome is 800 cubic feet. Start with the interval $[7, 8]$.

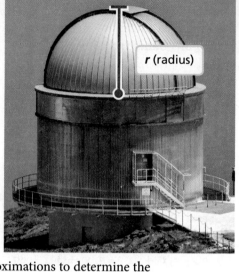

r (radius)

36. The vertical position of a particle with respect to its starting position is modeled by the function $s(t) = 2t^4 - 29t^3 + 125t^2 - 150t$, where t is measured in seconds.

    A. Write and solve a polynomial equation to determine the points in time when the particle returned to its starting vertical position.

    B. Write and solve a polynomial equation by successive approximations to determine the point in time to three decimal places when the particle reaches a vertical position of 64.

37. (Open Middle™) Using the integers -9 to 9, at most one time each, fill in the boxes to create a polynomial function and solutions whose x-intercepts are as close together as possible.

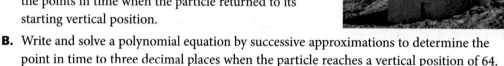

$$x^4 + \boxed{}\, x^2 + \boxed{}$$

$$x = \boxed{}\,, \boxed{}\,, \boxed{}\,, \text{ or } \boxed{}$$

Spiral Review • Assessment Readiness

38. What are the binomial factors of the quadratic function $f(x) = 2x^2 + 11x - 6$? Select all that apply.

    Ⓐ $2x - 6$

    Ⓑ $2x + 6$

    Ⓒ $x - 6$

    Ⓓ $x + 6$

    Ⓔ $2x - 1$

    Ⓕ $2x + 2$

39. What is the area of an isosceles triangle that has a height 3 less than twice its base?

    Ⓐ $2b^2 - 3b$ Ⓒ $3b - b^2$

    Ⓑ $b^2 - \frac{3}{2}b$ Ⓓ $\frac{3}{2}b - b^2$

40. The area of a rectangle is $A(x) = x^2 - 13x + 42$, and its width is $x - 7$. What is the rectangle's length?

    Ⓐ $x - 8$ Ⓒ $x - 6$

    Ⓑ $x + 8$ Ⓓ $x + 6$

41. Match each expression on the left with its equivalent expression on the right.

    A. $4x^2 - 4$ **1.** $(x + 2)(x - 2)$

    B. $4x^2 - 1$ **2.** $(x + 2)^2$

    C. $x^2 + 4x + 4$ **3.** $(2x + 1)(2x - 1)$

    D. $x^2 - 4$ **4.** $(x + 1)^2$

    E. $x^2 + 2x + 1$ **5.** $(2x - 2)(2x + 2)$

 I'm in a Learning Mindset!

What stress-management skills can I use to find solutions to polynomial equations?

The Fundamental Theorem of Algebra

(I Can) find the complex roots of polynomials and complex solutions to polynomial equations.

Spark Your Learning

The percent change in a housing cost index over time can be modeled by a polynomial function.

The model crosses the x-axis three times.

Year 0 of the model corresponds to 2005.

Complete Part A as a whole class. Then complete Parts B–D in small groups.

A. What is a mathematical question you can ask about this situation? What information would you need to know to answer your question?

B. What variables are involved in this situation? What unit of measurement would you use for each variable? How can you use the zeros to develop a polynomial model?

C. To answer your question, what strategy and tool would you use along with all the information you have? What answer do you get?

D. Does the answer make sense in the context of the situation? What is an appropriate domain for your model?

Turn and Talk Describe how the function modeling the situation would change if housing costs continued to increase and then decrease over time, so that the model crossed over the x-axis several more times.

Build Understanding

Investigate Complex Zeros of a Polynomial

A zero of a polynomial function can appear in the factorization of a polynomial more than once. The function $f(x) = x^2 + 10x + 25$ has a zero of -5 with **multiplicity** 2 because the corresponding factor $x + 5$ is raised to the second power when $f(x)$ is written in factored form. The power of a factor reveals the multiplicity of its corresponding zero, as you can see when $f(x)$ is rewritten as $f(x) = (x + 5)^2$. The multiplicity of a zero is important when looking for a pattern between the degree of a polynomial and the number of real and nonreal zeros.

1 ▶ Examine the relationship among zeros, multiplicities, degrees, and graphs of polynomial functions.

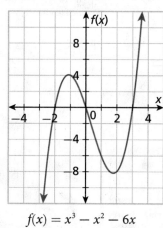 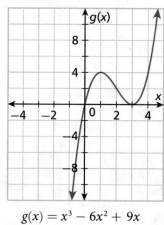 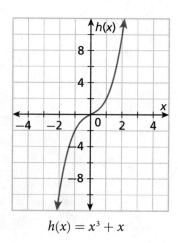

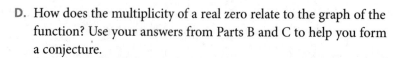

$$f(x) = x^3 - x^2 - 6x \qquad g(x) = x^3 - 6x^2 + 9x \qquad h(x) = x^3 + x$$

A. Write each of the functions $f(x)$, $g(x)$, and $h(x)$ in factored form.

B. Identify the real and complex zeros of each function and their multiplicities. What do you notice about the multiplicities of the zeros in relation to the degree of the functions?

C. What is the zero of the cubic function $f(x) = x^3$? What is the multiplicity of the zero? What do you notice about the graph of the function at the zero?

D. How does the multiplicity of a real zero relate to the graph of the function? Use your answers from Parts B and C to help you form a conjecture.

E. The figure shows the graph of a fourth-degree polynomial function. Use your findings about the relationship among multiplicities of zeros, the degree of the function, and the behavior of the graph around the zeros to predict the number of real and complex zeros of the function. Explain your reasoning.

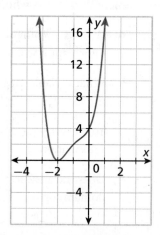

 Turn and Talk Based on your knowledge of the complex zeros of quadratic functions and the functions in this task, can a polynomial function have only one complex zero?

Step It Out

Apply the Fundamental Theorem of Algebra

The patterns you observed in the Build Understanding are reflected in the Fundamental Theorem of Algebra.

> ### The Fundamental Theorem of Algebra
>
> Every polynomial function of degree $n \geq 1$ has at least one zero, where a zero may be a complex number.
>
> **Corollary:** Every polynomial function of degree $n > 1$ has exactly n zeros, including multiplicities.

Because the zeros of a polynomial function $p(x)$ give the roots of the equation $p(x) = 0$, the theorem and its corollary also extend to finding all roots of a polynomial equation.

2 Solve the polynomial equation $x^3 + 7x^2 - 2x - 14 = 0$. You can use the Rational Roots Theorem to determine that since the leading coefficient is 1, all possible rational roots will be factors of -14. The factors of -14 are: $\pm 1, \pm 2, \pm 7, \pm 14$. Use a synthetic division table to test each factor.

Possible zeros	1	7	−2	−14
1	1	8	6	−8
2	1	9	16	18
7	1	14	96	658
14	1	21	292	4074
−1	1	6	−8	−6
−2	1	5	−12	10
−7	1	0	−2	0
−14	1	−7	96	−1358

A. How do you know -7 is the only rational root of the polynomial equation?

The degree of the polynomial $p(x) = x^3 + 7x^2 - 2x - 14$ is 3.

B. How do you determine the degree of $p(x)$?

Apply the Fundamental Theorem of Algebra to determine that $p(x)$ has 3 zeros.

A graph of $p(x)$ will show if the two zeros other than -7 are irrational or complex.

You can see that $p(x)$ crosses the x-axis three times, so all three zeros are real.

Factor $p(x)$ using the root -7 and set equal to 0: $0 = (x + 7)(x^2 - 2)$. The quadratic factor leads to the two other roots $x = -\sqrt{2}$ and $x = \sqrt{2}$.

The roots of $x^3 + 7x^2 - 2x - 14 = 0$ are $x = -7$, $x = -\sqrt{2}$, and $x = \sqrt{2}$.

D. Are the equation's roots real or complex? If they are real, are they rational or irrational?

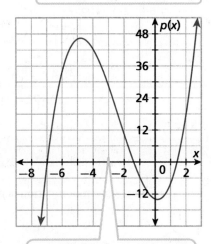

C. Describe where the zeros are located on the graph.

Write a Polynomial Function Given Its Zeros

For polynomial equations, irrational and complex roots come in pairs. In the previous task, two of the roots were $-\sqrt{2}$ and $\sqrt{2}$ which form a pair called **irrational conjugates**. These irrational root pairs can be written generally as $a + b\sqrt{c}$ and $a - b\sqrt{c}$, such as $4 + 3\sqrt{5}$ and $4 - 3\sqrt{5}$. When a polynomial equation has complex roots, these roots come in pairs called **complex conjugates** that can be written generally as $a + bi$ and $a - bi$, such as $3 + 6i$ and $3 - 6i$.

Irrational Root Theorem
If a polynomial $p(x)$ has rational coefficients and $a + b\sqrt{c}$ is a root of the equation $p(x) = 0$, where a and b are rational and $\sqrt{c}$ is irrational, then $a - b\sqrt{c}$ is also a root of $p(x) = 0$.

Complex Conjugate Root Theorem
If $a + bi$, where a and b are real numbers, is an imaginary root of the polynomial equation $p(x) = 0$ with real number coefficients, then $a - bi$ is also a root of $p(x) = 0$.

The product of irrational conjugates is a rational number because they are a sum and difference of terms. The product of complex conjugates is a real number because they are a sum and difference of terms.

Because the roots of the equation $p(x) = 0$ give the zeros of the polynomial function $p(x)$, the previous theorems also apply to identifying zeros of a polynomial function. You can use the zeros of a polynomial function to write the polynomial function.

3 ▶ Write the polynomial function in standard form that has a leading coefficient of 1 with the least degree for the given zeros 1, 4, and $2\sqrt{3}$.

Use the Irrational Root Theorem to identify $-2\sqrt{3}$ as another root of the polynomial.

$$p(x) = \left(x - 2\sqrt{3}\right)\left(x + 2\sqrt{3}\right)(x - 1)(x - 4)$$

$$= \left[x^2 - 4(3)\right](x - 1)(x - 4)$$

$$= \left(x^2 - 12\right)(x - 1)(x - 4)$$

$$= \left(x^3 - x^2 - 12x + 12\right)(x - 4)$$

$$= x^4 - 4x^3 - x^3 + 4x^2 - 12x^2 + 48x + 12x - 48$$

$$= x^4 - 5x^3 - 8x^2 + 60x - 48$$

A. Why do you write $p(x)$ in factored form?

B. What will be the degree of this polynomial? Explain how you know after writing the factored form.

The polynomial function is $p(x) = x^4 - 5x^3 - 8x^2 + 60x - 48$.

 Turn and Talk Can a polynomial function have only irrational zeros? Explain.

4 ▶ Write the polynomial function that has a leading coefficient of 1 with the least degree for the given zeros 6 and $5 - 3i$.

Write the function in factored form, and then multiply to write it in standard form.

A. Why are there 3 binomial factors of $p(x)$?

$p(x) = [x - (5 - 3i)][x - (5 + 3i)](x - 6)$

$\quad = [x^2 - (5 + 3i)x - (5 - 3i)x + (5 - 3i)(5 + 3i)](x - 6)$

$\quad = [x^2 - (5 + 3i + 5 - 3i)x + 25 - 9i^2](x - 6)$

$\quad = (x^2 - 10x + 34)(x - 6)$

B. What happens to all of the terms with the imaginary unit i?

$\quad = x^3 - 6x^2 - 10x^2 + 60x + 34x - 204$

$\quad = x^3 - 16x^2 + 94x - 204$

The polynomial function is $p(x) = x^3 - 16x^2 + 94x - 204$.

5 ▶ ## Solve a Real-World Problem by Graphing a Polynomial Model

The functions model the height for the first 60 seconds of each ride.

When polynomial functions do not have integer coefficients, you can use a graphing tool to locate or approximate zeros. Since this will only work for real zeros, this is a good strategy when finding zeros of polynomial models representing real-world situations.

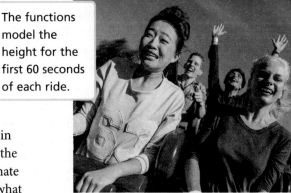

A polynomial function can be used to model the height H (in meters) of a roller coaster above the ground t seconds after the ride begins. The following polynomials model the approximate heights of the roller coasters Fear (*RF*) and Storm (*RS*). At what time(s) are the roller coasters at the same height?

$H_{RF}(t) = -0.000018t^4 + 0.0041t^3 - 0.3t^2 + 7.6t + 15$

$H_{RS}(t) = 0.000018t^4 - 0.0012t^3 - 0.08t^2 + 5.5t + 10$

A. Does it matter which function you subtract from the other? Explain.

Find the difference of the two functions $H_D(t)$ so that zeros of $H_D(t)$ represent the time when the roller coasters are at the same height.

$H_D(t) = -0.000018t^4 + 0.0041t^3 - 0.3t^2 + 7.6t + 15 - $

$\quad\quad (0.000018t^4 - 0.0012t^3 - 0.08t^2 + 5.5t + 10)$

$\quad = -0.000036t^4 + 0.0053t^3 - 0.22t^2 + 2.1t + 5$

Use a graphing calculator to graph $H_D(t)$ in order to approximate the zeros.

B. Why should you not include the zero that occurs close to $t = 80$?

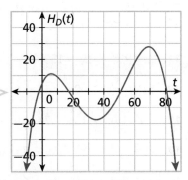

It appears from the graph that the roller coasters are at the same height after about 17 and 51 seconds.

🔄 **Turn and Talk** How can graphing each of the original equations on the same graph help you to find when the roller coasters are at the same height? Explain.

©jacoblund/iStock/Getty Images

Check Understanding

1. Explain how you can use the number of zeros of a polynomial function and their multiplicities to determine the degree of the polynomial function.

2. Find all of the zeros of $p(x) = x^3 + 8x^2 - 24x - 40$.

3. Write the polynomial function that has integer coefficients, a leading coefficient of 1, and the least degree for the given zeros 2 and $3 - \sqrt{7}$.

4. Write the polynomial function that has integer coefficients, a leading coefficient of 1, and the least degree for the given zeros -1, 2, and $-i$.

5. Mara created two different 'how to' videos and created a model L for each video to represent how many likes she gets each day, d days after releasing the videos.

   Birdhouse video: $L_B(d) = 0.08d^3 - 0.16d^2 - 5.12d + 490.44$

   Planter video: $L_P(d) = 0.4d^3 - 6.8d^2 + 25.6d + 222.6$

   Use a graphing calculator to find how many days after releasing the videos the number of likes is approximately the same.

On Your Own

6. (MP) **Reason** A teacher writes a fifth-degree polynomial equation on the board that had 2 real unique roots. Is it possible this polynomial has no complex roots? Is it possible this polynomial has complex roots? Explain.

7. (MP) **Use Structure** A polynomial $p(x)$ has a degree of 4. The graph of $p(x)$ is shown.

   A. What does the Fundamental Theorem of Algebra tell you about the number of zeros of $p(x)$?

   B. Does $p(x)$ have any irrational or complex zeros? Explain.

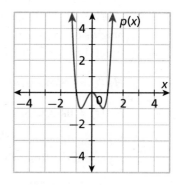

8. (MP) **Use Structure** You write a sixth-degree polynomial equation that has exactly 4 complex roots. Describe the other possible roots of the polynomial equation.

Find all the roots of each of the polynomial equations.

9. $x^3 - 2x^2 - 11x - 6 = 0$

10. $x^3 - 11x^2 + 36x - 26 = 0$

11. $2x^3 + x^2 + 4x - 15 = 0$

12. $x^3 - 5x^2 + 39x + 45 = 0$

13. $2x^3 + x^2 - 108x - 54 = 0$

14. $x^3 + 2x^2 - 23x + 6 = 0$

15. $x^3 + 10x^2 + 13x - 74 = 0$

16. $x^4 + 5x^3 + 23x^2 + 51x = 0$

17. $x^4 + 2x^3 - 2x^2 - 8x - 8 = 0$

18. $x^4 - 4x^3 - 26x^2 + 100x + 25 = 0$

19. $x^4 + 2x^3 - 5x^2 - 4x + 6 = 0$

20. $x^4 - x^2 - 20 = 0$

For each given set of zeros, write the polynomial function that has integer coefficients, a leading coefficient of 1, and the least degree.

21. $2\sqrt{2}, 3$

22. $-2, 1 + \sqrt{7}$

23. $3 - \sqrt{10}, 4$

24. $-1, 3 - \sqrt{2}$

25. $0, 1 - \sqrt{5}, 5$

26. $-\sqrt{3}, 3 + \sqrt{6}$

27. $9 - i, 4$

28. $-3, 2 - 4i$

29. $-5, 4 + i$

30. $1 - 4i, 2, 3$

31. $-2i, 1 + 3i$

32. $-3i, 2 + i$

33. (MP) **Use Structure** Use the graph of the polynomial function to answer the questions.

    A. Are the zeros of the polynomial function shown on the graph real or complex? Explain.

    B. What type of transformation on the polynomial function would change any complex zeros to real zeros?

    C. Can you transform this polynomial function so that it has no real zeros? Explain.

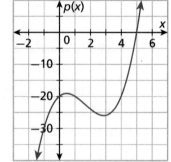

34. (MP) **Critique Reasoning** Ann says she wrote a third-degree polynomial function that has exactly 2 unique, real zeros. Is this possible? Why or why not?

35. (MP) **Use Structure** At most, how many complex roots can a seventh-degree polynomial have? Explain.

36. (MP) **Reason** Show that the Fundamental Theorem of Algebra and its corollary are true for quadratic polynomials.

37. Financial Literacy Keira purchased two different types of stocks, a transportation stock and an energy stock. She created a polynomial model P for each type of stock to represent the price of the stock m months after she purchased it.

    A. How can you combine these functions in order to find when the stocks were about the same price?

    B. Write the new function using the method you described in Part A.

    C. Use a graphing calculator to graph the function you wrote in Part B. When were the stocks about the same price?

Transportation stock:
$P_T(m) = -0.05m^4 + 0.5m^3 + 0.35m^2 - 8m + 107.2$

Energy stock: $P_E(m) = m^3 - 15m^2 + 54m + 24$

38. Two stores that sell clothing open in the same year. The annual revenue R (in millions of dollars) for each store t years after opening can be modeled by the polynomial functions $R_A(t)$ and $R_B(t)$.

   A. Use a graphing calculator to find when the revenues of the two stores were approximately equal.

   B. Describe the process you used to solve this problem.

   C. Describe a different way you could solve this problem.

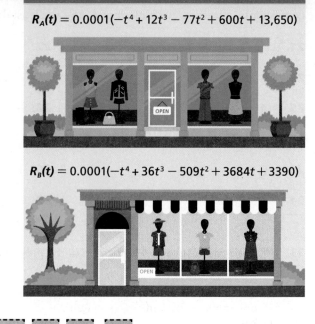

Annual revenue

$R_A(t) = 0.0001(-t^4 + 12t^3 - 77t^2 + 600t + 13{,}650)$

$R_B(t) = 0.0001(-t^4 + 36t^3 - 509t^2 + 3684t + 3390)$

39. (Open Middle™) Using the integers -9 to 9, at most one time each, fill in the boxes to create a polynomial function and solutions.

$$x^4 + \boxed{}x^3 + \boxed{}x^2 + \boxed{}x \qquad x = \boxed{}, \boxed{}, \boxed{}i, \boxed{}i$$

Spiral Review • Assessment Readiness

40. Determine the rational zeros for the polynomial function
$p(x) = 9x^3 + 33x^2 + 24x - 12$.
Select all that apply.

   (A) -3

   (B) -2

   (C) $-\dfrac{1}{3}$

   (D) $\dfrac{1}{3}$

   (E) 2

   (F) 3

41. The function $P(y) = y^3 + 6y^2 + 25y + 28$ represents the number of ponds a landscaping company installed each year, where y is the number of years after the company opened for business. How many years, after the company opened, did it install 110 ponds?

   (A) 1 year

   (B) 2 years

   (C) 4 years

   (D) 6 years

42. Match the equivalent expressions.

   A. $\sqrt[3]{64m^3n^3}$ **1.** $4mn$

   B. $\sqrt[3]{64m^6n^9}$ **2.** $8mn$

   C. $\sqrt{16m^6n^2}$ **3.** $4m^2n$

   D. $\sqrt[4]{256m^8n^4}$ **4.** $4m^3n$

   E. $\sqrt{64m^2n^2}$ **5.** $4m^2n^3$

 I'm in a Learning Mindset!

How does my stress level affect my ability to use the Fundamental Theorem of Algebra to determine complex solutions to polynomial equations?

Rational Zero Theorem

You can use the Rational Zero Theorem to find the rational zeros of the polynomial function $p(x) = x^3 + 4x^2 + x - 6$.

> The Rational Zero Theorem says that all rational zeros of a polynomial function can be written by dividing factors of the constant term by the leading coefficient.

Possible zeros: $\pm 1, \pm 2, \pm 3, \pm 6$

Use a synthetic division table to test possible zeros.

Possible zeros	1	4	1	−6
1	1	5	6	0

Rewrite $p(x)$ with $(x - 1)$ as a factor.

$p(x) = (x - 1)(x^2 + 5x + 6)$

Factor the quadratic to find the zeros -2 and -3.

The rational zeros of $p(x)$ are -3, -2, and 1.

> Because the entry in the last column is 0, 1 is a zero.

Rational Root Theorem

You can use the Rational Root Theorem to find the rational roots of the polynomial equation $0 = x^3 + 4x^2 + x - 132$.

> The Rational Root Theorem says that all rational roots of a polynomial equation can be written by dividing factors of the constant term by the leading coefficient.

Possible roots:

$\pm 1, \pm 2, \pm 3, \pm 4, \pm 6, \pm 11, \pm 12, \pm 22, \pm 33, \pm 44,$ $\pm 66, \pm 132$

Use a synthetic division table to test possible roots. The only rational root is 4.

> The other roots of this equation are complex.

The Fundamental Theorem of Algebra

Find all the zeros of the function $f(x) = x^3 - x^2 + 2x - 2$.

Use the Fundamental Theorem of Algebra to identify the number of zeros.

$f(x) = x^3 - x^2 + 2x - 2$

You can use a synthetic division table to test possible zeros: $\pm 1, \pm 2$.

The only rational zero is 1.

The other 2 zeros are $\sqrt{2}$ and $-\sqrt{2}$.

> Since the polynomial is degree 3, the polynomial function has 3 zeros.

> The Irrational Root Theorem tells you that if $\sqrt{2}$ is a zero, then $-\sqrt{2}$ is also a zero.

Write a Polynomial Function

Write the polynomial function with integer coefficients, a leading coefficient of 1, and with the least degree for the given zeros 3 and $2 + i$.

This polynomial function has three zeros: 3, $2 + i$, and $2 - i$.

> The Complex Conjugate Root Theorem tells you that if $2 + i$ is a zero, then $2 - i$ is also a zero.

$$p(x) = (x - 3)\big(x - (2 + i)\big)\big(x - (2 - i)\big)$$
$$= (x - 3)(x^2 - 4x + 5)$$
$$= x^3 - 7x^2 + 17x - 15$$

> A polynomial with 3 zeros has a least degree of 3.

Vocabulary

Choose the correct term from the box to complete each sentence.

1. The ___?___ of a zero describes how many times a zero of a function is a factor.

2. A ___?___ is a solution of the polynomial equation $f(x) = 0$.

3. Methods that systematically decrease the interval containing the actual zero until reaching a desired level of accuracy are called ___?___ .

4. A ___?___ of a function $f(x)$ is any value of x for which $f(x) = 0$.

Concepts and Skills

Use the Rational Zero Theorem to determine the rational zeros of each polynomial function.

5. $f(x) = x^3 + 2x^2 + 4x + 8$

6. $p(x) = x^3 - 3x^2 - 15x + 45$

7. $h(x) = x^4 - 2x^3 + 33x^2 - 72x - 108$

8. $t(x) = x^4 + x^3 - 9x^2 - 7x + 14$

Determine all roots of the polynomial equation.

9. $0 = 2x^4 - 5x^3 + 10x^2 - 20x + 8$

10. $0 = x^4 - 6x^2 + 5$

11. $53 = x^4 + 3x^2 - 55$

12. $14 = x^4 - 6x^3 + 13x^2 + 6x$

Write a polynomial function that has integer coefficients, a leading coefficient of 1, and the least degree for the given zeros.

13. $\sqrt{3}, 4$

14. $1, -2 + \sqrt{5}$

15. $-i, 8$

16. $2 + 4i, 3$

17. $\sqrt{5}, \sqrt{6}$

18. $\sqrt{3}, 2i$

19. $4i, 1 + i$

20. $4 + i, 4 - i$

21. The faculty at a school wanted to know which fundraiser might be more successful. The math department created polynomial models that represent the total amount earned for the school for two different fundraisers F if they occurred in m number of months where $m \geq 1$.

    Gourmet Pizza $F_P(m) = 0.15m^3 - 0.4m^2 - 0.8m + 868$

    Magazine Drive $F_M(m) = -0.25m^3 + 5m^2 + 15.6m + 564$

    A. Use the given functions to write a function that you can use to find when the fundraisers are predicted to earn about the same amount of money.

    B. (MP) **Use Tools** In how many months are the fundraisers predicted to earn about the same amount of money? State what strategy and tool you will use to answer the question, explain your choice, and then find the answer.

Rational Exponents and Radical Functions

Astronomer

Astronomers gather data about celestial objects using telescopes. They analyze and model this data using principles of physics and mathematics to learn more about our place in the universe.

©John Davis/Stocktrek Images/Getty Images

STEM Task

Apparent magnitude describes the brightness of celestial objects and relates the flux (amount of light received) of a star to a reference value. Each unit of apparent magnitude m corresponds to an increase in brightness by a factor of 2.5.

Object	Relative brightness	m
Moon	?	−13
Jupiter, Mars	1563%	?
Vega	100%	0
Spica	40%	1
Polaris	16%	?
Limit of human eye	?	7
Proxima Centauri	0.0042%	?

Learning Mindset

Perseverance Learns effectively

As you learn, it is important to recognize whether your efforts are proving to be effective or not. There are many things that can affect your learning, including organization, procrastination, and your relationship with your peers. You can improve the effectiveness of your learning by taking action early and checking in with your progress often. Here are some questions you can ask yourself to help you learn more effectively:

- How does procrastination affect my learning? How can I make sure that I get started early on?

- What organizational methods do I use? How do my organizational methods affect my learning?

- How can my relationships with others affect my learning in positive ways? How can they affect my learning in negative ways?

- What is preventing me from making my learning more effective? How can I change that?

©den-belitsky/iStock/Getty Images

Reflect

Q Think about an experience from the past when something wasn't working. Did you change your habits? How has that changed the way you work now?

Q Imagine you are an astronomer. How and why do astronomers build positive relationships with their colleagues and with their communities? How would that help them ensure that their efforts are effective?

6 Rational Exponents and Radical Operations

Module Performance Task: Focus on STEM

Geostationary Orbits of Satellites

The table shows two formulas for calculating a satellite's orbital speed depending on what information you know about the satellite.

Known information about the satellite	Satellite's orbital speed, v
• The mass M (in kilograms) of the astronomical object (such as Earth) being orbited • The radius r (in meters) of the satellite's approximately circular orbit	$v = \sqrt{\frac{GM}{r}}$ where G is the universal gravitational constant, approximately $6.67 \times 10^{-11} \frac{m^2}{kg \cdot s^2}$
• The satellite's period T, the time (in seconds) it takes the satellite to complete one orbit • The radius r (in meters) of the satellite's approximately circular orbit	$v = \frac{2\pi r}{T}$

A. Explain why the second formula makes sense.

B. Set the two expressions for v equal and solve for T. Express your result in both radical form and rational-exponent form.

C. Repeat Part B, but this time solve for r.

D. Earth's mass is approximately 5.98×10^{24} kg, and Earth's radius is approximately 6.38×10^6 m. A satellite in *geostationary orbit* around Earth remains in the same location above Earth if its period matches Earth's period of 23.9 hours. At what height above Earth must the satellite be positioned for its orbit to be geostationary?

Are You Ready?

Complete these problems to review prior concepts and skills you will need for this module.

Properties of Exponents

Simplify each expression.

1. $6^{-3} \cdot 6^5 \cdot 6^{-4}$

2. $\dfrac{5^3 \cdot 5^{-2}}{5^{-4} \cdot 5^6}$

3. $\left(4^{-2}\right)^5 \cdot 4^7$

4. $\dfrac{\left(7^{-3}\right)^4}{\left(7^5\right)^{-3}}$

Simplify Square Roots

Simplify each square root.

5. $\sqrt{20x^2}$

6. $\sqrt{48a^6b^5}$

7. $\sqrt{\dfrac{27x^2}{16y^2}}$

8. $\sqrt{\dfrac{28m^3n}{9m^7n^3}}$

9. $\sqrt{\dfrac{12x^3}{8x^5}}$

10. $\sqrt{\dfrac{108a^6b}{3a^2b^7}}$

Radicals and Rational Exponents

Simplify each expression.

11. $125^{\frac{2}{3}}$

12. $16^{\frac{5}{4}}$

13. $81^{-\frac{3}{4}}$

14. $32^{\frac{3}{5}}$

Connecting Past and Present Learning

Previously, you learned:

- to define integer exponents,
- to apply the properties of integer exponents to simplify expressions with integer exponents, and
- to solve real-world problems involving expressions with integer exponents.

In this module, you will learn:

- to define rational exponents and their connection to radicals,
- to apply the properties of rational exponents to simplify rational expressions and expressions involving radicals, and
- to solve real-world problems involving expressions with rational exponents.

Rational Exponents and *n*th Roots

(I Can) define rational exponents and *n*th roots and use them to solve real-world problems.

Spark Your Learning

Carmen is getting ready to walk to her train stop on a frigid day. She sees that the wind is blowing extremely hard and knows that she should dress for the wind chill temperature (the "feels like" temperature) instead of for the actual thermometer temperature.

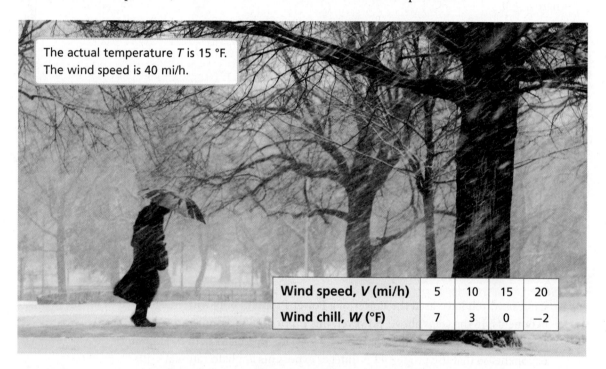

The actual temperature *T* is 15 °F.
The wind speed is 40 mi/h.

Wind speed, *V* (mi/h)	5	10	15	20
Wind chill, *W* (°F)	7	3	0	−2

Complete Part A as a whole class. Then complete Parts B–D in small groups.

A. What is a mathematical question you can ask about this situation? What information would you need to know to answer your question?

B. What variables are involved in this situation? What unit of measurement would you use for each variable?

C. To answer your question, what strategy and tool would you use along with all the information you have? What answer do you get?

D. Does your answer make sense in the context of the situation? How do you know?

Turn and Talk Notice that the wind chill formula is valid only for wind speeds *V* greater than 3 mi/h. Substitute *V* = 0 into the formula. Why does the resulting equation not make sense?

©Gillian Henry/Moment/Getty Images

Build Understanding

Define Rational Exponents in Terms of Roots

You know that 4 is a square root of 16 because $4^2 = 16$, and you can write this fact as $4 = \sqrt{16}$. Similarly, 2 is a cube root of 8 because $2^3 = 8$, and you can write $2 = \sqrt[3]{8}$. In general, for an integer n greater than 1, if $b^n = a$, then b is an **nth root** of a and is written as $b = \sqrt[n]{a}$. The expression is a **radical**, and n is the **index** of the radical. In the next task, you will see that an nth root of a can be written as a power of a.

 The steps below show how to find the value of k for which $\sqrt{a} = a^k$, where $a \geq 0$.

$\sqrt{a} = a^k$	Given
$\left(\sqrt{a}\right)^2 = \left(a^k\right)^2$	Square both sides.
$a = \left(a^k\right)^2$	Definition of square root
$a = a^{2k}$	Power of a Power Property
$a^1 = a^{2k}$	Definition of first power
$1 = 2k$	The bases are the same, so equate the exponents.
$\dfrac{1}{2} = k$	Solve for k.

So, $\sqrt{a} = a^{\frac{1}{2}}$.

A. What is the value of $81^{\frac{1}{2}}$? Explain.

B. Until now, you have used the Power of a Power Property only with integer exponents. In the steps above, however, this property was assumed to apply to an expression with a *rational* exponent, $\frac{1}{2}$. Mathematicians define rational exponents so that the properties of integer exponents apply to rational exponents as well. Using the Power of a Power Property, determine the value of k for which $\sqrt[3]{a} = a^k$.

C. In general, for what value of k is $\sqrt[n]{a} = a^k$, assuming that the nth root of a is a real number? Give a mathematical justification for your answer.

D. What are the values of $(-27)^{\frac{1}{3}}$ and $16^{\frac{1}{4}}$? Explain.

 Turn and Talk Let n be an integer greater than 1.

- For a positive number a, under what condition on n will there be only one real nth root? two real nth roots? Explain.
- For a negative number a, under what condition on n will there be no real nth root? one real nth root? Explain.

Step It Out

Translate Between Rational Exponents and Radical Expressions

In Task 1, you saw that a rational exponent $\frac{m}{n}$ with $m = 1$ represents an nth root, or that $a^{\frac{1}{n}} = \sqrt[n]{a}$ for positive values of a. This is also true for negative values of a when n is odd. To rewrite the expression $a^{\frac{m}{n}}$, where $m \neq 1$, you can think of the numerator m as the power and the denominator n as the root.

Rational Exponents		
For any natural number n, integer m, and real number a when the nth root of a is real:		
Words	**Numbers**	**Algebra**
The exponent $\frac{m}{n}$ indicates the mth power of the nth root of a quantity.	$16^{\frac{3}{4}} = \left(\sqrt[4]{16}\right)^3 = 2^3 = 8$	$a^{\frac{m}{n}} = \left(\sqrt[n]{a}\right)^m$
The exponent $\frac{m}{n}$ indicates the nth root of the mth power of a quantity.	$(-8)^{\frac{2}{3}} = \sqrt[3]{(-8)^2} = \sqrt[3]{64} = 4$	$a^{\frac{m}{n}} = \sqrt[n]{a^m}$

2 Kyla and Jean used different methods to simplify $(-27)^{\frac{4}{3}}$.

Kyla's method:

$$(-27)^{\frac{4}{3}} = \left(\sqrt[3]{-27}\right)^4$$
$$= (-3)^4$$
$$= 81$$

Jean's method:

$$(-27)^{\frac{4}{3}} = \sqrt[3]{-27^4}$$
$$= \sqrt[3]{531,441}$$
$$= 81$$

A. Are both Kyla's and Jean's methods valid? Explain.

B. Which method do you prefer? Why?

3 You can rewrite algebraic expressions with radicals as algebraic expressions with rational exponents, and vice versa. Some examples are shown.

Example 1:

$$\sqrt[4]{r^3} = r^{\frac{3}{4}}$$

Example 2:

$$(2xy)^{\frac{5}{3}} = \left(\sqrt[3]{2xy}\right)^5 \text{ or } \sqrt[3]{(2xy)^5}$$

A. In Example 1, can r be any real number? Explain.

B. In Example 2, can x and y each be any real number? Explain.

 Turn and Talk Colin says that the expressions $x^{\frac{4}{5}}$ and $\sqrt[4]{x^5}$ are equivalent. Is he correct? Explain.

Model with Rational Exponents

A *power function* has the form $y = ax^b$ where a is a real number and b is a rational number. Power functions are useful for modeling many mathematical and real-world quantities. The following are all examples of power functions.

$A = \pi r^2$ Formula for the area of a circle

$V = \dfrac{4}{3}\pi r^3$ Formula for the volume of a sphere

$T = 1.11 \cdot L^{\frac{1}{2}}$ Formula for the period T (in seconds) of a pendulum of length L feet

4   The *basal metabolic rate* for a mammal is the rate at which the mammal uses energy while at rest to maintain vital functions such as breathing. The function $R(m) = 73.3\sqrt[4]{m^3}$, known as Kleiber's Law, relates a mammal's basal metabolic rate R (in Calories per day) to its mass m (in kilograms). Rewrite this function with a rational exponent. Use the rewritten function to compare the basal metabolic rates of the cat and dog shown.

> The mass of the small dog is 3.5 kg. The mass of the large dog is 37 kg.

Rewrite the function with a rational exponent.

$R(m) = 73.3\sqrt[4]{m^3}$

$R(m) = 73.3m^{\frac{3}{4}}$

> **A.** Why is the exponent $\frac{3}{4}$ instead of $\frac{4}{3}$?

Compare the basal metabolic rates of the cat and dog.

One way to make a comparison is to find the ratio of the basal metabolic rates.

$$\frac{\text{dog's basal metabolic rate}}{\text{cat's basal metabolic rate}} = \frac{R(37)}{R(3.5)}$$

$$= \frac{73.3(37)^{\frac{3}{4}}}{73.3(3.5)^{\frac{3}{4}}}$$

$$= \frac{37^{\frac{3}{4}}}{3.5^{\frac{3}{4}}}$$

$$\approx \frac{15.0021}{2.5589}$$

$$\approx 5.9$$

> **B.** How can you find the values of the powers in the numerator and denominator?

The dog's basal metabolic rate is about 5.9 times the cat's basal metabolic rate.

 Turn and Talk About how many more Calories per day are used by the dog than by the cat to maintain vital functions? Explain how you found your answer.

©cynoclub/iStock/Getty Images

Check Understanding

1. Prove that $\sqrt[5]{a} = a^n$ can be rewritten as $\sqrt[5]{a} = a^{\frac{1}{5}}$.

2. Show two different ways to evaluate $216^{\frac{2}{3}}$.

Write each expression as a radical expression. If the expression is equivalent to an integer, write that integer.

3. $49^{\frac{7}{4}}$

4. $100^{\frac{3}{2}}$

Write each expression as an expression with a rational exponent. If the expression is equivalent to an integer, write that integer.

5. $\left(\sqrt[5]{243}\right)^3$

6. $\left(\sqrt[3]{-216}\right)^2$

7. The total wages W in a metropolitan area compared to its total population p can be approximated by the function $W = a \cdot p^{\frac{9}{8}}$, where a is a constant. What are the total wages for a metropolitan area with a population of 3,000,000 people in terms of a? Compare this to the total wages for a metropolitan area with a population of 750,000 people.

On Your Own

8. **(MP) Construct Arguments** Prove that $\sqrt[5]{b^8} = b^m$ can be rewritten as $\sqrt[5]{b^8} = b^{\frac{8}{5}}$. Can you use the same reasoning used in the proof shown in Task 1? Explain.

Solve for n in each expression.

9. $\sqrt[6]{a} = a^n$

10. $\sqrt[9]{a} = a^n$

11. $\sqrt[3]{a^7} = a^n$

12. $\sqrt[3]{a^2} = a^n$

13. $\sqrt[7]{a^6} = a^n$

14. $\sqrt[4]{a^5} = a^n$

15. $\sqrt[5]{a^6} = a^n$

16. $\sqrt[4]{a^9} = a^n$

17. $\sqrt{a^3} = a^n$

18. **(MP) Use Structure** Which of the expressions, $32^{\frac{1}{5}}$ or $243^{\frac{1}{5}}$, has a greater value? Do you need to calculate the values of the expressions in order to determine the answer? Explain.

19. **(MP) Use Tools** Use a calculator to evaluate $196^{\frac{1}{2}}$. Then write an equivalent expression that has a different base and a different rational exponent.

List the number of nth roots of each expression when n is odd and when n is even. The value of a is positive in each expression.

20. $4a$

21. $-8a$

22. $(-8)(-a)$

23. a^2

24. $-a^2$

25. $a + 1$

26. $a + a$

27. a^0

28. a^3

29. $(-a)^3$

30. $(a + 2)^2$

31. $(-a - 4)^3$

32. (MP) **Use Structure** Consider the quantity $a^{\frac{m}{n}}$ for any natural number n, integer m, and real number a. When the nth root of a is real, does it matter whether you take the nth root of a first or raise a to the power of m first? Explain.

Show two ways to evaluate each expression.

33. $4^{\frac{4}{2}}$ **34.** $9^{\frac{5}{2}}$ **35.** $8^{\frac{6}{3}}$

36. $27^{\frac{4}{3}}$ **37.** $64^{\frac{3}{2}}$ **38.** $16^{\frac{8}{4}}$

39. (MP) **Critique Reasoning** A student says that the value of the expression $64^{\frac{2}{6}}$ is 262,144 because the square root of 64 is 8 and $8^6 = 262{,}144$. What error did the student make when evaluating the expression? What is the correct answer?

Describe the root and the power for each expression.

40. $k^{\frac{5}{7}}$ **41.** $k^{\frac{7}{5}}$ **42.** $(-5b)^{\frac{9}{4}}$ **43.** $(-5b)^{\frac{4}{9}}$

44. $x^{\frac{2}{3}}$ **45.** $x^{\frac{1}{6}}$ **46.** $(7y)^{\frac{6}{5}}$ **47.** $(7y)^{\frac{7}{2}}$

48. $513^{\frac{2}{9}}$ **49.** $513^{\frac{4}{5}}$ **50.** $(1+m)^{\frac{8}{3}}$ **51.** $(1+m)^{\frac{4}{11}}$

Write each expression as a radical expression. Simplify the numerical expressions that are equivalent to integers. Assume all variables are positive.

52. $5^{\frac{3}{2}}$ **53.** $3^{\frac{7}{4}}$ **54.** $(-64)^{\frac{2}{3}}$

55. $81^{\frac{3}{4}}$ **56.** $t^{\frac{7}{6}}$ **57.** $(xy)^{\frac{9}{5}}$

58. $(16x)^{\frac{3}{4}}$ **59.** $(-25a)^{\frac{4}{9}}$ **60.** $\left(\dfrac{xy}{27}\right)^{\frac{5}{3}}$

61. The photo shows a C major chord on a guitar. The top finger is holding the G string to the third metal bar, or *fret*. This shortens the string's vibrating length and raises the pitch of the note it sounds. Each fret corresponds to a difference of one note in a scale. To find the distance a fret should be placed from a guitar's *bridge*, where the string begins on the guitar's body, multiply the full length of the vibrating portion of the string by $2^{-\frac{n}{12}}$ where n is the number of notes higher than the full string's note that you want to play.

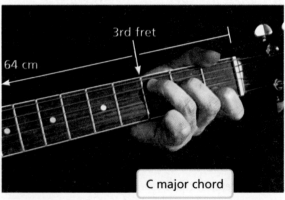

3rd fret

64 cm

C major chord

©StockImages/Alamy

A. How far should the third fret be placed from the bridge?

B. Is the distance between each fret constant? Justify your answer.

62. (MP) **Reason** Is it possible to determine when an expression written in rational exponent form is equivalent to an integer before evaluating? Explain.

63. (MP) **Reason** Is it possible to determine when an expression written in rational exponent form can be simplified before evaluating? Explain.

64. (MP) **Use Structure** Use the relationship between rational exponents and radical expressions to answer the following questions.

A. Are the expressions $(-27)^{\frac{2}{3}}$ and $-27^{\frac{2}{3}}$ equivalent? Explain.

B. Are the expressions $8x^{\frac{4}{3}}$ and $(8x)^{\frac{4}{3}}$ equivalent? Explain.

C. How do parentheses affect the evaluation of expressions with rational exponents?

65. (MP) **Use Structure** Are the expressions $6^{\frac{6}{3}}$ and $6^{\frac{8}{4}}$ equivalent? Explain. If the bases were -6 instead of 6, would your reasoning still hold true?

Write each radical expression as an expression with a rational exponent. Simplify the numerical expressions that are equivalent to integers. Assume all variables are positive.

66. $\left(\sqrt[3]{8}\right)^5$

67. $\sqrt[4]{49^3}$

68. $\left(\sqrt[4]{256}\right)^2$

69. $\sqrt[5]{9^2}$

70. $\sqrt[7]{r^8}$

71. $\left(\sqrt[4]{\dfrac{a}{b}}\right)^6$

72. $\left(\sqrt[9]{-27x}\right)^3$

73. $\left(\sqrt{\dfrac{xy}{4}}\right)^3$

74. $\left(\sqrt[6]{uv}\right)^7$

75. **STEM** The power functions $M_A(d) = 0.036\sqrt[5]{d^{13}}$ and $M_B(d) = 0.059\sqrt[10]{d^{23}}$ model two different data sets of trees. Each function can be used to estimate the biomass M (in kilograms) of a tree above ground, where d is the diameter (in centimeters) of the tree 4.5 feet above the ground. Biomass is the mass of all living things including the tree and anything living in the tree. Rewrite the functions using rational exponents. Then, determine how many times greater the biomass of a tree with a diameter of 20 centimeters from the data set of M_A is than a tree with the same diameter from the data set M_B.

The General Sherman Tree
Biomass: 1 million kg

76. **STEM** The power function $H(m) = 240m^{-\frac{1}{4}}$ models an animal's approximate resting heart rate H (in beats per minute) given its mass m (in kilograms). Consider a gorilla with a mass of 200 kilograms and a chimpanzee with a mass of 50 kilograms. Which animal has a faster heart rate when resting? How many times faster?

Gorilla
Mass: 200 kg

Chimpanzee
Mass: 50 kg

77. You can determine the ratio of the brightness of two stars by using the formula $\dfrac{B_2}{B_1} = \dfrac{2.512^{m_1}}{2.512^{m_2}}$ where B_1 and m_1 are the brightness and apparent magnitude of the dimmer star, and B_2 and m_2 are the brightness and apparent magnitude of the brighter star. (Note that the brighter a star, the lower its apparent magnitude.) Rigel and Betelgeuse are two stars in the constellation Orion. Which star is brighter? How many times as bright?

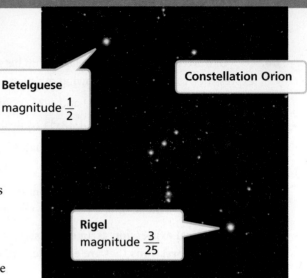

Betelguese magnitude $\dfrac{1}{2}$

Constellation Orion

Rigel magnitude $\dfrac{3}{25}$

78. (Open Middle™) Using the digits 1 to 9, at most one time each, fill in the boxes to create two true statements.

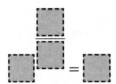

Spiral Review • Assessment Readiness

79. Which expression is a factor of the polynomial?

$$p(x) = x^3 - 4x^2 - 27x + 90$$

Ⓐ $x - 6$
Ⓑ $x + 1$
Ⓒ $x - 5$
Ⓓ $x + 2$

80. The functions each model the number of students S that played an online video game d days after each video game was released.

$$S_1(d) = 0.45d^3 - 3d^2 + 4.75d + 16$$
$$S_2(d) = 0.09d^3 - 1.31d^2 + 7.25d + 18$$

Use a graphing calculator to determine the number of days after the games' release that they were played by the same number of students.

Ⓐ 2
Ⓑ 6
Ⓒ 10
Ⓓ 18

81. Which polynomial function has the zeros $1 - 2i$ and 3?

Ⓐ $p(x) = x^3 - x^2 + x - 15$
Ⓑ $p(x) = x^3 + x^2 - x + 15$
Ⓒ $p(x) = x^3 - 5x^2 + 11x - 15$
Ⓓ $p(x) = x^3 + 5x^2 - 11x + 15$

82. Which expressions are equivalent to 6^4? Select all that apply.

Ⓐ $\left(6^2\right)^2$
Ⓑ $\dfrac{6^8}{6^2}$
Ⓒ $6^2 + 6^2$
Ⓓ $6^3 \cdot 6$
Ⓔ $\dfrac{6^7}{6^3}$
Ⓕ $6^6 - 6^2$

I'm in a Learning Mindset!

Did procrastination or lack of organization affect my learning outcomes? In what way?

6.2

Properties of Rational Exponents and Radicals

(I Can) simplify and rewrite expressions containing rational exponents and *n*th roots.

Spark Your Learning

A manufacturing company makes four different sized cylindrical cans. The volume doubles for each increase in size. The four sizes have volumes of 1896 cubic centimeters, 948 cubic centimeters, 474 cubic centimeters, and 237 cubic centimeters.

Although the cans being manufactured are different sizes, they are the same shape. The height of each can is twice its radius.

Complete Part A as a whole class. Then complete Parts B–D in small groups.

A. What is a mathematical question you can ask about this situation? What information would you need to know to answer your?

B. What variable(s) are involved in this situation? What unit of measurement would you use for each variable?

C. To answer your question, what strategy and tool would you use along with all the information you have? What answer do you get?

D. Does your answer make sense in the context of the situation? How do you know?

> **Turn and Talk** Predict the relationship of the surface areas between two different-sized cans with the same shape as the cans above given the following relationship between their volumes.
> - The volume of a can is 8 times the volume of another can.
> - The volume of a can is 32 times the volume of another can.
> - The volume of a can is 64 times the volume of another can.

©Andia/Alamy

Build Understanding

Investigate the Properties of Rational Exponents

You previously used properties to simplify and evaluate expressions with integer exponents. Some examples are shown below.

$$3^2 \cdot 3^3 = 3^{2+3} = 3^5 = 243 \qquad \frac{3^2}{3^3} = 3^{2-3} = 3^{-1} = \frac{1}{3} \qquad \left(3^2\right)^3 = 3^{2 \cdot 3} = 3^6 = 729$$

$$(3 \cdot 4)^2 = 3^2 \cdot 4^2 = 9 \cdot 16 = 144 \qquad \left(\frac{3}{4}\right)^2 = \frac{3^2}{4^2} = \frac{9}{16}$$

1 ▶ The table below shows the rules that apply to integer exponents.

A. Copy and complete the table by evaluating the given expression and the expression that has been rewritten using the rule.

Rule for integer exponents	Expression	Apply Rule	Simplify	Result
$a^m \cdot a^n = a^{m+n}$	$81^{\frac{1}{2}} \cdot 81^{\frac{3}{4}}$	?	$81^{\frac{5}{4}}$	?
$\dfrac{a^m}{a^n} = a^{m-n}$	$\dfrac{81^{\frac{9}{4}}}{81^{\frac{3}{2}}}$	?	$81^{\frac{3}{4}}$	?
$\left(a^m\right)^n = a^{mn}$	$\left(81^{\frac{3}{2}}\right)^{\frac{1}{2}}$	?	$81^{\frac{3}{4}}$	?
$(a \cdot b)^n = a^n \cdot b^n$	$(81 \cdot 16)^{\frac{3}{4}}$	?	$27 \cdot 8$	?
$\left(\dfrac{a}{b}\right)^n = \dfrac{a^n}{b^n}$	$\left(\dfrac{81}{16}\right)^{\frac{3}{4}}$	?	$\dfrac{27}{8}$	?

B. Show that $81^{\frac{1}{2}} \cdot 81^{\frac{3}{4}}$ and $81^{\frac{5}{4}}$ have the same value when simplified.

C. Based on your results for Part B, predict the rule for the Product of Powers Property for rational exponents. Does your work in Part B prove the Product of Powers Property for rational exponents? If not, what must be done to prove the property?

D. Based on your evaluations of $\left(81^{\frac{3}{2}}\right)^{\frac{1}{2}}$ and $81^{\frac{3}{4}}$, predict the rule for the Power of a Power Property for rational exponents.

 Turn and Talk How can repeated multiplication help you remember the properties of exponents?

Step It Out

Simplify Expressions Involving Rational Exponents

Rational exponents have the same properties as integer exponents. The table summarizes each property. The properties hold for all nonzero real numbers a and b and all rational numbers m and n.

Properties of Rational Exponents		
Property	**Example**	**Algebra**
Product of Powers Property	$5^{\frac{3}{4}} \cdot 5^{\frac{5}{4}} = 5^{\frac{3}{4}+\frac{5}{4}} = 5^2 = 25$	$a^m \cdot a^n = a^{m+n}$
Quotient of Powers Property	$\dfrac{25^{\frac{7}{2}}}{25^{\frac{6}{2}}} = 25^{\frac{7}{2}-\frac{6}{2}} = 25^{\frac{1}{2}} = 5$	$\dfrac{a^m}{a^n} = a^{m-n}$
Power of a Power Property	$\left(4^{\frac{3}{2}}\right)^{\frac{4}{3}} = 4^{\frac{3}{2} \cdot \frac{4}{3}} = 4^{\frac{12}{6}} = 4^2 = 16$	$(a^m)^n = a^{m \cdot n}$
Power of a Product Property	$(4 \cdot 25)^{\frac{1}{2}} = 4^{\frac{1}{2}} \cdot 25^{\frac{1}{2}} = 2 \cdot 5 = 10$	$(ab)^m = a^m b^m$
Power of a Quotient Property	$\left(\dfrac{9}{4}\right)^{\frac{1}{2}} = \dfrac{9^{\frac{1}{2}}}{4^{\frac{1}{2}}} = \dfrac{3}{2} = 1.5$	$\left(\dfrac{a}{b}\right)^m = \dfrac{a^m}{b^m}$

2 Simplify the expression $\dfrac{25^{\frac{5}{2}}}{25^{\frac{6}{2}}}$.

$\dfrac{25^{\frac{5}{2}}}{25^{\frac{6}{2}}} = 25^{\frac{5}{2}-\frac{6}{2}}$

> **A.** What property justifies rewriting $\dfrac{25^{\frac{5}{2}}}{25^{\frac{6}{2}}}$ as $25^{\frac{5}{2}-\frac{6}{2}}$?

$= 25^{\frac{(5-6)}{2}}$ Simplify.

$= 25^{-\frac{1}{2}}$ Simplify.

$= \dfrac{1}{25^{\frac{1}{2}}}$

> **B.** What justifies rewriting $25^{-\frac{1}{2}}$ as $\dfrac{1}{25^{\frac{1}{2}}}$?

$= \dfrac{1}{5}$ Simplify.

Turn and Talk

- What are the steps for simplifying the expression $\dfrac{y^{\frac{7}{5}}}{y^{\frac{2}{5}}}$?

- What are the steps for simplifying the expression $x^{\frac{1}{2}} \cdot x^{\frac{3}{4}}$?

You can apply multiple properties of rational exponents when simplifying an expression.

3 Simplify the expression $\left(\dfrac{y^{\frac{3}{4}}}{8y^{-\frac{1}{2}}}\right)^{\frac{2}{3}}$.

$$\left(\dfrac{y^{\frac{3}{4}}}{8y^{-\frac{1}{2}}}\right)^{\frac{2}{3}} = \left(\dfrac{y^{\frac{3}{4}}y^{\frac{1}{2}}}{8}\right)^{\frac{2}{3}} \qquad \text{Definition of a negative power}$$

$$= \left(\dfrac{y^{\frac{3}{4}+\frac{1}{2}}}{8}\right)^{\frac{2}{3}}$$

> **A.** What property justifies rewriting $\left(\dfrac{y^{\frac{3}{4}}y^{\frac{1}{2}}}{8}\right)^{\frac{2}{3}}$ as $\left(\dfrac{y^{\frac{3}{4}+\frac{1}{2}}}{8}\right)^{\frac{2}{3}}$?

$$= \left(\dfrac{y^{\frac{5}{4}}}{8}\right)^{\frac{2}{3}} \qquad \text{Simplify.}$$

$$= \dfrac{\left(y^{\frac{5}{4}}\right)^{\frac{2}{3}}}{8^{\frac{2}{3}}}$$

> **B.** What property justifies rewriting $\left(\dfrac{y^{\frac{5}{4}}}{8}\right)^{\frac{2}{3}}$ as $\dfrac{\left(y^{\frac{5}{4}}\right)^{\frac{2}{3}}}{8^{\frac{2}{3}}}$?

$$= \dfrac{y^{\frac{5}{4}\cdot\frac{2}{3}}}{8^{\frac{2}{3}}}$$

> **C.** What property justifies rewriting $\dfrac{\left(y^{\frac{5}{4}}\right)^{\frac{2}{3}}}{8^{\frac{2}{3}}}$ as $\dfrac{y^{\frac{5}{4}\cdot\frac{2}{3}}}{8^{\frac{2}{3}}}$?

$$= \dfrac{1}{4}y^{\frac{5}{6}} \qquad \text{Simplify.}$$

 Turn and Talk What are the steps for simplifying the expression $\left(36x^{\frac{4}{5}}\right)^{\frac{3}{2}}$?

Simplify Radical Expressions Involving *n*th Roots

The same properties that apply to square roots also apply to *n*th roots. The table summarizes these properties. The properties hold for all positive real numbers *a* and *b* and all positive integer values of *n*.

Properties of *n*th Roots		
Property	**Example**	**Algebra**
Product Property of Roots Property	$\sqrt[4]{48} = \sqrt[4]{16} \cdot \sqrt[4]{3} = 2\sqrt[4]{3}$	$\sqrt[n]{ab} = \sqrt[n]{a} \cdot \sqrt[n]{b}$
Quotient Property of Roots Property	$\sqrt[3]{\dfrac{125}{8}} = \dfrac{\sqrt[3]{125}}{\sqrt[3]{8}} = \dfrac{5}{2}$	$\sqrt[n]{\dfrac{a}{b}} = \dfrac{\sqrt[n]{a}}{\sqrt[n]{b}}$

4 ▸ Simplify the expression $\sqrt[3]{\frac{64}{y^2}}$.

$$\sqrt[3]{\frac{64}{y^2}} = \frac{\sqrt[3]{64}}{\sqrt[3]{y^2}}$$

> **A.** What property justifies rewriting $\sqrt[3]{\frac{64}{y^2}}$ as $\frac{\sqrt[3]{64}}{\sqrt[3]{y^2}}$?

$$= \frac{4}{\sqrt[3]{y^2}} \qquad \text{Simplify.}$$

$$= \frac{4}{\sqrt[3]{y^2}} \cdot \frac{\sqrt[3]{y}}{\sqrt[3]{y}} \qquad \text{Rationalize the denominator.}$$

$$= \frac{4\sqrt[3]{y}}{\sqrt[3]{y^3}}$$

> **B.** What property justifies rewriting $\frac{4}{\sqrt[3]{y^2}} \cdot \frac{\sqrt[3]{y}}{\sqrt[3]{y}}$ as $\frac{4\sqrt[3]{y}}{\sqrt[3]{y^3}}$?

$$= \frac{4\sqrt[3]{y}}{y} \qquad \text{Simplify.}$$

Real-World Models Having Rational Exponents

5 ▸ **Biology** The function $E(m) = (3.7 \times 10^8)m^{\frac{1}{5}}$ roughly models the life expectancy E (in seconds) of an animal in captivity that has a mass of m kilograms.

The function $R(m) = 3.8m^{-\frac{1}{4}}$ approximates the heart rate R (in beats per second) of an animal with a mass m (in kilograms). Approximately how many times will a greater kudu's heart beat over its expected lifetime in captivity?

> The mass of the greater kudu is 200 kilograms.

Since the units for $E(m)$ are seconds and the units for $R(m)$ are heartbeats per second, multiply the functions to determine the total number of heartbeats. For the greater kudu, replace m with 200.

$$(3.7 \times 10^8)(200^{\frac{1}{5}}) \times (3.8)(200^{-\frac{1}{4}})$$

$$= (3.7 \times 3.8 \times 10^8)(200^{\frac{1}{5}} \times 200^{-\frac{1}{4}})$$

> **A.** What property justifies rearranging the factors in the product here?

$$= (14.06 \times 10^8)(200^{-\frac{1}{20}})$$

> **B.** What property justifies rewriting $200^{\frac{1}{5}} \times 200^{-\frac{1}{4}}$ as $200^{-\frac{1}{20}}$?

$$= (1.406 \times 10^9)(2 \times 10^2)^{-0.05}$$

$$= (1.406 \times 10^9)(2)^{-0.05}(10^2)^{-0.05}$$

> **C.** What property justifies rewriting $(2 \times 10^2)^{-0.05}$ as $(2)^{-0.05}(10^2)^{-0.05}$?

$$= (1.406)(2^{-0.05})(10^9 \times 10^{-0.1})$$

$$= \frac{1.406}{2^{0.05}} \times 10^{8.9}$$

> **D.** What justifies writing $2^{0.05}$ in the denominator?

$$\approx 1.08 \text{ billion}$$

During a greater kudu's lifetime in captivity, its heart will beat about 1.08 billion times.

Check Understanding

1. Show that $6^{\frac{2}{3}} \cdot 6^{\frac{4}{3}} = \left(6^{\frac{1}{3}}\right)^6$.

Simplify each expression. Justify each step.

2. $8^{\frac{2}{3}} \cdot 8^{\frac{4}{3}}$

3. $\left(\dfrac{x^{\frac{3}{2}} y^{\frac{2}{3}}}{y^{\frac{1}{3}}}\right)^{\frac{3}{4}}$

4. $\sqrt[3]{\dfrac{32x^6}{x^4}}$

5. Annie and Sarah both invested money that earned interest compounded annually. Annie's investment (in dollars) can be represented by the expression $1000(1.02)^{\frac{11}{6}}$. Sarah's investment (in dollars) can be represented by the expression $500(1.02)^{\frac{27}{12}}$. How many times greater is Annie's investment than Sarah's? First express the actual comparison and then estimate to the nearest hundredths.

On Your Own

6. How can you rewrite the expression $\dfrac{8^6}{8^4}$ using rational exponents to show the Quotient of Powers Property is true for rational exponents?

Rewrite each expression using one of the properties of rational exponents, and then evaluate. Approximate to the nearest hundredth when appropriate.

7. $\left(49^{\frac{1}{2}}\right)^{\frac{3}{5}}$

8. $\dfrac{4^{\frac{3}{4}}}{4^{\frac{1}{4}}}$

9. $\left(\dfrac{27}{125}\right)^{\frac{4}{3}}$

10. $16^{\frac{7}{4}} \cdot 16^{-\frac{1}{2}}$

11. $(36 \cdot 64)^{\frac{3}{2}}$

12. $\left(\dfrac{9}{25}\right)^{\frac{5}{2}}$

13. $\dfrac{81^{\frac{5}{6}}}{81^{\frac{1}{3}}}$

14. $\left(\dfrac{64}{125}\right)^{\frac{4}{3}}$

15. $64^{\frac{3}{4}} \cdot 64^{-\frac{3}{2}}$

16. $\left(8^{\frac{1}{2}}\right)^{\frac{2}{3}}$

17. $\dfrac{3^{\frac{9}{2}}}{3^{\frac{3}{2}}}$

18. $\left(\dfrac{16}{81}\right)^{\frac{3}{2}}$

19. $25^{\frac{3}{2}} \cdot 25^{\frac{1}{4}}$

20. $\left(12^{\frac{4}{3}}\right)^{\frac{5}{2}}$

21. $(5 \cdot 20)^{\frac{3}{2}}$

22. $8^{\frac{5}{6}} \cdot 8^{\frac{2}{5}}$

23. $(16 \cdot 40)^{\frac{3}{8}}$

24. $\left(3^4\right)^{\frac{1}{3}}$

25. $\dfrac{32^{\frac{19}{20}}}{32^{\frac{3}{4}}}$

26. $(49 \cdot 9)^{-\frac{1}{2}}$

27. $\left(\dfrac{625}{16}\right)^{\frac{3}{4}}$

Simplify. Justify each step.

28. $y^{\frac{2}{5}}\left(x^{\frac{1}{2}}y\right)^{\frac{4}{5}}$

29. $\dfrac{4a^{\frac{1}{2}}}{4^{\frac{3}{2}}a^{\frac{3}{4}}}$

30. $\dfrac{81^{\frac{3}{4}} 27^{\frac{1}{3}} x^{\frac{6}{5}}}{x^{\frac{1}{5}}}$

31. $\left(x^{\frac{7}{4}} x^{-\frac{3}{4}} y^{\frac{1}{2}}\right)^{\frac{5}{2}}$

32. $\left(49m^{-\frac{4}{3}}\right)^{\frac{3}{2}}$

33. $\left(\dfrac{16^{\frac{1}{4}}}{16^{\frac{3}{4}}}\right)^{\frac{5}{2}}$

For Problems 34–45, simplify each expression.

34. $\left(64a^{\frac{4}{5}}\right)^{\frac{5}{6}}$

35. $\dfrac{(16y)^{\frac{7}{8}}}{16^{\frac{3}{8}}y^{\frac{1}{2}}}$

36. $\left(216 \cdot 8t^{\frac{7}{2}}\right)^{\frac{2}{3}}$

37. $\left(\dfrac{a^{\frac{1}{2}}b^{\frac{11}{3}}}{b^{\frac{5}{3}}c^{\frac{2}{3}}}\right)^{\frac{7}{4}}$

38. $\dfrac{64^{\frac{8}{3}} \cdot 64^{\frac{1}{6}}}{64^2}$

39. $\left[\dfrac{(81r)^{\frac{3}{4}}}{(9r)^{\frac{1}{2}}}\right]^{\frac{3}{2}}$

40. $\dfrac{81^{\frac{7}{4}}(uv)^{\frac{1}{2}}}{81u^{\frac{2}{3}}v^{\frac{3}{5}}}$

41. $\left(36x^{\frac{4}{3}}\right)^{\frac{1}{2}}\left(125x^{\frac{1}{2}}\right)^{\frac{2}{3}}$

42. $\left(m^{\frac{2}{5}}n^{\frac{1}{4}}\right)^2\left(m^2n^{\frac{3}{4}}\right)^{\frac{3}{2}}$

43. $\dfrac{16^{\frac{3}{4}}(mn)^{\frac{5}{3}}}{16^{\frac{1}{2}}mn^{\frac{2}{3}}}$

44. $\left(\dfrac{125a^{\frac{4}{3}}b^{\frac{5}{6}}}{5a^{\frac{2}{3}}b^{\frac{1}{2}}}\right)^{\frac{3}{2}}$

45. $\left(27x^{\frac{3}{4}}\right)^{\frac{2}{3}}\left(4x^{\frac{4}{5}}\right)^{\frac{5}{2}}$

46. **STEM** The power function $S(m) = 0.16m^{\frac{18}{25}}$ approximates the wing surface area S (in square meters) of a bird that has a mass of m (in kilograms). The wing surface area of an eagle with a mass of 5 kilograms is approximately how many times as great as that of a robin with a mass of 0.075 kilogram?

Eagle: mass of 5 kg

Robin: mass of 0.075 kg

Simplify. Justify each step.

47. $\sqrt[3]{\dfrac{32x^4}{54x}}$

48. $\sqrt[4]{128x^7}$

49. $\sqrt[5]{\dfrac{32a^3b^8}{a^{12}b}}$

For Problems 50–55, simplify each expression.

50. $\sqrt[4]{\dfrac{81u^8}{256}}$

51. $\sqrt[5]{96x^9y^6z^{10}}$

52. $\sqrt[3]{\dfrac{27a^4b^6}{8a^9b}}$

53. $\sqrt[4]{\dfrac{x^2y^{19}}{x^{12}y^2}}$

54. $\sqrt{\dfrac{50m^9}{m^{-6}n^5}}$

55. $\sqrt[5]{48r^{12}s^8t^6}$

56. **STEM** The function $T(a) = a^{\frac{3}{2}}$ models Kepler's Third Law. The period T (in Earth years) is the time it takes a planet to complete one orbit about the sun as a function of the planet's average distance a from the sun, measured in astronomical units (AU). What do you think are some key features of the graph of $T(a)$? Use a graphing calculator to graph $T(a)$ and examine its features. Then find the time it takes for Neptune, with an average distance from the sun of 30.06 AU, to complete its orbit of the sun.

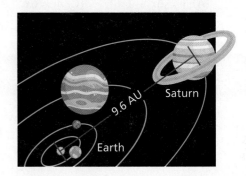

57. The volume of a sphere as a function of its surface area is given by $V(s) = \frac{4}{3}\pi\left(\frac{s}{4\pi}\right)^{\frac{3}{2}}$. How many times greater is the volume of a basketball than that of a golf ball when the approximate surface areas of a basketball and golf ball are 70 square inches and 9 square inches, respectively?

Basketball:
surface area: 70 in²
Golf ball:
surface area: 9 in²

 Construct Arguments For Problems 58–61, use the properties of rational exponents and the properties of *n*th roots to prove that each equality is true.

58. $\left(a^{2n} \cdot a^3\right)^{(n-4)} = a^{2n^2 - 5n - 12}$

59. $\left(\dfrac{a^{2m+3}}{a^{m-4}}\right)^3 = a^{3m+21}$

60. $\sqrt[n+1]{\dfrac{b^{2n+2}}{a^{n+1}}} = \dfrac{b^2}{a}$

61. $\sqrt[3n]{a^{7n} b^{9n}} = a^2 b^3 \sqrt[3n]{a^n}$

62. (Open Middle™) Using the digits 1 to 9, at most one time each, fill in the boxes to make three equivalent expressions.

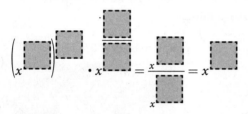

Spiral Review • Assessment Readiness

63. The volume V of a gift box (in cubic inches) is modeled by the function $V(w) = w^3 + 3w^2 - 10w$ where w is the width (in inches). What is the width of a gift box with volume 264 cubic inches?

Ⓐ 6 inches   Ⓒ 8 inches

Ⓑ 7 inches   Ⓓ 9 inches

64. For the functions $f(x)$ and $g(x)$, $f(x) = 3x - 5$ and $g(x) = 2x + 1$ The function $h(x) = 3 \cdot g(x) - 5$. Which equation is equivalent to $h(x)$?

Ⓐ $y = 6x + 1$ Ⓒ $y = 6x - 2$

Ⓑ $y = 6x + 3$ Ⓓ $y = 6x - 8$

65. Match equivalent expressions.

A. $\sqrt{(xy)^3}$ **1.** $(xy)^{\frac{2}{3}}$

B. $\sqrt[4]{xy}$ **2.** $(xy)^{\frac{1}{4}}$

C. $\sqrt[3]{(xy)^4}$ **3.** $(xy)^{\frac{3}{2}}$

D. $\left(\sqrt[3]{xy}\right)^2$ **4.** $(xy)^{\frac{1}{3}}$

E. $\sqrt[3]{xy}$ **5.** $(xy)^{\frac{4}{3}}$

66. Which is a zero of the function $p(x) = x^3 - x^2 + 4x - 4$?

Ⓐ 2   Ⓒ 0

Ⓑ 1   Ⓓ −2

 I'm in a Learning Mindset!

How did an initial failure with simplifying and evaluating expressions with rational exponents or radicals lead to learning growth?

©Nick Schlax/iStockPhoto.com

Rational Exponents and *n*th Roots

For any natural number *n*, integer *m*, and real number *a*, when the *n*th root of *a* is real:

- the exponent $\frac{m}{n}$ indicates the *m*th power of the *n*th root of a quantity.

$$a^{\frac{m}{n}} = \left(\sqrt[n]{a}\right)^m \Rightarrow \left(\frac{a}{b}\right)^{\frac{3}{7}} = \left(\sqrt[7]{\frac{a}{b}}\right)^3 \text{ and } 32^{\frac{4}{5}} = \left(\sqrt[5]{32}\right)^4 = 2^4 = 16$$

- the exponent $\frac{m}{n}$ indicates the *n*th root of the *m*th power of a quantity.

$$a^{\frac{m}{n}} = \sqrt[n]{a^m} \Rightarrow (xy)^{\frac{5}{6}} = \sqrt[6]{(xy)^5} \text{ and } (-8)^{\frac{4}{3}} = \sqrt[3]{(-8)^4} = \sqrt[3]{4096} = 16$$

Properties of Rational Exponents

The following properties are valid for all nonzero real numbers *a* and *b* and rational numbers *m* and *n*.

Product of Powers Property: $\quad a^m \cdot a^n = a^{m+n} \Rightarrow 5^{\frac{3}{4}} \cdot 5^{\frac{5}{4}} = 5^{\frac{3}{4}+\frac{5}{4}} = 5^2 = 25$

Quotient of Powers Property: $\quad \dfrac{a^m}{a^n} = a^{m-n} \Rightarrow \dfrac{25^{\frac{7}{2}}}{25^{\frac{6}{2}}} = 25^{\frac{7}{2}-\frac{6}{2}} = 25^{\frac{1}{2}} = 5$

Power of a Power Property: $\quad \left(a^m\right)^n = a^{m \cdot n} \Rightarrow \left(4^{\frac{3}{2}}\right)^{\frac{4}{3}} = 4^{\frac{3}{2} \cdot \frac{4}{3}} = 4^{\frac{12}{6}} = 4^2 = 16$

Power of a Product Property: $\quad \left(ab\right)^m = a^m b^m \Rightarrow (4 \cdot 25)^{\frac{1}{2}} = 4^{\frac{1}{2}} \cdot 25^{\frac{1}{2}} = 2 \cdot 5 = 10$

Power of a Quotient Property: $\quad \left(\dfrac{a}{b}\right)^m = \dfrac{a^m}{b^m} \Rightarrow \left(\dfrac{9}{4}\right)^{\frac{1}{2}} = \dfrac{9^{\frac{1}{2}}}{4^{\frac{1}{2}}} = \dfrac{3}{2}$

Properties of *n*th Roots

The following properties are valid for all positive values of *a* and *b*.

Product Property of Roots: $\quad \sqrt[n]{ab} = \sqrt[n]{a} \cdot \sqrt[n]{b} \Rightarrow \sqrt[4]{48} = \sqrt[4]{16} \cdot \sqrt[4]{3} = 2\sqrt[4]{3}$

Quotient Property of Roots: $\quad \sqrt[n]{\dfrac{a}{b}} = \dfrac{\sqrt[n]{a}}{\sqrt[n]{b}} \Rightarrow \sqrt[3]{\dfrac{125}{8}} = \dfrac{\sqrt[3]{125}}{\sqrt[3]{8}} = \dfrac{5}{2}$

Vocabulary

Choose the correct term from the box to complete each sentence.

1. For the equation $a = \sqrt[n]{b}$, a is the ___?___ of b.

2. The ___?___ of $\sqrt[m]{x}$ is m.

3. The expression $\sqrt[3]{27}$ is an example of a ___?___.

Concepts and Skills

Evaluate each expression.

4. $27^{\frac{1}{3}}$

5. $16^{\frac{1}{4}}$

6. $49^{\frac{1}{2}}$

7. $32^{\frac{1}{5}}$

8. $216^{\frac{1}{3}}$

9. $81^{\frac{1}{4}}$

Rewrite each expression as a radical expression.

10. $5^{\frac{3}{4}}$

11. $12^{\frac{7}{3}}$

12. $8^{\frac{6}{5}}$

13. $9^{\frac{5}{2}}$

14. $14^{\frac{4}{7}}$

15. $11^{\frac{7}{6}}$

Rewrite each radical expression using a rational exponent.

16. $\left(\sqrt[6]{2}\right)^7$

17. $\sqrt[5]{3^4}$

18. $\sqrt{15^3}$

19. $\sqrt[4]{6^5}$

20. $\sqrt[3]{2^{10}}$

21. $\left(\sqrt{6^5}\right)$

Evaluate each expression.

22. $(9 \cdot 4)^{\frac{3}{2}}$

23. $\left(\frac{27}{8}\right)^{\frac{2}{3}}$

24. $\dfrac{4^{\frac{1}{2}}}{4^{\frac{5}{2}}}$

For Problems 16–21, simplify each expression. Assume all variables are positive.

25. $\left(\frac{64}{125}\right)^{\frac{2}{3}}$

26. $\left(\frac{a^3 b}{ab^4}\right)^{\frac{5}{6}}$

27. $\left(m^{\frac{2}{3}} n^{\frac{1}{2}}\right)^{\frac{4}{3}}$

28. $\sqrt{\dfrac{36a^2 b^5}{49b^2}}$

29. $\sqrt[4]{16x^6 y^8}$

30. $\left(\sqrt[3]{6m}\right)^5 \left(\sqrt[3]{6m}\right)$

31. (MP) **Use Tools** The function $E(m) = \left(3.7 \times 10^8\right) m^{\frac{1}{5}}$ roughly models the life expectancy E (in seconds) of an animal in captivity that has a mass of m kilograms. The function $R(m) = 3.8m^{-\frac{1}{4}}$ roughly models the heart rate R (in beats per second) of an animal with a mass m (in kilograms). Approximately how many times greater is the number of heartbeats over the expected lifetime of a koala bear in captivity with a mass of 9 kilograms than that of a brown bear with a mass of 278 kilograms? State what strategy and tool you will use to answer the question, explain your choice, and then find the answer.

Module Performance Task: Focus on STEM

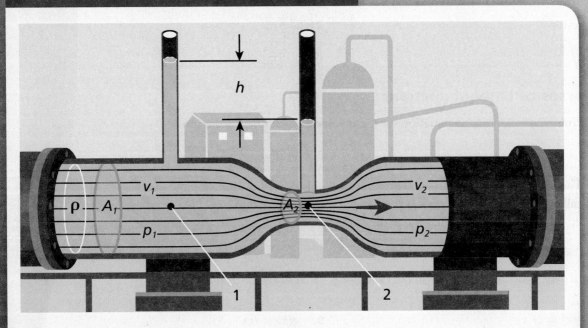

Fluid Flow

A Venturi meter measures the rate at which a fluid flows through a pipe by constricting the flow and observing the change in height h caused by the change in pressure.

Continuity equation	Bernoulli's equation	Pressure difference
$A_1 v_1 = A_2 v_2$ A_1 and A_2 are cross-sectional areas. v_1 and v_2 are velocities of the flow rate.	$p_1 + \dfrac{1}{2}\rho v_1{}^2 = p_2 + \dfrac{1}{2}\rho v_2{}^2$ p_1 and p_2 are pressures. ρ is the fluid density.	$p_1 - p_2 = \rho g h$ g is acceleration due to gravity. h is the observable difference in the heights of liquid in the vertical tubes.

A. What units are appropriate for the continuity equation? Use the units to interpret the meaning of the continuity equation in the context of fluid flow.

B. Letting gravity g, fluid density ρ, and the cross-sectional areas A_1 and A_2 remain constant, solve for v_1 as a function of the measured height h. Plot the function using graphing software, letting h be the independent variable.

C. Explain what happens to the function when $A_1 > A_2$, $A_1 = A_2$, and $A_1 < A_2$. Explain why it makes sense in this context.

D. Let $g = 9.8\ \frac{m}{s^2}$, $A_1 = 0.4\,m^2$, and $A_2 = 0.375m^2$. Determine the fluid velocity v_1 when the height is measured to be 50 cm. What height is needed to ensure the fluid is flowing faster than $10\ \frac{m}{s}$?

Are You Ready?

Complete these problems to review prior concepts and skills you will need for this module.

Square Roots and Cube Roots

Find each root.

1. $\sqrt{196}$

2. $\sqrt[3]{512}$

3. $\sqrt[3]{\dfrac{8}{27}}$

4. $\sqrt{\dfrac{324}{625}}$

Inverses of Linear Functions

For Problems 5–7, write an equation for the inverse of each linear function.

5. $f(x) = 3x - 5$

6. $g(x) = -\dfrac{1}{2}x + 4$

7. The function $C(h) = 35h + 60$ represents the total charge for Maria to make a house call and repair or upgrade computer systems where h is the number of hours it takes to do the job. State any restrictions on the domain and range of the inverse function.

Transformations of Functions

Identify the transformation of f to the function g. Then draw the graph of g.

8. $g(x) = 2f(x)$

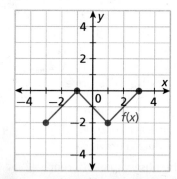

9. $g(x) = f(x - 3)$

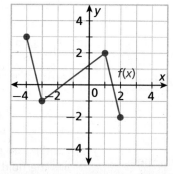

Connecting Past and Present Learning

Previously, you learned:

• to write the inverse of a linear function,

• to transform the graphs of quadratic functions, and

• to solve quadratic equations.

In this module, you will learn:

• to write the inverse of quadratic and cubic functions,

• to transform the graphs of square root and cube root functions, and

• to solve radical equations.

Inverse Functions and Function Composition

(I Can) **find the inverse of a function and use composition of functions to verify inverse functions.**

Spark Your Learning

Fencing will be used to enclose three square areas where horses will graze.

Area: 6400 square yards

Perimeter: 400 yards

Area: 2500 square yards

Complete Part A as a whole class. Then complete Parts B–D in small groups.

A. What is a mathematical question you can ask about this situation? What information would you need to know to answer your question?

B. What variables are involved in this situation? What unit of measurement would you use for each variable?

C. To answer your question, what strategy and tool would you use along with all the information you have? What answer do you get?

D. Does the answer make sense in the context of the situation? How do you know?

 Turn and Talk Predict how your work would change for each of the following changes in the situation:

- The pasture with an area of 6400 square yards is changed by increasing the length by 2 yards, and letting the width remain the same.
- The pasture with a perimeter of 400 yards is changed by decreasing the width by 4, and letting the length remain the same.
- The enclosures are all rectangular rather than square.

©fotoVoyager/E+/Getty Images

Build Understanding

Compose Functions

You learned how to combine two functions to create a new function using arithmetic operations. A composition of two functions is another way of combining two functions to create a new function.

To see how composition works, consider a bicycle with gears. The front gears (to which the bike's pedals are attached) have teeth, as do the rear gears (on the bike's rear wheel). A gear ratio is the ratio of the number of teeth on one of the front gears to the number of teeth on one of the rear gears. The gear ratio tells you how many times the rear wheel will turn for one revolution of the pedals.

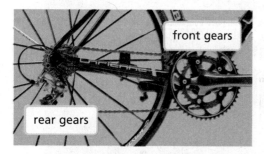

front gears

rear gears

rear wheel revolutions: $d = 26\pi w$

Suppose the gear ratio for a particular pairing of front and rear gears is 2:1. If p is the number of pedal revolutions and w is the number of rear-wheel revolutions, then w is a function of p: $w = 2p$.

If a bike's wheels are 26 inches in diameter, then the circumference of each wheel is 26π inches. The distance d (in inches) the bike travels is a function of w, the number of rear-wheel revolutions: $d = 26\pi w$.

1 **A.** Using the information above, write the distance d as a function of the number of pedal revolutions p. Explain your reasoning.

B. A composition of functions $f(x)$ and $g(x)$ is denoted by $(f \circ g)(x) = f(g(x))$. In the diagram, notice that $g(x)$ is substituted for x in $f(x)$. One requirement for the domain of the composite function $f \circ g$ is that x be an element of the domain of g. What other requirement must be imposed on the domain of $f \circ g$ for the composite function to be defined?

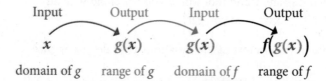

Input   Output   Input   Output

x $g(x)$ $g(x)$ $f(g(x))$

domain of g range of g domain of f range of f

C. Given the functions $f(x) = x^2$ and $g(x) = 2x$, what is the value of $(f \circ g)(-2)$? What is a rule for $(f \circ g)(x)$? What is the domain of the composite function?

Turn and Talk Is composition a commutative operation? In other words, is it true that for two functions f and g, $(f \circ g)(x) = (g \circ f)(x)$ for all values of x shared by the domains of $f \circ g$ and $g \circ f$? Use the functions in Part C to illustrate your reasoning.

Find Inverse Functions

An **inverse function**, denoted as $f^{-1}(x)$, is the function that "undoes" the operations of a function $f(x)$. This means that $f^{-1}(f(x)) = x$ for all values in the domain of $f(x)$.

The diagram shows the mapping from the domain to the range for the function $f(x)$ and then also for its inverse $f^{-1}(x)$. This shows that $f^{-1}(x)$ "undoes" the work of $f(x)$, returning the original domain values.

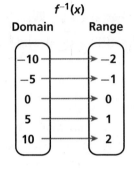

You can use algebra to determine the inverse of a given function. Having determined the inverse function, you can verify that the two functions are inverses by using composition to show that $f^{-1}(f(x)) = x$ and that $f(f^{-1}(x)) = x$.

2 ▶ Determine the inverse function for $g(x) = 2x + 4$.

Replace $g(x)$ with y.

$$y = 2x + 4$$

Solve for x.

$$y - 4 = 2x$$
$$\frac{y - 4}{2} = x$$

Switch x and y.

$$\frac{x - 4}{2} = y$$

Replace y with $g^{-1}(x)$.

$$g^{-1}(x) = \frac{x - 4}{2}$$

A. How does the order of operations when evaluating $g(x)$ for a given value of x compare to the order of operations when evaluating $g^{-1}(x)$ for a value of x?

B. Use composition to verify that $g(x)$ and $g^{-1}(x)$ are inverse functions.

C. The relationship between inverse functions can be visualized by graphing both functions on the same coordinate grid.

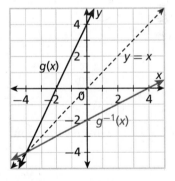

What relationship do you see between the graphs of $g(x)$ and $g^{-1}(x)$ in the figure at the right?

Turn and Talk

- If a function involves time as an input and gives distance as an output, what could you say about the inputs and outputs of the inverse function?
- When a function modeling a real-world situation has a restricted range like $\{y \mid y \geq 124\}$, what does this tell you about the corresponding inverse function?

Step It Out

Model a Real-World Situation Using an Inverse Function

In a model for a real-world situation, the variables have specific real-world meanings. It is helpful to choose the variable based on the quantity it represents. For example, using C for the cost of g gallons of gas makes it easy to connect the variables to their quantities.

The Mars Reconnaissance Orbiter is a NASA spacecraft orbiting Mars. The spacecraft captures images of the surface of Mars and sends those images back to Earth using radio waves. Radio waves travel at the speed of light.

The time it takes for images to reach Earth depends on how far apart the two planets are when the images are transmitted toward Earth.

When Mars and Earth are at their greatest distance apart, the function $D(s) = 380,000,000 - 300,000s$ gives the remaining distance D (in kilometers) that images sent by the Orbiter have left to travel s seconds after their transmission.

Suppose you want to know how long a group of images have been traveling if the radio wave containing the image data is currently 400,000 kilometers from Earth?

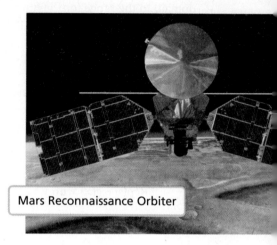

Mars Reconnaissance Orbiter

Create an inverse function for the given model.

The inverse of the given distance function will model the number of seconds s that the image data has been traveling as a function of the distance D left to reach Earth.

$$D = 380,000,000 - 300,000s$$

$$D - 380,000,000 = -300,000s$$

$$-\frac{D}{300,000} + \frac{3800}{3} = s$$

The inverse function is $s(D) = -\dfrac{D}{300,000} + \dfrac{3800}{3}$.

A. What is the speed of light? How do you know?

B. What is the greatest distance between Mars and Earth?

C. How long does it take data to travel to Earth from the orbiter when it is the farthest away? Justify your answer.

Use the inverse function.

Find $s(400,000)$.

$$s(400,000) = -\frac{400,000}{300,000} + \frac{3800}{3} = \frac{3796}{3} \text{ or } 1265\frac{1}{3}$$

The data has been traveling about $1265\frac{1}{3}$ seconds, or slightly more than 21 minutes.

D. What are the domain and range of the function $s(D)$? Explain.

Turn and Talk

- Which function would you use to determine the distance between Earth and the images 10 minutes after the transmission was sent out? Explain.
- Which function would you use to determine how long the data has been traveling when it is 200,000,000 kilometers from Earth? Explain.

Check Understanding

A clothing store is having a "40% off everything" sale. Ted has a $25 gift card. The function $T(c) = c - 25$ represents Ted's cost T (in dollars) for items that cost c dollars. The function $P(c) = 0.6c$ represents the purchase price P (in dollars) for items that originally cost c dollars.

1. Use the information from the problem to write Ted's cost T as a function of the purchase cost P. Then use the function to find Ted's cost when the original cost of his items is $54.

2. How can you write a function that applies the gift card first and then the discount? Use the function to evaluate what Ted pays when the original cost of his items is $54. Should he ask for the gift card to be applied before or after a discount? Explain.

At a local farm, people can pick their own strawberries to reduce the cost. The function $S(p) = 3p + 5$ models the total cost for picking p pounds of strawberries.

3. What is the inverse of the function $S(p) = 3p + 5$? Use function composition to verify that the two functions are inverses.

4. Describe the domain and range of the inverse function $p(S)$ in the context of the situation.

5. Given that the total cost was $23, which function would you use to determine how many pounds of strawberries were picked? How many pounds were picked?

On Your Own

For Problems 6–9, write the equation for each composition of functions $(f \circ g)(x)$ and $(g \circ f)(x)$, and express their domains and ranges in set notation.

6. $f(x) = 2x - 9$ and $g(x) = -5x + 6$

7. $f(x) = x^2 - 4$ and $g(x) = 6x + 2$

8. $f(x) = -x^2 + 5$ and $s(x) = -x^2 - 3$

9. $f(x) = x^2 - x - 6$ and $s(x) = 2x - 3$

For Problems 10–15, state the inverse of each function. Use composition of functions to verify the functions are inverse functions.

10. $j(x) = \frac{3}{5}x + 10$

11. $g(x) = 6x - \frac{1}{2}$

12. $h(x) = \frac{3}{4}x - 2$

13. $f(x) = 3x + 1$

14. $r(x) = -5x + 4$

15. $u(x) = -8x - 2$

16. A small rock is thrown into a pool from the shore, creating ripples in the water. The ripples form concentric circles. The function $r(t) = 14t$ models the radius (in inches) of the outer ripple t seconds after the rock enters the water. Write a function for the area (in square inches) of the outer ripple as a function of time (in seconds). What is the approximate area of the circle defined by the outer ripple 6 seconds after the rock was dropped?

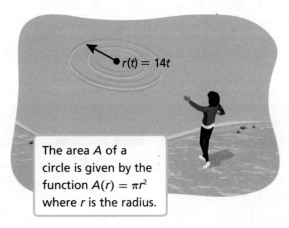

$r(t) = 14t$

The area A of a circle is given by the function $A(r) = \pi r^2$ where r is the radius.

17. Isla is flying from New Zealand to Canada and exchanges 100 New Zealand dollars for Canadian dollars. At the airport in Canada, she exchanges all her Canadian dollars for United States dollars. The exchange rates are 1 New Zealand dollar equals 0.9 Canadian dollar, and 1 Canadian dollar equals 0.76 United States dollar. Create a function that will determine how many United States dollars result from exchanging New Zealand dollars to Canadian dollars and then to United States dollars. Use your function to find the number of United States Isla will receive.

For Problems 18 and 19, Sally earns a weekly salary of $800 plus a 5% commission from her weekly sales. The function $E(s) = 0.05s + 800$ models Sally's total weekly earnings when her weekly sales are s dollars.

18. What is the inverse function of $E(s)$? Describe the domain and range of $s(E)$ in the context of the situation.

19. Determine Sally's weekly sales when she earns a total of $2000 for the week. Which function are you going to use to find her weekly sales? Explain.

20. The overall distance between the moon and Earth is changing because the moon is pulling away from us. The function $T(D) = \frac{D - 385,000}{38}$ gives the time T (in millions of years) from now that the moon will be D (in kilometers) from Earth. How far will the moon be from Earth in 1000 million years from now? Show the function you used to solve the problem.

How far away from Earth will the moon be in 1000 million years?

Spiral Review • Assessment Readiness

21. Which polynomial function has the zeros $-4i$ and -1?

Ⓐ $f(x) = x^3 + x^2 + 17x + 17$

Ⓑ $f(x) = x^3 + x^2 + 17x - 17$

Ⓒ $f(x) = x^3 + x^2 + 16x + 16$

Ⓓ $f(x) = x^3 + x^2 + 16x - 16$

22. Which statements are true? Select all that apply.

Ⓐ $\sqrt[5]{6x^2} = (6x)^{\frac{2}{5}}$

Ⓓ $\sqrt[3]{(7t)^2} = (7t)^{\frac{3}{2}}$

Ⓑ $\sqrt{(9y)^2} = 9y$

Ⓔ $\sqrt[4]{8x} = 2x$

Ⓒ $\sqrt[7]{(ab)^4} = (ab)^{\frac{4}{7}}$

Ⓕ $\sqrt[5]{(2m)^{10}} = 4m^2$

23. The function $T(a) = a^{\frac{3}{2}}$ models the time T (in years) it takes a planet to complete one orbit about the sun given its average distance a (in astronomical units) from the sun. About how long does Jupiter take to orbit the sun if its average distance to the sun is 5.2 astronomical units?

Ⓐ 3 years

Ⓒ 12 years

Ⓑ 9 years

Ⓓ 70 years

24. Solve $x = -2y + 6$ for y.

Ⓐ $y = -2x + 12$

Ⓒ $y = 2x - 12$

Ⓑ $y = -\frac{1}{2}x + 3$

Ⓓ $y = -\frac{1}{2}x - 3$

 I'm in a Learning Mindset!

Did procrastination affect my learning about composition of functions and inverse functions? In what way?

Inverses of Quadratic and Cubic Functions

(I Can) **find inverses of quadratic and cubic functions.**

Spark Your Learning

Maria is working on a science project. She needs to create a cube that has a volume of 512 cubic centimeters. She found an image of how to cut a cubic net from cardboard.

Complete Part A as a whole class. Then complete Parts B–D in small groups.

    A. What is a mathematical question you can ask about this situation? What information would you need to know to answer your question?

    B. What variables are involved in this situation? What unit of measurement would you use for each variable?

    C. To answer your question, what strategy and tool would you use along with all the information you have? What answer do you get?

    D. Does your answer make sense in the context of the situation? How do you know?

 Turn and Talk Predict how your work would change for each of the following changes in the situation:

- The volume of the cube is 343 cubic centimeters.
- The volume of the cube is 216 cubic inches.
- You are given the surface area of the cube instead of its volume.

Build Understanding

Find the Inverse of a Many-to-One Function

Some functions have the same value for different values in their domain. These functions are called *many-to-one functions*. Many-to-one functions do not have inverses that are functions. If the domain of a many-to-one function can be restricted so that the resulting function is one-to-one, then the inverse over that restricted domain is a function.

1 The function $f(x)$ is defined by the following ordered pairs.

$(7, 22), (8, 7), (9, -2), (10, -5), (11, -2), (12, 7), (13, 22)$

A. What is the inverse of $f(x)$?

B. Is the inverse of $f(x)$ a function? Justify your response.

Restrict the domain of $f(x)$ to only those ordered pairs that have values of $x \geq 10$.

$(10, -5), (11, -2), (12, 7), (13, 22)$

C. What is the inverse of $f(x)$ with the restricted domain?

D. Is the inverse of $f(x)$ with the restricted domain a function? Explain.

 Turn and Talk When the domain of $f(x)$ was restricted, did this change the range of $f(x)$?

The Square Root Function

Quadratic functions are many-to-one functions because there are numerous pairs of values of the independent variable whose function values are the same. For the quadratic function $f(x) = x^2$, the domain can be restricted so the inverse is a function.

Restrict the domain of $f(x)$.	$f(x) = x^2$ for $\{x \mid x \geq 0\}$
Replace $f(x)$ with y.	$y = x^2$
Solve for x.	$\sqrt{y} = \sqrt{x^2}$
	$\pm\sqrt{y} = x$
Switch x and y to write the inverse.	$\pm\sqrt{x} = y$
Replace y with $f^{-1}(x)$. Specify the domain.	$f^{-1}(x) = \sqrt{x}$ for $\{x \mid x \geq 0\}$
	$f^{-1}(x) = -\sqrt{x}$ for $\{x \mid x \leq 0\}$

The inverse of the parent quadratic function $f(x) = x^2$ for $\{x \mid x \geq 0\}$ is the **parent square root function** $g(x) = \sqrt{x}$ for $\{x \mid x \geq 0\}$. In general, the inverse of a quadratic function is a **square root function**.

2 The table shows some values of $f(x)$ and its inverse function.

x	−1	0	1	2	3	4	5	6	7	8	9	10
$f(x) = x^2$	1	0	1	4	9	16	25	36	49	64	81	100
$g(x) = \sqrt{f(x)}$	undef.	0	1	2	3	4	5	6	7	8	9	10

A. What is the range of $g(x) = \sqrt{x}$?

B. Is $g(x)$ an increasing or decreasing function? Is $g(x)$ a negative or positive function?

C. What are the intercepts of $g(x)$?

D. Sketch a graph of $g(x)$?

E. Confirm that $g(x)$ is the inverse of $f(x)$ for values of $x \geq 0$.

The Cube Root Function

The cubic function $f(x) = x^3$ is a one-to-one function because for every value of the function there is only one value of x. Therefore it is not necessary to restrict the domain of the parent cubic function in order to determine its inverse function.

Replace $f(x)$ with y. $y = x^3$

Solve for x. $\sqrt[3]{y} = \sqrt[3]{x^3}$

                                                                     $\sqrt[3]{y} = x$

Switch x and y to write the inverse. $\sqrt[3]{x} = y$

Replace y with $f^{-1}(x)$. $f^{-1}(x) = \sqrt[3]{x}$

The inverse of the parent cubic function $f(x) = x^3$ is the **parent cube root function** $g(x) = \sqrt[3]{x}$. In general, the inverse of a cubic function is a **cube root function**.

3 The table shows some values of $f(x)$ and its inverse function.

x	−5	−4	−3	−2	−1	0	1	2	3	4	5
$f(x) = x^3$	−125	−64	−27	−8	−1	0	1	8	27	64	125
$g(f(x)) = \sqrt[3]{f(x)}$	−5	−4	−3	−2	−1	0	1	2	3	4	5

A. What is the range of $g(x) = \sqrt[3]{x}$?

B. Is $g(x)$ an increasing or decreasing function? Where is the $g(x)$ positive or negative?

C. What are the intercepts of $g(x)$?

D. Sketch a graph of $g(x)$?

E. Confirm $g(x)$ is the inverse of $f(x)$.

 Turn and Talk Do all cubic functions have inverses that are functions? Why or why not?

Step It Out

Inverses of Quadratic Functions

4 Determine the inverse function of the function $p(x) = x^2 + 4$.

Since $p(x)$ is a quadratic function, you need to restrict the domain.

> **A.** Why must the domains of quadratic functions be restricted?

Let $p(x) = x^2 + 4$ for values $x \geq 0$.

Replace $p(x)$ with y. $\qquad\qquad\qquad y = x^2 + 4$

Solve for x. $\qquad\qquad\qquad\qquad y - 4 = x^2$

$$\pm\sqrt{y-4} = \sqrt{x^2}$$

$$\pm\sqrt{y-4} = x$$

> **B.** Why is the inverse equation $y = \sqrt{x-4}$ rather than $y = -\sqrt{x-4}$?

Switch x and y to write the inverse. $\qquad \sqrt{x-4} = y$

Replace y with $p^{-1}(x)$. Specify the domain. $\qquad p^{-1}(x) = \sqrt{x-4}$

> **C.** What is the domain of $p^{-1}(x)$? Why?

Use function composition to verify that $p(x)$ and $p^{-1}(x)$ are inverses.

$(p \circ p^{-1})(x)$

$= (\sqrt{x-4})^2 + 4$, for $x \geq 4$

$= x - 4 + 4$

$= x$

$(p^{-1} \circ p)(x)$

$= \sqrt{(x^2 + 4) - 4}$, for $x \geq 0$

$= \sqrt{x^2 + 4 - 4}$

$= \sqrt{x^2}$

$= x$

D. How does the work above show that $p(x)$ and $p^{-1}(x)$ are inverses?

The figure at the right shows the graphs of the functions $p(x)$ and $p^{-1}(x)$.

> **E.** Which curve is the graph of $p(x)$ and which curve is the graph of $p^{-1}(x)$? How do you know?

> **F.** How are the domains and ranges of $p(x)$ and $p^{-1}(x)$ related?

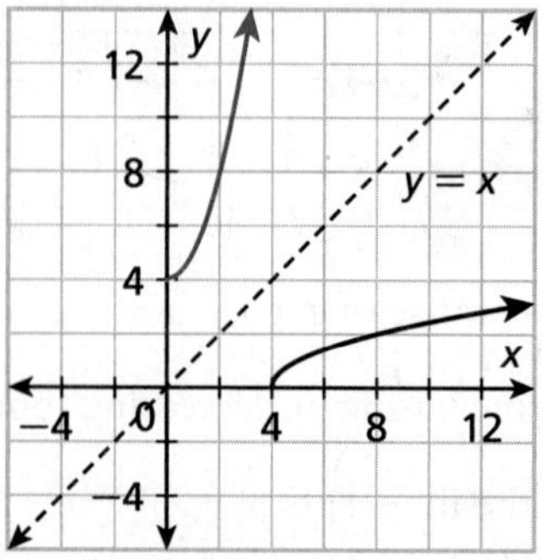

Turn and Talk How could you find the inverse of a square root function?

Inverses of Cubic Functions

5 ▸ Determine the inverse function of the function $p(x) = x^3 + 4$.

The function $p(x)$ is a vertical translation of the parent cubic function. There is no need to restrict the domain of $p(x)$ to find its inverse function.

> **A.** Why is it not necessary to restrict the domain?

Replace $p(x)$ with y. $y = x^3 + 4$

Solve for x. $y - 4 = x^3$

$$\sqrt[3]{y - 4} = \sqrt[3]{x^3}$$

$$\sqrt[3]{y - 4} = x$$

Switch x and y to write the inverse. $\sqrt[3]{x - 4} = y$

> **B.** What is the domain of $p^{-1}(x) = \sqrt[3]{x - 4}$?

Replace y with $p^{-1}(x)$. $p^{-1}(x) = \sqrt[3]{x - 4}$

The inverse of the function $p(x)$ is $p^{-1}(x) = \sqrt[3]{x - 4}$.

C. Use composition of functions to shows that $p(x)$ and $p^{-1}(x)$ are inverses.

 Turn and Talk How do you find the inverse of a cube root function?

Find the Inverse of a Real-World Cubic Model

In many instances, cubic functions are used to model real-world applications. It is often useful to find and interpret the inverse of cubic models. For real-world applications, it is more useful to use the notation $x(y)$ for the inverse of $y(x)$ instead of the notation $y^{-1}(x)$.

6 ▸ The function $m(L) = 0.00001L^3$ gives the mass m in kilograms of a red snapper of length L centimeters. Determine the inverse function $L(m)$ that gives the length L in centimeters of a red snapper as a function of its mass m in kilograms.

Find the inverse function.

Replace $m(L)$ with m. $m = 0.00001L^3$

Solve for L. $100{,}000m = L^3$

$$\sqrt[3]{100{,}000m} = \sqrt[3]{L^3}$$

$$\sqrt[3]{100{,}000m} = L$$

A 4-year old snapper weighs about 1.5 kg.

Replace L with $L(m)$. $\sqrt[3]{100{,}000m} = L(m)$

The inverse function is $L(m) = \sqrt[3]{100{,}000m}$.

> **A.** Why is it not necessary to switch the variables before making the replacement?

B. What is the length of the 4-year old snapper that weighs about 1.5 kilograms?

C. Suppose a snapper weighs 7.5 kilograms. What is its length?

Check Understanding

For Problems 1 and 2, the function $f(x)$ is defined by the following ordered pairs.

$(-4, -12), (-3, -9), (-2, -6), (-1, -3), (0, -6), (1, -9), (2, -12), (3, -15)$

1. Determine the inverse of $f(x)$.

2. How can you change $f(x)$ so that its inverse is a function? Show an example.

3. Describe the key features of $g(x)$ represented in the table of values.

x	−2	0	2	4	6	8	10	12	14	16	18	20
$f(x) = \dfrac{1}{4}x^2$	1	0	1	4	9	16	25	36	49	64	81	100
$g(x) = \sqrt{4f(x)}$	undef.	0	2	4	6	8	10	12	14	16	18	20

4. Describe the key features of $g(x)$ represented in the table of values.

x	−5	−4	−3	−2	−1	0	1	2	3	4	5
$f(x) = 2x^3$	−250	−128	−54	−16	−2	0	2	16	54	128	250
$g(x) = \sqrt[3]{\dfrac{1}{2}f(x)}$	−5	−4	−3	−2	−1	0	1	2	3	4	5

5. What is the inverse of $f(x) = \frac{1}{9}x^2$? of $g(x) = 8x^3$?

On Your Own

For each function $f(x)$ defined by the given set of ordered pairs, determine a restricted domain on $f(x)$ for an inverse function $f^{-1}(x)$ that contains the most possible ordered pairs. Then show the ordered pairs of the inverse function.

6. $(-1, 30), (0, 10), (1, -2), (2, -6), (3, -2), (4, 10), (5, 30), (6, 58)$

7. $(-7, 83), (-6, 56), (-5, 35), (-4, 20), (-3, 11), (-2, 8), (-1, 11)$

8. $(-9, 4), (-8, 0), (-7, -12), (-6, -32), (-5, -60), (-4, -96), (-3, -140)$

9. $(0, 44), (1, 8), (2, -4), (3, 8), (4, 44), (5, 104), (6, 188)$

For Problems 10 and 11, use the following table of values.

x	−2	0	2	4	6	8	10	12	14	16	18	20
$f(x) = \dfrac{1}{2}x^2$	2	0	2	8	18	32	50	72	98	128	162	200
$g(x) = \sqrt{2f(x)}$	undef.	0	2	4	6	8	10	12	14	16	18	20

10. What are the range and other key features of $g(x)$?

11. (MP) **Reason** According to the table of values, is $g(x)$ the inverse of $f(x)$? Explain. Let $h(f(x)) = \sqrt{f(x)}$. Why is $h(x)$ not the inverse of $f(x)$?

For Problems 12 and 13, use the following table of values.

x	−5	−4	−3	−2	−1	0	1	2	3	4	5
$f(x) = 4x^3$	−500	−256	−108	−32	−4	0	4	32	108	256	500
$g(x) = \sqrt[3]{\frac{1}{4}f(x)}$	−5	−4	−3	−2	−1	0	1	2	3	4	5

12. What are the range and other key features of $g(x)$?

13. **(MP) Reason** According to the table of values, is $g(x)$ the inverse of $f(x)$? Explain. Let $h\left(f(x)\right) = \sqrt[3]{f(x)}$. Why is $h(x)$ not the inverse of $f(x)$?

14. The *period* of a pendulum is how long it takes it to complete a full back-and-forth swing. Because a pendulum's period depends only on its length for a given gravitational strength, pendulums have long been used to keep time in clocks. On Earth's surface, the length l (in meters) of a pendulum with a period of T seconds is modeled by $l(T) = 9.8\left(\frac{T}{2\pi}\right)^2$.

   A. Find a model $T(l)$ for the period of a pendulum of a given length.

   B. What do you notice about the period of a pendulum that is 1 meter long?

For Problems 15–29, determine the inverse of each function.

15. $f(x) = 5x^2,\ x \geq 0$

16. $f(x) = \frac{1}{2}x^2 + 8,\ x \geq 0$

17. $f(x) = x^2 - 6,\ x \geq 0$

18. $f(x) = (4x)^2,\ x \geq 0$

19. $f(x) = (x + 2)^2,\ x \geq -2$

20. $f(x) = (3x - 9)^2,\ x \geq 3$

21. $f(x) = (-6x)^3$

22. $f(x) = \frac{1}{3}x^3 - 9$

23. $f(x) = \frac{1}{2}x^3$

24. $f(x) = 2x^3 - 8$

25. $f(x) = 4(x + 3)^3$

26. $f(x) = (x + 1)^3$

27. $f(x) = -(x - 2)^3$

28. $f(x) = 2x^3 + 4$

29. $f(x) = (x - 5)^3 + 2$

30. The kinetic energy of an object is the energy it has due to its motion. The kinetic energy E (in joules) of an object with a mass of m kilograms moving at v meters per second is modeled by the function $E(v) = \frac{1}{2}mv^2$.

   A. Find a model $V(e)$ for the velocity of an object with mass m and kinetic energy E joules.

   B. A top-speed professional baseball pitch can have a kinetic energy of 150 joules, while a professional bowling ball may impact the pins with a kinetic energy of 250 joules. The mass of a baseball is 0.149 kg. The mass of a bowling ball is 7.3 kg. How do the speeds of the baseball and bowling ball compare?

Kinetic enegy: $E(v) = \frac{1}{2}mv^2$

31. A company is opening and expanding a new headquarters in a school district over the next three years. The district had 6240 students just before the opening. If the district grows $r\%$ annually for this period, the student population P in three years will be $P(r) = 6240(1 + r)^3$. Find and interpret the inverse function $r(P)$. What annual growth rate will increase the student population to 7800 students?

Student population in three years:
$P(r) = 6240(1 + r)^3$

32. The volume of a sphere with radius r can be written as the function $V(r) = \frac{4}{3}\pi r^3$. Write the inverse of this function and use it to find the radius of a sphere with a volume of 50 cm³.

33. (Open Middle™) Using the digits −9 to 9, at most one time each, fill in the boxes to create a cube root function and its inverse function.

$$y = \sqrt[3]{x + \boxed{}} + \boxed{}$$

$$y = \boxed{}\left(x + \boxed{}\right)^3 + \boxed{}$$

Spiral Review • Assessment Readiness

34. Which expression is equivalent to $\sqrt[5]{(8a^2)^3}$?

(A) $(8a^2)^{\frac{5}{3}}$

(B) $(8a^2)^{\frac{3}{5}}$

(C) $(8a^2)^2$

(D) $\dfrac{1}{(8a^2)^2}$

35. The function $L = \frac{1}{200}p + 3$ models the total number of lives a player is given in a video game after scoring p points. The video game just gave Linda a fifth life. Which function determines the total number of points Linda scored in order to earn her fifth life?

(A) $p = \dfrac{1}{200}L + 3$

(B) $p = \dfrac{1}{200}L - 3$

(C) $p = 200L - 600$

(D) $p = 200L + 600$

36. Which expressions are equivalent to $4x^2$? Select all that apply.

(A) $\sqrt[3]{(2x)^6}$

(B) $\left(\sqrt[4]{4x^2}\right)^6$

(C) $\left(\sqrt[5]{\dfrac{16}{8x^{-1}}}\right)^{10}$

(D) $\sqrt[5]{(4x^2)^6}$

(E) $\left(\sqrt[8]{(4x^2)^4}\right)^2$

(F) $\left(\sqrt[4]{16x^4}\right)^2$

37. Recall transformations on the parent function $f(x) = x^2$. Which translation could transform the point $(0, 0)$ of the function $g(x) = \sqrt{x}$ to the point $(0, 2)$?

(A) translation 2 units up

(B) translation 2 units down

(C) translation 2 units right

(D) translation 2 units left

©Troy Aossey/Taxi/Getty Images

 I'm in a Learning Mindset!

How can I take advantage of working in small groups to improve my academic performance with inverses of quadratic and cubic functions?

Graph Square Root Functions

(I Can) graph square root functions.

Spark Your Learning

In a movie, the villain drops a hard drive that contains all the superhero's research from the top of a tall building. The superhero is flying toward the building and needs to know how much time she has before the hard drive reaches the height at which she is flying.

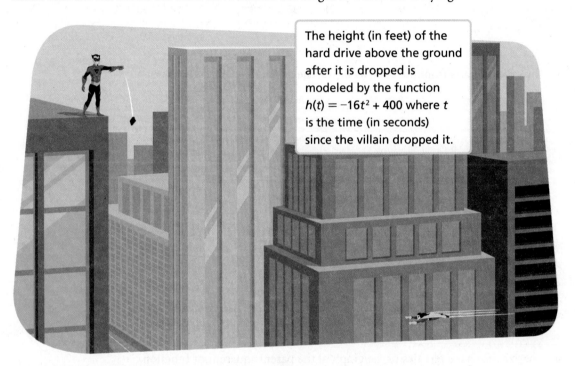

The height (in feet) of the hard drive above the ground after it is dropped is modeled by the function $h(t) = -16t^2 + 400$ where t is the time (in seconds) since the villain dropped it.

Complete Part A as a whole class. Then complete Parts B–D in small groups.

A. What is a mathematical question you can ask about this situation? What information would you need to know to answer your question?

B. What variables are involved in this situation? What unit of measurement would you use for each variable?

C. To answer your question, what strategy and tool would you use along with all the information you have? What answer do you get?

D. Does the answer make sense in the context of the situation? How do you know?

 Turn and Talk Predict how your work would change for each of the following changes in the situation:
- The hard drive is dropped from a height of 144 feet.
- The hard drive is dropped from a height of 784 feet.

Build Understanding

Graph the Parent Square Root Function

Recall that the parent square root function $g(x) = \sqrt{x}$ is the inverse function of the parent quadratic function $f(x) = x^2$ when the domain is restricted to $x \geq 0$. The parent square root function is also only defined for real values greater than or equal to 0.

The table of values represents the parent square root function $g(x) = \sqrt{x}$.

x	0	1	4	9	16	25	36	49	64	81	100	121	144
$g(x) = \sqrt{x}$	0	1	2	3	4	5	6	7	8	9	10	11	12

You can use the ordered pairs from the table to sketch the graph of $g(x)$.

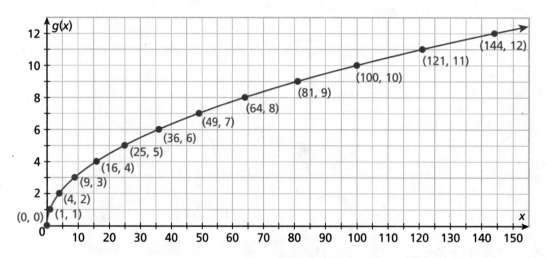

1 Summarize the characteristics of the graph of the parent square root function.

A. What are the domain and range of the parent square root function?

B. What are the x- and y-intercepts of the parent square root function?

C. Where is the function increasing or decreasing? Positive or negative?

D. Does the parent square root function have any maximum or minimum values? Explain your answer.

E. Describe the end behavior of the function.

F. Describe the rate of change of the function as x increases.

 Turn and Talk What can the key features of the graph of the function $f(x) = x^2$ tell you about the graph of the function $g(x) = \sqrt{x}$?

Transformations of the Parent Square Root Function

Recall that transformations of parent functions include vertical and horizontal translations, vertical and horizontal stretches or compressions, and reflections across the x- or y-axes. The specific transformations can be determined by identifying the parameters a, b, h, and k when a square root function is written in either of these forms:

$$g(x) = a\sqrt{x - h} + k \text{ or } g(x) = \sqrt{\frac{1}{b}(x - h)} + k.$$

The parent square root function $f(x) = \sqrt{x}$ is shown in each of the following figures.

Horizontal Translations	**Vertical Translations**	**Reflections Over Axes**
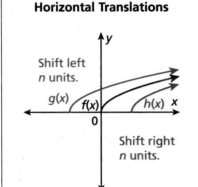	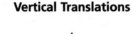 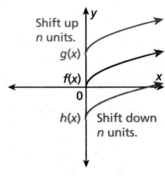	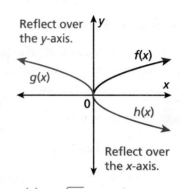
$g(x) = \sqrt{x + n}$ $h(x) = \sqrt{x - n}$	$g(x) = \sqrt{x} + n$ $h(x) = \sqrt{x} - n$	$g(x) = \sqrt{-x}$ $h(x) = -\sqrt{x}$

Vertical Stretches or Compressions	**Horizontal Stretches or Compressions**
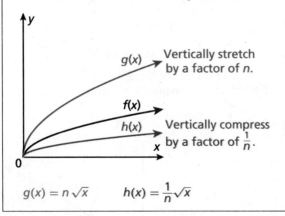	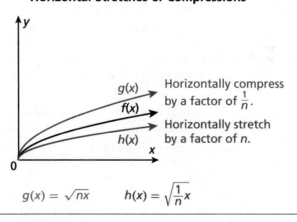
$g(x) = n\sqrt{x}$ $h(x) = \frac{1}{n}\sqrt{x}$	$g(x) = \sqrt{nx}$ $h(x) = \sqrt{\frac{1}{n}x}$

2 For each square root function, identify the values of a, b, h, and k. Then describe the effect that each parameter has on the graph of the function as compared to the parent square root function. Use a graphing tool to check your responses.

A. $g(x) = \sqrt{x} - 5$ B. $g(x) = \sqrt{x - 3}$ C. $g(x) = 3\sqrt{x}$

D. $g(x) = \sqrt{-4x}$ E. $g(x) = \sqrt{\frac{1}{4}x}$ F. $g(x) = -\frac{1}{5}\sqrt{x}$

 Turn and Talk Can you think of a pair of transformations that would map the graph of the parent square root function onto the graph of the parent quadratic function, its inverse?

Step It Out

Graph Square Root Functions

You can graph square root functions using transformations of the graph of the parent square root function $f(x) = \sqrt{x}$. It is helpful to analyze the effect of the transformations on the points $(0, 0)$ and $(1, 1)$ on the graph of the parent square root function.

For square root functions of the form $g(x) = a\sqrt{x - h} + k$,

$(0, 0)$ is mapped to (h, k) and $(1, 1)$ is mapped to $(h + 1, k + a)$.

For square root functions of the form $g(x) = \sqrt{\frac{1}{b}(x - h)} + k$,

$(0, 0)$ is mapped to (h, k) and $(1, 1)$ is mapped to $(h + b, k + 1)$.

Remember that you cannot take the square root of a negative number, so the expression appearing under the square root symbol leads to a restriction on the domain of the function. This restriction on the domain then determines the range of the function.

 Sketch the graph of $g(x) = 3\sqrt{x + 1} - 4$ using transformations of the graph of $f(x) = \sqrt{x}$.

Step 1: Rewrite g in the form $g(x) = a\sqrt{x - h} + k$. $g(x) = 3\sqrt{(x - (-1))} + (-4)$

Step 2: Identify the values of a, h, and k. $a = 3, h = -1, k = -4$

Step 3: Determine the mapping of $(0, 0)$ and $(1, 1)$ on the parent function f to their corresponding points on the graph of g.

> **A.** How does the mapping of $(0, 0)$ help to identify the domain and range of g?

$(0, 0)$ is mapped to (h, k): $(0, 0) \rightarrow (-1, -4)$

$(1, 1)$ is mapped to $(h + 1, k + a)$: $(1, 1) \rightarrow (-1 + 1, -4 + 3) = (0, -1)$

Step 4: Determine a few other points on the graph of g. The value of h indicates that the graph shifts 1 unit to the left. The points $(4, 2)$ and $(9, 3)$ are on the graph of the parent function f. Due to the 1-unit shift to the left, the corresponding points on the graph of g will have x-coordinates of 3 and 8. Use those values of x in g to determine their corresponding y-coordinates.

$g(3) = 3\sqrt{3 + 1} - 4 = 3(2) - 4 = 2$

$g(8) = 3\sqrt{8 + 1} - 4 = 3(3) - 4 = 5$

Step 5: To sketch the graph of g, plot the points $(-1, -4)$, $(0, -1)$, $(3, 2)$, and $(8, 5)$. Then draw a smooth curve starting from $(-1, -4)$ and passing through the other points.

> **B.** How can the graph be used to verify that the correct transformations are shown?

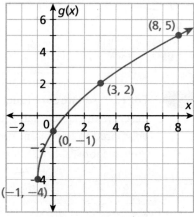

 Turn and Talk How is graphing transformations of the parent square root function similar to graphing transformations of other parent functions?

212

Write a Square Root Function for a Graph

Given the graph of a square root function, you can determine the parameters h, k, and a or b for the function by considering the mapping of the points $(0, 0)$ and $(1, 1)$ on the parent function to their corresponding points on the given graph.

- The coordinates of the endpoint of the graph correspond to the ordered pair (h, k).

- The parameter a can be determined by examining the vertical change from the point (h, k) to the second plotted point, if that point has x-coordinate $x = h + 1$.

- The parameter b can be determined by examining the horizontal change from the point (h, k) to the second plotted point, if that point has y-coordinate $y = k + 1$.

4 Write a square root function for the graph shown. The endpoint (h, k) is $(2, 1)$, so $h = 2$ and $k = 1$.

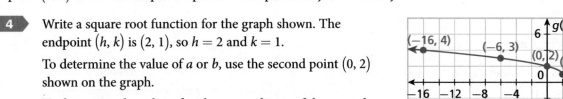

To determine the value of a or b, use the second point $(0, 2)$ shown on the graph.

To determine the value of a, the x-coordinate of the second point needs to be $h + 1 = 2 + 1 = 3$. But the x-coordinate of $(0, 2)$ is 0, so a cannot be determined.

To determine the value of b, the y-coordinate of the second point needs to be $k + 1 = 1 + 1 = 2$. But the y-coordinate of $(0, 2)$ is 2, so b can be determined.

Use the second point to determine the value of b.
$(h + b, k + 1) \rightarrow (0, 2)$, so $h + b = 0$; since $h = 2$, then $b = -2$.

> **A.** What can you do to verify that this is the correct function?

The equation of the function has the form $g(x) = \sqrt{\frac{1}{b}(x - h)} + k$.

Using the values of b, h, and k, the function is $g(x) = \sqrt{-\frac{1}{2}(x - 2)} + 1$.

> **B.** What are the domain and range of g?

 Turn and Talk How can you tell if the graph of a square root function has been compressed or stretched horizontally rather than vertically?

Model a Real-World Situation with a Square Root Function

5 The graph at the right shows the square root function $v(N) = \sqrt{\frac{24}{5}N}$, which models the speed v of a falling object (in meters per second) with an air resistance force of N (in newtons).

N	2	4	6	8	10	12	14	16	18
v(N)	3.1	4.4	5.4	6.2	6.9	7.6	8.2	8.8	9.3

A. What are the average rates of change for the first and last intervals in the table?

B. Using the graph, describe the overall rate of change in the context of the situation.

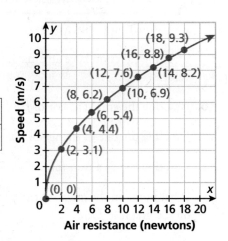

Check Understanding

1. What are the domain and range of the function $f(x) = \sqrt{x+2} - 5$?

2. What transformations of the graph of the parent square root function result in the graph of $f(x) = 10\sqrt{x} + 3$?

For Problems 3 and 4, use the function $g(x) = 2\sqrt{x-4} + 6$.

3. Where do the points $(0, 0)$ and $(1, 1)$ on the graph of the parent square root function get mapped to on the graph of g?

4. Draw the graph of g and use it to confirm that the domain of g is $\{x \mid x \geq 4\}$ and the range is $\{y \mid y \geq 6\}$.

5. What function of the form
$g(x) = \sqrt{\dfrac{1}{b}(x-h)} + k$ is represented
by the graph at the right?

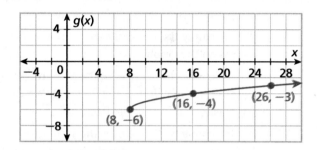

6. The function $S(w) = 60\sqrt{w} + 10$ models the weekly sales S, in thousands of dollars, for a national skateboard retailer during of a 12-week promotion from October 31 through December 18, where w is the number of the week of the promotion. Describe the overall rate of change shown in the table.

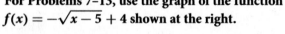

w	1	2	3	4	5	6	7	8	9	10	11	12
S(w)	70	95	114	130	144	157	169	180	190	200	209	218

On Your Own

For Problems 7–13, use the graph of the function $f(x) = -\sqrt{x-5} + 4$ shown at the right.

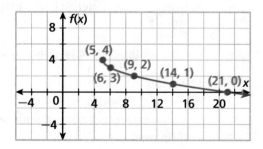

7. **(MP) Use Structure** What are the domain and range of f?

8. Is the function positive or negative for values of $x > 21$?

9. Does the function have any maximum or minimum values?

10. Describe the end behavior of f.

11. Describe the rate of change of $f(x)$ as x increases.

12. Describe $f(x)$ as a transformation of the parent square root function.

13. What point on the graph of the parent square root function corresponds to $(6, 3)$ on the graph of $f(x)$?

For Problems 14–19, describe the transformations of the graph of the parent square root function that result in the graph of the given function.

14. $f(x) = \sqrt{x+5} + 2$

15. $f(x) = -2\sqrt{x}$

16. $f(x) = \sqrt{4x}$

17. $f(x) = -\sqrt{2x} + 4$

18. $f(x) = \sqrt{-\frac{1}{2}x} - 6$

19. $f(x) = \frac{1}{4}\sqrt{x-3} + 8$

20. A car with good tires is traveling on a dry road. The speed s, in miles per hour, from which the car can stop in a given distance d, in feet, is given by the function $s(d) = \sqrt{96d}$. Create a table of values for the function by evaluating the speed for distances of 20, 40, 60, 80, and 100 feet. Calculate the average rates of change over the first and last intervals and explain what these rates of change represent.

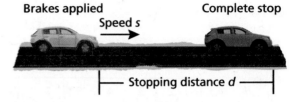

Brakes applied   Speed s Complete stop

— Stopping distance d —

Use the function $g(x) = \sqrt{\frac{1}{2}(x+8)} - 1$.

21. Where do the points $(0, 0)$ and $(1, 1)$ on the graph of the parent square root function get mapped to on the graph of g?

22. Where do the points $(49, 7)$ and $(64, 8)$ on the graph of the square root parent function get mapped to on the graph of g?

23. Draw the graph of g and use it to confirm that the domain of g is $\{x \mid x \geq -8\}$ and the range is $\{y \mid y \geq -1\}$.

Use the function $g(x) = \sqrt{-(x-1)} + 2$.

24. Where do the points $(0, 0)$ and $(1, 1)$ on the graph of the parent square root function get mapped to on the graph of g?

25. Where do the points $(36, 6)$ and $(100, 10)$ on the graph of the square root parent function get mapped to on the graph of g?

26. Draw the graph of g and use it to confirm that the domain of g is $\{x \mid x \leq 1\}$ and the range is $\{y \mid y \geq 2\}$.

For Problems 27 and 28, write a function of the form $g(x) = a\sqrt{x-h} + k$ that represents the graph.

27.

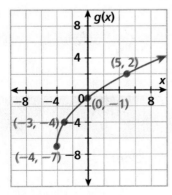

28.

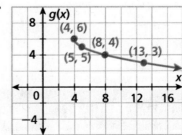

29. The table below shows values for the function $L(d) = 12\sqrt{d} + 4$. The function models the number of likes that Mara's video received on day d after she first posted it to her blog. Describe the overall rate of change in the values of $L(d)$ in the context of this situation.

Number of likes:
$L(d) = 12\sqrt{d} + 4$

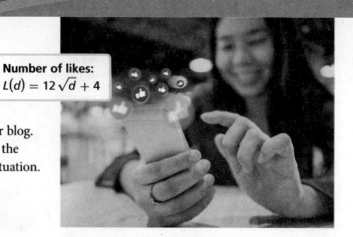

d	1	2	3	4	5	6	7	8	9	10	11	12	13	14	15	16
$L(d)$	16	21	25	28	31	33	36	38	40	42	44	46	47	49	50	52

30. (Open Middle™) Copy the material at the right onto your own paper, leaving the boxes blank. Using the integers -9 to 9, at most one time each, fill in the boxes to create a square root function, its domain, and the x-intercept.

$y = \boxed{}\sqrt{x + \boxed{}} + \boxed{}$

$\left\{x \mid x > \boxed{}\right\}$

x-intercept: $\left(\boxed{}, \boxed{}\right)$

Spiral Review • Assessment Readiness

31. How many times as bright one star is compared to another can be determined using the formula $\frac{B_2}{B_1} = \frac{2.512^{m_1}}{2.512^{m_2}}$, where B_1 and m_1 are the brightness and apparent magnitude of the fainter star and B_2 and m_2 are the brightness and the apparent magnitude of the brighter star. The star with the lower apparent magnitude is the brighter star. Which expression represents the brightness ratio $\frac{B_2}{B_1}$ if the apparent magnitude of Sirius A is $-\frac{73}{50}$ and that of Polaris is $\frac{48}{25}$?

Ⓐ $2.512^{-\frac{169}{50}}$ Ⓒ $2.512^{\frac{23}{50}}$

Ⓑ $2.512^{\frac{23}{50}}$ Ⓓ $2.512^{\frac{169}{50}}$

32. Which equation represents $(g \circ f)(x)$ when $f(x) = x^2 - 1$ and $g(x) = x + 2$?

Ⓐ $y = x^2 + 4x + 3$ Ⓒ $y = x^2 + 1$

Ⓑ $y = x^2 + 4x + 4$ Ⓓ $y = x^2 - 1$

33. Which function is the inverse of the function $f(x) = 2x^3 + 8$?

Ⓐ $f^{-1}(x) = \sqrt[3]{\frac{1}{2}x} - 4$

Ⓑ $f^{-1}(x) = \sqrt[3]{\frac{1}{2}x - 4}$

Ⓒ $f^{-1}(x) = \sqrt[3]{2x + 4}$

Ⓓ $f^{-1}(x) = \sqrt[3]{2x} + 4$

34. Let $f(x) = \sqrt[3]{x}$. A new function $g(x)$ translates $f(x)$ 6 units up. Which equation represents $g(x)$?

Ⓐ $g(x) = \sqrt[3]{x - 6}$

Ⓑ $g(x) = \sqrt[3]{x + 6}$

Ⓒ $g(x) = \sqrt[3]{x} + 6$

Ⓓ $g(x) = \sqrt[3]{x} - 6$

©marchmeena29/iStock/Getty Images

I'm in a Learning Mindset!

How am I prioritizing my learning of graphing square root functions?

Graph Cube Root Functions

(I Can) **graph cube root functions.**

Spark Your Learning

Sophia is pumping air into a spherical balloon to be used as part of her World Geography project. She does not want to overinflate and pop it, but she wants the balloon to be as large as possible so everyone in class can see it.

The package says the balloon can hold a maximum volume of 0.25 cubic meter of air when inflated.

Complete Part A as a whole class. Then complete Parts B–D in small groups.

A. What is a mathematical question you can ask about this situation? What information would you need to know to answer your question?

B. What variables are involved in this situation? What unit of measurement would you use for each variable?

C. To answer your question, what strategy and tool would you use along with all the information you have? What answer do you get?

D. How can you write a formula that could be used to find the radius of a spherical balloon for any given volume?

Turn and Talk How can you find the radius of the balloon for each of the following changes in the situation:
- The maximum volume of the balloon is 1 cubic meter.
- The maximum volume of the balloon is 8000 cubic inches.

Build Understanding

Graph the Parent Cube Root Function

Recall that the parent cube root function $g(x) = \sqrt[3]{x}$ is the inverse function of the parent cubic function $f(x) = x^3$. Both the domain and range of the parent cube root function are the set of all real numbers just like the parent cubic function.

The table represents some values of the parent cube root function $g(x) = \sqrt[3]{x}$.

x	−27	−8	−1	0	1	8	27
$g(x) = \sqrt[3]{x}$	−3	−2	−1	0	1	2	3

You can use the ordered pairs from the table to sketch a graph of g.

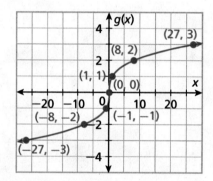

1. Summarize the characteristics of the graph of the parent cube root function.

   A. What are the domain and range of the parent cube root function?

   B. What are the intercepts of the parent cube root function?

   C. Is the function increasing or decreasing? Where is it positive? Where is it negative?

   D. Does the parent cube root function have any maximum or minimum values? Explain your answer.

   E. Describe the end behavior of the function.

   F. Describe the rate of change as x increases over the interval $(-\infty, 0)$. Describe the rate of change as x increases over the interval $(0, +\infty)$.

> **Turn and Talk** How does knowing the key features of the graph of the function $f(x) = x^3$ help you understand the graph of $g(x) = \sqrt[3]{x}$?

Transformations of the Parent Cube Root Function

The transformations discussed in the previous lesson have the same effect on the parent cube root function. The specific transformations can be determined by identifying the parameters a, b, h, and k when a cube root function is written in either of these forms:

$$g(x) = a\sqrt[3]{x - h} + k \text{ or } g(x) = \sqrt[3]{\frac{1}{b}(x - h)} + k.$$

The parent square root function $f(x) = \sqrt[3]{x}$ is shown in each of the following figures.

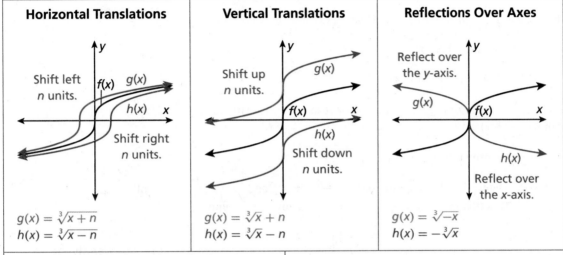

Horizontal Translations

Shift left n units.

Shift right n units.

$g(x) = \sqrt[3]{x + n}$
$h(x) = \sqrt[3]{x - n}$

Vertical Translations

Shift up n units.

Shift down n units.

$g(x) = \sqrt[3]{x} + n$
$h(x) = \sqrt[3]{x} - n$

Reflections Over Axes

Reflect over the y-axis.

Reflect over the x-axis.

$g(x) = \sqrt[3]{-x}$
$h(x) = -\sqrt[3]{x}$

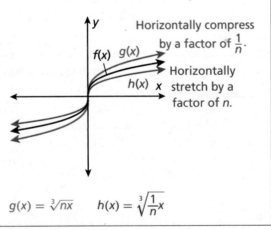

Vertical Stretches or Compressions

Vertically stretch by a factor of n.

Vertically compress by a factor of $\frac{1}{n}$.

$g(x) = n\sqrt[3]{x}$ $h(x) = \frac{1}{n}\sqrt[3]{x}$

Horizontal Stretches or Compressions

Horizontally compress by a factor of $\frac{1}{n}$.

Horizontally stretch by a factor of n.

$g(x) = \sqrt[3]{nx}$ $h(x) = \sqrt[3]{\frac{1}{n}x}$

2 For each cube root function, identify the values of a, b, h, and k. Then describe the effect that each parameter has on the graph of the function as compared to the parent cube root function. Use a graphing tool to check your responses.

A. $f(x) = \sqrt[3]{x} - 4$

B. $f(x) = \sqrt[3]{x - 1}$

C. $f(x) = 6\sqrt[3]{x}$

D. $f(x) = \sqrt[3]{\frac{1}{2}x}$

E. $f(x) = -\frac{1}{5}\sqrt[3]{x}$

F. $f(x) = \sqrt[3]{-x}$

Turn and Talk Could every graph of a function with a cube root be described as a transformation of the graph of the parent cube root function $f(x) = \sqrt[3]{x}$? Explain.

Step It Out

Graph Cube Root Functions

Analyzing the effect of transformations on the points $(-1, -1)$, $(0, 0)$, and $(1, 1)$ on the graph of the parent cube root function $f(x) = \sqrt[3]{x}$ identifies three corresponding points on the graph of any cube root function.

For cube root functions of the form $g(x) = a\sqrt[3]{x - h} + k$, the mappings are

$(-1, -1) \rightarrow (h - 1, k - a)$, $(0, 0) \rightarrow (h, k)$, and $(1, 1) \rightarrow (h + 1, k + a)$.

For cube root functions of the form $g(x) = \sqrt[3]{\frac{1}{b}(x - h)} + k$, the mappings are

$(-1, -1) \rightarrow (h - b, k - 1)$, $(0, 0) \rightarrow (h, k)$, and $(1, 1) \rightarrow (h + b, k + 1)$.

3 Sketch the graph of $g(x) = \sqrt[3]{\frac{1}{2}(x - 4)} + 1$ using transformations of the graph of $f(x) = \sqrt[3]{x}$.

Step 1: Identify the values of b, h, and k. $b = 2$, $h = 4$, $k = 1$

Step 2: Determine the mapping of $(-1, -1)$, $(0, 0)$, and $(1, 1)$ on the parent function f to their corresponding points on the graph of g.

$(-1, -1) \rightarrow (h - b, k - 1) = (4 - 2, 1 - 1) = (2, 0)$

$(0, 0) \rightarrow (h, k) = (4, 1)$

$(1, 1) \rightarrow (h + b, k + 1) = (4 + 2, 1 + 1) = (6, 2)$

> **A.** How does the mapping of $(0, 0)$ identify the translations of the parent graph needed to graph the function g?

Step 3: Determine a few other points on the graph of g. The value of k indicates that the graph shifts 1 unit up. The points $(-8, -2)$ and $(8, 2)$ are on the graph of the parent function f. Due to the 1-unit shift up, the corresponding points on the graph of g will have y-coordinates of -1 and 3. Use those values of y to determine their corresponding x-coordinates in the function g.

$$-1 = \sqrt[3]{\frac{1}{2}(x - 4)} + 1 \rightarrow (-2)^3 = \frac{1}{2}(x - 4) \rightarrow -16 = x - 4 \rightarrow -12 = x$$

$$3 = \sqrt[3]{\frac{1}{2}(x - 4)} + 1 \rightarrow (2)^3 = \frac{1}{2}(x - 4) \rightarrow 16 = x - 4 \rightarrow 20 = x$$

Step 4: To sketch the graph of g, plot the points $(2, 0)$, $(4, 1)$, $(6, 2)$, $(-12, -1)$, and $(20, 3)$. Then draw a smooth curve through the points.

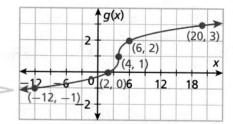

> **B.** How can the graph be used to verify that the correct transformations are shown?

> **Turn and Talk** How can you use the symmetry of the graph of a cube root function to verify the plotted points on the graph of the function g?

Write a Cube Root Function for a Graph

Given the graph of a cube root function, you can determine the parameters h, k, and a or b for the function by considering the mapping of the points $(-1, -1)$, $(0, 0)$, and $(1, 1)$ on the parent function to their corresponding points on the given graph.

- The point (h, k) is the mapping of the point $(0, 0)$ on the parent function. These points are the point of rotational symmetry for their respective graphs.

- Parameter a can be determined by examining the vertical change from the point (h, k) to the point $(h + 1, a + k)$, if that point is identified on the graph.

- Parameter b can be determined by examining the horizontal change from the point (h, k) to the point $(b + h, k + 1)$, if that point is identified on the graph.

4 ▶ Write the cube root function for the graph shown.

The point of rotational symmetry (h, k) is $(-2, -3)$; so $h = -2$ and $k = -3$.

To determine the value of a, look for a point with an x-coordinate of $h + 1 = -2 + 1 = -1$. Use the point $(-1, 7)$.

$(h + 1, a + k) \rightarrow (-1, -7)$, so $a + k = -7$; since $k = -3$, then $a = -4$.

> **A.** Can the value of b be determined? Explain.

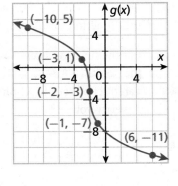

The equation of the function has the form $g(x) = a\sqrt[3]{x - h} + k$.

Using the values of a, h, and k, the function is $g(x) = -4\sqrt[3]{x + 2} - 3$.

> **B.** What transformations of the parent function created the graph of g?

 Turn and Talk Which types of transformations do you think are the most difficult to identify from the graph of a cube root function?

Model a Real-World Situation with a Cube Root Function

5 ▶ The graph at the right shows the cube root function $s(w) = \sqrt[3]{400w}$, which models the power w (in watts) for maintaining a constant cycling speed s (in kilometers per hour) when riding into a headwind.

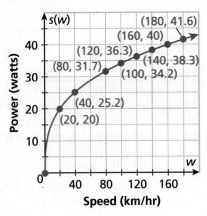

w	20	40	80	100	120	140	160	180
s(w)	20	25.2	31.7	34.2	36.3	38.3	40	41.6

A. What are the average rates of change for the first and last intervals in the table?

B. Using the graph, describe the overall rate of change in the context of the situation.

Check Understanding

For Problems 1–5, use the graph of the cube root function
$f(x) = \sqrt[3]{x-6} + 1$.

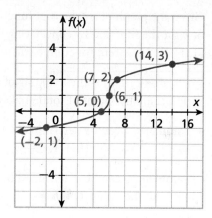

1. What are the domain and range of function f?

2. Is $f(x)$ positive or negative for values of $x < 5$?

3. Does the function f have any maximum or minimum values?

4. Describe the end behavior of f.

5. Describe the rate of change of $f(x)$ as x increases.

6. Describe each transformation of the graph of the parent cube root function for the graph of the function $g(x) = \sqrt[3]{\frac{1}{8}x} - 4$.

7. For the function $g(x) = 4\sqrt[3]{x+3} - 5$, identify the points to which the points $(-8, -2)$, $(-1, -1)$, $(0, 0)$, $(1, 1)$, and $(8, 2)$ of the parent cube root function are mapped. Then graph the function to verify your work.

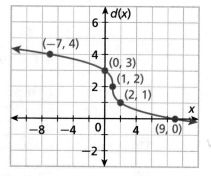

8. What function of the form $d(x) = a\sqrt[3]{x-h} + k$ is represented by the graph at the right?

9. The function $B(y) = 540\sqrt[3]{y+4}$ models the predicted number of bikes B sold in a year, where y is the number of years after the company started manufacturing bikes. Using the context of the situation, describe the overall rate of change shown in the table.

y	1	2	3	4	5	6	7	8	9	10
$B(y)$	923	981	1033	1080	1123	1163	1201	1236	1270	1301

On Your Own

For Problems 10–14, use the graph of the function
$h(x) = -\sqrt[3]{4x} - 6$ shown at the right.

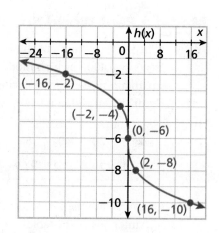

10. (MP) **Use Structure** What is the point of rotational symmetry?

11. Is $h(x)$ positive or negative for values of $x > 0$?

12. Is $h(x)$ increasing or decreasing?

13. Describe the end behavior of h.

14. What are the average rates of change between $x = 0$ and $x = 2$ and between $x = 2$ and $x = 16$?

For Problems 15–19, use the graph of the cube root function $j(x) = \sqrt[3]{-x+4} - 2$.

15. **(MP) Use Structure** What is the point of rotational symmetry?

16. Is $j(x)$ positive or negative for values of $x < -4$?

17. Is $j(x)$ increasing or decreasing?

18. Describe the end behavior of $j(x)$.

19. What are the average rates of change between $x = 3$ and $x = 5$ and between $x = 5$ and $x = 12$?

Describe the transformations of the graph of the parent cube root function that result in the graph of the given function.

20. $f(x) = -\dfrac{1}{6}\sqrt[3]{x} + 4$
21. $f(x) = \sqrt[3]{-4x} + 2$
22. $f(x) = 8\sqrt[3]{x+7} - 9$

For Problems 23–25, use the function $g(x) = -2\sqrt[3]{x-4} + 2$.

23. Where do the points $(0, 0)$, $(-1, -1)$, and $(1, 1)$ on the graph of the cube root parent function get mapped to on the graph of g?

24. Where do the points $(-8, -2)$ and $(8, 2)$ on the graph of the cube root parent function get mapped to on the graph of g?

25. Draw the graph of g and use it to confirm that the value of the function is negative for $x > 5$.

26. The height of an elephant is measured to its shoulder. The shoulder height h (in centimeters) of a particular elephant is modeled by the function $h(t) = 62.1\sqrt[3]{t} + 76$, where t is the age (in years) of the elephant.

    Create a table of values for the function by calculating the height for ages of 0, 10, 20, 30, and 40 years. Calculate the average rates of change over the first and last intervals, and explain what these rates of change represent.

For Problems 27–29, use the function $g(x) = \sqrt[3]{-(x+5)} - 6$.

27. Where do the points $(0, 0)$, $(-1, -1)$, and $(1, 1)$ on the graph of the cube root parent function get mapped to on the graph of g?

28. Where do the points $(-8, -2)$, and $(8, 2)$ on the graph of the cube root parent function get mapped to on the graph of g?

29. Draw the graph of g and use it to confirm that the value of the function is negative for $-13 < x < 3$.

30. Identify the values of a, b, h, and k for $g(x)$. Then describe the effect that each parameter has on the graph of $g(x)$ as compared to the parent cube root function.

31. The interior of Earth is composed of multiple layers. Because the layers differ in density, there is no single model for Earth's mass as a function of the distance from its center. However, an approximate model for a single layer can be developed. Modeling Earth's mass m (in kg) as a function of its radius r (in km) for values of r that give the boundary distances from Earth's center corresponding to the lower mantle and then taking the inverse gives the function $r(m) \approx 0.000036\sqrt[3]{m - 1.1 \times 10^{24}}$ for $2.0 \times 10^{24} \leq m \leq 5.1 \times 10^{24}$.

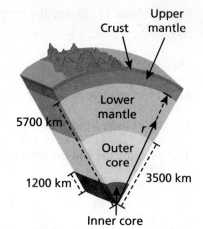

A. What does the function model mean in this context?

B. The core (outer core and inner core combined) has a mass of about 2×10^{24} kg. Substitute this value for m in $r(m)$. Why does the result make sense?

Write a cube root function that represents the graph.

32.

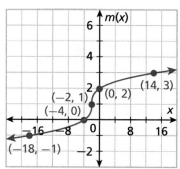

33.

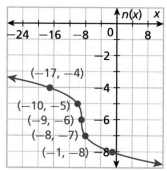

Spiral Review • Assessment Readiness

34. How many solutions does the equation $3 = \sqrt{8 + x}$ have?

  Ⓐ 0   Ⓒ 2

  Ⓑ 1   Ⓓ 3

35. The graph of $g(x)$ is obtained by translating the graph of $f(x) = \sqrt{x}$ two units to the right. What is $g(x)$?

  Ⓐ $g(x) = \sqrt{x - 2}$

  Ⓑ $g(x) = \sqrt{x} - 2$

  Ⓒ $g(x) = \sqrt{x + 2}$

  Ⓓ $g(x) = \sqrt{x} + 2$

36. Which function is the inverse of $f(x) = (x + 3)^2 + 5$?

  Ⓐ $f^{-1}(x) = \sqrt{x - 5} - 3$

  Ⓑ $f^{-1}(x) = \sqrt{x + 5} - 3$

  Ⓒ $f^{-1}(x) = \sqrt{x - 5} + 3$

  Ⓓ $f^{-1}(x) = \sqrt{x + 5} + 3$

37 Which equation represents the inverse of $f(x) = 6x - 5$?

  Ⓐ $y = 6x - 30$ Ⓒ $y = 6x + 30$

  Ⓑ $y = \frac{1}{6}x - 5$ Ⓓ $y = \frac{1}{6}x + \frac{5}{6}$

 I'm in a Learning Mindset!

How did an initial failure when writing an equation from the graph of a cubic function lead to learning growth?

Solve Radical Equations

(I Can) solve radical equations, including those with the variable on both sides.

Spark Your Learning

Two people jump off a platform in a lake and swim to shore at a right angle to one another. They swim to opposite ends of one of the lake's beach areas.

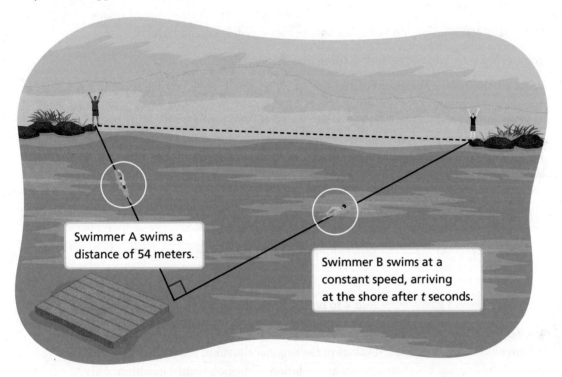

Swimmer A swims a distance of 54 meters.

Swimmer B swims at a constant speed, arriving at the shore after t seconds.

Complete Part A as a whole class. Then complete Parts B–D in small groups.

A. What is a mathematical question you can ask about this situation? What information would you need to know to answer your question?

B. What variables are involved in this situation? What unit of measurement would you use for each variable?

C. To answer your question, what strategy and tool would you use along with all the information you have? What answer do you get?

D. Does the answer make sense in the context of the situation? How do you know?

Turn and Talk Predict how the result would change for each of the following changes in the situation:

- The length of the beach area is 100 meters.
- Swimmer B swims at a speed of 1 meter per second.

Build Understanding

Solve Radical Equations

Recall that square root equations are inverses of quadratic equations. Equations involving a square root are just one type in a group of equations called radical equations. Radical equations have 0, 1, or 2 real solutions.

> **Connect to Vocabulary**
>
> You have worked with a variety of equation types. A **radical equation** is an equation that contains a variable within a radical.

1 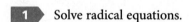 Solve radical equations.

A. How many real solutions do you think square root equations could have?

You can solve square root equations using inverse operations.

B. What are the inverse operations of addition, division, and taking a square root?

When you solve the radical equation $\sqrt{x-4} - 3 = 0$, you will be squaring both sides. Before squaring, you first want to isolate the radical. It is easier to square both sides of the equation $\sqrt{x-4} = 3$ than both sides of the equation $\sqrt{x-4} - 3 = 0$.

$\sqrt{x-4} - 3 = 0$	Given
$x - 4 = 3$	Add 3 to both sides of the equation.
$\left(\sqrt{x-4}\right)^2 = (3)^2$	Square both sides of the equation.
$x - 4 = 9$	Simplify.
$x = 13$	Add 4 to both sides of the equation.

The same algebraic steps that lead to easier polynomial equations can also eliminate information about the excluded values of the original equation. Sometimes an excluded value of the original equation appears as a solution of the polynomial equation. This excluded value is an extraneous solution of the polynomial equation. Extraneous solutions are not solutions of the original equation.

Check each solution to confirm it is a true solution and not extraneous. Substituting 13 for x in the original equation yields $\sqrt{13-4} - 3 = 0$, which is true. So, 13 is a solution.

C. How many solutions does the equation have? How do you know?

Solve Radical Equations Using Graphs

You can also use a graphing calculator to determine the solution of a radical equation.

2 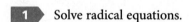 Enter each side of the equation $\sqrt{x-4} = 3$ as a function into a graphing calculator.

Enter: $y = 3$

Enter: $y = \sqrt{x-4}$

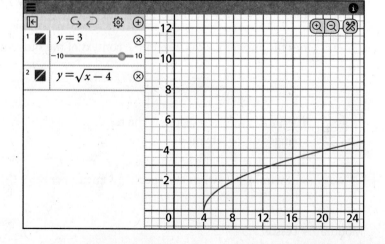

A. Does the graph show the same solution found in Task 1? Explain your answer.

The radical equation $\sqrt{x-2}+1=0$ can be solved algebraically.

$$\sqrt{x-2}+1=0$$

$$\sqrt{x-2}=-1$$

$$\left(\sqrt{x-2}\right)^{2}=(-1)^{2}$$

$$x-2=1$$

$$x=3$$

A solution found algebraically must be checked to be sure it is not an extraneous solution. Substitute 3 for x in the original equation.

$$\sqrt{3-2}+1=0 \rightarrow \sqrt{1}+1=0 \rightarrow 2\neq 0$$

B. How many solutions does the equation have? How do you know?

When using a graphing calculator to solve the equation $\sqrt{x-2}+1=0$, it can be helpful to isolate the radical. Then enter each side of the resulting equation into the graphing calculator.

Enter: $y=-1$

Enter: $y=\sqrt{x-2}$

[graphing calculator screen showing: 1. $y=-1$ with slider from -10 to 10; 2. $y=\sqrt{x-2}$; with a grid graph]

C. Does the graph show the same solution as the algebraic process? Explain.

Solve the equation $\sqrt{5x-6}-x=0$ algebraically.

$$\sqrt{5x-6}-x=0$$

$$\sqrt{5x-6}=x$$

$$0=x^{2}-5x+6$$

$$0=(x-2)(x-3)$$

$$x=2 \text{ or } x=3$$

Check the solutions: $\sqrt{5(2)-6}-2=0$ and $\sqrt{5(3)-6}-3=0$.

D. How many solutions does the equation have? How do you know?

Turn and Talk When solving a radical equation using a graphing calculator, is it mandatory that the radical be isolated? Explain.

Step It Out

Solve Square Root Equations

Algebraically, you can solve square root equations by isolating the radical expression and then squaring both sides of the equation. Squaring the expressions on both sides can introduce solutions that do not satisfy the original equation, so always remember to check each solution to see if it is an extraneous solution.

In Module 6, you learned to rewrite radical expressions using rational exponents. This skill can also be utilized when solving radical equations.

3 ▶ Here are two ways to write and solve the equation $\sqrt{4x + 9} - 1 = x$ algebraically.

$\sqrt{4x + 9} - 1 = x$	Given	$(4x + 9)^{\frac{1}{2}} - 1 = x$
$\sqrt{4x + 9} = x + 1$	Isolate the radical.	$(4x + 9)^{\frac{1}{2}} = x + 1$
$\left(\sqrt{4x + 9}\right)^2 = (x + 1)^2$	Square both sides.	$\left[(4x + 9)^{\frac{1}{2}}\right]^2 = (x + 1)^2$
$4x + 9 = x^2 + 2x + 1$	Definition of squaring	$4x + 9 = x^2 + 2x + 1$
$0 = x^2 - 2x - 8$	Combine like terms.	$0 = x^2 - 2x - 8$
$0 = (x + 2)(x - 4)$	Factor.	$0 = (x + 2)(x - 4)$
$x = -2$ or 4	Zero Product Rule	$x = -2$ or 4

Use both algebra and a graphing calculator to check for extraneous solutions.

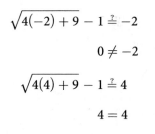

$\sqrt{4(-2) + 9} - 1 \overset{?}{=} -2$

$0 \neq -2$

$\sqrt{4(4) + 9} - 1 \overset{?}{=} 4$

$4 = 4$

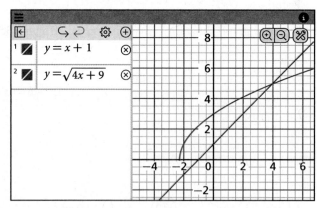

A. What can you conclude about the solution to the equation $\sqrt{4x + 9} - 1 = x$?

B. Describe how solving the equations written in different ways are similar and how they are different.

C. Which way of writing and solving the equation do you prefer? Justify your answer.

 Turn and Talk How does your approach to solving $\sqrt{x + 5} = a$ vary for different values of a?

Solve Cube Root Equations

4 ▶ Here are two ways to write and solve the equation $\sqrt[3]{2x+6}+4=0$

$\sqrt[3]{2x+6}+4=0$	Given	$(2x+6)^{\frac{1}{3}}+4=0$
$\sqrt[3]{2x+6}=-4$	Isolate the radical.	$(2x+6)^{\frac{1}{3}}=-4$
$\left(\sqrt[3]{2x+6}\right)^3=-4^3$	Cube both sides.	$\left[(2x+6)^{\frac{1}{3}}\right]^3=(-4)^3$
$2x+6=-64$	Definition of cubing	$2x+6=-64$
$2x=-70$	Combine like terms.	$2x=-70$
$x=-35$	Divide by 2.	$x=-35$

Use both algebra and a graphing calculator to check for extraneous solutions.

$\sqrt[3]{2(-35)+6}+4=0$

$\sqrt[3]{-70+6}+4=0$

$\sqrt[3]{-64}+4=0$

$-4+4=0$

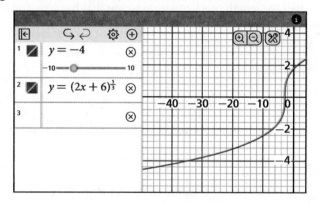

A. What can you conclude about the solution to the equation $\sqrt[3]{2x+6}+4=0$?

B. Describe how solving the equations is similar and how it is different.

C. Which way of writing and solving the equation do you prefer?

 Turn and Talk Can a cube root equation have any extraneous solutions?

Radical Equations in the Real-World

5 ▶ Ciera is building a rectangular shed with her mom. The length needs to be twice the width. They need to know the area of the base of the shed in order to estimate the cost of the foundation. They also need to know the length and the width to estimate the cost of a rubber mat. The function $P(a)=6\sqrt{\frac{a}{2}}$ gives the perimeter (in feet) of the shed based on its area a (in square feet).

Determine the area of the base of the shed when its perimeter is 48 feet.

$48=6\sqrt{\frac{a}{2}}$	Replace $P(a)$ with 48.
$8=\sqrt{\frac{a}{2}}$	Divide both sides by 6.
$(8)^2=\left(\sqrt{\frac{a}{2}}\right)^2$	Square both sides.
$64=\frac{a}{2}$	Simplify.
$128=a$	Multiply both sides by 2.

A. What does the solution mean in the context of the situation? Graph $P(a)$ and the line $y=48$ on a graphing calculator to verify the solution.

B. What are the width and length of the shed?

Check Understanding

1. Solve the equation $\sqrt{x+6} - 2 = 0$. Justify each step.

2. Solve the equation $\sqrt{2x} - 1 = 0$. What would a graph of the solution look like? Explain.

3. Solve the equation $\sqrt[3]{8x-3} + 3 = 0$. What would a graph of the solution look like? Explain.

4. Students are observing the effects of increasing and decreasing the length of a pendulum's string on the pendulum's period. The period of a pendulum is one back-and-forth swing. The function $P(L) = 1.11\sqrt{L}$ gives the period P (in seconds) of a pendulum as a function of the length L (in feet) of the pendulum's string. How many times greater is the length of a pendulum string that has a period of 2.72 seconds than the length of a pendulum string that has a period of 2.22 seconds? How do you know?

On Your Own

5. **(MP) Reason** What was done to $4\sqrt[3]{x-1} - 8 = 0$ to obtain $4\sqrt[3]{x-1} = 8$?

6. **(MP) Reason** What was done to $\sqrt[3]{x-1} = 2$ to obtain $x - 1 = 8$?

7. **(MP) Reason** What was done to $x - 1 = 8$ to obtain $x = 9$?

8. **(MP) Reason** Is $x = 9$ the solution to the equation $4\sqrt[3]{x-1} - 8 = 0$? Why or why not?

9. What possible number of solutions can a radical equation of the form $\sqrt{x-a} = b$ have? Use characteristics of graphs to support your reasoning.

10. Solve the equation $\sqrt{x-5} + 9 = 0$. Justify each step.

11. How many solutions does the equation $\sqrt{x-5} + 9 = 0$ have?

12. Does your solution for the equation $\sqrt{x-5} + 9 = 0$ in Problem 10 match the solution found using a graphing calculator as shown below? Explain.

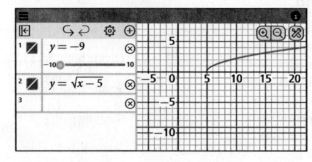

13. **(MP) Reason** Solve the equation $2\sqrt[3]{x-4} - 6 = 0$. Justify each step.

14. How many solutions does the equation $2\sqrt[3]{x-4} - 6 = 0$ have?

15. Does your solution for the equation $2\sqrt[3]{x-4}-6=0$ in Problem 13 match the solution found using a graphing calculator as shown below? Explain.

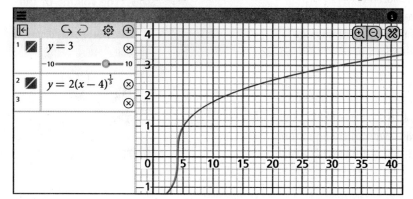

16. A. (MP) **Reason** Solve the equation $\sqrt{6x-8}-x=0$. Justify each step.

B. How many solutions does the equation $\sqrt{6x-8}-x=0$ have?

C. Does your solution for the equation $\sqrt{6x-8}-x=0$ match the solution found using a graphing calculator as shown at the right? Explain.

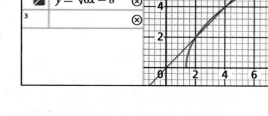

17. A cliff is eroding from wind damage. The function $v(d)=\sqrt{19.6d}$ gives the velocity in meters per second of a rock that has fallen d meters. If a certain rock travels faster than 60 meters per second, it will break into smaller pieces upon impact. Determine the maximum falling height at which the rock will stay intact. Justify each step. Explain how you can verify the solution using a graphing calculator.

For Problems 18–26, solve the equation.

18. $\sqrt{-x+1}-6=0$

19. $(2x-5)^{\frac{1}{2}}-7=0$

20. $\sqrt{3x-6}+4=0$

21. $(-5x+4)^{\frac{1}{2}}-8=0$

22. $\sqrt{x+6}-x=0$

23. $\sqrt{7x-9}+2=0$

24. $\sqrt[3]{x+4}-1=0$

25. $6(x+4)^{\frac{1}{3}}-24=0$

26. $(2x+10)^{\frac{1}{3}}-4=0$

27. Health and Fitness A triathlete is training for the swimming and running portions of an upcoming triathlon. She plans to swim and run a total of 10 miles today. She begins at the end of a jetty that extends out into the ocean and swims at an angle toward the beach, aiming for a point that she has estimated will make her time swimming and running approximately the same. Her expected rate of swimming is 2 mi/h and her expected rate of running is 8 mi/h. For what value of x will her time swimming and her time running be equal?

28. Janet's necklace has a fluorite crystal in the shape of a regular octahedron. The function $V(s) = \frac{\sqrt{2}}{3}s^3$ gives the volume (in cubic millimeters) of a regular octahedron as a function of the length of its edge (in millimeters). What is the length of one of the edges of Janet's fluorite crystal?

The volume of the crystal is 1290 mm³.

29. (Open Middle™) Copy the equations below on your own paper. Using the digits 1 to 9, at most one time each, fill in the boxes to create two radical equations, one with an extraneous solution and one with a real solution.

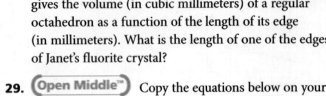

$$\sqrt{\left(\boxed{}x + \boxed{}\right)} + \boxed{} = \boxed{}$$

$$\sqrt{\left(\boxed{}x + \boxed{}\right)} + \boxed{} = \boxed{}$$

Spiral Review • Assessment Readiness

30. Lou is going to invest $500 for 3 years in a bank account that pays an annual interest rate compounded annually. The value V of the account after 3 years can be represented by the function $V(r) = 500(1 + r)^3$. Use the inverse function of $V(r)$ to determine the annual interest rate r needed for the value of the investment to be $562.

(A) 0.4%   (C) 4%

(B) 1.4%   (D) 14%

31. Which function represents a vertical stretch by a factor of 2 on the parent square root function?

(A) $g(x) = -\sqrt{2x}$ (C) $g(x) = 2\sqrt{x}$

(B) $g(x) = -\sqrt{\frac{1}{2}x}$ (D) $g(x) = \frac{1}{2}\sqrt{x}$

32. Which function represents a reflection across the x-axis on the cube root parent function?

(A) $g(x) = -\sqrt[3]{x}$ (C) $g(x) = \frac{-\sqrt[3]{x}}{3}$

(B) $g(x) = \sqrt[3]{-x}$ (D) $g(x) = \frac{\sqrt[3]{x}}{3}$

33. Which ordered pairs belong to the function $f(x) = 3(2)^x$? Select all that apply.

(A) $(0, 0)$

(B) $(1, 6)$

(C) $(3, 18)$

(D) $(4, 48)$

(E) $(5, 96)$

(F) $(6, 46{,}656)$

I'm in a Learning Mindset!

Where do I need to improve when working with square root and cube root functions?

Composition of Functions

Composition of two functions combines two functions by using the output of one function as the input of the other function.

The mapping below shows the process for evaluating the composition $(f \circ g)(x)$:

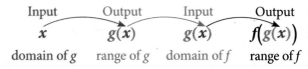

Inverses of Functions

Inverse functions undo each other because the domains and ranges are switched.

$f(x)$		$f^{-1}(x)$	
Domain	**Range**	**Domain**	**Range**

-2	-10	-10	-2
-1	-5	-5	-1
0	0	0	0
1	5	5	1
2	10	10	2

Inverse of a Quadratic Function

The inverse of the parent quadratic function $f(x) = x^2$ when $x \geq 0$ is the parent square root function $g(x) = \sqrt{x}$. In general, the inverse of a quadratic function is a square root function.

The graphs of the two parent functions are shown below.

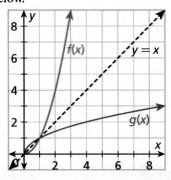

Inverse of a Cubic Function

The inverse of the parent cubic function $f(x) = x^3$ is the parent cube root function $g(x) = \sqrt[3]{x}$. In general, the inverse of a cubic function is a cube root function.

The graphs of the two parent functions are shown below.

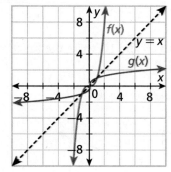

Solve Radical Equations

Radical equations can be solved algebraically by using inverse operations. When squaring both sides of a radical equation involving a square root, an extraneous root may result. So, all possible solutions must be checked in the original equation.

Radical equations can also be solved graphically by graphing both sides of the equation on a coordinate grid and using their point of intersection.

Vocabulary

Choose the correct term from the box to complete each sentence.

1. The ___?___ is the inverse function of the parent cubic function.

2. The ___?___ creates a new function by using the output of one function as the input of another function.

3. A ___?___ contains at least one term having a variable within a radical.

4. The ___?___ is the inverse function of the parent quadratic function.

Concepts and Skills

5. Let $h(x) = 2x^2 - 4x + 6$ and $k(x) = x - 7$. Evaluate $(h \circ k)(3)$ and $(k \circ h)(3)$.

6. Let $f(x) = -x^2 + 2x - 1$ and $g(x) = 2x + 4$. Evaluate $(f \circ g)(-2)$ and $(g \circ f)(-2)$.

7. Let $j(x) = 4x - 10$ and $k(x) = 5 - x^2$. Evaluate $(j \circ k)(4)$ and $(k \circ j)(4)$.

8. Let $f(x) = 3x - 4$ and $g(x) = x^2 + 10$. Write $(f \circ g)(x)$ and $(g \circ f)(x)$, and state their domains and ranges.

For Problems 9–12, determine the inverse function for each function.

9. $f(x) = 3x^2 - 6, x \geq 0$

10. $g(x) = -x^2 + 4, x \leq 0$

11. $h(x) = 4x^3 - 9$

12. $j(x) = -(x + 8)^3$

13. What transformations of $f(x) = \sqrt{x}$ result in the function $f(x) = \sqrt{\frac{1}{2}(x + 1)} - 4$?

14. What transformations of $f(x) = \sqrt[3]{x}$ result in the function $f(x) = 2\sqrt[3]{-x} + 3$?

For Problems 15 and 16, write the function whose graph is shown. Use the function form specified.

15. $g(x) = a\sqrt{x - h} + k$

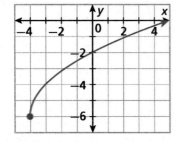

16. $g(x) = \sqrt[3]{\frac{1}{b}(x - h)} + k$

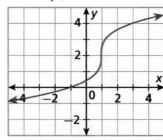

17. (MP) **Use Tools** The function $A(H) = 0.00718(W)^{0.425}(H)^{0.725}$ gives the area A (in square meters) of body surface where W is a person's weight (in kilograms) and H is the person's height (in centimeters). Jake weighs 90.7 kg and his body surface area is approximately 2.13 m². Use a graphing calculator to determine his height. State what strategy and tool you will use to answer the question, explain your choice, and then find the answer.

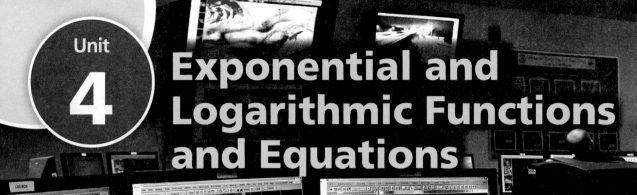

Unit 4
Exponential and Logarithmic Functions and Equations

(t) ©John Tlumacki/The Boston Globe/Getty Images; (b) ©Jaroslava V/Shutterstock

Meteorologist

Meteorologists study the continual changes in Earth's atmosphere to explain observed patterns of weather and predict future events. These scientists use data and physical principles to understand the relationship between the different measurable variables that impact weather trends over scales of mere minutes to over the span of several years.

STEM Task

Meteorologists approximate the dewpoint temperature in degrees Celsius, T_d, using the following rule:

> T_d decreases approximately 1 °C for every 5% decrease in the relative humidity, H.

Starting with the dry-bulb temperature of the air $T_d = C$ when $H = 100\%$, write a formula that approximates the dewpoint temperature $T_d(C, H)$.

Learning Mindset

Challenge-Seeking Sets Achievable Stretch Goals

It is important to identify goals for what you want to learn. These should include both short-term and long-term goals. Short-term goals help you stay positive by finding repeated success, while long-term goals provide motivation for self-improvement. You want to make sure that your goals challenge you to grow and learn but are not so challenging that they are unachievable. You may need to revise your goals as you move through the learning process. Here are some questions you can ask yourself as you set goals in your learning on this task:

- What is my long-term learning goal to improve my understanding of exponential and logarithmic functions? How will I grow as a result of this goal?

- What short-term goals can help me reach my long-term goal? How does each success with my short-term goals support my long-term learning goal?

- Are my goals achievable? Do I have enough time to reach each goal? How can I modify my goals to make sure they are achievable?

- How can I use goal-setting as I collaborate with others?

Reflect

Q What goals did you set to guide your learning? Did you meet those goals? Were they challenging enough?

Q Imagine you are a meteorologist. What are some short-term and long-term goals that might motivate your work?

8 Exponential Functions

Module Performance Task: *Spies and Analysts*™

Interest of Time

How much is $1,000,000 from
1960 worth now?

1960

Today

©Hero Images/Getty Images

Are You Ready?

Complete these problems to review prior concepts and skills you will need for this module.

Percent Increase and Decrease

Find each percent of increase or decrease.

1. A clothing store buys shirts for $15 and then sells them for $45. What is the percent increase in the price of the shirt?

2. Martin bought a basketball on sale for $38.50. The original price was $55. What is the percent decrease in price?

3. Jeanie made $10 an hour and received a $1.50-per-hour raise. What is the percent increase in her salary?

4. Ben scored 100% on his first test in science class. He scored 76% on the second test. What is the percent decrease in his scores?

Evaluate Expressions with Exponents

Evaluate each expression. Write your answer in exponential form.

5. $3^2 \cdot 3^5 \cdot 3^3$

6. $\dfrac{3^2 \cdot 3^5}{3^4}$

7. $\dfrac{x^4 \cdot y^3}{x^5 y^2}$

8. $x^4 \cdot y^3 \cdot x^2 \cdot y$

Graph Exponential Functions

Graph each exponential function.

9. $f(x) = 3(2)^x$

10. $f(x) = \dfrac{1}{3}(2)^x$

Connecting Past and Present Learning

Previously, you learned:

- to solve equations after using properties to rewrite them,
- to graph transformations of the parent function $f(x) = x$, and
- to graph exponential functions of the form $f(x) = ab^x$.

In this module, you will learn:

- to solve real-world problems involving exponential equations,
- to use exponential functions to model growth and decay,
- to use the natural base e to graph exponential functions, and
- to apply the compound interest formula in different real-world scenarios.

Exponential Growth and Decay Functions

(I Can) identify the effect of transformations on exponential functions to model situations of growth and decay.

Spark Your Learning

Chemical reactions occur at varying rates, depending on the molecules present, the pressure, the temperature, and other factors. Models for different reactions may belong to different function families.

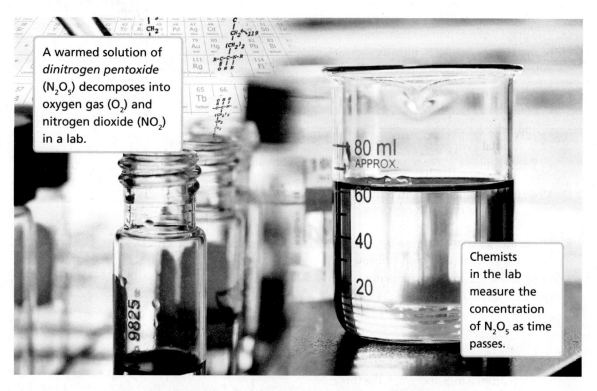

A warmed solution of *dinitrogen pentoxide* (N_2O_5) decomposes into oxygen gas (O_2) and nitrogen dioxide (NO_2) in a lab.

Chemists in the lab measure the concentration of N_2O_5 as time passes.

Complete Part A as a whole class. Then complete Parts B–D in small groups.

   A. What is a mathematical question you can ask about this situation? What information would you need to know to answer your question?

   B. How can you use the data to construct a model?

   C. To answer your question, what strategy and tool would you use along with all the information you have? What answer do you get?

   D. Does any kind of a polynomial model make sense? Justify your reasoning.

 Turn and Talk Select two points. What is the average rate of change? How does your choice of points affect the rate?

Build Understanding

Analyze Exponential Growth and Decay

An **exponential function** is a function of the form $f(x) = b^x$ where b is a positive constant other than 1 and the exponent x is a variable. The function represents **exponential growth** when $b > 1$ and **exponential decay** when $0 < b < 1$.

1 ▶ **A.** Consider the exponential functions $f(x) = 2^x$ and $g(x) = \left(\frac{1}{2}\right)^x$. Which function's values increase as the value of x increases? Which function's values decrease as the value of x increases?

B. Complete the tables of values shown at the right for $f(x)$ and $g(x)$.

C. The graphs of $f(x)$ and $g(x)$ are shown below. Use the graphs to identify the following key characteristics of each function:

- domain and range
- end behavior
- horizontal asymptote
- y-intercept

D. Describe the similarities and differences of the graphs of $f(x)$ and $g(x)$.

E. Using the key characteristics from Part C, what generalizations can you make about the general exponential function $f(x) = b^x$ where b is any positive real number other than 1?

F. For the functions $f(x) = 2x$, $g(x) = x^2$, and $h(x) = 2^x$, make a table of values for x-values from 0 to 5 and graph the three functions on the same coordinate plane. Describe what you observe as the values of x increase.

x	$f(x) = 2^x$
−3	$\frac{1}{8}$
−2	$\frac{1}{4}$
−1	$\frac{1}{2}$
0	?
1	?
2	?
3	?

x	$g(x) = \left(\frac{1}{2}\right)^x$
−3	8
−2	?
−1	?
0	1
1	$\frac{1}{2}$
2	?
3	?

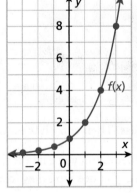

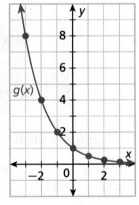

G. Find and compare the rate of change for $f(x)$ and the average rates of change for $g(x)$ and $h(x)$ for each two consecutive values of x in your table in Part F.

 Turn and Talk How would the graph of $h(x) = 10^x$ compare to the graph of $f(x) = 2^x$? How would the graph of $j(x) = \left(\frac{1}{10}\right)^x$ compare to the graph of $g(x) = \left(\frac{1}{2}\right)^x$?

Transform Exponential Growth Functions

The general form of an exponential function is $g(x) = a\left(b^{x-h}\right) + k$. The parameters a, h, and k in the general form indicate how the transformed function and its graph differ from the parent function $f(x) = b^x$ and its graph. The value of k identifies the vertical translation, the value of h indicates the horizontal translation, and the value of a indicates whether there is a vertical stretch or compression, and whether the graph is reflected across the x-axis.

 A. Consider the functions shown in the graph. How can you determine which is the parent function?

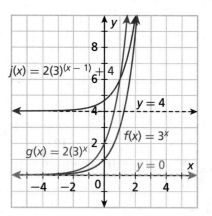

B. Compare the y-intercepts of the graphs of $f(x)$ and $g(x)$. How does the equation of the function for $g(x)$ indicate the change in the y-intercept from $f(x)$ to $g(x)$?

C. Compare the values of $f(1)$ and $g(1)$. What do you notice?

D. Compare the steepness of the graphs of $f(x)$ and $g(x)$. How is the equation of the function for $g(x)$ related to the difference in steepness between the graphs of $f(x)$ and $g(x)$?

E. Notice that the graphs of $f(x)$ and $g(x)$ have the same horizontal asymptote $\left(y = 0\right)$. How is the horizontal asymptote of the graph of $j(x)$ related to the horizontal asymptote of the graph of $g(x)$?

F. The table below shows the first and second reference points for a parent exponential function of any base b. Why do you think these are the reference points? Explain how you can use the parameters a, h, and k and the general form of an exponential function to write the ordered pairs that are the images of the two reference points on the parent function.

Function	First reference point	Second reference point
$f(x) = b^x$	$(0, 1)$	$(1, b)$
$g(x) = ab^{x-h} + k$	$(h, a + k)$	$(1 + h, ab + k)$

 Turn and Talk How do the following corresponding points reveal the translations that map a point on the graph of $g(x)$ to a point on the graph of $j(x)$?

- The point $(0, 2)$ on the graph of $g(x)$ has the corresponding point of $(1, 6)$ on the graph of $j(x)$.
- The point $(1, 60)$ on the graph of $g(x)$ has the corresponding point of $(2, 10)$ on the graph of $j(x)$.

Transform Exponential Decay Functions

As with other families of functions, it is helpful to use reference points when graphing transformations of exponential functions. The table below shows two key reference points and the asymptote for the parent function $f(x) = b^x$ and the corresponding information for the transformed function $g(x) = ab^{x-h} + k$.

Function	First reference point	Second reference point	Asymptote
$f(x) = b^x$	$(0, 1)$	$\left(-1, \frac{1}{b}\right)$	$y = 0$
$g(x) = ab^{x-h} + k$	$(h, a + k)$	$\left(h - 1, \frac{a}{b} + k\right)$	$y = k$

 Graph $g(x) = 2\left(\frac{1}{2}\right)^{x-4} - 1$.

Identify the parent function, the base, and the parameters.

The parent function is $f(x) = \left(\frac{1}{2}\right)^x$. The base is $b = \frac{1}{2}$.

The parameters are $a = 2$, $h = 4$, and $k = -1$.

> **A.** What transformations do these parameters represent?

Find the reference points and the asymptote for each function.

Function	First reference point	Second reference point	Asymptote
$f(x) = \left(\frac{1}{2}\right)^x$	$(0, 1)$	$(-1, 2)$	$y = 0$
$g(x) = 2\left(\frac{1}{2}\right)^{x-4} - 1$	$(h, a + k) = (4, 1)$	$\left(h - 1, \frac{a}{b} + k\right) = (3, 3)$	$y = -1$

> **B.** What is the image on the graph of g of the point $\left(1, \frac{1}{2}\right)$ on the graph of f?

Graph the transformed function.

> **C.** Why does part of the graph of g lie below the x-axis?

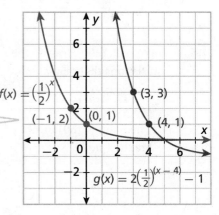

 Turn and Talk How does the average rate of change between corresponding pairs of points on the graphs of f and g compare?

242

Step It Out

Create an Exponential Function from a Graph

You can write the equation for an exponential function $g(x) = ab^{x-h} + k$ given the graph of the function, the reference points, and the asymptote.

4 ▶ Write the equation for the function shown in the graph $(b > 1)$.

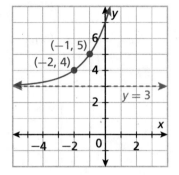

Identify the parameters.

> A. How do you know that $a = 1$?

Use the asymptote to identify k:
The asymptote is $y = 3$. So, $k = 3$.

Use the first reference point and k to find a and h:
$(-2, 4) = (h, a + k)$, so $h = -2$ and $a = 1$.

Use the second reference point, a, and k to find b:
$(-1, 5) = (1 + h, ab + k)$. So, $5 = 1(b) + 3$, and $b = 2$.

Write the equation: $g(x) = 2^{x+2} + 3$

> B. How are the values of a, b, h, and k related to the graph?

Model Depreciation with an Exponential Decay Function

An **exponential growth or decay function** has the form $f(t) = a(1 \pm r)^t$ where $a > 0$ is the initial amount and r is a constant percent increase or decrease for each unit increase in time t. The base $1 \pm r$ is the **growth or decay factor**, and r is the **growth or decay rate**.

	Function	Growth or decay rate	Growth or decay factor
Growth	$f(t) = a(1 + r)^t$	r is the percent *increase* (in decimal form)	$1 + r$
Decay	$f(t) = a(1 - r)^t$	r is the percent *decrease* (in decimal form)	$1 - r$

> A. How do you determine the initial value and the decay factor?

5 ▶ Delia paid $23,000 for a car. If its value decreases 11% per year, for what whole number of years will its value V remain above $6000?

Write a model for the car's value: $V(t) = 23{,}000(0.89)^t$

Graph the model and answer the question.

Use a calculator to graph the model along with the line $y = 6000$. Then identify the intersection point of the graphs, which is at approximately $(11.5, 6000)$.

> B. How does this ordered pair indicate the answer to the question?

Car Value

(graph showing V(t), y = 6000, and intersection point (11.5, 6022); Value ($) on vertical axis with 5000, 10000, 15000, 20000; Time (years) on horizontal axis with 4, 8, 12, 16)

Turn and Talk After what whole number of years will the value first drop below half the original value?

Check Understanding

1. How are the functions $f(x) = 4^x$ and $g(x) = \left(\frac{1}{4}\right)^x$ similar? How are they different?

2. How does the horizontal asymptote of $g(x) = 3^{x-h} - k$ compare to the horizontal asymptote of $f(x) = 3^{x-h} + k$ for $k > 0$?

3. The graph of a parent exponential decay function $f(x)$ is shown below. Graph the transformed function
$$g(x) = \left(\frac{1}{3}\right)^{x+2} - 4.$$

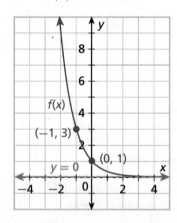

4. Write an equation for the exponential growth function graphed below.

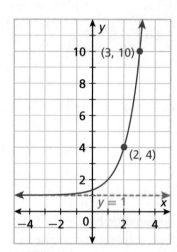

5. Jack purchases a new computer for $2500. The value of the computer depreciates by 24% each year. When will the value of the computer be less than $160?

On Your Own

6. How are the functions $f(x) = 3^x$ and $g(x) = 3^{-x}$ similar? How are they different?

7. How does the horizontal asymptote of $f(x) = \left(\frac{1}{2}\right)^x + 3$ compare to the horizontal asymptote of $5\left(\frac{1}{2}\right)^x + 3$?

8. Which transformations of $f(x) = b^x$ or $f(x) = \frac{1}{b}^x$ change the function's end behavior? Explain how you know.

Describe the effect of each transformation on the graph of the parent function whose base is the same as that of the given function. Then determine the domain, range, end behavior, and y-intercept of each function.

9. $g(x) = 2\left(\frac{1}{2}\right)^x - 1$

10. $g(x) = 3\left(\frac{1}{4}\right)^{x+1} + 2$

11. $g(x) = 4(3)^x + 1$

12. $g(x) = 2(2)^{x-3} - 1$

Identify the transformed values of the reference points and the asymptote from those of the parent function for each given function. Then graph the function.

13. $g(x) = 3(2)^{x+1} - 2$

14. $g(x) = 2(2)^{x-3} + 5$

15. $g(x) = 3\left(\frac{1}{2}\right)^{x+2} + 1$

16. $g(x) = 2\left(\frac{1}{2}\right)^{x-3} + 3$

For Problems 17–20, write the function represented by the graph.

17.
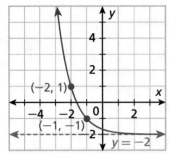

18.
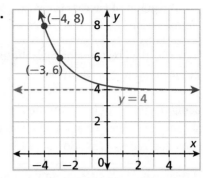

19.
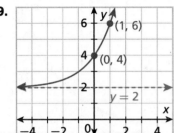

20.
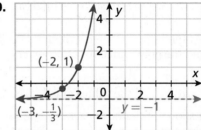

21. Trey invests $6000 in a savings bond that grows in value at 3% per year.

   A. Write a function that models the situation.

   B. Use a graphing calculator to find how many years it will take for the value of the bond to first exceed twice its initial value.

   C. Trey's friend Simone invests $5000 in a savings bond that grows at a rate of 5% per year. Write a function that models the growth of Simone's savings bond. When will Trey and Simone's bonds have the same value? Explain how you found your answer.

22. The function $V(x) = 650(0.77^x)$ models the change in yearly value for Anya's cellphone.

   A. What was the original value of the smartphone? What is the yearly depreciation of the smartphone?

   B. If Anya trades in her phone after 4 years toward a new phone that costs $750 and is given credit for her old phone's depreciated value, how much more will she have to pay for the new phone?

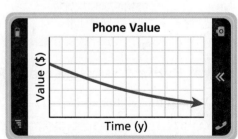

23. Use a graphing calculator to graph $f(x) = 8(2^x)$ and $g(x) = 2^{x+3}$. What do you notice about the two functions? (You may wish to use the Table feature to verify your observations.) Use the properties of exponents to verify your observations.

24. The image shows estimates of a local nesting population of monarch butterflies (in thousands) over two consecuive years. Write a model for the population after t years if it shows exponential growth. If this growth continued, after how many years would the population first pass one-half million butterflies?

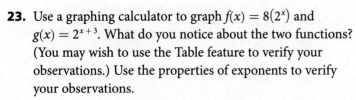

25. **(MP) Reason** Given $f(x) = 5^x$, explain how to write an exponential function whose graph is the reflection of the graph of f across the y-axis. Explain how to write an exponential function whose graph is a vertical compression of the graph of f.

26. Functions $f(x)$ and $g(x)$ are formed by transforming the exponential decay function with a base of $\frac{1}{3}$. To get the graph of $f(x)$, transform the parent function by shifting it 2 units to the right and 1 unit up. The graph of $g(x)$ contains the points shown in the table, with $(2, 4)$ being the image of $(0, 1)$ on the graph of the parent function. Write the functions $f(x)$ and $g(x)$. Then compare the two functions in terms of their asymptotes, end behavior, and range. What do you notice about the graphs?

x	g(x)
−1	82
0	28
1	10
2	4
3	2

27. The graph of $f(x) = 2^x$ is shown. What pattern do you notice about the average rate of change between the consecutive intervals indicated?

28. **(MP) Use Tools** Use a graphing calculator to graph the exponential function $f(x) = 1.5^x$ and the polynomial functions $g(x) = x^2$, $h(x) = x^3$, $j(x) = x^4$, and $k(x) = x^5$.

A. Do the values of f ever exceed the values of g, h, j, or k? Explain.

B. Create a table that shows the value of each function when x is 0, 1, 10, and 100. What do you notice?

C. Find and compare the rate of change for f and the average rate of change for the other four functions for each two consecutive values of x from your table in Part B. Round the average rates of change to the nearest hundredth, if necessary.

D. What can you conclude about exponential functions and polynomial functions?

29. **(Open Middle™)** Using the digits 1 to 9, at most one time each, fill in the boxes to make an exponential growth function and an exponential decay function.

 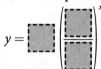

Spiral Review • Assessment Readiness

30. What is the solution to $14 + \sqrt{x + 1} = 20$?

Ⓐ 37   Ⓒ 5

Ⓑ 35   Ⓓ −7

31. Which function has the same y-intercept as $y = \sqrt[3]{x} + 1$? Select all that apply.

Ⓐ $y = x^3 + 1$ Ⓓ $y = x^3 - 1$

Ⓑ $y = (x + 1)^3$ Ⓔ $y = (x - 1)^3$

Ⓒ $y = \sqrt[3]{x} + 1$ Ⓕ $y = \sqrt[3]{x} - 1$

32. What is the domain of $y = \sqrt{x + 1} - 2$?

Ⓐ $(-\infty, +\infty)$ Ⓒ $(-2, +\infty)$

Ⓑ $[-1, +\infty)$ Ⓓ $(-2, -1)$

33. What is the approximate value of $\left(1 + \frac{1}{n}\right)^n$ for $n = 100$?

Ⓐ 2.7   Ⓒ 101

Ⓑ 3.1   Ⓓ 127

 I'm in a Learning Mindset!

What is my personal short-term learning goal for exponential functions?

The Natural Base e

(I Can) graph transformations of exponential functions having base e and use the graphs to solve real-world problems.

Spark Your Learning

This footbridge is a simple suspension bridge.

The footbridge forms a catenary curve.

A function that represents a catenary curve includes the constant e.

Complete Part A as a whole class. Then complete Parts B–D in small groups.

A. What is a mathematical question you can ask about this situation? What information would you need to know to answer your question?

B. Why would a graph of the function be helpful?

C. To answer your question, what strategy and tool would you use along with all the information you have? What answer do you get?

D. Does your answer make sense in the context of this situation? How do you know?

Turn and Talk A different footbridge can be modeled by the equation $y = 25\left(e^{\frac{x}{50}} + e^{-\frac{x}{50}}\right) - 53$. How many meters does this footbridge dip below its anchor points?

Build Understanding

Graph and Analyze the Function $f(x) = e^x$

The table shows the function $f(x) = \left(1 + \frac{1}{x}\right)^x$ for several values of x.

x	1	10	100	1000	10,000
$f(x)$	2	2.5937...	2.7048...	2.7169...	2.7181...

Notice that as the values of x increase, the value of $f(x)$ is approaching the decimal value 2.718.... This number is a special irrational number (like π) and is called e.

 A. Use a calculator to complete a table of values for the function $f(x) = e^x$ like the one shown.

x	$f(x) = e^x$
-2	0.135...
-1	?
0	?
1	?
2	?

B. Plot the points from the table on a graph and draw a smooth exponential curve connecting the points. How is this graph similar to other exponential graphs you have seen?

C. The value of e lies between the integers 2 and 3 on a number line. How would you expect the graphs of $g(x) = 2^x$ and $h(x) = 3^x$ to compare to the graph of $f(x) = e^x$?

D. The graph of $f(x)$ is shown below. Use a graphing calculator to graph $f(x) = e^x$, $g(x) = 2^x$, and $h(x) = 3^x$ on the same coordinate grid. What do you notice about the graphs?

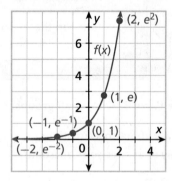

E. Use the graph from Part D to identify the following key characteristics of $f(x) = e^x$:

- domain and range
- end behavior
- y-intercept
- horizontal asymptote

How do these characteristics compare to the general graph of $f(x) = b^x$?

 Turn and Talk Explain why the number e is represented by a letter rather than being written out as a decimal or a fraction.

Step It Out

Transformations of the Graph of $f(x) = e^x$

The general form of the transformation of $f(x) = e^x$ is $g(x) = a \cdot e^{x-h} + k$ which is similar to the general form of the transformation of an exponential function with base b. The table shows two reference points and the asymptote of the parent function $f(x) = e^x$ as well as the corresponding values of the transformed function.

	First reference point	Second reference point	Asymptote
$f(x) = e^x$	$(0, 1)$	$(1, e)$	$y = 0$
$g(x) = a \cdot e^{x-h} + k$	$(h, a + k)$	$(h + 1, a \cdot e + k)$	$y = k$

Notice that these functions are identical to the exponential functions seen in the previous lesson $\left(f(x) = b^x \text{ and } g(x) = a(b)^{x-h} + k \right)$ when $b = e$.

2 ▶ Graph $g(x) = \frac{1}{2}(e)^{x+5} - 2$ using reference points and the asymptote.

Identify the parameters a, h, and k.

$a = \frac{1}{2}, h = -5, k = -2$

Use the parameters to find the reference points and the asymptote.

$\left(h, a + k \right) = \left(-5, -1\frac{1}{2} \right), \left(h + 1, a \cdot e + k \right) = \left(-4, \frac{1}{2}e - 2 \right), y = k = -2$

Graph g(x).

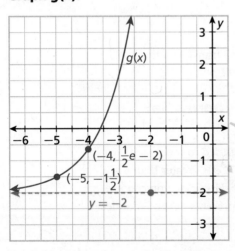

> **A.** How do you graph points such as $\left(-4, \frac{1}{2}e - 2 \right)$?

> **B.** Is transforming $f(x) = e^x$ a special case of transforming an exponential function with base b? Explain.

 Turn and Talk What are the similarities and differences between the graph of $g(x)$ and the graph of $h(x) = 2(e)^{x+5} - 2$? Do you need a graph in order to answer the question? Explain.

Create an Equation for a Transformation of $f(x) = e^x$

Given the graph of $g(x) = a \cdot e^{x-h} + k$, you can write its equation using the reference points $(h, a + k)$ and $(h + 1, a \cdot e + k)$.

3 ▶ Write the equation for the exponential function with base e shown in the graph. The two points shown on the grpah are the reference points.

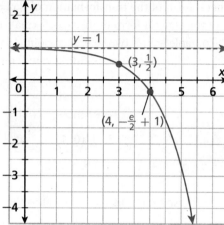

Use the asymptote and the given reference points to find the parameters.

Use the asymptote to identify k: The asymptote is $y = 1$. So, $k = 1$.

> **A.** How is k related to the asymptote? Is this always the case? Explain.

Use the first reference point and k to find a and h:
The first reference point is $(h, a + k)$, so $\left(3, \frac{1}{2}\right) = (h, a + k)$.

Set the corresponding coordinates equal to one another and solve for the missing values.

$3 = h$

$\dfrac{1}{2} = a + k$

$\dfrac{1}{2} = a + 1$

$-\dfrac{1}{2} = a$

> **B.** How do the coordinates of the reference point help you find h and a?

> **C.** What would your work look like if you used the second reference point to find h and a?

Write the equation.

$g(x) = -\dfrac{1}{2}(e)^{x-3} + 1$

> **D.** How could you use transformations to check your answer?

Model a Real-World Situation Using an Exponential Function with Base e

Transformations of the exponential function $f(x) = e^x$ can be used to model real-world situations involving exponential growth or decay. The value of e is greater than 1 and therefore, the general formula represents exponential growth. However, you can use the property of exponents to write $g(x) = e^{-x} = \frac{1}{e^x}$, which represents exponential decay, since $0 < \frac{1}{e} < 1$.

4 Carbon-14 is a radioactive isotope of carbon that decays at an exponential rate. The percent of original carbon-14 in the fossil after t years can be modeled by $N(t) = 100e^{-0.00012t}$, where t is the number of years after the living organism died. What is the decay rate r of the function? What is the age of the fossil?

A fossil contains 16% of its original carbon-14.

Find the value of r.

$N(t) = 100e^{-0.00012t}$

$= 100\left(e^{-0.00012}\right)^{t}$

A. How is this form of the equation related to the exponential decay formula?

Set the base of the function equal to the base of the exponential decay formula and solve for r.

$e^{-0.00012} = 1 - r$

$r = 1 - e^{-0.00012} \approx 0.00012$

So, the decay rate is about 0.012%.

Find the age of the fossil.

Use a graphing calculator to find the time t when 16% of the original 100% of the carbon-14 remains.

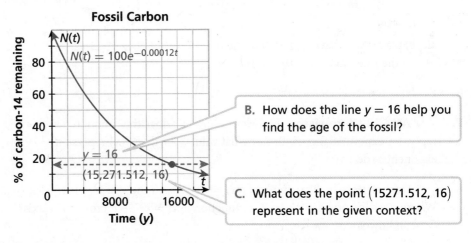

Fossil Carbon

$N(t) = 100e^{-0.00012t}$

$y = 16$

(15,271.512, 16)

% of carbon-14 remaining

Time (y)

B. How does the line $y = 16$ help you find the age of the fossil?

C. What does the point (15271.512, 16) represent in the given context?

The value of the function is about 16 when $t = 15{,}272$. So, the fossil is about 15,272 years old.

Turn and Talk As time passes between consecutive millennia, what happens to the average rate of decay of the carbon-14 in the fossil?

Check Understanding

1. How is the graph of $f(x) = e^x$ similar to the graph of an exponential function with base b? How is it different?

2. Identify the reference points and horizontal asymptote for the graph of $g(x) = 3e^{x+1} - 8$.

3. Write the equation for the function shown in the graph. The two points are reference points.

4. Suppose the population of a colony of bacteria is modeled by the exponential function $P(t) = 10,000e^{0.162t}$, where t is time in hours. What is the initial value and what does this mean for this situation? What is the growth rate of the bacteria colony? After how many hours will there be more than one million bacteria?

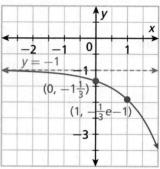

On Your Own

5. The graph shows the functions $f(x) = 2^x$, $f(x) = 4^x$, and $f(x) = e^x$.

    A. Identify which function generates which curve. Explain the strategies you used.

    B. Compare the value of $f(0)$ for all three functions.

    C. Explain the behavior of each of the functions on the intervals $(-\infty, 0)$ and $(0, +\infty)$.

6. Describe the end behavior of $f(x) = \left(1 + \frac{1}{x}\right)^x$.

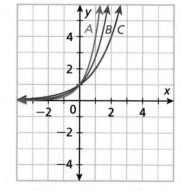

7. (MP) **Attend to Precision** For what values of c does the function $f(x) = e^{cx}$ represent exponential growth? For what values of c does $f(x)$ represent exponential decay?

8. (MP) **Use Structure** The graph of $f(x) = ce^x$ crosses the y-axis at the point $(0, 2)$. Where does the graph of the related function $g(x) = ce^x + d$ cross the y-axis? Explain how you know.

9. Write a transformation function $g(x)$ of the function $f(x) = e^x$ that has a vertical stretch, a horizontal translation to the right and a vertical translation down. Identify the end behavior and horizontal asymptote of your function.

Graph the function. Label the reference points and the horizontal asymptote.

10. $g(x) = (e)^x - 3$

11. $g(x) = 2(e)^x + 1$

12. $g(x) = \frac{1}{2}(e)^{x-1}$

13. $g(x) = \frac{1}{4}(e)^{x+1} - 2$

14. $g(x) = 3(e)^{x-4} + 1$

15. $g(x) = (e)^{x+3} + 2$

16. $g(x) = -2(e)^x - 1$

17. $g(x) = -\frac{1}{3}(e)^{x-2}$

Use the reference points and the asymptote to write the function whose graph is shown.

18.
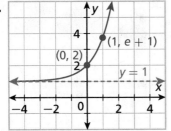

19.
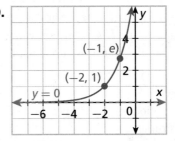

20.
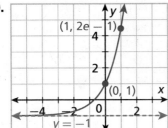

21.
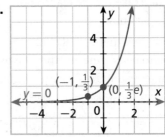

22.
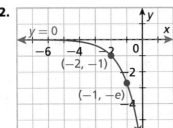

23.
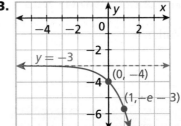

24. Radioactive isotopes are sometimes used in medical imaging. The amount of a radioactive isotope remaining (in milligrams) can be approximated by the function $A(t) = A_0 e^{-0.12t}$, where A_0 is the initial amount of the isotope and t is the time in hours. The initial amount of the isotope is shown. After how many hours will there be 50 milligrams of the isotope remaining? What is the rate of decay?

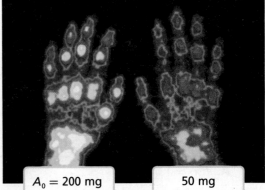

$A_0 = 200$ mg   50 mg

25. An archeological dig unearths a fossil that is determined to contain 21% of its original carbon-14. The percent of original carbon-14 in the fossil after t years can be modeled by $N(t) = 100e^{-0.00012t}$, where t is the number of years after the specimen died.

   A. What is the inital value? What does this mean?

   B. What is the rate of decay?

   C. What is the age of the fossil?

26. **STEM** Newton's law of cooling states that the temperature of an object can be modeled by the function $T(t) = T_A + (T_0 - T_A) e^{-kt}$, where T_0 is the initial temperature of the object, T_A is the ambient temperature, t is time in minutes, and k is a constant value given by the composition of the object. A cup of tea is 190 °F when it is served. The cooling constant k for the tea is approximately 0.04.

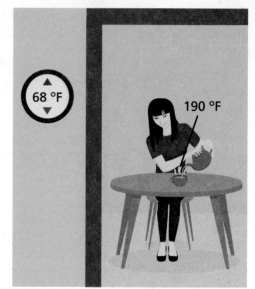

A. Write an equation for the temperature of the tea as a function of time.

B. How long will it take for the tea to cool to 60 °F? Explain how you know.

C. Graph the function that models the temperature of the tea and use it to determine whether the tea will ever cool to room temperature. Explain your answer.

D. Explain how the graph of $f(t) = e^{-0.04t}$ is transformed to produce the graph of the function you wrote in Part A.

Spiral Review • Assessment Readiness

27. What is the solution of the equation $\sqrt{x} + 2 = \sqrt{2x - 1}$?

Ⓐ $x = 25$

Ⓑ $x = 5$

Ⓒ $x = \sqrt{5}$

Ⓓ no real solution

28. Carlos invests $10,000 in a mutual fund that earns an annual simple interest rate of 4%. Which equation can be used to find the number of years he needs to invest the money to reach a balance of $15,000?

Ⓐ $15,000 = 10,000(1.04)^t$

Ⓑ $15,000 = 10,000(0.96)^t$

Ⓒ $10,000 = 15,000(1.04)^t$

Ⓓ $10,000 = 15,000(0.96)^t$

29. For each function, choose the number that indicates whether the function shows exponential growth, exponential decay, or neither.

Function	Exponential growth	Exponential decay	Neither
A. $f(x) = 1.6(x)^{3 + 0.1} - 5$	1	2	3
B. $f(x) = 6(0.3)^{x + 1} - 2$	1	2	3
C. $f(x) = \frac{1}{2}(2.1)^{x - 1} + 4$	1	2	3

 I'm in a Learning Mindset!

How did an initial struggle understanding base e lead to learning growth?

Keep Going to▶ Journal and Practice Workbook

Compound Interest

(I Can) model the value of an investment that earns compound interest.

Spark Your Learning

Cecil borrowed money to pay for his college education.

The bank allows Cecil to make no payments for the first 6 months after he graduates, but it still charges interest.

Cecil starts paying off his student loan 6 months after graduating.

Complete Part A as a whole class. Then complete Parts B–D in small groups.

A. What is a mathematical question you can ask about this situation? What information would you need to know to answer your question?

B. What type of function models the relationship between the amount A of money Cecil owes the bank and the time t in months since he graduated from college (where $t \leq 6$)?

C. To answer your question, what strategy and tool would you use along with all the information you have? What answer do you get?

D. Suppose the bank wants to express the interest rate on Cecil's loan as an annual rate instead of a monthly rate. What is an equivalent annual rate? Explain.

Turn and Talk Suppose the bank allows Cecil to make no loan payments for the first 2 years after he graduates, but still charges him interest. How much interest would Cecil owe after 2 years?

©Steve Debenport/E+/Getty Images

Build Understanding

Compare Simple and Compound Interest

Banks and other financial institutions often pay interest to people who leave their money in an account (or a person may pay a bank interest on money that the bank lends to the person). The bank may pay simple interest, where a certain percent of just the principle is paid at regular intervals. More commonly, banks pay **compound interest**, which is interest paid on both the principle and the accumulated interest.

1 Farah wants to deposit $500 she earned from her summer job into a savings account. Her local bank offers the two types of savings accounts shown below.

Basic Savings
- no minimum balance
- 3% annual simple interest

BANK

Rewards Savings
- $500 minimum balance
- 3% annual interest compounded yearly

Farah makes the spreadsheet shown below to compare the account balances she would have with the two types of savings accounts.

	A	B	C
	Years	**Basic savings**	**Rewards savings**
2	0	$500.00	$500.00
3	1	$515.00	$515.00
4	2	$530.00	$530.45
5	3	$545.00	$546.36
6	4	$560.00	$562.75
7	5	$575.00	$579.64

A. For each type of savings account, how is the balance after t years obtained from the balance after $(t-1)$ years for $t \geq 1$?

B. For each type of savings account, what is an equation that gives the amount A of money in the account as a function of the time t in years?

C. How much money would Farah have in each type of savings account after 10 years?

D. Which type of savings account should Farah choose? Explain.

Turn and Talk Which type of account do you think Farah should choose if the interest rate for the Rewards Savings account is lowered to 2.75%? Explain.

Step It Out

Model Interest Compounded Yearly

If an initial principle P is deposited into an account that pays interest compounded yearly, then the amount A of money in the account after t years is given by the exponential growth function,

$$A = P(1 + r)^t,$$

where r is the annual interest rate expressed as a decimal.

2 Juan has $400 in a savings account that pays 3.5% annual interest compounded yearly. He wants to use the money to buy a used mountain bike in 3 years. The current price of a new model of the bike Juan wants is shown, as is the expected rate at which the bike depreciates (loses value). Will Juan have enough money to buy a used model of this bike in 3 years?

> This bike costs $850 and is expected to depreciate by 20% per year.

Find the amount in Juan's saving account after 3 years.

Use the formula for the balance of an account with interest compounded yearly.

$A = P(1 + r)^t$

$= 400(1 + 0.035)^3$

> **A.** Why do you substitute 0.035 instead of 3.5 for r?

$= 400(1.035)^3$

≈ 443.49

Juan's account will have a balance of $443.49 after 3 years.

Estimate the cost of the bike Juan wants after 3 years.

The value V of the bike after t years can be modeled by the exponential decay function $V = 850(1 - 0.20)^t$, or $V = 850(0.8)^t$. Evaluate this function when $t = 3$.

$V = 850(0.8)^t$

$= 850(0.8)^3$

> **B.** Why is the base of this exponential function less than 1, while the base of the function for Juan's account balance is greater than 1?

$= 435.20$

The estimated cost of the bike in 3 years will be $435.20.

Answer the question.

Since Juan's account balance after 3 years, $443.49, is greater than the estimated cost of the bike after 3 years, $435.20, Juan will have enough money to buy the bike.

 Turn and Talk In Task 2, would Juan have enough money to buy the bike after 3 years if his saving account paid 2.5% annual interest compounded yearly? Explain.

©Shutterstock

Model Interest Compounded More than Once per Year

Interest may be earned more often than once a year. If interest is compounded n times per year, then the interest rate per compounding period is $\frac{r}{n}$ (where r is the annual interest rate), and the number of times interest is compounded in t years is nt. This leads to the following generalization of the formula $A = P(1 + r)^t$ for interest compounded yearly.

Formula for Compound Interest

If an initial principle P is deposited into an account that earns interest compounded n times per year, then the amount A of money in the account after t years is given by
$$A = P\left(1 + \frac{r}{n}\right)^{nt}$$
where r is the annual interest rate expressed as a decimal.

---

3 Lisa deposits \$1500 into an account that pays 4.8% annual interest compounded monthly. What is the account balance after 3 years? How much time does it take for the balance to reach \$2000?

To find the account balance after 3 years, substitute $P = 1500$, $r = 0.048$, $n = 12$, and $t = 3$ into the compound interest formula.

$A = P\left(1 + \frac{r}{n}\right)^{nt}$

$\quad = 1500\left(1 + \frac{0.048}{12}\right)^{12(3)}$

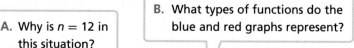
A. Why is $n = 12$ in this situation?

B. What types of functions do the blue and red graphs represent?

$\quad = 1500(1.004)^{36}$

$\quad \approx 1731.83$

The account balance after 3 years is \$1731.83.

To find the time it takes the balance to reach \$2000, use a graphing calculator to graph the function

$y = 1500\left(1 + \frac{0.048}{12}\right)^{12x}$, or

$y = 1500(1.004)^{12x}$, and the function $y = 2000$ on the same coordinate plane. Then find the x-coordinate of the point where the graphs intersect, which is $x \approx 6.01$.

The account balance reaches \$2000 after about 6 years.

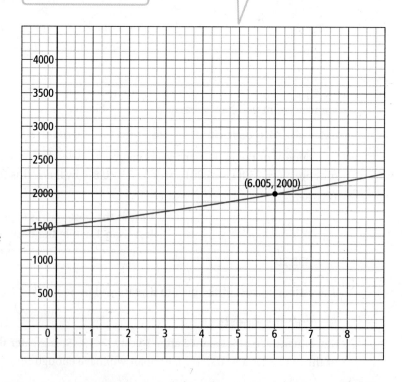

(6.005, 2000)

Turn and Talk Can the compound interest formula in Task 3 be used if interest is compounded yearly rather than more than once per year? Explain.

Model Interest Compounded Continuously

What happens to the compound interest formula $A = P\left(1 + \frac{r}{n}\right)^{nt}$ as the frequency of compounding n increases? By letting $m = \frac{n}{r}$, you can write the formula as

$A = P\left(1 + \frac{1}{m}\right)^{mrt}$, or $A = P\left[\left(1 + \frac{1}{m}\right)^{m}\right]^{rt}$, because $\frac{r}{n} = \frac{1}{m}$ and $nt = mrt$. If n increases

without bound, then m will also increase without bound, which means that $\left(1 + \frac{1}{m}\right)^{m}$ approaches e. This leads to the following formula for interest compounded *continuously*.

Formula for Continuously Compounded Interest

If an initial principle P is deposited into an account that earns interest compounded continuously, then the amount A of money in the account after t years is given by

$$A = Pe^{rt}$$

where r is the annual interest rate expressed as a decimal.

---

4 To pay for a trip to Machu Picchu in 4 years, Doug wants to deposit money into a savings account that earns 2.9% annual interest compounded continuously. Doug calculates the amount he needs to deposit as shown below.

Estimated trip cost: $2500

$$A = Pe^{rt}$$

$$2500 = Pe^{0.029(4)}$$

$$2500 = Pe^{0.116}$$

$$\frac{2500}{e^{0.116}} = P$$

$$2226.19 \approx P$$

So, Doug needs to deposit $2226.19 into his account.

A. In the formula for continuously compounded interest, why is the unknown value for this situation P rather than A?

B. How would the amount of money Doug needs to deposit change if his account earns interest compounded yearly instead of continuously?

Turn and Talk In Task 4, suppose Doug can afford to deposit only $2000 into his account. How many years must he wait until his account balance equals his estimated trip cost? Use a graphing calculator to find the answer.

Check Understanding

1. Louise has $1000 that she wants to deposit at her local credit union for 5 years. The credit union offers two types of savings accounts. Account A pays 2.5% annual simple interest. Account B pays 2% annual interest compounded yearly. Which account should Louise choose? Explain.

2. Ben deposits $600 into an account that pays 4% annual interest compounded yearly. Ben's brother Matt agrees to sell Ben the computer he just bought in 3 years. Matt paid $1700 for the computer, but its value is expected to decrease by 25% per year. Will Ben have enough money in his account after 3 years to buy the computer, assuming he pays Matt its fair market value? Explain.

For Problems 3–5, find the balance of the account after 6 years.

3. $250 is deposited into an account that pays 1.5% annual interest compounded yearly.

4. $4000 is deposited into an account that pays 3% annual interest compounded quarterly.

5. $800 is deposited into an account that pays 4.9% annual interest compounded continuously.

On Your Own

6. (MP) **Model with Mathematics** Kim sees the graphs shown in an online article about personal finance.

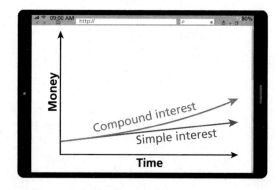

A. Suppose $300 is deposited into an account that pays 6% annual simple interest. Write an equation that gives the account balance A after t years. What type of function is the equation?

B. Suppose $300 is deposited into an account that pays 6% annual interest compounded yearly. Write an equation that gives the account balance A after t years. What type of function is the equation?

C. Are the shapes of the graphs shown in the personal finance article consistent with the equations you wrote? Explain.

7. The "rule of 72" shown approximates the number of years it takes an investment to double in value.

A. According to this rule, about how many years does it take an investment growing at 4% per year to double in value?

B. Use a graphing calculator to find the time it takes an investment of $100 to double in value if the investment grows at 4% per year. Compare your answer to the estimate given by the rule of 72.

> **Rule of 72**
>
> To find the approximate time t in years that it takes an investment to double, divide 72 by the investment's annual growth rate r expressed as a percent: $t = 72 \div r$.

8. **(MP) Critique Reasoning** Laura deposits $700 into a savings account that pays 3.6% annual interest compounded quarterly. She writes the equation $A = 700(1.036)^{4t}$ to model the account balance A after t years. Is Laura's equation correct? Explain.

For Problems 9–12, find the value of the investment after the specified time period.

9. a $250 investment that earns 4.5% annual interest compounded yearly for 7 years

10. a $375 investment that earns 1.2% annual interest compounded quarterly for 12 years

11. a $435 investment that earns 6% annual interest compounded monthly for 10 years

12. a $100 investment that earns 0.8% annual interest compounded continuously for 9 years

13. **Financial Literacy** For the 92-year period 1926–2017, the average annual growth rates for several types of investment assets are shown below.

U.S. large-company stocks: 10.2%

U.S. government bonds: 5.5%

Gold: 4.6%

Suppose a person invested $1000 in each asset type at the beginning of 1926. How much would each investment be worth at the end of 2017?

For Problems 14–17, use a graphing calculator to find the number of years it takes for the investment to grow to $3000. Round to the nearest tenth of a year.

14. an $1800 investment that earns 8% annual interest compounded yearly

15. a $2000 investment that earns 7.2% annual interest compounded monthly

16. a $2500 investment that earns 1.9% annual interest compounded daily

17. a $1000 investment that earns 4.3% annual interest compounded continuously

18. Rosa wants to have $10,000 saved to buy a used car in 5 years, so she plans to deposit money into an account that pays 4% annual interest. How much money must Rosa deposit now to reach her savings goal in 5 years if the interest is compounded yearly? How much must she deposit if the interest is compounded continuously?

19. Wanda deposits the money she saved from her summer job into a retirement account that earns 6.2% annual interest compounded quarterly. If she never deposits another cent in the account and the interest rate remains unchanged, how much money will be in the account after 50 years, when she expects to retire?

Wanda saved $2000 from her summer job.

20. Rochelle wants to have $15,000 saved for her child's college education in 15 years. She has an opportunity to invest in an account that will earn a fixed 4% annual interest rate compounded monthly for the 15-year term. How much money should she deposit now so that she will have $15,000 at the end of the 15 years?

21. (Open Middle™) Using the digits 1 through 9 at most once each, replace each box with a digit in the formula below for interest compounded quarterly so that the resulting amount of money A is as large as possible.

$$A = \boxed{}\left(1 + \frac{0.0\boxed{}}{4}\right)^{4 \cdot \boxed{}}$$

Spiral Review • Assessment Readiness

22. Which equation's graph is the graph of $y = e^x$ shifted left 2 units and down 6 units?

Ⓐ $y = e^{x+2} + 6$

Ⓑ $y = e^{x+2} - 6$

Ⓒ $y = e^{x-2} + 6$

Ⓓ $y = e^{x-2} - 6$

23. Mia buys a tablet for $500. She plans to sell it in 2 years. The tablet's value is projected to decrease by 40% per year. For how much can Mia expect to sell her tablet?

Ⓐ $420

Ⓑ $300

Ⓒ $180

Ⓓ $80

24. Match each function on the left with its inverse on the right.

A. $y = 3x^2$ for $x \geq 0$ **1.** $y = \sqrt{3x}$

B. $y = 3x^3$ **2.** $y = \sqrt[3]{3x}$

C. $y = \frac{1}{3}x^2$ for $x \geq 0$ **3.** $y = \sqrt{\frac{x}{3}}$

D. $y = \frac{1}{3}x^3$ **4.** $y = \sqrt[3]{\frac{x}{3}}$

I'm in a Learning Mindset!

What is my plan for improving my ability to solve problems involving compound interest?

Transformations of Exponential Growth and Decay Functions

The parent exponential function is $f(x) = b^x$, where b is a specific value. The general form of an exponential function is $g(x) = ab^{x-h} + k$. Identifying the values of a, h, and k in the general form of an exponential function provides the means for determining the transformation(s) of the parent function that produce a given exponential function.

	Exponential Growth $(b > 1)$		Exponential Decay $(0 < b < 1)$	
	$f(x) = b^x$	$g(x) = ab^{x-h} + k$	$f(x) = b^x$	$g(x) = ab^{x-h} + k$
First reference point	$(0, 1)$	$(h, a + k)$	$(0, 1)$	$(h, a + k)$
Second reference point	$(1, b)$	$(1 + h, ab + k)$	$\left(-1, \frac{1}{b}\right)$	$\left(h - 1, \frac{a}{b} + k\right)$
Asymptote	$y = 0$	$y = k$	$y = 0$	$y = k$

The value of h indicates a horizontal translation and the value of k indicates a vertical translation. The value of a identifies a vertical stretch or compression and also indicates if there is a reflection across the x-axis (when $a < 0$).

Exponential Growth and Decay: Rate and Factor

An exponential growth or decay function modeling a real-world situation has the form $f(t) = a(1 \pm r)^t$ where $a > 0$ and r is a constant percent change as a function of time t.

	Function	Rate	Factor
Growth	$f(t) = a(1 + r)^t$	percent increase, r	$1 + r$
Decay	$f(t) = a(1 - r)^t$	percent decrease, r	$1 - r$

Transformations of $f(x) = e^x$

The parent exponential function with base e is $f(x) = e^x$. The general form of an exponential function with base e is $g(x) = ae^{x-h} + k$.

Since $e > 1$, a table for $g(x) = ae^{x-h} + k$ has the same entries as the table for exponential growth $g(x) = ab^{x-h} + k$ shown above with $(1, b)$ replaced by $(1, e)$ and $(1 + h, ab + k)$ replaced by $(1 + h, ae + k)$.

Compound Interest

To find the value A of an investment or principal P earning compound interest, use the formula $A = P\left(1 + \frac{r}{n}\right)^{nt}$, where r is the annual rate (as a decimal), n is the number of times compounding occurs each year, and t is the number of years.

For principal compounded continuously, the formula becomes $A = Pe^{rt}$.

Vocabulary

Choose the correct term from the box to complete each sentence.

1. A(n) ___?___ is a function of the form $f(x) = b^x$, where b is a positive constant other than 1 and the exponent x is a variable.

2. The function $f(x) = b^x$ is a(n) ___?___ when $b > 1$.

3. The function $f(x) = b^x$ is a(n) ___?___ when $0 < b < 1$.

4. The percent increase r in the exponential growth function is called the ___?___.

5. The percent decrease r in the exponential decay function is called the ___?___.

6. Interest that is earned on principal as well as previous interest earned is called ___?___.

7. The expression $(1 + r)$ in an exponential growth function is called the ___?___.

8. The expression $(1 - r)$ in an exponential decay function is called the ___?___.

Concepts and Skills

For each function, describe the transformation(s) from the parent function. State the domain, range, end behavior, and y-intercept of each function.

9. $g(x) = 2\left(\dfrac{1}{2}\right)^x - 2$

10. $g(x) = 4(3)^x + 2$

Graph each function. Label the reference points and the horizontal asymptote.

11. $g(x) = e^x + 3$

12. $g(x) = 3e^x + 1$

13. $g(x) = \dfrac{1}{3}e^{x-1}$

14. $g(x) = -3e^x - 1$

(MP) Use Tools Find the value of each investment after the specified time period. State what strategy and tool you will use to answer the question, explain your choice, and then find the answer.

15. a $2500 investment compounded annually at a 5.5% interest rate for 8 years

16. a $3750 investment compounded quarterly at a 1.75% interest rate for 10 years

17. a $5000 investment compounded monthly at a 2.4% interest rate for 5 years

18. a $6500 investment compounded quarterly at a 4.1% interest rate for 15 years

Use a graphing calculator to find the number of years it takes for each investment to grow to $5000. Round to the nearest hundredth of a year.

19. a $3800 investment that earns 7% annual interest compounded yearly

20. a $2500 investment that earns 6.2% annual interest compounded monthly

21. a $1200 investment that earns 9% annual interest compounded quarterly

22. a $500 investment that earns 10% annual interest compounded monthly

Module Performance Task: *Spies and Analysts*™

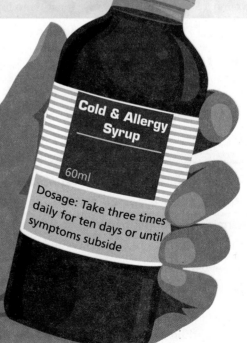

Patient **Patient**

How long will it take for the medicine to be effective?

Cold & Allergy Syrup

60ml

Dosage: Take three times daily for ten days or until symptoms subside

©Diego Cervo/Shutterstock

Are You Ready?

Complete these problems to review prior concepts and skills you will need for this module.

Scatter Plots and Lines of Fit

Find the equation of a line of fit for the data shown in each scatter plot. Then use it to answer the question.

1. How many visitors will attend during week eight?

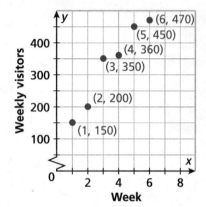

2. What is the number of hours per day for a 30 year old?

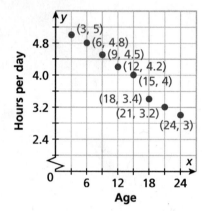

Inverses of Linear Functions

Write the inverse of each function.

3. $f(x) = 4 - 5x$

4. $f(x) = \frac{1}{2}x + 8$

5. Four friends went to a pizzeria for the Tuesday buffet night. They paid $38.60, including a 5% tax and a $5 tip. Write an inverse function to find the original cost of one buffet meal.

Radicals and Rational Exponents

Simplify each expression.

6. $\sqrt{4x^4y^2}$

7. $\left(27n^3\right)^{\frac{2}{3}}$

8. $\dfrac{1}{\left(16z^6\right)^{-\frac{1}{4}}}$

9. $\dfrac{t^{10}}{\sqrt{t^{12}}}$

Connecting Past and Present Learning

Previously, you learned:

- to determine the inverses of quadratic and cubic functions,
- to define exponential growth and decay functions, and
- to use exponential models in applied situations.

In this module, you will learn:

- to define and evaluate logarithmic functions,
- to graph logarithmic functions and analyze key features of their graphs, and
- to create logarithmic and exponential equations to model relationships between quantities found in real-world situations.

Logarithms and Logarithmic Functions

(I Can) **define and evaluate logarithms.**

Spark Your Learning

A skydiver uses an *altimeter* to observe the altitude, or height, above Earth's surface during a dive. As the skydiver is falling, the atmospheric pressure is increasing. The altimeter measures the atmospheric pressure and converts it into an altitude.

The skydiver will open the parachute at a predetermined altitude.

Complete Part A as a whole class. Then complete Parts B–D in small groups.

A. What is a mathematical question you can ask about this situation? What information would you need to know to answer your question?

B. What variables are involved in this situation? What unit of measurement would you use for each variable?

C. To answer your question, what strategy and tool would you use along with all the information you have? What answer do you get?

D. Given that the atmospheric pressure on Earth's surface is about 100 kPa, does your answer make sense in the context of the situation? Explain.

Turn and Talk In the model for pressure as a function of altitude, the *x*-axis is an asymptote of the graph. What does this mean for the graph of altitude as a function of pressure? Explain.

Build Understanding

Understand Logarithmic Functions as Inverses of Exponential Functions

In the exponential function $f(x) = b^x$, the exponent is the independent variable. The power of the base b with that exponent is the dependent variable. For example, the outputs of $f(x) = 2^x$ are powers of 2 for real number exponent values.

Since taking the inverse of a function reverses the inputs and outputs, the inverse of $f(x) = 2^x$ takes powers of 2 as inputs, and outputs exponents. The inverse of an exponential function is a **logarithmic function**. A **logarithm** is the exponent to which a base must be raised to produce a given number.

> **A logarithmic function:**
>
> - is written in the form $f(x) = \log_b x$ where $b \neq 1$ and $b > 0$; and
> - is read as "the logarithm with base b of x" or "log base b of x."

1 ▶ Use the exponential function $f(x) = 2^x$ to find values of its inverse, $f^{-1}(x) = \log_2 x$, the log base 2 of x, and to draw the graph of $f^{-1}(x)$.

Begin by creating a table of values for $f(x) = 2^x$ and drawing its graph.

x	$f(x) = 2^x$
-2	0.25
-1	0.5
0	1
1	2
2	4
3	8

A. How do the table and graph of $f(x) = 2^x$ reveal that its inverse will be a function?

B. Do you need to restrict the domain of $f(x) = 2^x$ for its inverse to be a function? What characteristic of $f(x) = 2^x$ allows you to make this conclusion?

C. How does the symmetry of a graph and its inverse help you predict the appearance of the graph of $f^{-1}(x) = \log_2 x$? How does this relate to the asymptotes?

D. How can you use the values in the table for $f(x)$ to find ordered pairs that satisfy $f^{-1}(x) = \log_2 x$? What are the resulting ordered pairs?

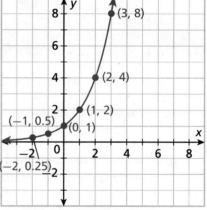

E. Copy the graph above and add the points you identified in Part D. Draw a smooth curve through the points. Does the graph confirm your answers to Parts A–C?

F. Find the average rate of change of $f(x)$ over the successive intervals defined by the ordered pairs. Repeat the process for $f^{-1}(x)$. What do you observe?

 Turn and Talk The definition of a logarithmic function, like that of an exponential function, includes "$b \neq 1$." Why is this restriction needed?

Convert Between Exponential and Logarithmic Equations

Since exponential and logarithmic functions are inverses, you can convert between exponential and logarithmic equations with the same base. That is, you can write a logarithmic equation from an exponential equation, and you can write an exponential equation from a logarithmic equation.

$$\textbf{Exponential equation} \rightarrow b^x = a \Leftrightarrow \log_b a = x \leftarrow \textbf{Logarithmic equation}$$

Similarly to how the equations $bx = a$ and $\frac{a}{b} = x$ are equivalent ways to express the same relationship (for $a \neq 0$), the equations $b^x = a$ and $\log_b a = x$ are equivalent ways to express the same relationship (for $b \neq 1$, $b > 0$).

2 Consider the exponential equations $5^3 = 125$ and $\left(\frac{6}{7}\right)^r = t$.

A. Complete the following to convert $5^3 = 125$ to a logarithmic equation.

The equation states that the base ___?___ raised to the exponent ___?___ gives the power ___?___, or that the ___?___ power of ___?___ is ___?___.

This is equivalent to saying that the exponent you must apply to the base ___?___ to write ___?___ as a power is ___?___.

So, $5^3 = 125 \Leftrightarrow \log_{\underline{\ ?\ }} \underline{\ ?\ } = \underline{\ ?\ }$.

B. Repeat the process of Part A to convert $\left(\frac{6}{7}\right)^r = t$ to a logarithmic equation.

C. To convert $b^x = a$ into a logarithmic equation, how can thinking, "a logarithm is an exponent" help you make the conversion correctly?

Consider the logarithmic equations $\log_4\left(\frac{1}{16}\right) = -2$ and $\log_{\frac{3}{5}} c = d$.

D. Complete the following to convert $\log_4\left(\frac{1}{16}\right) = -2$ to an exponential equation.

The equation states that the exponent you must apply to the base ___?___ to write ___?___ as a power is ___?___.

This is equivalent to saying that the base ___?___ raised to the exponent ___?___ gives the power ___?___, or that the ___?___ power of ___?___ is ___?___.

So, $\log_4\left(\frac{1}{16}\right) = -2 \Leftrightarrow \underline{\ ?\ }^{\underline{\ ?\ }} = \underline{\ ?\ }$.

E. Repeat the process of Part D to convert $\log_{\frac{3}{5}} c = d$ to an exponential equation.

Turn and Talk When you convert an exponential decay equation into a logarithmic equation, what can you say about the base of the related logarithmic equation?

Step It Out

Evaluate Logarithmic Functions by Converting to Exponential Form

A logarithmic function $f(x) = \log_b x$ takes a power of b as its input, and outputs an exponent. So, to be able to find an output, it helps when an input is a recognizable power of the base. For example, 25 is a recognizable power of 5, so it is easy to recognize that $f(x) = \log_5 x$ will output 2 for an input of 25.

To identify powers of the base, it can be helpful to let y represent an output of a logarithmic function $f(x)$, and then convert the equation to exponential form. Then you can rewrite the input as a power of the base and equate the exponents.

3 If $f(x) = \log_4 x$, find $f(64)$ and $f\left(\frac{1}{16}\right)$.

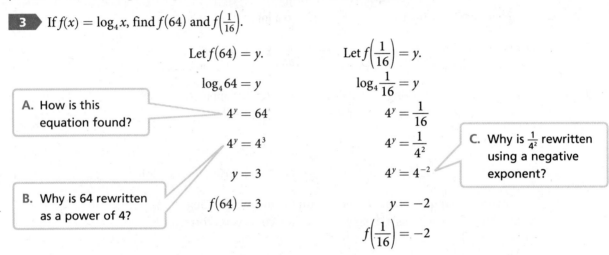

Let $f(64) = y$.

$\log_4 64 = y$

A. How is this equation found?

$4^y = 64$

$4^y = 4^3$

$y = 3$

B. Why is 64 rewritten as a power of 4?

$f(64) = 3$

Let $f\left(\frac{1}{16}\right) = y$.

$\log_4 \frac{1}{16} = y$

$4^y = \frac{1}{16}$

$4^y = \frac{1}{4^2}$

C. Why is $\frac{1}{4^2}$ rewritten using a negative exponent?

$4^y = 4^{-2}$

$y = -2$

$f\left(\frac{1}{16}\right) = -2$

Turn and Talk How can you use your knowledge of rational exponents to find $f(\sqrt{2})$ for the logarithmic function $f(x) = \log_4 x$?

Use a Logarithmic Model

Scientific and graphing calculators are designed to find the value of a logarithm directly when the base is 10 or e. Logarithms with a base of 10 are called **common logarithms**, and logarithms with a base of e are called **natural logarithms**.

When "log" is written without a number for the base, it is assumed to be a common logarithm; the common logarithm of a number x is written simply as "$\log x$." So, $\log 100 = 2$ because $10^2 = 100$. On a calculator, the "log" key evaluates common logarithms.

The expression "$\ln x$" (read as "l, n, x") indicates the natural logarithm of x. On a calculator, the "ln" key evaluates natural logarithms.

4 ▶ The loudness L (in decibels, dB) of a sound is modeled by $L = 10 \log \frac{I}{I_0}$ where I is the sound's intensity (in watts per square meter, W/m^2) and I_0 is 10^{-12} W/m^2, which is the approximate intensity of the softest hearable sound.

The photograph shows the intensity of the sound from a moderate rainfall and from a close lightning strike. What is the loudness in decibels of the moderate rainfall?

Loudness: $L = 10 \log \frac{I}{I_0}$

Using the loudness model, substitute the values for I and I_0.

$L = 10 \log \frac{I}{I_0}$

$= 10 \log \frac{10^{-4}}{10^{-12}}$

A. What property justifies rewriting $10 \log \frac{10^{-4}}{10^{-12}}$ as $10 \log 10^8$?

$= 10 \log 10^8$

$= 10 \cdot 8$

B. How do you know that $\log 10^8$ is 8?

$= 80$

Rainfall producing a sound intensity of 10^{-4} W/m^2 has a loudness level of 80 dB.

Turn and Talk For each increase in intensity by a factor of 10, how does the loudness L change? How can this help you find the loudness of a close lightning strike without going through all the steps of the substitution and simplification?

5 ▶ Radon is a radioactive gas that can accumulate in basements. The function $m = m_0 \left(\frac{1}{2}\right)^{\frac{t}{3.8}}$ describes the mass m of radon remaining after t days from an initial amount with mass m_0. After how long will 0.5 milligram of radon remain from an initial amount of 16 milligrams?

First substitute in $m = m_0 \left(\frac{1}{2}\right)^{\frac{t}{3.8}}$ to obtain $0.5 = 16\left(\frac{1}{2}\right)^{\frac{t}{3.8}}$, or $\frac{1}{32} = \left(\frac{1}{2}\right)^{\frac{t}{3.8}}$.

Now rewrite the exponential equation as a logarithmic equation so you can solve for t.

$\frac{1}{32} = \left(\frac{1}{2}\right)^{\frac{t}{3.8}} \Rightarrow \log_{\frac{1}{2}} \frac{1}{32} = \frac{t}{3.8}$

$3.8 \log_{\frac{1}{2}} \frac{1}{32} = t$

$3.8 \log_{\frac{1}{2}} \left(\frac{1}{2}\right)^5 = t$ ◁ **A.** Why is $\frac{1}{32}$ rewritten here as $\left(\frac{1}{2}\right)^5$?

$3.8(5) = t$, or $t = 19$

After 19 days, 0.5 milligram of the original 16 milligrams will remain.

Turn and Talk The quantity 3.8 represents the *half-life* of radon, or the time until only half of the original amount remains. How can does the original formula reveal this?

Check Understanding

1. Create a table of values or list of ordered pairs for $-2 \leq x \leq 2$ for the function $f(x) = 3^x$, and then draw its graph. Then use the values and graph to find ordered pairs and draw a graph for the function $g(x) = \log_3 x$. What is the relationship between the two functions and their graphs?

Write each exponential equation as a logarithmic equation.

2. $16^{\frac{1}{4}} = 2$

3. $(0.25)^5 = q$

Write each logarithmic equation as an exponential equation.

4. $\log_{12} 1728 = 3$

5. $\log_{\frac{3}{4}} x = y$

6. If $f(x) = \log_5 x$, find $f(625)$ and $f\left(\frac{1}{125}\right)$.

7. The loudness L (in decibels, dB) of a sound is modeled by $L = 10 \log \frac{I}{I_0}$ where I is the sound's intensity (in watts per square meter, W/m²) and I_0 is 10^{-12} W/m². What is the loudness in decibels of a subway whose sound intensity is 10^{-3} W/m²?

8. The amount of the radioactive isotope cesium-137 in the environment since 1950 is known. Plants take up cesium 137, which reveals information about when a plant was growing. The function $m = m_0 \left(\frac{1}{2}\right)^{\frac{t}{30.1}}$ describes the mass m of cesium-137 remaining after t years from an initial amount with mass m_0. After how long will 0.025 microgram of cesium-137 remain from an initial amount of 0.1 microgram?

On Your Own

9. (MP) **Use Structure** Consider the exponential function $f(x) = \left(\frac{1}{2}\right)^x$ and the logarithmic function $g(x) = \log_{\frac{1}{2}} x$.

   A. What is the relationship between the functions $f(x) = \left(\frac{1}{2}\right)^x$ and $g(x) = \log_{\frac{1}{2}} x$?

   B. Compare the domains and ranges of the functions $f(x)$ and $g(x)$. Is the domain of either function restricted? Explain.

   C. Compare the end behaviors and asymptotes of the graphs of $f(x)$ and $g(x)$.

   D. How does the average rate of change of $f(x)$ over the interval defined by the ordered pairs $(0, 1)$ and $\left(1, \frac{1}{2}\right)$ compare to the average rate of change of $g(x)$ over the interval defined by the ordered pairs $\left(\frac{1}{2}, 1\right)$ and $(1, 0)$?

   E. (MP) **Critique Reasoning** A student graphed the functions $f(x)$ and $g(x)$. His work is shown. Is the graph correct? Justify your reasoning. Make a sketch of a new graph if there is an error in the student's work.

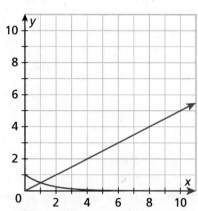

Write each given exponential equation in logarithmic form.

10. $e^8 = y$

11. $a^5 = b$

12. $9^y = 16$

13. $e^x = y$

14. $2^a = b$

15. $x^2 = y$

Write each given logarithmic equation in exponential form.

16. $\ln 10 = x$

17. $\log_{\frac{2}{5}} \frac{8}{125} = 3$

18. $\log_6 4 = t$

19. $\log_9 x = y$

20. $\ln x = y$

21. $\log x = \frac{1}{3}$

22. If $f(x) = \log_{\frac{1}{4}} x$, find $f(16)$ and $f\left(\frac{1}{64}\right)$.

23. If $f(x) = \log_8 x$, find $f(64)$ and $f\left(\frac{1}{512}\right)$.

24. If $f(x) = \log_{\frac{1}{10}} x$, find $f(1000)$ and $f(0.0001)$.

25. If $f(x) = \log_3 x$, find $f(81)$ and $f\left(\frac{1}{27}\right)$.

26. If $f(x) = \log_2 x$, find $f(64)$ and $f\left(\frac{1}{16}\right)$.

27. If $f(x) = \log_{\frac{1}{2}} x$, find $f(32)$ and $f\left(\frac{1}{8}\right)$.

28. (MP) **Reason** Evaluate each expression without using a calculator. Explain your reasoning.

　A. $\ln e^4$

　B. $10^{\log 9}$

　C. $e^{\ln 3}$

29. (MP) **Reason** Why do you think logarithms are commonly used to model physical quantities that have very large values?

Health and Fitness The logarithmic function $p(H) = \log_{10} \frac{1}{H}$ gives the acidity level or pH of a liquid where H (in moles per liter) is the concentration of hydrogen ions in a liquid. Use the function $p(H)$ to answer Problems 30–33.

Cranberry juice: 0.004 mol/L　　Grape juice: 0.0005 mol/L　　Apple juice: 0.0001 mol/L

30. What is the pH level in cranberry juice?

31. What is the pH level in grape juice?

32. What is the pH level in apple juice?

33. Based on your responses to Problems 28–31, is $p(H)$ an increasing or decreasing function?

34. Earthquakes are measured by instruments called seismographs. Their magnitudes are modeled by the logarithmic function $M = \log \frac{I}{I_0}$ where I_0 is movement that can barely be detected, and the intensity I is the amplitude of the largest waves recorded by seismographs. What is the magnitude of an earthquake that seismographs register as having intensity $I = 4012I_0$?

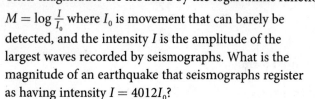

Magnitude: $M = \log\frac{I}{I_0}$

35. The population of frogs in a man-made pond can be modeled by the function $f(y) = 18(2)^{\frac{y}{6}}$ where y is the number of months since creating the pond. When will there be 144 frogs? Describe how you found your answer.

36. (Open Middle™) Using the integers −9 to 9, at most one time each, fill in the boxes and create two functions with the corresponding y-intercept.

$$y = \boxed{} \log_{\boxed{}} \left(x - \boxed{}\right) + \boxed{}$$

y-intercept $= \boxed{}$

Spiral Review • Assessment Readiness

37. The value of a car that costs $16,000 depreciates 15% per year. Which equation models the value of the car t years after its purchase?

Ⓐ $y = 16,000(0.85)^t$ Ⓒ $y = 16,000(1.5)^t$

Ⓑ $y = 16,000(1.15)^t$ Ⓓ $y = 16,000(0.15)^t$

38. The function $g(x) = a \cdot e^{x-h} + k$ is a transformation of the function $f(x) = e^x$. What does the value of k tell you about the graph of $g(x)$?

Ⓐ The horizontal asymptote is $x = k$.

Ⓑ The horizontal asymptote is $y = k$.

Ⓒ The x-coordinate of the first reference point is k.

Ⓓ The y-coordinate of the second reference point is k.

39. Which expression represents the balance of an account with an initial investment of $2,000 and a semi-annual interest rate of 2.8% over t years?

Ⓐ $2000(t + 1.014)$ Ⓒ $2000(1.028)^{2t}$

Ⓑ $2000(1.028)^t$ Ⓓ $2000(1.014)^{2t}$

40. Which equation represents $f(x) = 10^x$ shifted three units to the left?

Ⓐ $y = 10^{(x-3)}$ Ⓒ $y = 3 + 10^x$

Ⓑ $y = 10^{(x+3)}$ Ⓓ $y = -3 + 10^x$

I'm in a Learning Mindset!

What is my plan for improving my performance converting between exponential and logarithmic equations?

Graph Logarithmic Functions

(I Can) graph logarithmic functions.

Spark Your Learning

Duckweed, which ranges throughout the United States (except Hawaii), grows very rapidly. Although it is very common in nature, it is also grown commercially as animal food, for bioremediation, and even as a possible source for biomedicines.

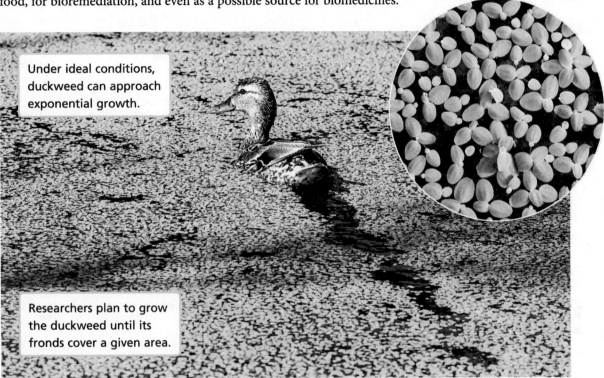

Under ideal conditions, duckweed can approach exponential growth.

Researchers plan to grow the duckweed until its fronds cover a given area.

Complete Part A as a whole class. Then complete Parts B–D in small groups.

 A. What is a mathematical question you can ask about this situation? What information would you need to know to answer your question?

 B. How can you represent the model that your teacher gave you with a graph?

 C. To answer your question, what strategy and tool would you use along with all the information you have? What answer do you get?

 D. Do your answer and graph make sense in the context? Explain.

 Turn and Talk In the Build Understanding task in the previous lesson, you used a table of values and graph of $f(x) = 2^x$ to graph $f^{-1}(x) = \log_2 x$. How is the graph you made for the duckweed model related to the graph of f^{-1}?

Build Understanding

Graph Logarithmic Functions

As is true for exponential functions, there is a parent logarithmic function $f(x) = \log_b x$ for each value of b. You are already familiar with the graph of the parent function $f(x) = \log_2 x$ shown at the right. Since you will commonly encounter logarithmic functions with base 10 and with base e, you should be familiar with the graphs of the parent logarithmic functions $f(x) = \log x$ and $f(x) = \ln x$.

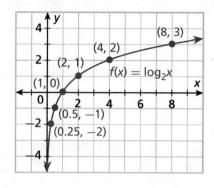

1 ▶ Compare and contrast the graphs of the parent logarithmic functions with base 10, $f(x) = \log x$, and with base e, $f(x) = \ln x$.

A. Complete the table of values for $f(x) = \log x$.

x	?	?	1	10	?	?
$f(x) = \log x$	−2	−1	0	1	2	3

Now complete the table of values for $f(x) = \ln x$. Remember that $e \approx 2.718$.

x	?	$\frac{1}{e} \approx 0.37$	1	$e \approx 2.72$	?	?
$f(x) = \ln x$	−2	−1	0	1	2	3

You can see that the tables and the plotted ordered pairs in the graph of $f(x) = \log_2 x$ all have range values of $-2 \le f(x) \le 3$. Complete the corresponding domain values for each function below.

$$f(x) = \log_2 x: 0.25 \le x \le 8$$

$$f(x) = \log x: 0.01 \le x \le \underline{}$$

$$f(x) = \ln x: 0.135 \le x \le \underline{}$$

What do these domain values indicate about what scale you would need to use on the x-axis to graph logarithmic functions for the same range values as the base b increases? Explain.

B. What do the three functions have in common regarding the range values as x decreases from 1 toward 0? How does the relationship between exponential functions and logarithmic functions explain this?

The graphs of $f(x) = \log x$ and $f(x) = \ln x$ are shown below. From them, you can identify key features of the graphs of parent logarithmic functions where $b > 1$. Since the functions are undefined for $x \le 0$, there is no end behavior as $x \to -\infty$, but you can describe their behavior as x approaches 0. In general, x can approach 0 in two ways:

- "$x \to 0^+$" indicates as "x approaches 0 from the right" (the positive direction)
- "$x \to 0^-$" indicates as "x approaches 0 from the left" (the negative direction)

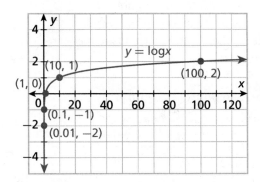 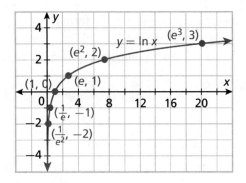

C. Find each for $f(x) = \log x$ and $f(x) = \ln x$: the domain and range, the end behavior, and any asymptotes. How do these compare to each other for the two functions, and to the same features of $f(x) = \log_2 x$?

D. Find each for $f(x) = \log x$ and $f(x) = \ln x$: any intercepts, the intervals over which the function is positive or negative, and the intervals over which it is increasing or decreasing. How do these compare to each other for the two functions, and to the same features of $f(x) = \log_2 x$?

E. Complete the table of average rates of change over the given intervals (use a calculator for $f(x) = \log x$ and $f(x) = \ln x$, and round to the nearest 0.01.)

Function	$0.5 \le x \le 1$	$1 \le x \le 2$	$2 \le x \le 4$	$4 \le x \le 8$
$f(x) = \log x$	0.60	?	0.15	?
$f(x) = \ln x$	?	0.69	?	0.17
$f(x) = \log_2 x$	2	?	?	0.25

What do you observe about the average rates of change for each function? What do you observe about the average rates of change as the value of b increases when you compare the three functions to each other? How do your observations relate to the graphs?

F. What can you conclude about the key features of the graphs of functions of the form $f(x) = \log x$ where $b > 1$?

 Turn and Talk Remembering that logarithmic functions and exponential functions are inverses, why will the key features of $f(x) = \log_b x$ where $0 < b < 1$ be much different than when $b > 1$? What key features will remain the same?

Step It Out

Transformations of Logarithmic Functions

You've seen graphs of $f(x) = \log_2 x$, $f(x) = \log x$, and $f(x) = \ln x$. Graphing transformations of these parent functions and of parent logarithmic functions with other bases works in the same way that you have seen before.

Recall that the reference points $(0, 1)$ and $(1, b)$ helped you graph transformations of parent exponential functions of the form $f(x) = b^x$. Because of the inverse relationship between logarithmic and exponential functions, this means that $(1, 0)$ and $(b, 1)$ are the corresponding reference points for logarithmic functions.

Function	Reference point	Reference point	Asymptote
$f(x) = \log_b x$	$(1, 0)$	$(b, 1)$	$x = 0$
$g(x) = a\log_b(x - h) + k$	$(1 + h, k)$	$(b + h, a + k)$	$x = h$

2   Graph $g(x) = 3\log_4(x - 2) + 8$.

Identify the parent function, its base, and the parameters.

Parent function: $f(x) = \log_4 x$, with base $b = 4$

$a = 3$: vertical stretch by a factor of 3

$h = 2$: translation right 2 units

> **A.** Why is h equal to 2, and not -2?

$k = 8$: translation up 8 units

Find the reference points and the asymptote for the parent function and for $g(x)$.

$f(x) = \log_4 x$: reference points $(1, 0)$ and $(b, 1) = (4, 1)$; asymptote $x = 0$

$g(x) = 3\log_4(x - 2) + 8$: reference points $(1 + h, k) = (3, 8)$ and $(6, 11)$; asymptote $x = 2$

Graph the transformed function.

> **B.** How can you find the coordinates of the second reference point of $g(x)$?

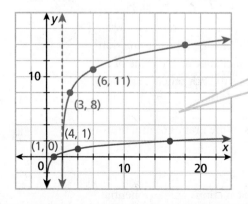

> **C.** This point has coordinates $(16, 2)$. How can you verify that the unlabeled point on the graph of $g(x)$ is its image?

 Turn and Talk How would changing the parameter from $a = 3$ to $a = -\frac{1}{3}$ change the graph of $g(x)$? Would it change the domain and range? Explain.

Graph Logarithmic Models

3 The velocity of a flying bat involves many factors, including wingbeat frequency, or how quickly the bat flaps its wings, and wingbeat amplitude, or the angle through which the wings flap. Across certain species of bats, the relationship between flight velocity and wingbeat frequency for a bat with a mass of 10 grams can be approximated by $f(V) = -3\log V + 12$ where V is the velocity in meters per second and $f(V)$ is the wingbeat frequency per second.

Relationship between flight velocity and wingbeat frequency: $f(V) = -3\log V + 12$

Use transformations to describe and graph $f(V)$. Then describe the relationship shown over the appropriate domain for the model, which is approximately $2 \le V \le 10$.

Compare $f(V) = -3\log V + 12$ to the transformations model for common logarithms, $g(x) = a\log(x - h) + k$.

- $a = -3$: vertical stretch by a factor of 3 and reflection across the x-axis
- $k = 12$: vertical shift up 12 units

> **A.** Why does the asymptote not change?

Algebraically identify the asymptote and images of the reference points.

Function	Reference point	Reference point	Asymptote
$f(x) = \log x$	$(1, 0)$	$(10, 1)$	$x = 0$
$f(V) = -3\log V + 12$	$\left(1, -3(0) + 12\right) = (1, 12)$	$\left(10, -3(1) + 12\right) = (10, 9)$	$V = 0$

Use the coordinates of the reference points and the graph of the parent function to graph the model. You can use a calculator to find a few other ordered pairs, such as $(3, 10.6)$, $(5, 9.9)$, and $(8, 9.3)$, to graph $f(V)$.

> **B.** How does the graph reveal the vertical stretch?

> **C.** Since $f(V)$ includes a reflection of $f(x) = \log x$ across the x-axis, why aren't the point at $(10, 1)$ and its image at $(10, 9)$ on opposite sides of the x-axis?

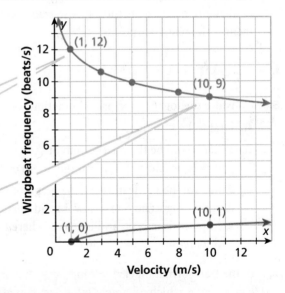

Over the domain $2 \le V \le 10$, the model shows that as the velocity increases, the wingbeat frequency decreases from about 11 per second to 9 per second. At the lower velocities, the wingbeat frequency is decreasing more quickly than at the higher velocities.

> **Turn and Talk** Is it surprising that the wingbeat frequency is lower at higher velocities? How could this be related to the fact that wingbeat amplitude is greater at higher velocities?

Check Understanding

1. For what values of x is the graph of $y = \log x$ above the graph of $y = \ln x$? below the graph of $y = \ln x$?

2. What point, if any, do the graphs of $y = \log x$ and $y = \ln x$ share with the graph of any logarithmic function $y = \log_b x \, (b > 0, b \neq 1)$? Why is this true?

3. Copy and complete the table of values for the function $f(x) = \log_6 x$.

x	?	?	1	?	?	?
$f(x) = \log_6 x$	−2	−1	0	1	2	3

4. Answer the following questions about the graph of $g(x) = -\log_2(x + 4) - 1$.

   A. What are the parent function, its base, and the parameters of the transformation?

   B. What transformations of the graph of the parent function does the graph of $g(x) = -\log_2(x + 4) - 1$ represent?

   C. What are the coordinates of the reference points on the parent graph and of their image points on the transformed graph?

5. Monique's video is still gaining "likes," though not as quickly as it once was. The total number of likes the video has received can be approximated over the last 100 days by the function $l(t) = 50 \log_3 t + 300$ where l represents the number of likes and t represents the day. Use transformations to describe and graph $l(t)$. Include the reference points.

On Your Own

6. Consider the logarithmic parent function with base 5, $f(x) = \log_5 x$.

   A. Graph the function.

   B. What would be the relationship of the graph of $f(x) = \log_5 x$ to the graphs of $f(x) = \log x$ and $f(x) = \ln x$ if they were on the same coordinate grid?

   C. Compare the key features of the graph of $f(x) = \log_5 x$ with those of the graphs of $f(x) = \log x$ and $f(x) = \ln x$. Include the domain, range, end behavior, asymptote, intercept, and intervals where the graphs are positive or negative and increasing or decreasing.

7. In the transformation $g(x) = a \log_b(x - h) + k \, (b > 1)$ of a parent function $f(x) = \log_b x$, which parameter(s), if any, can affect the following? Describe the effects.

   A. the domain, range, and asymptote(s)

   B. the end behavior

   C. the intercept(s)

   D. the intervals where the function is positive or negative and increasing or decreasing

   E. the average rate of change on an interval

Identify the transformations of the graph of the parent function that produce the graph of the given function $g(x)$. Identify the asymptote of the graph of $g(x)$.

8. $g(x) = 0.5 \log_{12} x - 3$

9. $g(x) = \log(x - 3) + 4$

10. $g(x) = -5 \ln(x + 1)$

11. $g(x) = -\log_{\frac{1}{2}}\left(x + \frac{1}{2}\right) - 8$

Identify the coordinates of the reference points on the graph of the parent function and their images on the graph of the given function $g(x)$.

12. $g(x) = \log(x - 2) + 6$

13. $g(x) = 3 \log_6(x - 1) - 5$

14. $g(x) = \frac{1}{2} \log_4(x + 1)$

15. $g(x) = 10 \ln x - 2$

16. $g(x) = 2 \ln(x + 1)$

17. $g(x) = -\log_3 x + 5$

18. $g(x) = \log_4(2x) + 3$

19. $g(x) = \ln\big(2(x + 1)\big)$

Identify the transformations of the graph of the parent function that produce the graph of the given function $g(x)$. Graph each function $g(x)$ along with the graph of its parent function. Include the reference points.

20. $g(x) = 2 \ln x + 1$

21. $g(x) = \frac{1}{2} \log(x - 5) - 2$

22. $g(x) = -2 \log_5(x - 4) + 3$

23. $g(x) = -\log_2(x + 2) - 1$

24. After the age of about 25 years, the average size of the pupils in a person's eyes decreases. An approximate model for the average pupil diameter d (in millimeters) under low-light conditions as a function of age a (in years) is shown in the photo.

> **Pupil diameter as a function of age:** $d(a) = -2.1 \ln a + 13.7$

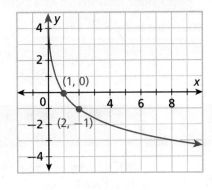

Use transformations (include reference points) to describe and graph $d(a)$. Then describe the relationship shown over the domain $25 \le a \le 70$. At about what age does the average diameter fall below 6 millimeters?

25. The graph of $f(x) = \log_{\frac{1}{2}} x$ is shown.

A. Graph the function $g(x) = -\log_2 x$.

B. How do the graphs of $f(x)$ and $g(x)$ compare?

C. Write $\log_{\frac{1}{2}} x = y$ and $-\log_2 x = y$ in exponential form. Next, use the properties of exponents to rewrite the exponential form of $\log_{\frac{1}{2}} x = y$ using a negative exponent. What do you notice? How is this related to your answer to Part B?

26. A small bookstore starts a customer loyalty program. Over the first year, the total number of customers who have signed up can be modeled by the function shown in the photo, where c is the number of customers and w is how many weeks the program has been in effect.

A. Graph $c(w)$. Include the reference points.

B. What is a reasonable domain for this context? Explain.

C. The first 75 customers sign up the first week. How many additional weeks does it take for the second 75 customers to sign up? the third 75? the fourth 75? What do you notice? Why might this make sense in the context?

D. From the model, would you predict that at least 410 people will have signed up by the end of the year? Explain your reasoning.

> **Customers who signed up:**
> $c(w) = 75 \log_2(w + 1)$

27. (Open Middle™) Using the integers -9 to 9, at most one time each, fill in the boxes to create a function with the greatest possible y-intercept.

$$y = \boxed{} \log_{\boxed{}} \left(x - \boxed{}\right) + \boxed{}$$

$$y\text{-intercept} = \boxed{}$$

Spiral Review • Assessment Readiness

28. What transformations of the parent function $f(x) = e^x$ does $g(x) = 4e^{x-1} + 3$ represent? Select all that apply.

Ⓐ translation 4 units up

Ⓑ translation 3 units up

Ⓒ translation 1 unit left

Ⓓ translation 1 unit right

Ⓔ vertical stretch by a factor of 4

Ⓕ horizontal stretch by a factor of 4

29. What is $\log_5 r = s$ written in exponential form?

Ⓐ $s^5 = r$

Ⓑ $r^5 = s$

Ⓒ $5^s = r$

Ⓓ $s^r = 5$

30. If you invest $5000 at an annual interest rate of 3% compounded continuously, about how much will you have after 4 years?

Ⓐ $5,038

Ⓑ $5,637

Ⓒ $16,601

Ⓓ $281,305

31. Solve $1600 = 200(2)^{\frac{x}{4}}$ for x.

Ⓐ $x = 4$

Ⓑ $x = 8$

Ⓒ $x = 12$

Ⓓ $x = 16$

 I'm in a Learning Mindset!

What is my personal short-term learning goal for graphing logarithmic functions?

9.3

Create Exponential and Logarithmic Functions

(I Can) create logarithmic and exponential equations to represent relationships between quantities.

Spark Your Learning

The population of a town has grown in recent years since a company moved its headquarters nearby.

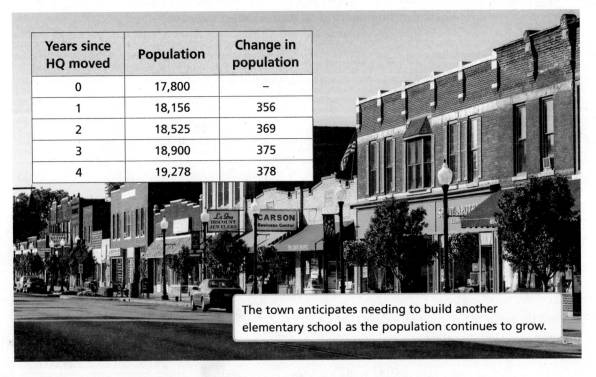

Years since HQ moved	Population	Change in population
0	17,800	–
1	18,156	356
2	18,525	369
3	18,900	375
4	19,278	378

The town anticipates needing to build another elementary school as the population continues to grow.

Complete Part A as a whole class. Then complete Parts B–D in small groups.

A. What is a mathematical question you can ask about this situation? What information would you need to know to answer your question?

B. What variables are involved in this situation? What unit of measurement would you use for each variable?

C. To answer your question, what strategy and tool would you use along with all the information you have? What answer do you get?

D. Does your answer make sense in the context of the situation? Explain why or why not.

Turn and Talk How would the data values in the *Change in population* column of the table be different if the town's population growth was linear instead of exponential? Explain.

Build Understanding

Create an Exponential Model from a Data Set

For an exponential function $f(x) = ab^x$, the function value of the next integer value of x is given by $f(x+1) = ab^{x+1}$. Using the Product of Powers Property, you can rewrite $ab^{x+1} = a(b^x \cdot b^1) = ab^x \cdot b = f(x) \cdot b$. Increasing the value of x by 1 multiplies the value $f(x)$ by b. This means that for successive integer values of x, each value of $f(x)$ is b times the value that precedes it.

You can see if a given set of data would best be modeled by an exponential or decay function by testing for a common ratio. For example, you can determine the base of the decay function $f(x)$ by dividing the function values of successive integer values of x.

$f(1) = 1.5$

$f(2) = 1.125$ $\dfrac{1.125}{1.5} = \dfrac{0.84375}{1.125} = \dfrac{3}{4}$ The base of $f(x)$ is $\dfrac{3}{4}$.

$f(3) = 0.84375$

Rarely do models fit real-world data sets perfectly. An exponential model can still be a good model for a data set if ratios are approximately equivalent.

1 The table shows the number of newly built housing units sold each year in the United States for the years 2011 through 2017.

Let $H(t)$ represent the number of newly built housing units sold (in thousands). Instead of using the year for the t-values, let t represent the number of years after 2011.

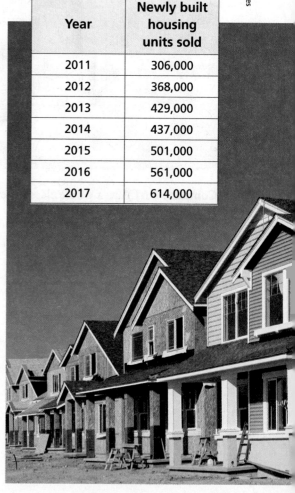

Year	Newly built housing units sold
2011	306,000
2012	368,000
2013	429,000
2014	437,000
2015	501,000
2016	561,000
2017	614,000

Find the ratios of the function values $H(t)$ for all consecutive integer values of t.

$\dfrac{H(1)}{H(0)} = \dfrac{368}{306} \approx 1.20$ $\dfrac{H(2)}{H(1)} = \dfrac{429}{368} \approx 1.17$

$\dfrac{H(3)}{H(2)} = \dfrac{437}{429} \approx 1.02$ $\dfrac{H(4)}{H(3)} = \dfrac{501}{437} \approx 1.15$

$\dfrac{H(5)}{H(4)} = \dfrac{561}{501} \approx 1.12$ $\dfrac{H(6)}{H(5)} = \dfrac{614}{561} \approx 1.09$

Although the ratios are not all exactly the same, you can find the average of the ratios to approximate the base of a exponential function modeling the data.

$$\dfrac{1.20 + 1.17 + 1.02 + 1.15 + 1.12 + 1.09}{6} = \dfrac{6.75}{6}$$

$$= 1.125$$

$$= \dfrac{9}{8}$$

Write an exponential model $H(t) = ab^t$. Use the average ratio $\frac{9}{8}$ for b. Then determine the initial value a for the function. The value a occurs when $t = 0$, which represents the year 2011. The number of newly constructed housing units (in thousands) sold in 2011 was 306.

An exponential model for this data is $H(t) = 306\left(\frac{9}{8}\right)^t$.

Use a graphing calculator to graph the function $H(t)$ and plot the points from the table.

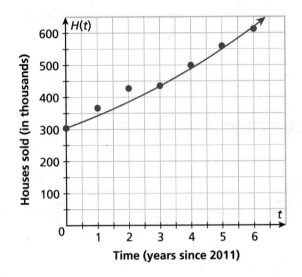

A. Does the exponential model for this data show exponential growth or exponential decay? Explain how you know.

B. Describe how the function values of an exponential function $f(x) = ab^x$ change from one integer value of x to the next. Why is an exponential function a good model for data set if ratios of consecutive function values are nearly constant?

C. Why might you use the average of the ratios to identify the base of the exponential function when the ratios are similar, but not all exactly the same?

D. Is the value of a in the exponential model $f(x) = ab^x$ always equivalent to the function value when $x = 0$? Explain why or why not.

E. Do you think $H(t) = 306\left(\frac{9}{8}\right)^t$ is a good model for the data in the table? Explain why or why not.

 Turn and Talk How would the exponential function $H(t) = 306\left(\frac{9}{8}\right)^t$ change if the common ratio was $\frac{7}{8}$ instead? Describe what this would tell you about how the number of newly built housing units sold was changing over time.

Step It Out

Create an Exponential Model Using Technology

2 ▶ You can use a graphing calculator to find an exponential model of best fit for the data set from Task 1.

- Enter the data in a table. For this data set, the x_1 corresponds to the t-values and the y_1 corresponds to the $H(t)$-values.

- Then enter the general form for an exponential function using y_1 and x_1: $y_1 \sim ab^{x_1}$. Select Log Mode.

The graphing calculator will show the data values from the table plotted as points and the exponential function. You can graph the equation of the model you created in Task 1 for easy comparison.

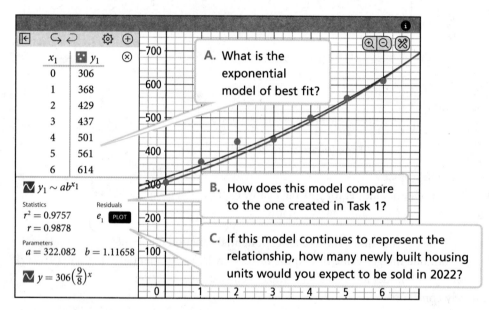

x_1	y_1
0	306
1	368
2	429
3	437
4	501
5	561
6	614

$y_1 \sim ab^{x_1}$

Statistics
$r^2 = 0.9757$
$r = 0.9878$

Residuals
e_1 PLOT

Parameters
$a = 322.082$ $b = 1.11658$

$y = 306\left(\frac{9}{8}\right)^x$

A. What is the exponential model of best fit?

B. How does this model compare to the one created in Task 1?

C. If this model continues to represent the relationship, how many newly built housing units would you expect to be sold in 2022?

Create a Logarithmic Model

You can create a logarithmic model for real-world data if an exponential model is already known, or by performing a logarithmic regression.

3 ▶ Create a logarithmic model for a given set of data already modeled by an exponential model.

Gray wolves were reintroduced back into some of the states where they once lived before being put on the Endangered Species list. One of these populations of wolves was tracked for a period of time so that scientists could monitor the growth of the population.

$P = 81(1.09)^t$ models the wolf population P.

The exponential model shown was developed from a set of data where P is the wolf population at time t (in years since the tracking began). A researcher studying wolf populations throughout the United States wants to create a new model that gives the time it takes the wolf population to reach a certain number so that she can compare it to other data.

In order to write a model, find the inverse of the exponential model. In other words, convert the exponential model to a logarithmic model.

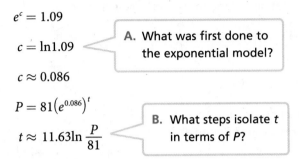

$e^c = 1.09$

$c = \ln 1.09$

A. What was first done to the exponential model?

$c \approx 0.086$

$P = 81\left(e^{0.086}\right)^t$

$t \approx 11.63\ln \dfrac{P}{81}$

B. What steps isolate t in terms of P?

The table below shows the original set of data that was collected.

Years since study began, t	0	1	2	3	4	5	6	7	8	9	10	11	12
Wolf population, P	82	90	99	105	113	124	134	146	162	176	194	207	239

Evaluate whether the logarithmic function is a good model for the data. Use a graphing calculator to graph the data points from the table, being sure to use the population numbers for x-values and the years for y-values. Then graph the logarithmic function $t = 11.63\ln\dfrac{P}{81}$.

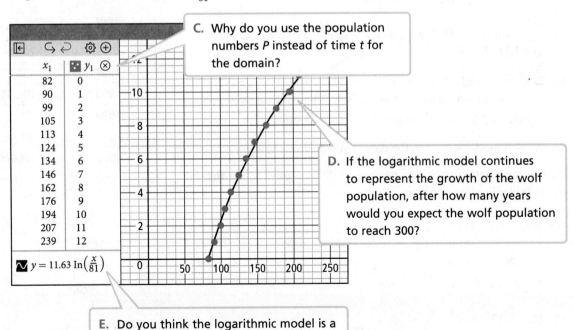

C. Why do you use the population numbers P instead of time t for the domain?

D. If the logarithmic model continues to represent the growth of the wolf population, after how many years would you expect the wolf population to reach 300?

E. Do you think the logarithmic model is a good fit for the data? Explain.

Turn and Talk If you were to perform a regression on the data in the table using the P-values for the domain and the t-values for the range, what type of regression would you perform? How does this type of model relate to the original exponential model? Use a graphing calculator to perform this new regression. What is the regression model?

Check Understanding

1. Explain how you can use ratios to determine whether or not an exponential model might be a good fit for a data set.

Use the table of values for Problems 2–5.

2. Create a best fit exponential model for the data set.

3. Use a graphing calculator to perform an exponential regression on the data set. What is the exponential regression? Round each value to the nearest hundredth.

4. Which model better fits the data? How do you know?

5. Use the model you created in Problem 2 to create a logarithmic model that gives the time it takes the number of paintings sold to reach a certain number.

Year	Paintings sold
2009	9
2010	12
2011	15
2012	25
2013	38
2014	49
2015	58

On Your Own

6. Using ratios, you determine that an exponential model is a good model for a data set. What are two different ways that you can find the value of a of an exponential model $f(x) = ab^x$ for the given set of data?

Use the table of values for Problems 7–9.

7. **(MP) Model with Mathematics** Create a best fit exponential model for the data set.

8. **(MP) Use Tools** Use a graphing calculator to perform an exponential regression on the data set. What is the exponential regression? Round each value to the nearest hundredth.

9. Which model better fits the data? How do you know?

Year	Profit in dollars
1996	209,847
1997	150,726
1998	106,565
1999	74,209
2000	54,880
2001	38,640
2002	27,850

Determine whether each exponential model is a good fit for the data in the table. Explain your reasoning.

10. $f(x) = 65(7.2)^x$

x	0	1	2	3	4	5	6
f(x)	65	468	1,872	7,675	29,932	119,728	478,912

11. $f(x) = 12(0.86)^x$

x	0	1	2	3	4	5	6
f(x)	30	26	21	19	16	14	12

12. **(MP) Use Structure** The inverse of an exponential function is a logarithmic function. Describe what this means for the domain and range of a data set when writing a logarithmic model from an existing exponential model.

13. (MP) **Use Structure** Describe two different ways to find an exponential model for a set of data.

14. (MP) **Use Structure** Describe two different ways to find a logarithmic model for a set of data.

The function $P(t) = 2557(1.09)^t$ models the data in the table showing the number of eagle pairs t years since 1988. Use the given information for Problems 15–19.

Number of years since 1988, t	Eagle pair population, $P(t)$
0	2475
1	2680
2	3035
3	3399
4	3749
5	4015
6	4449
7	4712
8	5094
9	5295
10	5748
11	6404
12	6471
13	7066
14	9789

15. Use the given exponential function to write a function that gives the time it takes the eagle pair population to reach a certain number. What is your model?

16. Use the given table to create a table showing the domain and range of the model you wrote in Problem 15.

17. Graph your function from Problem 15. What else should you graph in order to check whether the model is a good fit for the data?

18. Do you think that logarithmic model is a good fit for the data? How do you know?

19. If the model continues to represent the growth of the eagle population, during which year would you expect the eagle population to reach 12,000?

The function $G(t) = 3.13(1.53)^t$ models the data in the table showing the worldwide capacity (in gigawatts) of installed solar panels t years since 2004. Use the given information for Problems 20–25.

Years since 2004, t	0	1	2	3	4	5	6	7	8	9
Solar panel capacity (in gigawatts), $G(t)$	3.7	5.1	7	9	16	23	40	70	100	139

20. Write a function model that gives the time it takes the capacity of solar panels to reach a certain number.

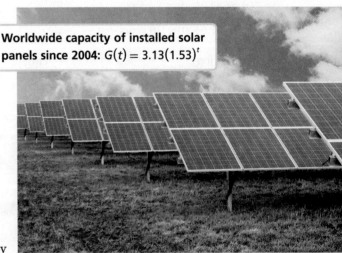

Worldwide capacity of installed solar panels since 2004: $G(t) = 3.13(1.53)^t$

21. Graph your model from Problem 20. Do you think the logarithmic model is a good fit for the data? How do you know?

22. Create a table using your logarithmic model or its graph where the capacity in gigawatts is 20, 40, 60, 80, 100, 120, and 140.

23. Using your table from Problem 22, determine the rate of change for each interval of 20 gigawatts.

24. How does the time it takes to increase the capacity by 20 gigawatts change as the capacity increases?

25. If the model continues to represent the increase in the solar panel capacity, will the capacity reach 200 gigawatts before 2020? Explain your reasoning.

The data in the table shows the approximate number of mobile cellular subscriptions S in the world per 100 people t years after 2008. A model for the data is shown with the photo. Use the given information for Problems 26–29.

Mobile cellular subscriptions (per 100 people), S	Years since 2008, t
59.45	0
67.58	1
76.14	2
83.69	3
87.90	4
92.42	5
96.01	6
97.38	7
100.72	8
104.49	9

$t = 0.031(1.056)^s$

26. Write a model that gives the number of subscriptions per 100 people, S, as a function of time, t.

27. Graph your model from Problem 26. Do you think the model is a good fit for the data? How do you know?

28. Describe how you found the model you wrote in Problem 26. What is another way you could find a model for the data?

29. If the model continues to represent growth for subscriptions, during which year would you expect the subscriptions to be double the initial number of subscriptions? Explain your reasoning.

Spiral Review • Assessment Readiness

30. You invest $100 at an annual interest rate of 2.4% compounded continuously. Which statements are true about the balance of the account given the scenario? Assume that money is never withdrawn. Select all that apply.

    Ⓐ $107.47 after 3 years

    Ⓑ $231.64 after 35 years

    Ⓒ $1102.31 after 10 years

    Ⓓ $682.09 after 8 years

    Ⓔ $161.61 after 20 years

31. What is $\log_{\frac{1}{5}} a = b$ written as an exponential equation?

    Ⓐ $a^b = \frac{1}{5}$

    Ⓒ $\left(\frac{1}{5}\right)^b = a$

    Ⓑ $\left(\frac{1}{5}\right)^a = b$

    Ⓓ $b^{\frac{1}{5}} = a$

32. Which statement is true for the graph of $f(x) = 3\log(x - 7) + 1$?

    Ⓐ It contains the point $(8, 0)$.

    Ⓑ It contains the point $(17, 4)$.

    Ⓒ The function has a domain of all real numbers.

    Ⓓ The function is decreasing.

33. Which expression is equivalent to $\log 100$?

    Ⓐ $(\log 4)(\log 25)$

    Ⓑ $\log 10 + \log 2$

    Ⓒ $(\log 10)^2$

    Ⓓ $\log 20 + \log 5$

I'm in a Learning Mindset!

How can my success with modeling exponential and logarithmic functions support my long-term goals?

Review

Logarithmic Functions

A lily pad in a pond reproduces itself each month. The total population of lily pads created from this 1 lily pad is modeled by the exponential function $L = 2^m$ where m is the number of months the lily pad has reproduced.

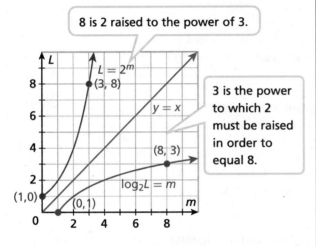

8 is 2 raised to the power of 3.

3 is the power to which 2 must be raised in order to equal 8.

The logarithmic function $\log_2 L = m$ is the inverse of the exponential function $L = 2^m$.

Graph Logarithmic Functions

A micro-organism was found in the pond. The total population per drop of water is modeled by the logarithmic function $P(d) = 10 \log(d + 1) + 5$ where d is the number of days since it was taken from the pond.

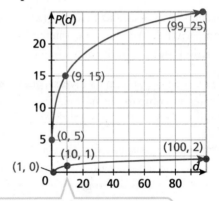

$(1, 0)$ and $(10, 1)$ are reference points of the parent function.

$P(d)$ stretches the parent function vertically by a factor of 10, then translates it 5 units up and 1 unit to the left.

Exponential and Logarithmic Models

The table represents the pond's total frog population in t number of years since 2008.

Years since 2008	0	1	2	3	4	5	6	7	8	9	10
Number of Frogs	10,006	9805	9600	9405	9220	9053	8854	8687	8500	8331	8164

An exponential model models the frogs population, $P = 10{,}006(0.98)^t$.

the initial population

the common ratio between successive years

Knowing the population of the frogs, the logarithmic function $t \approx -49.5 \ln\left(\frac{P}{10,006}\right)$ outputs the year.

$\frac{1}{\ln(0.98)}$

Other logarithms could also be used.

Vocabulary

Choose the correct term from the box to complete each sentence.

1. A logarithm with a base of e is called a ___?___.

2. A ___?___ is the power to which a value must be raised in order to get a certain value.

3. A ___?___ is a value raised to a power.

4. A logarithm with a base of 10 is called a ___?___.

Concepts and Skills

5. Graph $f(x) = 3^x$ and its inverse, $g(x) = \log_3 x$. Use the graphs you created to compare the domain, range, intercepts, asymptotes, and rate of change of one function to those of the other function.

6. Graph $f(x) = \left(\frac{1}{4}\right)^x$ and its inverse, $g(x) = \log_{\frac{1}{4}} x$. Use the graphs you created to compare the domain, range, intercepts, asymptotes, and rate of change of one function to those of the other function.

7. Graph the logarithmic function $g(x) = -2\log_6(x - 4) + 1$. Use the graph to describe the sequence of transformations performed on the parent function $f(x) = \log_6 x$ in order to graph $g(x)$.

8. (MP) **Use Tools** The total population P of the bacteria that turns milk into yogurt can be determined by the function $P(t) = 2000(2)^{\frac{t}{73}}$ where t is in minutes. How long does it take the population to grow to 64,000? State what strategy and tool you will use to answer the question, explain your choice, and then find the answer.

9. Forest rangers studied a population of deer over a period of time.

Year of study	0	1	2	3	4	5	6	7	8
Deer population	85	110	130	165	200	254	320	412	503

A. Create an exponential model for the data set. Compare your model with an exponential regression model performed on the data.

B. When will the deer population reach 1000?

C. Describe the end behavior of your model. Does this accurately describe the deer population? Explain your reasoning.

10. The forest rangers also studied a fox population and determined the function $P(t) = 42(1.18)^t$ models the fox population at time t (in years) since their study began. A research team of biologists are interested in a model that gives the time it takes the fox population to reach a certain level. Graph your model and describe what the graph shows about the growth.

Exponential and Logarithmic Equations

Module Performance Task: *Spies and Analysts*™

OUR NATIONAL DEBT:
21,195,005,572,456

YOUR *Family share* 261,040

THE NATIONAL DEBT CLOCK

All in the Family

DEBT

How many years would it take to pay off the national debt if each family contributed the same amount each year?

Are You Ready?

Complete these problems to review prior concepts and skills you will need for this module.

Properties of Exponents

Simplify each expression using properties of exponents.

1. $2^4(2^5)$

2. $\left(4 \cdot 3^2 \cdot 5^3\right)^2$

3. $\dfrac{6 \cdot 7^5 \cdot 3^3}{2 \cdot 6^4 \cdot 7^3 \cdot 3^7}$

4. $\left(\dfrac{3(-2)(9)^2}{5(-2)^2(9)^3(-1)^4}\right)^2$

Justify Steps for Solving Equations

Write the justification for each step in the solution of $7(x + 3) - 3(x + 2) = 23$.

$7(x + 3) - 3(x + 2) = 23$

5. $\rightarrow\ 7x + 21 - 3x - 6 = 23$

6. $\rightarrow\quad\quad 4x + 15 = 23$

7. $\rightarrow\quad\quad\quad\quad 4x = 8$

8. $\rightarrow\quad\quad\quad\quad\quad x = 2$

Solve Radical Equations

Solve each radical equation.

9. $\sqrt{3 - 2x} = x$

10. $\sqrt{x - 7} = 9$

11. $\sqrt{x - 15} = 3 - \sqrt{x}$

12. $\sqrt{x} - 2 = \sqrt{x - 5}$

13. $\sqrt{6x - 5} = x$

14. $3 + \sqrt{x - 6} = x - 5$

Connecting Past and Present Learning

Previously, you learned:
- to simplify expressions using properties of exponents including products, quotients, and powers of powers,
- to define and create exponential and logarithmic functions, and
- to use exponential and logarithmic models in applied situations.

In this module, you will learn:
- to simplify expressions using properties of logarithms,
- to model with and solve exponential equations, and
- to model with and solve logarithmic equations.

Properties of Logarithms

(I Can) **develop and apply the properties of logarithms to simplify expressions.**

Spark Your Learning

Pedro works for the city of Phoenix, Arizona. To help the city with its urban planning, he needs to determine or predict the years when the population increases by increments of 10% from the 2010 population.

Pedro finds the population of Phoenix in 2010.

Pedro researches the rate of population growth for the city in recent years.

Complete Part A as a whole class. Then complete Parts B–D in small groups.

A. What is a mathematical question you can ask about this situation? What information would you need to know to answer your question?

B. What variable(s) are involved in this situation? What unit of measurement would you use for each variable?

C. To answer your question, what strategy and tool would you use along with all the information you have? What answer do you get?

D. Does your work make sense in the context of the situation? How do you know?

Turn and Talk If a logarithmic model were used to relate the time and population, how would it be related to the exponential model?

©dszc/E+/Getty Images

Build Understanding

Investigate the Properties of Logarithms Numerically

Scientific calculators have a LOG button and LN button that can be used to find decimal equivalents or approximations of logarithmic expressions.

 1 Use a scientific calculator to evaluate the expressions in each set.

    A. What is the value of each logarithm shown in the table?

    B. Match each expression in Set A to its equivalent expression in Set B. For any expressions that do not have a match, write an inequality statement.

Set A	Set B
$\log 1$	$\ln e$
$\log 10$	$\ln e^5$
$\log 10^4$	$\ln 1$

    C. How can you check the results of evaluating the expressions in Set B? Use your method to check the results.

    D. What general statement seems to be true about the expression $\log 10^b$?

    E. What general statement seems to be true about the expression $\ln e^a$?

> **Turn and Talk** How might you use a similar approach to generalize an equality statement inferred by the logarithmic expressions $\log 10e$ and $1 + \log e$?

Investigate the Properties of Logarithms Graphically

Graphing calculators can be used to graph and analyze functions involving common logarithms as well as natural logarithms.

2 Consider the graphs of $y = \log 2x$ and $y = \log 2 + \log x$.

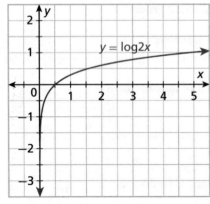 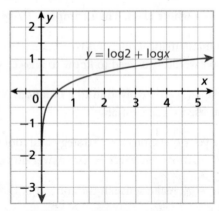

    A. Compare the two graphs visually. What do you observe about the curves?

    B. Graph the functions $y = \log 2x$ and $y = \log 2 + \log x$ together on a graphing calculator. Use the table feature to compare the y-values of the two functions.

C. Write two other functions that you believe have the same relationship. Use a graphing calculator to check that your functions are related in the same way as the pair of functions graphed in this task. Explain your results.

D. What general statement seems to be true about functions of the form $y = \log_b mn$?

 Turn and Talk How are the functions $y = \log 6x$, $y = \log 3(2x)$, and $y = \log 2(3x)$ related? Are the functions $y = \log 6x$ and $y = \log 2 + \log 3 + \log x$ equivalent? Explain.

Logarithmic functions can include different types of expressions including sums, differences, products, and quotients.

3 Consider the graphs of $y = \log \frac{x}{2}$ and $y = \log x - \log 2$.

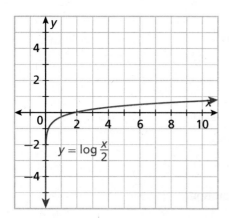 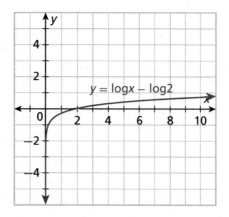

A. Compare the two graphs visually. What do you observe about the curves?

B. Graph the functions $y = \log \frac{x}{2}$ and $y = \log x - \log 2$ together on a graphing calculator. Use the table feature to compare the y-values of the two functions.

C. Write two other functions that you believe have the same relationship. Use a graphing calculator to check that your functions are related in the same way as the pair of functions graphed above. Explain your results.

D. What general statement seems to be true about functions of the form $y = \log_b \frac{m}{n}$?

 Turn and Talk How are the functions $y = \log \frac{x}{6}$ and $y = \log \frac{2x}{12}$ related? Are the functions $y = \log \frac{x}{6}$ and $y = \log x - \log 2 - \log 3$ equivalent? Explain.

Step It Out

Prove the Properties of Logarithms

A **logarithm** is the exponent to which a base must be raised in order to obtain a given number, so $\log_b b^m = m$. It follows that $\log_b b^0 = 1$, so $\log_b 1 = 0$. Also, $\log_b b^1 = 1$, so $\log_b b = 1$. Additional properties of logarithms are shown in the table.

Properties of Logarithms	
For any positive numbers *a, m, n, b* $(b \neq 1)$, and *c* $(c \neq 1)$, the following properties hold.	
Definition-Based Properties	$\log_b b^m = m$ $\qquad$ $\log_b 1 = 0$ $\qquad$ $\log_b b = 1$
Product Property of Logarithms	$\log_b mn = \log_b m + \log_b n$
Quotient Property of Logarithms	$\log_b \dfrac{m}{n} = \log_b m - \log_b n$
Power Property of Logarithms	$\log_b m^n = n\log_b m$
Change of Base Property of Logarithms	$\log_c a = \dfrac{\log_b a}{\log_b c}$

4 ▶ Prove the Power Property of Logarithms, $\log_b m^n = n\log_b m$.

A. Write the proof statements in the correct order.

$$\log_b b^{xn} = xn$$

$$\left(\log_b m\right)n = n\log_b m$$

$$\log_b m^n = \log_b \left(b^x\right)^n$$

Let $x = \log_b m^n$.
Then $m = b^x$.

$$\log_b \left(b^x\right)^n = \log_b b^{xn}$$

$$xn = \left(\log_b m\right)n$$

B. Write the proof reasons in the correct order.

Substitution

Definition of logarithm

Commutative Property of Multiplication

Power of a Power Property of Exponents

Substitution

Definition of logarithm

Turn and Talk What connections do you see between properties of logarithms and properties of exponents?

298

Use Properties of Logarithms to Evaluate Expressions

The properties of logarithms can be used to rewrite logarithmic expressions. Sometimes an expression can be simplified to a numerical value without needing to use a calculator.

5 Simplify each expression.

$\log_{12} 9 + \log_{12} 16$

$\log_{12} 9 + \log_{12} 16 = \log_{12}(9 \cdot 16)$

$= \log_{12} 144$

$= \log_{12} 12^2$

$= 2\log_{12} 12$

$= 2$

$\log_6 90 - \log_6 9$

$\log_6 90 - \log_6 9 = \log_6 \dfrac{90}{9}$

$= \log_6 10$

$= \dfrac{\log_{10} 10}{\log_{10} 6}$

≈ 1.2851

> **A.** Justify each step of the simplifications.

B. What single property of logarithms could you apply in order to verify these simplifications using only a calculator? Verify the results.

Use a Logarithmic Model to Solve a Real-World Problem

6 The population of the country Liberia has been increasing at about the same rate over the past several years. If this rate continues, how long will it take for the population to increase by 50%?

The exponential growth model is $P = P_0(1 + r)^t$, where P is the population (in millions) after t years, P_0 is the population in 2017, and r is the average growth rate (as a decimal).

$P_0 = 4.7 \qquad P = 1.5P_0 = 7.05 \qquad r = 0.025$

Liberia Population:
- 4.7 million (2017)
- annual increase: 2.5%

AFRICA

LIBERIA

Gulf of Guinea

ATLANTIC OCEAN

Find the inverse model of $P = P_0(1 + r)^t$.

$P = P_0(1 + r)^t$

$\dfrac{P}{P_0} = (1 + r)^t$ Divide both sides by P_0.

$\log_{1 + r}\left(\dfrac{P}{P_0}\right) = t$ Take the log base-$(1 + r)$ of both sides.

$\dfrac{\log \dfrac{P}{P_0}}{\log(1 + r)} = t$

> **A.** Which definition-based property was used to rewrite the right side as just t in this step?

> **B.** What property justifies this step?

Substitute the known values. Use a calculator to evaluate the expression for t.

$t = \dfrac{\log\left(\dfrac{P}{P_0}\right)}{\log(1 + r)} = \dfrac{\log\left(\dfrac{7.05}{4.7}\right)}{\log(1 + 0.025)} = \dfrac{\log 1.5}{\log 1.025} \approx 16.42$

C. In what year will the population of Liberia be 50% greater than it was in 2017?

Check Understanding

For Problems 1 and 2, evaluate each logarithm.

1. $\log \dfrac{1}{100,000}$

2. $\ln e^3$

3. Prove the Quotient Property of Logarithms: $\log_b \dfrac{m}{n} = \log_b m - \log_b n$.

    A. Start with $x = \log_b m$ and $y = \log_b n$ and then rewrite these two equations using the definition of logarithms.

    B. Complete the proof using substitution, properties of exponents, and the definition of logarithms.

For Problems 4 and 5, simplify the expression as a single logarithm. Then evaluate the expressions, without a calculator if possible.

4. $2\log_3 9 + \log_3 3 - 3\log_3 3$

5. $4\log 2 + 4\log 5$

6. Assume that a small town with a current population of 5500 is growing at a rate of 2% annually.

    A. Write a logarithmic model for the population of the town t years from now.

    B. Write a function for t, the number of years it will take for the population to increase by 20% from its current level.

    C. How many years will it take for the population to increase by 20%?

On Your Own

For Problems 7–10, evaluate each logarithm.

7. $\log 0.01$

8. $\ln e^6$

9. $\log_4 0.25$

10. $\log_5 625$

11. (MP) **Reason** Prove the Change of Base Property: $\log_c a = \dfrac{\log_b a}{\log_b c}$.

    Hint: Begin by letting $\log_c a = y$.

Rewrite each expression as a single logarithm. Then evaluate the resulting logarithm without using a calculator.

12. $\log_6 9 + \log_6 4$

13. $\log_3 405 - \log_3 5$

14. $3\log 5 + \log 8$

15. $\log_9 1.5 + \log_9 18$

16. $\log_8 3 - 2\log_8 6$

17. $2\log_{12} 4 + 3\log_{12} 3 + 2\log_{12} 2$

For Problems 18–23, rewrite each expression as a single logarithm. Then use a calculator to evaluate the resulting logarithm.

18. $\log_7 5 + \log_7 8$

19. $\log_8 72 - \log_8 4$

20. $4\log 3 + \log 2$

21. $\log_9 3.4 + \log_9 15$

22. $\log_6 12 - 3\log_6 4$

23. $2\log_5 4 + 3\log_5 3 + 2\log_5 2$

24. After many years of increases, the number of runners registering for road races in the United States has decreased slightly.

2016 participation:
18.5 million

Rate of change from 2016 to 2017:
1.1% decrease

    A. Write an expression for the number of registered runners in millions. Let t be the number of years after 2016.

    B. Write an equation in terms of t, the time it takes for the number of registered runners to decrease 10% from the 2016 participation levels.

    C. If the pattern continues, in what year will overall participation decrease by 10% of the 2016 participation levels?

25. (MP) **Critique Reasoning** A student estimated the logarithmic expression $\log_4 32 - \log_5 125 \approx -1$, explaining that it is true because $\log_4 \frac{32}{125} \approx \log_4 \frac{1}{4}$ and $\log_4 \frac{1}{4} = -1$. Explain and correct the student's error.

26. Suppose that the population of one endangered species is decreasing at an average rate of 5% per year throughout all of its natural habitats. In one of its habitats, the current population of the species is 108. After how many years will the population in that habitat fall below 50?

27. **Open Ended** Write a logarithmic expression that can be simplified using the Quotient Property and Power Property of Logarithms. Simplify the expression.

28. (MP) **Model with Mathematics** The population of North Carolina has been growing faster than the rest of the United States in recent years.

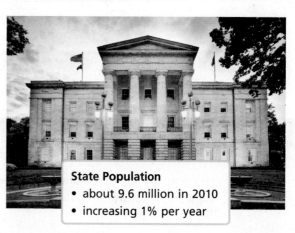

    A. Write a logarithmic equation for t, the time in years for the population to be 25% greater than the 2010 population.

    B. If the population continues growing at its current rate, in what year will the population be 25% greater than the 2010 population?

State Population
- about 9.6 million in 2010
- increasing 1% per year

29. (MP) **Model with Mathematics** The owners of a café have seen its income grow by the same percent over the past few years.

A. Write a function for t, the number of years it will take for the café's income to increase by 30% from its current income I if the income continues to grow at its current rate.

B. How many years will it take for the income to increase by 30% over its current level?

Income Model:
$I(t) = 150,000(1.045)t$

30. **STEM** The formula $M = \frac{2}{3}\log\left(\frac{E}{10^{11.8}}\right)$ gives the Richter magnitude M of an earthquake as a function of the energy released E, in ergs. Write a formula for E as a function of M. Then use the new formula to find the energy released by the earthquake that occurred near Anchorage, Alaska on January 13, 2019.

ALASKA

CANADA

Magnitude: 5.0

Anchorage

Gulf of Alaska

31. **Open Middle™** Using the digits 1 to 9, at most one time each, fill in the boxes to make an equivalent statement with the least possible value for the expressions.

$$\boxed{}\log\boxed{} + \log\boxed{} - \log\boxed{} = \log\boxed{}$$

Spiral Review • Assessment Readiness

32. Match each exponential equation with is logarithmic form.

   A. $8^x = y$ 1. $\ln 8 = y$

   B. $8^y = x$ 2. $\log_8 y = x$

   C. $e^y = 8$ 3. $\ln y = 8$

   D. $e^8 = y$ 4. $\log_8 x = y$

33. What is the x-intercept of the graph of $y = -2\log_3(x - 5) + 2$?

   (A) 3   (C) 7

   (B) 5   (D) 8

34. Which equation represents an initial population of 2.5 million that shrinks by 3% annually?

   (A) $y = 2.5(0.7)^x$

   (B) $y = 2.5(1.03)^x$

   (C) $y = 2.5(0.97)^x$

   (D) $y = 2.5(1.3)^x$

35. What is the x-value of the intersection of $y = 0.5$ and $y = 4^x$? Use a graphing calculator.

   (A) -2 (C) -0.5

   (B) -1 (D) 0.125

I'm in a Learning Mindset!

How can my success in understanding and using the properties of logarithmic support my long term goals?

Solve Exponential Equations

(I Can) use logarithms to find missing values for exponential models.

Spark Your Learning

A piano has 88 keys. Each key is tuned to a specific frequency of sound waves in order to produce a unique musical note. From left to right, the keys produce notes that increase in frequency.

$f(n)$ = frequency of note played
n = position of key to the right or left of concert A on the piano

Complete Part A as a whole class. Then complete Parts B–D in small groups.

A. What is a mathematical question you can ask about this situation? What information would you need to know to answer your question?

B. What are the limitations on the domain of the function relating the position of a piano key to the frequency of the note it plays?

C. To answer your question, what strategy and tool would you use along with all the information you have? What answer do you get?

D. Does your answer make sense in the context of the situation? How do you know?

Turn and Talk What does a negative value for n mean in this situation? What is the relationship between keys that have a 2:1 relationship in frequency? between keys with a 2:3 relationship in frequency?

Build Understanding

Estimate Solutions of Exponential Equations from Tables

One method to estimate the solution of an exponential equation is to use a table of values. You can substitute different input values until you find your answer to the specificity that is asked for in the given situation.

By carefully choosing input values, you can "narrow down" the possible input values, bracketing the solution between an upper bound and a lower bound.

You can use what you know about the function to choose appropriate values and to interpret the solution using a table like the one below.

 1 Let $f(x) = 250(1.02)^{3x}$. Estimate a value for x such that the output is 1000.

A. Write an equation to represent this problem. To estimate the solution, start with convenient values of x. What starting values do you think make sense for this problem?

B. Examine the columns in each row of the table below. How does the entry in the center column of a row lead to the entry in the last column, and ultimately to the choice of a value for x for the next row?

x	$f(x) = 250(1.02)^{3x}$	Next guess for x
0	250	$x > 0$
5	336.467	$x > 5$
10	452.840	$x > 10$
15	609.464	$x > 15$
20	820.258	$x > 20$
30	1485.783	$20 < x < 30$
25	1103.959	$20 < x < 25$
23	980.284	$23 < x < 25$
24	1040.285	_____?_____

C. How can you use the table of values to determine the nearest whole number value of x that results in a function value closest to 1000?

D. To the nearest whole number, what is the solution of the equation you wrote in Part A? Explain.

E. If you wanted to find the value of x to the nearest tenth, what would be your next guess for x? Explain.

 Turn and Talk When using a table to estimate the solution, why is it important to know whether the graph is always increasing or always decreasing?

Solve an Exponential Equation Graphically

Another way to solve exponential equations is to use a graphical approach. You have solved several different types of equations in one variable using graphs, including quadratic and other polynomial equations.

Recall that the technique for solving an equation graphically involves setting the expressions on each side of the equation equal to y and graphing the resulting functions together on the same coordinate plane. Whether using graph paper or a graphing calculator, you then locate any point (or points) of intersection. The x-coordinate of any point of intersection is a solution of the original equation. The graph at the right shows how this method works for the equation $x^2 - 8x + 13 = 1$. The graph shows that the equation has two solutions, $x = 2$ and $x = 6$.

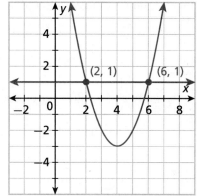

This graphical method can be used to solve an exponential equation in one variable.

2 Solve the equation $6000 = 8000(0.95)^x$ using a graphical approach.

A. What two functions will be graphed together on a graphing calculator?

B. What will the graphs of the two functions look like? How do you know?

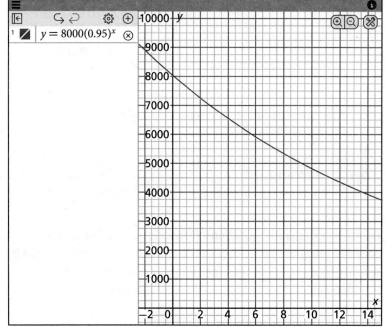

C. The graph of the function $y = 8000(0.95)^x$ is shown below. How can you use the gridlines in the figure to estimate the solution of the given exponential equation?

D. Graph the functions $y = 8000(0.95)^x$ and $y = 6000$ together on a graphing calculator. Use the graphing calculator to identify the point of intersection. What are the coordinates of this point?

E. What does the point of intersection reveal as the solution of the original equation? How can you verify that this value is indeed the solution of the equation?

F. What are the benefits of graphing with technology to solve the exponential equation over graphing using graph paper?

 Turn and Talk How do you know there is only one solution to the equation? How else could you solve this equation graphically?

Step It Out

Solve an Exponential Equation Algebraically

In addition to estimating solutions of exponential equations using a table and solving them graphically, you can also solve exponential equations algebraically. Some exponential equations can be solved directly by rewriting them so that both sides of the equation are exponential expressions with the same base.

> **Property of Equality for Exponential Equations**
>
> For all real numbers b $(b \neq 1)$, x, and y, $b^x = b^y$ if and only if $x = y$.

3 ▶ Solve the equation $3(2^{x+3}) = 96$.

$3(2^{x+3}) = 96$ Given

$2^{x+3} = 32$ Divide both sides by 3.

$2^{x+3} = 2^5$ Write 32 as a power of 2.

$x + 3 = 5$

$x = 2$ **A.** What reasons justify the last two steps of the solution?

B. Why is the first step of the solution process division by 3? Why is it not possible to use the Property of Equality for Exponential Equations as the first step of the process?

 Turn and Talk What advantage does solving an equation algebraically have over the techniques of using a table or graphing?

For many exponential equations, it will not be possible to rewrite the two sides of the equation using the same base. To complete the solution when this is the case, you can rewrite the exponential equation using the definition of a logarithm and then solve the resulting equation using the properties of logarithms.

4 ▶ Solve the equation $5(3^x) - 7 = 43$.

$5(3^x) - 7 = 43$

$5(3^x) = 50$ **A.** Why can't the Property of Equality for Exponential Equations be used now?

$3^x = 10$

$x = \log_3 10$ Definition of logarithm

B. What property justifies this step? What further simplification could you make here before using a calculator?

$x = \dfrac{\log 10}{\log 3}$

$x \approx 2.096$ Use a calculator; round to the nearest thousandth.

 Turn and Talk How is the solution process different when the base of the logarithmic expression is something other than 10 or e?

Real-World Problems Modeled by Exponential Equations

You can use algebra to solve real-world problems that are modeled by exponential equations. For example, the amount of medicine that remains in a body decreases exponentially over time as the body processes the medicine. So the amount of medication remaining in a person or animal's bloodstream at any given time since the medication was administered is modeled by an exponential decay function.

5 ▸ During an annual check-up, a veterinarian diagnoses arthritis in the hips of Marissa's dog. The veterinarian instructs Marisa to give her dog one 300-mg tablet of a medicine per day to treat the arthritis and then administers the first tablet.

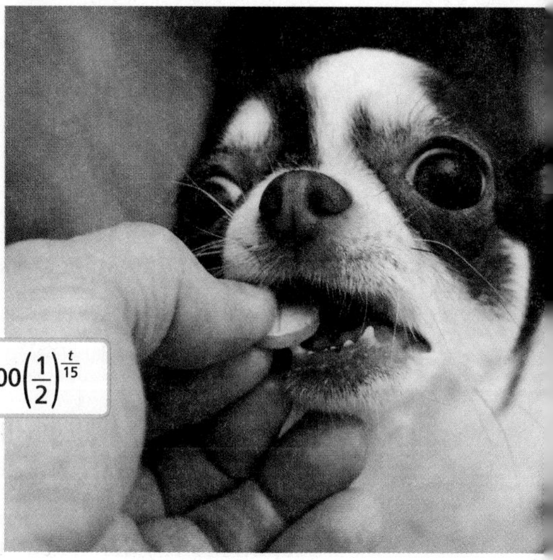

The amount of medicine A remaining in the dog's bloodstream after t minutes can be expressed by an exponential decay function. How long will it take for the amount of medicine to drop to 75 mg?

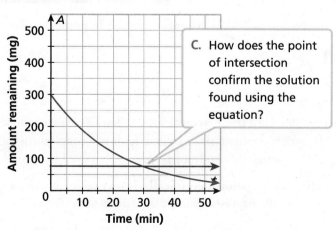

$$A = 300\left(\frac{1}{2}\right)^{\frac{t}{15}}$$

$A = 300\left(\frac{1}{2}\right)^{\frac{t}{15}}$ Given equation

$75 = 300\left(\frac{1}{2}\right)^{\frac{t}{15}}$ Substitute 75 for A.

$\frac{1}{4} = \left(\frac{1}{2}\right)^{\frac{t}{15}}$ Divide both sides by 300.

$\left(\frac{1}{2}\right)^{2} = \left(\frac{1}{2}\right)^{\frac{t}{15}}$ **A. What has been done in this step of the solution? What alternative way could this have been done?**

$2 = \frac{t}{15}$ **B. What is the justification for this step?**

$30 = t$ Multiply both sides by 15.

So, it will take 30 minutes for the amount of medicine to drop to 75 mg.

This result can be verified by graphing the two sides of the equation $75 = 300\left(\frac{1}{2}\right)^{\frac{t}{15}}$ on the same coordinate grid and then finding the point of intersection.

C. How does the point of intersection confirm the solution found using the equation?

Graph: vertical axis "Amount remaining (mg)" marked 100, 200, 300, 400, 500; horizontal axis "Time (min)" marked 10, 20, 30, 40, 50.

Turn and Talk Would you be able to solve the problem algebraically if the medicine tablet was 325 mg? How else might you solve this problem?

Check Understanding

1. Solve $750 = 130(1.03)^{2x}$ to the nearest whole number. Complete a table of values that shows increasingly closer upper and lower bounds.

For Problems 2 and 3, solve each equation either graphically or algebraically. Round to the nearest whole number.

2. $1350 = 100(1.4)^x$

3. $4.5 = 80\left(\frac{1}{2}\right)^x$

4. Solve the equation $237 = 3(2)^x - 6$ using a logarithm. Round your answer to the nearest thousandth.

5. The amount of a radioactive substance y that is left from an original mass of P after x days of decaying is found by the decay equation $y = P(0.9986)^x$. How many days will it take for 240 milligrams of radioactive material to decay to 7.5 milligrams?

On Your Own

6. A local minor league baseball team has seen its attendance increase steadily during the season. The equation models the increase in attendance. Let g be the number of the game and A be the attendance at that game.

   Attendance at game g:
   $A = 3000(1.08)^{\frac{g}{3}}$

   A. How could you use a table to find which game would first have attendance over 8000?

   B. What is the first game that would have attendance over 8000? Show your work in a table.

   ©Cheryl Casey/Shutterstock

For Problems 7–10, solve each equation by graphing. Round to the nearest tenth.

7. $5e^{2x} = 75$

8. $24e^{0.3x} = 7$

9. $28e^{5x} + 6 = 10$

10. $6e^{0.11x} - 18 = 72$

11. (MP) **Construct Arguments** When solving an exponential equation of the form $ab^{cx} = d$ graphically, a student finds two solutions to the equation. How do you know that this student has incorrectly solved the equation?

Solve each equation algebraically. Justify each step. Use a calculator and round to the nearest thousandth, if necessary.

12. $8^{4x+3} + 9 = 521$

13. $6\left(\frac{1}{2}\right)^{1-2x} = 24$

14. $e^{6x} - 11 = 104$

15. $e^{0.25x} + 35 = 215$

16. $2(9)^{-0.4x} + 23 = 87$

17. $5(3)^{8x} - 1020 = 945$

18. (MP) **Critique Reasoning** Sunil solved an exponential equation. His work is shown at the right.

   A. What mistake did Sunil make when solving the equation?

   B. What is the correct solution to the equation? Round your answer to the nearest thousandth. Show your work.

$$6^{3y} + 7 = 234$$
$$6^{3y} = 227$$
$$\ln 6^{3y} = \ln 227$$
$$3y = \ln 227$$
$$y = \frac{\ln 227}{3}$$
$$y \approx 1.808$$

19. (MP) **Model with Mathematics** A young worker has started to save for retirement. She has heard that investing in the stock market for the long term is her best option. Annual growth in the stock market over many decades has averaged about 6% per year, though this is not a constant growth rate.

   A. Assuming that the growth rate is constant, create a model for the value of an investment that was made in the stock market several decades ago.

   B. Write an exponential equation to represent the time t for a $10,000 investment in the stock market to be worth $100,000.

   C. How long will it take for the investment to be worth $100,000? Solve the equation you wrote in Part B. Justify each step. Round your answer to the nearest hundredth.

20. A consumer group released new data on how vehicles lose value after purchase. Assume that the rates of decrease are constant.

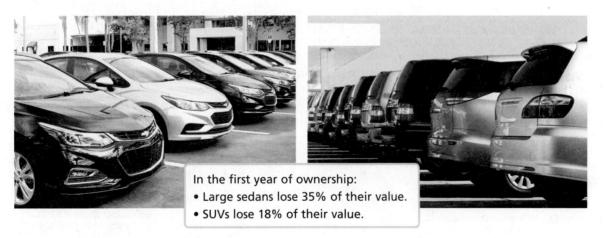

In the first year of ownership:
• Large sedans lose 35% of their value.
• SUVs lose 18% of their value.

   A. How many years will it take until an SUV loses 60% of its value? Round your answer to the nearest tenth.

   B. How many years will it take until a large sedan loses 60% of its value? Round your answer to the nearest tenth.

   C. A new SUV is sold in January 2019 for $28,500. When will the value of this SUV be $10,000? Round your answer to the nearest month.

   D. A new large sedan is sold in July 2019 for $34,500. When will the value of this large sedan be $10,000? Round your answer to the nearest month.

   E. How would your answers change if the rate of decrease in value for the large sedan decreased after the first year to 11% per year?

21. (MP) **Model with Mathematics** While researching the cost of schooling, Eliza found that the average school in her state spent $12,756 per student in 2018. This was an increase of 2.5% over the previous year.

A. Assuming that the growth rate is constant, write an exponential equation to represent the time x in years until the per-student spending will be $18,000.

B. How long will it take for the per-student spending to exceed $18,000? Round your answer to the nearest whole number.

22. (MP) **Model with Mathematics** A neighborhood bank is advertising a special interest rate for customers who open a new savings account.

A. Write an equation for A, the value of an account with principal P invested for x years.

B. How long will it take for an initial investment of $500 to earn enough interest that the value of the account will become $2500? Show your work. Round to the nearest hundredth.

TOWN BANK — Limited Time!

Open a new Savings Account and receive **4.5%** interest compounded monthly!

23. (Open Middle™) Using the digits 1 to 9, at most one time each, fill in the boxes to make an exponential equation whose solution is the least possible value.

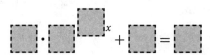

$$\boxed{} \cdot \boxed{}^{\boxed{}x} + \boxed{} = \boxed{}$$

Spiral Review • Assessment Readiness

24. Match each exponential equation with is logarithmic form.

A. $y = 5^3$ **1.** $y = \ln 7$

B. $7 = e^y$ **2.** $3 = \log_5 y$

C. $3 = 5^y$ **3.** $7 = \ln y$

D. $y = e^7$ **4.** $y = \log_5 3$

25. What is the y-intercept of the graph of $y = 3\log_5(x + 5) - 2$?

Ⓐ -5 Ⓒ 1

Ⓑ -2 Ⓓ 3

26. Which equation represents an initial population of 475 that grows by 1.3% annually?

Ⓐ $y = 475(1.3)^x$ Ⓒ $y = 475(1.13)^x$

Ⓑ $y = 475(0.13)^x$ Ⓓ $y = 475(1.013)^x$

27. Evaluate the logarithm $\log_2 28 - \log_2 7$.

Ⓐ -4 Ⓒ 2

Ⓑ -2 Ⓓ 4

I'm in a Learning Mindset!

How did I use goal-setting skills when collaborating on solving exponential equations?

Solve Logarithmic Equations

(I Can) solve logarithmic equations.

Spark Your Learning

The Richter scale is used to express the magnitude of an earthquake. In the formula, M is the magnitude of the earthquake and E is the amount of energy released in ergs. In a one-month period during the fall of 2018, five medium-sized earthquakes were recorded off the coast of Oregon.

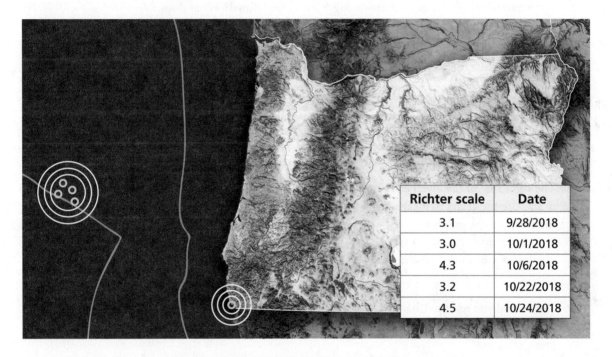

Richter scale	Date
3.1	9/28/2018
3.0	10/1/2018
4.3	10/6/2018
3.2	10/22/2018
4.5	10/24/2018

Complete Part A as a whole class. Then complete Parts B–D in small groups.

A. What is a mathematical question you can ask about this situation? What information would you need to know to answer your question?

B. What variable(s) are involved in this situation? What unit of measurement would you use for each variable?

C. To answer your question, what strategy and tool would you use along with all the information you have? What answer do you get?

D. Can you represent an equation like this with a graph? Show how or explain why not.

 Turn and Talk How could you combine the logarithms in the formula, and find the zeros of its graph?

Build Understanding

Solve a Logarithmic Equation Graphically

You solved exponential equations by graphing both sides of the equation as separate functions on the same coordinate plane and finding the point of intersection. You can solve logarithmic equations using the same graphical approach.

1 Use a graph to solve the equation $\log_2(x + 1) = 3.5$ to the nearest integer.

The expression on the left side of the equation involves a logarithm with base 2.

A. For what values of x is the expression $\log_2(x + 1)$ undefined? What does this mean for the graph of $y = \log_2(x + 1)$?

B. What are some values of x that produce integer values of $\log_2(x + 1)$? Explain.

The integer values of $\log_2(x + 1)$ and their corresponding values of x have been used to sketch the graph of $y = \log_2(x + 1)$.

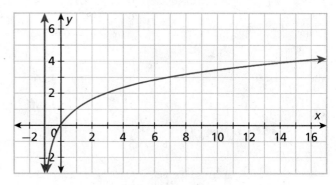

C. The right side of the given equation is 3.5. Use the graph to locate the point on the graph where y is approximately 3.5. What is the x-value of this point to the nearest integer?

D. How could you use the Change of Base Property for Logarithms in order to graph $y = \log_2(x + 1)$ and $y = 3.5$ on a graphing calculator to solve the given equation?

2 Solve the equation $5\ln(x + 2) = 9$ using a graphing calculator.

A. What two functions will be graphed together on the graphing calculator?

B. What will the graphs of the two functions look like?

C. Use a graphing calculator to graph the two functions on the same coordinate plane. Rounding to the nearest hundredth, what are the coordinates of the point of intersection of the two functions?

D. To the nearest hundredth, what is the solution of the equation?

Turn and Talk Which of the equations in Tasks 1 and 2 do you find more difficult to solve graphically? Explain your choice.

Step It Out

Solve a Logarithmic Equation Algebraically

In addition to solving logarithmic equations graphically, you can also solve them algebraically. Some logarithmic equations can be solved directly if they can be rewritten so that both sides of the equation are logarithmic expressions with the same base.

> **Property of Equality for Logarithmic Equations**
>
> For all real numbers b $(b \neq 1)$, x, and y, $\log_b x = \log_b y$ if and only if $x = y$.

3 Solve $\log_6(3x + 7) = \log_6(5x - 1)$.

$\log_6(3x + 7) = \log_6(5x - 1)$ **A.** What justifies this first step of the solution?

$3x + 7 = 5x - 1$

$7 = 2x - 1$ **B.** What property justifies the second step?

$8 = 2x$ Add 1 to both sides.

$4 = x$ Divide both sides by 2.

C. What is the result when you check the solution in the original equation? How can you find the actual numerical value of each side?

The logarithmic equation in the next task also involves two logarithmic expressions with the same base. However, this equation contains a constant term. The Property of Equality for Logarithmic Equations cannot be applied.

4 Solve $\log 8x + \log(20 + x) = 3$.

$\log 8x + \log(20 + x) = 3$ **A.** What property justifies this step?

$\log[8x(20 + x)] = 3$

$8x(20 + x) = 10^3$ **B.** How does this step follow from the line above?

$8x^2 + 160x = 1000$ Multiply.

$8x^2 + 160x - 1000 = 0$ Subtract 1000 from both sides.

$8(x^2 + 20x - 125) = 0$ Factor out the common factor.

$(x + 25)(x - 5) = 0$ Divide both sides by 8 and factor the trinomial.

$x + 25 = 0$ or $x - 5 = 0$

$x = -25$ or $x = 5$

C. What happens when you check the solution $x = -25$ in the original equation? What is the result when you check the solution $x = 5$? Explain what these results mean.

 Turn and Talk Why is it always important to check your answers when solving an equation algebraically?

Real-World Problems Modeled by Logarithmic Equations

When solving a real-world problem algebraically, always check that your solution makes sense in the context of the situation. For example, distance in the real world is not negative. However, sometimes a negative value for a distance does make sense in the context of the situation because it means below, to the left, or behind the starting point. As an example, in some contexts a negative value for altitude can mean below sea level. Often the real world restricts values to positive numbers. For example, if a box can be modeled with dimensions x, $10 - 2x$, and $15 - 2x$, the volume is modeled by the function $V = x(10 - 2x)(15 - 2x)$ with the domain being $0 < x < 5$. For any other values of x, at least one of the dimensions of the box is negative, which does not make sense.

5 The brightness of a star as measured from Earth is its apparent magnitude m. The absolute magnitude M is the brightness of the star from a standard distance of 10 parsecs. These measures are related by the formula $m - M = 5\log\frac{d}{10}$, where d is the distance of the star from Earth measured in parsecs. How far is the star Pollux from Earth?

> **Pollux:**
> apparent magnitude: 1.14
> absolute magnitude: 0.70

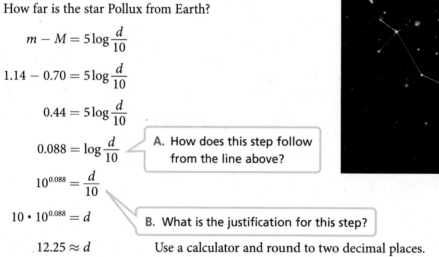

$$m - M = 5\log\frac{d}{10}$$

$$1.14 - 0.70 = 5\log\frac{d}{10}$$

$$0.44 = 5\log\frac{d}{10}$$

$$0.088 = \log\frac{d}{10}$$

> **A.** How does this step follow from the line above?

$$10^{0.088} = \frac{d}{10}$$

$$10 \cdot 10^{0.088} = d$$

> **B.** What is the justification for this step?

$$12.25 \approx d \qquad \text{Use a calculator and round to two decimal places.}$$

The star Pollux is about 12.25 parsecs from Earth.

C. How can you use a graphing calculator to verify the answer?

D. If 10 parsecs are equivalent to approximately 32.6 light-years, how would you calculate the distance between Pollux and Earth in light-years?

E. Is it reasonable to say that Pollux is 40 light-years away from Earth? Explain.

F. Review the steps used in the solution above. Using the given formula, what is a general equation for d in terms of m and M?

Turn and Talk Does an approximation work well for this situation? Explain your answer.

© EREEE/iStock/Getty Images

Check Understanding

1. Use a graph to solve the equation $\log_2(3x - 4) = 4.5$ to the nearest integer.

For Problems 2 and 3, solve each logarithmic equation algebraically.

2. $\log x + \log(x + 3) = 1$

3. $\log_8(7x - 5) = \log_8(4x + 9)$

4. An equation for the loudness of a sound in decibels is $L = 10 \log R$, where R is the relative intensity of the sound.

   A. The loudness of the music at a concert is about 115 decibels. What is the relative intensity of this sound?

   B. A regular conversation is found to have a loudness of 62 decibels. What is the relative intensity of this sound? How many times greater is the intensity of the concert than the conversation?

On Your Own

5. (MP) **Use Tools** Nadia is solving the logarithmic equation $\log_4(6x + 3) = 2.5$ using a graphing calculator. She graphs the equation $y = \log_4(6x + 3)$ and finds the x-intercept of this equation. Did Nadia solve the equation? If not, how should she use the graphing calculator to solve the equation?

Solve each logarithmic equation graphically. Round your answer to the nearest hundredth.

6. $10 \log(5x + 9) = 15$

7. $6 = 3 \log(7x - 1)$

8. $12 \ln(8x + 3) = 30$

9. $\ln(3x - 2) = 4$

For problems 10–15, solve each logarithmic equation algebraically.

10. $\log_3 3x + \log_3(x - 2) = 2$

11. $\log_{15}(x + 13) = \log_{15}(9x - 5)$

12. $\log(4x - 10) - \log 2 = 1$

13. $\log_6(4x + 7) + \log_6 3 = \log_6 9$

14. $\log 6x + \log 5 = 2 \log x$

15. $\log_8(x + 5) = \dfrac{2}{3}$

16. (MP) **Critique Reasoning** Holly solved the logarithmic equation $\log_6(x - 5) = 2 - \log_6 x$ and found two solutions. Her work is shown at the right. How can you help her to find the correct solution to this equation? What is the correct solution? Explain your answer.

$$\log_6(x - 5) = 2 - \log_6 x$$
$$\log_6(x - 5) + \log_6 x = 2$$
$$\log_6(x^2 - 5x) = 2$$
$$6^2 = x^2 - 5x$$
$$0 = x^2 - 5x - 36$$
$$0 = (x - 9)(x + 4)$$
$$x - 9 = 0 \text{ or } x + 4 = 0$$
$$x = 9 \quad \text{or} \quad x = -4$$

17. The daily sales of two products during a month are modeled by logarithmic functions. The number of units of product A sold is modeled by $s_A = 50 \log_2(0.125t + 2)$, where t is the number of days since the beginning of the month. The number of units of product B sold is modeled by $s_B = 60 \log_5(0.5t + 5)$. How can you use a graphing calculator to determine the day when the same number of units were sold? What day was it?

18. The San Francisco earthquake of 1906 devastated the city. Estimates of its magnitude have varied, but current science seems to agree on how strong it was. Using the formula $M = \frac{2}{3}\left[\log E - \log 10^{11.8}\right]$, write an equation with one unknown and one logarithm, then find the amount of energy released by the earthquake.

Estimated Magnitude: 7.9

19. The pH of a substance tells how acidic or basic the substance is. You can use special strips to test the pH of a liquid.

A. The formula relates the pH of a substance to H, the moles of hydrogen ions in the substance. Write a logarithmic equation, without a fraction, for the number of moles of hydrogen in a sample with a pH of 5.8.

B. How many moles of hydrogen ions are in the sample?

pH Formula: $pH = \log\frac{1}{H}$

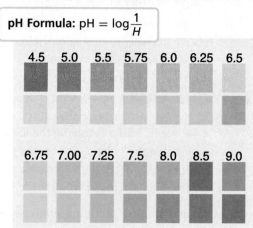

20. Open Ended Write a logarithmic equation with logarithmic expressions on both sides that can be solved algebraically without using a calculator. Find the solution.

Spiral Review • Assessment Readiness

21. Which equation models the amount of radioactive material that remains from 80 grams of a substance with a half-life of 5 years?

Ⓐ $y = 80(0.5)^{5x}$ Ⓒ $y = 80(0.5)^{x-5}$

Ⓑ $y = 80(0.5)^{x+5}$ Ⓓ $y = 80(0.5)^{\frac{x}{5}}$

22. Solve the exponential equation $5 = 8(2)^{x+3} - 4$. Round to the nearest hundredth if necessary

Ⓐ -6 Ⓒ -3

Ⓑ -3.67 Ⓓ -2.83

23. Match each expression with its simplified form.

Ⓐ $3\log 2 + 3\log 5$ **1.** 1

Ⓑ $4\ln e - \ln 1$ **2.** 2

Ⓒ $-2\log_2 0.5$ **3.** 3

Ⓓ $\log_3 21 - \log_3 7$ **4.** 4

24. Which equation models a direct variation relationship?

Ⓐ $y = 3x + 4$ Ⓒ $y = 2x^2$

Ⓑ $y = -4x$ Ⓓ $y = 10^x$

⬡ **I'm in a Learning Mindset!**

What is my plan for improving my performance with logarithmic and exponential equations?

Properties of Logarithms

Definition of logarithm: If $a^b = c$, then $\log_a c = b$.

These three properties follow directly from the definition:

$$\log_b b = 1$$
$$\log_b 1 = 0$$
$$\log_b b^m = m$$

For any positive numbers $a, m, n, b \left(b \neq 1\right)$, and $c \left(c \neq 1\right)$, the following properties hold.

Product Property of Logarithms:
$\log_b mn = \log_b m + \log_b n$

Quotient Property of Logarithms:
$\log_b \dfrac{m}{n} = \log_b m - \log_b n$

Power Property of Logarithms:
$\log_b m^n = n\log_b m$

Change of Base Property: $\log_b m = \dfrac{\log_a m}{\log_a b}$

Solve Exponential Equations

Solve $18 = 6e^{2x}$ algebraically.

$18 = 6e^{2x}$ — Take the natural logarithm of both sides.

$3 = e^{2x}$

$\ln(3) = \ln\left(e^{2x}\right)$ — Power Property

$\ln(3) = 2x\ln(e)$

$\ln(3) = 2x$ — $\ln(e) = 1$

$\dfrac{\ln(3)}{2} = x$

$0.549 \approx x$

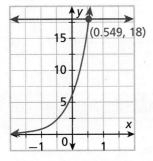

(0.549, 18)

Solve Logarithmic Equations

Solve $6 = 3\log_4(x + 1)$ algebraically.

$6 = 3\log_4(x + 1)$

$2 = \log_4(x + 1)$

$4^2 = 4^{\log_4(x + 1)}$ — Rewrite in exponential form.

$16 = x + 1$ — $4^{\log_4(x + 1)} = x + 1$

$15 = x$

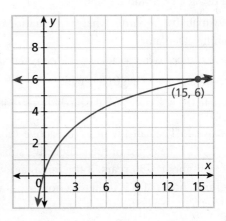

(15, 6)

Vocabulary

Choose the correct term from the box to complete each sentence.

1. When solving a logarithmic equation, rewriting both sides of the equation in ___?___ is one of the steps.

2. The change of base property for logarithms allows you to rewrite a logarithm with base 5 as the ratio of two ___?___.

3. The definition of logarithm can be used to rewrite an exponential equation as a(n) ___?___.

Concepts and Skills

Use the properties of logarithms to simplify each expression.

4. $\log_8(16)$

5. $\log_6 18 + \log_6 12$

6. $\log_8 4^{3x} - \log_5 125^3$

Rewrite each logarithm in terms of natural logarithms.

7. $\log_3 128$

8. $\log_4(96) - \log_4 8$

9. $\log_5 30 + \log_5 70$

For Problems 10–15, solve each equation. Round your answer to the nearest thousandth, if necessary.

10. $5 \cdot 3^{2x+1} = 415$

11. $9^{4x+5} = 3^{2(x-4)}$

12. $4^{x-6} = 3^{x+2}$

13. $\log_3(x - 3) = -2$

14. $\log(2x + 3) = 1.23$

15. $\log_2(3x - 2) = 6$

16. Donita considers the exponential equation $11^{x-3} = 78.2$. She first estimates the solution using a table and a graph.

A. To estimate by graphing, what two equations should she graph together on her graphing calculator?

B. If she wants to estimate by using a table, what two consecutive integer values of x should she use to begin her table?

C. Estimate the solution to the nearest hundredth using a table.

17. (MP) **Use Tools** The half-life of a radioactive substance is the amount of time it takes for half of the atoms of the radioactive substance to decay. The half-life of Carbon-14 is about 5730 years. If the initial amount of Carbon-14 in a substance was 10 grams, how old is it if there is now 4.2 grams remaining? Round to the nearest hundred years. State what strategy and tool you will use to answer the question, explain your choice, and then find the answer.

18. In one layer of Earth's atmosphere, the temperature is relatively constant at $-57\,°C$. The atmospheric pressure in this layer can be modeled by the function $f(h) = 128(10)^{-0.0682h}$, where f is the pressure in kilopascals (kPa) and h is the altitude in kilometers above sea level. What is the altitude, to the nearest kilometer, where the pressure is 4.92 kPa?

Rational Functions and Equations

Chemical Engineer

©Traimak_Ivan/iStock/Getty Images

Chemical engineers translate processes developed in the lab into practical applications for the commercial production of products and then work to maintain and improve those processes. They need to be able to reliably predict how matter will react on both micro and macro scales. Chemical engineers develop functions to model the behavior of materials in different states of matter.

STEM
POWERING INGENUITY

STEM Task

Under ideal conditions, the pressure, volume, and temperature of an ideal gas are related through the ideal-gas equation, $pV = nRT$.

p	pressure
V	volume
T	temperature
n	number of moles
R	Constant of proportionality, 8.31 $\frac{J}{K \cdot mol}$

What is the volume of a container that holds 1 mole of an ideal gas at temperature 273.15 K and pressure of 1.00 atm = 101325 $\frac{J}{m^3}$?

Learning Mindset

Strategic Help-Seeking Asks Questions

While learning a new concept or skill, it's important to learn how to ask questions that will help you progress in your learning. Asking and sequencing targeted questions about underlying details will lead you to your learning goal. Don't hesitate to ask your classmates about their understanding. Friendly and positive collaboration will promote growth and learning for all. Here are some ideas about how to ask questions in order to get the appropriate answer for the situation:

- What questions can I ask my teacher to help me understand the concepts that will support my learning about rational functions?

- What questions can I ask to encourage my classmates to share their knowledge about rational functions and equations?

- How can I use the knowledge I have already acquired to help me refine my questions? What questions can help clarify my understanding?

- Did I make any assumptions? Are they valid? Are my assumptions helpful? How might I think about the problem differently?

Reflect

Q What questions do you have about rational functions and equations? What question does your overall learning goal answer? How can you sequence your questions to reach your learning goal?

Q Imagine you are a chemical engineer. What series of small questions might you ask to help you determine the temperature of an ideal gas?

Rational Functions

Module Performance Task: *Spies and Analysts*™

FULL OF HOT AIR

How long will it take two people to fill the room with balloons?

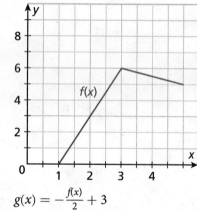

Are You Ready?

Complete these problems to review prior concepts and skills you will need for this module.

Write Equations for Proportional Relationships

Write an equation to represent each proportional relationship.

1. distance while driving at a speed of 65 mi/h

2. learning 10 new vocabulary words per night

3.

x	3	5	12
y	39	65	156

4.

x	2	7	20
y	−50	−175	−500

Transformations of Functions

Graph each transformed function $g(x)$.

5.

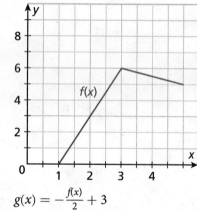

$g(x) = -\dfrac{f(x)}{2} + 3$

6.

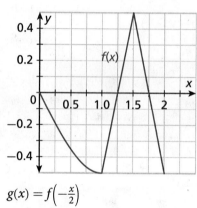

$g(x) = f\left(-\dfrac{x}{2}\right)$

Graph Logarithmic Functions

Graph each function and identify its vertical asymptote.

7. $f(x) = 3\log_3 x$

8. $f(x) = \log_5(x + 4)$

Connecting Past and Present Learning

Previously, you learned:

• to find the inverse of quadratic, cubic, and exponential functions and

• to graph exponential and logarithmic functions using asymptotes.

In this module, you will learn:

• to use inverse variation to model real-world situations and

• to graph rational functions using intercepts and asymptotes.

Inverse Variation

(I Can) recognize when two quantities show inverse variation and write an equation to model the relationship between the quantities.

Spark Your Learning

Jackson is a cyclist who is competing in an individual time trial, which is a type of race in which cyclists race alone against the clock.

Jackson's average speed for the race is 32 mi/h. He takes 1.5 min more than the winner does to finish.

©Neil Tingle/Alamy

Complete Part A as a whole class. Then complete Parts B–D in small groups.

A. What is a mathematical question you can ask about this situation? What information would you need to know to answer your question?

B. What variables are involved in this situation? How are the variables related?

C. To answer your question, what strategy and tool would you use along with all the information you have? What answer do you get?

D. Suppose Jackson races in several time trials that are each 50 miles long. How does his finishing time change if his average speed increases from one trial to the next? How does his finishing time change if his average speed decreases from one trial to the next? Why is the product of his average speed and finishing time useful to know?

> **Turn and Talk** Suppose a cyclist completes two time trials that each cover the same distance. How would a cyclist's average finishing time change if the cyclist's average speed for the second time trial increased by 10%? Explain.

Build Understanding

Investigate Inverse Variation

Previously, you learned that two quantities x and y show *direct variation* if $y = ax$ where $a \neq 0$. Two quantities x and y show **inverse variation** if $y = \frac{a}{x}$ where $a \neq 0$. The constant a is the **constant of variation**, and y is said to *vary inversely with x*.

1 ▶ Amelia walks for exercise on two consecutive days. Her walking speed r on Day 1 and the distance d she walks on Day 2 are shown in the photo.

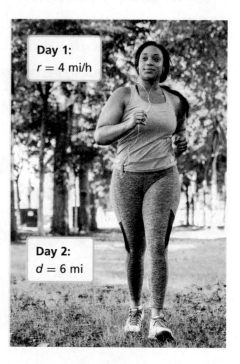

Day 1:
$r = 4$ mi/h

Day 2:
$d = 6$ mi

A. Write an equation giving Amelia's distance d walked on Day 1 as a function of the time t that she walks. Is the relationship between t and d direct variation or inverse variation?

B. What happens to the distance Amelia walks on Day 1 if her walking time doubles? Explain.

C. Write an equation giving the time t it takes Amelia to complete her walk on Day 2 as a function of her walking speed r. Is the relationship between r and t direct variation or inverse variation?

D. What happens to the time it takes Amelia to complete her walk on Day 2 if she jogs at double her walking speed? Explain.

Investigate Graphs of Inverse Variation Functions

The inverse variation function $f(x) = \frac{a}{x}$ is defined for all nonzero real numbers x. However, in this lesson you will be looking at real-world situations in which the domain is restricted to positive numbers and the constant of variation a is positive.

2 ▶ A. The graph of $f(x) = \frac{1}{x}$ for $x > 0$ is shown. As x approaches $+\infty$, what happens to the value of $f(x)$? What is a horizontal asymptote of the graph?

B. As x approaches 0, what happens to the value of $f(x)$? What is a vertical asymptote of the graph?

C. Use a graphing calculator to graph the functions $f(x) = \frac{1}{x}$, $g(x) = \frac{2}{x}$, and $h(x) = \frac{0.5}{x}$ on the same coordinate plane for $x > 0$. How are the graphs alike? How are they different?

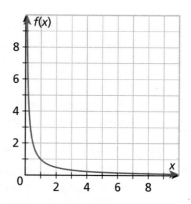

Turn and Talk What is a line of symmetry for the graphs from Part C of Task 2? What does this imply about the inverse of each function? Is your conclusion about the inverse true for any inverse variation function? Explain.

Step It Out

Write an Inverse Variation Equation

If you know that two quantities x and y vary inversely, you can use one pair of data values (x, y) to find the constant of variation a and write an equation $y = \frac{a}{x}$ relating x and y. You can then use this equation to determine other pairs of data values.

3 The quantities x and y vary inversely, and $y = 12$ when $x = 3$. Write an equation relating x and y. Then find the value of y when $x = 42$ and the value of x when $y = 4$.

Write an equation relating x and y.

$y = \dfrac{a}{x}$ Write the general inverse variation equation.

$12 = \dfrac{a}{3}$ Substitute 3 for x and 12 for y.

$36 = a$ Solve for a.

$y = \dfrac{36}{x}$ Write an equation relating x and y.

Find the value of y when $x = 42$.

$y = \dfrac{36}{x}$ Equation relating x and y

$y = \dfrac{36}{42}$ Substitute 42 for x.

$y = \dfrac{6}{7}$ Simplify.

Find the value of x when $y = 4$.

$y = \dfrac{36}{x}$ Equation relating x and y

$4 = \dfrac{36}{x}$ Substitute 4 for y.

$4x = 36$ Multiply each side by x.

$x = 9$ Divide each side by 4.

A. What is always true about the product of x and y if y varies inversely with x? How could you use this fact to find the constant of variation in Task 3?

B. How would the equation relating x and y in Task 3 change if $y = 12$ when $x = 3$ but y varies directly with x rather than inversely with x?

 Turn and Talk Suppose $y = 12$ when $x = 0$. Can the relationship between x and y be represented by an inverse variation equation? Explain.

Check Data for Inverse Variation

You can rewrite an inverse variation equation $y = \frac{a}{x}$ as $xy = a$. So, a set of data pairs (x, y) shows inverse variation if the products xy are constant or approximately constant.

4 When water falls from a spout, the speed of the water increases as it falls, and the column of water becomes narrower. For the water column shown, the water's speed v and the column's cross-sectional area A are given at four different locations along the column. Determine whether cross-sectional area varies inversely with water speed. If so, write an equation that models this relationship, and find the cross-sectional area when the water speed is 5 ft/s.

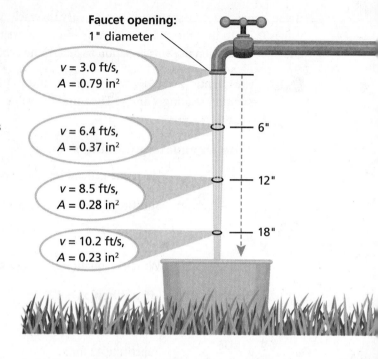

Faucet opening:
1" diameter

$v = 3.0$ ft/s,
$A = 0.79$ in²

$v = 6.4$ ft/s,
$A = 0.37$ in²
— 6"

$v = 8.5$ ft/s,
$A = 0.28$ in²
— 12"

$v = 10.2$ ft/s,
$A = 0.23$ in²
— 18"

Find the product $v \cdot A$ for each data pair (v, A) in the diagram.

$3.0(0.79) = 2.37$

$6.4(0.37) \approx 2.37$

$8.5(0.28) = 2.38$

$10.2(0.23) \approx 2.35$

The products are approximately constant, so the water column's cross-sectional area varies inversely with the water speed.

Write an equation that models the relationship between v and A.
Based on the products above, a good approximation for the constant of variation is $a = 2.4$. An equation relating v and A is $v \cdot A = 2.4$, or $A = \frac{2.4}{v}$.

Find the cross-sectional area when the water speed is 5 ft/s.

$A = \frac{2.4}{v}$ \quad\quad Equation for cross-sectional area

$= \frac{2.4}{5}$ \quad\quad Substitute 5 for v.

$= 0.48$ \quad\quad Use a calculator.

When the water speed is 5 ft/s, the cross-sectional area of the water column is about 0.48 in².

A. Can you write an inverse variation equation that gives the water's speed v as a function of the water column's cross-sectional area A? If so, what is the equation?

B. Suppose that when the water hits the bottom of the container shown, the cross-sectional area of the water column is 0.18 in². What is the water's speed when it hits the bottom of the container?

Turn and Talk If each possible cross section of the water column in Task 4 is a circle, what equation gives the water speed v as a function of the column's radius r?

Model with Inverse Variation

5 ▸ The amount of gasoline used on a trip varies inversely with the fuel efficiency of the vehicle. Samuel and Parvati both rent more fuel-efficient vehicles for a 400-mile road trip instead of driving their own vehicles.

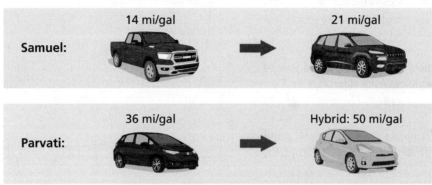

| **Personal vehicle** | | **Rental vehicle** |

Samuel: 14 mi/gal → 21 mi/gal

Parvati: 36 mi/gal → Hybrid: 50 mi/gal

Write and graph a function to model the amount of gasoline y (in gallons) used during the trip while driving a vehicle with fuel efficiency x (in miles per gallon). Which rental will save more gas?

Write a function.

The amount of gasoline y used varies inversely with the fuel efficiency x, so the model is:

$$y = \frac{400}{x}.$$

A. Why is the constant of variation equal to 400?

B. What are the graph's asymptotes? What do they mean in this situation?

Graph the function.

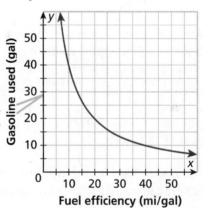

Answer the question.

Samuel's personal vehicle would use $\frac{400}{14} \approx 28.6$ gal of gas, while his rental will use $\frac{400}{21} \approx 19$ gal.

Parvati's personal vehicle would use $\frac{400}{36} \approx 11.1$ gal of gas, while her rental will use $\frac{400}{50} = 8$ gal.

Samuel's gas savings: $28.6 - 19 = 9.6$ gal

Parvati's gas savings: $11.1 - 8 = 3.1$ gal

Therefore, Samuel's rental saves more gas for the 400-mile trip.

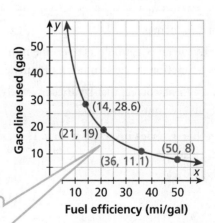

C. Compare the average rates of change between the red points and between the green points. How does this help answer the question?

Check Understanding

1. Which equations below represent inverse variation? Explain your reasoning.

$$y = \frac{4}{x} \qquad x + y = 4 \qquad xy = 7 \qquad y = \frac{x}{7}$$

2. The graph of $f(x) = \frac{6}{x}$ is shown for $x > 0$. What are the asymptotes of the graph? Does the graph have any x-intercepts or y-intercepts? Explain.

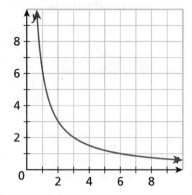

3. The quantities x and y vary inversely, and $y = 14$ when $x = 2$. Write an equation relating x and y. Then find the value of y when $x = 5$.

4. The table shows the force needed to loosen a bolt using wrenches with handles of various lengths.

Handle length, ℓ (in.)	6	9	12	15
Force, F (lb)	300	200	150	120

   A. Does force vary inversely with handle length? Explain.

   B. Predict the force required to loosen the bolt using a wrench with a handle length of 18 in.

5. The frequency (in vibrations per second) of a vibrating violin string varies inversely with the string's length (in centimeters). Suppose a violin string that is 30 cm long vibrates 280 times per second. Write an equation that gives the frequency f as a function of the string length ℓ. What is the frequency for a violin string 25 cm long?

On Your Own

6. (MP) **Critique Reasoning** Anna received a gift card worth $100 to use at her favorite restaurant. Each Saturday Anna uses the gift card to buy lunch for $10. Anna claims that the remaining balance on the card varies inversely with the number of lunches she buys because the balance decreases as the number of lunches increases.

   A. Write an equation that gives the remaining gift card balance b (in dollars) as a function of the number n of lunches Anna buys.

   B. Is Anna correct that b varies inversely with n? Use the equation you wrote to justify your answer.

Tell whether y varies inversely with x. If so, state the constant of variation and draw the graph.

7. $y = \frac{2}{x}$

8. $x = \frac{y}{3}$

9. $y = \frac{1}{3x}$

10. $y = \frac{2}{5x}$

11. $xy = 6$

12. $xy = \frac{1}{7}$

13. $y = \frac{x}{8}$

14. $y = \frac{0.4}{x}$

15. $7 = \frac{y}{x}$

16. The graphs of three different inverse variation functions are shown for $x > 0$. Order the functions from least to greatest constant of variation.

A.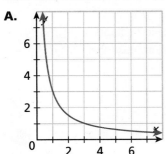

B.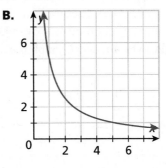

C.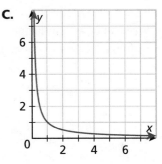

For Problems 17–20, y varies inversely with x. Write an equation relating x and y. Then find the indicated value.

17. $y = 6$ when $x = 2$. Find the value of y when $x = 4$.

18. $y = 3$ when $x = 10$. Find the value of y when $x = 6$.

19. $y = 12$ when $x = 7$. Find the value of x when $y = 21$.

20. $y = 2.5$ when $x = 24$. Find the value of x when $y = 30$.

21. (MP) **Model with Mathematics** For a certain carpentry project, the time t (in hours) needed to finish the project depends on the number of carpenters c assigned to it, as shown in the table.

A. Does the time to finish the project vary inversely with the number of carpenters? Explain.

B. Write an equation that gives t as a function of c.

C. If the project needs to be finished in at most 3 days and the carpenters work 8 hours per day, what is the minimum number of carpenters that must be assigned to the project?

Number of carpenters, c	Time to finish project, t (h)
1	72
2	36
4	18
6	12
8	9

22. STEM Boyle's Law states that for a given mass of confined gas at a constant temperature, the pressure P the gas exerts varies inversely with the volume V the gas occupies. At 100 °F, a given mass of gas exerts a pressure of 125 lb/in² when placed in a tank with a volume of 2 ft³. If the same mass of gas at the same temperature is placed in a tank with a volume of 5 ft³, what pressure will the gas exert? Graph the function, and use the graph to justify your answer.

23. Emilio weighs 150 pounds. When he stands on snow, the average pressure that he exerts on the snow (in pounds per square inch) is his weight divided by the area of the bottom of his footwear (in square inches).

A. Write an equation that gives the pressure as a function of the area. Does the pressure Emilio exerts on the snow vary inversely with his footwear area? Explain.

B. Compare the pressure Emilio exerts on the snow when wearing the boots shown with the pressure he exerts when wearing the snowshoes shown. How do your answers explain why Emilio is less likely to sink into the snow when he wears the snowshoes?

$A = 60$ in²

$A = 600$ in²

24. Mia measures the *apparent height* of a tree 300 feet away by holding a ruler in front of her eye and observing that the tree appears to be 6 inches tall. The apparent height h (in inches) varies inversely with Mia's distance d (in feet) from the tree. Write an equation that gives h as a function of d. How far would Mia need to stand from the tree for its apparent height to be 4 inches? Graph the function, and use the graph to justify your answer.

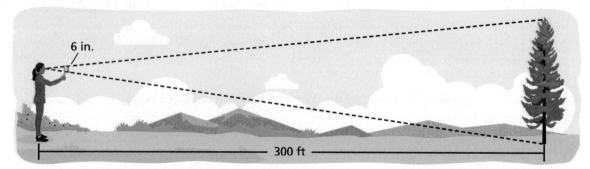

6 in.

300 ft

25. The graphs of $y = x$ and $y = \frac{1}{x}$ are shown for $x > 0$.

  A. What is the intersection point of the two graphs?

  B. Graph $y = x$, $y = \frac{4}{x}$, and $y = \frac{9}{x}$ on the same coordinate plane for $x > 0$. What is the intersection point of the graphs of $y = x$ and $y = \frac{4}{x}$? What is the intersection point of the graphs of $y = x$ and $y = \frac{9}{x}$?

  C. Make a conjecture about the intersection point of the graphs of $y = x$ and $y = \frac{a}{x}$ ($a > 0$) in the first quadrant of the coordinate plane. Then prove your conjecture.

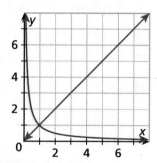

Spiral Review • Assessment Readiness

26. Which expression is equivalent to $\log x + 3 \log y$?

  Ⓐ $3(\log x)(\log y)$

  Ⓑ $\log 3xy$

  Ⓒ $\log xy^3$

  Ⓓ $3 \log xy$

27. Katy deposits $1000 into a savings account that earns 5% annual interest compounded continuously. After about how many years will the account balance reach $1500?

  Ⓐ 1.4 years   Ⓒ 8.3 years

  Ⓑ 8.1 years   Ⓓ 10 years

28. What are the solutions of $\log 5x + \log(x - 1) = 2$?

  Ⓐ only -4

  Ⓑ only 5

  Ⓒ -4 and 5

  Ⓓ no solution

29. The graph of which equation is a translation of the graph of $y = x^2$?

  Ⓐ $y = -x^2$

  Ⓑ $y = 3x^2$

  Ⓒ $y = x^3 + 1$

  Ⓓ $y = (x - 3)^2$

 I'm in a Learning Mindset!

What questions can I ask my teacher to help me understand inverse variation?

Graph Simple Rational Functions

(**I Can**) graph the rational function $f(x) = \frac{1}{x}$ and use the graph's key features to graph transformations of this function.

Spark Your Learning

Jordan wants to take a trip with some friends for spring break. They plan on flying to their destination and staying for a week.

"Each person will need to buy a round-trip airplane ticket."

"We can rent a condo for a week and split the cost equally among everyone who goes."

Complete Part A as a whole class. Then complete Parts B–D in small groups.

   A. What is a mathematical question you can ask about this situation? What information would you need to know to answer your question?

   B. To answer your question, what strategy and tool would you use along with all the information you have? What answer do you get?

   C. What is the total cost per person if 4 people go on the trip?

   D. How does the total cost per person change as the number of people who go on the trip increases?

 Turn and Talk How would the the total cost per person change if the airfare drops $30 but the cost of renting the condo for a week increases by $100?

©Undrey/Shutterstock

Build Understanding

Graph and Analyze $f(x) = \dfrac{1}{x}$

A **rational function** has the form $f(x) = \dfrac{p(x)}{q(x)}$ where $p(x)$ and $q(x)$ are polynomials and $q(x) \neq 0$. You have already graphed rational functions of the form $f(x) = \dfrac{a}{x}$ that model real-world situations for which $a > 0$ and the domain is restricted to $\{x \mid x > 0\}$. Such graphs lie in the first quadrant. In the next task, you will graph the rational function $f(x) = \dfrac{1}{x}$ when the function's domain is not restricted by real-world considerations.

 A. Is the function $f(x) = \dfrac{1}{x}$ an odd function, an even function, or neither? Give a mathematical justification for your answer, and explain what your answer implies about the graph of f.

B. The part of the graph of $f(x) = \dfrac{1}{x}$ that lies in the first quadrant is shown. Use your answer from Part A to draw the complete graph of f in a coordinate plane that shows all four quadrants.

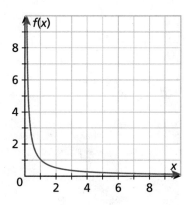

C. Identify the following key features of the function f.

Key Features of $f(x) = \dfrac{1}{x}$	
Domain	?
Range	?
Vertical asymptote	?
Horizontal asymptote	?

D. Describe the end behavior of the function f.

E. Identify the intervals where $f(x)$ is positive and the intervals where $f(x)$ is negative.

F. Identify the intervals where the function f is increasing and the intervals where it is decreasing.

 Turn and Talk What is a line of symmetry for the graph of $f(x) = \dfrac{1}{x}$? What does the line of symmetry imply about the inverse of f?

Graph Simple Rational Functions

You can apply transformations to the graph of $f(x) = \frac{1}{x}$ to produce a new rational function $g(x) = a\left(\dfrac{1}{\frac{1}{b}(x-h)}\right) + k$. The table describes the information you can gather from each parameter in $g(x)$. Notice that the asymptotes are affected only by h and k, while the reference points are affected by all four parameters.

Key Features of Graphs of Simple Rational Functions		
Feature	$f(x) = \dfrac{1}{x}$	$g(x) = a\left(\dfrac{1}{\frac{1}{b}(x-h)}\right) + k$
Vertical asymptote	$x = 0$	$x = h$
Horizontal asymptote	$y = 0$	$y = k$
Reference point	$(-1, -1)$	$(-b + h, -a + k)$
Reference point	$(1, 1)$	$(b + h, a + k)$

2 ▶ Consider the function $g(x) = 3\left(\dfrac{1}{x-1}\right) + 2.$

    A. What transformations can you apply to the graph of $f(x) = \frac{1}{x}$ to produce the graph of g?

    B. What are the reference points on the graph of g corresponding to the reference points $(-1, -1)$ and $(1, 1)$ on the graph of $f(x) = \frac{1}{x}$?

    C. What are the asymptotes of the graph of g?

    D. What are the domain and range of g?

    E. Sketch the graph of g. How is the graph of g similar to the graph of $f(x) = \frac{1}{x}$? How is it different?

Turn and Talk Consider the graph of $h(x) = -\dfrac{1}{x}$.
- How is the graph of h related to the graph of $f(x) = \frac{1}{x}$?
- What are the reference points and asymptotes of the graph of h?
- Suppose 3 is replaced by -3 in the equation for $g(x)$ in Task 2. How could you obtain the graph of this new function by apply transformations to the graph of h?

Step It Out

Rewrite Rational Functions in Order to Graph Them

When given a rational function of the form $g(x) = \frac{mx + n}{px + q}$ where $m \neq 0$ and $p \neq 0$, you can use long division to rewrite the function in one of the general forms $g(x) = a\left(\frac{1}{x - h}\right) + k$ or $g(x) = \frac{1}{\frac{1}{b}(x - h)} + k$ in order to identify the key features and graph the function.

3 ▶ Use long division to rewrite the function $g(x) = \frac{2x + 3}{x + 1}$ in one of the two general forms given above. Then graph the function.

$$
\begin{array}{r}
2 \\
x + 1 \overline{) 2x + 3} \\
\underline{2x + 2} \\
1
\end{array}
$$

> **A.** What steps were used to find the quotient and remainder?

The quotient is 2 and the remainder is 1. Use the relationship among the dividend, divisor, quotient, and remainder to rewrite the equation for $g(x)$.

$$\frac{\text{dividend}}{\text{divisor}} = \text{quotient} + \frac{\text{remainder}}{\text{divisor}}$$

$$\frac{2x + 3}{x + 1} = 2 + \frac{1}{x + 1}$$

$$g(x) = \frac{1}{x + 1} + 2$$

> **B.** Why is this form of the equation for $g(x)$ more useful for graphing the function?

The parameters for $g(x)$ are $a = 1$, $h = -1$, and $k = 2$. Identify the key features of the graph of g and sketch the graph.

Vertical asymptote: $x = -1$

Horizontal asymptote: $y = 2$

Reference points:

$(-1 - 1, -1 + 2) = (-2, 1)$

$(1 - 1, 1 + 2) = (0, 3)$

Domain: $\{x \mid x \neq -1\}$

Range: $\{y \mid y \neq 2\}$

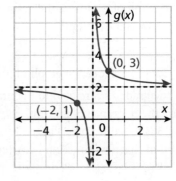

 Turn and Talk What transformations of the graph of $f(x) = \frac{1}{x}$ would produce the graph of g in Task 3?

Write Simple Rational Functions from Graphs

When presented with the graph of a rational function, you can use the features of the graph to write an equation for the function. The function can be written in the form $g(x) = a\left(\dfrac{1}{x-h}\right) + k$ or in the form $g(x) = \dfrac{1}{\frac{1}{b}(x-h)} + k$.

4 Write an equation of the graph shown. Use the form $g(x) = a\left(\dfrac{1}{x-h}\right) + k$.

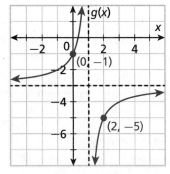

You can identify a vertical asymptote at $x = 1$, so the parameter h is 1. There is a horizontal asymptote at $y = -3$, so the parameter k is -3.

Substitute these values into the general form of the equation.

$g(x) = a\left(\dfrac{1}{x-1}\right) - 3$

> **A.** Why does h appear negative in the equation when the parameter is positive?

Finally, choose either reference point shown on the graph, such as $(0, -1)$. Substitute the x-coordinate of the reference point for x and the y-coordinate for $g(x)$. Then solve to find the value of the parameter a.

$g(x) = a\left(\dfrac{1}{x-1}\right) - 3$

$-1 = a\left(\dfrac{1}{0-1}\right) - 3$

> **B.** Why can either reference point be used?

$-1 = a(-1) - 3$

$2 = -a$

$a = -2$

Substitute -2 for a to complete the equation for $g(x)$.

$g(x) = a\left(\dfrac{1}{x-1}\right) - 3$

$g(x) = -2\left(\dfrac{1}{x-1}\right) - 3$

> **C.** How can you check that your equation is correct?

 Turn and Talk What is an equation of the form $g(x) = \dfrac{1}{\frac{1}{b}(x-h)} + k$ for the graph in Task 4?

Model with Simple Rational Functions

When a real-world situation involves both a shared cost and a per-person or per-item cost, you can model the situation using a rational function of the form $g(x) = \frac{a}{x} + k$. In this model, $g(x)$ is the total cost per person or per item, a is the shared cost, x is the number of people or items that share the cost a, and k is the per-person or per-item cost.

5 ▷ A group of friends is traveling to see a concert in a nearby city. Each person will pay for their own ticket, and the group will split the $20 cost for gas and tolls. How many people need to travel together for the total cost per person to be at most $44?

Tickets to concert: $40 each

Organize the information.
- The cost per person for a ticket is $40.
- The cost of gas and tolls to split is $20.
- Each person can pay a maximum of $44.

Write and graph a function.
Let p = the number of people who go to the concert, and let $c(p)$ = the total cost per person.

Total cost per person	=	Cost of gas and tolls / Number of people	+	Ticket cost
$c(p)$	=	$\dfrac{20}{p}$	+	40

Graph this rational function and the horizontal line representing the maximum cost per person, $c = 44$, in the first quadrant of the coordinate plane.

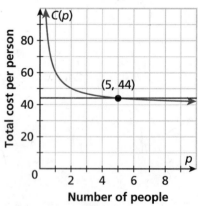

Answer the question.
The two graphs intersect at the point $(5, 44)$, and the graph of the function $c(p)$ for the total cost per person is on or below the line $c = 44$ for $p \geq 5$. This means that at least 5 people need to go to the concert in order for the total cost per person to be $44 or less.

A. Emmet thinks that the function giving the total cost per person should be $c(p) = \frac{20 + 40}{p}$, or $c(p) = \frac{60}{p}$. How would you explain to Emmet why this function is incorrect?

B. Can the total cost per person ever be $40? Explain.

C. Can the total cost per person ever be $46? Explain.

Turn and Talk Suppose the friends also share the cost of parking at the concert, which is $15. How does the function for the total cost per person change?

©PeopleImages/Getty Images

Check Understanding

1. Describe the symmetries of the graph of $f(x) = \frac{1}{x}$. What do these symmetries tell you about the function?

2. What transformations can you apply to the graph of $f(x) = \frac{1}{x}$ to produce the graph of $g(x) = 5\left(\frac{1}{x-2}\right) - 4$? What are the asymptotes and reference points of the graph of g?

3. What is an equation of the graph shown?

4. Write $g(x) = \frac{3x+19}{x+5}$ in the form $g(x) = a\left(\frac{1}{x-h}\right) + k$. Then graph g, showing the asymptotes and reference points.

5. Kyle spent $100 buying mixing bowls and pans for making muffins. His cost for the ingredients for each muffin is $0.75. Write an equation giving Kyle's total cost per muffin as a function of the number of muffins he makes. How many muffins must he make for the total cost per muffin to be at most $1.25?

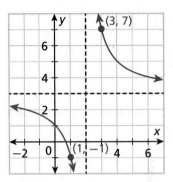

On Your Own

6. **(MP) Construct Arguments** Explain why the function $f(x) = \frac{1}{x}$ has no zeros.

7. Compare the graphs of $f(x) = \frac{1}{x}$ and $g(x) = \left(\frac{1}{2}\right)^x$ by describing two ways in which the graphs are similar and two ways in which they are different.

8. **(MP) Reason** Do the graphs of $f(x) = \frac{1}{x}$ and $g(x) = \frac{2}{x}$ ever intersect? Explain your reasoning.

9. **Open Ended** Write an equation for a rational function g whose domain is all real numbers except 5 and whose range is all real numbers except -3.

Identify the transformations you can apply to the graph of $f(x) = \frac{1}{x}$ to produce the graph of g. Use a graphing calculator to verify each transformation.

10. $g(x) = \dfrac{1}{(3x)}$

11. $g(x) = -\dfrac{1}{x}$

12. $g(x) = \dfrac{1}{x} + 5$

13. $g(x) = \dfrac{1}{x-3}$

14. $g(x) = 6\left(\dfrac{1}{x}\right)$

15. $g(x) = \dfrac{1}{x+1} - 2$

16. $g(x) = -\dfrac{2}{x}$

17. $g(x) = \dfrac{1}{x+2} + 3$

18. $g(x) = \dfrac{1}{3x-6}$

19. $g(x) = -\dfrac{1}{2x-4} + 1$

20. $g(x) = 4\left(\dfrac{1}{x+5}\right) + 2$

21. $g(x) = -2\left(\dfrac{1}{x-4}\right) - 3$

Identify the domain and range of the function g.

22. $g(x) = 2\left(\dfrac{1}{x}\right) - 4$

23. $g(x) = \dfrac{1}{x + 6}$

24. $g(x) = \dfrac{1}{x - 5} + 3$

25. $g(x) = 4\left(\dfrac{1}{x + 2}\right) + 1$

26. $g(x) = -\dfrac{3}{x + 1}$

27. $g(x) = \dfrac{5}{x + 2} - 1$

28. $g(x) = \dfrac{1}{2x + 4}$

29. $g(x) = -\dfrac{1}{x + 30}$

Graph the function g. Show the asymptotes and reference points for the graph.

30. $g(x) = \dfrac{1}{x - 1} + 1$

31. $g(x) = \dfrac{1}{x + 4} + 2$

32. $g(x) = 3\left(\dfrac{1}{x + 2}\right) - 1$

33. $g(x) = 2\left(\dfrac{1}{x}\right) - 5$

Rewrite the function in the form $g(x) = a\left(\dfrac{1}{x - h}\right) + k$ and graph it. Show the asymptotes and reference points for the graph.

34. $g(x) = \dfrac{3x - 4}{x - 2}$

35. $g(x) = \dfrac{4x - 5}{x - 1}$

36. $g(x) = \dfrac{5x + 11}{x + 3}$

37. $g(x) = \dfrac{-2x - 1}{x + 1}$

Write an equation of the graph shown. Use the form $g(x) = a\left(\dfrac{1}{x - h}\right) + k$.

38.

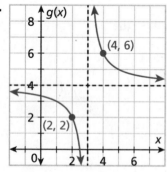

39.

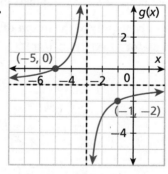

40.

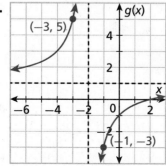

41.

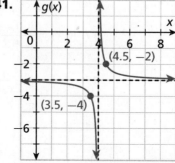

42. Let f be the rational function defined by the equation $f(x) = 3\left(\dfrac{1}{x+2}\right) + 5$, and let g be the rational function whose graph is shown.

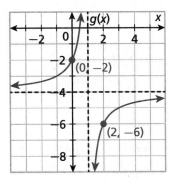

  A. The graphs of both f and g have a vertical asymptote with an equation of the form $x = h$. For which function is the value of h greater? Explain.

  B. Both functions approach a value k as $x \to +\infty$. For which function is the value of k greater? Explain.

43. Financial Literacy Lacy buys a cell phone for $300 and pays $40 per month for cellular service.

  A. Write an equation that gives Lacy's average monthly cost $c(m)$ of owning the cell phone as a function of the number of months m she owns it.

  B. Find Lacy's average monthly cost after she has owned the phone for 2 months. Explain why this cost is so high.

  C. For how many months must Lacy own the phone in order for her average monthly cost to fall to $60? Use a graph to find the answer.

  D. If Lacy owns the phone for 3 years before buying a new one, what is her average monthly cost over her ownership period?

44. The function shown gives a kayaker's speed s (t) in feet per second, where t is the number of seconds after the kayaker leaves the river's edge.

$$s(t) = -18\left(\frac{1}{t+3}\right) + 13$$

  A. Make a table of values showing the first 10 seconds and each corresponding kayaker's speed.

  B. Sketch a graph of the data represented in the table.

  C. Compare the kayaker's average rate of change in speed during the first 5 seconds with the average rate of change in speed during the next 5 seconds. Interpret your results in the context of the situation.

  D. What speed does the kayaker eventually approach?

45. (MP) **Model with Mathematics** Rosa purchased a silk-screening kit for applying designs to fabric. The kit costs $200. She plans to buy T-shirts for $10 each, apply a design that she creates to the T-shirts, and then sell them for $18 each.

  A. Write an equation that gives Rosa's average profit per T-shirt as a function of the number of T-shirts that she sells.

  B. How many T-shirts must Rosa sell for her average profit per T-shirt to reach $3? Use a graph to find the answer.

  C. Can Rosa's average profit per T-shirt ever reach $10? Explain why or why not.

46. (MP) **Critique Reasoning** A student was asked to graph the function $g(x) = \frac{-4x + 10}{x - 2}$. Did the student graph the function correctly? Explain.

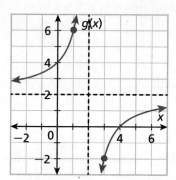

47. STEM To breathe safely, divers working in deep water use air containing less oxygen than Earth's atmosphere. The recommended percent p of oxygen (by volume) in the air a diver breathes is given by the equation shown, where d is the depth (in feet) at which the diver is working.

A. What is the recommended percent of oxygen for a diver working at a depth of 100 feet?

B. What value does the recommended percent of oxygen approach as the diver's depth increases?

$$p = \frac{660}{d + 33}$$

48. (Open Middle™) Using the integers −9 to 9, at most one time each, fill in the boxes to create a rational function and identify its vertical asymptote and zero.

Function: $y = \boxed{}\left(\dfrac{1}{x + \boxed{}}\right) + \boxed{}$ Vertical asymptote: $x = \boxed{}$ Zero: $x = \boxed{}$

Spiral Review • Assessment Readiness

49. What is the solution of the equation $4 + 9^{x + 1.5} = 7$?

(A) −1

(C) 0

(B) −0.5

(D) 0.5

50. What is the solution of the equation $\log_3(3x - 1) = \log_3(2x + 5)$?

(A) 3

(C) 6

(B) 4

(D) 12

51. Suppose y varies inversely with x, and $y = 12$ when $x = 4$. What is the value of y when $x = 6$?

(A) 2

(C) 14

(B) 8

(D) 18

52. What is the factored form of $x^2 + 4x - 32$?

(A) $(x + 4)(x + 8)$

(C) $(x - 4)(x + 8)$

(B) $(x + 4)(x - 8)$

(D) $(x - 4)(x - 8)$

©Alexis Rosenfeld/Getty Images

 I'm in a Learning Mindset!

What questions can I ask to encourage my classmates to share their knowledge of how to graph simple rational functions?

Graph More Complicated Rational Functions

(I Can) identify key characteristics of more complicated rational functions and use these characteristics to graph the functions.

Spark Your Learning

In professional baseball, the radius and volume of the baseball are strictly regulated.

The radius of each baseball must be within regulation standards.

Complete Part A as a whole class. Then complete Parts B–D in small groups.

A. What is a mathematical question you can ask about this situation? What information would you need to know to answer your question?

B. What formula(s) will be needed to answer your question?

C. To answer your question, what strategy and tool would you use along with all the information you have? What answer do you get?

D. Does your answer make sense in the context of the situation? What level of accuracy is needed in measuring the baseballs to determine whether they meet the regulation standards?

> **Turn and Talk** How would your answers change for a basketball used in the Women's National Basketball Association (WNBA) where the regulations are as follows:
> - The diameter can vary by only 0.16 inch.
> - The smallest allowable basketball has a volume that is 95% of the volume of the largest allowable basketball.

Build Understanding

Investigate Domains and Vertical Asymptotes of More Complicated Rational Functions

From the previous lesson, you know that for the rational function $f(x) = \frac{1}{x-h} + k$, the value of $x = h$ is excluded from its domain. You also know that the graph of this function has a vertical and a horizontal asymptote as shown in the image. In the following tasks, you will investigate the behavior of more complicated rational functions, which can have variables in the numerator as well as the denominator.

Graph of $f(x) = \frac{1}{x-h} + k$

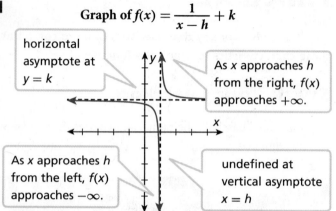

horizontal asymptote at $y = k$

As x approaches h from the right, $f(x)$ approaches $+\infty$.

As x approaches h from the left, $f(x)$ approaches $-\infty$.

undefined at vertical asymptote $x = h$

1

A. Consider the rational function $f(x) = \frac{x+2}{x-1}$. For what values of x do you expect the graph of the function to be undefined? Explain your answer. Use a graphing calculator to graph $f(x)$. How does the behavior of the graph relate to your expectation?

B. Consider the following rational functions.

$$g(x) = \frac{x-1}{(x-2)(x-3)} \qquad h(x) = \frac{(x-1)(x-2)}{x-3} \qquad j(x) = \frac{x^2 - 8x + 16}{(x+2)(x-4)}$$

Do you think the graphs of these functions have any vertical asymptotes? If so, describe the number of asymptotes and the location of the asymptotes.

C. Use a graphing calculator to graph each of the functions $g(x)$, $h(x)$, and $j(x)$. Compare the vertical asymptotes in the graph with your expectations. Are the asymptotes where you expected? Explain.

D. Use the table feature to examine $g(x)$ and $h(x)$ at their excluded domain values. What do you notice? How are these results related to the graph of each function?

E. Use the table feature to examine $j(x)$ at $x = -2$ and $x = 4$. Then use the trace feature to examine the graph at the same values. What do you notice? How would you summarize the behavior of the graph near and at these points?

F. Is the graph of $j(x)$ identical to the graph of $k(x) = \frac{x-4}{x+2}$? Use a graph or a table of values to support your answer.

Turn and Talk How would you expect the graphs to behave as they approach the vertical asymptotes of the function?

Identify the Breaks in the Graph of a Rational Function

The functions discussed in Task 1 have breaks in their graph at values that are excluded from the domain. The two types of breaks in a graph of a rational function are vertical asymptotes and holes.

2 Consider the graphs of the rational functions below.

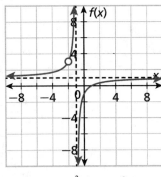 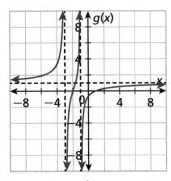

$$f(x) = \frac{x^2 + x - 2}{x^2 + 3x + 2} \qquad\qquad g(x) = \frac{x^2 + x - 2}{x^2 + 4x + 3}$$

A. What are the values that are excluded from the domain of $f(x)$? How do these excluded values relate to breaks in the graph of the function?

B. What are the values that are excluded from the domain of $g(x)$? How do these excluded values relate to breaks in the graph of the function?

C. Factor the numerator and denominator of $f(x)$. Are any of the factors the same? If so, what type of break in the graph is at the related excluded value?

D. Factor the numerator and denominator of $g(x)$. Are any of the factors the same? If so, what type of break in the graph is at the related excluded value?

E. How do you think the type of break in the graph is related to whether or not a factor appears in both the numerator and denominator of a rational function?

F. The graph of a rational function $h(x)$ is shown. What types of breaks do you see in the graph of this function? Do you think the numerator and denominator of this rational function have any common linear factors? Explain.

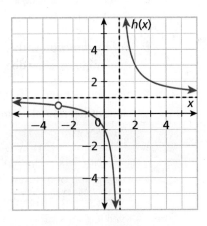

 Turn and Talk How can you determine where the graph of a rational polynomial function has a break and what type of break occurs at that point?

Identify the Horizontal and Slant Asymptotes of the Graph of a Rational Function

In addition to having vertical asymptotes, the graph of a rational function $f(x) = \frac{p(x)}{q(x)}$ can also have horizontal or slant asymptotes. **Slant asymptotes** are linear asymptotes that are neither vertical nor horizontal.

3 Consider the graphs of the rational functions below.

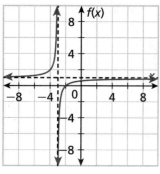

$$f(x) = \frac{x + 2}{x + 3}$$

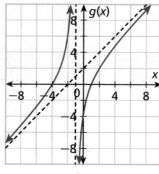

$$g(x) = \frac{x^2 + 3x - 4}{x + 1}$$

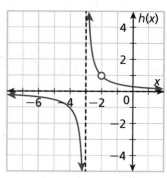

$$h(x) = \frac{x + 2}{x^2 + 5x + 6}$$

A. For each function, identify the following:
- the types of asymptotes that appear in the graph,
- the degree of $p(x)$ for each function, and
- the degree of $q(x)$ for each function.

B. What do you notice about the degree of $p(x)$ and the degree of $q(x)$ for the functions that have horizontal asymptotes?

C. When the degrees of $p(x)$ and $q(x)$ are equal, the rational function has a horizontal asymptote at $y = \frac{a}{b}$, where a is the leading coefficient of $p(x)$ and b is the leading coefficient of $q(x)$. Write a rational function that has a horizontal asymptote of $y = 5$.

D. What do you notice about the degree of $p(x)$ and the degree of $q(x)$ for the function that has a slant asymptote?

E. For the function with the slant asymptote, divide the numerator by the denominator. How does the quotient relate to the slant asymptote?

F. Do all functions with the degree of $p(x) >$ the degree of $q(x)$ have either a slant or horizontal asymptote? Justify your answer.

Turn and Talk Which of the following combinations of asymptotes are possible for the graph of different rational functions? Explain your answer.
- vertical and horizontal
- vertical and slant
- horizontal and slant
- vertical, horizontal, and slant

Step It Out

Graph More Complicated Rational Functions

To sketch the graph of a rational function you will first need to identify any vertical asymptotes, holes, horizontal asymptotes, and slant asymptotes. The zeros and excluded values can be used to establish intervals on the x-axis. You can check the sign of the factors of the numerator and of the denominator to determine whether the graph is above or below the x-axis in each interval.

 Graph the rational function $f(x) = \frac{x^2 + 5x + 4}{x + 2}$.

Identify vertical asymptotes and holes.
The function is undefined when the denominator $x + 2 = 0$, or when $x = -2$. There are no holes, but $x = -2$ is a vertical asymptote.

Identify horizontal or slant asymptotes.
The degree of the numerator is 1 more than the degree of the denominator, so the graph has a slant asymptote. Divide the numerator by the denominator to find the slant asymptote.

$$
\begin{array}{r}
x + 3 \\
x + 2 \overline{)\, x^2 + 5x + 4} \\
\underline{x^2 + 2x} \\
3x + 4 \\
\underline{3x + 6} \\
-2
\end{array}
$$

Rewrite $f(x)$ as $f(x) = x + 3 - \frac{2}{x+2}$. As x gets large, $\frac{2}{x+2}$ approaches 0. This means that as x increases, the function resembles the line $y = x + 3$, which is the slant asymptote.

Identify the x-intercepts.
Set the numerator equal to 0 and solve for x. The numerator is 0 when $x + 4 = 0$ or $x + 1 = 0$. So, the x-intercepts are -4 and -1.

> A. How do you determine the sign of each polynomial over each interval?

Create a sign table.
Use the vertical asymptote and the x-intercepts to create test intervals.

Interval	$x < -4$	$-4 < x < -2$	$-2 < x < -1$	$x > -1$
Sign of $(x + 4)$	$-$	$+$	$+$	$+$
Sign of $(x + 1)$	$-$	$-$	$-$	$+$
Sign of $(x + 2)$	$-$	$-$	$+$	$+$
Sign of $f(x) = \dfrac{(x+4)(x+1)}{x+2}$	$\dfrac{(-)(-)}{(-)} = -$	$\dfrac{(+)(-)}{(-)} = +$	$\dfrac{(+)(-)}{(+)} = -$	$\dfrac{(+)(+)}{(+)} = +$

Sketch the graph.

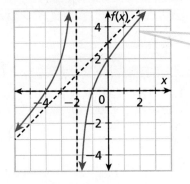

> B. How does the information about the asymptotes, intercepts, and interval signs relate to the graph of $f(x)$?

5 Graph the rational function $f(x) = \frac{x^2 - 2x - 8}{x^2 + x - 2}$.

Identify vertical asymptotes and holes.

Factor the trinomials and find the zeros of the denominator.

$$f(x) = \frac{x^2 - 2x - 8}{x^2 + x - 2} = \frac{(x-4)(x+2)}{(x-1)(x+2)}$$

The function is undefined when $x = 1$ or $x = -2$.

There is a vertical asymptote at $x = 1$.

There is a hole at $x = -2$ because $x + 2$ is a common factor of the numerator and denominator.

Identify horizontal or slant asymptotes.

Since the numerator and denominator have the same degree, there is a horizontal asymptote at $y = \frac{1}{1} = 1$.

> **A.** How do you find the values of the numerator and denominator of the horizontal asymptote?

Identify the x-intercepts.

Set the numerator equal to 0 and solve for x. The numerator is 0 when $x - 4 = 0$ or $x + 2 = 0$. So, the x-intercept is 4.

> **B.** Why is -2 not an x-intercept?

Create a sign table.

Use the vertical asymptote and the x-intercept to create test intervals.

Interval	$x < 1$	$1 < x < 4$	$x > 4$
Sign of $(x - 4)$	$-$	$-$	$+$
Sign of $(x - 1)$	$-$	$+$	$+$
Sign of $f(x) = \frac{(x-4)\cancel{(x+2)}}{(x-1)\cancel{(x+2)}}$	$\frac{(-)}{(-)} = +$	$\frac{(-)}{(+)} = -$	$\frac{(+)}{(+)} = +$

Sketch the graph.

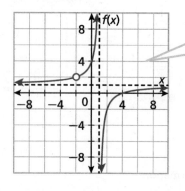

> **C.** What do you graph first? How do you use the test intervals to graph the function?

 Turn and Talk Why is a common factor in the numerator and denominator of a rational function not used in the sign table?

Model with a More Complicated Rational Function

Some real-world situations involve a comparison of two variable quantities using a ratio or rate. This comparison can be represented with a rational function. You can use a graph of the rational function to answer questions about the situation.

6 ▶ Tony records the number of first serves hit in play during a tennis match.

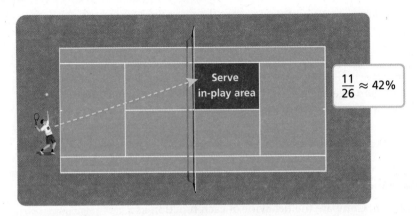

How many consecutive first serves does he need to hit in play in order for his percentage to reach 70%? Write a rational function to represent the situation. Then graph the rational function to solve the problem. What does the horizontal asymptote of the graph represent?

Write an equation.
Let h represent the number of consecutive successful first serve hits made after his initial 26 hits. Tony's first serve in-play percentage as a function of h is then:

$$p(h) = \frac{11 + h}{26 + h}.$$

A. What quantities do the expressions in the numerator and denominator represent? What does this ratio represent?

Graph the function.
Use a graphing calculator to graph the function $p(h)$ and the line $p(h) = 0.7$. Find the point of intersection.

Interpret.
Tony's first serve in-play percentage will be 70% if he successfully hits the next 24 consecutive hits. The horizontal asymptote $p(h) = 1$ indicates that the success rate will approach 100% but never actual reach 100%.

B. What does the line $p(h) = 0.7$ represent?

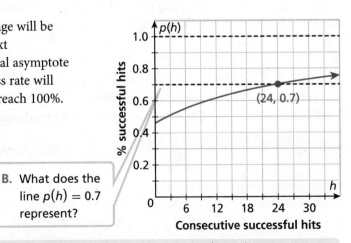

Turn and Talk What is the average rate of change for the function on the interval $0 \leq h \leq 24$? What does this average change represent?

Check Understanding

1. How are the domains and vertical asymptotes of rational functions related?

2. How is the behavior of the graph of a rational function different when approaching a hole compared to approaching a vertical asymptote?

3. What does it mean for a function to be asymptotic to more than one line? How does this behavior help you sketch the graph of the function?

4. Graph $g(x) = \dfrac{x^2 + 4x + 3}{x^2 - 2x - 8}$.

5. A football team has won 6 of the 11 games played. How many consecutive wins does the team need to raise their winning percentage to 75%?

On Your Own

6. (MP) **Reason** The graphs of the rational functions $f(x) = \dfrac{x - 1}{50(x + 1)(x + 2)}$ and $g(x) = \dfrac{x + 1}{50(x + 1)(x + 2)}$ are shown. Compare the behavior of each function as x approaches -2 from the left and from the right. Compare the behavior of each function as x approaches -1 from the left and the right. How does this behavior relate to the type of breaks of each graph?

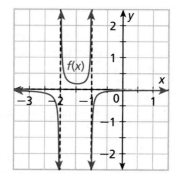 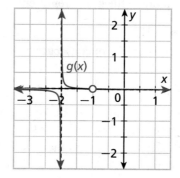

7. (MP) **Use Structure** Explain why common factors in the numerator and denominator cause a hole in the graph of a rational function instead of a vertical asymptote.

8. (MP) **Use Structure** Do the graphs of all rational functions have at least one vertical asymptote or hole? Explain why or why not.

For each rational function, identify any excluded values of the domain. At any excluded value, tell whether the type of break in the graph is a vertical asymptote or a hole.

9. $f(x) = \dfrac{x + 3}{x + 4}$

10. $f(x) = \dfrac{x + 1}{x^2 + 3x + 2}$

11. $f(x) = \dfrac{x^2 - 5x + 6}{x^2 - 3x + 2}$

12. $f(x) = \dfrac{x^2 + 3x + 4}{x + 2}$

13. $f(x) = \dfrac{4}{x^2 - 4}$

14. $f(x) = \dfrac{x + 3}{2x^2 - 18}$

15. $f(x) = \dfrac{x^3}{x^2 + x}$

16. $f(x) = \dfrac{x + 1}{x^2 + 1}$

17. Consider the equation of the rational function $f(x) = \frac{3x+1}{x-2}$ and the graph of the rational function $g(x)$, which is shown. Compare the types of asymptotes, the domains, and the ranges of $f(x)$ and $g(x)$.

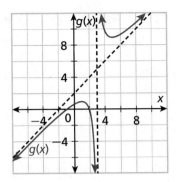

For each function, write the equation of any asymptotes.

18. $f(x) = \dfrac{x-5}{x+1}$

19. $f(x) = \dfrac{2x-1}{2x-2}$

20. $f(x) = \dfrac{x+1}{x^2+6x+5}$

21. $f(x) = \dfrac{(x+2)(x+1)}{x-2}$

Sketch the graph of each rational function. State any excluded values of the domain and identify the type of break in the graph at that value of x. Use dotted lines to represent any asymptotes of the graph. Use an open circle to represent any holes of the graph.

22. $f(x) = \dfrac{x-2}{x+2}$

23. $f(x) = \dfrac{x-1}{x+3}$

24. $f(x) = \dfrac{x-1}{(x+2)(x-3)}$

25. $f(x) = \dfrac{x(x-1)}{x^2-1}$

26. $f(x) = \dfrac{2(x-2)}{x^2+3x-10}$

27. $f(x) = \dfrac{x^2-4x+4}{2x^2-4x}$

28. $f(x) = \dfrac{x^2-x+2}{x-2}$

29. $f(x) = \dfrac{x^2-3x+4}{x+1}$

30. Tiana paddles a canoe at an average rate of 4 miles per hour in still water. Her trip takes 4 hours and the distance she travels upstream and downstream is shown. The rational function $t(c) = \frac{5}{4-c} + \frac{8}{4+c} = \frac{52-3c}{16-c^2}$, where c is the average rate of the current (in miles per hour), represents the time t (in hours) spent canoeing the entire trip. Use a graph to find the average rate of the current.

31. The graph shows the average cost (in dollars per unit) of manufacturing a new smart prosthetic as a function of the number of units manufactured. How does the average rate of change for the function on the interval $200 \le x \le 400$ compare to the average rate of change on the interval $600 \le x \le 800$? Interpret your answer in the context of the problem.

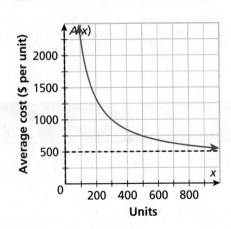

32. (MP) **Model with Mathematics** A manufacturer makes and sells fitness trackers. The average profit per fitness tracker $A(x)$ can be calculated using the ratio of the profit to the number of fitness trackers sold: $A(x) = \frac{P(x)}{x}$.

Average profit for fitness trackers: $A(x) = \frac{P(x)}{x}$

A. The profit is equal to the revenue of the fitness trackers $R(x) = 120x$ minus the cost of the fitness trackers $C(x) = 1250 - 55x$. Write a rational function to model the average profit $A(x)$ in terms of x.

B. State the domain of the function for the situation it represents.

C. Sketch a graph of the average profit per fitness tracker. After how many sales will the average profit be $120 per fitness tracker?

D. What does the horizontal asymptote tell you about the average profit per fitness tracker?

33. Open Ended Write a rational function that has all of the following characteristics.

- vertical asymptote at $x = 2$
- hole at $x = -4$
- graph passes through $(0, -3)$

34. (Open Middle™) Using the digits 1 to 9, at most one time each, fill in the boxes to create a rational function with no zeros.

$$y = \frac{\left(x + \boxed{}\right)}{x^2 + \boxed{}x + \boxed{}}$$

Spiral Review • Assessment Readiness

35. For what value of x is $\log_3 8 = \log_3 x + \log_3 4$?

- (A) 2
- (B) 4
- (C) 8
- (D) 64

36. The graph of which rational function is a vertical stretch of the graph $f(x) = \frac{1}{x}$ by a factor of 2?

- (A) $g(x) = \frac{2}{x}$
- (B) $g(x) = \frac{1}{2x}$
- (C) $g(x) = \frac{1}{x+2}$
- (D) $g(x) = \frac{1}{x} + 2$

37. The value of y varies inversely with the value of x. The value of y is 5 when x is 2. What is the value of x when y is 30?

- (A) 18
- (B) 6
- (C) $\frac{1}{3}$
- (D) $\frac{1}{18}$

38. Which expression is equivalent to $\frac{8}{3}\left(\frac{x}{3}\right) \div \frac{4}{5}$?

- (A) $\frac{8}{3}\left(\frac{x}{3}\right)\left(\frac{5}{4}\right)$
- (B) $\frac{4}{5} \div \frac{8}{3}\left(\frac{x}{3}\right)$
- (C) $\frac{8}{3}\left(\frac{4}{5}\right) \div \frac{3}{x}$
- (D) $\frac{4}{5} \div 8x$

 I'm in a Learning Mindset!

How can I refine my questions to clarify my understanding of graphing more complicated rational functions?

Inverse Variation

The relationship between the length and width of a rectangle with constant area represents inverse variation.

w	l
1	28
2	14
4	7
7	4
8	3.5
14	2
28	1

the constant of variation

$$l = \frac{a}{w} = \frac{28}{w}$$

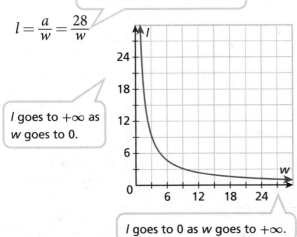

l goes to $+\infty$ as *w* goes to 0.

l goes to 0 as *w* goes to $+\infty$.

Graphs of Simple Rational Functions

Consider the function $y = \frac{a}{x}$, where $x \neq 0$ and $a \neq 0$ and a is the constant of variation.

vertical asymptote at $x = 0$

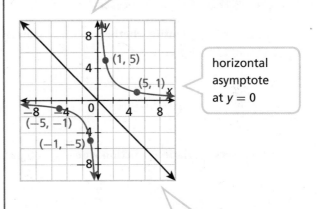

horizontal asymptote at $y = 0$

Reflect over $y = -x$ if a is positive and $y = x$ if a is negative.

Plot reference points and each asymptote, then sketch the function.

Graphs of More Complicated Rational Functions

Consider the rational function

$$f(x) = \frac{x^3 - 4x^2 - 11x + 30}{x^2 + 3x - 10}$$

Notice that the degree of the numerator is one more than the degree of the denominator, so the function has a slant asymptote and no horizontal asymptote.

To find the vertical asymptote and any holes, we must first factor the numerator and denominator.

$$f(x) = \frac{(x - 2)(x - 5)(x + 3)}{(x - 2)(x + 5)}$$

a hole at $x = 2$

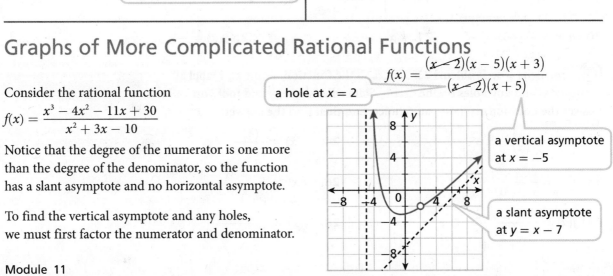

a vertical asymptote at $x = -5$

a slant asymptote at $y = x - 7$

Vocabulary

Choose the correct term from the box to complete each sentence.

1. A(n) ___?___ is a function of the form $f(x) = \frac{p(x)}{q(x)}$ where $p(x)$ and $q(x)$ are polynomials and $q(x) \neq 0$.

2. A(n) ___?___ is a function of the form $y = \frac{a}{x}$.

3. In the function $y = \frac{a}{x}$, a is the ___?___.

4. An asymptote that is neither horizontal nor vertical is a(n) ___?___.

Concepts and Skills

For Problems 5–7, identify whether y varies inversely with x. If so, state the value of the constant of variation.

5. $y = \frac{3}{x}$

6. $y = \frac{2x}{3x}$

7. $y = \frac{1}{5x}$

8. $xy = 10$

9. $y = \frac{1}{x + 2}$

10. $y = \frac{x}{8}$

Write an inverse variation function whose graph passes through the given point, and then determine the missing value.

11. $(6, 2), (8, ?)$

12. $(2, 0.25), (?, 0.1)$

13. $(6, 3), (-9, ?)$

14. $(1, 5), (?, 2)$

15. $(-3, 4), (2, ?)$

16. $(7, 4), (10, ?)$

Describe how each graph is related to the parent function $f(x) = \frac{1}{x}$.

17. $z(x) = \frac{1}{x} - 5$

18. $m(x) = \frac{1}{2(x + 3)}$

19. $g(x) = 2\left(\frac{1}{x}\right) + 4$

20. $h(x) = \frac{5}{x} - 3$

21. $k(x) = \frac{1}{x - 6} + 2$

22. $y(x) = -\frac{2}{x}$

(MP) **Use Tools** For Problems 23–28, graph the function. Draw and label all asymptotes and any holes on the graph. State what strategy and tool you will use to answer the question, explain your choice, and then find the answer.

23. $g(x) = 3\left(\frac{1}{x}\right) - 5$

24. $g(x) = \frac{1}{x - 6}$

25. $f(x) = \frac{x + 2}{x^2 + 3x + 2}$

26. $f(x) = \frac{x^2 + 3x - 4}{x - 2}$

27. $f(x) = \frac{x^2 + 7x + 12}{x^2 + 5x - 6}$

28. $f(x) = \frac{x^2 + 2x}{x^2 - 6x - 27}$

12 Rational Expressions and Equations

Module Performance Task: Focus on STEM

Doppler Effect

The sound of a vehicle will change in pitch as it passes by an observer. As a source of sound moves, the distance between successive wave-fronts can be compressed or expanded, causing an observer to perceive a change in observed frequency.

- Given f_s, the frequency at the source, c, the speed of sound, v_o, the velocity of the observer, and v_s, the velocity of the source, then the observed frequency is $f_o = \frac{c \pm v_o}{c \pm v_s} f_s$.
- v_s is positive when the source moves away from the observer.
- v_o is positive when the observer moves toward the source.

A. Create and graph a function that models each scenario:

1) The source is stationary, and the observer is moving toward the source at a rate of x.

2) The observer is stationary, and the source is moving toward the observer at a rate of x.

3) The observer is stationary, and the source is moving away from the observer at a rate of x.

4) Both the observer and source are moving in the same direction at the same rate of x.

B. Describe the shape, domain, and range of each function in context.

C. Explain why the observed frequency for scenario 1 is different from scenario 2.

D. Describe, in context, what happens to f_o in each scenario as x approaches the speed of sound.

Are You Ready?

Complete these problems to review prior concepts and skills you will need for this module.

Solve Multi-Step Equations

Solve each equation.

1. $5 = 5x + 1$

2. $7(x - 6) = 56$

3. $5(x + 8) - 4 = 3x - 5$

4. $11x - 9 = 3(4x - 8)$

5. $3x + 2 = 6x - 4$

6. $-4(2x - 5) = -12x + 8$

Factor Quadratic Expressions

Factor each expression.

7. $3x^2 + 15x$

8. $x^2 - x - 20$

9. $2x^2 + 13x + 21$

10. $3x^2 + 12x - 36$

11. $2x^2 + 7x - 4$

12. $5x^2 - 25x + 30$

Solve Quadratic Equations by Factoring

Solve each equation by factoring.

13. $x^2 = 4x$

14. $x^2 - 6x - 16 = 0$

15. $6x^2 - 12x + 6 = 0$

16. $-5x^2 = 6x + 1$

17. $x^2 - 5x - 36 = 0$

18. $2x^2 + 6 = 7x$

Connecting Past and Present Learning

Previously, you learned:

• to simplify fractional expressions,

• to apply function operations to polynomial expressions, and

• to understand that polynomials form a system analogous to the integers.

In this module, you will learn:

• to understand that rational expressions form a system analogous to the rational numbers,

• to add, subtract, multiply, divide, and rewrite rational expressions, and

• to construct and solve rational equations.

Multiply and Divide Rational Expressions

(I Can) **multiply and divide rational expressions.**

Spark Your Learning

The women's and men's track teams have the same number of meets remaining. Jen, a sports reporter, wonders what winning percentage each team will have if both teams win their remaining meets.

Women's track team:
12 wins so far

Men's track team:
11 wins so far

Complete Part A as a whole class. Then complete Parts B–D in small groups.

A. What is a mathematical question you can ask about this situation? What information would you need to know to answer your question?

B. How can you write an algebraic expression to represent each team's winning percentage?

C. To answer your question, what strategy and tool would you use along with all the information you have? What answer do you get?

D. Does your answer make sense in the context of the situation? How do you know?

Turn and Talk How would the answer to your question change if the men's track team has 12 wins and 4 losses so far? Explain.

Build Understanding

Simplify Rational Expressions

You have learned to rewrite some numerical fractions by dividing out common factors from the numerator and denominator. For example:

$$\frac{36}{48} = \frac{3 \cdot \cancel{12}}{4 \cdot \cancel{12}} = \frac{3}{4}$$

When simplifying a rational expression, a similar procedure is applied. Recall that division by 0 is undefined.

1 The graph of the rational function $y = \frac{(x+1)(x+4)}{x+4}$ is shown below.

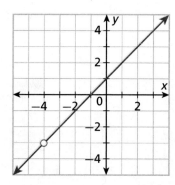

A. Describe the graph of the function.

B. What is the domain of the function?

C. What value of x must be excluded so that division by 0 does not occur in the rational expression $\frac{(x+1)(x+4)}{x+4}$?

D. Simplify the rational function shown above. Since the domain of the function does not change due to the simplification, how must the simplified function be written?

2 Consider the rational expression $\frac{4x^3 - 12x^2 - 160x}{4x^3 + 12x^2 - 40x}$.

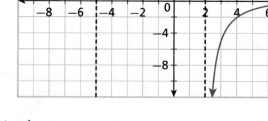

A. Factor the expression completely. Then simplify it by dividing out any common factors from the numerator and denominator.

B. What are the excluded values of the given expression?

C. The graph of the related rational function is shown at the right. Write a description of the graph.

D. What is the domain of the function? How do the excluded values of the rational expression impact the graph of the related rational function?

E. Write the simplified form of the rational function whose graph is shown above.

Turn and Talk How do you simplify a rational expression with trinomials in the numerator and the denominator? How do you determine the excluded values of the simplified expression?

Step It Out

Multiply Rational Expressions

Multiplying two rational expressions is like multiplying two numerical fractions. First, multiply the numerators, then multiply the denominators. Simplify the product by dividing out any common factors appearing in both the numerator and the denominator.

3 Multiply $\frac{x^2 - 3x - 10}{x^2 + x - 20}$ by $\frac{x^2 - 16}{x^2 - 4}$.

$$\frac{x^2 - 3x - 10}{x^2 + x - 20} \cdot \frac{x^2 - 16}{x^2 - 4} = \frac{(x^2 - 3x - 10)(x^2 - 16)}{(x^2 + x - 20)(x^2 - 4)}$$

B. Explain how the factors shown in the numerator and denominator here were determined.

$$= \frac{(x - 5)(x + 2)(x + 4)(x - 4)}{(x + 5)(x - 4)(x + 2)(x - 2)}$$

A. What are the excluded values for this multiplication?

$$= \frac{(x - 5)\cancel{(x + 2)}(x + 4)\cancel{(x - 4)}}{(x + 5)\cancel{(x - 4)}\cancel{(x + 2)}(x - 2)}$$

$$= \frac{(x - 5)(x + 4)}{(x + 5)(x - 2)}$$

C. What equivalent expression for the product could be given?

Divide with Rational Expressions

Just as when dividing two numerical fractions, dividing rational expressions involves multiplying by the reciprocal of the divisor. The remaining steps of the process are those for multiplying two rational expressions.

4 Divide $\frac{x^3 + 6x^2 + 12x + 8}{x^2 - 12x + 32}$ by $\frac{x^3 + 8}{x^2 - 64}$.

$$\frac{x^3 + 6x^2 + 12x + 8}{x^2 - 12x + 32} \div \frac{x^3 + 8}{x^2 - 64} = \frac{x^3 + 6x^2 + 12x + 8}{x^2 - 12x + 32} \cdot \frac{x^2 - 64}{x^3 + 8}$$

B. Explain how the factors shown here were determined.

$$= \frac{(x + 2)(x^2 + 4x + 4)(x + 8)(x - 8)}{(x - 8)(x - 4)(x + 2)(x^2 - 2x + 4)}$$

A. What are the excluded values for this division? How is determining these values different than for a product of two rational expressions?

$$= \frac{(x + 2)(x + 2)(x + 2)(x + 8)(x - 8)}{(x - 8)(x - 4)(x + 2)(x^2 - 2x + 4)}$$

$$= \frac{(x + 2)(x + 2)\cancel{(x + 2)}(x + 8)\cancel{(x - 8)}}{\cancel{(x - 8)}(x - 4)\cancel{(x + 2)}(x^2 - 2x + 4)}$$

$$= \frac{(x + 2)(x + 2)(x + 8)}{(x - 4)(x^2 - 2x + 4)}$$

 Turn and Talk Consider the graph of this quotient as a function. Does the graph have any holes? Does it have vertical asymptotes? Identify any holes or vertical asymptotes.

Multiply and Divide with Rational Expressions in the Real World

The fastest train in the United States is the Acela train. It can maintain its top speed for only a short section of its tracks between Boston and New York City.

5 The expression $\dfrac{d_1 r_2 + d_2 r_1}{r_1 r_2}$ represents the time (in hours) it takes for the Acela train to travel from Boston to New York City, where r_1 is the top speed (in miles per hour) of the train during the trip, r_2 is the average speed of the train on the remainder of the trip (including stops), and d_1 and d_2 are the corresponding distances (in miles) at those speeds.

Create an expression for the average speed r of the Acela trip from Boston to New York if the average speed when it is not at its top speed is 60 miles per hour.

Top speed: 150 mi/h
Boston to New York City: 231 mi

The total distance traveled is equal to the product of the average speed (rate) and the total time for the trip. So the average speed is the total distance divided by the total time.

$$\text{average speed} = \text{total distance} \div \text{total time}$$

$$r = 231 \div \frac{d_1 r_2 + d_2 r_1}{r_1 r_2}$$

    A. Explain the substitutions that have been made in this step.

$$= 231 \cdot \frac{r_1 r_2}{d_1 r_2 + d_2 r_1}$$

    B. What has happened in this step?

$$= \frac{231 r_1 r_2}{d_1 r_2 + d_2 r_1}$$

$$= \frac{231(150)(60)}{60 d_1 + 150 d_2}$$

    C. Justify the substitutions that have been made in this step.

$$= \frac{231(150)(60)}{60x + (150)(231 - x)}$$

    D. What does x represent here? Justify the replacement of d_2 by $231 - x$.

$$= \frac{2{,}079{,}000}{-90x + 34{,}650}$$

So the average speed for the trip depends on the distance the train can travel at top speed.

E. If the train can only travel at top speed for 33.9 miles, what is the average speed of the train from Boston to New York City?

F. How long does the train take to travel from Boston to New York City?

 Turn and Talk How would the solution process change if you had a rational expression for the average speed (rate) and wanted to find the total distance?

Check Understanding

1. Simplify the expression $\frac{8x - 24}{x^2 + 7x - 30}$.

2. Find the product and list all excluded values of $\frac{x^2 - 81}{x + 81} \cdot \frac{x^2 + 81x}{x^3 - 81x}$.

3. Explain all steps for dividing and simplifying the quotient $\frac{x^2 + 4x}{x - 2} \div \frac{x^2 + 2x - 8}{x^2 - 2x - 8}$.

4. **A.** Express the ratio of the surface area of a sphere with radius r to its volume.

   B. Express the ratio of the surface area to the volume of a cube with side length r.

   C. Write and simplify a rational expression of the ratio of the volume of a sphere with radius r to the volume of a cube with side length r.

On Your Own

5. Describe the steps to simplify the rational expression $\frac{x^4 + 72x^2 + 1296}{x^4 - 1296}$.

6. Can the rational expression $\frac{(x^2 + 1)}{(x^2 - 1)}$ be simplified? If so, describe the steps. If not, explain your reasoning.

Find each product and list all excluded values.

7. $\frac{-35xy}{24z} \cdot \frac{18z^2}{15x^2y}$

8. $\frac{7p^2}{4rs} \cdot \frac{20q^2r^3}{21p^2s}$

9. $\frac{8 - x}{x^4 - 100x^2} \cdot \frac{x^2 + 10}{x^2 + 2x - 80}$

10. $\frac{x^2 + 12x + 36}{x^3 + 216} \cdot \frac{x^3 - 216}{x^2 - 36}$

For Problems 11–16, find each quotient and list all excluded values.

11. $\frac{5xy}{8z^2} \div \frac{x^2y}{4z}$

12. $\frac{x + 10}{10x^2} \div \frac{x^2 - 10x}{x^2 - 100}$

13. $\frac{x}{x + 4} \div \frac{x^2 + 3x}{x^2 + x - 12}$

14. $\frac{8x}{x + 6} \div \frac{x^2 - 6x}{x^2 + 3x - 18}$

15. $\frac{6x^2 + 14x + 8}{9x^2 - 16} \div \frac{x^2 + 2x + 1}{x^2 - 5x + 4}$

16. $\frac{x^3 - 27}{3x^2 - 24x + 45} \div \frac{x^2 + 3x + 9}{x^2 - 25}$

17. (MP) **Reason** When dividing two rational expressions, why is it insufficient to consider only their denominators when checking for excluded values?

18. (MP) **Model with Mathematics** The height of a rectangular prism is 2.5 times its length. The product of the length and width of the prism is 72 square inches. Let the width of the prism be w.

   A. Write an expression for the length and another expression for the height of the prism in terms of w.

   B. Write an equation for the area of one face of the prism formed by its length and height.

   C. Write an equation for the volume of the prism.

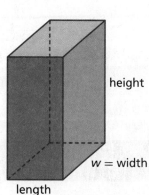

height

w = width

length

19. Starting with the records shown, the soccer team goes on to win half of their remaining games while the softball team wins all of theirs. By the end of their seasons, both teams have won the same number of games. Assume there were no ties by either team during their seasons.

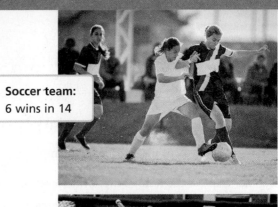

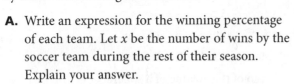

Soccer team:
6 wins in 14

A. Write an expression for the winning percentage of each team. Let x be the number of wins by the soccer team during the rest of their season. Explain your answer.

B. Write and simplify an expression for the ratio of the winning percentage of the softball team to the winning percentage of the soccer team.

Softball team:
8 wins in 13

C. Write an equation that shows that the winning percentage of the softball team was 50% greater than that of the soccer team.

20. A. Simplify the rational function $f(x) = \frac{4x^2 + 8x - 60}{5x - 15}$.

B. Graph the function using a graphing calculator. Describe any holes or asymptotes of the graph.

21. (Open Middle™) Using the digits 1 to 9, at most one time each, fill in the boxes to create a true statement.

$$\frac{x^2 - x - 6}{x^2 + 4x + 3} \div \frac{x^2 + \boxed{}x + \boxed{}}{x^2 + \boxed{}x + \boxed{}} = \frac{x - 3}{x + 4}$$

Spiral Review • Assessment Readiness

22. Which equation has a graph that is shifted 3 units left, 5 units up, and vertically stretched by a factor of 2 from the graph of $y = \frac{1}{x}$?

Ⓐ $y = \frac{2}{x - 3} + 5$ Ⓒ $\frac{1}{2}y = \frac{1}{x - 3} + 5$

Ⓑ $y = \frac{2}{x + 3} + 5$ Ⓓ $\frac{1}{2}y = \frac{1}{x + 3} + 5$

23. What is the x-intercept of the graph of $f(x) = -\frac{x - 4}{(x + 3)^2}$?

Ⓐ -4 Ⓑ $-\frac{4}{9}$ Ⓒ $\frac{4}{9}$ Ⓓ 4

24. What is the least common denominator of $\frac{3}{24x^2}$ and $\frac{5}{90x^2}$?

Ⓐ $360x$ Ⓒ $360x^4$

Ⓑ $360x^2$ Ⓓ $720x$

⬡ **I'm in a Learning Mindset!**

What is my plan for improving my performance with multiplying and dividing rational expressions?

Add and Subtract Rational Expressions

(I Can) add and subtract rational expressions.

Spark Your Learning

A company hires two independent truck drivers to make a long-distance delivery.

One of the trucks averages 2.5 miles per gallon of fuel more than the other truck.

The length of the trip is 2000 miles.

©Carolyn Franks/Alamy

Complete Part A as a whole class. Then complete Parts B–D in small groups.

A. What is a mathematical question you can ask about this situation? What information would you need to know to answer your question?

B. What expressions can be written for the fuel efficiency of each of the trucks?

C. To answer your question, what strategy and tool would you use along with all the information you have? What answer do you get?

D. Does your answer make sense in the context of the situation? How do you know?

 Turn and Talk How would your work and the result change if, instead of being told the fuel efficiency of the more fuel-efficient truck, you had been told that the less fuel efficient truck averages 16 miles per gallon?

Build Understanding

Investigate Sums and Differences of Rational Expressions

The addition and subtraction of rational expressions is very similar to adding and subtracting numerical fractions.

1 ▶ Compare finding the sum $\frac{x+4}{x-4} + \frac{2x-16}{x-4}$ to finding the sum $\frac{3}{8} + \frac{1}{8}$.

    A. For numerical fractions, having like denominators means the fractions have the same number in their denominators. What does this mean for rational expressions?

    B. Since both addition problems involve like denominators, what will be the first step in finding each sum?

    C. The first two steps for finding the sums are shown below. The resulting numerical fraction can be simplified further. Can the resulting rational expression also be simplified? If so, explain how to simplify it. If not, explain why not.

$$\frac{3}{8} + \frac{1}{8} = \frac{3+1}{8} \qquad\qquad \frac{x+4}{x-4} + \frac{2x-16}{x-4} = \frac{(x+4)+(2x-16)}{x-4}$$

$$= \frac{4}{8} \qquad\qquad\qquad\qquad\qquad\qquad = \frac{3x-12}{x-4}$$

    D. Simplifying $\frac{3x-12}{x-4}$ requires factoring. How is factoring used to simplify $\frac{4}{8}$?

2 ▶ Compare finding the difference $\frac{x+2}{x-3} - \frac{3x+16}{x^2-x-6}$ to finding the difference $\frac{11}{12} - \frac{3}{8}$.

The first step in both subtraction problems is to find a common denominator.

    A. How is determining a common denominator for the numerical fractions the same as determining a common denominator for the rational expressions? How is it different?

    B. The steps for finding the differences are shown below. How is subtracting in the numerators of the rational expressions different than for the numerical fractions?

$$\frac{11}{12} - \frac{3}{8} = \frac{11(2)}{12(2)} - \frac{3(3)}{8(3)} \qquad \frac{x+2}{x-3} - \frac{3x+16}{x^2-x-6} = \frac{(x+2)(x+2)}{(x-3)(x+2)} - \frac{3x+16}{(x-3)(x+2)}$$

$$= \frac{22}{24} - \frac{9}{24} \qquad\qquad\qquad\qquad = \frac{(x^2+4x+4)-(3x+16)}{(x-3)(x+2)}$$

$$= \frac{22-9}{24} \qquad\qquad\qquad\qquad = \frac{x^2+4x+4-3x-16}{(x-3)(x+2)}$$

$$= \frac{13}{24} \qquad\qquad\qquad\qquad\qquad = \frac{x^2+x-12}{(x-3)(x+2)}$$

    C. The resulting numerical fraction cannot be simplified. Can the resulting rational expression be simplified? If so, explain how to simplify it. If not, explain why not.

 Turn and Talk In Task 2, one factor of the denominator $x^2 - x - 6$ was the denominator of the other rational expression. How would the work differ if this had not been the case?

Step It Out

Add and Subtract Rational Expressions

When adding and subtracting numerical fractions with unlike denominators, if you find the least common denominator (LCD) of the fractions then the resulting sum or difference is usually a fraction in simplest form. The same is often true when adding and subtracting rational expressions.

3 ▶ Determine the sum: $\frac{x-1}{x^2-x} + \frac{x+2}{x+1}$.

$$\frac{x-1}{x^2-x} + \frac{x+2}{x+1} = \frac{x-1}{x(x-1)} + \frac{x+2}{x+1}$$

$$= \frac{1}{x} + \frac{x+2}{x+1}$$

$$= \frac{1(x+1)}{x(x+1)} + \frac{x(x+2)}{x(x+1)}$$

$$= \frac{x+1+x^2+2x}{x(x+1)}$$

$$= \frac{x^2+3x+1}{x(x+1)}$$

> **A.** How is it beneficial to have factored the denominator of the first rational expression as the first step?

> **B.** What would the LCD have been here if the common binomial factor had not been divided out in the previous steps?

> **C.** Why is it a good idea to leave the denominator factored in this step?

D. Is it possible to simplify the rational expression shown in the last step above? Explain.

 Turn and Talk How does the work of adding two rational expressions differ if you simply use the product of the two denominators as the common denominator?

4 ▶ Determine the difference: $\frac{x+2}{x^2-2x-15} - \frac{5x}{2x^2+7x+3}$.

A. Arrange the steps of the subtraction process in the correct order.

$$= \frac{x+2}{x^2-2x-15} - \frac{5x}{2x^2+7x+3}$$

$$= \frac{(x+2)(2x+1) - 5x(x-5)}{(x-5)(x+3)(2x+1)}$$

$$= \frac{-3x^2+30x+2}{(x-5)(x+3)(2x+1)}$$

$$= \frac{2x^2+5x+2-5x^2+25x}{(x-5)(x+3)(2x+1)}$$

$$= \frac{(x+2)(2x+1)}{(x-5)(x+3)(2x+1)} - \frac{5x(x-5)}{(2x+1)(x+3)(x-5)}$$

$$= \frac{x+2}{(x-5)(x+3)} - \frac{5x}{(2x+1)(x+3)}$$

B. Arrange the justifications for the steps in the correct order.

Subtract the numerators.

Combine like terms.

Distributive Property

Factor the denominators.

Use the common denominator.

Investigate Closure

Recall that a set of numbers is closed under a given operation if the result of the operation on any two numbers in the set is also included in the set. The table shows the closure properties of the set of whole numbers, the set of integers, and the set of rational numbers under the four basic operations.

	Addition	Subtraction	Multiplication	Division (nonzero)
Whole numbers	Closed	Not Closed	Closed	Not Closed
Integers	Closed	Closed	Closed	Not Closed
Rational numbers	Closed	Closed	Closed	Closed
Rational expressions	?	?	?	?

5 **A.** Make predictions about the closure of the set of rational expressions for each of the operations listed in the table above.

Using the rational expressions $\frac{p(x)}{q(x)}$ and $\frac{r(x)}{s(x)}$, where $p(x)$, $q(x)$, $r(x)$, and $s(x)$ are nonzero polynomial expressions, perform each of the four operations.

Addition:
$$\frac{p(x)}{q(x)} + \frac{r(x)}{s(x)} = \frac{s(x)}{s(x)} \cdot \frac{p(x)}{q(x)} + \frac{r(x)}{s(x)} \cdot \frac{q(x)}{q(x)}$$

$$= \frac{s(x)p(x) + r(x)q(x)}{q(x)s(x)}$$

> **B.** Is this final expression a rational expression? Explain.

Subtraction:
$$\frac{p(x)}{q(x)} - \frac{r(x)}{s(x)} = \frac{s(x)}{s(x)} \cdot \frac{p(x)}{q(x)} - \frac{r(x)}{s(x)} \cdot \frac{q(x)}{q(x)}$$

$$= \frac{s(x)p(x) - r(x)q(x)}{q(x)s(x)}$$

> **C.** Is the final expression a rational expression? Explain.

Multiplication:
$$\frac{p(x)}{q(x)} \cdot \frac{r(x)}{s(x)} = \frac{p(x)r(x)}{q(x)s(x)}$$

> **D.** Is this expression rational? Explain.

Division:
$$\frac{p(x)}{q(x)} \div \frac{r(x)}{s(x)} = \frac{p(x)}{q(x)} \cdot \frac{s(x)}{r(x)}$$

$$= \frac{p(x)s(x)}{q(x)r(x)}$$

> **E.** Is this final expression a rational expression? Explain.

F. State whether the set of rational expressions is closed under each of the four operations. How do these results compare to your predictions?

Turn and Talk Now look back at your predictions. If you predicted that the set of rational expressions is not closed for some operations, discuss how your thinking led you to that decision. If you predicted correctly that the set of rational expressions is closed for all four operations, discuss how you reached that conclusion.

Add and Subtract Rational Models

Rational expressions can be used to model and explore many real-world situations. For example, when several people share a job equally in order to complete the work, a rational expression can model the portion of the work assigned to each of them.

6 ▶ Two groups of local citizens volunteer to clean up 5 miles of a beach shoreline each. Both groups divide up their 5-mile stretch of beach equally among the persons in their group, assigning each group member to a specific section.

Write and simplify an expression that represents the difference between the distance each person in group A must clean up and the distance each person in group B must clean up.

Group B has 8 more people than group A.

Use a verbal model.

Let x represent the number of people in group A.

Shoreline miles to be cleaned by group A		Number of people in group A		Shoreline miles to be cleaned by group B		Number of people in group B
5	÷	x	−	5	÷	$x + 8$

Write an expression using the model.

$$\frac{5}{x} - \frac{5}{x + 8}$$

Simplify the expression.

$$\frac{5}{x} - \frac{5}{x + 8} = \frac{5(x + 8)}{x(x + 8)} - \frac{5x}{x(x + 8)}$$

$$= \frac{5x + 40 - 5x}{x(x + 8)}$$

$$= \frac{40}{x(x + 8)}$$

A. Why does the model show the distance per person in group B being subtracted from the distance per person in group A rather than the other way around?

B. What property justifies this step?

So, each person in group A must clean $\frac{40}{x(x + 8)}$ mile(s) more than each person in group B.

C. Suppose there are 12 people in group B. What is the difference in shoreline distance to be cleaned?

Turn and Talk If the verbal model had shown the subtraction in the opposite order, how would it have been evident that the resulting expression was an impossible model of the situation?

Check Understanding

1. How does adding two rational expressions with like denominators differ from adding two rational expressions with unlike denominators?

2. How is subtracting two rational expressions with unlike denominators similar to subtracting two numerical fractions with unlike denominators?

Determine each sum. Write the answer in simplest form.

3. $\dfrac{3x+5}{2x-6} + \dfrac{7x-3}{2x-6}$

4. $\dfrac{5}{x+2} + \dfrac{2x}{x^2-4}$

For Problems 5 and 6, determine each difference. Write the answer in simplest form.

5. $\dfrac{5x-11}{6x+4} - \dfrac{3x-5}{6x+4}$

6. $\dfrac{x}{x^2+2x} - \dfrac{2x+1}{3x+6}$

7. With respect to closure, is the set of rational expressions most like the set of whole numbers, the set of integers, or the set of rational numbers? Explain your answer.

8. For a community service project, volunteers from the junior and senior classes at a high school are cleaning the shoreline of a local lake. The classes will each clean approximately 3 miles along the lake. There are 16 more volunteers from the senior class than from the junior class. Let n represent the number of volunteers from the junior class. Write and simplify an expression that represents the difference between the lakeshore distance each junior volunteer must clean and the lakeshore distance each senior volunteer must clean.

On Your Own

9. **(MP) Use Structure** Explain how finding the difference $\dfrac{3x+2}{x+5} - \dfrac{2x-3}{x+5}$ is similar to finding the difference $\dfrac{4}{5} - \dfrac{2}{5}$.

10. **(MP) Use Structure** Explain how finding the sum $\dfrac{4x}{x+2} + \dfrac{x-4}{x-5}$ is similar to finding the sum $\dfrac{5}{6} + \dfrac{2}{5}$.

11. Explain the similarities and differences in the strategies used to add two rational expressions and to subtract two rational expressions.

For Problems 12–23, determine each sum or difference. Write the answer in simplest form.

12. $\dfrac{1}{x} + \dfrac{1}{x-1}$

13. $\dfrac{2}{x+3} - \dfrac{5}{x}$

14. $\dfrac{1}{x-1} + \dfrac{1}{x+1}$

15. $\dfrac{x}{3-x} + \dfrac{2}{3-x}$

16. $\dfrac{4x}{2x+1} - \dfrac{4x+1}{2x+1}$

17. $\dfrac{x^2}{x-1} - \dfrac{2x-7}{1-x}$

18. $\dfrac{x+3}{x^2+8} + \dfrac{2-x}{x^2+8}$

19. $\dfrac{-1}{x+2} - \dfrac{x+1}{x+4}$

20. $\dfrac{5}{x+3} + \dfrac{4}{x^2+3x}$

21. $\dfrac{5}{x+8} - \dfrac{3x}{x^2+5x-24}$

22. $\dfrac{x+2}{x^2+2x+1} + \dfrac{3}{x+1}$

23. $\dfrac{x}{x^2-x-6} - \dfrac{1}{x^2-9}$

24. The graphs of $p(x) = \frac{1}{x+2}$ and $q(x) = \frac{1}{x-3}$ are shown below.

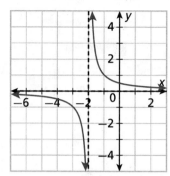 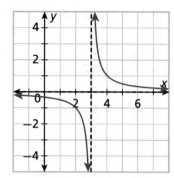

The sum of two functions represents the sum of the y-values for all corresponding values of x. For example, $p(0) + q(0) = \frac{1}{0+2} + \frac{1}{0-3} = \frac{1}{6}$.

So the point $\left(0, \frac{1}{6}\right)$ lies on the graph of the function representing the sum of $p(x)$ and $q(x)$. Use this information to sketch a graph of $p(x) + q(x)$. What are the vertical asymptotes of the graph? How do they relate to the original functions?

Let $p(x) = \frac{x}{x-2}$ and $q(x) = \frac{2}{x+1}$. Perform each operation using the rational expressions and simplify the result to show that the result is also a rational expression.

25. $p(x) + q(x)$ **26.** $p(x) - q(x)$

27. $q(x) - p(x)$ **28.** $q(x) \cdot p(x)$

29. $p(x) \div q(x)$ **30.** $q(x) \div p(x)$

For Problems 31 and 32, write and simplify an expression for the situation.

31. The junior class and the senior class at a high school each pledge to raise $200 towards a new school water fountain. There are 25 more students in the junior class than there are in the senior class. If the students in each class raise the same amount per person, how much more will each senior need to raise than each junior needs to raise? Let x represent the number of students in the senior class at the high school.

32. A bicycle courier averages r miles per hour traveling to his delivery point. On the return trip, he averages 3 miles per hour faster. If the distance from the courier office to the delivery destination was 4 miles, what is the bicycle courier's total travel time (in hours) for the round trip?

Delivery destination: 4 miles

For Problems 33 and 34, write and simplify an expression for the situation.

33. A snowboarder rides the ski lift up to the top of a ski slope and then snowboards back down to the base of the lift. The average rates of the snowboarder going up the ski lift and down the hill are shown. What is the total time (in hours) it takes the snowboarder to complete one round trip? Let d represent the distance from the base of the ski lift to the top of the hill.

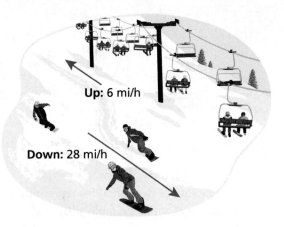

Up: 6 mi/h

Down: 28 mi/h

34. Jim and Maria run a city relay race. The race consists of 8 laps around a planned city route. Jim runs 3 of the laps at an average speed that is 0.5 mile per hour faster than Maria's average speed for the remaining 5 laps. What is Jim and Maria's combined race time? Let r represent Maria's average speed.

35. Let $p(x) = \dfrac{a}{(x-b)}$ and $q(x) = \dfrac{c}{(x-d)}$. In general how do the vertical asymptotes of $p(x) + q(x)$ compare to the vertical asymptotes of $p(x)$ and $q(x)$?

36. (Open Middle™) Using the integers -9 to 9, at most one time each, fill in the boxes to create a true statement.

$$\left(\frac{\boxed{}\,x}{x^2 - \boxed{}}\right) - \left(\frac{\boxed{}}{x + \boxed{}}\right) = \left(\frac{\boxed{}\,x + \boxed{}}{x^2 + \boxed{}}\right)$$

Spiral Review • Assessment Readiness

37. Which equation represents the horizontal asymptote of the graph of $f(x) = \frac{3}{x}$?

   Ⓐ $x = 3$ Ⓒ $x = 0$

   Ⓑ $y = 3$ Ⓓ $y = 0$

38. Which function has a graph with the same vertical asymptote as the graph of $f(x) = \frac{4}{x+1} + 2$?

   Ⓐ $g(x) = \dfrac{7}{x+1}$ Ⓒ $g(x) = \dfrac{6}{x-3} + 2$

   Ⓑ $g(x) = \dfrac{2}{x-1}$ Ⓓ $g(x) = \dfrac{x^2-1}{x+1} - 2$

39. If $p(x) \cdot q(x) = 1$ and $p(x) = \frac{x}{x^2+3}$, which expression is equivalent to $q(x)$?

   Ⓐ $\dfrac{-x}{x^2+3}$ Ⓒ $\dfrac{x^2-3}{x}$

   Ⓑ $\dfrac{x}{x^2-3}$ Ⓓ $\dfrac{x^2+3}{x}$

40. For what values of x does $\frac{3x}{4} = x + 2$?

   Ⓐ $x = -8$ Ⓒ $x = 2$

   Ⓑ $x = -2$ Ⓓ $x = 8$

⬡ I'm in a Learning Mindset!

How can I refine my questions to clarify my understanding of adding and subtracting rational expressions and find new learning opportunities?

Solve Rational Equations

(I Can) solve rational equations graphically and algebraically.

Spark Your Learning

An airplane travels from New York City to Los Angeles and back.

The round-trip time in the air is 10 hours.

While traveling to Los Angeles, the plane flies against a headwind. While traveling back, the plane flies with a tailwind.

Complete Part A as a whole class. Then complete Parts B–D in small groups.

A. What is a mathematical question you can ask about this situation? What information would you need to know to answer your question?

B. What do you know about each leg of the trip? How does this relate to the information you want to find?

C. To answer your question, what strategy and tool would you use along with all the information you have? What answer do you get?

D. Does your answer make sense in the context of the situation? Explain why or why not.

 Turn and Talk Predict how the following situations would change the problem:
- The round-trip time in the air is 12 hours.
- The tailwind is 150 miles per hour and the headwind remains 100 miles per hour.
- The headwind is 150 miles per hour and the tailwind remains 100 miles per hour.

Build Understanding

Solve Rational Equations Graphically

You have previously worked with rational expressions. A rational equation is an equation with one or more rational expressions. These equations can be solved algebraically or graphically.

 A. Consider the rational equation $\frac{3}{x+1} = 3$. Rewrite the equation so that one side is zero. Let the nonzero side of the equation represent $g(x)$. What transformation(s) map the graph of the function $f(x) = \frac{1}{x}$ to the function related to the nonzero side of the equation?

B. For what values of x is $\frac{3}{x+1} = 3$ undefined? How does this relate to the transformation in Part A?

C. The graph of $g(x) = \frac{3}{x+1} - 3$ is shown. What is the x-intercept(s)? Is the value of the x-intercept(s) an excluded value?

D. How can you use the graph of $g(x)$ to identify the solution(s) of $\frac{3}{x+1} = 3$? What is the solution?

E. Consider the rational equation $\frac{2}{x-4} - x = -3$. Notice that if you add x to both sides of the equation, you have a simple rational expression on the left and a linear expression on the right. Rewrite each of these expressions as a function. How could you use a graph of the two functions to solve for x?

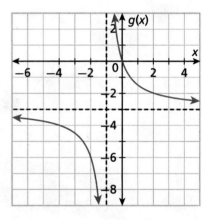

F. The graphs of $f(x) = \frac{2}{x-4}$ and $g(x) = x - 3$ are shown. For what values of x does $\frac{2}{x-4} = x - 3$? Are these values excluded values? How can you check your answer?

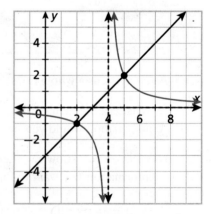

 Turn and Talk How could you use the table feature of a graphing calculator to solve rational equations? Explain.

Step It Out

Solve Rational Equations Algebraically

You can solve rational equations algebraically by multiplying each term by the LCD and solving for the unknown value. This method may result in solution values that are identified as excluded values in the given equation. These values are called **extraneous solutions** and are not part of the solution.

 2 Solve $\frac{x+4}{5x-5} = \frac{x+7}{3x-3}$ algebraically.

Identify any excluded values.

$5x - 5 = 0 \qquad 3x - 3 = 0$

$\qquad x = 1 \qquad\qquad x = 1$

> **A.** Why are the numerators not used to identify excluded values?

The excluded value is $x = 1$.

Factor the denominators, if possible, and identify the LCD.

$$\frac{x+4}{5(x-1)} = \frac{x+7}{3(x-1)}$$

The LCD is $15(x-1)$.

> **B.** How did you find the LCM of $5(x-1)$ and $3(x-1)$?

Use the LCD to eliminate the denominators.

$$\frac{x+4}{5(x-1)} \cdot 15(x-1) = \frac{x+7}{3(x-1)} \cdot 15(x-1) \qquad \text{Multiply each term by the LCD.}$$

$$\frac{x+4}{5(x-1)} \cdot \overset{3}{\cancel{15}}\cancel{(x-1)} = \frac{x+7}{3(x-1)} \cdot \overset{5}{\cancel{15}}\cancel{(x-1)} \qquad \text{Divide out common factors.}$$

$$3(x+4) = 5(x+7) \qquad \text{Simplify.}$$

$$3x + 12 = 5x + 35 \qquad \text{Use the Distributive Property.}$$

$$-2x = 23 \qquad \text{Solve for } x.$$

$$x = -11.5$$

Check whether the solution found is an excluded value. Since $x = -11.5$ is not an excluded value, it is the solution of the equation.

> **C.** What would the solution be if the value were an excluded value?

Check your answer by writing each side of the original equation as a function and then graphing the two functions.

> **D.** What part of the graph corresponds to the solution?

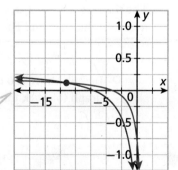

 Turn and Talk Previously, you may have solved proportions like $\frac{1}{2} = \frac{x}{10}$ using cross multiplication. Could you use cross multiplication to solve rational equations? Explain.

You can use the same technique to algebraically solve rational equations that are not proportions. Find the LCD and use that to eliminate denominators.

3 Solve $\frac{2x+5}{x-3} + \frac{x}{7} = \frac{11}{x-3}$ algebraically.

Identify any excluded values.

$x - 3 = 0$

> **A.** Explain how to determine any excluded values.

$x = 3$

The excluded value is $x = 3$.

The denominators cannot be factored, so identify the LCD.

The LCD is $7(x - 3)$.

> **B.** How was the LCD found?

Use the LCD to eliminate the denominators.

$\frac{2x+5}{x-3} \cdot 7(x-3) + \frac{x}{7} \cdot 7(x-3) = \frac{11}{x-3} \cdot 7(x-3)$ Multiply each term by the LCD.

$\frac{2x+5}{\cancel{x-3}} \cdot 7(\cancel{x-3}) + \frac{x}{\cancel{7}} \cdot \cancel{7}(x-3) = \frac{11}{\cancel{x-3}} \cdot 7(\cancel{x-3})$ Divide out common factors.

$(2x+5)7 + x(x-3) = (11)7$ Simplify.

$14x + 35 + x^2 - 3x = 77$ Use the Distributive Property.

$x^2 + 11x - 42 = 0$ Write in standard form.

$(x - 3)(x + 14) = 0$ Factor.

$x - 3 = 0 \text{ or } x + 14 = 0$ Use the Zero Product Property.

$x = 3 \text{ or } x = -14$ Solve for x.

The solution $x = 3$ is extraneous because it is an excluded value. The only solution is $x = -14$.

> **C.** What happens when you substitute an extraneous solution into the equation?

> **D.** Describe how you could use a graph to check the solution.

 Turn and Talk How does an extraneous solution come about when solving a rational equation?

Solve Rational Equations in the Real World

In the previous lesson, you worked with some real-world rational expressions. Modeling these same types of situations with rational equations allows you to solve for a unknown value.

4 The motorboat shown in the image travels 30 miles upstream and 30 miles downstream. The total trip takes 2.75 hours. What is the average speed of the current?

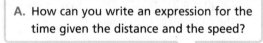

Boat speed: 22 mph

Formulate a Plan

Let c represent the speed of the current (in miles per hour). When the boat travels upstream, the speed is equal to the speed of the boat minus the speed of the current. When the boat travels downstream, the speed is equal to the speed of the boat plus the speed of the current.

Recall that distance = rate · time or time = $\frac{\text{rate}}{\text{distance}}$.

You can organize the given information in a table.

Write an equation for the total time.

total time = time upstream + time downstream

$$2.75 = \frac{30}{22 - c} + \frac{30}{22 + c}$$

A. How can you write an expression for the time given the distance and the speed?

B. Why aren't the times traveled upstream and downstream equal?

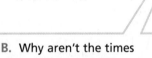

	Distance (mi)	Average speed (mi/h)	Time (h)
Upstream	30	$22 - c$	$\frac{30}{22 - c}$
Downstream	30	$22 + c$	$\frac{30}{22 + c}$

Solve

The excluded values occur when $22 - c = 0$ and when $22 + c = 0$, or when $c = 22$ and $c = -22$.

$$2.75(22 - c)(22 + c) = (22 - c)(22 + c) \cdot \frac{30}{(22 - c)} + \frac{30}{(22 + c)} \cdot (22 - c)(22 + c)$$

$$2.75(22 - c)(22 + c) = 30(22 + c) + 30(22 - c)$$

$$2.75(484 - c^2) = 660 + 30c + 660 - 30c$$

$$484 - c^2 = 480$$

$$0 = c^2 - 4$$

$$c + 2 = 0 \text{ or } c - 2 = 0$$

$$c = -2 \text{ or } c = 2$$

C. Explain how to get to this step from the previous step.

D. Are either of the values extraneous? Explain.

Interpret

The solution $c = -2$ is unviable in the given context because the speed of the current cannot be negative. If the speed of the current is 2 miles per hour, it would take the motor boat 1.5 hours to go 30 miles upstream and 1.25 hours to go 30 miles downstream, which is a total of 2.75 hours.

Check Understanding

1. What are two different ways you can use a graph to solve a rational equation? Explain how you can check your answers.

Solve each rational equation algebraically.

2. $\dfrac{-3}{x+2} = \dfrac{2x}{x^2-4}$

3. $\dfrac{1}{x} = 1 + \dfrac{6}{5x}$

4. Amber paddles a canoe at a constant rate of 3 miles per hour in still water. She travels 28 miles downstream in the same amount of time that it takes her to travel 20 miles upstream. What is the speed of the current? Explain how you can verify your answer by graphing.

On Your Own

5. **(MP) Use Structure** Describe two different ways you could use a graph to solve the equation $\dfrac{5}{x+7} + 1 = x - 1$.

6. The graph of $f(x) = \dfrac{x}{x+2} - 2$ is shown. Explain how you can use the graph to find the solution(s) of the equation $\dfrac{x}{x+2} = 2$. What is the solution of the equation?

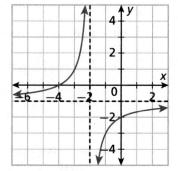

7. **(MP) Use Structure** How does rewriting a rational equation so that one side is 0 help with solving the equation?

8. **(MP) Attend to Precision** Use a graphing calculator to solve $\dfrac{2x}{x-3} = x + 5$. Is your solution exact or approximate? Explain.

9. The formula $t = \dfrac{d}{(b-c)} + \dfrac{d}{(b+c)}$ gives the total time t (in hours) needed for a boat to travel upstream a distance of d miles and then back downstream the same distance, where b is the speed of the boat in still water and c is the speed of the river's current (both in miles per hour). How can you write a formula that gives the speed of the current in terms of the other variables? What is the formula?

Solve each rational equation by graphing.

10. $\dfrac{1}{x-5} + 8 = 7$

11. $\dfrac{1}{x+4} = 1$

12. $\dfrac{x}{x-2} = x - 2$

13. $\dfrac{3x}{x-1} - 2 = x - 2$

Solve each rational equation algebraically. Justify each step of the solution.

14. $\dfrac{1}{2x} = \dfrac{x+1}{x+3}$

15. $\dfrac{x}{x^2-x} = \dfrac{3+6x}{x^2-x}$

16. $\dfrac{1}{x-2} = \dfrac{1}{x^2+3x-10} + \dfrac{3}{x+5}$

17. $\dfrac{x-6}{x+1} + \dfrac{x+5}{x^2+x} = \dfrac{1}{x^2+x}$

18. $\dfrac{2x}{x^2-4} = \dfrac{1}{x+2} - \dfrac{1}{x-2}$

19. $\dfrac{4}{x^2+5x+6} + \dfrac{2}{x+2} = \dfrac{3}{x+3}$

20. The combined gas law $\frac{P_1 V_1}{T_1} = \frac{P_2 V_2}{T_2}$ shows the relationship among pressure P_1 and P_2, volume V_1 and V_2, and temperature T_1 and T_2 for a fixed mass of gas. Rewrite the formula so that it gives T_2 in terms of the other variables.

21. The total resistance R for a parallel circuit can be found using the formula $\frac{1}{R} = \frac{1}{R_1} + \frac{1}{R_2}$, where R_1 and R_2 are each the resistance for a parallel path. Rewrite the formula so that it gives R_2 in terms of the other variables.

22. Printer A can print a company's weekly sales reports in 60 minutes. Printer B can print the weekly sales reports in 40 minutes.

 A. Describe how you can use a rational equation to represent how long it would take both printers working together to print the sales reports.

 B. How long would it take the two printers working together to print the sales reports?

23. Marina walks the length of an airport terminal at an average pace of 80 meters per minute. Returning, she walks at the same pace on a moving walkway for the entire distance. It takes her a total of 12 minutes to walk from one end of the terminal to the other and back.

560 meters

 A. Write a rational equation you can use to find the speed of the moving walkway.

 B. What is the speed of the moving walkway?

24. A baseball player's batting average is the ratio of the number of hits to the number of times the player is at bat. During spring training, a player has 50 at bats and 13 hits. Partway through the regular season, the player has 46 hits in 200 at bats.

 A. How could you use a graph to find the number of consecutive hits the player would need to raise his season batting average above his spring training average?

 B. Describe how you could use an equation to solve the problem described in Part A.

 C. Which method would you choose? Explain why.

 D. What is the number of consecutive hits the player would need so that his season batting average is greater than his spring training average?

Completion time: 4 hours

25. Joann and an apprentice are professional roofers. Joann can work twice as fast as the apprentice. The time it takes for them to complete the job together is shown.

 A. How long would it take Joann working alone to complete the roofing job?

 B. How long would it take the apprentice working alone to complete the roofing job?

©sturti/iStock/Getty Images

26. Tom averages a speed of 6 kilometers per hour during the first half of a race. How much faster does he need to run during the second leg of the race to complete the total 5 kilometers in less than 40 minutes?

27. Phuong's driving rate in his car is 40 miles per hour faster than his rate on his bicycle. He travels each given distance in the same amount of time. Find Phuong's average driving speed and average bicycling speed.

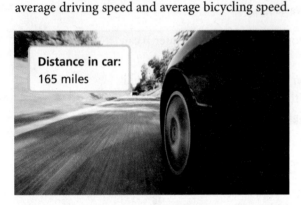

Distance in car:
165 miles

Distance on bicycle:
45 miles

28. The time it takes a pharmacist to compile and fill a customer's prescription is given by the equation $t = 3 + \frac{4n}{r}$, where t is time in minutes, n is the number of prescriptions, and r is the average speed (in prescriptions per minute) at which the pharmacist fills prescriptions. If it takes 15 minutes for a pharmacist to compile and fill an order for a customer with 4 prescriptions, what is the average speed of the pharmacist?

29. (MP) **Construct Arguments** Danny states that $x = 0$ is always an excluded value for a rational function with x in the denominator since it is not possible to divide by zero. Is Danny's claim correct? Give an example to support your argument.

Spiral Review • Assessment Readiness

30. What are the asymptotes of the graph of $f(x) = \frac{x}{x+1} + 5$? Select all that apply.

Ⓐ $x = -1$ Ⓓ $y = 0$

Ⓑ $x = 1$ Ⓔ $y = 5$

Ⓒ $x = 5$ Ⓕ $y = 6$

31. Which product is equal to x for $x \neq -1$?

Ⓐ $\frac{x}{x+1} \cdot \frac{1}{x}$ Ⓒ $\frac{1}{x+1} \cdot \frac{x+1}{x}$

Ⓑ $\frac{1}{x+1} \cdot \frac{x}{x+1}$ Ⓓ $\frac{x}{x+1} \cdot \frac{x+1}{1}$

32. How many excluded values does the expression $\frac{x+2}{x-2} - \frac{1}{x^2-4}$ have?

Ⓐ 0   Ⓒ 2

Ⓑ 1   Ⓓ 3

33. What number comes next in the pattern?
$-2, 4, -8, 16, \ldots$

Ⓐ -32 Ⓒ 8

Ⓑ -4 Ⓓ 64

I'm in a Learning Mindset!

What questions can I ask my teacher to help me understand solving rational equations?

Multiply and Divide Rational Expressions

Consider the function.

> Factor.

$$\frac{(x^2 + 3x - 10)}{(x^2 - x - 20)} \cdot \frac{x + 4}{x - 2} = \frac{(x + 5)(x - 2)(x + 4)}{(x - 5)(x + 4)(x - 2)}$$

Simplify the product.

$$\frac{(x + 5)(x - 2)(x + 4)}{(x - 5)(x + 4)(x - 2)} = \frac{(x + 5)}{(x - 5)}$$

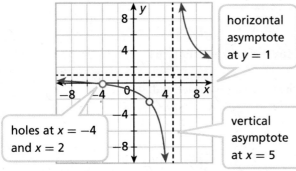

> horizontal asymptote at $y = 1$

> holes at $x = -4$ and $x = 2$

> vertical asymptote at $x = 5$

Rational expressions are closed under multiplication and division, just like the rational numbers.

Add and Subtract Rational Expressions

Find the difference.

$$\frac{x - 1}{x^2 - x - 6} - \frac{x + 4}{3x + 9} = \frac{x - 1}{(x + 2)(x - 3)} - \frac{x + 4}{3(x + 3)}$$

Rewrite the expression using the common denominator and subtract.

> Factor the denominators.

$$= \frac{3(x + 3)}{3(x + 3)} \cdot \frac{x - 1}{(x + 2)(x - 3)} - \frac{x + 4}{3(x + 3)}$$

$$\cdot \frac{(x + 2)(x - 3)}{(x + 2)(x - 3)}$$

> Multiply by a form of 1.

$$= \frac{3(x + 3)(x - 1)}{3(x + 3)(x + 2)(x - 3)}$$

$$- \frac{(x + 4)(x + 2)(x - 3)}{3(x + 3)(x + 2)(x - 3)}$$

$$= \frac{3x^2 + 6x - 9 - (x^3 + 3x^2 - 10x - 24)}{3(x + 3)(x + 2)(x - 3)}$$

$$= \frac{-x^3 + 16x + 15}{3(x + 3)(x + 2)(x - 3)}$$

> Collect like terms.

Rational expressions are closed under addition and subtraction, just like the rational numbers.

Solve Rational Equations Graphically

To solve $\frac{1}{(x - 4)} = 2$, graph each expression and then identify any points of intersection.

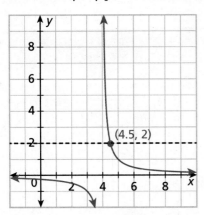

(4.5, 2)

Solve Rational Equations Algebraically

Solve $\frac{x + 5}{3x + 3} = \frac{x - 7}{5x + 5}$ algebraically.
What values of x are excluded? $x = -1$

$$\frac{x + 5}{3(x + 1)} = \frac{x - 7}{5(x + 1)}$$

> Factor the denominators.

$$\frac{x + 5}{3(x + 1)}\left(15(x + 1)\right) = \frac{x - 7}{5(x + 1)}\left(15(x + 1)\right)$$

$$5(x + 5) = 3(x - 7)$$

$$5x + 25 = 3x - 21$$

$$2x = -46$$

$$x = -23$$

> Multiply both sides by the LCD.

Vocabulary

Choose the correct term from the box to complete each sentence.

1. A(n) ___?___ sets two expressions equal to one another, where at least one expression involves a fraction that has a numerator and denominator that are polynomials.

2. A(n) ___?___ is a value that is identified as an excluded value in the given equation.

3. A(n) ___?___ is a fraction in which the numerator and the denominator are polynomials.

Concepts and Skills

Find each product. Identify any values of x for which the product is undefined.

4. $\dfrac{-18xy}{15z} \cdot \dfrac{35z^2}{24x^2y}$

5. $\dfrac{20p^2}{21rs} \cdot \dfrac{7q^2r^3}{4p^2s}$

6. $\dfrac{x+9}{x-1} \cdot \dfrac{x^2+9x-10}{x^2+8x-9}$

7. $\dfrac{x-8}{x^2+16x+64} \cdot \dfrac{x^2-64}{x^2-16x+64}$

Find each quotient. Identify any values of x for which the quotient is undefined.

8. $\dfrac{8z^2}{5xy} \div \dfrac{4z}{x^2y}$

9. $\dfrac{x+9}{9x^2} \div \dfrac{x^2-9x}{x^2-81}$

10. $\dfrac{x}{x-4} \div \dfrac{x^2-3x}{x^2-x-12}$

11. $\dfrac{8x}{x-6} \div \dfrac{x^2+6x}{x^2-3x-18}$

(MP) Use Tools Find each sum or difference. Write each answer in simplest form and identify any values of x for which the sum or difference is undefined. State what strategy and tool you will use to answer the question, explain your choice, and then find the answer.

12. $\dfrac{-1}{x+2} + \dfrac{x+1}{x+4}$

13. $\dfrac{5}{x+3} - \dfrac{4}{x^2+3x}$

14. $\dfrac{1}{x-2} + \dfrac{1}{x+2}$

15. $\dfrac{2x}{x^2+5x+4} - \dfrac{2}{x+4}$

Solve each rational equation by graphing.

16. $\dfrac{1}{x-4} + 6 = 7$

17. $\dfrac{1}{x+5} = 2$

18. $\dfrac{1}{2x-3} = 4$

19. $\dfrac{2}{x+5} + 1 = 0$

Solve each rational equation algebraically.

20. $\dfrac{-1}{2x} = \dfrac{x-1}{x-3}$

21. $\dfrac{x}{x^2-x} = \dfrac{3-x}{x^2-x}$

22. $\dfrac{x+1}{x+3} = \dfrac{2}{x}$

23. $\dfrac{x+2}{x^2-1} = \dfrac{2x-6}{x+1}$

24. Explain the relationship between the set of rational expressions and the set of rational numbers with respect to the four basic arithmetic operations.

Computer Programmer

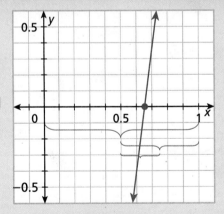 STEM
POWERING INGENUITY

Computer programmers develop code for computer software and applications. They use a variety of computer languages and algorithms to direct how computers function and expand upon existing programs. They must be precise with the code to prevent bugs and crashes and to minimize the amount of processing power required.

©REDPIXEL.PL/Shutterstock

STEM Task

The *bisection method* can be used to approximate a root of a function. To find the root of a continuous function $f(x)$, choose a and b such that $f(a) < 0$ and $f(b) > 0$.

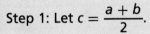

Step 1: Let $c = \dfrac{a + b}{2}$.

Step 2: Find $f(c)$. If it is zero, you have your root.

Step 3: If $f(c) > 0$, then replace b with c and go back to Step 1. If $f(c) < 0$, then replace a with c and go back to Step 1.

Approximate the root of the function $f(x) = x^3 - 2x^2 + 7x - 4$. Explain why your root is a good approximation of the zero.

Learning Mindset

Perseverance Checks for Understanding

```
            = array();
          = mysql::query("SELECT DISTINCT(studio) as studio, COUNT(*) as count FROM image WHERE day_id =           ->id' AND enabled='y' GROUP BY studio");
while(studio_list = mysql::fetch(        )) {
          = metadate::day_info(    ->shot_date,      ->studio,"quick");
          [] = array("studio" =>              ->studio, "count" =>         ->count, "title" =>       ->title);
}
    ->studio_list =                ;
    [    ->shot_date] =      ;
}

return        ;
}

static function day_images_list(            ) {
    global            ;
    if(!in_array(         )) die("error studio");
      = mysql::escape(    );
    if(mysql::count("image_date","shot_date =       '")            ('date not found');
    studio = intval(    );

      array();

      = mysql::query("SELECT image.id as image                   image_date WHERE image_date.id=image.day_id AND image_date.shot_date='       ' AND image.enabled='y' AND
while(      = mysql::fetch(        )) {
```

As you explore a new subject area, take time to check in with yourself to make sure that you are progressing in your understanding. Look for evidence that your understanding is meeting your own learning goals, as well as those of your teacher, classmates, or teammates. Here are some questions you can ask yourself to help you assess your understanding:

- What is my learning goal for sequences and series? How is this shaped by myself, teachers, and classmates?

- Is my understanding of sequences and series progressing as I anticipated? What adjustments, if any, do I need to make to enhance my learning and understanding?

- What adjustments do I need to make to enhance my learning?

- What evidence do I have that my work is meeting expectations? How can I make sure that I meet expectations?

Reflect

Q How can you check that your understanding is meeting your own and your teacher's expectations? How can you use this assessment of your understanding to continue to advance your learning?

Q Imagine you are a computer programmer. What evidence might you look for to see whether your work meets expectations? How would you use that evidence to assess your work?

©Africa Studio/Shutterstock

Explicit Formulas for Sequences and Series

Breaking the Bank

How much should I borrow compared to a bank loan?

Monthly Payments

$ _____

Loan Amount

Loan Term $

Interest Rate $

Total Principal Paid $

Total Interest Paid $

Compare Loan Rates $

©TippyTortue/Shutterstock

Are You Ready?

Complete these problems to review prior concepts and skills you will need for this module.

Evaluate Algebraic Expressions

Evaluate each algebraic expression for $a = 4$, $b = -2$, and $c = \frac{1}{2}$.

1. $2a - 3b + 5$

2. $c(4a + 6b) - 2$

3. $b(-4c - 5a) + 3$

4. $\dfrac{20(5ac - bc)}{ab}$

5. $\dfrac{2ab - 4}{b + c}$

6. $\dfrac{a(b - c)}{6c + 1}$

Graph Linear Equations in Slope-Intercept Form

Graph each line.

7. $y = -2x + 5$

8. $y = \dfrac{1}{2}x - 4$

9. $y = -\dfrac{3}{5}x - 1$

10. $y = -12x + 240$

Graph Exponential Functions

Graph each function.

11. $h(x) = 3^x$

12. $m(x) = \left(\dfrac{1}{2}\right)^x$

13. $g(x) = 3(2)^x - 1$

14. $q(x) = -25\left(\dfrac{4}{5}\right)^x - 10$

Connecting Past and Present Learning

Previously, you learned:

- to compare functions across representations,
- to determine and interpret the domain, range, and end behavior of sequences defined as functions, and
- to model real-world scenarios with exponential functions.

In this module, you will learn:

- to describe sequences and series as functions, and
- to write arithmetic and geometric sequences and series that model real-world situations.

Define Sequences and Series

(I Can) write sequences, series, and find general terms.

Spark Your Learning

If your teacher asked you to place a flat object like a block so that it extends as far as possible out over the desk's edge, you would intuitively place it so that just about half of its length extends over the edge. This keeps the object's *center of gravity* over the desk. Extending this idea has some surprising results.

> The stack is balanced even though the entire top block is past the desk's edge.

> To extend the top block as far as possible, you must start from the bottom. The more layers you want, the less the bottom layer can overhang.

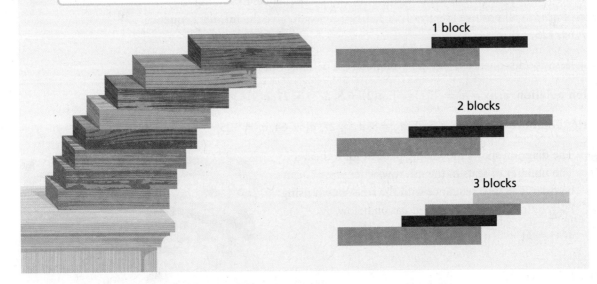

1 block

2 blocks

3 blocks

Complete Part A as a whole class. Then complete Parts B–D in small groups.

A. What is a mathematical question you can ask about this situation?

B. What variables are involved in this situation? What unit of measurement would you use for each variable?

C. To answer your question, what strategy and tool would you use along with all the information you have? What answer do you get?

D. How can you find the smallest number of blocks for which the top block is completely beyond the desk's edge? What is this number?

 Turn and Talk Using the rule you found in Part C and the process you used in Part D, create a spreadsheet to calculate how many block lengths the top block can extend beyond the desk in a stack of *n* blocks. How many blocks high must the stack be for the top block to extend 2 block lengths beyond the desk? 3 lengths? 4 lengths?

Build Understanding

Define a Mathematical Sequence

When you do things *in sequence*, you do them in order: first, second, third, and so on. A **sequence** is an ordered list of numbers, each called a **term** of the sequence. Because a sequence maps a set of ordered integers to the terms of the sequence, a sequence is a function whose domain is a subset of the integers and whose range is the set of values of the terms.

A sequence is often described by an equation, or **rule**. The domain for the rule often begins with the position number $n = 1$, though it doesn't have to. Consider the sequence $a(n)$ describing the cubes of the first 5 positive integers:

$a(n) = n^3$: Domain: $\{1, 2, 3, 4, 5\}$; Range: $\{1, 8, 27, 64, 125\}$

Because $a(n)$ has a limited number of terms, it is a **finite sequence**. Extending the domain of $a(n)$ to all positive integers 1, 2, 3, 4, 5, . . . would give the **infinite sequence** 1, 8, 27, 64, 125, ...

You can describe a sequence using function notation or subscript notation.

Function notation: $a(n) = n^3 \Rightarrow a(1) = 1, a(2) = 8, a(3) = 27, a(4) = 64, a(5) = 125$

Subscript notation: $a_n = n^3 \Rightarrow a_1 = 1, a_2 = 8, a_3 = 27, a_4 = 64, a_5 = 125$

1 The diagram shows the seating pattern for a theater. The number of seats in the *n*th row, where $n \geq 1$, can be described by a sequence with the rule shown using both function and subscript notation below.

$a(n) = 11 + 3(n - 1)$ or $a_n = 11 + 3(n - 1)$

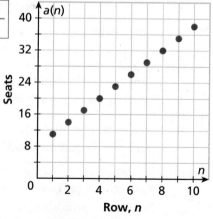

n = 14 rows

a(1) = 11

A. Complete the partial table of values for $a(n)$.

n	1	2	3	4	5
$a(n) =$ $11 + 3(n - 1)$	?	?	?	?	?

The domain of the sequence is $\{1, 2, 3, \ldots, 14\}$. What is the range? How do you know?

B. How does the rule represent the pattern in the number of seats in the diagram? Why do you think the rule is not simplified by combining like terms?

C. The graph shows the first 10 terms of the sequence. Describe the graph. Could you show the graph of the entire sequence? Explain.

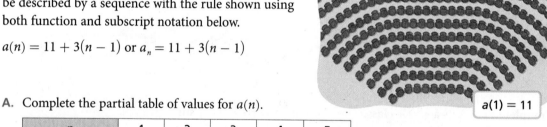

Turn and Talk How can you rewrite the rule for the sequence to begin with $n = 0$? What does this change for the function, its graph, and how you interpret the rule?

Define a Mathematical Series

There are many times that it is useful to know the sum of the terms in a sequence. A **series** is the expression formed by adding the terms of the sequence. For example, $5 + 10 + 15 + 20 + 25$ is the series formed by adding the terms of the sequence $\{5, 10, 15, 20, 25\}$.

The series above has a finite number of addends, 5 to be specific, and so is a **finite series**. An **infinite series** expresses the sum of the terms of an infinite sequence, and so has infinitely many addends.

To represent a series efficiently, you can use **sigma notation**, named for the Greek letter for S, which is represented by the symbol $\sum$.

For example, the terms of the sequence above can be expressed by the rule $5n$ where $1 \le n \le 5$. Sigma notation uses the **index of summation** using the letter k or another letter, to count the terms from the **lower limit of summation** (in this case 1) to the **upper limit of summation** (in this case 5).

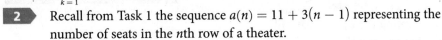

$$\sum_{k=1}^{5} 5k \quad\begin{matrix} \longleftarrow \text{ upper limit of summation} \\ \longleftarrow \text{ sequence rule using index } k \\ \longleftarrow \text{ lower limit of summation} \end{matrix}$$

So, $\displaystyle\sum_{k=1}^{5} 5k = 5(1) + 5(2) + 5(3) + 5(4) + 5(5) = 5 + 10 + 15 + 20 + 25$.

Note that changing the upper limit above to n gives the series $\displaystyle\sum_{k=1}^{n} 5k$, which represents the sum of the first n multiples of 5. Changing the upper limit to ∞ gives the series $\displaystyle\sum_{k=1}^{\infty} 5k$, which represents the infinite series $5 + 10 + 15 + \dots$.

2 ▶ Recall from Task 1 the sequence $a(n) = 11 + 3(n - 1)$ representing the number of seats in the nth row of a theater.

A. What does the series $\displaystyle\sum_{k=1}^{14} [11 + 3(k - 1)]$ represent in the context of the theater seating? Explain. Include the role of the index and the limits of summation in your explanation.

B. Write out the series in Part A, simplifying each addend. What is the sum of the series?

C. For a special show, the first six rows of the theater, containing $\displaystyle\sum_{k=1}^{6} [11 + 3(k - 1)]$ seats, are reserved for season subscribers. Find the sum of the series. Then find the sum of the series $\displaystyle\sum_{k=7}^{14} [11 + 3(k - 1)]$.

What do you notice? Why does this make sense?

Turn and Talk How can you create a spreadsheet to verify the sum you found for the series in Part B?

Step It Out

Create and Use Rules for Sequences

Because sequences are functions whose domain is a subset of the integers, you can simply substitute domain values to create a sequence from a rule.

Consider the sequence $a(n) = n^2 + n$ with domain $\{1, 2, 3, 4\}$. Substitute:

$$a(1) = 1^2 + 1 = 2 \quad a(2) = 2^2 + 2 = 6 \quad a(3) = 3^2 + 3 = 12 \quad a(4) = 4^2 + 4 = 20$$

The first four terms are 2, 6, 12, 20.

Often, you will need to look for a pattern to write a rule for a sequence.

Consider the sequence $-12, -6, -4, -3, -2.4, \ldots$.

Creating a table can help reveal a pattern:

n	1	2	3	4	5
$a(n)$	−12	−6	−4	−3	−2.4

From the table, it is easy to see that the sequence represents an inverse variation relationship. The rule can be written as $a(n) = -\dfrac{12}{n}$ or as $a_n = -\dfrac{12}{n}$.

---

3 ▶ Practice ranges for professional golfers often stack the balls in a pyramid as shown. Write a rule for the sequence that represents the number of balls in each row of the front triangular face of the pyramid. Then write a rule for the sequence that gives the total number of balls in each layer, and graph the sequence.

From the top down, the number of balls on the front face is the sequence 1, 2, 3, 4, 5, 6, 7. So, starting at the top with $n = 1$, a rule for the sequence is simply $a(n) = n$, or $a_n = n$.

To write a sequence representing the number of balls in each layer, start at the top again with $n = 1$.

> **A.** How did you determine the number of balls in each layer?

Write the ordered pairs in the sequence:

$(1, 1), (2, 4), (3, 9), (4, 16), (5, 25), (6, 36), (7, 49)$

The number of balls in each layer is the square of the layer number.

The rule for the sequence is $a(n) = n^2$. The graph is shown.

> **B.** What is the rule for the nth term of the sequence written in subscript form?

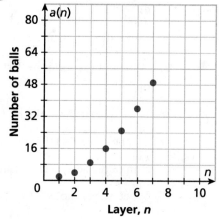

Turn and Talk Suppose that $n = 1$ is used to represent the bottom row of the pyramid instead of the top row. Can you still write rules for the sequences? If so, what are they?

4 The table shows all possible handshakes for each person when $n = 2, 3,$ or 4 people shake hands with each other. For example, Person A shakes hands with Person B, Person B shakes hands with Person A, and so on.

How many *distinct* handshakes are in a group of 20 people?

$n = 2$	$n = 3$	$n = 4$
A: AB	A: AB, AC	A: AB, AC, AD
B: BA	B: BA, BC	B: BA, BC, BD
	C: CA, CB	C: CA, CB, CD
		D: DA, DB, DC

Find a rule for the number of *distinct* handshakes in a group of *n* people. How many possible handshakes is there for a group of 20 people?

Look for a pattern: Notice that for $n = 2$, $2 = 2(1)$ letter pairs are listed, for $n = 3$, $6 = 3(2)$ pairs are listed, and for $n = 4$, $12 = 4(3)$ pairs are listed.

A rule $\left(\text{for } n \geq 2\right)$, is $a_n = \dfrac{n(n - 1)}{2}$.

A. Why is $n(n - 1)$ divided by 2?

In a group of 20 people, there are $a_{20} = \dfrac{20(20 - 1)}{2} = 190$ possible handshakes.

 Turn and Talk If you add 1 person, that person shakes hands with everyone already in the group. How can you use this pattern to generate the sequence without the formula?

Use a Formula for the Sum of a Series

While you can find the sum of a short, simple series by adding each term of the sequence it represents, some series have convenient formulas for their sums.

Sum of first *n* positive integers: $\displaystyle\sum_{k=1}^{n} k = \dfrac{n(n + 1)}{2}$

Sum of squares of first *n* positive integers: $\displaystyle\sum_{k=1}^{n} k^2 = \dfrac{n(n + 1)(2n + 1)}{6}$

5 Suppose a pyramid of golf balls like the one in Task 3 is made with 12 layers of balls. How many balls are on the front triangular face? How many balls are there altogether?

Identify the sequences. Then apply the formulas for the series.

Balls in *n*th row of front face: $a_n = n$

Total balls in front face: $\displaystyle\sum_{k=1}^{12} k = \dfrac{12(12 + 1)}{2} = 78$ balls

A. How do you know you can apply the formulas above to find the sums of the series?

Balls in *n*th layer: $a_n = n^2$

Total balls in pyramid: $\displaystyle\sum_{k=1}^{12} k^2 = \dfrac{12(12 + 1)(2 \cdot 12 + 1)}{6} = 2(13)(25) = 650$ balls

 Turn and Talk How can you find how many layers high the pyramid would have to be for the front face to contain 300 balls? What is this number of layers?

Check Understanding

1. In a section of a needlepoint design, the rule $a(n) = 8 + 2(n-1)$ gives the number of stitches in the nth row of the section, which contains 12 rows.

   A. How can you interpret the rule in the context of the needlepoint design?

   B. What are the domain and range of the sequence?

   C. Graph the sequence.

2. What does the series $\sum\limits_{k=1}^{12} [8 + 2(k-1)]$ mean in the context of Problem 1? Write out the series, simplifying each addend, then find the sum of the series.

3. The diagram shows the top and side views of a tower of blocks as it is being built where n is the layer number counting from the top. Write a list of ordered pairs representing the number of blocks in each of the top 5 layers. Use the list to write a rule for the number of blocks in the nth layer of the tower using both function notation and sequence notation. How many blocks would be in the 10th layer?

   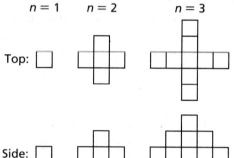

4. Represent the series for the sum of the first 30 positive integers and for the sum of the squares of the first 30 positive integers using sigma notation. Then use the formulas

   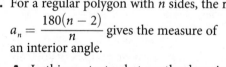

   $$\sum_{k=1}^{n} k = \frac{n(n+1)}{2} \text{ and } \sum_{k=1}^{n} k^2 = \frac{n(n+1)(2n+1)}{6} \text{ to find the sums.}$$

On Your Own

5. What is the difference between a finite sequence and an infinite sequence?

6. How are function notation and subscript notation for sequences related?

Write the first six terms of each sequence, beginning with $n = 1$.

7. $a(n) = 132 - 11n$

8. $a(n) = \dfrac{60}{n}$

9. $a(n) = n - n^2$

10. $a_n = 5^{n+1}$

11. $a_n = \dfrac{n+1}{n}$

12. $a_n = (n+2)^3$

13. For a regular polygon with n sides, the rule $a_n = \dfrac{180(n-2)}{n}$ gives the measure of an interior angle.

   A. In this context, what are the domain and range of the sequence that this rule describes? Explain.

   Measure of an interior angle of a regular polygon:
   $$a_n = \frac{180(n-2)}{n}$$

   B. Write the first 10 terms of the sequence. What is the measure of the interior angle shown in the image?

   C. Graph $a(n) = \dfrac{180(n-2)}{n}$ for $3 \le n \le 10$.

Write out the expression for each series. Then find the sum.

14. $\sum_{k=1}^{10} 2k - 10$ **15.** $\sum_{k=1}^{6}(k-3)^2$ **16.** $\sum_{k=1}^{6}\frac{1}{k}$ **17.** $\sum_{k=0}^{5}-k^4$

18. Write a rule for the sequence that the table represents. If the sequence continues in the same pattern, what will the tenth term of the sequence be?

n	a_n
0	100
1	121
2	144
3	169
4	196
5	225

19. Write a rule in function notation for the sequence represented by the table. What numbers does the sequence represent?

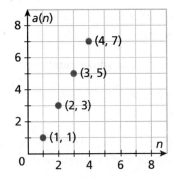

20. The number of rolled hay bales in each layer of the stack shown, starting from the top, is described by the sequence 2, 6, 12, 20, 30.

A. What pattern do you see in the sequence? What are the next three terms?

B. Complete the table below:

Row, n	1	2	3	4
Bales	2 • ___?___	3 • ___?___	4 • ___?___	5 • ___?___

C. Using the table above, what function rule can you write for the sequence? If the stack were 10 layers high, how many bales would be in the bottom layer?

Stacking sequence of hay bales: 2, 6, 12, 20, 30.

Write the series using sigma notation.

21. $12 + 24 + 36 + 48 + 60 + 72$ **22.** $14 + 8 + 2 - 4 - 10 - 16$

23. $20 - 40 + 80 - 160 + 320$ **24.** $\frac{2}{3} + \frac{3}{4} + \frac{4}{5} + \frac{5}{6} + \frac{6}{7} + \frac{7}{8} + \frac{8}{9}$

25. The number of cans in each layer of the stack shown, starting from the top, is described by the sequence 6, 20, 42, 72.

A. What pattern do you see in the number you must add to get from one term of the sequence to the next? What is the next term?

B. Complete the table below:

Row, n	1	2	3	4
Cans	2 • ___?___	4 • ___?___	6 • ___?___	8 • ___?___

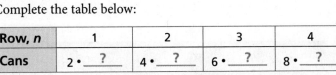

C. Using the table above, what function rule can you write for the sequence? If the stack were 8 layers high, how many cans would be in the bottom layer?

D. Use sigma notation to represent the total number of cans in a stack 8 layers high, then write out the series. How many cans are in a stack 8 layers high?

26. A formula for finding the sum of the series $2^0 + 2^1 + 2^2 + 2^3 + \ldots + 2^n$ is $\sum_{k=0}^{n} 2^k = 2^{n+1} - 1$. What is the value of $\sum_{k=0}^{9} 2^k$? Describe what this formula means in terms of finding sums of whole number powers of 2.

27. The formula $\dfrac{n^2(n+1)^2}{4}$ gives the sum of the terms of the sequence $a_n = n^3$.

   A. Use sigma notation to write the series representing the sum of the first 5 terms of a_n. Then verify that the formula is correct for $n = 5$.

   B. What is the sum of the cubes of the first 1000 positive integers? Show how you used the formula.

28. Let a_n be the sequence of whole number powers of 10: $a_n = 10^n$ ($n = 0, 1, 2, \ldots$).

   How can you write the sum of the series $\sum_{k=0}^{n} 10^k$ for any whole number n? Explain your reasoning.

29. You can form a new sequence from two sequences a_n and b_n by adding a_n and b_n term by term. The sum of the terms of the new sequence is the same as the sum of the series for the individual sequences: $\sum_{k=1}^{n}(a_k + b_k) = \sum_{k=1}^{n} a_k + \sum_{k=1}^{n} b_k$.

   A. Verify the formula for the first 5 terms of $a_n = n$ and $b_n = n^2$. What properties of equality did you use?

   B. Use the sum formulas for $\sum_{k=1}^{n} k$ and $\sum_{k=1}^{n} k^2$ to write a formula for $\sum_{k=1}^{n}(k + k^2)$.

Spiral Review • Assessment Readiness

30. Which is equivalent to $\dfrac{2x}{x-1} - \dfrac{4}{x+6}$?

   Ⓐ $\dfrac{2x^2 + 8x + 4}{x^2 + 5x - 6}$ Ⓒ $\dfrac{2x^2 - 6x - 24}{x^2 + 5x - 6}$

   Ⓑ $\dfrac{2x^2 + 8x - 4}{x^2 + 5x - 6}$ Ⓓ $\dfrac{2x^2 - 6x + 24}{x^2 + 5x - 6}$

31. A riverboat traveling at an average speed of 18 miles per hour travels 12 miles upstream and 12 miles downstream in a total of 1.35 hours. What is the average speed of the current?

   Ⓐ 1.25   Ⓑ 1.75   Ⓒ 2   Ⓓ 2.25

32. Which statements are true for the expression? Select all that apply.

   $$\dfrac{x^2 + 2x - 3}{4x} \div \dfrac{x^2 - 1}{6x}$$

   Ⓐ $x \neq 0$ Ⓑ $x \neq 2$ Ⓒ $x \neq -1$

   Ⓓ It is equivalent to $\dfrac{3x + 9}{2x - 2}$.

   Ⓔ It is equivalent to $\dfrac{3x + 9}{2x + 2}$.

   Ⓕ It is equivalent to $\dfrac{3x - 3}{2x - 2}$.

33. Which value is a term of the sequence $a_n = a_1 + 6(n - 1)$ when $a_1 = 100$?

   Ⓐ 92   Ⓑ 118   Ⓒ 144   Ⓓ 156

 I'm in a Learning Mindset!

Is my understanding of sequences and series progressing as I anticipated?
What, if any, adjustments do I need to make to enhance my learning?

Arithmetic Sequences and Series

(I Can) write arithmetic sequences and series, and use them to model real-world situations.

Spark Your Learning

Look closely at this picture of the Louvre pyramid. The top of the Paris art museum visible above ground is made entirely of glass panes. The glass panes are in the shape of rhombuses except for the triangular panes along the bottom.

Complete Part A as a whole class. Then complete Parts B–D in small groups.

  A. What is a mathematical question you can ask about this situation?

  B. What variable(s) are involved in this situation? How can you express the relationship between a row in the pyramid and how many panes are in that row?

  C. To answer your question, what strategy and tool would you use along with all the information you have? What answer do you get?

  D. Does your answer make sense in the context of the situation? How do you know?

> **Turn and Talk**
> - Is the pattern for the oblique rows the same as the pattern for the horizontal rows?
> - Suppose all four sides of the pyramid are identical. How could you use your rule to determine how many rhombus-shaped panes are in each row of the entire pyramid?

Build Understanding

Investigate Arithmetic Sequences

In the world around us, there are situations that involve adding or subtracting the same number repeatedly, resulting in a sequential pattern.

An **arithmetic sequence** is a sequence whose successive terms differ by the same number, called the **common difference**. Using subscript notation, the general rule for an arithmetic sequence is $a_n = a_1 + (n - 1)d$, where a_n is the nth term of the sequence, a_1 is the first term, and d is the common difference. Using function notation, the general rule is written as $a(n) = a(1) + (n - 1)d$, where $a(n)$ is the nth term, $a(1)$ is the first term, and d is again the common difference.

1 Some plastic chairs are designed to be stackable. After the first chair in the stack, each additional chair adds the same amount to the overall height of the stack. How can you model the height of a stack of n chairs?

The table below shows the total height of the stack when there are 1, 2, 3, and 4 chairs in the stack.

Number of chairs, n	Height of stack (in.)
1	28
2	31
3	34
4	37

Each chair is 28 inches tall.

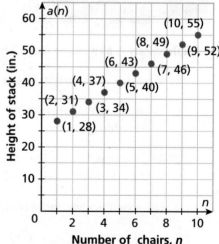

A. Look at the table. Do you notice any patterns in the stack height values?

In function notation, the rule for the arithmetic sequence that models the height of the stack of n chairs is $a(n) = 28 + (n - 1)3$.

B. In general, what are the domain and range of $a(n)$? In the real world, why might the domain and range be restricted? Give an example of what those restrictions might be.

C. The graph at the right models the arithmetic sequence $a(n) = 28 + (n - 1)3$. How are the domain and range of the sequence apparent in the graph?

D. Imagine drawing a line through the points on the graph. What key feature of the sequence does the slope of this line model? What type of function is modeled by an arithmetic sequence?

Graph: Height of stack (in.) vs. Number of chairs, n, showing points (1, 28), (2, 31), (3, 34), (4, 37), (5, 40), (6, 43), (7, 46), (8, 49), (9, 52), (10, 55).

©oilkili/Stock/Getty Images

Turn and Talk How would the rule for the sequence change if each chair was 32 inches tall? if each chair added 5 inches to the overall height of the stack? if both occurred?

Determine a Term in an Arithmetic Sequence

If you know that a sequence is arithmetic and you can determine both its first term and the common difference, you can determine the value of any term in the sequence.

2 The table of values at the right gives the first four terms of an arithmetic sequence. What is the 11th term of the sequence?

To write a rule for the sequence, you need to know the first term and the common difference.

n	$a(n)$
1	-6
2	-1
3	4
4	9

A. What reasoning can you use to justify that the first term of the sequence is -6?

B. How do you determine the common difference of the sequence? How can you verify that the difference is correct?

Using the first term and the common difference, the general rule (using subscript notation) for the arithmetic sequence is $a_n = -6 + (n - 1)5$.

C. How would you write the rule in function notation?

Use the rule to determine the 11th term by substituting 11 for n: $a_{11} = -6 + (11 - 1)5 = 44$.

3 An arithmetic sequence has a common difference of -10 and its 7th term is 140. Write a rule for the sequence. What is the 19th term?

The common difference is given. In order to write the rule, you just need to determine the first term of the sequence.

A. Can the first term be found directly using the 7th term and the common difference? Explain.

Using the general rule $a(n) = a(1) + (n - 1)d$ for an arithmetic sequence,

$140 = a(1) + (7 - 1)(-10)$
$140 = a(1) - 60$
$200 = a(1)$

Using function notation, the rule is $a(n) = 200 + (n - 1)(-10)$.

B. How is the rule written in subscript notation?

Use either form of the rule to determine the 19th term:
$a(19) = 200 + (19 - 1)(-10) = 20$.

4 The 12th term of an arithmetic sequence is 33 and the 16th term is 41. What is a rule for the sequence, written in both subscript and function notation?

A. Use the general rule along with the given information to find two expressions for the first term, a_1. Explain how to determine the common difference d using the two expressions for a_1.

B. How you can use the equation $33 = a_1 + (12 - 1)2$ to finish the work needed to write the general rule for the arithmetic sequence?

C. Write the general rule in both function and subscript notation.

Step It Out

Derive the Formula for the Sum of a Finite Arithmetic Series

The sum of a finite arithmetic series can be determined since the number of addends is finite. The sum of an infinite arithmetic series cannot be found because the number of addends is infinite and the sum will always continue increasing (or decreasing).

> **Connect to Vocabulary**
>
> An **arithmetic series** is the sum of the terms of an arithmetic sequence.

5 ▶ The formula for the sum of a finite arithmetic series can be derived by adding a general arithmetic series to itself, with one of the series written in reverse order, and then dividing both sides of the resulting equation by 2.

Let S_n be the sum of the first n terms of an arithmetic sequence.

$$S_n = a_1 + a_2 + a_3 + \ldots + a_{n-1} + a_n$$

You know that each term in an arithmetic sequence is found by adding d to the previous term. Rewrite the sum above with each intermediate term expressed using a_1 and d.

$$S_n = a_1 + (a_1 + d) + (a_1 + 2d) + \ldots + (a_1 + (n-2)d) + a_n$$

> **A.** How can the fact that $a_3 = a_2 + d$ be used to explain that $a_3 = a_1 + 2d$?

Now write the expression for S_n with the terms in the reverse order.

$$S_n = a_n + a_{n-1} + a_{n-2} + \ldots + a_2 + a_1$$
$$= a_n + (a_n - d) + (a_n - 2d) + \ldots + (a_n - (n-2)d) + a_1$$

> **B.** When the terms are in reverse order, why do the intermediate terms involve subtraction?

Add the two expressions for S_n.

$$\begin{aligned}
S_n &= a_1 & + (a_1 + d) &+ (a_1 + 2d) + \ldots + (a_1 + (n-2)d) + a_n \\
+\; S_n &= a_n & + (a_n - d) &+ (a_n - 2d) + \ldots + (a_n - (n-2)d) + a_1 \\
\hline
2S_n &= (a_1 + a_n) + (a_1 + a_n) + (a_1 + a_n) + \ldots + (a_1 + a_n) & + (a_1 + a_n)
\end{aligned}$$

$(a_1 + a_n)$ is added n times.

So, $2S_n = n(a_1 + a_n)$.

> **C.** How do you know that the quantity $(a_1 + a_n)$ appears n times?

Now divide both sides by 2 to find the expression for S_n.

Therefore, $S_n = \dfrac{n(a_1 + a_n)}{2}$ or $S_n = n\left(\dfrac{a_1 + a_n}{2}\right)$.

 Turn and Talk How is the formula for the sum of a finite arithmetic series related to the formula for the arithmetic mean of two numbers?

Calculate the Sum of a Finite Arithmetic Series

The formula for the sum of a finite arithmetic series is particularly useful when the number of terms is great.

While the sum of an infinite arithmetic series cannot be found, the sum of a specified number of consecutive terms from an infinite arithmetic sequence can be found since those terms form a finite arithmetic series.

6 Consider the arithmetic sequence $\{2, 5, 8, 11, 14, \ldots\}$. What is the sum of the first 25 terms of this sequence?

The arithmetic series formed by the first 25 terms of the sequence is a finite series, so its sum can be found using the formula $S_n = n\left(\dfrac{a_1 + a_n}{2}\right)$.

> **A.** What values are needed when using the formula?

The first term is 2. The common difference is $5 - 2 = 3$. These two values can be used to determine the value of the 25th term.

Use the general rule for an arithmetic sequence.

$$a_n = a_1 + (n - 1)d$$

$$a_{25} = 2 + (25 - 1)3 \qquad \text{Substitute 25 for } n, \text{ 2 for } a_1, \text{ and 3 for } d.$$

$$= 2 + (24)3$$

> **B.** How is the order of operations used to evaluate a_{25}?

$$= 2 + 72$$

$$= 74$$

So, the 25th term is 74.

Now use the formula for the sum of a finite arithmetic series to determine the sum of the first 25 terms.

$$S_n = n\left(\frac{a_1 + a_n}{2}\right)$$

$$S_{25} = 25\left(\frac{2 + 74}{2}\right) \qquad \text{Substitute 25 for } n, \text{ 2 for } a_1, \text{ and 74 for } a_n.$$

$$= \frac{25(76)}{2}$$

> **C.** How is the order of operations used to evaluate S_{25}?

$$= \frac{1900}{2}$$

$$= 950$$

The sum of the first 25 terms of the sequence $\{2, 5, 8, 11, 14, \ldots\}$ is 950.

 Turn and Talk How would the work change if the question had asked for the sum of 25 consecutive terms beginning with the 10th term of the sequence?

Model with an Arithmetic Series

  Kiera is a senior this year. She just won a regional math award that provides an amount of money now and additional money during the next four years while she is in college. She is given two options for receiving the money, as shown. Based on total cash value, which award option should Kiera choose?

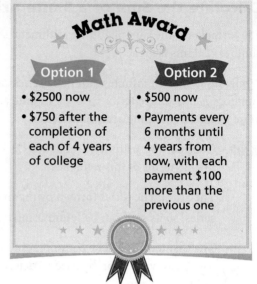

Math Award

Option 1	Option 2
• $2500 now	• $500 now
• $750 after the completion of each of 4 years of college	• Payments every 6 months until 4 years from now, with each payment $100 more than the previous one

Determine the total cash value of the award if Option 1 is chosen.

This option provides $2500 now plus four future payments of $750.

$$2500 + 4(750) = 2500 + 3000 = 5500$$

The total cash value of Option 1 is $5500.

Determine the total cash value of the award if Option 2 is chosen.

This option is more complicated. There is a $500 payment now followed by payments that increase in their amount over the next 4 years.

Create a table of values to organize the payments. Record when the payments occur and the amount of each payment.

Payment number, n	1	2	3	...	n
Months from now	0	6	12	...	48
Payment amount ($)	500	600	700	...	?

A. Can the value of n be determined? If so, what is it?

B. Why is there an entry of 48 here in the last column?

The payment amounts in the last row of the table form an arithmetic sequence with a first term of 500 and a common difference of 100. The cash value of Option 2 is the sum of these payment amounts. This sum is an arithmetic series.

To use the formula $S_n = n\left(\frac{a_1 + a_n}{2}\right)$, the values of n, a_1, and a_n are needed.

$$a_n = a_1 + (n - 1)d$$

$$a_9 = 500 + (9 - 1)100 \qquad \text{Substitute 9 for } n, \text{ 500 for } a_1, \text{ and 100 for } d.$$

$$= 500 + 800$$

$$= 1300$$

Now use the formula for the sum of a finite arithmetic series.

$$S_9 = 9\left(\frac{500 + 1300}{2}\right) = 9(900) = 8100$$

The total cash value of Option 2 is $8100.

So, Kiera should choose Option 2 since its cash value is greater.

C. Could there be a reason for Kiera to choose Option 1 instead? Explain.

Check Understanding

1. Robert's dad is in the military and has been all over the world. Robert and his dad collect 8 postcards each month from different countries. They started with 2 postcards. How can you model how many postcards Robert and his dad will own in n months?

2. The table of values represents an arithmetic sequence $a(n)$. What is the 20th term of the sequence?

n	1	2	3	4
$a(n)$	54	53	52	51

3. The fourth term of an arithmetic sequence is 7 and the common difference is 9. What is the 17th term of the sequence?

4. The 8th term of an arithmetic sequence is 24 and the 14th term is 60. What is a rule for the sequence?

5. The set of numbers $\{1, -3, -7, -11, \ldots\}$ are the terms of an arithmetic sequence. What is the sum of the first 10 terms? What is the sum of the next 10 terms (that is, the 11th through the 20th terms)? Explain what you did differently in order to determine both sums.

6. Jared is creating a pyramid using a computer program. The bottom row of the pyramid will be 280 pixels. The next row will be 245 pixels, and the next row will be 210 pixels. Keep repeating this pattern until the top row is 35 pixels. What type of model gives the total number of pixels used to create the pyramid? Explain. How many pixels are used to create the pyramid?

On Your Own

7. For one size of flowerpot sold at a garden store, the rim is 2 inches tall. So when the flowerpots are stacked, each additional flowerpot after the first one adds 2 inches to the height of the stack. The possible heights of a stack of n flowerpots can be modeled by an arithmetic sequence.

   A. What is the first term of the sequence?

   B. What is the common difference?

   C. What is a rule for the sequence?

   D. What are the domain and range? How are the domain and range affected if the space available on the shelving at the garden store is 30 inches high?

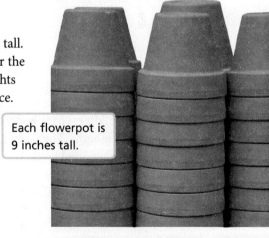

Each flowerpot is 9 inches tall.

8. Shopping carts are manufactured so they can be nested to save space when not in use. The graph shows the length, in inches, of a row of nested shopping carts with various numbers of carts. The length of a row of n shopping carts can be modeled by an arithmetic sequence.

   A. What information is needed in order to write a rule for the sequence?

   B. What is a rule for the sequence?

   C. What are the domain and range?

   D. Is the sequence finite or infinite? Explain.

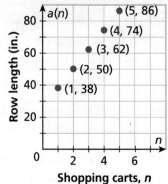

9. The graph below shows an infinite arithmetic sequence $a(n)$. What is the 72nd term of the sequence? Explain.

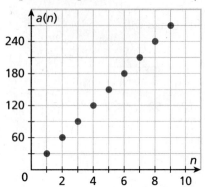

10. Does the graph below show an arithmetic sequence? Why or why not?

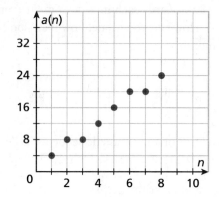

11. Determine whether an arithmetic sequence is an appropriate model for the table of values. If it is, write its rule and determine the 2nd term of the sequence.

n	9	10	11	12
$a(n)$	271	306	341	376

12. Is an arithmetic sequence an appropriate model for the table of values? If so, write its rule and determine the 25th term of the sequence.

n	4	5	6	7
$a(n)$	−417	−435	−453	−471

For Problems 13–16, use the given information about the arithmetic sequence to find the value of the specified term.

13. 11th term: 685
common difference: 68
What is the 28th term?

14. 19th term: 4190
common difference: 45
What is the 29th term?

15. 4th term: −200
8th term: −408
What is the 29th term?

16. 5th term: 613
15th term: 1103
What is the 34th term?

17. The office building where Isabella works holds a fire drill every 6 months. The floor where she works is 125 feet above ground level. The height above ground level of her shoe after going down n steps can be modeled by an arithmetic sequence.

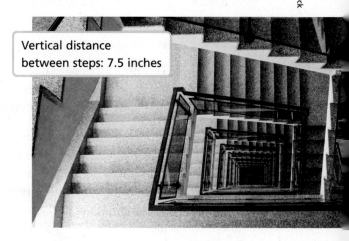

Vertical distance between steps: 7.5 inches

A. What is the common difference, converted to feet, for the sequence?

B. What is a rule for the sequence?

C. Is the sequence finite or infinite? Explain.

D. What is the last term of the sequence? How many terms are in the sequence?

18. Consider the arithmetic sequence whose rule is $a_n = 6 + (n - 1)18$. What is the sum of the first 17 terms of the sequence?

19. What is the sum of the first 16th terms of the arithmetic sequence $\{-4, 19, 42, 65, 88, \ldots\}$?

20. D'ante is buying a new cell phone. He will pay for the phone in equal monthly payments over the next 24 months.

The price of the phone is $450.

   A. Can the amount remaining to be paid after n months be modeled by an arithmetic sequence? Explain.

   B. How can you find the common difference? Will it be positive or negative? Explain.

   C. Why is the first term not 450? What is the first term?

   D. Write a rule for the sequence that models this situation.

21. The sum of the first 36 terms of an arithmetic sequence is 4950. The first term of the sequence is 15. What is the rule for the arithmetic sequence?

22. The sum of the first 28 terms of an arithmetic sequence is -1736. The 28th term of the sequence is -116. What is the rule for the arithmetic sequence?

23. Andres is preparing for a foreign language advanced placement exam. He studied for 1 hour today. Andres plans to increase his study time by 10 minutes each day for the two weeks he has remaining to study before the exam.

   A. What is an arithmetic sequence that models this situation?

   B. What is the last term of the sequence?

   C. What is the total amount of time Andres will study for his exam?

24. What is the sum of the first 20 terms of the sequence whose rule is $f(n) = 540 + (n - 1)(-36)$?

25. (MP) **Use Structure** In a video game you have to retrieve different artifacts in order to advance to the next level. In the first level you have to retrieve 2 artifacts, in the next level you have to retrieve 4 artifacts, in the next level you have to retrieve 6 artifacts, and so on, until the end of the game.

There are 8 levels in the video game.

   A. Would an arithmetic sequence or an arithmetic series give the total number of artifacts you must retrieve to complete all the levels and win the game?

   B. What is the model?

   C. What are the domain and range of the model?

   D. What type of function is the model based on when the rate of change is constant?

   E. What is the total number of artifacts you must collect in order to win the game? How do you know?

26. 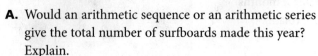 **Use Structure** A company that manufactures surfboards plans to increase production by an additional 25 surfboards each month for the next 12 months.

Last month's production total: 300 surfboards

A. Would an arithmetic sequence or an arithmetic series give the total number of surfboards made this year? Explain.

B. What is an arithmetic sequence that models the company's monthly output?

C. How many surfboards does the company plan to produce during the next 12 months?

27. What is the sum of the first 30 terms of an arithmetic sequence whose first term is k with a common difference of 16?

28. **(Open Middle™)** Using the digits 0 to 9, at most one time each, fill in the boxes to create an arithmetic sequence and its common difference.

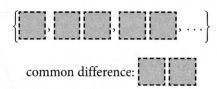

common difference: ⬛⬛

Spiral Review • Assessment Readiness

29. Which expression is equivalent to $\frac{3x-6}{x^2-4} \div \frac{x}{4x+8}$?

 Ⓐ $\frac{x}{12}$

 Ⓒ $\frac{x}{12}, x \neq -2, 2$

 Ⓑ $\frac{12}{x}, x \neq -2, 0, 2$

 Ⓓ $\frac{12}{x}, x \neq 0, 4$

30. Traveling at the same rate of speed, it takes Maria's family 1.5 hours more to travel 292.5 miles to her brother's college than it takes them to travel 195 miles to her sister's college. How long does it take to get to her brother's college?

 Ⓐ 3

 Ⓒ 4

 Ⓑ 3.5

 Ⓓ 4.5

31. What is the sum of the series

$$\sum_{k=1}^{6} 12k + 5?$$

 Ⓐ 282

 Ⓒ 77

 Ⓑ 205

 Ⓓ 65

32. Consider the function $f(n) = 3 \cdot 2^n$. What are the first four terms of the sequence?

 Ⓐ {6, 36, 216, 1296}

 Ⓑ {6, 12, 24, 48}

 Ⓒ {3, 6, 12, 24}

 Ⓓ {3, 9, 27, 81}

©Mikolette/E+/Getty Images

⬡ **I'm in a Learning Mindset!**

Does my work show I can write arithmetic sequences and series and use them to model real-world situations?

Geometric Sequences and Series

(I Can) **write geometric sequences and series, and use them to model real-world situations.**

Spark Your Learning

This tree fractal shows how simple rules can quickly lead to complex images. Animated movies look more realistic because of computer-generated fractals.

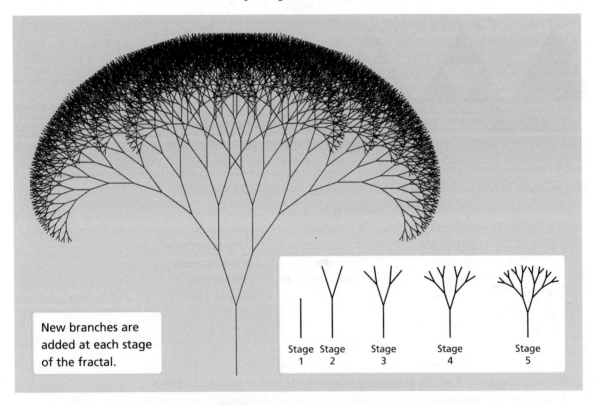

New branches are added at each stage of the fractal.

Stage 1   Stage 2   Stage 3   Stage 4   Stage 5

Complete Part A as a whole class. Then complete Parts B–D in small groups.

   A. What is a mathematical question you can ask about this situation? How can you organize the information so you can see a pattern?

   B. What variable(s) are involved in this situation? How can you use a table of values to see the relationship between one fractal and the next?

   C. To answer your question, what strategy and tool would you use along with all the information you have? What answer do you get?

   D. Does your answer make sense in the context of the situation? How do you know?

Turn and Talk
- How many new branches would there be in a forest of t trees?
- How would your rule change if each branch split into 3 new branches at each stage?

Build Understanding

Investigate Geometric Sequences

A **geometric sequence** is a sequence in which the ratio of successive terms is constant. The constant ratio r, called the **common ratio**, where $r \neq 0$ and $r \neq 1$. You can write a rule for a geometric sequence using function notation: $a(n) = a(1) \cdot r^{n-1}$ where $a(1)$ is the first term and r is the common ratio. In subscript notation, the general rule is $a_n = a_1 \cdot r^{n-1}$.

Waclaw Sierpinski designed the triangle fractal shown below.

Sierpinski began with a solid triangle. In each subsequent stage of the fractal, he removed a smaller triangle from the center of each solid triangle appearing in the previous stage.

 The table shows the number of solid congruent triangles and the number of removed congruent triangles for each stage n.

Stage, n	Number of congruent solid triangles	Number of congruent removed triangles	Total number of congruent triangles
1	1	0	1
2	3	1	4
3	9	7	16

For each stage, the fraction of the area that is shaded is the number of solid congruent triangles over the total number of congruent triangles.

A. The fraction for the first triangle is $\frac{\text{solid}}{\text{total}} = \frac{1}{1} = 1$. What fraction of the second triangle is shaded?

B. Notice that the large "removed" triangle in the third stage can be viewed as being formed by four of the smaller "removed" triangles. What fraction of the triangle is shaded?

C. What is the rule between consecutive fractions in the list?

The sequence that models the area of the shaded region of stage n is $a(n) = \left(\frac{3}{4}\right)^{n-1}$, or $a_n = \left(\frac{3}{4}\right)^{n-1}$ when written in subscript notation. The first ten terms of the sequence $a(n)$ are shown on the graph.

D. If you continue the graph of $a(n)$, how would you describe its end behavior? What type of function has a graph whose shape is similar to the graph of a geometric sequence?

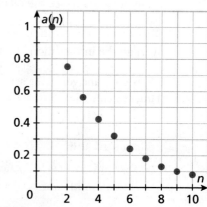

Determine a Term in a Geometric Sequence

Recall that there are two parts when writing a general rule for a geometric sequence. You need to know the first term of the sequence and the common ratio. You can use the general rule for a geometric sequence to determine any nth term.

2 ▶ Consider the geometric sequence $\{6, -18, 54, -162, 486, \ldots\}$. To write a rule for the sequence, you need to know the first term and the common ratio. By looking at the sequence of numbers, you can identify the first term as 6.

A. What do you notice about the signs of the terms of the sequence? What does this suggest about the common ratio?

The common ratio of the sequence is $-18 \div 6 = -3$.

B. Will the 12th term of the sequence be positive or negative? Explain.

Now use the general rule for a geometric sequence $a(n) = a(1) \cdot r^{n-1}$ where the first term is $a(1)$ and the common ratio is r to write a rule for the sequence.

The rule (in function notation) is $a(n) = 6(-3)^{n-1}$. In subscript notation, it is $a_n = 6(-3)^{n-1}$.

Determine the 12th term by substituting 12 for n: $a(12) = 6(-3)^{12-1} = -1{,}062{,}882$.

3 ▶ A geometric sequence has a 5th term that is 125 and a common ratio of 5. Write a rule for the sequence. What is the 15th term?

A. Can the 10th term be found directly using the 5th term and the common ratio? Explain.

In order to write the rule for the geometric sequence you need to determine the value of the first term.

$$125 = a_1 \cdot (5)^{5-1}$$
$$125 = a_1 \cdot (625)$$

The general rule $a_n = a_1 \cdot r^{n-1}$ for a geometric sequence and the common ratio can be used to find the value of a_1.

$$\frac{1}{5} = a_1$$

B. How is the rule written in subscript notation? in function notation?

Use either form of the rule to determine the 10th term:
$$a_{10} = \tfrac{1}{5}(5)^{10-1} = 390{,}625.$$

4 ▶ The 7th term of a geometric sequence is 192 and the 12th term is 6144. What is a rule for the sequence, written in both function and subscript notation?

Solve for $a(1)$ in two ways:

$$192 = a(1) \cdot r^{7-1} \qquad 6144 = a(1) \cdot r^{12-1}$$
$$\frac{192}{r^6} = a(1) \qquad\qquad \frac{6144}{r^{11}} = a(1)$$

Use the results to solve for r:

$$\frac{192}{r^6} = \frac{6144}{r^{11}}$$
$$192 r^{11} = 6144 r^6$$
$$r^5 = 32$$
$$r = 2$$

A. Explain the process above for determining the common ratio r.

B. How can you use $a(1) \cdot (2)^{7-1} = 192$ to write the rule for the sequence?

C. Write the rule for the sequence in both function and subscript notation.

Step It Out

Derive the Formula for the Sum of a Finite Geometric Series

Just as a finite arithmetic series has a sum, the sum of a finite geometric series can be determined and a formula can be derived to find this sum.

> **Connect to Vocabulary**
>
> A **geometric series** is the sum of the terms of a geometric sequence.

In the previous lesson, the formula for the sum of a finite arithmetic series was derived by carefully pairing terms when adding a general arithmetic series to itself. To derive the formula for the sum of a finite geometric series, a similar approach is used.

5 Let S_n be the sum of the first n terms of a geometric sequence.

$$S_n = a_1 + a_1r + a_1r^2 + \dots + a_1r^{n-3} + a_1r^{n-2} + a_1r^{n-1}$$

Multiply S_n by r, the common ratio of the sequence, to obtain an expression for rS_n.

$$rS_n = a_1r + a_1r^2 + a_1r^3 + \dots + a_1r^{n-2} + a_1r^{n-1} + a_1r^n$$

> **A.** Why is the exponent of the last term of rS_n just the variable n?

Now subtract rS_n from S_n.

$$S_n = a_1 + \quad a_1r \quad + \quad a_1r^2 \quad + \dots + \quad a_1r^{n-2} \quad + \quad a_1r^{n-1}$$
$$(-)\ rS_n = \qquad\quad a_1r \quad + \quad a_1r^2 \quad + \dots + \quad a_1r^{n-2} \quad + \quad a_1r^{n-1} \quad + a_1r^n$$

$$S_n - rS_n = a_1 + (a_1r - a_1r) + (a_1r^2 - a_1r^2) + \dots + (a_1r^{n-2} - a_1r^{n-2}) + (a_1r^{n-1} - a_1r^{n-1}) - a_1r^n$$

Simplify the expression for $S_n - rS_n$.

$$S_n - rS_n = a_1 - a_1r^n$$

> **B.** Why is there a subtraction symbol preceding the last term?

Rewrite both sides using the Distributive Property, and then solve for S_n.

$$S_n - rS_n = a_1 - a_1r^n$$
$$S_n(1 - r) = a_1(1 - r^n)$$
$$S_n = \frac{a_1(1 - r^n)}{1 - r}$$

> **C.** What properties justify the final two steps of the derivation?

The formula for the sum of a finite geometric series is $S_n = a_1\left(\frac{1 - r^n}{1 - r}\right)$.

D. Examine the formula. To find the sum of a geometric series, what key values of the series are needed to use the formula?

Turn and Talk Now that you have seen the derivation of the formula, why was it necessary to multiply the general form of a geometric series by r during the process?

Calculate the Sum of a Finite Geometric Series

The formula that was just derived can be used for a finite geometric series with any number of terms, but it is particularly useful when there are a great number of terms or when the terms themselves are great.

6 Consider the geometric sequence $\{4, 12, 36, 108, \ldots\}$. How much less is the sum of the first 8 terms of this sequence than the sum of the 12 terms of the sequence? The series formed by the first 8 terms and the first 12 terms of the geometric sequence are both finite series, so their sums can be found using the formula $S_n = a_1\left(\frac{1-r^n}{1-r}\right)$.

> **A.** What values are needed when using the formula?

Determine the sum of the first 8 terms.

The first term is 4, so $a_1 = 4$.

The common ratio is $12 \div 4 = 3$, so $r = 3$.

There are 8 terms in the series, so $n = 8$.

Using these values in the formula,

$$S_8 = 4\left(\frac{1-3^8}{1-3}\right) = -2(1-3^8) = 13{,}120.$$

Determine the sum of the first 12 terms.

The first term and the common ratio are again 4 and 3, respectively.

There are 12 terms in this series, so $n = 12$.

> **B.** Why is only the value of n different when finding the second sum?

Using these values in the formula,

$$S_{12} = 4\left(\frac{1-3^{12}}{1-3}\right) = -2(1-3^{12}) = 1{,}062{,}880.$$

Determine the difference.

$1{,}062{,}880 - 13{,}120 = 1{,}049{,}760$

So the sum of the first 8 terms of this sequence is 1,049,760 less than the sum of the first 12 terms of the sequence.

C. Finding the sums of the two series and then subtracting them is not the only way to determine the answer to the question. What alternative solution method could be used? Test your method to verify that the result is the same.

 Turn and Talk How could you represent the sum of the first 8 terms using summation notation? How could you represent the sum of the first 12 terms this way?

Model with a Geometric Series

Many phenomena in the real world can be modeled by a geometric sequence and its related geometric series.

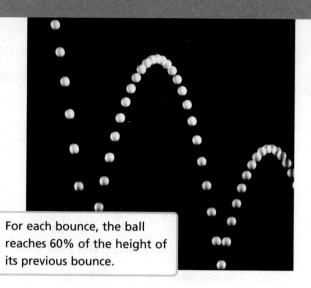

7 An experiment involves dropping a ball from a height of 60 inches and measuring the height the ball reaches on each bounce. The experiment is recorded in order to facilitate the measurements. On the first bounce it reaches a height of 36 inches. How much vertical distance (not including the initial drop) has the ball traveled by the end of the 6th bounce?

> For each bounce, the ball reaches 60% of the height of its previous bounce.

Determine if the situation is modeled by a geometric series.

The height that the ball reaches on every bounce is 60% of the height of the previous bounce. So the sequence of heights is a geometric sequence with a common ratio of 0.6.

However, the discussion here is about the total vertical distance traveled. Since each bounce is an up-and-down motion, the vertical distance for each bounce is twice the height reached by the ball.

> **A.** If the sequence of heights is geometric, would the sequence of heights of a ball that bounces twice as high also be geometric? Explain.

Determine the vertical distance traveled.

Method 1: Use the formula for the sum of a finite geometric series.

$$S_6 = 72\left(\frac{1 - 0.6^6}{1 - 0.6}\right) = 72\left(\frac{1 - 0.6^6}{0.4}\right) = 180(1 - 0.6^6) \approx 171.6$$

> **B.** Why are $a_1 = 72$ and $n = 6$?

Method 2: Set up a table of values to find the total vertical distance traveled.

Bounce number	Vertical distance traveled (inches)	Total vertical distance traveled (inches)
1	$2 \cdot 36 = 72$	72
2	$72(0.6) = 43.2$	115.2
3	$72(0.6)^2 = 25.92$	141.12
4	$72(0.6)^3 = 15.552$	156.672
5	$72(0.6)^4 = 9.3312$	166.0032
6	$72(0.6)^5 = 5.59872$	171.60192

> **C.** Does the table method yield the same result as the formula? Explain.

The ball travels vertically a total of approximately 171.6 inches during 6 bounces.

Turn and Talk How would your work change if each of these changes occurred.
- The height of the first bounce is 48 inches.
- The ball reaches only 25% of the height of its previous bounce.

Check Understanding

1. The Ladies' Singles and the Men's Singles Wimbledon Championship each begin with 128 players. Each match is between 2 players, with the winner moving on to the next round. There are 64 matches in the first round. How can you model the number of players in each round?

For Problems 2–4, use the given information about the geometric sequence to find the value of the specified term.

2. $a(1) = 4$

   $r = -1$

   Find $a(7)$.

3. $a_3 = \frac{1}{4}$

   $r = -\frac{1}{8}$

   Find a_5.

4. $a(1) = -2$

   $a(4) = -250$

   Find $a(10)$.

5. The rule $a(n) = \frac{1}{125}(5)^{n-1}$ models a geometric sequence. What is the formula for the sum of the first 5 terms of the sequence?

6. What is the sum of the first 8 terms of the infinite geometric sequence $a(n) = -2(4)^{n-1}$

7. Mark is creating a tree fractal on a computer. The program starts with a single branch. When he clicks on the tip of a branch, the program draws three smaller branches from it. In each stage of the program, Mark continues to click on each branch, adding three new branches on the end of each existing branch. What is the total number of branches after 6 stages, if the single branch at the start is stage 1?

On Your Own

8. The first four stages of the Sierpinski carpet fractal are shown in the illustration at the right. For this fractal design, the center of each solid square is removed in each stage after the first stage.

   A. What information is needed to write a geometric sequence to model the shaded area of the nth stage of Sierpinski's carpet?

   B. What is the general rule for the geometric sequence?

   C. Is the geometric sequence finite? Why or why not?

   D. What are the domain and range of the geometric sequence?

   E. Graph the geometric sequence. Describe the end behavior as n increases.

9. Suppose the expected rate of inflation for a large $12 pizza with one topping is 5% per year.

   A. What information is needed to model the expected cost of a large pizza in n years?

   B. What is the general rule for the geometric sequence?

   C. Is the geometric sequence finite? Why or why not?

   D. What are the domain and range of the geometric sequence?

   E. Graph the geometric sequence. Describe the end behavior as n increases.

10. Is the graph of the discrete function $a(n)$ shown at the right the graph of a geometric sequence? Why or why not?

11. Describe the key characteristics of the graph of a geometric sequence.

12. Is the domain of an infinite geometric sequence always the same? Explain.

13. Darah sells handmade bracelets at craft shows and online. She is planning to raise the price of the bracelets by 15 cents at the beginning of each year. Can a geometric sequence model the price of her handmade bracelet in n years? Explain.

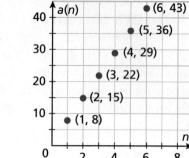

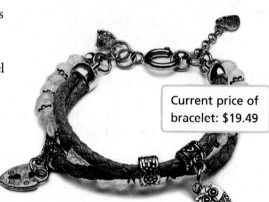

Current price of bracelet: $19.49

For Problems 14 and 15, each graph models an infinite geometric sequence.

14. What is the 17th term of the sequence?

15. What is its 14th term of the sequence?

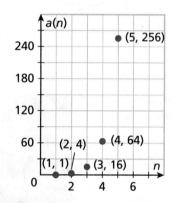

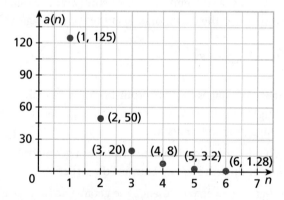

For Problems 16–24, use the given information about the geometric sequence to find the value of the specified term. Round to the nearest thousandth if necessary.

16. $a(1) = 125$

$r = 0.8$

Find $a(9)$.

17. $a_1 = -4$

$r = \dfrac{7}{4}$

Find a_{20}.

18. $a(1) = 64$

$r = -\dfrac{3}{8}$

Find $a(11)$.

19. $a_4 = 128$

$r = 8$

Find a_6.

20. $a(3) = 3.125$

$r = 1.25$

Find $a(8)$.

21. $a_7 = -93{,}750$

$r = 5$

Find a_{12}.

22. $a(3) = 8$

$a(6) = 512$

Find $a(8)$.

23. $a_5 = 80$

$a_9 = 1280$

Find a_{16}.

24. $a(3) = -36$

$a(5) = -972$

Find $a(7)$.

25. **(MP) Use Structure** Consider the geometric sequence $\{1, 2, 4, 8, \ldots\}$. What is a simplified formula for the sum of the first n terms of the geometric series?

26. **(MP) Critique Reasoning** Consider the geometric sequence $\{1, r, r^2, r^3, \ldots\}$. John simplified the formula for the sum of the first n terms of the geometric series as shown. Is he correct? Explain why or why not.

$$S_n = 1\left(\frac{1 - r^n}{1 - r}\right) = r^{n-1}$$

For Problems 27–32, use the given information about each geometric sequence to find the sum of the first n terms specified.

27. $a(n) = \left(\frac{3}{10}\right)^{n-1}$

    Find S_{10}.

28. $a_n = 6^{n-1}$

    Find S_5.

29. $a(n) = -2(3)^{n-1}$

    Find S_6.

30. $a_n = 3(-3)^{n-1}$

    Find S_6.

31. $a(n) = 2(4)^{n-1}$

    Find S_8.

32. $a(n) = 9\left(-\frac{1}{2}\right)^{n-1}$

    Find S_4.

33. **Music** The frequencies produced by playing C notes in ascending octaves make up a geometric sequence. C0 is the lowest C note audible to the human ear.

    A. The note commonly called middle C is C4. What is the frequency of middle C?

    B. Write a geometric sequence for the frequency of C notes in hertz where $n = 1$ represents C1.

    C. Humans cannot hear sounds with frequencies greater than 20,000 Hz. What is the first C note that humans cannot hear?

Scale of C's	
Note	**Frequency (Hz)**
C0	16.24
C1	32.7
C2	65.4
C3	130.8
C4	?

34. **Health and Fitness** During a flu outbreak, a hospital recorded 16 cases the first week, 56 cases the second week, and 196 cases the third week.

    A. Write a rule for a geometric sequence to model the flu outbreak.

    B. If these patients had not come to the hospital and they remained untreated, in which week would the total number infected exceed 10,000?

35. **Financial Literacy** A movie earned $202 million in its first week of release and $26.6 million in the fifth week of release. The weekly earnings can be modeled by a geometric sequence.

    A. What information do you need to know in order to write the rule for the model?

    B. Estimate the movie's earnings in its second week of release.

    C. By what approximate ratio did the earnings decrease each week?

    D. Estimate the movie's total earnings during its first 10 weeks of release.

36. A cracker was accidentally dropped along a sidewalk by a pedestrian. During the first hour, 4 ants found the cracker, and during the fourth hour, 500 ants found the cracker. The number of ants that have found the discarded cracker after n hours can be modeled by a geometric sequence.

    A. Write a rule for a geometric sequence to model the number of ants that found the cracker.

    B. How many ants found the cracker during the third hour?

37. Financial Literacy Bethany saved 10 cents the first day of last month and then doubled her daily savings each day for 11 straight days.

Day 1: 10 cents

Day 2: 20 cents

Day 3: 40 cents

    A. Would a geometric sequence or a geometric series give the total daily savings for the 12 days?

    B. What information do you need to know in order to write the rule for the model?

    C. What are the first four terms of the model?

    D. How much did Bethany save on the 12th day?

    E. What were her total daily savings for the 12 days? How do you know?

38. (Open Middle™) Using the digits 0 to 9, at most one time each, fill in the boxes to create a geometric sequence and the greatest possible common ratio.

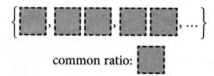

common ratio: ☐

Spiral Review • Assessment Readiness

39. Cara and Janelle work at a beachside hotel. Cara can paint a cabana alone in 8.2 hours. Janelle can paint the same cabana in 6.5 hours. Janelle paints the cabana for 2 hours alone before Cara joins her to complete the job. How long did Cara paint?

    Ⓐ 6 h 21 min   Ⓒ 4 h 31 min

    Ⓑ 5 h 21 min   Ⓓ 2 h 31 min

40. What is the sum $\sum_{k=1}^{5} k(k+3)$?

    Ⓐ 100   Ⓒ 51

    Ⓑ 60   Ⓓ 40

41. What is the 100th term of the arithmetic sequence $\{-8, -5, -2, 1, \ldots\}$?

    Ⓐ 103   Ⓒ 292

    Ⓑ 289   Ⓓ 305

42. The function $a_n = a_{n-1} \cdot 4$ is a geometric sequence where $a_1 = 7$. What is a_3?

    Ⓐ 12   Ⓒ 112

    Ⓑ 28   Ⓓ 448

I'm in a Learning Mindset!

What evidence supports my understanding of geometric sequences and series?

Review

Arithmetic Sequence

Find the common difference between terms and the first term of the sequence.

2, 5, 8, 11, 14, …

First term: 2

Common difference:
$14 - 11 = 11 - 8 = 8 - 5 = 5 - 2 = 3$ Linear

General explicit rule:
$f(n) = a_1 + d(n - 1)$ or $a_n = a_1 + d(n - 1)$

Explicit rule (n is the term number):
$f(n) = 2 + 3(n - 1)$ or $a_n = 2 + 3a_{n-1}$

Both forms of the rule include the common difference $d = 3$ and the first term $a_1 = 2$.

Arithmetic Series

An arithmetic series is a sum of the terms in an arithmetic sequence.

$$S_n = \sum_{k=1}^{n} a_n = a_1 + a_2 + a_3 + \ldots + a_n$$

Sigma notation for a series can include the explicit rule.

$$\sum_{k=1}^{13} 2 + 3(k - 1) = 2 + [2 + 3(2 - 1)] + \ldots + [2 + 3(13 - 1)]$$

Find the sum of the first 13 terms of 2, 5, 8,….

$$a_n = 2 + 3(n - 1)$$
$$a_{13} = 2 + 3(13 - 1)$$
$$= 38$$

$$S_n = \frac{n(a_1 + a_n)}{2}$$
$$S_{13} = \frac{13(2 + 38)}{2}$$
$$= 260$$

Geometric Sequence

Find the common ratio between terms and the first term of the sequence.

2, 10, 50, 250, 1250, …

First term: 2

Common ratio: $\dfrac{1250}{250} = \dfrac{250}{50} = \dfrac{50}{10} = \dfrac{10}{2} = 5$

Exponential

General explicit rule:
$f(n) = a_1 \cdot (r)^{n-1}$ or $a_n = a_1 \cdot (r)^{n-1}$

Explicit rule (n is the term number):
$f(n) = 2 \cdot 5^{(n-1)}$ or $a_n = 2 \cdot 5^{(n-1)}$

Both forms of the rule include the common ratio $r = 5$ and the first term $a_1 = 2$.

Geometric Series

A geometric series is a sum of the terms in a geometric sequence.

$$S_n = \sum_{k=1}^{n} a_n = a_1 + a_2 + a_3 + \ldots + a_n$$

Sigma notation for a series can include the explicit rule.

$$\sum_{k=1}^{13} 2 \cdot 5^{(k-1)} = 2 + 2 \cdot 5^{(2-1)} + \ldots + 2 \cdot 5^{(13-1)}$$

Find the sum of the first 13 terms of 2, 10, 50, 250,….

$$S_n = a_1\left(\frac{1 - r^n}{1 - r}\right)$$

$$S_{13} = 2\left(\frac{1 - 5^{13}}{1 - 5}\right) = 610{,}351{,}562$$

Vocabulary

Choose the correct term from the box to complete each sentence.

1. The sum of the numbers in a sequence is a(n) ___?___.

2. A set of numbers where the same number is added to each previous number is a(n) ___?___.

3. A(n) ___?___ is a set of numbers where each number, or ___?___, is given in a particular order.

4. A set of ordered numbers that terminates is a(n) ___?___, and one that continues forever is a(n) ___?___.

5. A(n) ___?___ is a set of ordered numbers with a constant ratio between numbers.

Concepts and Skills

6. How does the pattern of numbers in an arithmetic sequence compare with the pattern of numbers in a geometric sequence?

Determine whether each sequence is arithmetic or geometric and whether it is finite or infinite.

7. $4, 1.9, -0.2, -2.3, \ldots$

8. $-60, 30, -15, 7.5, \ldots, 0.1171875$

Write an explicit rule for each sequence. Use the table for Problems 9 and 10.

Year	1	2	3	4	5	6
Visitors	2900	3350	3800	4250	4700	5150
Revenue	$50,000	$55,000	$60,500	$66,550	$73,205	$80,525.50

9. the sequence of the number of visitors each year

10. the sequence of the revenue each year

11. an arithmetic sequence with a 5th term of 289 and a 12th term of 170

Find the sum of each series.

12. $\displaystyle\sum_{k=1}^{9}(5-3k)$

13. $\displaystyle\sum_{k=1}^{10}6\left(\frac{1}{2}\right)^{k}$

(MP) Use Tools Write an explicit rule to model each scenario. State what strategy and tool you will use to answer the question, explain your choice, and then find the answer.

14. Monica deposited $40 in a savings account at the end of January. She increases the amount she deposits by the same amount each month. She deposited $69.75 at the end of August. How much will she deposit at the end of December?

15. Jared has a 4-year-old car that is currently worth $15,000. The value of his car is projected to decline by 12% per year. How much will his car be worth when it is 10 years old?

14 Recursive Formulas for Sequences

Module Performance Task: *Spies and Analysts*™

One Step at a Time

What is the height of the tower after *n* levels?

Are You Ready?

Complete these problems to review prior concepts and skills you will need for this module.

Percent Increase and Decrease

Find each percent of increase or decrease. Round to the nearest tenth.

1. The price of a bicycle decreased from $280 to $255.

2. The price of a shirt was marked up from $25 to $32.

3. The total of a bill before sales tax was $76.21 and after sales tax was $81.16.

4. The value of a stock changed from $45.12 to $43.86.

5. The number of students in a class increased from 24 to 30.

Add and Subtract Rational Numbers

Find each sum or difference. Simplify the result.

6. $\frac{3}{4}+\frac{1}{3}$

7. $\frac{5}{8}-\frac{1}{6}$

8. $1\frac{1}{2}+2\frac{2}{5}$

9. $9\frac{5}{6}-4\frac{1}{2}$

10. $6\frac{2}{3}+3\frac{4}{5}$

11. $7\frac{1}{8}-2\frac{3}{4}$

Multiply and Divide Rational Numbers

Find each product or quotient. Simplify the result.

12. $\frac{7}{8}\cdot\frac{3}{5}$

13. $\frac{2}{7}\div\frac{1}{3}$

14. $\frac{3}{10}\cdot\frac{5}{6}$

15. $\frac{11}{12}\div\frac{8}{9}$

16. $2\frac{5}{6}\cdot3\frac{3}{4}$

17. $8\frac{1}{3}\div4\frac{1}{6}$

Connecting Past and Present Learning

Previously, you learned:
- to identify common differences and ratios in series,
- to create and apply explicit formulas for arithmetic sequences and series, and
- to create and apply explicit formulas for geometric sequences and series.

In this module, you will learn:
- to create and apply recursive formulas of arithmetic and geometric sequences,
- to translate between explicit and recursive formulas of arithmetic and geometric sequences, and
- to model real-world scenarios using recursive formulas.

Recursive Formulas for Arithmetic Sequences

(**I Can**) write a recursive formula for an arithmetic sequence and translate between explicit and recursive formulas for arithmetic sequences.

Spark Your Learning

A mixed-use building is being constructed that will have shops, offices, and restaurants on the first floor and apartments on the other floors.

All floors above the first floor will have the same height. The first floor will be taller.

Complete Part A as a whole class. Then complete Parts B–D in small groups.

A. What is a mathematical question you can ask about this situation? What information would you need to know to answer your question?

B. The additional information your teacher gave you includes a formula for a sequence. How is this formula different from the formulas you have seen before for sequences?

C. To answer your question, what strategy and tool would you use along with all the information you have? What answer do you get?

D. How would the formula your teacher gave you change if the first floor of the building is 12 feet tall and the other floors are each 9 feet tall?

 Turn and Talk Can you write a formula that gives the height of the building to the top of the nth floor as a function of the floor number n? If so, what is the formula?

Build Understanding

Explore Recursive Formulas for Arithmetic Sequences

In the previous module, you used *explicit formulas* such as $a(n) = 2 + 3n$ to represent sequences. An **explicit formula** gives the nth term $a(n)$ as a function of the term's position number n in the sequence. In this lesson, you will learn how to define a sequence using a *recursive formula*. A **recursive formula** gives the beginning term or terms of a sequence and then a *recursive equation* that tells how the nth term $a(n)$ is related to one or more preceding terms.

 Use this recursive formula for a sequence: $a(1) = 3$, $a(n) = a(n-1) + 5$.

A. Explain in words how to find a term of the sequence using one or more of the preceding terms.

B. Enter the term numbers 1, 2, 3, ..., 10 in column A of a spreadsheet as shown. In cell B2, enter the first term of the sequence, 3. In cell B3, enter the formula "=B2+5" for finding the second term. Fill down the formula from cell B2 to cell B11 in order to find the first ten terms of the sequence. What type of sequence do the terms form? How do you know?

	A	B	C
1	Term number	Term (recursive formula)	Term (explicit formula)
2	1	3	
3	2	= B2 + 5	
4	3		
5	4		
6	5		
7	6		
8	7		
9	8		
10	9		
11	10		

C. What is an explicit formula for the sequence?

D. Use the explicit formula to write a formula in cell C2 of the spreadsheet for calculating the first term of the sequence. The formula in cell C2 should use the term number in cell A2. Fill down the formula from cell C2 to cell C11 to find the first ten terms of the sequence. Do the terms you found in column C using the explicit formula match the terms you found in column B using the recursive formula?

E. In general, what is the recursive equation for an arithmetic sequence with common difference d?

F. Suppose you need to find the 200th term of a sequence without a spreadsheet or calculator. Which type of formula for the sequence—an explicit formula or a recursive formula—would be more helpful? Why?

G. What is the 200th term of the sequence you worked with in this task?

 Turn and Talk Consider the sequence defined by $a(1) = 4$, $a(n) = a(n-1) - 3$. Is this an arithmetic sequence? If so, what is the common difference?

Step It Out

Write Recursive Formulas for Arithmetic Sequences

A recursive equation for an arithmetic sequence with common difference d is $a(n) = a(n-1) + d$ in function notation, or $a_n = a_{n-1} + d$ in subscript notation. You can write a recursive formula for an arithmetic sequence given a graph, a table, or two terms.

2 ▶ Write a recursive formula for the sequence whose graph is shown.

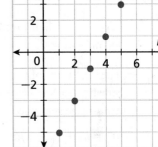

The terms of the sequence are the y-coordinates of the points: $-5, -3, -1, 1, 3, 5$.

There is a common difference of 2, so the sequence is arithmetic.

Using subscript notation, you can write a recursive formula for the sequence as $a_1 = -5, a_n = a_{n-1} + 2$.

A. How can you tell from the graph that the sequence is arithmetic?

B. How can you write the recursive formula in function notation?

3 ▶ Write a recursive formula for the sequence shown in the table.

There is a common difference of -4, so the sequence is arithmetic.

Using function notation, you can write a recursive formula for the sequence as $a(1) = 27, a(n) = a(n-1) - 4$.

n	$a(n)$
1	27
2	23
3	19
4	15
5	11
6	7

A. How can you use the recursive formula to find the 7th term?

B. How can you write the recursive formula in subscript notation?

4 ▶ Write a recursive formula for the arithmetic sequence with terms $a_5 = 10$ and $a_{22} = 61$.

Find the common difference d. Because $22 - 5 = 17$, it follows that:

$a_5 + 17d = a_{22}$

$10 + 17d = 61$

> **A.** Why can you find a_{22} by adding $17d$ to a_5?

$17d = 51$

$d = 3$

Find the first term a_1. Because $5 - 1 = 4$, it follows that:

$a_1 + 4d = a_5$

$a_1 + 4(3) = 10$

> **B.** Why do you need to find a_1 in addition to the common difference d?

$a_1 = -2$

Therefore, a recursive formula for the sequence is $a_1 = -2, a_n = a_{n-1} + 3$.

Translate Between Formulas for Arithmetic Sequences

Given an explicit formula for an arithmetic sequence, you can write a recursive formula, and vice versa. The table below shows how to translate between these two representations of an arithmetic sequence.

	Function notation	Subscript notation
Explicit formula	$a(n) = a(1) + (n-1)d$	$a_n = a_1 + (n-1)d$
Recursive formula	$a(1) =$ value of 1st term, $a(n) = a(n-1) + d$	$a_1 =$ value of 1st term, $a_n = a_{n-1} + d$

5 Write an explicit formula for the arithmetic sequence defined by the recursive formula $a_1 = 2$, $a_n = a_{n-1} - 7$.

The first term of the sequence is 2, and the common difference is -7. Substitute these values into the general form of the explicit formula for an arithmetic sequence.

$a_n = a_1 + (n-1)d$

$a_n = 2 + (n-1)(-7)$

$a_n = 2 - 7n + 7$

$a_n = 9 - 7n$

An explicit formula for the sequence is $a_n = 9 - 7n$.

A. How do you know that the common difference of the sequence is -7 instead of 7?

B. Kim says that because the first term of the sequence is 2, the explicit formula should be $a_n = 2 - 7n$. Why is Kim mistaken?

 Turn and Talk How can you write an explicit formula for the arithmetic sequence defined by $a(1) = -3.5$, $a(n) = a(n-1) + 1.5$? Use function notation.

6 Write a recursive formula for the arithmetic sequence defined by the explicit formula $a(n) = -8 + 12n$.

Find the first term of the sequence: $a(1) = -8 + 12(1) = 4$.

The common difference is the coefficient of n in the explicit formula: 12.

A recursive formula for the sequence is $a(1) = 4$, $a(n) = a(n-1) + 12$.

A. What is another way you can use the explicit formula to find the common difference?

B. How can you check that the recursive formula is correct?

 Turn and Talk How can you write a recursive formula for the arithmetic sequence defined by $a_n = \frac{4}{3} - \frac{1}{3}n$? Use subscript notation.

Apply Recursive Formulas for Arithmetic Sequences

7 Lisa and Aaron each received a gift card for an online company that offers streaming movie and music subscriptions.

Lisa's gift card is for $100. She uses it to buy a movie subscription that costs $10 per month.

Aaron's gift card is for $75. He uses it to buy a music subscription that costs $8 per month.

For each gift card, write a recursive formula giving the remaining balance on the card after n months. What is the balance on each gift card after 5 months? Are Lisa and Aaron able to use up the entire values of their gift cards with their subscriptions?

Let $L(n)$ = Lisa's gift card balance after n months, and let $A(n)$ = Aaron's gift card balance after n months. For these sequences, the first term corresponds to $n = 0$ (rather than $n = 1$) and represents the initial balance on the gift card. The recursive formulas are as follows.

Lisa: $L(0) = 100$, $L(n) = L(n - 1) - 10$

Aaron: $A(0) = 75$, $A(n) = A(n - 1) - 8$

A. Are these arithmetic sequences? If so, what is the common difference for each sequence, and what does it represent?

Use the recursive formulas and a spreadsheet to find the terms of each sequence.

	A	B	C
1	Number of months, n	Lisa's gift card balance, $L(n)$	Aaron's gift card balance, $A(n)$
2	0	100	75
3	1	90	67
4	2	80	59
5	3	70	51
6	4	60	43
7	5	50	35
8	6	40	27
9	7	30	19
10	8	20	11
11	9	10	3
12	10	0	−5

B. What formulas would you enter in cells B3 and C3?

C. What does this negative number tell you about the situation?

After 5 months, Lisa's gift card balance is $50 and Aaron's gift card balance is $35.

Lisa has a balance of $0 after 10 months, so she is able to use up the entire value of her gift card. However, Aaron has a balance of $3 after 9 months, which is not enough to purchase a 10th month of service. So, Aaron cannot use up the entire value of his card.

 Turn and Talk What are explicit formulas for the sequences $L(n)$ and $A(n)$?

Check Understanding

1. How is a recursive formula for a sequence different from an explicit formula for a sequence?

Write a recursive formula for the arithmetic sequence defined by the graph or table.

2.

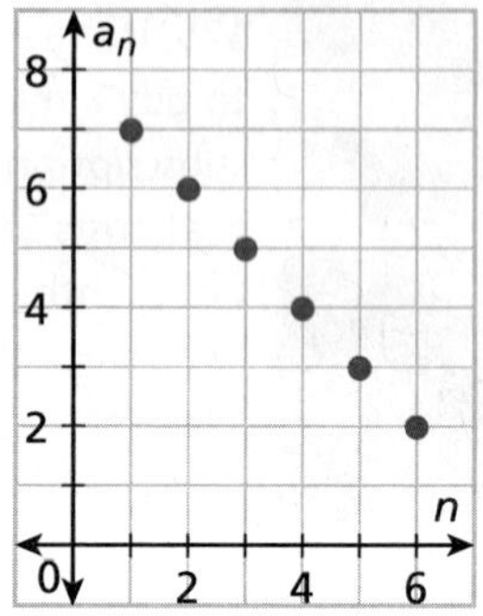

(graph: points plotted descending — a_n vertical axis with markings 2, 4, 6, 8; n horizontal axis with markings 2, 4, 6)

3.

n	a(n)
1	−7
2	−2
3	3
4	8
5	13

4. Write a recursive formula for the arithmetic sequence with terms $a_6 = 60$ and $a_{18} = -24$.

5. Write a recursive formula for the arithmetic sequence defined by the explicit formula $a_n = 3.5 + 0.2n$.

6. There are 15 seats in the row nearest the stage of a theater. Each row after the first has 2 more seats than the row before it. Using function notation, write a recursive formula for the number of seats in the nth row. Translate the recursive formula into an explicit formula, and find the number of seats in the 12th row.

On Your Own

Find the first 5 terms of the sequence defined by the given recursive formula. Then tell whether the sequence is an arithmetic sequence.

7. $a(1) = 12, a(n) = a(n - 1) + 8$

8. $a(1) = 5, a(n) = 2 \cdot a(n - 1)$

9. $a_1 = 2, a_n = (a_{n-1})^2$

10. $a_1 = -\dfrac{5}{2}, a_n = a_{n-1} - \dfrac{3}{2}$

11. **(MP) Reason** Recursive formulas for two sequences are given below. Without doing any calculations, how do you know that $b(n) > a(n)$ for $n \geq 1$?

$$a(1) = 3, a(n) = a(n - 1) + 5$$

$$b(1) = 4, b(n) = b(n - 1) + 5$$

12. **(MP) Model with Mathematics** The photo shows the cost of a large pizza at a pizzeria.

   A. Let n be the number of toppings on a large pizza, and let $c(n)$ be the cost of the pizza. Is the starting term for the sequence of possible costs $c(0)$ or $c(1)$? Explain.

   B. Write a recursive formula for $c(n)$.

   C. Write an explicit formula for $c(n)$.

Large cheese pizza: $15
Toppings: $2 each

Write a recursive formula for the arithmetic sequence whose graph is shown.

13.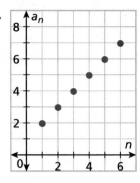

14.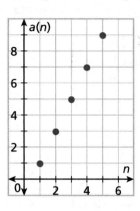

15.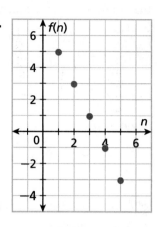

Write a recursive formula for the arithmetic sequence defined by the table.

16.

n	a_n
1	6
2	10
3	14
4	18
5	22

17.

n	$a(n)$
1	9
2	−2
3	−13
4	−24
5	−35

18.

n	$f(n)$
1	−3
2	1.5
3	6
4	10.5
5	15

Write a recursive formula for the arithmetic sequence with the two given terms.

19. $a_2 = 5, a_6 = 13$

20. $a_3 = 40, a_{17} = -2$

21. $a(5) = -11, a(10) = -16$

22. $f(7) = 5, f(20) = 36.2$

Translate the given recursive formula into an explicit formula, or the given explicit formula into a recursive formula.

23. $a_1 = 9, a_n = a_{n-1} + 6$

24. $a(1) = 14, a(n) = a(n-1) - 5$

25. $a_n = -80 + 10n$

26. $f(n) = 24 - 3n$

27. Financial Literacy A car dealership is offering 0% financing for new cars. Jane decides to buy the car shown. She negotiates $2000 off the car's sticker price and makes a down payment of $3000. She takes out a loan for the remaining balance and agrees to pay off the loan in equal monthly installments over 5 years.

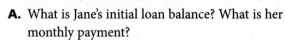

A. What is Jane's initial loan balance? What is her monthly payment?

B. Write a recursive formula that gives Jane's loan balance $b(n)$ after n months.

C. Write an explicit formula for $b(n)$.

D. If Jane decides to sell the car for $13,000 after 3 years and pay off the loan with part of the sales proceeds, how much money does she have left from the sale after paying off the loan?

28. Write a recursive formula and an explicit formula for the number of squares S_n in the nth figure. Is the sequence defined by the formulas an arithmetic sequence? Explain.

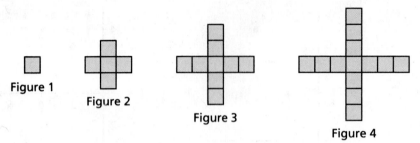

Figure 1

Figure 2

Figure 3

Figure 4

29. **(MP)** **Use Structure** The *Fibonacci sequence* is 1, 1, 2, 3, 5, 8, 13, 21, 34, ...

A. Is the Fibonacci sequence an arithmetic sequence? Explain.

B. Describe the pattern in the list of terms of the Fibonacci sequence.

C. Write a recursive formula for the sequence. Then find the next five terms.

30. **(Open Middle™)** Using the digits 1 to 9, at most one time each, fill in the boxes (with one digit per box) to make an arithmetic sequence and its recursive equation.

Sequence: ⬚ , ⬚ , ⬚⬚ , . . .

Recursive equation: $a_n = a_{n-1} + $ ⬚

Spiral Review • Assessment Readiness

31. What is the value of $\sum\limits_{k=1}^{4} k^3$?

Ⓐ 64

Ⓒ 100

Ⓑ 65

Ⓓ 13,824

32. Which sequences are arithmetic sequences? Select all that apply.

Ⓐ 0, 2, 4, 6, 8, 10, . . .

Ⓑ 1, 4, 9, 16, 25, 36, . . .

Ⓒ 1, 2, 4, 7, 11, 16, . . .

Ⓓ 3, 6, 12, 24, 48, 96, . . .

Ⓔ −8, −11, −14, −17, −20, −23, . . .

Ⓕ 4.3, 4.7, 5.1, 5.5, 5.9, 6.3, . . .

33. What is a formula for the nth term of this sequence?

2, −6, 18, −54, 162, −486, . . .

Ⓐ $a_n = 10 - 8n$

Ⓒ $a_n = 3(-2)^{n-1}$

Ⓑ $a_n = -3n$

Ⓓ $a_n = 2(-3)^{n-1}$

34. The function $P = 1350(1.07)^t$ models the population of bison at a wildlife refuge t years after the refuge is established. What is the approximate bison population 3 years after the refuge is established?

Ⓐ 1546

Ⓒ 4334

Ⓑ 1654

Ⓓ 3.014×10^9

 I'm in a Learning Mindset!

Does my work demonstrate an understanding of recursive formulas for arithmetic sequences? What evidence supports that claim?

Recursive Formulas for Geometric Sequences

(I Can) write a recursive formula for a geometric sequence and translate between explicit and recursive formulas for geometric sequences.

Spark Your Learning

The Koch snowflake is a *fractal*, which is a special kind of shape created by repeating the same pattern. The first stage of the Koch snowflake is an equilateral triangle, and the number of sides of the snowflake increases from one stage to the next. Can you see the pattern?

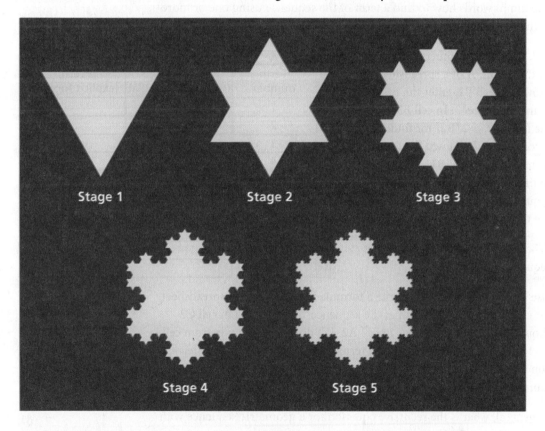

Stage 1   Stage 2   Stage 3

Stage 4   Stage 5

Complete Part A as a whole class. Then complete Parts B and C in small groups.

A. What is a mathematical question you can ask about this situation? What information would you need to know to answer your question?

B. Why is the generation of the Koch snowflake a recursive process?

C. To answer your question, what strategy and tool would you use along with all the information you have? What answer do you get?

 Turn and Talk Why do the numbers of sides of the stages of the Koch snowflake form a geometric sequence?

Build Understanding

Explore Recursive Formulas for Geometric Sequences

In the last lesson, you learned how to write recursive formulas for arithmetic sequences. With an arithmetic sequence, the recursive formula expresses the fact that you always *add* the same number to each term in order to obtain the next term.

With a geometric sequence, however, you *multiply* each term by the same number to obtain the next term. You can use this fact to create a recursive formula for a geometric sequence.

 Use this recursive formula for a sequence: $a(1) = 3$, $a(n) = 2 \cdot a(n - 1)$.

A. Explain in words how to find a term of the sequence using one or more of the preceding terms.

B. Enter the term numbers 1, 2, 3, ..., 10 in column A of a spreadsheet as shown. In cell B2, enter the first term of the sequence, 3. In cell B3, enter the formula "=2*B2" for finding the second term. Fill down the formula from cell B2 to cell B11 in order to find the first ten terms of the sequence. What type of sequence do the terms form? How do you know?

	A	B	C
1	Term number	Term (recursive formula)	Term (explicit formula)
2	1	3	
3	2	= 2*B2	
4	3		
5	4		
6	5		
7	6		
8	7		
9	8		
10	9		
11	10		

C. What is an explicit formula for the sequence?

D. Use the explicit formula to write a formula in cell C2 of the spreadsheet for calculating the first term of the sequence. The formula in cell C2 should use the term number in cell A2. Fill down the formula from cell C2 to cell C11 to find the first ten terms of the sequence. Do the terms you found in column C using the explicit formula match the terms you found in column B using the recursive formula?

E. In general, what is the recursive equation for a geometric sequence with common ratio r?

F. What is the 20th term of the sequence? Which formula did you use to find this term—the recursive formula or the explicit formula? Why?

 Turn and Talk Consider the sequence defined by $a(1) = 400$, $a(n) = \frac{a(n - 1)}{2}$. Is this a geometric sequence? If so, what is the common ratio?

Step It Out

Write Recursive Formulas for Geometric Sequences

A recursive equation for a geometric sequence with common ratio r is $a(n) = r \cdot a(n-1)$ in function notation, or $a_n = r \cdot a_{n-1}$ in subscript notation. You can write a recursive formula for a geometric sequence given a graph, a table, or two terms.

2 Write a recursive formula for the sequence whose graph is shown. The terms of the sequence are the y-coordinates of the points: 32, 16, 8, 4, 2. Find the ratios of consecutive terms:

$$\frac{16}{32} = \frac{1}{2}, \frac{8}{16} = \frac{1}{2}, \frac{4}{8} = \frac{1}{2}, \text{ and } \frac{2}{4} = \frac{1}{2}.$$

There is a common ratio of $\frac{1}{2}$, so the sequence is geometric. Using subscript notation, you can write a recursive formula for the sequence as $a_1 = 32, a_n = \frac{1}{2} \cdot a_{n-1}$.

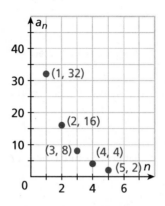

A. How can you tell from the graph that the sequence is *not* arithmetic?

B. How can you write the recursive formula in function notation?

3 Write a recursive formula for the sequence shown in the table. Find the ratios of consecutive terms in the second column:

$$\frac{6}{2} = 3, \frac{18}{6} = 3, \frac{54}{18} = 3, \frac{162}{54} = 3, \text{ and } \frac{486}{162} = 3.$$

There is a common ratio of 3, so the sequence is geometric.

Using function notation, you can write a recursive formula for the sequence as $a(1) = 2, a(n) = 3 \cdot a(n-1)$.

n	$a(n)$
1	2
2	6
3	18
4	54
5	162
6	486

A. How can you use the recursive formula to find the 7th term?

B. How can you write the recursive formula in subscript notation?

4 Write a recursive formula for the geometric sequence with terms $a_2 = -10$ and $a_5 = -80$. Find the common ratio r. Because $5 - 2 = 3$, it follows that:

$$a_2 \cdot r^3 = a_5$$

> A. Why can you find a_5 by multiplying a_2 by r^3?

$$-10 \cdot r^3 = -80$$

$$r^3 = 8$$

$$r = 2$$

> B. Why is it true that $a_2 = 2 \cdot a_1$?

Find the first term a_1. Because $a_2 = 2 \cdot a_1$, or $-10 = 2 \cdot a_1$, it follows that $a_1 = -5$. Therefore, a recursive formula for the sequence is $a_1 = -5$, $a_n = 2 \cdot a_{n-1}$.

Translate Between Formulas for Geometric Sequences

Given an explicit formula for a geometric sequence, you can write a recursive formula, and vice versa. The table below shows how to translate between these two representations of a geometric sequence.

	Function notation	Subscript notation
Explicit formula	$a(n) = a(1) \cdot r^{n-1}$	$a_n = a_1 \cdot r^{n-1}$
Recursive formula	$a(1) =$ value of 1st term, $a(n) = r \cdot a(n-1)$	$a_1 =$ value of 1st term, $a_n = r \cdot a_{n-1}$

5 Write an explicit formula for the geometric sequence defined by the recursive formula $a_1 = 7$, $a_n = 4 \cdot a_{n-1}$.

The first term of the sequence is 7, and the common ratio is 4. Substitute these values into the general form of the explicit formula for a geometric sequence.

$a_n = a_1 \cdot r^{n-1}$

$a_n = 7 \cdot 4^{n-1}$

An explicit formula for the sequence is $a_n = 7 \cdot 4^{n-1}$.

A. How can you check that the explicit formula gives the correct first term of the sequence?

B. Nicolas says that the explicit formula should be $a_n = 4 \cdot 7^{n-1}$. What mistake did Nicolas make?

 Turn and Talk How can you write an explicit formula for the geometric sequence defined by $a(1) = 60$, $a(n) = \frac{2}{3} \cdot a(n-1)$? Use function notation.

6 Write a recursive formula for the geometric sequence defined by the explicit formula $a(n) = 10(-6)^{n-1}$.

Find the first term of the sequence: $a(1) = 10(-6)^{1-1} = 10(-6)^0 = 10$.

The common ratio is the base of the power in the explicit formula: -6.

A recursive formula for the sequence is $a(1) = 10$, $a(n) = -6 \cdot a(n-1)$.

A. What is another way you can use the explicit formula to find the common ratio?

B. How can you check that the recursive formula is correct?

 Turn and Talk How can you write a recursive formula for the geometric sequence defined by $a_n = -80(0.4)^{n-1}$? Use subscript notation.

Apply Recursive Formulas for Geometric Sequences

 7 A standard piano has 88 keys, which include 52 white keys and 36 black keys. If you number the keys 1 through 88 from left to right, you can develop a formula for the frequency (in hertz) of the note made by the nth key. The greater the note's frequency, the higher its pitch.

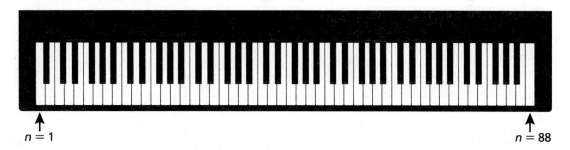

$n = 1$ $n = 88$

The frequency of the note made by the first key is 27.5 hertz, and the frequency for each key after the first is $2^{\frac{1}{12}}$ times the previous key's frequency. Write both a recursive formula and an explicit formula for the frequency $f(n)$ of the note made by the nth key on a piano. Then find the frequency made by the last (88th) key.

Write a recursive formula for $f(n)$.

Because each key's frequency is $2^{\frac{1}{12}}$ times the previous key's frequency, the frequencies form a geometric sequence with common ratio $r = 2^{\frac{1}{12}}$. The first term of the sequence is the frequency of the first key, 27.5 hertz. So a recursive formula for $f(n)$ is:

$$f(1) = 27.5, f(n) = 2^{\frac{1}{12}} \cdot f(n-1).$$

Write an explicit formula for $f(n)$.

Substitute the first term and the common ratio into the general form of the explicit formula for a geometric sequence.

$$f(n) = f(1) \cdot r^{n-1}$$
$$f(n) = 27.5 \left(2^{\frac{1}{12}}\right)^{n-1}$$
$$f(n) = 27.5 \left(2^{\frac{n-1}{12}}\right)$$

> **A.** What property of exponents was used to simplify the explicit formula?

Find the frequency of the note made by the last (88th) key.

Use the explicit formula to find $f(88)$.

$$f(88) = 27.5 \left(2^{\frac{88-1}{12}}\right) = 27.5 \left(2^{\frac{87}{12}}\right)$$

> **B.** Why does it make sense to use the explicit formula instead of the recursive formula to find the frequency for the last key?

$$\approx 27.5(152.219)$$
$$\approx 4186$$

The frequency produced by the last (88th) key is about 4186 hertz.

Check Understanding

1. How is a recursive formula for a geometric sequence similar to a recursive formula for an arithmetic sequence? How is it different?

Write a recursive formula for the geometric sequence defined by the graph or table.

2.

3.

n	$a(n)$
1	243
2	81
3	27
4	9
5	3
6	1

4. Write a recursive formula for the geometric sequence with terms $a_2 = -45$ and $a_5 = 1215$.

5. Write an explicit formula for the geometric sequence defined by the recursive formula $a(1) = 8$, $a(n) = 10 \cdot a(n-1)$.

6. Write a recursive formula for the geometric sequence defined by the explicit formula $a_n = -80\left(\frac{3}{4}\right)^{n-1}$.

7. A professional tennis tournament has 128 players who play a match in round 1. In each successive round, the number of players who play a match is half the number from the previous round. The rounds continue until there is only one player remaining (the tournament winner). Write a recursive formula and an explicit formula for the number of players $p(n)$ who play a match in the nth round. After how many rounds is a winner determined?

On Your Own

Find the first 5 terms of the sequence defined by the given recursive formula. Then tell whether the sequence is a geometric sequence.

8. $a_1 = 9$, $a_n = a_{n-1} + 2$

9. $a_1 = 9$, $a_n = 2 \cdot a_{n-1}$

10. $a(1) = -48$, $a(n) = \dfrac{a(n-1)}{4}$

11. $a(1) = 2$, $a(n) = 3 \cdot a(n-1) - 5$

12. $a_1 = -1$, $a_n = 2(a_{n-1})^2$

13. $a(1) = 256$, $a(n) = \dfrac{3}{2} \cdot a(n-1)$

14. **(MP) Critique Reasoning** Bryce and Kelli each try to write a recursive formula for a geometric sequence with given terms $a(3) = 54$ and $a(7) = 4374$. Bryce writes the formula $a(1) = 6$, $a(n) = 3 \cdot a(n-1)$. Kelli writes the formula $a(1) = 6$, $a(n) = -3 \cdot a(n-1)$. Whose formula is correct? Explain.

Write a recursive formula for the geometric sequence whose graph is shown.

15.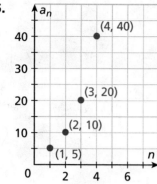

16.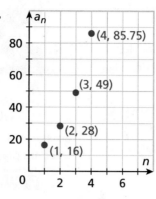

17.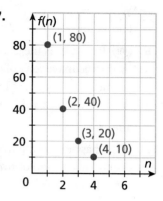

Write a recursive formula for the geometric sequence defined by the table.

18.

n	a_n
1	3
2	15
3	75
4	375
5	1875

19.

n	$a(n)$
1	81
2	54
3	36
4	24
5	16

20.

n	$f(n)$
1	−2
2	6
3	−18
4	54
5	−162

Write a recursive formula for the geometric sequence with the two given terms.

21. $a_2 = 50, a_3 = 125$

22. $a_3 = 81, a_6 = 3$

23. $a(4) = -500, a(7) = 62{,}500$

24. $f(3) = 200, f(8) = \dfrac{25}{4}$

Translate the given recursive formula into an explicit formula, or the given explicit formula into a recursive formula.

25. $a_1 = 9, a_n = 4 \cdot a_{n-1}$

26. $a(1) = 11, a(n) = -2 \cdot a(n-1)$

27. $a_n = 600\left(\dfrac{3}{4}\right)^{n-1}$

28. $f(n) = -34(0.8)^{n-1}$

29. STEM A pendulum is released to swing freely. The distance traveled by the *bob* (the weight at the end of the pendulum) is 50 centimeters on the first swing. On each successive swing, the bob's distance traveled is 90% of the distance traveled on the previous swing.

A. Write a recursive formula and an explicit formula that give the distance $d(n)$ traveled by the pendulum's bob on the nth swing.

B. On what swing is the distance traveled by the bob first less than half its distance traveled on the first swing?

Swing 1: 50 cm
Swing 2: 50(0.9) cm
Swing 3: 50(0.9)² cm

30. A tree farm initially has 5000 trees.

    A. Write a recursive formula that gives the farm's number of trees $t(n)$ after n years.

    B. (MP) **Reason** Is the sequence modeled by the recursive formula arithmetic, geometric, or neither? Explain.

    C. How many trees does the farm have after 3 years?

    D. What happens to the tree population over a long period of time? Use a spreadsheet or calculator to help you.

Each year 15% of the trees are harvested and 600 new trees are planted.

31. (Open Middle™) Using the digits 1 to 9, at most one time each, fill in the boxes (with one digit per box) to make a geometric sequence and its recursive equation.

Sequence: ⬚ , ⬚ , ⬚⬚ , . . .

Recursive equation: $a_n = $ ⬚ $\cdot a_{n-1}$

Spiral Review • Assessment Readiness

32. What is a formula for the arithmetic sequence with terms $a_5 = -8$ and $a_{11} = 34$?

    Ⓐ $a_n = -43 + 7n$

    Ⓑ $a_n = -36 + 7n$

    Ⓒ $a_n = -8 + 7n$

    Ⓓ $a_n = -8 + 42n$

33. Which sequences are geometric sequences? Select all that apply.

    Ⓐ 0, 3, 6, 9, 12, 15, . . .

    Ⓑ 4, 8, 16, 32, 64, 128, . . .

    Ⓒ 1, 8, 27, 64, 125, 216, . . .

    Ⓓ $\frac{1}{2}, \frac{1}{4}, \frac{1}{6}, \frac{1}{8}, \frac{1}{10}, \frac{1}{12}, \ldots$

    Ⓔ $-54, 36, -24, 16, -\frac{32}{3}, \frac{64}{9}, \ldots$

    Ⓕ 1, −2, 3, −4, 5, −6, . . .

34. The height $h(n)$ in centimeters of a stack of n plates is given by:

$$h(1) = 1.5, \quad h(n) = h(n-1) + 0.5$$

How many plates are in a stack that is 12 centimeters tall?

    Ⓐ 8 plates   Ⓒ 22 plates

    Ⓑ 21 plates   Ⓓ 24 plates

35. The measure of angle A is 45°. The measure of angle B is $\frac{\pi}{3}$ radians. Which angle has the greater measure?

    Ⓐ angle A

    Ⓑ angle B

    Ⓒ The angles have equal measure.

    Ⓓ The answer cannot be determined.

©Douglas Sacha/E+/Getty Images

I'm in a Learning Mindset!

Is my understanding of recursive formulas progressing as I anticipated?
What adjustments, if any, do I need to make to enhance my learning?

Recursive Functions

The recursive rule for a function tells how to find one term in a sequence from previous terms. The recursive rule must include at least two equations, one for the first term and one for how to find additional terms.

$$f(1) = 2$$
$$f(n) = \left[f(n-1) \right]^2$$
or
$$a_1 = 2$$
$$a_n = \left(a_{n-1} \right)^2$$
both represent 2, 4, 16, 256, ...

The recursive rule for a function may depend on more than one previous term. In this case there must be more than two equations in the rule.

$$f(1) = 1, f(2) = 1$$
$$f(n) = f(n-1) + f(n-2)$$
or
$$a_1 = 1, a_2 = 1$$
$$a_n = a_{n-1} + a_{n-2}$$
both represent 1, 1, 2, 3, 5, 8, 11, ...

Recursive Rules for Arithmetic Sequences

In the formulas below, a is the first term of the sequence, d is the common difference, and n is the number of the term.

Recursive rule:

$$f(1) = a_1$$
$$f(n) = d + f(n-1)$$

Explicit rule:

$$f(n) = a_1 + d(n-1)$$

OR

$$a_1 = a$$
$$a_n = d + a_{n-1}$$

$$a_n = a_1 + d(n-1)$$

Each form of the rule includes the common difference d and the first term a_1.

Example:

Sequence: $a_1 = 2, d = 3$

Recursive rule:

$$f(1) = 2$$
$$f(n) = 3 + f(n-1)$$

Explicit Rule:

$$f(n) = 2 + 3(n-1)$$

Recursive Rules for Geometric Sequences

In the formulas below, a is the first term of the sequence, r is the common ratio, and n is the number of the term.

Recursive rule:

$$f(1) = a_1$$
$$f(n) = r \cdot f(n-1)$$

Explicit rule:

$$f(n) = a_1 \cdot (r)^{n-1}$$

OR

$$a_1 = a$$
$$a_n = r \cdot a_{n-1}$$

$$a_n = a_1 \cdot (r)^{n-1}$$

Each form of the rule includes the common ratio r and the first term a_1.

Example:

Sequence: $a_1 = 2, r = 3$

Recursive rule:

$$f(1) = 2$$
$$f(n) = 3 \cdot f(n-1)$$

Explicit Rule:

$$f(n) = 2 \cdot (3)^{n-1}$$

Vocabulary

Choose the correct term from the box to complete each sentence.

1. A(n) __?__ describes a set of ordered numbers by how they differ from the previous number.

2. A(n) __?__ is a set of ordered numbers that have a constant difference between consecutive numbers.

3. A(n) __?__ is a set of ordered numbers that have a constant ratio between consecutive numbers.

4. A(n) __?__ describes how to find a specific number in a set of ordered numbers directly.

Concepts and Skills

5. How does the domain of the function of an explicit rule of a sequence relate to the domain of the function of a recursive rule of a sequence?

The population of two small cities continues to grow beyond the years shown in the table. Write a recursive rule for each sequence.

Year	1	2	3	4	5	6
Greenville	45,250	46,375	47,500	48,625	49,750	50,875
Riverside	44,000	45,320	46,680	48,080	49,522	51,008

6. the population of Greenville

7. the population of Riverside

Write a recursive rule for each sequence described with an explicit rule.

8. $f(n) = 2.5(15)^{n-1}$

9. $f(n) = 4 - 3(n - 1)$

Write an explicit rule for each sequence described with a recursive rule.

10. $f(n) = \frac{3}{8} \cdot f(n - 1), f(1) = \frac{3}{4}$

11. $f(1) = -8, f(n) = -\frac{5}{6} + f(n - 1)$

(MP) **Use Tools Write a recursive rule to model each scenario and find a solution. State what strategy and tool you will use to answer the question, explain your choice, and then find the answer.**

12. Ever since Smallville reached a population of 25,000, it has been growing at a rate of 5% per year. If this growth trend continues, how many years will it take for the population to exceed 40,000?

13. Jason has $39.50 of credit on his bus pass. If each ride costs $1.75, how many rides can he take without adding more to his bus pass?

Trigonometric Functions and Identities

Solar Engineer

The goal of a solar engineer is to convert energy from the sun's rays to electricity. They must have a solid understanding of physics, chemistry, electronics, and mechanical engineering. They calculate the expected efficiency of solar panels at a given location and align them to maximize collection.

STEM Task

In the northern hemisphere, solar panels are typically oriented to face due south with the angle of tilt set approximately equal to the latitude of the location.

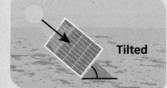 Tilted

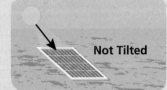 Not Tilted

Consider a solar panel that is 65 inches long by 39 inches wide.

For your latitude, compare the collection area of a module that is tilted with one that is not tilted.

Learning Mindset

Resilience Manages the Learning Process

As you continue to develop your understanding, paying attention to your mindset enables you to manage your learning. Mindful practices like reading, notetaking, studying, writing, and revising can help you to learn better. The key is to believe in yourself and your potential. All your work is enhanced when you understand how it serves your personal development. Here are some questions you can ask yourself as you manage your learning process:

- Where do I fall within the growth-mindset spectrum with respect to trigonometric functions and identities?

- What steps am I taking to direct my own learning on trigonometric functions and identities?

- How can I modify my mindset to increase my performance?

- How do my decisions about studying impact my achievement?

Reflect

Q Think about experiences you have had when you made mistakes. What did you learn from the mistakes you made? Were your mistakes because of your own level of preparedness or the challenge of the task? What can you do differently next time?

Q Imagine you are a solar engineer. How would your mindset affect your learning of current methods? How can your mindset affect the development of new technologies?

15 Unit-Circle Definition of Trigonometric Functions

Module Performance Task: Focus on STEM

Total Internal Refraction

Light travels at different speeds depending on the medium it travels through. The refractive index describes the speed of light in a medium relative to a vacuum, $n = \frac{c}{v}$, where v is the velocity of light in the medium and c is the speed of light in a vacuum. As light travels between mediums, it bends according to the law of refraction, $n_1 \sin(\theta_1) = n_2 \sin(\theta_2)$.

A. Within a fiber optic cable, an incident angle of 30 degrees is refracted to an angle of 46.1 degrees in air. Determine the ratio between the index of refraction for fiber optic cable and air, $n_c : n_a$.

B. Approximate the speed of light in a fiber optic cable if the index of refraction for air is approximately 1 and the speed of light is approximately 3×10^8 m/s.

C. Describe what happens when the refracted angle is 90° and what happens when the refracted angle is greater than 90°.

D. The critical angle for total internal reflection occurs when the refracted angle is 90°. Determine the critical angle for total internal reflection in a fiber optic cable.

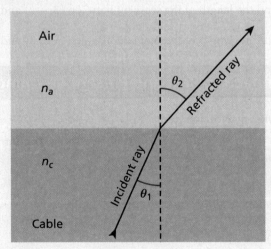

Are You Ready?

Complete these problems to review prior concepts and skills you will need for this module.

Write Equations for Proportional Reasoning

Write an equation to represent each relationship.

1.

x	16	20	24
y	64	80	96

2.

x	2	7	9
y	18	63	81

The Pythagorean Theorem and Its Converse

Find the missing side lengths in the right triangles.

3.

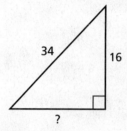

4.

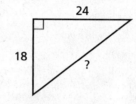

Determine whether each set of side lengths forms a right triangle.

5. 3, 4, 6

6. 18, 24, 30

Distance and Midpoint Formulas

Use the Distance Formula or Midpoint Formula to describe each line segment.

7. Find the midpoint of the segment between $(-4, 4)$ and $(2, 4)$.

8. Find the midpoint of the segment between $(1, -2)$ and $(-5, -2)$.

9. Find the length of the segment between $(3, -2)$ and $(3, 3)$.

10. Find the length of the segment between $(-2, 3)$ and $(-2, -1)$.

Connecting Past and Present Learning

Previously, you learned:

- to understand that by similarity, side ratios in right triangles are properties of the angles,
- to use the Pythagorean Theorem to solve problems, and
- to define trigonometric ratios for acute angles.

In this module, you will learn:

- to define the radian measure of an angle,
- to extend the definition of trigonometric functions using the unit circle, and
- to prove and use the trigonometric identity $\sin^2 \theta + \cos^2 \theta = 1$.

15.1

Angles of Rotation and Radian Measure

(I Can) mathematically express the relationship between the unit circle and radian measure.

Spark Your Learning

At an air force base, pilots train on a human centrifuge.

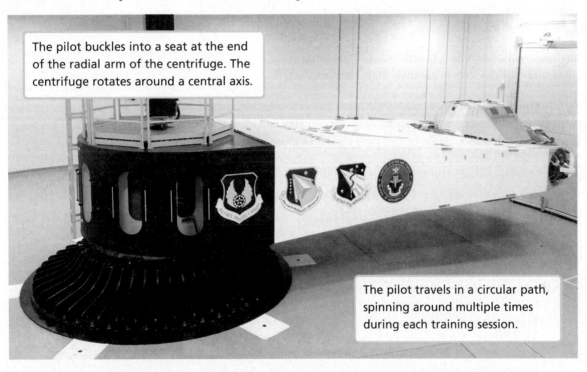

The pilot buckles into a seat at the end of the radial arm of the centrifuge. The centrifuge rotates around a central axis.

The pilot travels in a circular path, spinning around multiple times during each training session.

Complete Part A as a whole class. Then complete Parts B–D in small groups.

A. What is a mathematical question you can ask about this situation? What information would you need to know to answer your question?

B. What formula(s) will be needed to answer your question?

C. To answer your question, what strategy and tool would you use along with all the information you have? What answer do you get?

D. Does your answer make sense in the context of the situation? How does the speed relate to a car on a highway traveling 60 mph?

Turn and Talk How would your answer change if the pilot's seat on the centrifuge were moved closer to the central axis? Explain your answer.

©U.S. Department of Defense

Module 15 • Lesson 15.1

437

Build Understanding

Analyze Angles of Rotation and Identify Coterminal Angles

In trigonometery, an **angle of rotation** θ is an angle formed by the starting and ending positions of a ray that rotates about its endpoint. In *standard position*, the endpoint of the ray is at the origin of a coordinate plane and the *initial side* of the angle lies along the positive *x*-axis. A curved arrow is used to indicate the direction of rotation from the starting position to the ending position of the ray. The ending position of the ray is called the *terminal side* of the angle.

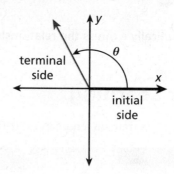

The angle of rotation can be counterclockwise (positive angle measures) or clockwise (negative angle measures).

When the terminal sides of two angles of different measure coincide, they are called **coterminal angles**. The angles you encountered in geometry had measures between 0° and 180°. Angles of rotation however, can have measures greater than 180° or less than 0°.

1 The angles with measures of 214° and −146° are shown.

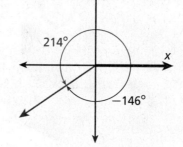

- **A.** Identify the initial side and terminal side of each angle. How are the angles related? How are they different?

- **B.** Are there any other angles that would be coterminal with the angles shown? Explain how you know.

- **C.** Sketch a pair of coterminal angles in Quadrant I. Explain the relationship between your angles.

The angle with 431° is shown.

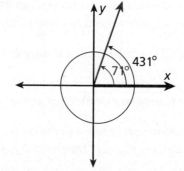

- **D.** What does the curved arrow tell you about the angle?

- **E.** How could you find a positive coterminal angle? How could you find a negative coterminal angle?

- **F.** Is it possible to identify other coterminal angles? Draw a sketch to support your answer.

 Turn and Talk How could you find several coterminal angles for a 102° angle of rotation? Write expressions to model the measures of all such coterminal angles.

Investigate the Relationship Between Arc Length and Radius

Recall that the radius of a circle is the distance from the center to a point on the circle, and an arc is a portion of the circumference of a circle.

 The diagram shows three circles with radii 1 unit, 2 units, and 3 units, centered at the origin. A central angle of 200° creates arcs $\overset{\frown}{ABC}$, $\overset{\frown}{DEF}$, and $\overset{\frown}{GHI}$ between the initial side and the terminal side of the angle.

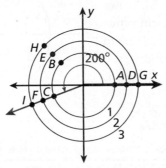

A. What are the similarities and differences of $\overset{\frown}{ABC}$, $\overset{\frown}{DEF}$, and $\overset{\frown}{GHI}$?

B. Compare the lengths of $\overset{\frown}{ABC}$, $\overset{\frown}{DEF}$, and $\overset{\frown}{GHI}$ without any calculations. What do you notice about the relationship between the corresponding radius and the arc length?

C. What is the ratio of the number of degrees in the central angle given to the number of degrees in a full circle? What does this ratio represent?

D. The length of an arc is the portion of the entire circumference represented by the arc. What do each of the following calculations represent? Explain how you know.

$$\left(2\pi(1)\right)\left(\frac{5}{9}\right) = \frac{10\pi}{9} \qquad \left(2\pi(2)\right)\left(\frac{5}{9}\right) = \frac{20\pi}{9} \qquad \left(2\pi(3)\right)\left(\frac{5}{9}\right) = \frac{30\pi}{9}$$

E. Find the ratio of the arc length to the radius for $\overset{\frown}{ABC}$, $\overset{\frown}{DEF}$, and $\overset{\frown}{GHI}$. What do you notice?

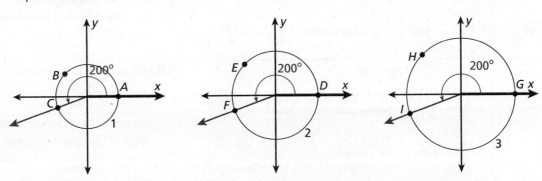

 Turn and Talk Suppose the central angle were 135° instead of 200°. Compare the ratios of the arc length to the radius for the arcs $\overset{\frown}{ABC}$, $\overset{\frown}{DEF}$, and $\overset{\frown}{GHI}$.

Step It Out

Convert Between Degree Measure and Radian Measure

Previously you have worked with degree measurements such as 360° in a full circle and 180° degrees in a straight angle. Angles can also be measured using the ratio of the arc of length s to the radius r of the circle on which the arc lies, giving the **radian measure** $\theta = \frac{s}{r}$. The diagram shows a **unit circle**, which is a circle centered at the origin with radius 1. The angle that creates an arc equal in measure to the radius is called 1 *radian*. On a unit circle, 1 radian is the measure of an angle that intercepts the arc of length 1.

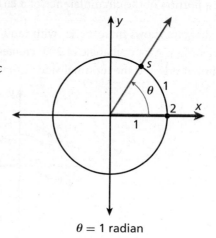

$\theta = 1$ radian

There are 360° in a full circle and the arc length of a full circle is equal to the circumference, $s = 2\pi r$. So there are $\frac{2\pi r}{r} = 2\pi$ radians in a full circle. This gives a conversion factor of $\frac{360°}{2\pi \text{ radians}} = \frac{180°}{\pi \text{ radians}}$ as shown in the table below.

Convert Angle Measure	
Convert degrees to radians	**Convert radians to degrees**
(measure of angle in degrees)$\left(\dfrac{\pi \text{ radians}}{180°}\right)$	(measure of angle in radians)$\left(\dfrac{180°}{\pi \text{ radians}}\right)$

3 Convert each measure from degrees to radians or from radians to degrees.

Degree measure	Radian measure
15°	$15° \cdot \dfrac{\pi}{180°} = \dfrac{\pi}{12}$
700°	$700° \cdot \dfrac{\pi}{180°} = \dfrac{35\pi}{9}$
−315°	$-315° \cdot \dfrac{\pi}{180°} = -\dfrac{7\pi}{4}$
$\dfrac{\pi}{3} \cdot \dfrac{180°}{\pi} = 60°$	$\dfrac{\pi}{3}$
$-\dfrac{4\pi}{3} \cdot \dfrac{180°}{\pi} = -240°$	$\dfrac{4\pi}{3}$
$\dfrac{11\pi}{6} \cdot \dfrac{180°}{\pi} = 330°$	$\dfrac{11\pi}{6}$

A. Why is a conversion factor with degrees in the denominator used when converting 15° to radians? How do you know when to use the different conversion factors?

B. What do you notice about the sign of the angle in the equivalent degree and radian measures? Explain what the sign of the angle indicates.

Turn and Talk What are the radian measures for each angle with a multiple of 30° found in a unit circle?

Solve a Real-World Problem Involving Arc Length

The equation $\theta = \frac{s}{r}$ describes the relationship among three variables: a central angle θ, the arc length created by that angle s, and the radius r. Rewriting this equation gives the arc length formula $s = r\theta$.

Arc Length Formula (radians)
For a circle of radius r, the arc length s intercepted by a central angle θ (in radians) is given by the formula: $$s = r\theta$$

Real-world problems involving circular rotation about a center point may involve arc length, or the distance an object travels. Real-world problems may also describe *angular velocity*, or the rotational speed of an object. The angular velocity of an object may be expressed as the angle measure through which an object rotates over the time it takes the object to travel along the arc.

 4 Jupiter has a radius of about 71,500 kilometers at its equator. What is the angular velocity (in radians per hour) of a point on Jupiter's equator? How far around Jupiter's axis does the point travel in one hour? How does this distance compare with the distance of about 40,075 kilometers traveled by a point on Earth's equator in one day?

Find the angular velocity.

The point travels 2π radians in one revolution. So a point on Jupiter's equator travels $\frac{2\pi}{9.9}$ radians per hour. This measure provides the angle of rotation in one hour.

A point on Jupiter's equator makes a full revolution once every 9.9 hours.

Find the distance traveled.

The distance the point travels is the length of the arc s intercepted by the angle of rotation θ for the given interval of time.

A. How many radians does the point travel in half of a revolution?

$s = r\theta$

$= 71,500\left(\dfrac{2\pi}{9.9}\right)$

B. What are the units of arc length? How do you know?

$\approx 45,378.6$

So, a point on Jupiter's equator travels about 45,378.6 kilometers around Jupiter's axis in one hour.

This is almost the same distance that a point travels around Earth's equator in one *day* on Earth. Since there are 24 hours in a day, this means that a point on Jupiter's equator travels more than 24 times as fast as a point on Earth's equator.

 Turn and Talk How would your answer change if the angle of rotation were measured in degrees?

Check Understanding

1. Identify the following statements about coterminal angles as *sometimes*, *always*, or *never true*. Explain your answer.

   A. The terminal side lies in the same quadrant.

   B. The direction of rotation is the same.

   C. The sum of the angle measures is 360°.

2. Describe the relationship between the radius of a circle centered at the origin and the length of an arc intercepted by a central angle.

3. What is the radian measure for a central angle of 180°?

4. The minute hand on a clock is 4 inches long. The hour hand is 3.5 inches long. What is the difference in the distance traveled by the tip of the hour hand and the tip of the minute hand each hour?

On Your Own

5. **MP** **Reason** Is it possible for two different acute angles to be coterminal? Is it possible for two different obtuse angles to be coterminal? Explain why or why not.

Determine whether each pair of given angles in standard position are coterminal. Sketch a graph to support your answer.

6. 65°, 425°

7. 122°, 842°

8. 33°, −337°

9. 75°, −285°

10. −15°, −375°

11. −114°, −474°

Sketch a graph of each indicated angle for the given angle in standard position.

12. a negative coterminal angle

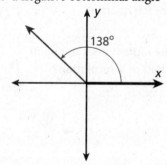

13. a positive coterminal angle

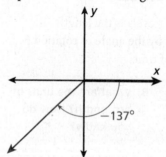

14. a negative coterminal angle

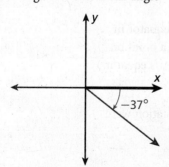

15. a positive coterminal angle

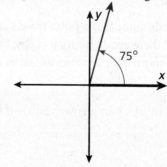

For each given angle, find the nearest two positive coterminal angles and the nearest two negative coterminal angles.

16. 40°

17. 220°

18. −130°

19. (MP) **Use Structure** There are two circles such that one has a radius that is twice the radius of the other. Each circle has an arc with the same central angle. What is the relationship between the arc lengths in the two circles? Explain.

Convert each measure from degrees to radians or from radians to degrees.

20. 50°

21. 270°

22. −340°

23. −36°

24. $\dfrac{4\pi}{3}$

25. $-\dfrac{9\pi}{4}$

26. $-\dfrac{\pi}{9}$

27. $\dfrac{4\pi}{5}$

28. 3π

29. Music A metronome is a device used by musicians to maintain a steady beat. The pendulum creates repeated clicking sounds (beats), at an adjustable pace, as the weight swings from side to side.

A. What is the per beat length of the arc traveled by the weight when it is positioned 4 centimeters from the point of rotation?

B. What is the distance the weight travels each beat when the weight is moved an additional 2 centimeters toward the top of the metronome?

C. Will the tempo (time between beats) increase or decrease when the weight is moved away from the point of rotation? Explain.

30. What is the angular velocity (in radians per second) of a gear turning at 30 revolutions per minute (rpm)?

31. Use the clock shown at the right.

A. What is the angle (in radians) between the hour hand and minute hand of a clock at 10:15?

B. What is the angular velocity of the minute hand in radians per minute? What is the angular velocity of the hour hand in radians per minute?

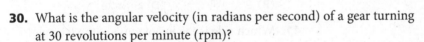

32. A Ferris wheel is circular with passenger cars positioned along the circumference of the circle. The distance from the center of a Ferris wheel to a passenger car is 70 feet. It takes 40 seconds for the Ferris wheel to complete one full rotation.

A. What is the length of the arc each passenger car travels in one minute?

B. How would the distance traveled change if the cars were moved closer to the center of the Ferris wheel? How would this affect the angular velocity? Explain.

C. (MP) **Reason** Are larger Ferris wheels always faster than smaller Ferris wheels? Explain why or why not.

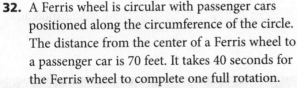

33. STEM Mars completes one rotation about its axis every 24.6 hours. The equatorial circumference is about 13,263 miles. How far does a point on the equator of Mars travel in one hour?

34. A 90-horsepower outboard motor rotates its propeller at different speeds (in revolutions per minute) based on the throttle setting as shown. How does the angular velocity (in radians per minute) of the propeller at full throttle compare to the angular velocity at reduced throttle?

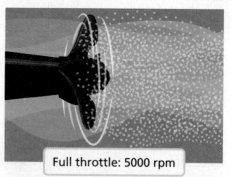

Full throttle: 5000 rpm

35. (MP) **Use Structure** Which quantity is greater: 1 radian or 1 degree? Explain.

36. (MP) **Reason** Shane reads an angle measure of 34.5. He claims that the unit of measure must be degrees since the measure is a decimal. Is Shane correct? Explain why or why not.

37. (MP) **Use Structure** How can you tell when an angle using degree measure is greater than a full revolution in the positive or negative direction? How can you tell the same when the angle is expressed in radian measure?

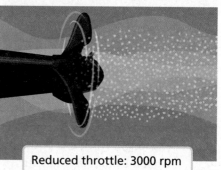

Reduced throttle: 3000 rpm

Spiral Review • Assessment Readiness

38. What is a recursive rule for the sequence defined by the points $(1, 7)$, $(2, 14)$, $(3, 28)$, $(4, 56)$?

Ⓐ $a_1 = 1, a_n = 7a_{n-1}$

Ⓑ $a_1 = 7, a_n = 2a_{n-1}$

Ⓒ $a_1 = 2, a_n = 7a_{n-1}$

Ⓓ $a_1 = 7, a_n = a_{n-1} + 7$

39. Which values are terms in the sequence below? Select all that apply.

$a_n = a_{n-1} + 10$
$a_1 = 29$

Ⓐ 9   Ⓓ 38

Ⓑ 19   Ⓔ 68

Ⓒ 29   Ⓕ 99

40. What is the sum of the infinite geometric series $1 + 0.5 + 0.25 + 0.125\ldots$?

Ⓐ 1.9   Ⓒ 2.25

Ⓑ 2   Ⓓ infinite

41. Which side is the hypotenuse of the triangle?

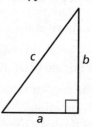

Ⓐ a Ⓒ c

Ⓑ b Ⓓ There is no hypotenuse.

I'm in a Learning Mindset!

How do my decisions about studying angles of rotation and radian measure impact my achievement?

Define and Evaluate the Basic Trigonometric Functions

(I Can) use the unit circle to define the trigonometric functions for all real numbers.

Spark Your Learning

Jonah is riding a Ferris wheel.

For half of the ride, Jonah is above the hub of the Ferris wheel.

Jonah's car

Hub

The height of Jonah's car changes as the angle it makes with the horizontal axis changes.

Complete Part A as a whole class. Then complete Parts B–D in small groups.

A. What is a mathematical question you can ask about this situation? What information would you need to know to answer your question?

B. What formula(s) will be needed to answer your question?

C. To answer your question, what strategy and tool would you use along with all the information you have? What answer do you get?

D. Does your answer make sense in the context of this situation? How do you know?

 Turn and Talk How would your solution pathway change if the Ferris wheel had a smaller radius? How would your work change if the car was below the *x*-axis?

© Wicki58/E+/Getty Images

Build Understanding

Use Special Right Triangles in a Unit Circle

When studying right triangle trigonometry in geometry, the functions sine, cosine, and tangent each represented a ratio of side lengths of a right triangle.

Sine, Cosine, and Tangent (for acute angle θ in a right triangle)		
$\sin\theta = \dfrac{\text{opposite}}{\text{hypotenuse}}$	$\cos\theta = \dfrac{\text{adjacent}}{\text{hypotenuse}}$	$\tan\theta = \dfrac{\text{opposite}}{\text{adjacent}}$

You also studied the relationship between the side lengths of special right triangles with angles of $45°-45°-90°$ and $30°-60°-90°$ as shown.

When one of these triangles has a hypotenuse that is 1 unit long, you can inscribe the triangle in the unit circle. You can use these triangles to find the value of the trigonometric functions for the angles 30°, 45°, and 60°.

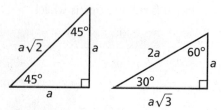

1 ▶ The special triangles shown below are each inscribed in a unit circle. A $30°-60°-90°$ triangle is shown in two different orientations. For each triangle, the coordinates of the point where the hypotenuse intersects the unit circle are given.

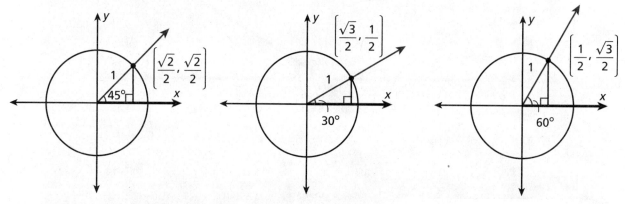

A. In each of the triangles shown above, how does the hypotenuse of the triangle relate to the radius of the circle?

B. How can you use the relationship between the sides of a $45°-45°-90°$ triangle or of a $30°-60°-90°$ triangle to determine the coordinates of the point where the hypotenuse of each triangle intersects the unit circle as shown?

C. Use the triangles to find the value of the trigonometric functions for the angle of rotation θ and complete the table.

D. How do the values of the trigonometric functions relate to the coordinates of the point of intersection of the hypotenuse and the unit circle?

E. Define each coordinate x and y of a point (x, y) on the unit circle in terms of a trigonometric function of the angle of rotation θ.

Angle (θ)		Values of trigonometric functions		
Degrees	Radians	$\sin\theta$	$\cos\theta$	$\tan\theta$
30°	$\dfrac{\pi}{6}$	?	?	?
45°	$\dfrac{\pi}{4}$	?	?	?
60°	$\dfrac{\pi}{3}$	?	?	?

Explore Basic Trigonometric Functions for Special Angles

In the previous task, you defined the coordinates (x, y) of the point on the unit circle where the radius intersects it as $x = \cos\theta$ and $y = \sin\theta$ based on your observations of special triangles in the first quadrant.

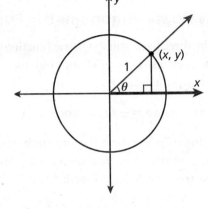

Now you use reflections to explore trigonometric functions of angles that have a terminal side in Quadrants II, III, and IV.

 A. A $45°-45°-90°$ triangle is inscribed in a unit circle in the first quadrant with one leg along the x-axis. The triangle is then reflected into each of the other three quadrants as shown. What are the coordinates of each of the points labeled A, B, and C? How could these coordinates be used to find sine, cosine, and tangent of the reflected angles in Quadrants II, III, and IV?

B. What is the value of the angle of rotation θ in a counterclockwise direction with a terminal side that passes through point A? Explain how you know. Then find the values of θ for the angles of rotation in a counterclockwise direction with a terminal side passing through point B and passing through point C.

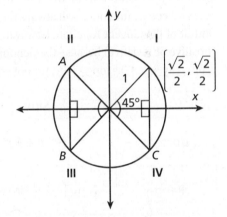

C. For a $30°-60°-90°$ triangle inscribed in a unit circle so that $\theta = 30°$, reflect the triangle into each of the other three quadrants. What are the coordinates of the point of intersection of the hypotenuse and the unit circle for each triangle? Use these coordinates to find sine, cosine, and tangent of the reflected angles in Quadrants II, III, and IV.

D. Repeat Part C for a $30°-60°-90°$ triangle inscribed in a unit circle so that $\theta = 60°$.

E. Identify the counterclockwise angles of rotation that result in the terminal side of the angle passing through the points identified in Parts C and D.

F. What do you notice about the signs of the values of sine, cosine, and tangent in each of the four quadrants? Use the coordinates of the points you identified in Parts A, C, and D to justify the information shown in the table.

Quadrant	Sign		
	sin	cos	tan
I	+	+	+
II	+	−	−
III	−	−	+
IV	−	+	−

 Turn and Talk What are the values of sine, cosine, and tangent of the angle $\frac{7\pi}{6}$? Explain how you can use reflections of a special triangle to determine these values.

Step It Out

Evaluate Trigonometric Functions Given a Point

The three basic trigonometric functions can be defined using the coordinates (x, y) of any point on a circle centered at the origin with radius r.

$$\sin\theta = \frac{y}{r} \qquad \cos\theta = \frac{x}{r} \qquad \tan\theta = \frac{y}{x}, x \neq 0$$

Using coordinates on the unit circle, you can determine that the sine and cosine functions can be defined for any angle θ. However, the tangent function is not defined when $x = 0$. This occurs when $\theta = -\frac{\pi}{2}, \frac{\pi}{2}, \frac{3\pi}{2}, \ldots, \frac{(2n+1)\pi}{2}$, where n is all integers. Because the values of the sine and cosine functions are coordinates of points on the unit circle, the output of the sine and cosine functions will always range from -1 to 1. The output of the tangent function, however, can be arbitrarily large (positive or negative) because the denominator can become arbitrarily small (as long as it does not equal 0).

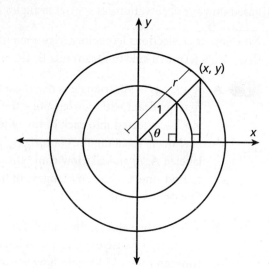

	Sine	Cosine	Tangent
Domain	$\{\theta \mid \theta \in \mathbb{R}\}$	$\{\theta \mid \theta \in \mathbb{R}\}$	$\left\{\theta \mid \theta \neq \dfrac{(2n+1)\pi}{2}, n \in \mathbb{Z}\right\}$
Range	$\{\sin\theta \mid -1 \leq \sin\theta \leq 1\}$	$\{\cos\theta \mid -1 \leq \cos\theta \leq 1\}$	$\{\tan\theta \mid \tan\theta \in \mathbb{R}\}$

Given a point on the terminal side of an angle of rotation, you can use the definitions above to evaluate the sine, cosine, or tangent ratios of any angle on the three corresponding trigonometric function's domain.

3   Find the values of sine, cosine, and tangent of θ.

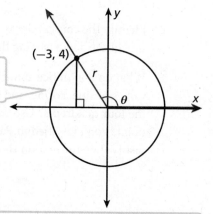

Find the value of r.

$r = \sqrt{x^2 + y^2}$

$= \sqrt{(-3)^2 + (4)^2}$

$= \sqrt{25}$

$= 5$

> **A.** Is this angle on the domain of all three functions? Explain.

> **B.** What theorem can you use to find the value of r?

Substitute.

Substitute the values for x, y, and r into the definitions of the trigonometric functions.

$$\sin\theta = \frac{y}{r} = \frac{4}{5} \qquad \cos\theta = \frac{x}{r} = -\frac{3}{5} \qquad \tan\theta = \frac{y}{x} = -\frac{4}{3}$$

> **C.** Explain how you can determine the sign of the value of each function before substitution.

 Turn and Talk What are the values of sine, cosine, and tangent of θ given that a point on the terminal side of the angle θ is $(-5, -12)$?

Use Trigonometric Functions to Solve a Real-World Problem

You can use trigonometric functions to solve real-world problems involving right triangles or circular rotation.

4 An airplane begins its scheduled descent at an angle of $-3°$ to the horizontal. What is its change in elevation after it flies 6000 feet horizontally toward the runway? If the plane begins at an elevation of 3200 feet, at what horizontal distance from the runway must it begin its descent?

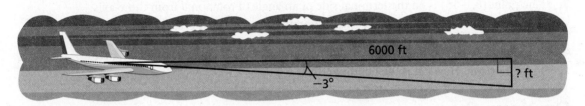

Use the position of the plane at the beginning of its descent as the origin. The horizontal distance traveled by the plane is then the x-coordinate and the vertical change in elevation is the y-coordinate.

You can use the relationship among the angle of descent, the elevation change, and the horizontal distance to find the change in elevation.

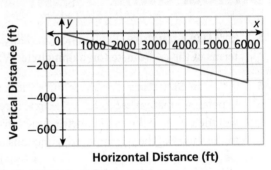

$$\tan\theta = \frac{y}{x}$$

$$\tan(-3°) = \frac{y}{6000}$$

$$6000\tan(-3°) = y$$

$$y \approx -314.447$$

A. Why is the tangent function used instead of sine or cosine?

B. What mode of angle measurement should you use with your calculator? How do you know?

Over 6000 horizontal feet, the plane's elevation decreases about 314 feet.

The elevation change will be -3200 feet by the time the plane reaches the runway. Use the relationship among the angle of descent, the elevation change, and the horizontal distance.

$$\tan\theta = \frac{y}{x}$$

$$\tan(-3°) = \frac{-3200}{x}$$

$$x = \frac{-3200}{\tan(-3°)}$$

$$x \approx 61{,}060$$

C. Why is the unknown in the denominator?

So, the plane will need to begin its descent at a horizontal distance of about 61,060 feet, or about 11.6 miles, from the runway.

Turn and Talk What would the change in elevation be if the plane was descending at an angle of $-4°$ and the plane flew 4000 feet horizontally?

Check Understanding

1. Why is a 30°–60°–90° triangle inscribed in a unit circle in two different orientations in Task 1?

2. Consider the point of intersection (x, y) of a unit circle and the terminal side of any given angle θ. Explain how the signs of the basic trigonometric functions in all four quadrants are justified by the signed values of the coordinates of this point.

3. The point $(8, -15)$ is on the terminal side of an angle of rotation θ from the x-axis. What are the values of the three basic trigonometric functions of the angle θ?

4. A building casts a 24-meter long shadow when the sun is at an angle of 75° relative to the horizon. How tall is the building?

On Your Own

5. (MP) **Use Structure** Explain how to define the sine and cosine of an angle in terms of the coordinates on a unit circle. Why does this definition work?

6. (MP) **Use Structure** A right triangle with one leg along the x-axis and a hypotenuse that intersects the unit circle is reflected into the third quadrant. How will the values of the trigonometric functions of the new angle of rotation be related to the values of the trigonometric functions of the original angle of rotation?

7. (MP) **Use Structure** A right triangle with side lengths of 3, 4, and 5 units has an angle of 36.9°. A similar right triangle with an angle of approximately 36.9° is inscribed in the first quadrant of the unit circle as shown. Use reflections to complete the table for the three basic trigonometric functions.

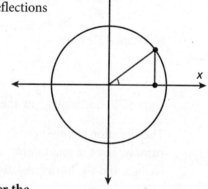

Angle of rotation, θ	36.9°	143.1°	216.9°	323.1°
$\sin \theta$	?	?	?	?
$\cos \theta$	?	?	?	?
$\tan \theta$	?	?	?	?

Without actually evaluating the trigonometric function, state whether the result will be positive or negative.

8. $\sin 225°$

9. $\cos 300°$

10. $\tan 150°$

11. $\sin \dfrac{11\pi}{6}$

12. $\cos\left(-\dfrac{\pi}{4}\right)$

13. $\tan \dfrac{5\pi}{3}$

Identify the quadrant of the terminal side of each angle that has the following trigonometric values.

14. Sine is positive and tangent is negative.

15. Cosine and sine are negative.

16. Cosine and tangent are positive.

Use the given point on the terminal side of an angle of rotation θ to evaluate the three basic trigonometric functions of θ.

17.

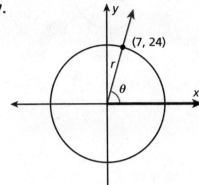

18.

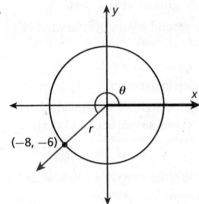

19.

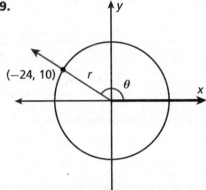

20.

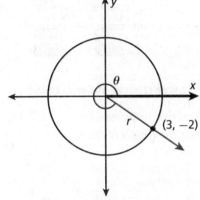

21. (MP) **Use Structure** Use the unit circle and quadrant locations to prove that $\cos(-\theta) = \cos\theta$ for any angle θ.

22. (MP) **Critique Reasoning** Jenna says that the tangent of the angle of rotation θ from the *x*-axis with a terminal side that passes through the point $(-3, 1)$ is -3. Describe the error in her reasoning and find the correct value of $\tan\theta$.

Use a calculator to evaluate the trigonometric function of each angle given in degrees or radians. Round to the nearest thousandth, if necessary.

23. $\sin(-340°)$

24. $\tan 125°$

25. $\cos(-100°)$

26. $\sin\dfrac{\pi}{12}$

27. $\cos\dfrac{4\pi}{5}$

28. $\tan\left(-\dfrac{3\pi}{5}\right)$

29. Two scuba divers are diving at different depths along the same line of sight to the boat as shown. Diver A is 120 feet deep and Diver B is 150 feet deep.

   A. Which trigonometric function would you use to find the distance each diver is from the boat along the line of sight? Explain why.

   B. How much farther from the boat along the line of sight is Diver B than Diver A?

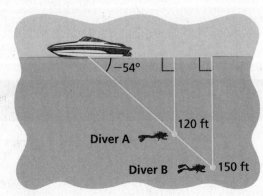

30. Amy swings back and forth on a swing. The ropes of the swing are 3 meters long and the seat of the swing sits 0.5 meter above the ground when at rest.

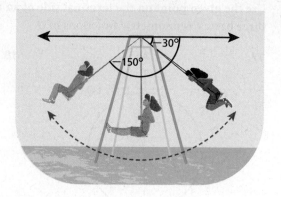

A. How far from the ground is Amy at either end of her swing?

B. What horizontal distance does Amy travel from one end of the swing to the other?

C. How much will her vertical and horizontal distances change if Amy swings back and forth from $-135°$ to $-45°$?

31. (Open Middle™) Using the integers -9 to 9, at most one time each, fill in the boxes to find the function's least possible value.

$$\sin \frac{\square \pi}{\square} = \frac{\sqrt{\square}}{\square}$$

Spiral Review • Assessment Readiness

32. A right triangle has legs that measure 8 cm and 6 cm. What is the length of the hypotenuse?

Ⓐ 4 cm

Ⓑ 10 cm

Ⓒ 12 cm

Ⓓ 14 cm

33. What is a recursive rule for the sequence 5, 15, 45, 135, . . .?

Ⓐ $a(1) = 5; a(n) = a(n - 1) + 10$

Ⓑ $a(1) = 5; a(n) = 3 \cdot a(n - 1)$

Ⓒ $a(1) = 3; a(n) = 5 \cdot a(n - 1)$

Ⓓ $a(1) = 5; a(n + 1) = 3 \cdot a(n - 1)$

34. Match each angle to the quadrant in which its terminal side lies.

Angle	Quadrant
A. $\frac{9\pi}{4}$	**1.** Quadrant I
B. $-\frac{\pi}{4}$	**2.** Quadrant II
C. $194°$	**3.** Quadrant III
D. $-557°$	**4.** Quadrant IV

I'm in a Learning Mindset!

What steps am I taking to direct my own learning with trigonometric functions?

Use a Pythagorean Identity

(I Can) use a given trigonometric function value to calculate the values of other trigonometric functions by means of a Pythagorean identity.

Spark Your Learning

The Leaning Tower of Pisa was reinforced in 1990 to help support the structure.

The tower was built in the 12th century on ground that was unable to support the tower's weight.

The tower slowly tilted over time, beginning even while it was being constructed.

Complete Part A as a whole class. Then complete Parts B–D in small groups.

A. What is a mathematical question you can ask about this situation? What information would you need to know to answer your question?

B. What formula(s) will be needed to answer your question?

C. To answer your question, what strategy and tool would you use along with all the information you have? What answer do you get?

D. Does your answer make sense in the context of the situation? How do you know?

 Turn and Talk How would your work change for a slope of 15? for a horizontal overhang of 4.2 meters?

Build Understanding

Prove a Pythagorean Identity

When the terminal ray of an angle θ intersects the unit circle at a point (x, y), then $x = \cos\theta$ and $y = \sin\theta$, and therefore the ratio $\frac{y}{x} = \tan\theta$. Combining these facts yields the trigonometric identity $\tan\theta = \frac{\sin\theta}{\cos\theta}$, which is true for all values of θ where $\cos\theta \neq 0$.

The following task derives another identity using the Pythagorean Theorem, which is why this trigonometric identity is known as a *Pythagorean identity*.

1 ▶ In the figure at the right, angle θ is drawn with its terminal side intersecting the unit circle at the point (a, b). Drawing a vertical segment from the point down to the x-axis creates a right triangle.

A. How are the lengths of the legs of the right triangle, a and b, related to the value of θ? Explain how you determined your answers.

Now that a right triangle has been created, the Pythagorean Theorem can be used to write an equation relating the lengths of the sides of the triangle. Using the expressions for the lengths determined in Figure 1 leads to an equation relating the sine and cosine functions.

B. How would you justify each of the steps shown in the calculations below?

$$a^2 + b^2 = c^2$$

$$(\cos\theta)^2 + (\sin\theta)^2 = 1^2$$

$$\cos^2\theta + \sin^2\theta = 1$$

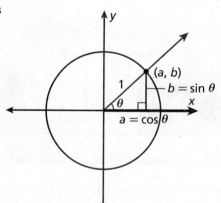

In the final step, notice how the power of a trigonometric function, such as $(\cos\theta)^2$, can also be written without using parentheses: $(\cos\theta)^2 = \cos^2\theta$.

C. The final step of the calculation above is typically written as $\sin^2\theta + \cos^2\theta = 1$. Which algebraic property justifies rewriting the equation in this form?

 Turn and Talk How would your reasoning be affected if the point (a, b) had been in Quadrant II, Quadrant III, or Quadrant IV, where either or both of a and b would be negative?

Step It Out

Find the Value of Trigonometric Functions Given the Value of $\sin\theta$ or $\cos\theta$

By rewriting the Pythagorean identity, you can express both $\sin\theta$ and $\cos\theta$ in terms of the other. Each version involves both positive and negative square roots. The sign is determined by the quadrant in which the terminal side of the angle θ lies.

Pythagorean Identities		
Standard form	**Solved for $\sin\theta$:**	**Solved for $\cos\theta$:**
$\sin^2\theta + \cos^2\theta = 1$	$\sin\theta = \pm\sqrt{1 - \cos^2\theta}$	$\cos\theta = \pm\sqrt{1 - \sin^2\theta}$

2 ▶ Given that $\sin\theta \approx 0.434$ where $0 < \theta < \frac{\pi}{2}$, find the value of $\cos\theta$.

$$\cos\theta = \pm\sqrt{1 - \sin^2\theta}$$

A. In what quadrant does θ lie?

$$= \pm\sqrt{1 - (0.434)^2}$$

B. How would sketching the triangle help you choose the correct sign here?

$$\approx \pm 0.901$$

Since the value of the cosine function is positive in Quadrant I, $\cos\theta \approx 0.901$.

 Turn and Talk How would your solution response change if the domain were changed to $\frac{\pi}{2} < \theta < \pi$?

Find the Value of Trigonometric Functions Given the Value of $\tan\theta$

The identity $\tan\theta = \frac{\sin\theta}{\cos\theta}$ can be used to write two additional identities. Multiplying both sides of the identity by $\cos\theta$ gives $\sin\theta = \cos\theta\tan\theta$, and then dividing both sides of $\sin\theta = \cos\theta\tan\theta$ by $\tan\theta$ gives $\cos\theta = \frac{\sin\theta}{\tan\theta}$.

3 ▶ Given that $\tan\theta \approx 0.482$ where $\pi < \theta < \frac{3\pi}{2}$, find the value of $\sin\theta$ and $\cos\theta$.

Use the identity $\sin\theta = \cos\theta\tan\theta$ to write $\sin\theta$ in terms of just $\cos\theta$.

$$\sin\theta = \cos\theta\tan\theta \approx \cos\theta(0.482)$$

Now use the Pythagorean identity $\sin^2\theta + \cos^2\theta = 1$ to find $\cos\theta$. Then find $\sin\theta$.

A. Could the work have begun by writing $\cos\theta$ in terms of $\sin\theta$? Explain.

$$(0.482\cos\theta)^2 + \cos^2\theta \approx 1$$

$$0.232\cos^2\theta + \cos^2\theta \approx 1$$

B. What justifications can be given for the steps of the solution?

$$1.232\cos^2\theta \approx 1$$

$$\cos^2\theta \approx 0.812$$

$$\cos\theta \approx \pm 0.901$$

C. How do you know that the terminal side of θ lies in Quadrant III?

The terminal side of θ lies in Quadrant III, where cosine is negative.
So, $\cos\theta \approx -0.901$ and therefore $\sin\theta \approx \cos\theta(0.482) \approx -0.434$.

Check Understanding

1. How can you use a Pythagorean identity to relate the three basic trigonometric functions?

2. If $\cos\theta \approx 0.972$, can you show that $\sin\theta \approx 0.235$? Explain why or why not.

3. Given that $\tan\theta \approx -1.522$ where $\frac{3\pi}{2} < \theta < 2\pi$, explain how to find the values of $\sin\theta$ and $\cos\theta$.

On Your Own

4. Why does the Pythagorean identity only make sense for a reference angle that intersects a point on a unit circle?

5. (MP) **Use Structure** The coordinates of any point that lies on the unit circle where the terminal ray of an angle θ intersects the circle are $(x, y) = (\cos\theta, \sin\theta)$. Copy the figure at the right and use $\tan\theta = \frac{\sin\theta}{\cos\theta}$ to specify which trigonometric functions have positive values in each quadrant.

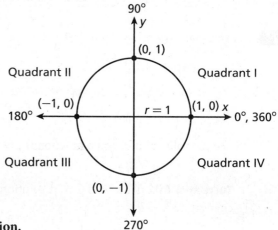

6. If the value of $\sin^2\theta$ is 0.143, what are the values of $\cos^2\theta$ and $\cos\theta$?

Find the approximate value of the trigonometric function.

7. Given that $\sin\theta \approx -0.345$ where $\pi < \theta < \frac{3\pi}{2}$, find the value of $\cos\theta$.

8. Given that $\sin\theta \approx 0.921$ where $0 < \theta < \frac{\pi}{2}$, find the value of $\cos\theta$.

9. Given that $\cos\theta \approx -0.993$ where $\frac{\pi}{2} < \theta < \pi$, find the value of $\sin\theta$.

10. Given that $\cos\theta \approx -0.817$ where $\pi < \theta < \frac{3\pi}{2}$, find the value of $\sin\theta$.

11. Given that $\sin\theta \approx -0.032$ where $\frac{3\pi}{2} < \theta < 2\pi$, find the value of $\cos\theta$.

12. Given that $\sin\theta \approx 0.829$ where $0 < \theta < \frac{\pi}{2}$, find the value of $\cos\theta$.

13. Given that $\cos\theta \approx 0.645$ where $\frac{3\pi}{2} < \theta < 2\pi$, find the value of $\sin\theta$.

14. Given that $\cos\theta \approx -0.719$ where $\frac{\pi}{2} < \theta < \pi$, find the value of $\sin\theta$.

15. Given that $\sin\theta \approx 0.974$ where $\frac{\pi}{2} < \theta < \pi$, find the value of $\cos\theta$.

16. Given that $\cos\theta \approx 0.139$ where $\frac{3\pi}{2} < \theta < 2\pi$, find the value of $\sin\theta$.

17. Given that $\sin\theta \approx 0.921$ where $0 < \theta < \frac{\pi}{2}$, find the value of $\cos\theta$.

18. Given that $\cos\theta \approx -0.985$ where $\pi < \theta < \frac{3\pi}{2}$, find the value of $\sin\theta$.

19. Given that $\sin\theta \approx 0.326$ where $\frac{\pi}{2} < \theta < \pi$, find the value of $\cos\theta$.

Find the approximate value of each trigonometric function.

20. Given that $\tan\theta \approx 1.876$ where $\pi < \theta < \frac{3\pi}{2}$, find the values of $\sin\theta$ and $\cos\theta$.

21. Given that $\tan\theta \approx 2.345$ where $0 < \theta < \frac{\pi}{2}$, find the values of $\sin\theta$ and $\cos\theta$.

22. Given that $\tan\theta \approx -0.549$ where $\frac{\pi}{2} < \theta < \pi$, find the values of $\sin\theta$ and $\cos\theta$.

23. Given that $\tan\theta \approx -6.430$ where $\frac{3\pi}{2} < \theta < 2\pi$, find the values of $\sin\theta$ and $\cos\theta$.

24. Given that $\tan\theta \approx -3.711$ where $\frac{\pi}{2} < \theta < \pi$, find the values of $\sin\theta$ and $\cos\theta$.

25. Given that $\tan\theta \approx 8.026$ where $\pi < \theta < \frac{3\pi}{2}$, find the values of $\sin\theta$ and $\cos\theta$.

26. Given that $\tan\theta \approx 2.773$ where $0 < \theta < \frac{\pi}{2}$, find the values of $\sin\theta$ and $\cos\theta$.

27. Given that $\tan\theta \approx -1.559$ where $\frac{3\pi}{2} < \theta < 2\pi$, find the values of $\sin\theta$ and $\cos\theta$.

For Problems 28–31, show that the Pythagorean identity $\sin^2\theta + \cos^2\theta = 1$ is true for the given angle.

28. $\theta = \dfrac{5\pi}{3}$

29. $\theta = -\dfrac{3\pi}{4}$

30. $\theta = \dfrac{11\pi}{6}$

31. $\theta = \dfrac{\pi}{4}$

32. Different NASCAR racetracks are banked at various degrees to allow the driver of the racecar to navigate the turns at a greater velocity. The mass of a racecar m, gravity g, coefficient of friction μ for the track surface, and the banking angle θ play a part in the physics behind the forces that keep the car on the track. At the instant when the tires of the car would begin to slide, the weight component, $mg \sin\theta$, is equal to the resistive force of friction, $\mu mg \cos\theta$.

A. Find the value of μ to the nearest hundredth for the track in Martinsville.

B. Is the coefficient of friction μ for the track in Talladega greater or less than that of Martinsville? Justify your answer.

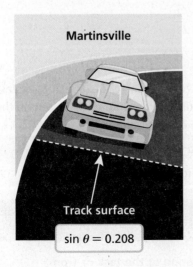

Martinsville

Track surface

$\sin\theta = 0.208$

Talladega

Track surface

$\sin\theta = 0.545$

33. A large stone block is placed on an inclined plane with an incline angle of θ. What is the approximate value of $\sin \theta$ when $\cos \theta \approx 0.543$?

34. Caden claims that he can use a Pythagorean identity to find the exact value instead of an approximation of $\sin \theta$ and $\cos \theta$ given $\tan \theta = \sqrt{3}$. Do you agree or disagree? Explain.

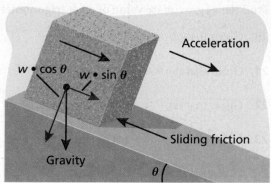

35. (MP) **Use Structure** The terminal side of θ intersects the unit circle in Quadrant I as shown. Complete the table and find the values of $\sin \theta$, $\cos \theta$, and $\sin^2 \theta + \cos^2 \theta$ using the reference angle in each of the four quadrants. What do you notice about the values of $\sin \theta$ and $\cos \theta$?

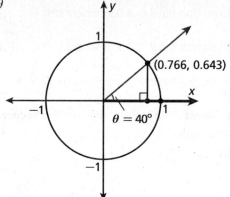

θ	$\sin \theta$	$\cos \theta$	$\sin^2 \theta + \cos^2 \theta$
40°	?	?	?
140°	?	?	?
220°	?	?	?
320°	?	?	?

36. (Open Middle™) Using the digits 0 to 9, at most one time each, fill in the boxes to make a true statement. Find at least two different sets of answers with different reference angles.

$$\sin \frac{\square \square \pi}{\square} = \cos \frac{\square \square \pi}{\square}$$

Spiral Review • Assessment Readiness

37. What is the third term in the sequence $a(n) = a(n-1) - 20$, where $a(1) = 15$?

Ⓐ −45   Ⓒ −10

Ⓑ −25   Ⓓ −5

38. What is the value of $y = \sin \theta$, when $\theta = \frac{\pi}{6}$?

Ⓐ $-\frac{\sqrt{2}}{2}$ Ⓒ $\frac{1}{2}$

Ⓑ $-\frac{1}{2}$ Ⓓ $\frac{\sqrt{3}}{2}$

39. What is the value of $\sin \frac{15\pi}{4}$?

Ⓐ $-\frac{\sqrt{2}}{2}$ Ⓒ $\frac{\sqrt{2}}{2}$

Ⓑ $-\frac{1}{2}$ Ⓓ $\frac{\sqrt{3}}{2}$

40. A tire with a diameter of 16 inches rotates 270°. Approximately how far does a point on the outside of the tire travel?

Ⓐ 8 in.   Ⓒ 38 in.

Ⓑ 19 in.   Ⓓ 75 in.

I'm in a Learning Mindset!

Did the mistakes I made stem from the level of challenge of the task or from my prior knowledge skill? What can I do differently next time?

Angles of Rotation

An angle of rotation θ is an angle formed by the initial and terminal positions of a ray that rotates about its endpoint.

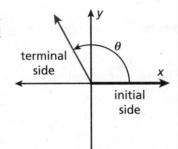

Coterminal angles are two angles with different measures whose terminal sides coincide when written in standard position.

Additional rotations of 360° create coterminal angles.

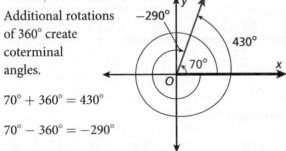

$70° + 360° = 430°$

$70° - 360° = -290°$

$70° \pm n \cdot 360°$, where n is an integer, describes all angles coterminal with 70°.

Radian Measure

A natural system for measuring angles compares the ratio of the arc length s to the radius r of the circle on which the arc lies.

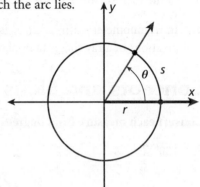

Radian measure $\theta = \dfrac{s}{r}$

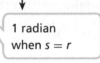

1 radian when $s = r$

Convert 60° to radians.

$(60°)\left(\dfrac{\pi \text{ radians}}{180°}\right) = \dfrac{\pi}{3} \text{ radians}$

Convert $\dfrac{\pi}{4}$ radians to degrees.

$\left(\dfrac{\pi}{4} \text{ radians}\right)\left(\dfrac{180°}{\pi \text{ radians}}\right) = 45°$

Trigonometric Functions

Trigonometric ratios are extended to non-acute angles through the unit circle.

$\cos(\theta)$ is the x-coordinate on the unit circle.

$\sin(\theta)$ is the y-coordinate on the unit circle.

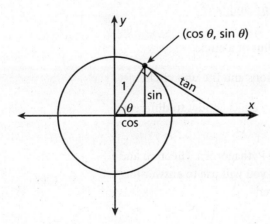

Pythagorean Identity

Considering the unit circle, $\sin\theta$ and $\cos\theta$ are related through the Pythagorean Identity.

$$a^2 + b^2 = r^2$$

$$\sin^2\theta + \cos^2\theta = 1$$

You can evaluate $\sin\theta$ knowing $\cos\theta$.

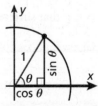

$$\sin^2\theta + \cos^2\theta = 1$$

$$\sin^2\theta = 1 - \cos^2\theta$$

$$\sin\theta = \pm\sqrt{1 - \cos^2\theta}$$

Substitute the known value of $\cos\theta$, such as $\cos\theta = 0.545$.

$$\sin\theta = \pm\sqrt{1 - \cos^2\theta}$$

$$= \pm\sqrt{1 - (0.545)^2}$$

The sign depends on the quadrant.

$$\approx \pm 0.838$$

Vocabulary

Choose the correct term from the box to complete each sentence.

Vocabulary
angle of rotation
coterminal angles
radian measure
reference angle

1. The ___?___ of an angle is measured as $\theta = \frac{s}{r}$.

2. When the terminal sides of two angles of different measure coincide, the angles are ___?___.

3. The ___?___ of a rotated angle is the acute angle from the terminal side of the rotation angle to the x-axis.

4. In trigonometery, a(n) ___?___ is an angle formed by the starting and ending positions of a ray that rotates about its endpoint.

Concepts and Skills

Convert each measure from degrees to radians or from radians to degrees.

5. $150°$

6. $\frac{4\pi}{9}$ radians

Determine whether the given angles in standard position are coterminal. Explain.

7. $30°, -300°$

8. $122°, -598°$

Find the nearest two positive coterminal angles and the nearest two negative coterminal angles.

9. $59°$

10. $192°$

Find the exact value of each trigonometric function.

11. $\sin \frac{3\pi}{4}$

12. $\tan \frac{11\pi}{6}$

Find the approximate value of each trigonometric function.

13. Given that $\sin\theta \approx -0.345$ where $\pi < \theta < \frac{3\pi}{2}$, find $\cos\theta$ and $\tan\theta$.

14. Given that $\cos\theta \approx -0.75$ where $\pi < \theta < \frac{3\pi}{2}$, find $\sin\theta$ and $\tan\theta$.

15. Explain the relationship between a radian and the radius of a circle.

16. Explain the relationship between trigonometric functions and the unit circle.

17. Use transformations to explain why the same reference angle applies to different positions on the unit circle.

18. (MP) **Use Tools** Explain the relationship between the Pythagorean Theorem and the Pythagorean Identity. State what strategy and tool you will use to answer the question, explain your choice, and then find the answer.

Graph Trigonometric Functions

Module Performance Task: *Spies and Analysts*™

Making **Waves**

How long is a paddle under water?

Are You Ready?

Complete these problems to review prior concepts and skills you will need for this module.

Fit Exponential Functions to Data

Create an exponential function that passes through each set of points.

1. $(1, 10), (2, 2), (4, 0.08)$

2. $(-4, 1), (-2, 9), (-1, 27)$

3. $\left(-2, \dfrac{1}{9}\right), (1, 24), (3, 864)$

4. $(-4, -512), (-1, -8), \left(2, -\dfrac{1}{8}\right)$

Transformations of Functions

Graph each function, $g(x)$, given the graph of $f(x)$.

5. $g(x) = f(x) - 3$

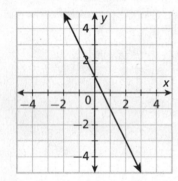

6. $g(x) = 2f(x + 2)$

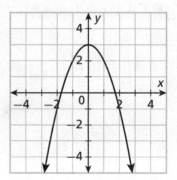

Graph Rational Functions

Graph each function.

7. $f(x) = \dfrac{4}{x}$

8. $f(x) = \dfrac{1}{x - 4} - 1$

Connecting Past and Present Learning

Previously, you learned:

• to compare two functions each represented a different way,

• to graph functions and identify key features of the graph, and

• to extend the domain of trigonometric functions using the unit circle.

In this module, you will learn:

• to graph trigonometric functions, showing period, midline, and amplitude,

• to transform trigonometric functions, and

• to model periodic phenomena with trigonometric functions.

Graph Sine and Cosine Functions

(I Can) identify the key features of the graphs of the sine and cosine functions.

Spark Your Learning

The pendulum swings back and forth.

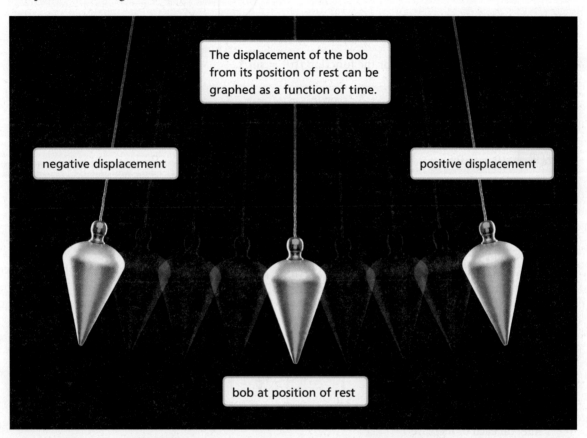

The displacement of the bob from its position of rest can be graphed as a function of time.

negative displacement

positive displacement

bob at position of rest

Complete Part A as a whole class. Then complete Parts B–D in small groups.

A. What is a mathematical question you can ask about this situation? What information would you need to know to answer your question?

B. What variables are involved in this situation? What unit of measurement would you use for each variable?

C. To answer your question, what strategy and tool would you use along with all the information you have? What answer do you get?

D. Does your answer make sense in the context of the situation? How do you know?

Turn and Talk How would your work change if the bob was moving twice as fast it does in the given data?

Build Understanding

Graph the Basic Sine and Cosine Functions

In the previous module, you learned that the coordinates (x, y) of any point on the unit circle are given by $(\cos\theta, \sin\theta)$ as shown.

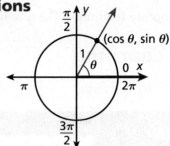

1 ▶ The table shows several values for the function $f(\theta) = \sin\theta$.

$\sin\theta$									
θ	0	$\dfrac{\pi}{6}$	$\dfrac{\pi}{2}$	$\dfrac{5\pi}{6}$	π	$\dfrac{7\pi}{6}$	$\dfrac{3\pi}{2}$	$\dfrac{11\pi}{6}$	2π
$f(\theta)$	0	0.5	1	0.5	0	−0.5	−1	−0.5	0

A. Look at the unit circle above and the values in the table. What appears to be the domain of $f(\theta) = \sin\theta$? What appears to be the range of $f(\theta) = \sin\theta$? What are the x- and y-intercepts of $f(\theta) = \sin\theta$?

B. How can you use the unit circle, the table, and your knowledge of coterminal angles to describe the values of $f(\theta) = \sin\theta$ over the domain $2\pi \le \theta \le 4\pi$ and over the domain $-2\pi \le \theta \le 0$?

C. The graph shows $f(\theta) = \sin\theta$ for $-2\pi \le \theta \le 4\pi$. Use the graph to identify the domain, range, maxima, minima, intercepts, at least one interval each of increase and decrease, end behavior, and whether the sine function is an even or odd function.

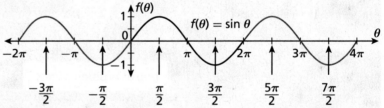

> **Turn and Talk** How can analysis of the unit circle figure help you verify the intervals where the graph is increasing and decreasing?

2 ▶ The table shows several values for the function $g(\theta) = \cos\theta$.

$\cos\theta$									
θ	0	$\dfrac{\pi}{3}$	$\dfrac{\pi}{2}$	$\dfrac{2\pi}{3}$	π	$\dfrac{4\pi}{3}$	$\dfrac{3\pi}{2}$	$\dfrac{5\pi}{3}$	2π
$g(\theta)$	1	0.5	0	−0.5	−1	−0.5	0	0.5	1

A. Look at the unit circle above and the values in the table. What appears to be the domain of $g(\theta) = \cos\theta$? What appears to be the range of $g(\theta) = \cos\theta$? What are the x- and y-intercepts of $g(\theta) = \cos\theta$?

B. How can you use the unit circle, the table, and your knowledge of coterminal angles to describe the values of $g(\theta) = \cos\theta$ over the domain $2\pi \leq \theta \leq 4\pi$ and over the domain $-2\pi \leq \theta \leq 0$?

C. The graph shows $g(\theta) = \cos\theta$ for $-2\pi \leq \theta \leq 4\pi$. Use the graph to identify the domain, range, maxima, minima, intercepts, at least one interval each of increase and decrease, end behavior, and whether the cosine function is an even or odd function.

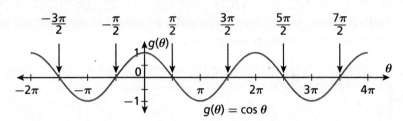

Turn and Talk Compare and contrast the graphs of the sine and cosine functions. What transformation of the graph of $g(\theta) = \cos\theta$ would make it coincide with the graph of $f(\theta) = \sin\theta$?

Graph $f(x) = a\sin\left(\frac{1}{b}x\right)$ or $g(x) = a\cos\left(\frac{1}{b}x\right)$

The sine and cosine functions are called **periodic functions** because they repeat their values over regular intervals on the horizontal axis. The length of this interval is called the function's **period**.

The graphs of the sine and cosine functions are shaped like waves. These waves have "crests" (where the function's maximum value occurs) and "troughs" (where the function's minimum value occurs). Halfway between these "crests" and "troughs" is the **midline** of the graph. The distance that the "crest" rises above the midline or the distance that the "trough" falls below the midline is called the graph's **amplitude**.

A. What are the period and amplitude of the basic sine and cosine graphs shown in the previous task?

B. Which type of transformations do you think will affect the period and the amplitude of a sine or cosine graph? Explain your reasoning.

C. The graphs of $f(x) = -4\sin(2x)$ and $g(x) = \frac{2}{3}\cos\left(-\frac{x}{4}\right)$ are shown below. What is the period and amplitude of each graph?

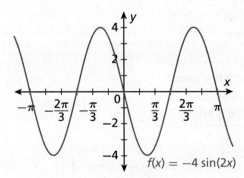

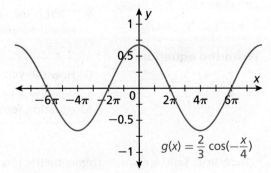

D. How do the period and the amplitude appear to relate to the variables a and b in the transformed functions $f(x) = a\sin\left(\frac{1}{b}x\right)$ and $g(x) = a\cos\left(\frac{1}{b}x\right)$?

Step It Out

Create $f(x) = a\sin\left(\frac{1}{b}x\right)$ or $g(x) = a\cos\left(\frac{1}{b}x\right)$ from a Graph

In the previous task, you saw that a and b are related to the amplitude and period of the functions $f(x) = a\sin\left(\frac{1}{b}\right)x$ and $g(x) = a\cos\left(\frac{1}{b}\right)x$.

Amplitude and Period of Sine and Cosine

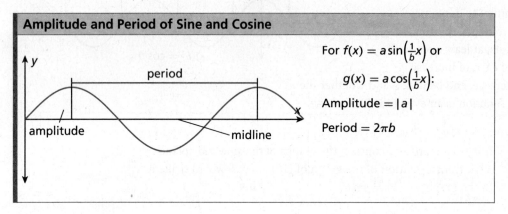

For $f(x) = a\sin\left(\frac{1}{b}x\right)$ or

$g(x) = a\cos\left(\frac{1}{b}x\right)$:

Amplitude $= |a|$

Period $= 2\pi b$

4 ▶ Given the graph of a trigonometric function, you can write its equation by using its key characteristics.

Identify the parent function.
Compare the y-intercept of the graph to the y-intercept of the graphs of sine and cosine. If no horizontal translation was performed, then the parent function is $y = \sin x$.

Identify the amplitude.
From the graph you can see that the maximum value is $\frac{1}{2}$ and the minimum value is $-\frac{1}{2}$. Halfway between these values is the midline, which is at $y = 0$. The amplitude a of the graph is $\frac{1}{2}$.

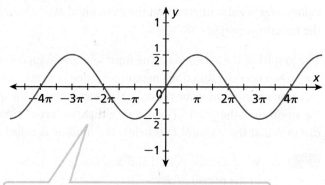

A. Is this a reflection of $y = \sin x$ or $y = \cos x$ over the x-axis? How would a reflection over the x-axis affect the value of a?

Identify the period.
The graph repeats itself in intervals of 4π. So, the period of the graph is 4π.

$2\pi b = 4\pi$

$b = 2$

B. What is the value of b in the parent function $y = \sin x$?

Write the equation.

$y = \frac{1}{2}\sin\left(\frac{1}{2}x\right)$

C. How can you use the values of a and b to write the equation for the graph?

 Turn and Talk For which trigonometric function would a reflection about the y-axis be indistinguishable from the graph of the function? Explain.

Create Models with Sine and Cosine Functions

Sine and cosine functions are useful for modeling real-world phenomena involving periodic behavior, such as sound waves. Each sound has a **frequency**, which is the number of cycles completed in a given unit of time. Since the period represents the amount of time it takes to complete one cycle, the frequency is the reciprocal of the period. The standard measure of frequency is Hertz (Hz), which is equivalent to one cycle per second.

A tuning fork is a simple metal prong that, when struck, emits a constant tone. Musicians use them to tune their instruments. Different size tuning forks vibrate at different speeds and cause fluctuations in the air pressure. This fluctuation has a maximum that is related to the sound wave's amplitude. The change in air pressure is typically measured in pascals.

$$\text{frequency} = \frac{1}{\text{period}}$$

5 For each sound wave, determine the frequency, write an equation to model the air pressure P (in pascals) as a function of time t (in seconds), and graph the function.

Use a sine function to model a sound wave with a period of 0.0025 second and an amplitude of 3 pascals.

Identify the frequency.

$$\text{frequency} = \frac{1}{\text{period}} = \frac{1}{0.0025} = 400\text{Hz}$$

Write equation.

$$P(t) = 3\sin\left(\left(\frac{2\pi}{0.0025}\right)t\right) = 3\sin 800\pi t$$

Graph function.

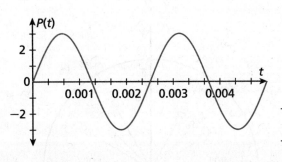

Use a cosine function to model a sound wave with a period of 0.005 second and an amplitude of 2 pascals.

Identify the frequency.

$$\text{frequency} = \frac{1}{\text{period}} = \frac{1}{0.005} = 200\text{Hz}$$

Write equation.

$$P(t) = 2\cos\left(\left(\frac{2\pi}{0.005}\right)t\right) = 2\cos 400\pi t$$

Graph function.

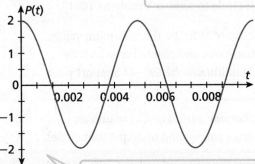

A. How are the period, frequency, and equation related?

B. How do you use the period and amplitude to graph each function?

Turn and Talk Suppose a sound wave had a period of 0.001 second and an amplitude of 4 pascals. What would the new frequency, equation, and graph of the sine function be?

Check Understanding

1. How are the intervals of increasing and decreasing behavior for the graphs of $f(x) = \sin x$ and $g(x) = \cos x$ similar? How are they different?

2. How can you use the symmetry of $g(\theta) = \cos\theta$ to graph the function for $\theta \leq 0$?

3. What type of transformation is related to the amplitude of a sine or cosine function? Explain.

4. The graph of a trigonometric function is shown.

   Write a cosine function to represent the graph.

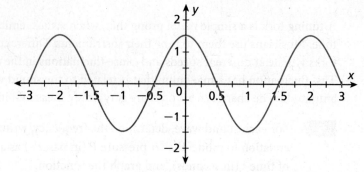

5. Use a sine function to graph a sound wave with a period of 0.003 second and an amplitude of 1.5 pascals. What is the frequency of the sound wave?

On Your Own

Identify each statement as true or false. If the statement is false, correct the statement to form a true statement.

6. The distance between consecutive x-intercepts for the graph of $f(x) = \sin x$ is $\frac{\pi}{2}$.

7. $\sin x < \cos x$ for all real values of x.

8. The graph of $f(x) = \cos x$ intercepts the y-axis at $(0, 1)$.

9. The graph of $f(x) = \sin x$ repeats on each interval of π.

Use the unit circle to answer Problems 10–13.

10. (MP) **Reason** Why are the maximum values of the basic sine and cosine curve 1? Why are their minimum values -1? Support your answer.

11. What does one period of $f(x) = \sin x$ or $f(x) = \cos x$ correspond to on the unit circle?

12. How does the unit circle relate to the periodic behavior of the sine and cosine functions?

13. How can the unit circle be used to explain why $g(x) = \cos 4x$ is a horizontal compression of the parent graph $f(x) = \cos x$?

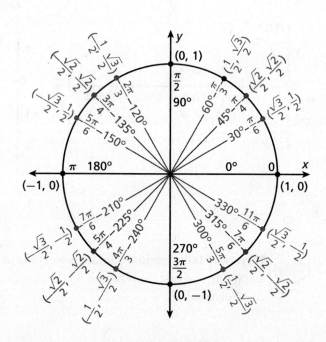

14. How does the period of the graph of a sine or cosine function relate to the value of b? Write an expression to find the period of a sine or cosine function given the value of b.

15. Describe a rotation that will map the graph of $f(\theta) = \sin\theta$ onto itself. How does this information help you to graph $f(-\theta)$?

16. (MP) **Critique Reasoning** Vera says that the equation of a sine function with a vertical stretch of 3 and a horizontal compression of $\frac{1}{3}$ is $y = 3\sin\frac{1}{3}x$. Explain her error and write the correct equation.

Identify the vertical stretch or compression a and the horizontal stretch or compression b for each trigonometric function. Then graph the function and identify the amplitude and period.

17. $y = 2\sin x$

18. $y = \frac{1}{2}\sin 4x$

19. $y = \cos\left(\frac{1}{5}x\right)$

20. $y = -3\cos 2\pi x$

Write an equation for each graph using the sine or cosine function.

21.

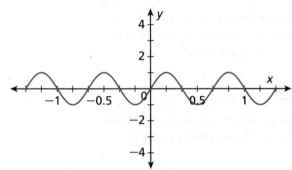

22.

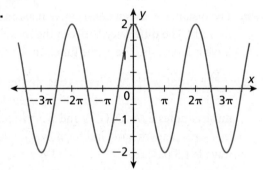

23.

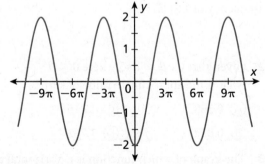

24.

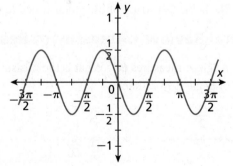

25. Scientists use ocean buoys to measure wave height and the time it takes the buoy to go from the highest point of a wave to the highest point of the next wave. Write an equation that represents the vertical position v, in feet, of the buoy shown as a function of time t, in seconds. Let $t = 0$ when the buoy is at its highest point.

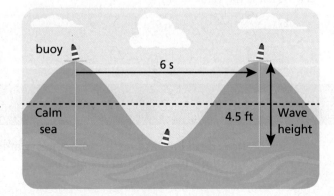

26. **A.** Write a cosine function to represent a sound wave with a period of 0.005 second and an amplitude of 5 pascals. Graph the function.

  B. Write a sine function to graph the same sound wave. Graph the function.

27. **STEM** A mass on a spring rests at its equilibrium position. The mass is pulled down vertically to the lowest position as shown before being released. Every 2 seconds, the mass oscillates from down to up to down again.

  A. Write a cosine function to represent the mass's vertical displacement relative to its equilibrium position over time.

  B. What is the amplitude of the function? What is the period of the function?

  C. Graph the cosine function you wrote in Part A.

  D. What are the points on the graph when the time after the mass is released is 0 seconds, 2.5 seconds, and 7 seconds? What do these points represent in the context of the mass?

28. The distance between consecutive maximum values of a sound wave is 0.004 seconds. The difference between the maximum and minimum displacement of the wave is 2 pascals. Use a sine function to model and graph the sound wave.

29. **(MP) Model with Mathematics** In the standard tuning, each of the six strings on a guitar are tightened so that the frequencies at which the strings vibrate create the musical notes E, A, D, G, B, and E. On a particular guitar, the 5th string vibrates so that string moves back and forth every 0.0096 second. The amplitude of the sound wave is 1.5 pascals.

  A. Use a sine function to model the sound wave for the 5th string.

  B. Is the 5th string of the guitar tuned to the correct frequency of 110 Hz?

Spiral Review • Assessment Readiness

30. Angle A measures 60°. What is the measure of angle A in radians?

  (A) $\frac{\pi}{2}$ (C) $\frac{\pi}{6}$

  (B) $\frac{\pi}{3}$ (D) $\frac{\pi}{60}$

31. What is the value of $\sin\left(\frac{5\pi}{6}\right)$?

  (A) $\frac{\sqrt{3}}{2}$ (C) $\frac{1}{2}$

  (B) $\frac{\sqrt{2}}{2}$ (D) $-\frac{\sqrt{2}}{2}$

32. Given that $\tan\theta \approx 1.45$ where $0 \leq \theta \leq \frac{\pi}{2}$, what is the approximate value of $\sin\theta$?

  (A) 0.568   (C) 1.215

  (B) 0.823   (D) 1.761

33. The graph of which function is a horizontal and vertical translation of the graph of $f(x)$?

  (A) $g(x) = -2f(-3x)$ (C) $g(x) = f(x+2) - 3$

  (B) $g(x) = f(2x) + 3$ (D) $g(x) = 2f(x+3)$

 I'm in a Learning Mindset!

How can I increase my performance related to graphing sine and cosine functions by modifying my mindset?

Graph Tangent Functions

(I Can) identify the key features of the graph of a tangent function.

Spark Your Learning

You can use a sundial to tell time by observing the shadow it casts.

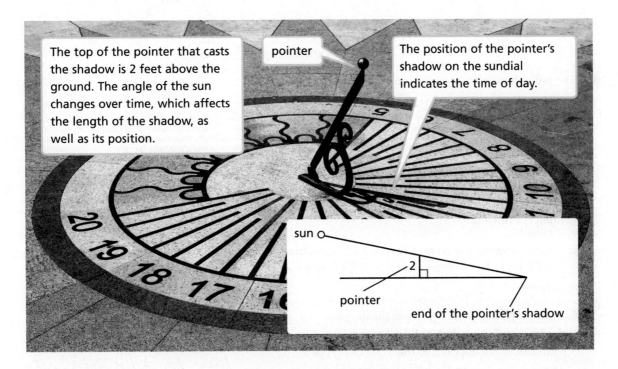

The top of the pointer that casts the shadow is 2 feet above the ground. The angle of the sun changes over time, which affects the length of the shadow, as well as its position.

pointer

The position of the pointer's shadow on the sundial indicates the time of day.

sun

2

pointer

end of the pointer's shadow

Complete Part A as a whole class. Then complete Parts B–D in small groups.

A. What is a mathematical question you can ask about this situation? What information would you need to know to answer your question?

B. What variables are involved in the situation? What unit of measurement would you use for each variable?

C. To answer your question, what strategy and tool would you use along with all the information you have? What answer do you get?

D. Does your answer make sense in the context of the situation? How do you know?

Turn and Talk Predict how your work would change if:
- The pointer was 3 feet above the ground.
- The angle changed by 10° per hour.

Build Understanding

Graph the Basic Tangent Function

Recall that $\tan \theta = \frac{\sin \theta}{\cos \theta}$. Using the coordinates of a point on the unit circle $(x, y) = (\cos \theta, \sin \theta)$, you can find the value of the tangent function from the ratio $\frac{y}{x}$.

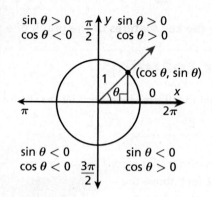

1 The table shows values for $f(\theta) = \tan \theta$.

θ	$-\frac{\pi}{2}$	$\frac{-\pi}{4}$	0	$\frac{\pi}{4}$	$\frac{\pi}{2}$
$f(\theta) = \tan \theta$	undefined	-1	0	1	undefined

A. Using the unit circle and the values in the table, what do you observe about the range of the tangent function? What appears to be the domain of the tangent function?

B. Some values of the tangent function are undefined. What do you think the graph looks like at those values of θ? Use the unit circle to support your answer.

C. The graph of $f(x) = \tan x$ over the domain $-2\pi \leq x \leq 2\pi$ is shown. Recall that x is in radians. What happens to the value of $f(x)$ as x approaches $\frac{\pi}{2}$ from the left? from the right? Does this support your prediction from Part B?

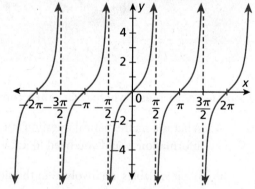

D. Identify the major characteristics of the tangent function: domain, range, intercepts, intervals of increase and decrease, positive and negative intervals, and end behavior.

E. What is the location of the two vertical asymptotes closest to the y-axis? How is the period of the function related to the vertical asymptotes? Explain.

F. Is the tangent function odd, even, or neither? Explain.

 Turn and Talk Compare the period of the graph of $f(x) = \tan x$ to the periods of the graphs of $f(x) = \sin x$ and $f(x) = \cos x$.

Graph $f(x) = a \tan\left(\frac{1}{b}x\right)$

You can use transformations such as reflections and vertical and horizontal stretches and compressions on the parent function $f(x) = \tan x$ to graph tangent functions of the form $f(x) = a \tan\left(\frac{1}{b}x\right)$. These transformations have the same effect on the graph of the parent tangent function as they do on graphs of other parent functions.

Vertical Asymptotes and Reference Points of $f(x) = a\tan\left(\frac{1}{b}x\right)$

For $f(x) = a\tan\left(\frac{1}{b}x\right)$:

- The vertical asymptotes closest to the y-axis are $x = \frac{-b\pi}{2}$ and $x = \frac{b\pi}{2}$.
- Reference points are located at $\left(\frac{-b\pi}{4}, -a\right)$ and $\left(\frac{b\pi}{4}, a\right)$, which correspond to the points $\left(\frac{-\pi}{4}, -1\right)$ and $\left(\frac{\pi}{4}, 1\right)$ on the graph of $f(x) = \tan x$.

2 Let $g(x) = -3\tan(2x)$ and $h(x) = \frac{2}{3}\tan\left(\frac{x}{3}\right)$.

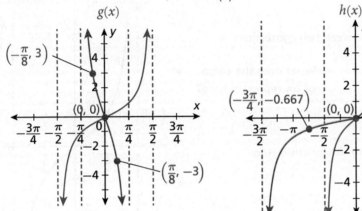

A. How is the transformed function $g(x)$ different from the parent function $f(x) = \tan x$? Describe how the period, domain, range, and locations of vertical asymptotes and reference points have changed.

B. How is the transformed function $h(x)$ different from the parent function $f(x) = \tan x$? Describe how the period, domain, range, and locations of vertical asymptotes and reference points have changed.

C. What are the values of a and b in $g(x)$? What are the values of a and b in $h(x)$? How do they appear to be related to any vertical or horizontal stretches or compressions or any reflections needed to produce this graph from the parent function?

D. When will the distance between the vertical asymptotes of a transformed tangent function of the form $g(x) = a\tan\left(\frac{1}{b}x\right)$ be greater than the distance between the vertical asymptotes of the parent tangent function $f(x) = \tan x$? When will the distance be less? Explain.

Turn and Talk Why is the vertical stretch parameter a referred to as the amplitude when transforming sine and cosine functions, but not tangent functions?

Step It Out

Create $f(x) = a\tan\left(\frac{1}{b}x\right)$ from a Graph

From its graph, you can write a tangent equation in the form $f(x) = a\tan\left(\frac{1}{b}x\right)$.

Identify the value of b from the spacing between the asymptotes. The separation between any two consecutive asymptotes is $b\pi$. Once you identify b, determine a by evaluating $\tan\left(\frac{x}{b}\right)$ at a recognizable point on the graph and then solving $f(x) = a\tan\left(\frac{1}{b}x\right)$ for a.

3 ▶ Look at the graph of a tangent function. Write an equation for the graph in the form $f(x) = a\tan\left(\frac{1}{b}x\right)$.

Find b from the distance between two consecutive asymptotes.

$$\pi - (-\pi) = b\pi$$
$$2\pi = b\pi$$
$$2 = b$$

> **A.** What does the value of $b\pi$ represent here?

Substitute the value of b into the function rule.

$$f(x) = a\tan\left(\frac{1}{2}x\right)$$

Use the point $\left(-\frac{\pi}{2}, 2\right)$ on the graph to find a.

$$2 = a\tan\left(\frac{-\frac{\pi}{2}}{2}\right)$$

> **B.** Could you use any point on the graph? Explain.

$$2 = a\tan\left(\frac{-\pi}{4}\right)$$

> **C.** How can you find the value of $\tan\left(-\frac{\pi}{4}\right)$?

$$2 = a(-1)$$

$$a = -2$$

The equation is $f(x) = -2\tan\left(\frac{x}{2}\right)$.

> **D.** How can you use the values of a and b to check that your equation $f(x) = -2\tan\left(\frac{x}{2}\right)$ for the graph is correct?

 Turn and Talk What is the value of b when two consecutive asymptotes are at $x = -\frac{1}{2}$ and $x = \frac{1}{2}$? What else do you need to know about the graph to write the equation of the function $f(x) = a\tan\left(\frac{1}{b}x\right)$?

Compare Tangent Functions Represented Differently

To compare tangent functions represented differently, identify key characteristics of each function. For example, asymptotes are easy to identify from graphs, equations, or tables. You can determine the period from the location of two consecutive asymptotes.

4 Compare the tangent functions by comparing their periods. The table shows $f(x)$ and the graph shows $g(x)$.

x	$-\dfrac{5\pi}{8}$	$-\dfrac{3\pi}{8}$	0	$\dfrac{3\pi}{8}$	$\dfrac{5\pi}{8}$
$f(x)$	undefined	-4	0	4	undefined

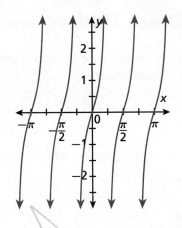

A. How can you identify the vertical asymptotes of a tangent function from a table?

Subtract two consecutive asymptotes to find the period of the tangent function.

$f(x)$ period:

$$\frac{5\pi}{8} - \left(-\frac{5\pi}{8}\right) = \frac{10\pi}{8} = \frac{5\pi}{4}$$

$g(x)$ period:

$$\frac{\pi}{4} - \left(-\frac{\pi}{4}\right) = \frac{2\pi}{4} = \frac{\pi}{2}$$

B. How can you identify the vertical asymptotes of a tangent function from a graph?

The period of $f(x)$ is greater than the period of $g(x)$.

Create Models with Tangent Functions

You can use a tangent function to model real-world problems that involve a perpendicular measure expressed as a function of a changing angle.

5 A rock climber is ascending the face of a 500-foot high vertical cliff. A friend is observing from 150 feet away. Write the climber's height as a function of the angle of elevation of the observer's line-of-sight to the climber.
Does the viewing angle ever reach 75°?

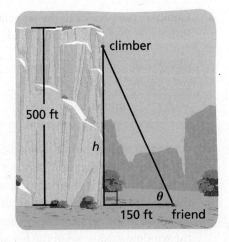

From the diagram, you can see that the height h of the climber and the distance 150 feet form two legs of a right triangle. Use this information to write $\tan\theta = \frac{h}{150}$.

A. Why do you use h instead of 500 in this equation?

The tangent function $h = 150\tan\theta$ gives the height of the climber as a function of the observer's viewing angle.

B. How can you find the maximum viewing angle?

C. In the context of the situation, what does the dashed line at $x = 90$ represent? What does the point $(0, 0)$ represent?

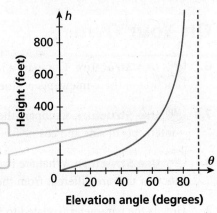

Check Understanding

1. Compare the domain and range of the tangent function to those of the sine and cosine functions.

2. Is the graph of $f(x) = -a\tan\left(\frac{1}{b}x\right)$ the same as the graph of $g(x) = a\tan\left(-\frac{1}{b}x\right)$ when the values of a and b are the same for both functions? Explain.

3. Use the graph to write a tangent function of the form $f(x) = a\tan\left(\frac{1}{b}x\right)$.

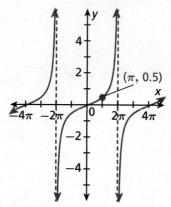

4. Compare the periods of the tangent functions expressed differently. $f(x)$ is shown in the table and $g(x) = 2\tan\left(\frac{\pi}{4}x\right)$.

x	$-\frac{\pi}{4}$	$-\frac{\pi}{8}$	0	$\frac{\pi}{8}$	$\frac{\pi}{4}$
$f(x)$	undefined	$-\frac{1}{4}$	0	$\frac{1}{4}$	undefined

5. A window washer is on a hydraulic-powered platform that is ascending the face of a 200-foot skyscraper at 25 feet per minute. A person 50 feet away from the base of the skyscraper is observing the ascent of the window washer. Write an equation that describes the height of the scaffolding platform as a function of the angle of elevation of the person's line-of-sight to the scaffolding platform. At what height is the window washer when the person's viewing angle is 62°?

On Your Own

6. **(MP) Use Structure** Compare and contrast the x-intercepts of the tangent function to the x-intercepts of sine and cosine functions.

7. **(MP) Use Structure** Compare the y-intercepts of the tangent function to the y-intercepts of sine and cosine functions.

8. **(MP) Use Structure** What are two key features of the graph of the tangent function that are different from the graphs of the sine and cosine functions?

9. How is the parameter b related to the period of the function $f(x) = a\tan\left(\frac{1}{b}x\right)$? How is b related to the asymptotes of $f(x)$?

10. Compare and contrast the effect that a has on the amplitude of sine and cosine functions with the effect that a has on the vertical stretch of tangent functions.

Graph each tangent function.

11. $f(x) = \frac{3}{4}\tan(4x)$

12. $f(x) = 4\tan\left(-\frac{x}{5}\right)$

13. $f(x) = 6\tan(\pi x)$

14. (MP) **Use Structure** If a tangent function's asymptotes are more spread out than those of its parent function, what does that tell you about a? about b?

15. (MP) **Use Structure** If the halfway points of a tangent function's graph are closer together vertically than those of its parent function's graph, what does that tell you about a? about b?

Write the tangent function in the form $f(x) = a\tan\left(\frac{1}{b}x\right)$ for each graph.

16.

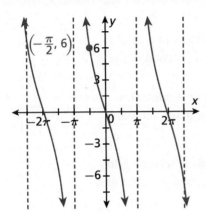

17.

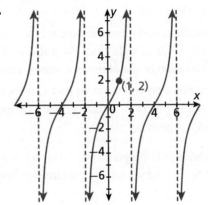

18. Compare the tangent functions $f(x)$ and $g(x)$ by comparing their periods. The graph of $f(x)$ is shown and $g(x) = -8\tan(4x)$.

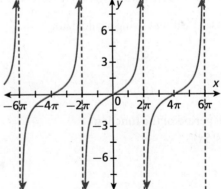

19. The horizontal field of view (HFOV) h (in mm) of a lens is related to the working distance w (in mm) from the lens to the object and the angle a of the field of view in degrees.

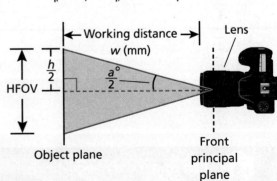

A. Write a function that gives h in terms of w and a. Then write the function when the working distance is 10 mm.

B. What limitations, if any, are there on values of a in this context? Explain.

C. Graph the function when the working distance is 10 mm. Take into account any limitations you discussed in Part B. Describe how the limitations are represented in your graph.

20. The CN Tower in Canada has several elevators that can be seen from outside the building's glass wall as they carry people up 1136 feet at 22 feet per second. A person is 600 feet from the base of the tower and looking through a pair of binoculars at these high-speed glass elevators.

elevator →

h ft

observer

θ

600 ft

A. Write an equation that gives the height of the glass elevator as a function of the angle of elevation of an observer's line-of-sight to the glass elevator.

B. At what height is the glass elevator if the person's viewing angle is 55°?

C. Write a function that gives the time it takes for the glass elevator to ascend to the observer's line of sight from the bottom of the tower as a function of the angle of elevation of the observer's line-of-sight.

D. Graph the function you wrote in Part C. What restriction to the domain is relevant to the situation? What vertical asymptote does your graph show and what does it represent?

21. How could you sketch the graph of $y = \tan x$ on a coordinate plane with no grid lines (except the x- and y-axes) that is already showing the graphs of $y = \sin x$ and $y = \cos x$?

Spiral Review • Assessment Readiness

22. Evaluate $\cos\left(\frac{\pi}{3}\right)$ without using a calculator.

(A) 1

(C) $\frac{\sqrt{2}}{2}$

(B) $\frac{\sqrt{3}}{2}$

(D) $\frac{1}{2}$

23. What is the period of the function $f(x) = 2\cos(5x)$?

(A) $\frac{\pi}{5}$

(B) $\frac{2\pi}{5}$

(C) $\frac{5\pi}{2}$

(D) 5π

24. A pendulum is released at a point 6 inches to the right of its position at rest. Write a cosine function that represents the pendulum's horizontal displacement relative to its position at rest if it completes one back-and-forth swing every 3 seconds.

(A) $y = 6\cos\left(\frac{2\pi x}{3}\right)$

(C) $y = 6\cos\left(\frac{\pi x}{3}\right)$

(B) $y = 3\cos\left(\frac{\pi x}{3}\right)$

(D) $y = 3\cos\left(\frac{\pi x}{6}\right)$

25. Given that $\sin\theta \approx 0.624$ for some θ between 0 and $\frac{\pi}{2}$, which most closely approximates the value of $\cos\theta$?

(A) 0.7814

(C) 0.3894

(B) 0.6106

(D) 0.2186

 I'm in a Learning Mindset!

What steps am I taking to direct my own learning about graphing tangent functions?

Translations of Trigonometric Graphs

I Can identify how $f(x + h)$ and $f(x) + k$ will shift the graph of a trigonometric function $f(x)$ for constants h and k.

Spark Your Learning

The ocean rises and falls over the course of the day. Many people, such as the owners of the fishing boats at this harbor, make their daily plans based on the predictable cycling of the depth of the seawater at their location.

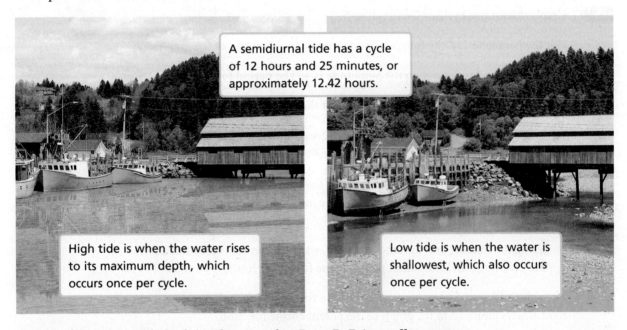

A semidiurnal tide has a cycle of 12 hours and 25 minutes, or approximately 12.42 hours.

High tide is when the water rises to its maximum depth, which occurs once per cycle.

Low tide is when the water is shallowest, which also occurs once per cycle.

Complete Part A as a whole class. Then complete Parts B–D in small groups.

A. What is a mathematical question you can ask about this situation? What information would you need to know to answer your question?

B. What variables are involved in the situation? What unit of measurement would you use for each variable?

C. To answer your question, what strategy and tool would you use along with all the information you have? What answer do you get?

D. Does your answer make sense in the context of the situation? How do you know?

Turn and Talk Discuss how your work would change for each of the following changes in the situation:
- The coefficient of the cosine function in $d(t)$ is increased or decreased.
- The constant at the end of the given function $d(t)$ is increased or decreased.

©gvictoria/Shutterstock

Build Understanding

Graph General Trigonometric Functions

Vertical compressions and stretches of the graphs of the sine and cosine parent functions change the amplitude, but the midline remains on the x-axis. Horizontal compressions and stretches change the period of the graphs of all three trigonometric parent functions.

Horizontal and vertical translations of the trigonometric parent functions are indicated by the parameters h and k in their equations. The general forms of the functions are $f(x) = a\sin\frac{1}{b}(x - h) + k$, $f(x) = a\cos\frac{1}{b}(x - h) + k$, and $f(x) = a\tan\frac{1}{b}(x - h) + k$, where h indicates the horizontal translation and k indicates the vertical translation.

1 ▶ Graph at least one cycle of the function $f(x) = \frac{1}{2}\cos 4\left(x - \frac{\pi}{4}\right) + 3$.

Use the parameters of the function to identify the key features of the graph of f.

In the equation for f, $a = \frac{1}{2}$ so the amplitude is $\frac{1}{2}$. The period for f is $2\pi \cdot \frac{1}{4} = \frac{\pi}{2}$.

A. Why is $\frac{1}{4}$ used to determine the period of the function f?

B. What do the amplitude and period of f reveal about how its graph compares to the graph of the parent cosine function?

The midline of a trigonometric function has the equation $y = k$. So the midline for f is $y = 3$. While not part of the graph, the midline acts as a guide when drawing the graph.

C. Using the midline and the amplitude of f, what will be the y-coordinates of the maximum and minimum points of the function? Justify your answers.

The value of h in the equation for $f(x)$ is $\frac{\pi}{4}$, so the graph of f is shifted $\frac{\pi}{4}$ unit right when compared to the graph of the parent cosine function.

For the parent cosine function, $(0, 1)$ is a maximum point and $(\pi, -1)$ is a minimum point. These points correspond to $\left(\frac{\pi}{4}, \frac{7}{2}\right)$ and $\left(\frac{\pi}{2}, \frac{5}{2}\right)$, respectively, on the graph of f.

D. How were the parameters of f used to determine these maximum and minimum points?

E. How can the maximum and minimum points above and the period of f be used to find some of the points where the graph of f crosses the midline?

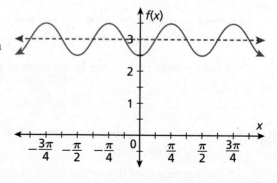

Since the minimum value of the function is 2.5, there are no x-intercepts. When $x = 0$, $f(0) = \frac{1}{2}\cos 4\left(-\frac{\pi}{4}\right) + 3 = \frac{1}{2}\cos(-\pi) + 3 = 2.5$, so the y-intercept is 2.5.

The graph of the function is shown at the right.

Create General Trigonometric Functions from Graphs

You can write equations for sine, cosine, and tangent graphs using the general forms of the functions by determining the parameters a, b, h, and k from examining the key features of the graphs.

2 ▶ Write a tangent function for the graph shown. The halfway points are plotted on the tangent graph along with points on the midline.

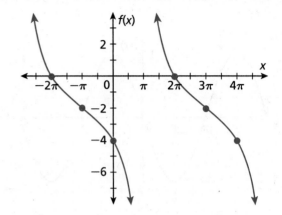

The equation of the midline is $y = -2$, so $k = -2$.

  A. What type of transformation is associated with the midline?

The period is 4π. So, $\pi \cdot b = 4\pi$ and $b = 4$.

  B. How do you know the period is 4π?

A comparison of the midline location to the halfway points shows that $a = -2$.

  C. How was the value of a determined and what types of transformations occurred on the parent tangent function because $a = -2$?

The graph of the parent tangent function has its midline at $y = 0$ and one branch of the graph crosses the midline at the origin. The graph shown here has a midline at $y = -2$, so you already know that points are shifted 2 units down. Focus on the point on the midline at $(-\pi, -2)$. This point shows a shift of π units to the left, indicating that $h = -\pi$.

  D. Can h be a different value? Explain.

One possible equation for the graph is $f(x) = -2\tan\frac{1}{4}(x + \pi) - 2$.

3 ▶ Write a sine function for the graph shown.

The amplitude is 3, so $a = 3$.

  A. How was the amplitude calculated?

The midline of the graph is $y = 5$, so $k = 5$.

  B. How is the value $b = \frac{4}{\pi}$ determined?

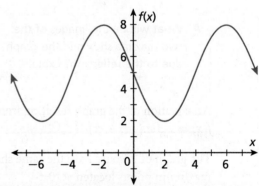

To determine the value of h, examine where the point $(0, 0)$ of the parent sine function shifted. Since $k = 5$, the point $(0, 0)$ shifted up 5 units. On the parent graph, the point $(0, 0)$ is on a part of the curve that is rising, so look to the right of $(0, 5)$ for the next point at $y = 5$ that is on a rising portion of the graph. This is the point $(4, 5)$. So $h = 4$.

  C. Can h be a different value? Explain.

One possible sine function is $f(x) = 3\sin\frac{\pi}{4}(x - 4) + 5$.

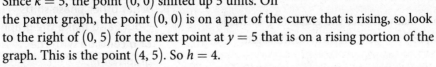

Turn and Talk How could you rewrite this sine function as a cosine function?

Step It Out

Determine Phase Shifts of Sine and Cosine Functions

Recall the graphs of the parent functions $f(x) = \sin x$ and $g(x) = \cos x$.

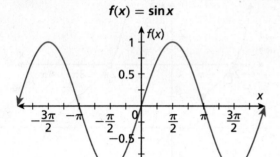

The two curves would coincide through a simple horizontal translation, called a *phase shift*, of either graph. For the sine function, notice that a translation $\frac{\pi}{2}$ units to the left would have its graph coincide with the graph of the cosine function. Similarly, shifting the cosine graph $\frac{\pi}{2}$ units to the right would make it coincide with the sine graph.

4 The graph of $f(x) = 3\sin\frac{1}{2}(x - \pi) + 2$ is shown at the right. Using a reflection and a phase shift, create another sine function whose graph coincides with this graph.

Suppose the graph of f is reflected over its midline.

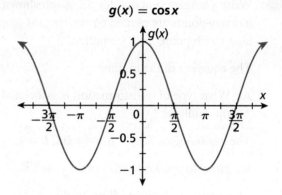

> **A.** What will be the images of the two maxima shown in the graph due to the reflection? Explain.

An equation of the graph resulting from the reflection would be
$f(x) = -3\sin\frac{1}{2}(x - \pi) + 2$.

The graph of g would have the same shape as the graph of f but it has one of its maximum points located at $(0, 5)$.

One phase shift that will have the graph of g coincide with the graph of f is a shift 2π units to the right.

> **B.** What other phase shifts would also make the graph of g coincide with the graph of f?

This phase shift will map the maximum point $(0, 5)$ on the graph of g to the maximum point $(2\pi, 5)$ on the graph of f.

Use the phase shift to write the equation of a function $h(x)$ whose graph coincides with the graph of f.

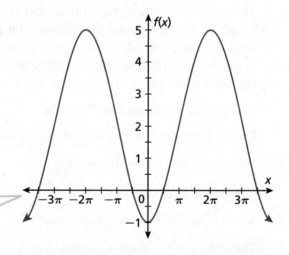

$$h(x) = -3\sin\frac{1}{2}\left(x - (\pi + 2\pi)\right) + 2$$
$$= -3\sin\frac{1}{2}(x - 3\pi) + 2$$

> **C.** Why is the sum of π and 2π shown in parentheses?

482

Trigonometric Models for Real-World Phenomena

Many real-world phenomena that exhibit repeating, periodic patterns can be modeled by trigonometric functions.

5 ▷ Each gondola on a Ferris wheel travels the same circular path during the ride. Suppose the height h (in feet) of the pivot point of a gondola above the ground is modeled by the function given, where t is the time in seconds since the ride began with a chosen gondola nearest the ground.

Identify the key parameters of the function.

period: $2\pi \cdot \dfrac{60}{\pi} = 120$

A. How was the period determined?

midline: $h(t) = 37$

amplitude: 30

$$h(t) = -30\cos\frac{\pi}{60}t + 37$$

maximum: $37 + 30 = 67$

minimum: $37 - 30 = 7$

B. How were the maximum and minimum values found?

Determine the points where the graph intersects the midline.

$h(t) = 37$ when $\cos\frac{\pi}{60}t = 0$; the value of the cosine function is 0 for $\frac{\pi}{2}, \frac{3\pi}{2}, \frac{5\pi}{2}, \ldots$.

$$\frac{\pi}{60}t = \frac{\pi}{2} \qquad\qquad \frac{\pi}{60}t = \frac{3\pi}{2}$$

$$t = 30 \qquad\qquad\qquad t = 90$$

C. What does one cycle of the graph represent in the context of the situation?

The graph intersects the midline twice during one cycle, at the points $(30, 37)$ and $(90, 37)$.

Determine the maximum and the minimum points of the graph.

The cycle begins with the gondola nearest the ground, so one minimum point is $(0, 7)$. A second occurs at the end of the cycle (the period) at the point $(120, 7)$. The only maximum point occurs midway through the cycle at $(60, 67)$.

Interpret these five key points in terms of the real-world setting.

$(0, 7)$: The Ferris wheel begins with the gondola's pivot point at a height of 7 feet.

$(30, 37)$: The pivot point reaches the height of the wheel's axle, 37 feet, in 30 seconds.

$(60, 67)$: At 60 seconds, the pivot point reaches its maximum height of 67 feet at the top of the wheel.

$(90, 37)$: The pivot point comes back down to the height of the axle, 37 feet, in 90 seconds.

$(120, 7)$: One trip around the Ferris wheel takes 120 seconds, ending with the gondola's pivot point back at a height of 7 feet.

The graph at the right models the height of one gondola's pivot point on the Ferris wheel.

D. Does the function $h(t)$ indicate the position of the gondola's point with respect to the axle of the Ferris wheel? Explain.

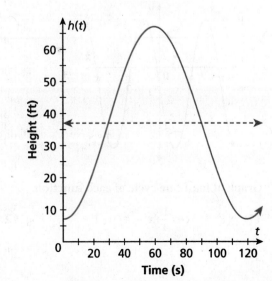

Check Understanding

1. Consider the functions $f(x) = 2\tan 4\left(x - \frac{\pi}{2}\right) + 1$ and $g(x) = 2\cos 4\left(x - \frac{\pi}{2}\right) + 1$. Are the periods of these functions the same? Explain.

2. When writing a function rule in the form $f(x) = a\tan\frac{1}{b}(x - h) + k$ for the graph of a tangent function, how can you determine the values of h and k?

3. You are given the graph of a cosine function but not the function. Explain why you could write both a cosine function and a sine function for the graph.

4. Do the functions $f(x) = 3\cos 2\left(x - \frac{\pi}{2}\right) + 4$ and $g(x) = 3\cos 2\left(x - \frac{\pi}{2}\right) - 4$ have the same graph? Explain.

5. A water wheel is rotated by a moving water source. Suppose the motion of a point on the outer edge of one blade is modeled by the function $h(t) = 10\sin\frac{\pi}{6}(t - 3) + 8$, where h is the height (in feet) measured from the water line and t is the time (in seconds). Let $t = 0$ be the time when the point is at the bottom of the water wheel. Graph one cycle of the function and use the graph to describe what is happening in the context of the situation.

On Your Own

6. **(MP) Use Structure** How do the parameters h and k in the general forms of the trigonometric functions affect the graphs of those functions?

7. **(MP) Use Structure** If you know the coordinates of the five key points of the graph of $f(x) = 6\sin 2x$, how can you use h and k to find the five key points of the graph of $g(x) = 6\sin 2(x - \pi) - 4$?

8. A transformation was performed on the parent cosine function that changed the range to $[-4, -6]$. Write the equation of the new function $g(x)$.

For Problems 9 and 10, write the trigonometric function specified for each graph.

9. Write a sine function.

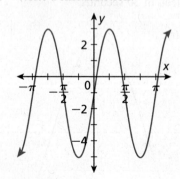

10. Write a cosine function.

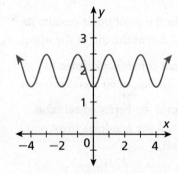

Graph at least one cycle of each function.

11. $g(x) = 3\cos\frac{1}{4}(x - \pi) - 1$

12. $h(x) = -\sin 4\left(x - \frac{\pi}{2}\right) + 2$

13. Graph at least one cycle of the function $j(x) = 2\tan\frac{1}{2}(x + 2\pi) + 8$.

14. How are the asymptotes of the graph of $f(x) = a\tan\frac{1}{b}(x)$ affected by h and k when the graph is transformed to $f(x) = a\tan\frac{1}{b}(x - h) + k$?

15. What is the maximum value of the function $f(x) = a\cos\frac{1}{b}(x - h) + k$? Explain.

16. What are the y-values at the halfway points on the graph of $f(x) = a\tan\frac{1}{b}(x - h) + k$? Explain.

For Problems 17 and 18, write a tangent function for each graph.

17.

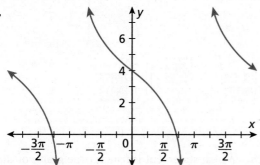

18.

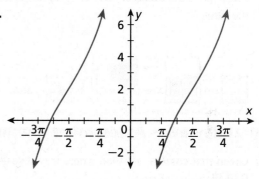

19. Can you write a cosine function rule for a sine function? Explain.

20. How many sine functions are represented by the same graph? Explain.

21. Why can you write a tangent function with different tangent function rules?

22. Write two different sine functions for the graph.

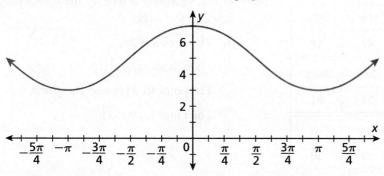

23. Write two different cosine functions for the graph.

24. For one particular model of a wind turbine, the blades rotate whenever the wind blows from 8 to 56 miles per hour. For a certain wind speed, the height h (in feet) of the tip of each blade of the wind turbine can be modeled by the function $h(t)$ shown, where t is the time in seconds and $t = 0$ when the tip of one blade is at its lowest point. Graph one cycle and use it to describe the height of the tip of that one blade as it rotates through one cycle.

$$h(t) = -116 \cos \frac{\pi}{2} t + 212$$

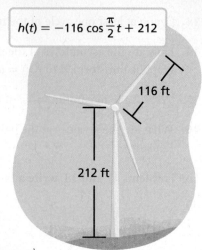

116 ft

212 ft

25. (Open Middle™) Using the digits 1 to 9, at most two times each, fill in the boxes so that the graphs of the two functions are the same.

$$\boxed{} \sin\left(\boxed{}\left(x + \frac{\boxed{}}{2}\pi\right)\right) + \boxed{} \quad \text{and} \quad \boxed{} \sin\left(\boxed{}\left(x + \frac{\boxed{}}{2}\pi\right)\right) + \boxed{}$$

Spiral Review • Assessment Readiness

26. Given that $\cos\theta = -0.4965$ where $\pi \leq \theta \leq \frac{3\pi}{2}$, find the value of $\sin\theta$.

Ⓐ -0.8680 Ⓒ 0.7535

Ⓑ -0.7532 Ⓓ 0.8680

27. The table shows average monthly high temperatures in degrees Fahrenheit for Cleveland, Ohio.

Month	Jan.	Feb.	Mar.	Apr.
Temp.	34	38	47	59
Month	May	June	July	Aug.
Temp.	69	79	83	81
Month	Sept.	Oct.	Nov.	Dec.
Temp.	74	62	51	38

Which parameter models the data for the function $y = a\sin\frac{1}{b}(x - h) + k$?

Ⓐ $b = \frac{1}{12}$ Ⓒ $k = 58.5$

Ⓑ $a = 4$ Ⓓ $h = 24.5$

28. Which statement is true for the graph of the function $f(x) = \frac{1}{4}\sin(2x)$?

Ⓐ The range is $\left[-\frac{1}{4}, \frac{1}{4}\right]$.

Ⓑ The domain is $[-2, 2]$.

Ⓒ The graph repeats itself every 2π.

Ⓓ $\left(-\frac{\pi}{2}, -1\right)$ lies on the graph.

29. Which statement is true for the parent tangent function $f(x) = \tan x$?

Ⓐ The period is 2π.

Ⓑ There is an asymptote at $x = \frac{\pi}{2}$.

Ⓒ The point $(0, 1)$ lies on the graph.

Ⓓ The range is $[-1, 1]$.

I'm in a Learning Mindset!

How do my decisions about studying translations of trigonometric graphs impact my achievement?

Model Periodic Phenomena with Trigonometric Functions

(I Can) use sine functions to model periodic phenomena and solve real-world problems.

Spark Your Learning

Influenza (flu) can make a person very sick. Managers at healthcare facilities make plans in preparation for the periodic changes in their patient numbers due to the flu.

The rate at which people contract the virus that causes the flu has a natural tendency to be cyclical throughout the year.

Complete Part A as a whole class. Then complete Parts B–D in small groups.

A. What is a mathematical question you can ask about this situation? What information would you need to know to answer your question?

B. What variables are involved in the situation? What unit of measurement would you use for each variable?

C. To answer your question, what strategy and tool would you use along with all the information you have? What answer do you get?

D. Does your answer make sense in the context of the situation? How do you know?

Turn and Talk Predict how your work would change for each of the following changes in the situation:
- Each percentage is increased by 10 percent.
- Only the greatest, second greatest, and third greatest percentages are increased by 5 percent.

Build Understanding

Fit a Trigonometric Function to Data Without Using Technology

Some real-world data exhibit a cyclical pattern. The graph of the general sine function $f(x) = a \sin \frac{1}{b}(x - h) + k$ or the general cosine function $f(x) = a \cos \frac{1}{b}(x - h) + k$ provides a good model for this type of data.

1 ▶ The table shows the average monthly high temperature, in degrees Fahrenheit, for Washington, D.C. Write a trigonometric function that models this real-world situation.

Month, m	1	2	3	4	5	6
Average high temperature (°F), T	42	44	53	64	75	83

Month, m	7	8	9	10	11	12
Average high temperature (°F), T	87	84	78	67	55	45

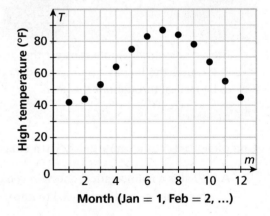

$$T = a \sin \frac{1}{b}(m - h) + k$$

Use a scatter plot of the data points to help determine the parameters a, b, h, and k in the general sine function. The period of the general sine function is $2\pi b$. The period for the given data is 12 months, so $12 = 2\pi b$ and therefore $b = \frac{6}{\pi}$.

A. How does the value of b transform the graph of the parent function $f(x) = \sin x$?

The midline for the graph of the general sine function is $y = k$. One method to identify the midline for real-world data is to average the y-coordinates of the greatest and least data points. The maximum temperature is 87 °F and the minimum is 42 °F. The average of these values is 64.5. Therefore the midline is $T = 64.5$, and the value of k is 64.5.

B. How does the value of k transform the graph of the parent sine function?

The amplitude a is one-half the vertical distance between the highest and lowest data points in the scatter plot. So $a = \frac{87 - 42}{2} = 22.5$.

The graph of the general sine function crosses its midline at $x = h$. The first time the temperature passes 64.5° F is during month 4, so $h \approx 4$.

Substituting in the values for each parameter, the model is $T = 22.5 \sin \frac{\pi}{6}(m - 4) + 64.5$.

C. What can you do to determine how well the model fits the data?

D. How could you use the maximum on the scatter plot to write a cosine function to model the situation? Write a cosine function to model the data.

Step It Out

Fit a Sine Function to Data Using Technology

A sine function model can be found by performing a sine regression on a graphing calculator, just as linear, quadratic, and other regressions were used in earlier lessons.

2 ▶ The table below repeats the average monthly high temperature data for Washington, D.C. given in Task 1. Use a graphing calculator to perform a sine regression on the data.

Month, m	1	2	3	4	5	6	7	8	9	10	11	12
Average high temperature (°F), T	42	44	53	64	75	83	87	84	78	67	55	45

Begin by entering the data in the graphing calculator and plotting the points.

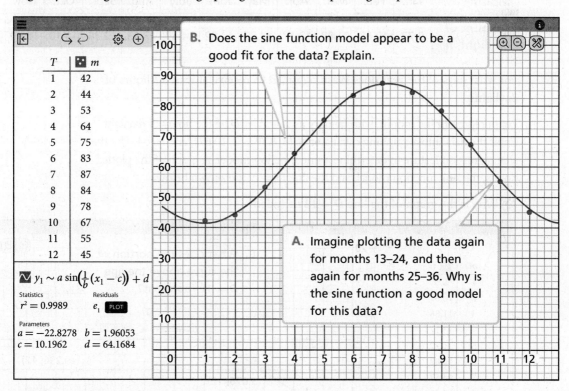

B. Does the sine function model appear to be a good fit for the data? Explain.

A. Imagine plotting the data again for months 13–24, and then again for months 25–36. Why is the sine function a good model for this data?

Calculator display:

T	m
1	42
2	44
3	53
4	64
5	75
6	83
7	87
8	84
9	78
10	67
11	55
12	45

$y_1 \sim a \sin\left(\frac{1}{b}(x_1 - c)\right) + d$

Statistics
$r^2 = 0.9989$

Residuals
e_1 PLOT

Parameters
$a = -22.8278$ $b = 1.96053$
$c = 10.1962$ $d = 64.1684$

Now use the sine regression feature to find a sine function that models the data.

$$T = -22.8 \sin \frac{1}{2.0}(m - 10.2) + 64.2$$

C. What does the value of R^2 tell you about the fit of the curve to the data?

 Turn and Talk Compare the graphs and the equations of the sine function found using technology to those of the sine function found by determining the parameters in Task 1.

Solve a Real-World Problem Using a Sine Model

You can use the graph of a sine function model to identify values of interest.

3 The table below shows the average daily amount of daylight (in hours) in Washington, D.C. for each month of the year.

Dawn

Dusk

Month	Jan.	Feb.	Mar.	Apr.	May	June	July	Aug.	Sept.	Oct.	Nov.	Dec.
Amount of daylight, h	9.77	10.67	11.88	13.17	14.27	14.82	14.57	13.63	12.38	11.10	10.00	9.48

For what days of the year does Washington, D.C. receive at least 12 hours of daylight?

Let m represent the month, with January as 1, and let D be the hours of daylight. Enter the data into a graphing calculator as $(1, 9.77)$, $(2, 10.67)$, and so on. Use the sine regression feature to determine a sine function model. A graph of the plotted points, the sine function model, and the line $D = 12$ are shown below.

A. Why is the graph of the line $D = 12$ included?

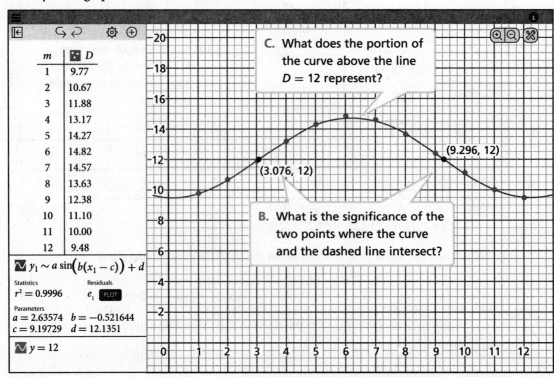

C. What does the portion of the curve above the line $D = 12$ represent?

(9.296, 12)

(3.076, 12)

B. What is the significance of the two points where the curve and the dashed line intersect?

m | D
1 | 9.77
2 | 10.67
3 | 11.88
4 | 13.17
5 | 14.27
6 | 14.82
7 | 14.57
8 | 13.63
9 | 12.38
10 | 11.10
11 | 10.00
12 | 9.48

$y_1 \sim a \sin\big(b(x_1 - c)\big) + d$

Statistics   Residuals
$r^2 = 0.9996$ e_1 [PLOT]

Parameters
$a = 2.63574$ $b = -0.521644$
$c = 9.19729$ $d = 12.1351$

$y = 12$

The model gives about March 17 as the first day with at least 12 hours of daylight.

Check Understanding

1. How do you find the value of b in order to determine a trigonometric function that will model a set of data?

2. How can you use technology to determine a function that best models a set of data in which its graph displays a wave-like pattern?

3. How can you use a graph of a sine regression model to determine the maximum value of the data?

4. How can you use the equation of a sine regression model to determine the maximum value of the data?

On Your Own

5. (MP) **Use Structure** The table shows the average number of wet days per month in Las Vegas, Nevada. Would a trigonometric function be a good fit for the data? Explain.

Month	Jan.	Feb.	Mar.	Apr.	May	June	July	Aug.	Sept.	Oct.	Nov.	Dec.
Average number of wet days	3	3	2	2	1	0	3	2	1	2	2	3

The table shows the average daily high temperature (in degrees Fahrenheit) for each month in Denver, Colorado and in Memphis, Tennessee.

Month	Jan.	Feb.	Mar.	Apr.	May	June	July	Aug.	Sept.	Oct.	Nov.	Dec.
Average daily high temperature Denver (°F)	45	46	54	61	72	82	90	88	79	66	52	45
Average daily high temperature Memphis (°F)	50	55	64	73	81	89	92	91	85	74	63	52

6. Create a trigonometric function that models the data for Denver without using technology.

7. Use a graphing calculator to find a sine function that models the data for Denver.

8. Compare the two models for Denver.

9. What does the value of R^2 tell you about the model found using the calculator?

10. For what days of the year does Denver average a high temperature of at least 60 °F?

11. Create a trigonometric function that models the data for Memphis without using technology.

12. How can you use your models to determine when the two cities have the same average daily high temperature?

13. Is there a month when the two cities have the same average daily high temperature? Explain.

The table shows the average monthly precipitation (in inches) for Seattle, Washington.

$$y = a\sin\frac{1}{b}(x - h) + k$$

Month	Jan.	Feb.	Mar.	Apr.	May	June
Average daily precipitation (in.)	0.18	0.12	0.12	0.09	0.06	0.05

Month	July	Aug.	Sept.	Oct.	Nov.	Dec.
Average daily precipitation (in.)	0.02	0.03	0.05	0.11	0.22	0.17

14. Create a trigonometric function model of the data without using technology.

15. Use a graphing calculator to find a sine function model for the data in the table.

16. Compare the two models for the data.

17. What does the value of R^2 tell you about the model found using the calculator?

18. For what days of the year does Seattle average 0.1 inch or more of rain?

Spiral Review • Assessment Readiness

19. A series of transformations were performed on $f(x) = \sin x$ to obtain the function $g(x) = \frac{1}{2}\sin 3(x - \pi) + 4$.

   Which of these transformations was part of the series?

   Ⓐ vertical compression

   Ⓑ vertical translation down

   Ⓒ horizontal stretch

   Ⓓ horizontal translation to the left

20. Which statement is true for the parent tangent function $f(x) = \tan x$?

   Ⓐ The set is the domain of all real numbers.

   Ⓑ The point $\left(\frac{-\pi}{2}, 1\right)$ is on the graph.

   Ⓒ There is an asymptote at $x = 0$.

   Ⓓ The period is π.

21. A pendulum is released at a point 4 inches to the right of its position at rest. Select the function that models its horizontal displacement relative to its rest position if it completes one back-and-forth swing every 1.5 sec.

   Ⓐ $y = \frac{3}{2}\cos\frac{2x}{\pi}$

   Ⓑ $y = \frac{3}{2}\cos\frac{\pi x}{2}$

   Ⓒ $y = 4\cos\frac{4\pi x}{3}$

   Ⓓ $y = 4\cos\frac{3x}{4\pi}$

22. You roll a number cube. Event A is rolling an odd number and event B is rolling a number less than 5. What is the probability of event A and B $P(A \cap B)$?

   Ⓐ $\frac{1}{6}$ Ⓑ $\frac{1}{3}$ Ⓒ $\frac{1}{2}$ Ⓓ $\frac{5}{6}$

I'm in a Learning Mindset!

What did I learn from the mistakes I make creating sine functions to model periodic phenomenon in the real world?

Review

Graph a Sine or Cosine Function

a vertical stretch

a horizontal compression

$g(x) = 3 \sin (2x)$ is a transformation of the parent function.

- Maxima and minima occur when $2x = (2n + 1)\frac{\pi}{2}$, or $x = (2n + 1)\frac{\pi}{4}$.
- Zeros occur when $2x = m\pi$, or $x = m\frac{\pi}{2}$.
- The amplitude is 3.

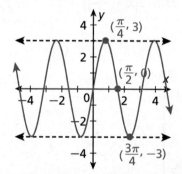

Cosine functions are phase shifted sine functions. $g(x) = 3 \cos \left(2x - \frac{\pi}{2}\right)$

Graph a Tangent Function

a vertical stretch

a horizontal stretch

$f(x) = 2 \tan \left(\frac{x}{2}\right)$ is a transformation of the parent function.

- Asymptotes occur when $\frac{x}{2} = (2n + 1)\frac{\pi}{2}$, or $x = (2n + 1)\pi$.
- Zeros occur when $\frac{x}{2} = m\pi$, or $x = 2m\pi$.

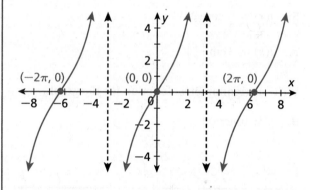

Fit a Sine Function to Data

A city tracks its average high temperature each month to make predictions for the following year.

Month	1	3	5	7	9	11
Average high temperature (°F)	33	43	66	80	72	49

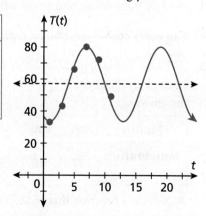

$T(t) = 23.5 \sin \left(\frac{2\pi}{12}(t - 4)\right) + 57.17$

The midline is the average value, so $h = 57.17$.

The amplitude is half of the range, so $A = 23.5$.

The frequency is determined by the timescale, so $f = \frac{2\pi}{12}$.

Assume it repeats every 12 months

Vocabulary

Choose the correct term from the box to complete each sentence.

1. The ___?___ of a periodic function is the number of cycles per unit of time.

2. A(n) ___?___ is a function that repeats exactly in regular intervals.

3. The ___?___ of a periodic function is half the distance of the maximum and minimum values.

4. The ___?___ of a periodic function is the length of a cycle.

Concepts and Skills

Graph each function.

5. $f(x) = \frac{1}{3} \cos (2x)$

6. $f(x) = 4 \sin \left(\frac{x}{2}\right)$

7. $f(x) = 3 \tan \left(\frac{x}{4}\right)$

8. $f(x) = 2 \sin \left(2\left(x + \frac{3\pi}{2}\right)\right) - 1$

Write a trigonometric function for the graph.

9. sine function

10. cosine function

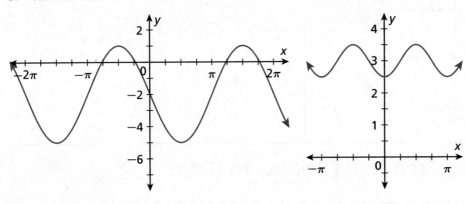

11. How do the midline and amplitude relate to transformations of sine and cosine functions?

12. Can every cosine function be represented by a sine function? Explain your reasoning.

13. (MP) **Use Tools** The table shows the average water temperature for Lake Erie. State what strategy and tool you will use to answer the question, explain your choice, and then find the answer.

Month	Jan.	Feb.	Mar.	Apr.	May	June	July	Aug.	Sept.	Oct.	Nov.	Dec.
Temperature (°F)	37	36	36	39	46	59	70	72	66	57	48	41

   A. Create a function that models the data.

   B. What does the midline represent in this context?

   C. What does the amplitude represent in this context?

   D. How often does the cycle repeat? Explain your reasoning.

Unit 8

Probability

Archaeologist

Archaeologists reconstruct human history by interpreting material evidence. They survey sites, taking detailed notes while recovering artifacts of ancient societies. They carefully clean, classify, and preserve artifacts, allowing them to make reasonable, evidence-based arguments.

©Openfinal/Shutterstock

STEM POWERING INGENUITY

STEM Task

An archaeologist allocates an effective sweep width while searching a site for artifacts.

Effective sweep width

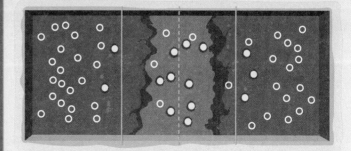

How successful was the sweep?

Learning Mindset
Perseverance Getting Unstuck

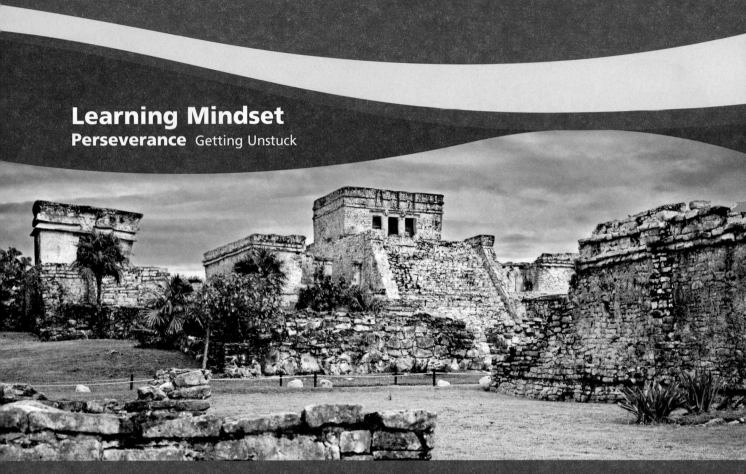

©Nataliya Hora/Shutterstock

What do you do when you don't know what to do? Despite out best intentions, we sometimes need help to get unstuck and moving again. Having a plan for when you get stuck can help you develop your understanding quicker. Determining what resources are available to help you at the beginning of a project will allow you to explore different strategies and progress. It is also helpful to change your mindset and think about the problem from a fresh perspective. Here are some questions you can ask yourself to get unstuck while learning.

- How can I proactively seek to fill gaps in my knowledge or understanding?

- What resources do I have to help me get unstuck? Who can help me get unstuck?

- What has slowed me down in the past? How can that experience be used when I need to get unstuck again?

- How can I look at this situation from a new perspective? What other approaches can help me see the problem from a different viewpoint?

Reflect

Q Have you ever found yourself stuck while working on a task? How did you get unstuck? Did you share your situation with a teacher or classmate? How did you benefit from this experience?

Q As an archaeologist, why would you reach out to others for different viewpoints? Why would you want to go back and refine your initial inferences as new evidence is introduced?

Probability of Compound Events

Building **Character**

What makes a strong password?

Create a password

••••••••••••

Confirm your password

Password strength   Poor 😟
Your password is easily
guessable. You can do better.

Password strength   Poor 😟
Your password is easily
guessable. You can do better.

Password strength   Average 😐
Your password is easily
guessable. You can do better.

Password strength   Strong 😀
Your password is great.
Nice work!

©mimagephotography/Shutterstock

Are You Ready?

Complete these problems to review prior concepts and skills you will need for this module.

Write Decimals and Fractions as Percents

Express each number as a percent.

1. 0.39

2. 0.0048

3. $\frac{3}{25}$

4. $\frac{7}{500}$

Probability of Simple Events

Find the theoretical probability of each event.

5. A number cube labeled 1–6 is rolled. What is the probability that a prime number is rolled?

6. A spinner with equal sections labeled 1–8 is spun. What is the probability that the result is a multiple of 3?

7. Suppose that each letter from the word "PROBABILITY" is written on a separate piece of paper. What is the probability of randomly selecting a B?

Probability of Compound Events Involving *Or*

Find the theoretical probability of each compound event.

8. Suppose that a number cube labeled 1–6 is rolled. What is the probability that a prime number or an even number is rolled?

9. Suppose that a spinner with equal sections labeled 1–8 is spun. What is the probability that the result is an even number or a number less than 4?

10. Suppose that each letter from the word "MATHEMATICS" is written on a separate piece of paper. What is the probability of randomly selecting an M or a vowel?

Connecting Past and Present Learning

Previously, you learned:

- to define theoretical probability in terms of sets and set operations,
- to summarize data in two-way frequency and relative frequency tables, and
- to recognize associations between categorical data in two-way frequency tables.

In this module, you will learn:

- to calculate theoretical and experimental probabilities within a given sample space,
- to use two-way tables as a sample space to determine if events are independent, and
- to use two-way tables to approximate conditional probabilities.

Theoretical and Experimental Probability

(I Can) calculate the theoretical or experimental probability of an event.

Spark Your Learning

A school district purchased two brands of laptop computers three years ago and is planning to buy more laptops this year. The district's IT manager would like to standardize on a single brand and wants to buy the brand that has been more reliable.

Three years ago, the school district purchased 2000 laptops of Brand A and 3000 laptops of Brand B.

Complete Part A as a whole class. Then complete Parts B and C in small groups.

A. What is a mathematical question you can ask about this situation? What information would you need to know to answer your question?

B. To answer your question, what strategy and tool would you use along with all the information you have? What answer do you get?

C. Jamie says that since fewer Brand A laptops than Brand B laptops needed repair, the school district should buy Brand A. Do you agree with Jamie's reasoning? Explain.

Turn and Talk What is the probability that a Brand A laptop did *not* need repair during the 3-year period? What is the probability that a Brand B laptop did *not* need repair? Do your results support how you answered the Spark Your Learning question?

Build Understanding

Investigate Theoretical Probability

A **probability experiment** is an activity that involves chance, such as rolling a number cube. Each repetition of the experiment is a **trial**, and each possible result of the experiment is an **outcome**. The set of all possible outcomes of the experiment is the **sample space**, and a subset of outcomes from the sample space is an **event**.

For example, the sample space S for rolling a number cube is the set of outcomes $S = \{1, 2, 3, 4, 5, 6\}$. The event A of rolling an odd number is the set of outcomes $A = \{1, 3, 5\}$. You can use the notation $n(S)$ or $n(A)$ to represent the number of outcomes in the sample space or an event. In this case, $n(S) = 6$ and $n(A) = 3$.

Theoretical Probability
When all outcomes of a probability experiment are equally likely, the **theoretical probability** of an event A is given by: $$P(A) = \frac{\text{number of outcomes in the event } A}{\text{number of outcomes in the sample space } S} = \frac{n(A)}{n(S)}$$

1 ▶ Suppose you spin the green spinner shown below.

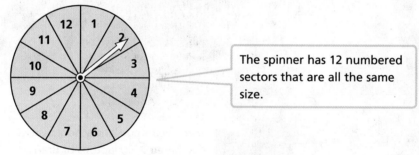

The spinner has 12 numbered sectors that are all the same size.

A. What is the sample space S for this probability experiment?

B. Are all of the outcomes in the sample space equally likely? Why or why not?

C. What is the set of outcomes A for the event of spinning a prime number?

D. What is the theoretical probability of spinning a prime number? Explain.

E. What is an event for spinning the spinner whose theoretical probability is $\frac{1}{4}$? whose theoretical probability is 0? whose theoretical probability is 1?

F. Carol and two friends spin the blue spinner shown to decide who gets to pick the next movie they watch. Carol gets to pick if the spinner lands on 1. Carol says the process is fair because the probability of getting each number is $\frac{1}{3}$. Do you agree? If not, explain why not, and tell how you would modify the process to make a fair decision.

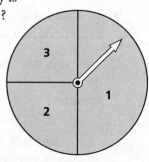

 Turn and Talk Are you more likely to spin a prime number or a composite number using the green spinner in Task 1? Explain.

Investigate Experimental Probability

The theoretical probability of getting a 3 when rolling a number cube is $\frac{1}{6}$, which means that you can expect to get a 3 one time for every six times you roll the cube. However, if you roll a number cube 600 times, you probably will not get a 3 *exactly* 100 times. The ratio of the number of times you actually get a 3 to your number of rolls is your *experimental probability* of getting a 3.

> **Experimental Probability**
>
> When a probability experiment is conducted for a certain number of trials, the **experimental probability** of an event *A* is given by:
>
> $$P(A) = \frac{\text{number of trials where event } A \text{ occurs}}{\text{total number of trials}}$$

2 ▶ Fabiola spins the green spinner shown 60 times and records the outcomes in a table.

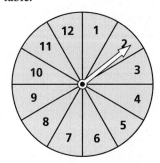

Outcomes for 60 Spins
8, 3, 8, 11, 12, 12, 6, 11, 8, 11, 1, 12, 9, 11, 6, 1, 12, 12, 3, 2, 1, 2, 5, 7, 5, 2, 4, 2, 12, 1, 8, 4, 12, 8, 6, 4, 6, 1, 10, 10, 7, 12, 11, 9, 3, 2, 6, 1, 5, 11, 12, 10, 9, 4, 11, 9, 7, 8, 10, 6

A. What is the theoretical probability of spinning an 11?

B. How many times would you expect to spin an 11 in 60 spins? Explain your reasoning.

C. How many times did Fabiola actually spin an 11 in 60 spins? What is her experimental probability of spinning an 11?

D. Compare the theoretical and experimental probabilities of spinning an 11. Does the experimental probability overestimate or underestimate the theoretical likelihood of spinning an 11?

E. Suppose Fabiola had spun the spinner 600 times instead of 60 times. Would you expect her experimental probability of spinning an 11 to be closer to or farther from the theoretical probability? Explain.

F. What is an event whose theoretical probability is greater than the experimental probability calculated from Fabiola's results? Justify your answer mathematically.

G. Recall that in Task 1 Carol thought the theoretical probability of getting a 1 when spinning the blue spinner shown is $\frac{1}{3}$. How could you use experimental probability to convince Carol that she is mistaken?

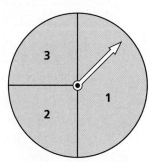

H. What is an example of a question that can be answered more easily using experimental probability than theoretical probability? Explain.

Explore Intersections, Unions, and Complements

The **intersection** of two events A and B, written as $A \cap B$ or as "A and B," is the set of outcomes that are in both A and B. The **union** of A and B, written as $A \cup B$ or as "A or B," is the set of outcomes that are in A or B. The **complement** of A, written as A^C or as "not A," is the set of outcomes in the sample space that are not in A. These concepts are illustrated in the Venn diagrams below.

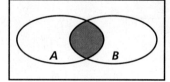
$A \cap B$ is shaded.

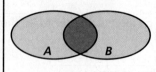
$A \cup B$ is shaded.

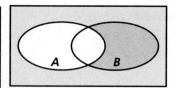
A^C is shaded.

3 Suppose you spin the spinner shown below. Let event A be getting a multiple of 3, and let event B be getting a number less than 8. The events A and B are represented by the Venn diagram, where S is the sample space.

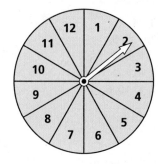
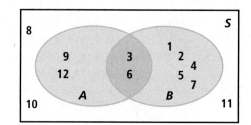

A. Write A and B as sets of outcomes.

B. Describe in words what the events $A \cap B$, $A \cup B$, A^C, and B^C mean.

C. Write $A \cap B$, $A \cup B$, A^C, and B^C as sets of outcomes.

D. What are $P(A \cap B)$, $P(A \cup B)$, $P(A^C)$, and $P(B^C)$?

E. Verify that the following equation is true for the given event A.

$$P(A) + P(A^C) = 1$$

Then show that this equation is true for *any* event A in a sample space S that consists of equally likely outcomes.

F. The equation in Part E can be rewritten in either of the following forms.

$$P(A) = 1 - P(A^C)$$
$$P(A^C) = 1 - P(A)$$

How can the first equation help you find the probability of an event when it is more convenient to find the probability of its complement?

Turn and Talk What is an event A related to the spinner in Task 3 for which $P(A) = P(A^C)$? Explain.

Step It Out

Calculate Probabilities

4 The table shows information about a DJ's music library.

> A DJ is using a 200-song library of music for a party.

Genre	Country	Hip hop	Pop	R&B
Number of songs	26	60	72	42

A guest at the party selects a song at random from the DJ's library. Find the probability of each event expressed as a percent.

- The song is a country song.
- The song is a hip hop or pop song.
- The song is not an R&B song.

$P(\text{country}) = \dfrac{26}{200} = 0.13 = 13\%$

$P(\text{hip hop or pop}) = \dfrac{60 + 72}{200} = \dfrac{132}{200} = 0.66 = 66\%$

$P(\text{not R\&B}) = 1 - P(\text{R\&B}) = 1 - \dfrac{42}{200} = \dfrac{158}{200} = 0.79 = 79\%$

A. Why is the numerator of this fraction $60 + 72$?

B. What is another way you could find $P(\text{not R\&B})$?

5 A 20-sided die has faces numbered from 1 to 20, as shown in the photo. If you roll a 20-sided die, what is the probability that you get a number that is prime and greater than 10?

Let A be the event that the number rolled is prime, and let B be the event that the number rolled is greater than 10.

$A = \{2, 3, 5, 7, 11, 13, 17, 19\}$

$B = \{11, 12, 13, 14, 15, 16, 17, 18, 19, 20\}$

You can use the Venn diagram shown to represent events A and B within the sample space S. The desired probability is $P(A \cap B)$. Notice that $A \cap B = \{11, 13, 17, 19\}$.

$P(A \cap B) = \dfrac{n(A \cap B)}{n(S)} = \dfrac{4}{20} = \dfrac{1}{5}$

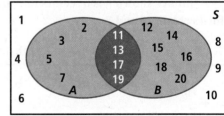

So the probability of rolling a number that is prime and greater than 10 is $\frac{1}{5}$.

A. What region of the Venn diagram represents $A \cap B$?

B. What is the probability that you roll a number that is prime and at most 10 with a 20-sided die? What region of the Venn diagram represents this event?

> **Turn and Talk** Why is $P(A \cap B) \leq P(A)$ and $P(A \cap B) \leq P(B)$ for any events A and B?

Check Understanding

1. How is the experimental probability of an event different from the theoretical probability of an event?

   A number cube like the one shown is rolled 30 times. The outcomes of the rolls are given in the table. Let event _A_ be rolling a multiple of 3, and let event _B_ be rolling a number less than 5. Use this information for Problems 2 and 3.

Outcomes for 30 Rolls
6, 2, 3, 6, 4, 5, 4, 4, 1, 5,
4, 5, 4, 3, 4, 2, 1, 1, 4, 1,
4, 2, 1, 3, 5, 5, 2, 3, 5, 6

2. Find each theoretical probability.

   A. $P(A)$ **B.** $P(B)$ **C.** $P(A \cap B)$

   D. $P(A \cup B)$ **E.** $P(A^C)$ **F.** $P(B^C)$

3. Find each experimental probability.

   A. $P(A)$ **B.** $P(B)$ **C.** $P(A \cap B)$

   D. $P(A \cup B)$ **E.** $P(A^C)$ **F.** $P(B^C)$

4. A kicker on a professional football team has made 153 out of the 180 field goals he has attempted so far in his career. What is the experimental probability that the kicker makes his next field goal? What is the experimental probability that the kicker misses his next field goal? Write your answers as percents.

On Your Own

5. (MP) **Construct Arguments** Explain how you can find the probability of an event by using the event's complement.

The spinner shown has 8 sectors that are all the same size. Use the spinner for Problems 6 and 7.

6. Find the theoretical probability that the spinner lands on the indicated color.

   A. red   **B.** blue

   C. green   **D.** red or blue

   E. not blue   **F.** blue and green

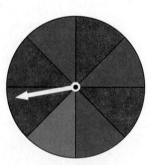

7. Matt spins the spinner shown 40 times and records whether the spinner lands on red (R), blue (B), or green (G). The results of his spins are shown in the table. Find the experimental probability that the spinner lands on the indicated color.

   A. red   **B.** green

   C. not blue   **D.** not red

   E. red or blue   **F.** blue or green

Outcomes for 40 Spins
R, R, B, R, R, G, R,
B, B, R, B, R, R, B, B,
R, G, B, R, R, R, B,
R, B, B, R, R, B, B, B,
R, R, B, B, B, R, G,
R, R, R

8. Liam has 150 ebooks stored on his tablet. The table shows the number of ebooks he owns by genre. Liam randomly chooses an ebook to read during his school's spring break. Find the probability of each event.

Genre	Ebooks
Fantasy	21
Horror	12
Mystery	30
Science fiction	48
Thriller	39

A. Liam chooses a science fiction ebook.

B. Liam chooses a horror or mystery ebook.

C. Liam chooses an ebook that is not a thriller.

D. Liam chooses an ebook from a genre other than mystery or fantasy.

9. A movie studio has made 50 movies during its existence. Let P be the set of movies that have been profitable for the studio, and let A be the set of movies that have won a major award. The Venn diagram shows how many of the studio's movies are in each set or in neither set.

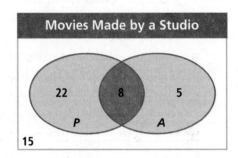

Movies Made by a Studio

A. What is the probability that a randomly selected movie from the studio was profitable *and* won a major award?

B. What is the probability that a randomly selected movie from the studio was profitable *or* won a major award?

C. What is the probability that a randomly selected movie from the studio was *not* profitable?

D. What does the set $P \cap A^C$ represent? What is the probability that a randomly selected movie from the studio is in this set?

10. A high school basketball game was attended by 400 people. The Venn diagram shows the number of people at the game who bought a beverage (B), food (F), team merchandise (M), or none of these items.

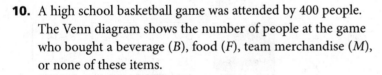

Basketball Game Purchases

A. What is the probability that a randomly selected person at the game bought a beverage *and* food?

B. What is the probability that a randomly selected person at the game bought food *or* team merchandise?

C. What is the probability that a randomly selected person at the game did *not* buy a beverage?

D. What does the set $(B \cap F) \cap M$ represent? What is the probability that a randomly selected person at the game belongs to this set?

11. Open Ended Suppose you spin a spinner that has 10 sectors of the same size numbered 1 through 10. Describe an event with a theoretical probability of $\frac{2}{5}$.

12. (MP) **Reason** Suppose you roll a 20-sided die. Is there an event related to your roll that has a theoretical probability of 48%? Explain.

13. (MP) **Reason** Ben and Pete are brothers whose family is going out to eat on Friday night. Ben wants to go to an Italian restaurant, while Pete wants to go to a Chinese restaurant. Their mother suggests that they roll a number cube to decide on a restaurant, with Ben getting to choose if the number is prime and Pete getting to choose if the number is not prime. Will this process lead to a fair decision? Explain.

14. **(MP) Model with Mathematics** Out of 200 seniors in a high school, there are 75 who are in the chess club, drama club, or robotics club. There are 4 seniors who are in just the chess club and drama club, 9 seniors who are in just the chess club and robotics club, 5 seniors who are in just the drama club and robotics club, and 2 seniors who are in all three clubs.

A. Draw a Venn diagram with regions labeled C, D, and R that represent the chess club, drama club, and robotics club, respectively. Fill in each part of the diagram with the number of seniors that the part represents.

B. Find the probability that a randomly selected senior is in the chess club *or* the robotics club.

C. Find the probability that a randomly selected senior is in the drama club *and* the robotics club.

D. Find the probability that a randomly selected senior is *not* in the chess club.

E. Find the probability that a randomly selected senior is in only the drama club.

23 seniors are in the chess club.
40 seniors are in the drama club.
34 seniors are in the robotics club.

©Monkey Business Images/Shutterstock

Spiral Review • Assessment Readiness

15. How can you translate the graph of $y = \cos x$ to produce the graph of $y = \cos(x + 2) + 3$?

Ⓐ right 2 units and up 3 units

Ⓑ right 2 units and down 3 units

Ⓒ left 2 units and up 3 units

Ⓓ left 2 units and down 3 units

16. The frequency table shows how many rides the members of a tour group went on at an amusement park. How many people went on at least 5 rides?

Rides	0–4	5–9	10–14
People	13	11	6

Ⓐ 11   Ⓑ 13   Ⓒ 17   Ⓓ 24

17. The table shows the average daily high temperature in Madison, Wisconsin, for each month of the year, where month 1 = January, month 2 = February, and so on. Which function best fits the data?

Month number, x	1	2	3	4	5	6	7	8	9	10	11	12
Average high temperature (°F), y	26	31	43	57	68	78	82	79	72	59	44	30

Ⓐ $y = 1.8 \sin(0.48x - 29) + 53$

Ⓑ $y = 0.48 \sin(29x - 1.8) + 53$

Ⓒ $y = 53 \sin(0.48x - 1.8) + 29$

Ⓓ $y = 29 \sin(0.48x - 1.8) + 53$

 I'm in a Learning Mindset!

How did I seek to fill any gaps in my understanding of theoretical and experimental probability?

Two-Way Tables and Probability

(I Can) construct two-way tables and use them to calculate probabilities.

Spark Your Learning

Residents of a town voted on an initiative to increase funding for the local library. The initiative passed, but voters in the town's two precincts were split on it, with Precinct 1 supporting the initiative and Precinct 2 opposing it. A reporter standing in the town center plans to interview residents about why they voted the way they did.

The reporter wants to talk with a voter from Precinct 2 who opposed the initiative. The reporter approaches a woman wearing a pin that says "I voted!"

Complete Part A as a whole class. Then complete Parts B and C in small groups.

A. What is a mathematical question you can ask about this situation? What information would you need to know to answer your question?

B. Look at the table your teacher gave you. How does the table show that voters in Precinct 1 supported the initiative, that voters in Precinct 2 opposed the initiative, and that the initiative passed?

C. To answer your question, what strategy and tool would you use along with all the information you have? What answer do you get?

Turn and Talk How can we tell if a voter that the reporter interviews is more likely to be from Precinct 1 or Precinct 2?

Build Understanding

Investigate Two-Way Tables

A **two-way frequency table** gives frequencies (counts) of people or objects based on two categories. For example, the two-way frequency table from the Spark Your Learning gives frequencies of voters based on their location and how they voted on an initiative. A **two-way relative frequency table** shows relative frequencies instead of frequencies. Recall that a frequency can be converted to a relative frequency by dividing the frequency by the total number of people or objects being categorized in the table.

Two-way frequency table

Location	Vote on Initiative		
	Yes	No	Total
Precinct 1	495	405	900
Precinct 2	270	330	600
Total	765	735	1500

Two-way relative frequency table

Location	Vote on Initiative		
	Yes	No	Total
Precinct 1	0.33	0.27	0.60
Precinct 2	0.18	0.22	0.40
Total	0.51	0.49	1.00

In the relative frequency table, each number in a green-shaded cell is a **joint relative frequency**, which is the ratio of the number of people or objects in a particular category to the total number of people or objects. Each number in a purple-shaded cell is a **marginal relative frequency**, which is the sum of the joint relative frequencies in a row or column. Joint and marginal relative frequencies are useful for determining probabilities.

1 Use the two-way frequency table and two-way relative frequency table shown above.

A. What number were the frequencies in the first table divided by to obtain the relative frequencies in the second table? What does this number represent?

B. What is the probability that a randomly selected voter lives in Precinct 1 and supported the initiative? Is this probability a joint relative frequency or a marginal relative frequency?

C. What is the probability that a randomly selected voter lives in Precinct 2? Is this probability a joint relative frequency or a marginal relative frequency?

D. What is the probability that a randomly selected voter supported the initiative? Is this probability a joint relative frequency or a marginal relative frequency?

E. What is the probability that a randomly selected voter was *not* a supporter of the initiative who lives in Precinct 2?

Turn and Talk Let V_1 be the set of voters who live in Precinct 1, and let V_y be the set of voters who voted "yes" on the initiative. Copy the Venn diagram shown. Then fill in each part of the diagram with the number of voters the part represents.

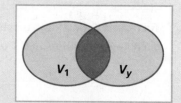

Step It Out

Compute Probabilities from Two-Way Tables

2 A wildlife biologist captures, tags, and releases a sample of two species of snapping turtles as part of her research. The sample includes 50 male and 62 female common snapping turtles, as well as 46 male and 42 female alligator snapping turtles.

Common snapping turtle

Alligator snapping turtle

Make a two-way frequency table and a two-way relative frequency table of the data. Then find the probability that a turtle the biologist tagged meets each condition.

- The turtle is a male common snapping turtle.
- The turtle is female.
- The turtle is an alligator snapping turtle.

Make a two-way frequency table and a two-way relative frequency table.

The two categorical variables for the tables are gender (male or female) and species of snapping turtle (common or alligator).

Two-way frequency table

Species		Gender		
		Male	Female	Total
	Common	50	62	112
	Alligator	46	42	88
	Total	96	104	200

Two-way relative frequency table

Species		Gender		
		Male	Female	Total
	Common	0.25	0.31	0.56
	Alligator	0.23	0.21	0.44
	Total	0.48	0.52	1.00

Use the two-way relative frequency table to find the probabilities.

P(male common snapping turtle) $= 0.25$

A. How was this probability obtained?

P(female) $= 0.52$

P(alligator snapping turtle) $= 0.44$

B. Is this probability a joint or marginal relative frequency?

Turn and Talk How can we tell which combination of gender and species is least likely to be selected at random from the snapping turtles that the biologist tagged?

Check Understanding

The two-way frequency table shows the numbers of small, medium, and large pizzas that a pizzeria sold for takeout and for delivery during the past week. Use the table for Problems 1–6.

		Type of Order		
		Takeout	**Delivery**	**Total**
Pizza Size	**Small**	80	160	240
	Medium	56	88	144
	Large	120	296	416
	Total	256	544	800

1. Make a two-way relative frequency table for the pizza data.

2. What is the probability that a pizza sold during the week was a large pizza that was delivered? Is this probability a joint relative frequency or a marginal relative frequency?

3. What is the probability that a pizza sold during the week was a takeout order? Is this probability a joint relative frequency or a marginal relative frequency?

4. What is the probability that a pizza sold during the week was a medium pizza? Is this probability a joint relative frequency or a marginal relative frequency?

5. What is the probability that a pizza sold during the week was *not* a small pizza that was a takeout order?

6. What is the probability that a pizza sold during the week was *not* a large pizza?

On Your Own

7. (MP) **Use Structure** Consider a two-way relative frequency table in which one categorical variable has m possible values and the other categorical variable has n possible values. How many joint relative frequencies does the table contain? How many marginal relative frequencies does the table contain?

8. **Health and Fitness** Jean manages a sporting goods store and wants to know whether the store should stock more soccer equipment. To gauge her customers' interest in soccer, one Saturday she asks every person who enters the store whether or not they watch soccer and whether or not they play soccer. The Venn diagram shows how many people responded each way to Jean's questions.

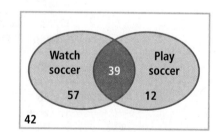

A. Make a two-way frequency table of the data.

B. Make a two-way relative frequency table of the data.

C. What is the probability that a person who visited the store on Saturday watches soccer but does not play soccer? Is this probability a joint relative frequency or a marginal relative frequency?

D. What is the probability that a person who visited the store on Saturday plays soccer? Is this probability a joint relative frequency or a marginal relative frequency?

E. What is the probability that a visitor to the store on Saturday is *not* someone who both watches and plays soccer?

People visiting a downtown shopping center one afternoon were asked how they got there and where they live. The photo shows the breakdown of responses. Use this information for Problems 9–14.

9. Make a two-way frequency table of the data.

10. Make a two-way relative frequency table of the data.

11. What is the probability that a person surveyed lives in the city and took public transit? Is this probability a joint relative frequency or a marginal relative frequency?

Live in the city, took public transit: 125
Live in the city, took no public transit: 65
Live outside the city, took public transit: 40
Live outside the city, took no public transit: 270

12. What is the probability that a person surveyed lives outside the city? Is this probability a joint relative frequency or a marginal relative frequency?

13. What is the probability that a person surveyed did not take public transit? Is this probability a joint relative frequency or a marginal relative frequency?

14. Show how you can represent the data using a Venn diagram.

15. **(MP) Reason** In several problems in this lesson, you have used a two-way frequency table to make a two-way relative frequency table. Given a two-way relative frequency table, can you reverse the process and find the two-way frequency table that produced it? Why or why not?

A city conducted a census to determine the types of schools attended by the city's students. Hannah finds some of the data from the census on different websites and constructs the partial two-way frequency table shown. Use the table for Problems 16–19.

		Type of School			
		Public non-charter	Public charter	Private	Total
Grade Level	Elementary	2098	392	?	?
	Middle school	1834	?	418	2531
	High school	?	435	?	2364
	Total	5208	?	1577	?

16. Copy and complete the two-way frequency table by determining the missing values.

17. Make a two-way relative frequency table. Express the relative frequencies as percents. Round to the nearest tenth if necessary.

18. What is the probability (expressed as a percent) that a student in the city attends a public non-charter high school?

19. What is the probability (expressed as a percent) that a student in the city attends an elementary school?

20. (MP) **Model with Mathematics** The Venn diagram shows, by grade level, the number of students at a certain high school who are taking an art class.

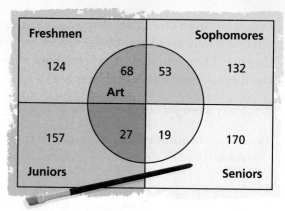

Freshmen			Sophomores
124	68	53	132
	Art		
157	27	19	170
Juniors			Seniors

  A. Describe how you could use a two-way frequency table to display the data shown in the Venn diagram. Include in your description the categorical variables you would use and the possible values of those variables.

  B. Make a two-way frequency table of the data shown in the Venn diagram.

  C. Make a two-way relative frequency table of the data. Express the relative frequencies as percents. Round to the nearest tenth if necessary.

  D. What is the probability (expressed as a percent) that a student at the high school is a freshman who is taking an art class?

Spiral Review • Assessment Readiness

21. Which equation represents the graph of $y = \sin x$ translated 1 unit right and 2 units down?

  (A) $y = \sin(x + 1) - 2$

  (B) $y = \sin(x - 1) - 2$

  (C) $y = \sin(x + 2) + 1$

  (D) $y = \sin(x - 2) + 1$

22. Mark draws a tile at random from a bag containing twelve tiles numbered 1 through 12. The Venn diagram shows the event A of drawing an odd number and the event B of drawing a multiple of 4. What is $P(A \cup B)$?

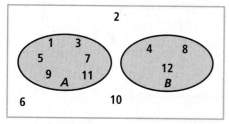

2

1 3
5 7
9   11
  A

4   8
  12
  B

6   10

  (A) 0   (B) $\frac{1}{4}$ (C) $\frac{2}{3}$ (D) $\frac{3}{4}$

23. An observation wheel allows passengers to see a city from a maximum height of 200 feet. Passengers enter a gondola attached to the wheel at a height of 10 feet above the ground. The wheel makes one complete revolution in 8 minutes. Which function gives the height h in feet of the gondola t minutes after the wheel starts moving?

  (A) $h = 95 \sin \frac{\pi}{4}(t - 2) + 105$

  (B) $h = 100 \sin \frac{\pi}{4}(t - 2) + 105$

  (C) $h = 190 \sin \frac{\pi}{4}(t - 2) + 10$

  (D) $h = 200 \sin \frac{\pi}{4}(t - 2) + 10$

24. A spinner has eight sectors of the same size numbered 1 through 8. What is the probability of spinning a prime number?

  (A) $\frac{1}{8}$ (B) $\frac{1}{4}$ (C) $\frac{1}{2}$ (D) $\frac{3}{4}$

I'm in a Learning Mindset!

Is my understanding of two-way tables and probability progressing as I anticipated? What adjustments, if any, do I need to make to enhance my learning?

17.3

Mutually Exclusive and Inclusive Events

(I Can) use probabilities to identify events as either mutually exclusive or inclusive.

Spark Your Learning

At Lincoln High School, many of the students choose to participate in the band and sports programs that are available there.

Some students participate in both the band program and the sports program.
Some students do not play a sport nor do they perform in the band program.

Complete Part A as a whole class. Then complete Parts B–D in small groups.

A. What is a mathematical question you can ask about this situation? What information would you need to know to answer your question?

B. How else could you display the data your teacher gave you?

C. To answer your question, what strategy and tool would you use along with all the information you have? What answer do you get?

D. Does your answer make sense in the context of the situation? How do you know?

Turn and Talk How would you expect your answer to change if the high school eliminated some of its sports programs? If it added a symphonic orchestra to its band programs? Why?

©B Christopher/Alamy

Build Understanding

Explore Probabilities Involving Mutually Exclusive Events

Two events are said to be **mutually exclusive** if both events cannot occur at the same time. For example, flipping a coin results in one of two mutually exclusive outcomes: it comes up either heads or tails.

 1. The Venn diagram shows the possible outcomes for selecting a random tile out of a bag of tiles numbered 10 through 30. Event A is drawing a tile with an odd number, and event B is drawing a tile with a number that is divisible by 4.

$A = \{11, 13, 15, 17, 19, 21, 23, 25, 27, 29\}$

$B = \{12, 16, 20, 24, 28\}$

Make a two-way frequency table to show how many of the drawings are of odd- or even-numbered tiles, and how many are divisible by 4 or not divisible by 4.

	Odd (A)	Even (A^c)	Total
Divisible by 4 (B)	0	5	5
Not divisible by 4 (B^c)	10	6	16
Total	10	11	21

A. Why is there a 0 in in the two-way frequency table?

Find the probabilities of choosing an odd-numbered tile, choosing a tile whose number is divisible by 4, and choosing either an odd-numbered tile or a tile whose number is divisible by 4.

$$P(A) = \frac{\text{number of odd-numbered tiles}}{\text{total number of tiles}} = \frac{10}{21}$$

$$P(B) = \frac{\text{number of tiles with numbers divisible by 4}}{\text{total number of tiles}} = \frac{5}{21}$$

$$P(A \cup B) = \frac{\text{number of odd-numbered tiles or tiles with numbers divisible by 4}}{\text{total number of tiles}} = \frac{15}{21}$$

B. How can you express the probability of choosing an even-numbered tile with a number that is not divisible by 4 using symbols? What is that probability?

C. What equation relates the values $P(A)$ and $P(B)$ to the value of $P(A \cup B)$?

D. Explain why your equation relating $P(A)$ and $P(B)$ to $P(A \cup B)$ is true.

 Turn and Talk Could there be a third event that is mutually exclusive to both events A and B? If not, explain why not. If so, describe such an event and explain its effect on the two-way frequency table. Could there be more than three events, all mutually exclusive from each other?

514

Explore Probabilities Involving Inclusive Events

Two events are **overlapping events** if they have one or more outcomes in common. Overlapping events are sometimes called **inclusive events**.

2 Consider again randomly choosing a tile out of a bag of tiles numbered 10 through 30.

Let A be the event of drawing a tile with an odd number and B be the event of drawing a tile with a prime number. The Venn diagram shows the possible outcomes for the two events.

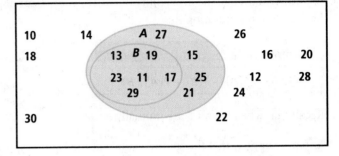

$A = \{11, 13, 15, 17, 19, 21, 23, 25, 27, 29\}$

$B = \{11, 13, 17, 19, 23, 29\}$

Make a two-way frequency table to show how many of the numbers are odd, how many are even, how many are prime, and how many are composite.

	Odd (A)	Even (A^c)	Total
Prime (B)	6	0	6
Composite (B^c)	4	11	15
Total	10	11	21

A. Why is there a 0 in this two-way frequency table?

Find the probabilities of choosing an odd-numbered tile, choosing a tile whose number is prime, choosing a tile whose number is both odd and prime, and choosing a tile whose number is either odd or prime.

$$P(A) = \frac{\text{number of odd-numbered tiles}}{\text{total number of tiles}} = \frac{10}{21}$$

$$P(B) = \frac{\text{number of prime-numbered tiles}}{\text{total number of tiles}} = \frac{6}{21}$$

$$P(A \cap B) = \frac{\text{number of tiles that are both odd AND prime}}{\text{total number of tiles}} = \frac{6}{21}$$

$$P(A \cup B) = \frac{\text{number of tiles that are either odd OR prime}}{\text{total number of tiles}} = \frac{10}{21}$$

B. Why is $P(A \cap B) = P(B)$? Why is $P(A \cup B) = P(A)$?

C. Why does the rule for mutually exclusive events, $P(A \cup B) = P(A) + P(B)$, not hold when events A and B are inclusive?

D. What equation relates the values of $P(A)$, $P(B)$, and $P(A \cap B)$ to the value of $P(A \cup B)$ for inclusive events?

 Turn and Talk Given only its unlabeled data cells, could you determine whether a two-way frequency table represented overlapping events? Explain.

Step It Out

Calculate the Probability of Two Events

For any two events, the probability of either event occurring for a single trial can be found using the Addition Rule.

Addition Rule
$P(A \cup B) = P(A) + P(B) - P(A \cap B)$

Recall that when A and B are mutually exclusive events, $P(A \cap B) = 0$.

3 ▶ Suppose that the spinner shown at the right is spun one time. What is the probability that the spinner lands on blue or D?

Applying the Addition Rule:

$$P(\text{blue or D}) = P(\text{blue} \cup D)$$

$$= P(\text{blue}) + P(D) - P(\text{blue} \cap D)$$

$$= \frac{2}{5} + \frac{1}{5} - 0$$

$$= \frac{3}{5}$$

A. Can the spinner land on both blue and D? What type of events are these?

B. Why is $P(\text{blue}) = \frac{2}{5}$?

C. Why is $P(D) = \frac{1}{5}$?

D. Examine the spinner. How can you verify that the probability found above is correct?

4 ▶ The table shows the number of stocks in each of four distinct industry sectors that increased in price and the number that decreased in price on one particular day last fall. What is the probability that a randomly selected stock from those represented was either a technology stock or one that increased in price?

	Technology	Energy	Transportation	Healthcare	Total
Increase	9	21	13	32	75
Decrease	50	13	25	17	105
Total	59	34	38	49	180

Applying the Addition Rule:

$$P(\text{technology or increased in price}) = P(\text{tech} \cup \text{increase})$$

$$= P(\text{tech}) + P(\text{increase}) - P(\text{tech} \cap \text{increase})$$

$$= \frac{59}{180} + \frac{75}{180} - \frac{9}{180}$$

$$= \frac{125}{180}$$

A. Why is $P(\text{tech}) = \frac{59}{180}$?

B. Why is $P(\text{increase}) = \frac{75}{180}$?

C. Why is this not 0? What type of events are these?

Check Understanding

Suppose a bag contains tiles numbered 41 through 60.

1. Write two mutually exclusive events *A* and *B* with $P(A \text{ or } B) = 1$.

2. Write two inclusive events *C* and *D* with $P(C \text{ or } D) < 1$.

Consider a number cube whose sides are labeled 1 through 6.

3. What is the probability of rolling a number less than 3 or a number greater than 4?

4. What is the probability of rolling a prime number or an even number?

On Your Own

5. **(MP) Reason** How can you determine from a two-way frequency table whether two events are mutually exclusive?

Consider the spinner shown at the right. Find each probability and describe the pairs of events as *mutually exclusive* or *inclusive*.

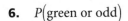

6. $P(\text{green or odd})$

7. $P(\text{green or even})$

8. $P(\text{even or blue})$

9. $P(8 \text{ or pink})$

10. $P(\text{white or red})$

11. $P(\text{prime or odd})$

12. $P(\text{blue or } 1)$

13. $P(\text{even or not blue})$

14. $P(\text{odd or not green})$

15. $P(\text{gray or pink})$

The table below shows the number of sophomores and juniors at a high school that took various science courses last year.

	Chemistry	Physics	Biology	Earth Science	Total
Sophomores	24	5	144	26	199
Juniors	106	25	16	14	161
Total	130	30	160	40	360

For Problems 16–18, two events are described.

a. Determine whether the events are mutually exclusive or inclusive.

b. Explain how to calculate $P(F \text{ or } G)$.

c. Find $P(F \text{ or } G)$.

16. Let *F* be the event of randomly selecting a student who took earth science. Let *G* be the event of randomly selecting a student who took physics.

17. Let *F* be the event of randomly selecting a student who was a junior. Let *G* be the event of randomly selecting a student who took chemistry.

18. Let *F* be the event of randomly selecting a student who was a junior. Let *G* be the event of randomly selecting a student who did not take biology.

Consider the spinner shown at the right. Find the
probability of each union of events and describe
the events as *mutually exclusive* or *inclusive*.

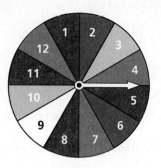

19. $P(\text{green or odd})$

20. $P(\text{green or even})$

21. $P(\text{odd or blue})$

22. $P(8 \text{ or pink})$

23. $P(\text{white or red})$ **24.** $P(\text{prime or odd})$

25. $P(\text{blue or } 1)$ **26.** $P(\text{even or not blue})$

27. $P(\text{odd or not green})$ **28.** $P(3 \text{ or pink})$

Twenty game tokens numbered 51 through 70 are placed in a box. Let A be the
event that a multiple of 3 is randomly chosen from the box. Let B be the event that
a multiple of 8 is randomly chosen from the box. The Venn diagram below shows
which numbers are elements of event A and which are elements of event B.

29. Find $P(A \text{ or } B)$.

30. Find $P(A \text{ or } B^C)$.

31. Find $P(A^C \text{ or } B)$.

32. Find $P(A^C \text{ or } B^C)$.

33. Make a two-way frequency table
to represent A, B, A^C, and B^C.

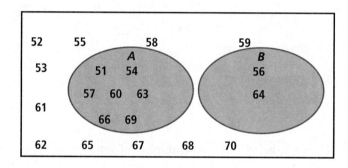

34. Make a two-way relative frequency table to represent A, B, A^C, and B^C.

Suppose the situation described for **Problems 29–34** is changed so that B is the event
that an even-numbered token is randomly chosen from the box. Event A remains the
same. The Venn diagram below models this new situation.

35. Find $P(A \text{ or } B)$.

36. Find $P(A \text{ or } B^C)$.

37. Find $P(A^C \text{ or } B)$.

38. Find $P(A^C \text{ or } B^C)$.

39. Find $P((A \text{ or } B)^C)$.

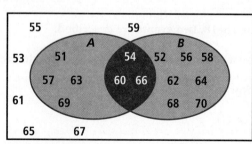

40. Make a two-way frequency table to represent A, B, A^C, and B^C.

41. Make a two-way relative frequency table to represent A, B, A^C, and B^C.

Geography Martina is learning about the 50 states of the United States. To help her learn their locations, she created the Venn diagram shown at the right, using the postal codes of the states. Set *A* includes states that border Canada or Mexico, and set *B* includes the states that border an ocean or the Gulf of Mexico. Note that Pennsylvania and Ohio share a water border with Canada, but Wisconsin does not.

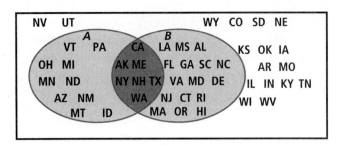

42. What is the probability that a randomly selected state borders Canada or Mexico or an ocean or the Gulf of Mexico?

43. What is the probability that a randomly selected state borders Canada or Mexico or does not border an ocean or gulf?

44. What is the probability that a randomly selected state borders an ocean or gulf or does not border Canada or Mexico?

45. What is the probability that a randomly selected state does not border Canada or Mexico or does not border the ocean or the Gulf of Mexico?

A bag contains 100 lettered tiles. The table below shows the frequency of each letter. Consider Y as a consonant.

Letters	J, K, Q, X, Z	B, C, F, P, V, W, Y	G, H, M	D, L, S, U	N, R, T	O	A, I	E
Number of tiles	1	2	3	4	6	8	9	12

For Problems 46–51, two events are described.

a. Determine whether the events are mutually exclusive or inclusive.

b. Find $P(A \text{ or } B)$.

46. Let *A* be the event of randomly selecting a vowel. Let *B* be the event of randomly selecting a consonant.

47. Let *A* be the event of randomly selecting an E. Let *B* be the event of randomly selecting a letter in the word "mathematics."

48. Let *A* be the event of randomly selecting a vowel. Let *B* be the event of randomly selecting a letter in the word "probability."

49. Let *A* be the event of randomly selecting a consonant. Let *B* be the event of randomly selecting a letter in the word "mathematics."

50. Let *A* be the event of randomly selecting a letter in the word "probability." Let *B* be the event of randomly selecting a letter in the word "even."

51. Let *A* be the event of randomly selecting a letter in the word "exclusive." Let *B* be the event of randomly selecting a letter in the word "inclusive."

52. **(MP) Attend to Precision** Two events that overlap are *inclusive* events, but two events that do not overlap are not called *exclusive* events. Rather, they are called *mutually exclusive* events. Why is the word *mutually* added to the term describing non-overlapping events?

53. Jorge has a 12-sided number cube with sides labeled 1–12. When the cube is rolled, each side is equally likely to face up. What is the probability of rolling an even number or a prime number?

54. **Open Ended** Think of two events A and B that are mutually exclusive and $P(A \text{ or } B) < 1$. Describe inclusive events C and D such that $P(C \text{ or } D) = P(A \text{ or } B)$.

Spiral Review • Assessment Readiness

55. Consider the spinner shown. How much greater is the probability of spinning a prime number than the probability of spinning a multiple of 4?

Ⓐ $\frac{1}{10}$ Ⓒ $\frac{3}{10}$

Ⓑ $\frac{1}{5}$ Ⓓ $\frac{1}{2}$

56. In the Venn diagram, A is the event that a student got an A or a B on their last algebra test. B is the event that a student got an A or a B on their last paper for English class. What is the probability that a randomly selected student got an A or a B on either their last algebra test or their last paper for English class?

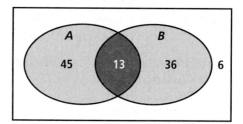

Ⓐ 6%   Ⓒ 13%

Ⓑ 58%   Ⓓ 94%

57. The two-way table shows the results of a survey of what people were wearing on a fall day. Match each outfit combination with its probability to the nearest tenth of a percent.

	Belt	No belt	Total
Sweater	27	21	48
No sweater	8	69	72
Total	35	85	120

A. belt

B. no sweater

C. sweater and no belt

D. belt and no sweater

1. 6.7%

2. 17.5%

3. 29.2%

4. 60%

 I'm in a Learning Mindset!

How did I proactively seek to fill any gaps in knowledge or understanding?

Theoretical Probability

Theoretical probability is used to predict the likelihood of different events. Before an experiment or trial occurs, the results can be predicted based on given information.

The theoretical probability of rolling a multiple of 3 on a number cube labeled 1–6 is shown.

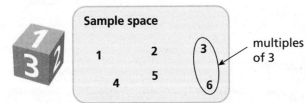

multiples of 3

$$\text{probability} = \frac{\text{\# of outcomes for a given event}}{\text{total \# of possible outcomes}}$$
$$= \frac{2}{6} = \frac{1}{3}$$

Experimental Probability

After running an experiment multiple times, you can calculate the experimental probability by relating the number of successes and the number of trials.

> Experimental probability is based on what happens, not what is expected to happen.

When rolling a number cube 10 times, the cube shows a multiple of 3 twice. So, the experimental probability of rolling a multiple of 3 is shown below.

$$\text{probability} = \frac{\text{\# of successes}}{\text{\# of trails}} = \frac{2}{10} = 20\%$$

Contingency Table

A two-way table, or contingency table, can show data for two related variables for the same situation.

Data was collected about rolling a number cube 75 times.

	≤ 3	> 3	Total
Even	10	29	39
Odd	26	10	36
Total	36	39	75

This table can be written with frequencies, as above, or relative frequencies, by dividing each frequency by the overall total.

	≤ 3	> 3	Total
Even	0.13	0.39	0.52
Odd	0.35	0.13	0.48
Total	0.48	0.52	1.00

Exclusivity of Events

Two related events are either mutually exclusive or inclusive. If two events cannot both happen at the same time, like prime and not prime, they are mutually exclusive.

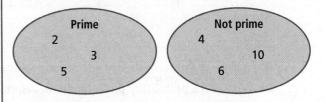

If two events overlap, like odd numbers and multiples of 3, they are inclusive.

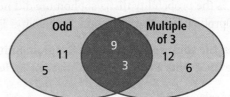

Vocabulary

Choose the correct term from the box to complete each sentence.

1. A two-way table is also called a(n) ___?___.

2. The likelihood of an event using the results of multiple trials is called ___?___.

3. Two events that cannot happen at the same time are ___?___.

4. The likelihood of an event using given information about a situation is called ___?___.

5. The set of possible outcomes for a probability situation is the ___?___.

Concepts and Skills

6. Why is the sum of a probability and its complement always 1?

7. Let A be the event that a person was in a car yesterday. Let B be the event that a person washed dishes yesterday.

   A. Find $P(A \text{ or } B)$ and describe what this probability represents.

   B. Find $P(A^C \text{ and } B^C)$ and describe what this probability represents.

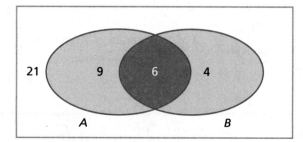

8. (MP) **Use Tools** A high school kept track of which students took a music class last year. State what strategy and tool you will use to answer the question, explain your choice, and then find the answer.

	Freshmen	Sophomores	Juniors	Seniors	Total
Music class	166	167	165	204	702
No music class	44	39	35	23	141
Total	210	206	200	227	843

   A. What is the probability that a randomly selected student took a music class?

   B. What is the probability that a randomly selected student was not a junior?

   C. What is the probability that a randomly selected student was a freshman who did not take a music class?

   D. Is the probability that a sophomore did not take a music class a theoretical probability or experimental probability? Explain your reasoning.

Consider the spinner shown. Find the probability of each union of events and describe the events as *mutually exclusive* or *inclusive*.

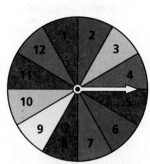

9. $P(\text{purple } or \text{ odd})$

10. $P(\text{blue } or \text{ even})$

11. $P(\text{tan } or \text{ even})$

12. $P(\text{red } or \text{ even})$

13. $P(\text{green } or \text{ prime})$

14. $P(\text{tan } or \text{ prime})$

18 Probability and Decision Making

Module Performance Task: *Spies and Analysts™*

4ᵗʰ Down and What

How can you decide if you should go for it on 4th down with one yard to go?

Are You Ready?

Complete these problems to review prior concepts and skills you will need for this module.

Multiply and Divide Rational Numbers

Simplify each expression.

1. 0.4×6

2. $\dfrac{4}{7} \cdot \dfrac{3}{8}$

3. $-\dfrac{8}{18} \cdot \dfrac{12}{9}$

4. $1.08 \div 1.2$

5. $\dfrac{5}{18} \div \left(-\dfrac{15}{9}\right)$

6. $3 \div \dfrac{1}{10}$

Probability of Simple Events

Given a set of 10 cards numbered 1 to 10, calculate each probability.

7. What is the probability that you randomly choose a card with an even number?

8. What is the probability that you randomly choose a card with a number less than 4?

9. What is the probability that you randomly choose a card with a number divisible by 4?

10. What is the probability that you randomly choose a card with a multiple of 3?

Probability of Compound Events Involving *And*

Given a set of 10 cards numbered 1 to 10, calculate each probability.

11. What is the probability that you randomly choose a card with a number greater than 3 and less than or equal to 8?

12. What is the probability that you randomly choose a card with a number less than 4 and greater than 7?

13. What is the probability that you randomly choose a card that is an even number greater than 5?

Connecting Past and Present Learning

Previously, you learned:

- to compute probabilities using two-way tables,
- to contrast theoretical and experimental probabilities, and
- to determine if events were mutually exclusive or inclusive.

In this module, you will learn:

- to calculate conditional probabilities using two-way tables and formulas,
- to understand that two events *A* and *B* are independent if the probability of *A* and *B* occurring together is the product of each individual probability, and
- to use conditional probability to analyze real-world decisions.

Conditional Probability

(I Can) calculate conditional probabilities using two-way tables and formulas.

Spark Your Learning

Tina is going to a "fee-to-fish" recreation park that has two different ponds, Clear Water Pond and Big Fish Pond. The park guarantees that you will catch a fish and stocks both ponds with bass, perch, bluegill, and catfish.

> Tina flips a coin to decide where to fish: "heads" for Clear Water and "tails" for Big Fish. She hopes to catch a bass.

Complete Part A as a whole class. Then complete Parts B–D in small groups.

  A. What is a mathematical question you can ask about this situation? What information would you need to know to answer your question?

  B. What must you know to find the probability of an event?

  C. To answer your question, what strategy and tool would you use along with all the information you have? What assumption must you first make about the likelihood of catching any particular fish? What answer do you get?

  D. Does your answer make sense in the context of the situation? How do you know? How does it compare to the answer if Tina's coin had landed "tails" instead of "heads"?

 Turn and Talk Suppose you were asked the probability that Tina catches a bass without knowing the result of the coin toss. How would you find this probability? What is the relationship between the sample space for this situation and the sample space you used to answer the original question?

Build Understanding

Find Conditional Probabilities from a Two-Way Frequency Table

In Lesson 17.1 you calculated the probability $P(A)$ which is the probability event A occurs. In this lesson, you will calculate the **conditional probability** $P(A \mid B)$ which is the probability event A occurs given that event B has already occurred.

1 ▶ Student council surveyed 240 upperclassmen on whether or not they attended the homecoming football game. The two-way frequency table shows the results.

	Attended	Did not attend	Total
Juniors	74	36	110
Seniors	82	48	130
Total	156	84	240

Event A = attended football game.
Event B = junior.

Let event A be "attended the homecoming football game." Let event B be a junior.

A. First consider the probability that a junior attended the homecoming football game. This is asking for the conditional probability $P(A \mid B)$ where you assume event B, a junior, is true and you want to know the likelihood that event A, attended the homecoming football game, is also true.

How many upperclassmen surveryed are juniors? How many of those juniors attended the homecoming football game?

$$P(A \mid B) = \frac{\text{number of juniors who attended}}{\text{number of juniors}} \approx 67\%$$

Why is the probability $P(A \mid B)$ different from the probability $P(A)$?

B. Next consider the probability that an upperclassman who attended the homecoming football game is a junior. This is asking for the conditional probability $P(B \mid A)$ where you assume event B, attended the homecoming football game, is true and you want to know the likelihood that event A, a junior, is also true.

How many upperclassmen surveryed attended the homecoming football game? How many of those attendees are juniors?

$$P(B \mid A) = \frac{\text{number that attended who are juniors}}{\text{number that attended}} \approx 47\%$$

Why is the probability $P(B \mid A)$ different from the probability $P(A \cap B)$?

C. Are conditional probabilities commutative? In other words, does $P(A \mid B) = P(B \mid A)$? Explain.

Turn and Talk For the question "What is the probability that a senior did not attend the homecoming football game?", what event is assumed to have already occurred?

Find Conditional Probabilities from a Two-Way Relative Frequency Table

A frequency is the number of times something occurs. A relative frequency is the fraction of times something occurs which is also the probability that something occurs. To find relative frequencies, divide each frequency by the total number in the sample.

 In the scenario from Task 1, a student council surveyed 240 upperclassmen on whether or not they attended the homecoming football game. You can use a relative frequency table to find conditional probabilities.

A. Copy and complete the relative frequency table for the data from Task 1.

	Attended	Did not attend	Total
Juniors	$\frac{74}{240} \approx 0.31$	?	?
Seniors	?	?	?
Total	?	?	$\frac{240}{240} = 1.00$

B. Recall from Task 1 that event A is "attended the homecoming football game" and event B is a junior. Consider the probability that a junior attended the homecoming football game. You can find this conditional probability $P(A \mid B)$ from the two-way relative frequency table.

What is the probability an upperclassmen surveryed is a junior? What is the probability an upperclassmen is a junior and attended the football game?

$$P(A \mid B) = \frac{P(A \cap B)}{P(B)} \approx 67\%$$

Is the probability $P(A \mid B)$ found from using a frequency table in Task 1 the same as the probability $P(A \mid B)$ found here from using a relative frequency table? Explain why this makes sense.

C. You can prove that finding probabilities using relative frequency tables is the same as finding probabilities using frequency tables.

Let $n(S)$ represent the number of elements in the sample space. What does $n(B)$ represent? What does $n(A \cap B)$ represent?

What is a formula for $P(A \cap B)$ using $n(A \cap B)$ and $n(S)$? What is a formula for $P(B)$ using $n(B)$ and $n(S)$?

$$P(B \mid A) = \frac{\text{number that attended who are juniors}}{\text{number that attended}} \approx 47\%$$

Using these formulas, show that $P(A \mid B) = \frac{P(A \cap B)}{P(B)}$ and $P(A \mid B) = \frac{n(A \cap B)}{n(B)}$ are equivalent.

 Turn and Talk When calculating a conditional probability from a two-way table, explain why it doesn't matter whether the table gives frequencies or relative frequencies

Find Conditional Probabilities from a Formula

You do not have to create a table to find conditional probabilities. Instead, you can use a formula.

Conditional Probability
The conditional probability of *A* given *B* (that is, the probability that event *A* occurs given that event *B* occurs) is as follows: $$P\left(A\mid B\right) = \frac{P(A \cap B)}{P(B)}$$

3 ▶ A standard number cube is rolled. Consider the probability that the number rolled is an odd number greater than or equal to 3.

A. The probability that the number rolled is an odd number greater than or equal to 3 is a conditional probability.

What is event *B* which is assumed to have occurred?

What is event *A*?

B. The numbers on a standard number cube are {1, 2, 3, 4, 5, 6}.

What is the set of odd numbers?

What is the set of numbers greater than or equal to 3?

What is the set of numbers that is both odd and greater than or equal to 3?

Therefore $n(S) = 6$, $n(B) = 3$, and $n(A \cap B) = 2$.

C. Use the formula to find the conditional probability.

What is $P\left(A \cap B\right)$?

What is $P\left(B\right)$?

Use these probabilities to find the conditional probability $P\left(A \mid B\right)$.

$$P\left(A \mid B\right) = \frac{\frac{2}{6} \cdot 6}{\frac{3}{6} \cdot 6} = \frac{2}{3}$$

D. According to how a relative frequency table is used to determine a conditional probability, does $P\left(A \mid B\right) = \frac{P(A \cap B)}{P(B)}$ make sense? Explain.

 Turn and Talk Under what conditions would $P\left(A \mid B\right) = P\left(B \mid A\right)$?

Step It Out

Find Conditional Probabilities

You can find conditional probabilities using frequency tables, relative frequency tables, and the conditional probability formula.

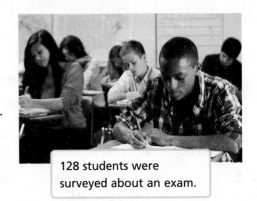

128 students were surveyed about an exam.

4 A teacher surveyed all 128 of her students anonymously about an exam they took mid-semester. Let event A be "passed the exam," event B be "did not pass the exam," event C be "studied 3 hours or less," and event D be "studied more than 3 hours."

Use a frequency table.

The results of the survey are shown in the relative frequency table.

	Passed exam	Did not pass exam	Total
Studied 3 hours or less	33	27	60
Studied more than 3 hours	59	9	68
Total	92	36	128

A. How could you find the totals for each row and column if they were not given?

What is the probability that a student who passed the exam studied more than 3 hours?

$$P(D \mid A) = \frac{n(D \cap A)}{n(A)} = \frac{59}{92} = 64\%$$

B. Why is this probability $P(D|A)$ and not $P(A|D)$?

Use a relative frequency table.

Create a relative frequency table.

	Passed exam	Did not pass exam	Total
Studied 3 hours or less	0.26	0.21	0.47
Studied more than 3 hours	0.46	0.07	0.53
Total	0.72	0.28	1.00

C. How are the values in the table determined?

What is the probability that a student who studied more than 3 hours passed the exam?

$$P(A \mid D) = \frac{n(A \cap D)}{n(D)} = \frac{0.46}{0.53} \approx 87\%$$

D. Why is the denominator $P(D)$ and not $P(A)$?

Use a formula.

What is the probability that a student who did not pass the exam studied 3 hours or less?

$$P(D \mid B) = \frac{P(D \cap B)}{P(B)} = \frac{\frac{27}{128}}{\frac{36}{128}} = 75\%$$

E. Explain how $P(D \cap B)$ and $P(B)$ were found.

Check Understanding

A group of 300 sophomores and juniors were asked if they want to live in a city or live elsewhere. The results of the survey are shown in the two-way frequency table.

1. Using the frequency table, what is the probability that a sophomore wants to live in a city?

2. Create a relative frequency table for the data. Using this table, what is the probability that a student who wants to live elsewhere is a sophomore?

	Live in a city	Live elsewhere	Total
Sophomores	156	18	174
Juniors	66	60	126
Total	222	78	300

3. Using the formula for conditional probability, what is the probability that a student who wants to live elsewhere is a junior?

4. Using any method, what is the probability that a junior wants to live in a city?

On Your Own

(MP) Use Structure A school store surveyed its customers, students and teachers, to determine if they use gel pens. The results of the survey are shown in the two-way frequency table.

	Uses gel pens	Does not use gel pens	Total
Students	139	49	188
Teachers	23	36	59
Total	162	85	247

5. What is the probability that a student uses gel pens?

6. What is the probability that a teacher does not use gel pens?

7. What is the probability that a customer who does not use gel pens is a student?

(MP) Use Structure A wireless provider surveyed a group of underclassmen to see if they prefer a smaller smartphone of under 5 inches or a larger smartphone of over 5 inches. The results of the survey are shown in the two-way frequency table.

	Prefer smaller smartphone	Prefer larger smartphone	Total
Freshman	32	60	92
Sophomores	36	62	98
Total	68	122	190

8. What is the probability that a sophomore prefers a smaller smartphone?

9. What is the probability that a freshman prefers a smaller smartphone?

10. Is the probability that a person is a freshman and prefers a larger smartphone the same as the probability that a freshman prefers a larger smartphone? Explain.

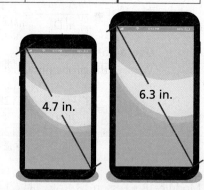

4.7 in.

6.3 in.

Use Structure The operators of the roller coasters and water rides at an amusement park were asked if they like roller coasters. The results of the survey are shown in the two-way relative frequency table.

	Likes roller coasters	Dislikes roller coasters	Total
Roller coaster operators	0.45	0.10	0.55
Water ride operators	0.28	0.17	0.45
Total	0.73	0.27	1.00

11. What is the probability that a water ride operator likes roller coasters?

12. What is the probability that an operator who likes roller coasters runs a water ride?

13. **Critique Reasoning** A student made the following calculation. Explain the student's error, and find the correct probability.

$$P(\text{likes roller coaster rides} \mid \text{roller coaster operator}) = \frac{0.45}{0.73} \approx 62\%$$

14. A fitness center had its annual fundraiser for the Special Olympics. Participants either biked or ran. After studying the data of the participants, one of the organizers of the fundraiser said, "The conditional probability of a participant choosing to bike for the fundraiser given that the participant is over 30 is greater than the conditional probability of a participant choosing to run for the fundraiser given that the participant is over 30." Explain what the statement means in everyday language so that the organizers can share this information with people who have no statistics background.

15. **Open Ended** Describe two events in your everyday life where one event might affect the likelihood of the other. Describe how you think the probability is affected in terms of likelihood.

Problems 16–18 refer to a standard deck of playing cards.

16. What is the probability that a black card drawn from the deck is an ace?

17. What is the probability that a face card (a king, queen, or jack) drawn from the deck is a heart?

18. What is the probability that a spade drawn from the deck is a queen?

Use Structure The cafeteria recently offered pizza or a sub for lunch. The upperclassmen were asked which they preferred. The results of the survey are shown in the two-way frequency table. Use the table for Problems 20–22.

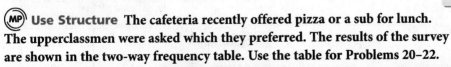

	Prefers pizza	Prefers a sub
Juniors	98	64
Seniors	105	41

19. Complete the frequency table. Then create a relative frequency table of the data.

20. Using any method, what is the probability that a junior prefers pizza?

21. Using any method, what is the probability that an upperclassman who prefers subs is a senior?

Problems 22–24 refer to a standard number cube.

22. What is the probability that an odd number rolled on a number cube is a 1?

23. What is the probability of rolling a prime number that is less than 3?

24. Is the probability that an even number rolled is 4 or more and the probability that a number 4 or more rolled is an even number the same? Explain.

(MP) Use Structure Some of the students at a high school were interviewed to see if they would be interested in playing soccer or taking a science class. The results of the survey are shown in a two-way frequency table.

25. Add totals for the rows and columns to finish the frequency table. Then create a relative frequency table of the data.

26. Using any method, what is the probability that a soccer player is taking science?

27. Using any method, what is the probability that a student who is not interested in science is also not interested in soccer?

	Soccer	No soccer
Science	63	501
No science	21	167

Spiral Review • Assessment Readiness

28. You roll a number cube. Event A is rolling an even number and event B is rolling a number greater than 3. What is $P(A \cup B)$?

Ⓐ $\frac{1}{3}$ Ⓑ $\frac{1}{2}$ Ⓒ $\frac{2}{3}$ Ⓓ $\frac{5}{6}$

29. Let event A be teachers and event B be owns plants. Which statement is true?

	Owns plants	No plants
Teachers	58	34
Administrators	21	23

Ⓐ $P(A \cap B) = P(A) \cdot P(B \mid A)$

Ⓑ $P(A \cap B) = P(A) \cdot P(A \mid B)$

Ⓒ $P(A \cap B) = P(A) \cdot P(B)$

Ⓓ $P(A^C \cap B) = P(A^C) \cdot P(B)$

30. From the frequency data in the table, which probability is a marginal probability?

	Art class	Music class
Sophomore	38	26
Junior	16	20

Ⓐ 58%   Ⓑ 54%   Ⓒ 38%   Ⓓ 26%

31. Using the frequency data in the table, what is $P(\text{Sophomore or No glasses})$?

	Glasses	No glasses
Freshman	21	39
Sophomore	17	38

Ⓐ $\frac{38}{77}$ Ⓑ $\frac{76}{115}$ Ⓒ $\frac{38}{55}$ Ⓓ $\frac{94}{115}$

©Flashon Studio/Shutterstock

⬡ I'm in a Learning Mindset!

What do I do when I do not know if I should apply the formula for the conditional probability to determine a probability?

Dependent and Independent Events

(I Can) determine if events are independent or dependent and calculate probabilities of the events accordingly.

Spark Your Learning

A skydiving team has been using two different practice targets in their training: a plain tan target and a brightly-colored target.

The team keeps detailed records of all jumps, including hits or misses and the target used.

©Dreamframer/Shutterstock

Complete Part A as a whole class. Then complete Parts B–D in small groups.

A. What is a mathematical question you can ask about this situation? What information would you need to know to answer your question?

B. How could you represent the information you need using the notation of probability?

C. To answer your question, what strategy and tool would you use along with all the information you have? What answer do you get?

D. Does your answer make sense in the context of the situation? How do you know?

 Turn and Talk What kind of result would make you conclude that the target's color and whether or not the team hit it were not independent of each other?

Build Understanding

Determine the Independence of Events

Recall that a conditional probability calculates the probability that some event A occurs given that some event B has already occurred. Sometimes one event occurring or not occurring affects the outcome of the other event. For example, consider the probabilities of drawing even- or odd-numbered tiles when choosing two of the number tiles shown below, one at a time, from a bag.

| 1 | 2 | 3 | 4 | 5 |

If you replace the first tile before drawing the second one, you have restored the original sample space ahead of drawing the second tile. That makes the two tile draws **independent events**: the occurrence or non-occurrence of one event will not affect the probability of the other event.

Now consider drawing the second tile without first replacing the first tile. The first draw having occurred now affects the probability of the second event because the sample space has changed. This makes the two tile draws **dependent events**: the occurrence or non-occurrence of one event *does* affect the probability of the other event.

1 ▶ A survey was given to 100 students. Two of the survey questions asked students if they drink milk and if they like yogurt. The results of the survey for these two questions are shown in the two-way frequency table.

	Likes yogurt	Dislikes yogurt	Total
Drinks milk	44	36	80
Does not drink milk	11	9	20
Total	55	45	100

The probability that a student who likes yogurt also drinks milk is the conditional probability $P(A \mid B)$ where event A is drinks milk and event B is likes yogurt. First find that the total number of students who like yogurt is 55. Of the students who like yogurt, 44 drink milk. Write the probability that a student who likes yogurt also drinks milk: $P(A \mid B) = \frac{44}{55} = 80\%$.

The probability that a student drinks milk, $P(A)$ is $\frac{80}{100} = 80\%$.

A. What do you notice about the probabilities $P(A \mid B)$ and $P(A)$?

B. For the same events A and B, find the probabilities $P(B \mid A)$ and $P(B)$. What do you notice about these probabilities?

C. Do you think one event affects the probability of the other event? Explain. Are the events that a student likes yogurt and that a student drinks milk independent?

 Turn and Talk Are the events that a student does not drink milk and that a student dislikes yogurt independent events? Explain.

Show Events Are Independent

You observed in the previous task that when A and B are independent events, then $P(A \mid B) = P(A)$. The following formula can be used to test whether two events are independent.

Probability of Independent Events

Events A and B are independent if and only if $P(A \cap B) = P(A) \cdot P(B)$.

---

2 ▶ You studied the formula for conditional probability in the previous lesson. Given that when A and B are independent events $P(A \mid B) = P(A)$, you can derive the formula for the Probability of Independent Events from the formula for conditional probability. A and B are independent events.

$$P(A \mid B) = \frac{P(A \cap B)}{P(B)} \qquad \text{Conditional Probability Formula}$$

$$P(A) = \frac{P(A \cap B)}{P(B)} \qquad \text{Replace } P(A \mid B) \text{ with } P(A) \text{ because the events are independent.}$$

$$P(A) \cdot P(B) = P(A \cap B) \qquad \text{Multiply both sides by } P(B) \text{ and simplify.}$$

A. How can you use the formula $P(A) \cdot P(B) = P(A \cap B)$ to show that $P(B \mid A) = P(B)$ when A and B are independent events?

B. Describe how you can use the formula for the Probability of Independent Events to determine whether two events are independent.

C. If $P(A) \cdot P(B) \neq P(A \cap B)$, what do you know about events A and B?

A survey of 187 college freshman and sophomores were asked if they were taking any early morning classes. The results of the survey are shown in the two-way relative frequency table. Use the table for Part D.

	Early classes	No early classes	Total
Freshmen	0.144	0.385	0.529
Sophomores	0.128	0.343	0.471
Total	0.272	0.728	1

D. Let event A represent a student taking early morning classes and let event B represent a student being a freshman. If events A and B are independent events, what should be true about the relative frequencies? Verify your prediction.

Turn and Talk What are two ways of showing that two events are independent?

Find the Probability of Dependent Events

When two events are dependent instead of independent, you cannot simply multiply the probabilities of the events to find the probability of their intersection. Instead, because the probability of one event depends on the other event, you must use a formula that involves conditional probability.

Multiplication Rule

For events A and B, given that event A has occurred, $P(A \cap B) = P(A) \cdot P(B \mid A)$.

---

3 Consider drawing a marble without looking from the bag shown. The probability that the first marble drawn is red is $P(R) = \frac{5}{5+3} = \frac{5}{8}$, and the probability that the first marble drawn is blue is $P(B) = \frac{3}{5+3} = \frac{3}{8}$. If the first marble drawn is replaced in the bag before a second is drawn, then the events of drawing one marble and then another are independent. So, for example, $P(R \cap B) = \frac{5}{8} \cdot \frac{3}{8} = \frac{15}{64}$.

If the first marble is not replaced before drawing the second, however, the sample space for the second draw changes in two ways: the number of marbles remaining in the bag is reduced, and the ratios of the remaining marble colors changes. In general, drawing without replacement leads to dependent events.

A. Suppose a red marble is drawn and not replaced in the bag.

What are the elements of the new sample space for the second draw? How does this help you find the probability of drawing a red marble and then a blue one (without replacement)?

Complete the statement: $P(R \cap B) = P(R) \cdot P(B \mid R) = \frac{5}{8} \cdot \frac{3}{?} = \frac{15}{?}$

B. How does your result for Part A compare with $P(R \cap B)$ with replacement? Why does this make sense?

C. Now suppose that a blue marble is drawn from the bag, not replaced, and then a red marble is drawn.

What are the elements of the new sample space for the second draw?

Complete the statement: $P(B \cap R) = P(B) \cdot P(R \mid B) = \frac{3}{8} \cdot \frac{?}{7} = \frac{?}{56}$

D. Compare your results for Parts A and B. What do you notice? How can you use this result to write an alternate expression for the Multiplication Rule for the Probability of Dependent Events?

Turn and Talk How can you extend what you did above to find the probability of drawing a red marble, then a blue one, and then another blue one (all without replacement)? What is this probability?

Step It Out

Find the Probability of Two Independent or Dependent Events

While you can apply the rule for the probability of independent events A and B, $P(A \cap B) = P(A) \cdot P(B)$, only when you know that two events are independent, you can apply the Multiplication Rule, $P(A \cap B) = P(A) \cdot P(B \mid A)$, to any two events A and B.

To see this, remember that for independent events A and B, $P(A) = P(A \mid B)$ and $P(B) = P(B \mid A)$. Substituting $P(B)$ for $P(B \mid A)$ in the Multiplication Rule then gives $P(A \cap B) = P(A) \cdot P(B \mid A) = P(A) \cdot P(B)$, which is just the rule for finding the probability of independent events.

4 One hundred sixty high school juniors and seniors at a school were asked if they were working part-time jobs during the current school semester. The results of the survey are shown in the table below.

	Employed	Not employed	Total
Juniors	8	72	80
Seniors	51	29	80
Total	59	101	160

Use the Multiplication Rule in two ways to find the probability that a student is a senior and is employed part-time this semester. Are these events independent? How do you know?

To apply the Multiplication Rule, use an expression for $P(\text{senior} \mid \text{employed})$ or an expression for $P(\text{employed} \mid \text{senior})$.

> **A.** How is this probability related to the frequencies in the two-way table?

$P(\text{senior} \cap \text{employed})$
$= P(\text{senior}) \cdot P(\text{employed} \mid \text{senior})$

$= \dfrac{80}{160} \cdot \dfrac{51}{80}$

$= \dfrac{51}{160}$ or 31.875%

$P(\text{senior} \cap \text{employed})$
$= P(\text{employed}) \cdot P(\text{senior} \mid \text{employed})$

$= \dfrac{59}{160} \cdot \dfrac{51}{59}$

$= \dfrac{51}{160}$ or 31.875%

> **B.** If the events were independent, what would you expect the probability that a student is a junior and is employed to be? Explain. What is the probability?

Now notice that $P(\text{senior}) \cdot P(\text{employed})$
$= \frac{80}{160} \cdot \frac{59}{160} = \frac{59}{320}$ or 18.4375%.

Since $P(A \cap B) \neq P(A) \cdot P(B)$, events A and B are not independent, but are dependent. The probability that a student is a senior and is employed is about 32%.

Turn and Talk If the events were independent, how would you expect the following to be related?

- $P(\text{employed} \mid \text{junior})$, $P(\text{employed} \mid \text{senior})$, $P(\text{employed})$
- $P(\text{junior} \mid \text{employed})$, $P(\text{junior} \mid \text{not employed})$, $P(\text{junior})$

Check Understanding

The results of a survey of employees of a manufacturing company are shown in the relative frequency table. Let *A* represent the event of an employee being age 40 or under and let *B* represent the event that an employee likes basketball. Use the table to answer Problems 1 and 2.

	Likes basketball	Dislikes basketball	Total
Ages 40 and under	0.39	0.26	0.65
Age over 40	0.21	0.14	0.35
Total	0.60	0.40	1

1. What do you notice about the probabilities $P(A \mid B)$ and $P(A)$? about the probabilities $P(B \mid A)$ and $P(B)$? What does this mean about the events?

2. Use the formula for the probability of independent events to show that events *A* and *B* are independent.

3. Suppose a bag contains the letter tiles shown below.

A	M	T	A	T	O	H	M

   A. A tile is drawn from the bag, and the letter is recorded. The tile is then returned to the bag, the bag is shaken, and a second tile is drawn. Are the events independent or dependent? What is $P(\text{vowel} \cap \text{vowel})$?

   B. Suppose that the process in Problem A is carried out, but without replacing the first tile before drawing the second. Are the events independent or dependent? What is $P(\text{vowel} \cap \text{vowel})$?

4. Using a two-way table for two events *A* and *B* and their complements, what are three different ways to determine $P(A \cap B)$?

On Your Own

5. When drawing more than one item in a row at random from a collection of items, which represents independent events, and which represents dependent events: drawing one item, recording it, and returning it before drawing a second item, or drawing one item, recording it, and then drawing a second item without first replacing the first item drawn?

6. **(MP) Use Structure** Students at a high school were asked whether they had ever made dinner for their families. The result of the survey are shown in the table below. Let *A* represent the event "Haven't made" dinner and let *B* represent the event "Freshman."

A = "Haven't made"
B = Freshman

	Have made	Haven't made	Total
Freshman	0.51	0.17	0.68
Senior	0.24	0.08	0.32
Total	0.75	0.25	1

A. Find the probabilities $P(B \mid A)$ and $P(B)$. What do you notice?

B. Find the probabilities $P(A \mid B)$ and $P(A)$. What do you notice?

C. What can you conclude about the events?

7. **(MP) Use Structure** Juniors and seniors at a rural high school were asked if they ever listen to country music. The results are shown in the table.

	Listen	Don't listen	Total
Junior	0.33	0.22	0.55
Senior	0.27	0.18	0.45
Total	0.60	0.40	1

A. How can you use the table to find $P(\text{junior} \cap \text{listen})$? What is this probability?

B. How can you use the table to find $P(\text{junior})$ and $P(\text{listen})$? What are these probabilities?

C. What is $P(\text{junior}) \cdot P(\text{listen})$? What can you conclude? Explain.

D. Explain what the product in Part C means in terms of the relationship between being a junior in the school and the junior's probability of listening to country music. Use language so that someone who has not studied statistics could understand.

A bag contains 4 green, 3 yellow, 2 purple, and 1 blue marble. You draw a marble, put it aside, and then draw another marble. Find each probability.

8. You draw the blue marble, and then a green marble or a yellow marble.

9. You draw six marbles in succession, and none of these marbles is green.

In a standard deck of 52 playing cards, there are 4 aces (A), 4 kings (K), 4 queens (Q), and 4 jacks (J). All other cards have number values. The kings, queens, and jacks are called "face cards." You are dealt two cards in sequence. Find each probability.

10. $P(\text{ace, then king})$

11. $P(\text{ace, then ace})$

12. $P(\text{two face cards})$

13. $P(\text{two number cards})$

14. Students at a school were asked whether they would be interested in free guitar lessons. They were also asked whether they were left- or right-handed. The results of are shown in the table below.

	Interested	Not interested
Left-handed	6	10
Right-handed	16	88

A. Use the multiplication rule to find the probability that a student is left-handed and is interested in taking the guitar lessons.

B. Are the events of being left-handed and being interested in guitar lessons independent or dependent? Explain.

15. When you roll two number cubes, each has six sides that can face up, so there are 36 pairs of sides that face up. Of these 36 pairs, 6 have a sum of 7, as shown below:

$(1, 6), (2, 5), (3, 4), (4, 3), (5, 2),$ and $(1, 6)$

Suppose you roll a red number cube and a black number cube. Let A be the event that that the red cube shows a 2. Let B be the event that the sum of the numbers showing on the two cubes is 7.

A. What is $P(B)$? What is $P(B \mid A)$? What is $P(A \cap B)$?

B. Are events A and B independent or dependent? Explain your reasoning.

16. (Open Middle™) Using the digits 0 to 9, at most one time each, fill in the boxes to create two probabilities of independent events and their corresponding compound probability.

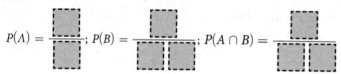

Spiral Review • Assessment Readiness

17. Using the data in the table, which probability is a joint probability?

	Likes volleyball	Dislikes volleyball
Freshman	60	43
Sophomore	85	41

Ⓐ $\dfrac{41}{229}$ Ⓒ $\dfrac{60}{145}$

Ⓑ $\dfrac{84}{229}$ Ⓓ $\dfrac{126}{229}$

18. What is $P(\text{Junior} \cap \text{Prefers summer})$?

	Prefers summer	Does not prefer summer
Junior	73	31
Senior	88	29

Ⓐ $\dfrac{145}{221}$ Ⓑ $\dfrac{30}{52}$ Ⓒ $\dfrac{73}{161}$ Ⓓ $\dfrac{73}{221}$

19. What is the probability that a senior dislikes science classes?

	Likes science classes	Dislikes science classes
Junior	60	43
Senior	85	41

Ⓐ 18%   Ⓒ 49%

Ⓑ 33%   Ⓓ 76%

20. Consider events A and B and the conditional probabilities $P(A \mid B)$ and $P(B \mid A)$. Which expression is equivalent to $P(A \cap B)$?

Ⓐ $\dfrac{P(A \mid B)}{P(B)}$ Ⓒ $P(B) \cdot P(A \mid B)$

Ⓑ $\dfrac{P(A \mid B)}{P(B \mid A)}$ Ⓓ $P(B) \cdot P(B \mid A)$

 I'm in a Learning Mindset!

How did I proactively seek to fill in any gaps between conditional probabilities and understanding independent and dependent events?

Analyze Decisions

(I Can) use conditional probability to analyze real-world decisions.

Spark Your Learning

Michelle's friend texts and invites her over, but Michelle must hurry to take the 4:10 train to catch the last ferry to where her friend lives. Michelle wants to go, but she doesn't want to risk wasting time and money if she will probably miss the ferry.

> The 4:10 train is often delayed to wait for another train.

> The ferry's departure time varies within a 20-minute "window."

Complete Part A as a whole class. Then complete Parts B–D in small groups.

A. What is a mathematical question you can ask about this situation? What information would you need to know to answer your question?

B. How could you represent the information you need using a two-way relative frequency table?

C. To answer your question, what strategy and tool would you use along with all the information you have? What answer do you get?

D. Does your answer make sense in the context of the situation? How do you know?

> **Turn and Talk** As Michelle is about to leave home, she gets a text alert that the 4:10 train will be delayed. If Michelle thinks it is worth the risk of missing the ferry if she has at least a 1 in 3 chance of making it to her friend's house, should she still go? Explain.

©Martin Shields/Alamy

Build Understanding

Analyze Decisions Using Probability

Finding the probability that an event will occur under different conditions is extremely important in real-world contexts for making decisions. For example, for medical testing that isn't 100% reliable, you need to be able to find accurate probabilities to make the best possible decisions.

1 ▶ Suppose scientists have created a new test for a virus that is carried by 8% of the population. They have determined that 88% of people who carry the virus test positive for the virus, and 96% of people who don't carry the virus test negative for the virus.

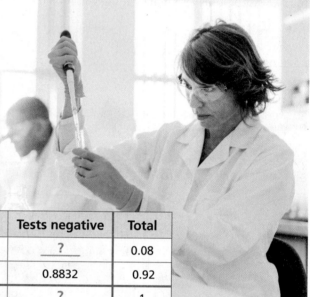

A. A two-way relative frequency table for the test is shown below. Describe how the relative frequencies shown were found, then complete the table.

	Tests positive	Tests negative	Total
Carries virus	0.0704	?	0.08
Doesn't carry virus	?	0.8832	0.92
Total	?	?	1

Because the result of a person taking the test is simply "positive" or "negative," this result is what any decisions must be based upon.

B. How can you find the conditional probability that a person actually carries the virus given a positive test result? What is the probability? Is the test reliable for determining who carries the virus? Explain.

C. How can you find the conditional probability that a person does not actually carry the virus given a negative test result? What is the probability? Is the test reliable for determining who doesn't carry the virus? Explain.

D. If you needed to make some kind of decision based on your test result, in which case would you feel more confident in your decision—you tested positive, or you tested negative? Explain. In which case would you want to get more information before making any decisions?

Turn and Talk A *false positive* is an error in a test result in which the test incorrectly indicates that a condition or disease is present when it actually is not. A *false negative* is an error in a test result in which the test incorrectly indicates that a condition or disease is not present when it actually is. Which of these errors is a larger concern for this particular test? Explain.

Derive Bayes' Theorem

In the previous task, you were given one set of conditional probabilities, and then you used a two-way relative frequency table to another set of conditional probabilities.

Bayes' Theorem gives a general formula for working with conditional probabilities. You can derive Bayes' Theorem using the definition of conditional probability,

$$P(B \mid A) = \frac{P(A \cap B)}{P(A)} \text{ or } P(A \mid B) = \frac{P(A \cap B)}{P(B)}.$$

2 ▶ Both expressions above contain $P(A \cap B)$. Solve the first one for $P(A \cap B)$:

$$P(B \mid A) = \frac{P(A \cap B)}{P(A)} \Rightarrow P(A \cap B) = P(A) \cdot P(B \mid A)$$

Now substitute the expression for $P(A \cap B)$ into the one for $P(A \mid B)$:

$$P(A \mid B) = \frac{P(A \cap B)}{P(B)} \Rightarrow P(A \mid B) = \frac{P(A) \cdot P(B \mid A)}{P(B)} \leftarrow \text{Bayes' Theorem}$$

A. Could you also write Bayes' Theorem as $P(B \mid A) = \dfrac{P(B) \cdot P(A \mid B)}{P(A)}$? Explain.

B. You can use a probability tree diagram to write and apply an expanded form of Bayes' Theorem. Remember that a two-way table represents the intersections of four events, that is, four joint events. The four events represented are event A, event A's complement A^C, event B, and event B's complement B^C.

	A	A^C	Total
B	$A \cap B$	$A^C \cap B$	B
B^C	$A \cap B^C$	$A^C \cap B^C$	B^C
Total	A	A^C	1

In the tree diagram, follow the branches down from the top to find the joint probabilities at the bottom. For example, look at the leftmost branches: Event A has a probability, as does Event B given Event A. The product of these probabilities, $P(A) \cdot P(B \mid A)$, is equivalent to $P(A \cap B)$, as you saw at the start of the task.

The two-way table represents the four possible joint events in the non-totals cells of the table. How are the corresponding probabilities represented in the tree diagram?

C. In the table, the row total for Event B is $(A \cap B) + (A^C \cap B)$. In the tree diagram, the total probability of Event B is $P(A \cap B) + P(A^C \cap B)$. Complete the statement:

$$P(B) = P(A \cap B) + P(A^C \cap B) = P(A) \cdot P(B \mid A) + \underline{\quad ? \quad}$$

Now you can expand Bayes' Theorem: $P(A \mid B) = \dfrac{P(A) \cdot P(B \mid A)}{P(B)} = \dfrac{P(A) \cdot P(B \mid A)}{\underline{\quad ? \quad}}.$

Turn and Talk How is $P(A)$ represented in the last row of the tree diagram?

Step It Out

Use Bayes' Theorem

Using Bayes' Theorem, you can find the conditional probabilities needed to make an informed decision from a small amount of initial information.

Bayes' Theorem
Given two events A and B with $P(B) \neq 0$, $P(A \mid B) = \dfrac{P(A) \cdot P(B \mid A)}{P(B)}$.
Another form is $P(A \mid B) = \dfrac{P(A) \cdot P(B \mid A)}{P(A) \cdot P(B \mid A) + P(A^c) \cdot P(B \mid A^c)}$.

3 ▶ A plant manager receives a complaint about a shipment with too many defective items. The items were made by two different machines, an older one that has an error rate of 0.4%, and a newer one that has an error rate of 0.15%. The newer machine produced 72% of the items in the shipment. The plant manager assumes that the older, more error-prone machine is to blame for the defective items. Is she correct to draw this conclusion? Explain.

Organize the information in a tree diagram to help you apply Bayes' Theorem.

> **A.** In each case, why can you just subtract from 1 to find the unknown probability?

- $P(\text{made by new}) = 0.72$, so $P(\text{made by old}) = 1 - 0.28 = 0.72$.
- $P(\text{error} \mid \text{old}) = 0.004$, so $P(\text{no error} \mid \text{old}) = 1 - 0.004 = 0.996$.
- $P(\text{error} \mid \text{new}) = 0.0015$, so $P(\text{no error} \mid \text{new}) = 1 - 0.0015 = 0.9985$.

Use the probabilities to fill in the branches of the tree diagram. Multiply the probabilities along the branches to find the probabilities of the joint events in the bottom row.

> **B.** Why is the sum of the probabilities in the bottom row equal to 1? How does this relate to two-way tables?

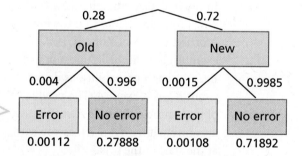

To evaluate whether the plant manager was correct to blame the old machine for the defects, find the probability that the old machine made a given error, $P(\text{old} \mid \text{error})$.

$$P(\text{old} \mid \text{error}) = \frac{P(\text{old}) \cdot P(\text{error} \mid \text{old})}{P(\text{error})}$$

$$= \frac{0.28 \cdot 0.004}{0.00112 + 0.00108} \approx 0.509$$

She was not correct: A defect was almost equally likely produced by either machine.

Turn and Talk What is the advantage of using the tree diagram to find the probabilities of the joint events instead of using the probability notation?

4 The plant manager from the previous task receives a request for large order on a tight schedule and must increase production to fill it. She cannot increase the new machine's output, but she can increase the output of the old machine to 40% of total output. Doing so, however, will increase its error rate from 0.4% to 0.6%.

- How do these changes affect the likelihood that the old machine will be responsible for an error in the new order?

- How would the change in production change the overall error rate? Should the manager agree to accept the order? Explain

Organize the updated information in a tree diagram.

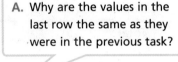
A. Why are the values in the last row the same as they were in the previous task?

- $P(\text{made by old}) = 0.40$, so $P(\text{made by new}) = 1 - 0.40 = 0.60$.
- $P(\text{error} \mid \text{old}) = 0.006$, so $P(\text{no error} \mid \text{old}) = 1 - 0.006 = 0.994$.
- $P(\text{error} \mid \text{new}) = 0.0015$, so $P(\text{no error} \mid \text{new}) = 1 - 0.0015 = 0.9985$.

Use the probabilities to fill in the branches of the tree diagram. Multiply the probabilities along the branches to find the probabilities of the joint events in the bottom row.

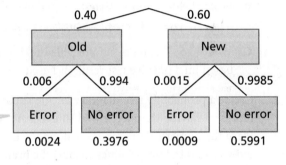

B. The probability of an error is the sum of two probabilities. Describe these probabilities.

Find the probability that the old machine will produce a defective item, $P(\text{old} \mid \text{error})$, in the new production arrangement.

$$P(\text{old} \mid \text{error}) = \frac{P(\text{old}) \cdot P(\text{error} \mid \text{old})}{P(\text{error})} = \frac{0.40 \cdot 0.006}{0.0024 + 0.0009} \approx 0.727$$

With the new production, the old machine will be responsible for almost 73% of defective items, instead of about 51%.

C. How does $P(\text{error})$ for the new production schedule compare to $P(\text{error})$ in the original production schedule?

Note that the overall error probability is represented by the denominator in the expression for Bayes' Theorem above:

$$P(\text{error}) = 0.0024 + 0.0009 = 0.0033 = 0.33\%$$

D. Why is $P(\text{error})$ in the denominator just this simple sum? What is the relationship to the longer form of Bayes' Theorem?

In the new production arrangement, $P(\text{error}) \approx \frac{1}{3}\%$. This means that a shipment of 10,000 items would be expected to have about 33 defective items. Because for most purposes this is a very small error rate, it seems likely that any negative impacts will be limited, so it seems reasonable for the manager to accept the order.

Turn and Talk Look back at the longer form of Bayes' Theorem. Compare the numerator and denominator of the expression. What about them makes the formula easier to remember? Explain.

Check Understanding

1. Suppose there is a test for a certain allergy found in 5% of the population. The test correctly identifies people who have the allergy 90% of the time. The test correctly identifies people who don't have the allergy 94% of the time. The relative frequency table represents this situation.

	Tests positive	Tests negative	Total
Has allergy	0.045	0.005	0.05
Doesn't have allergy	0.057	0.893	0.95
Total	0.102	0.898	1

   A. From the description, $P(\text{tests} + \mid \text{allergy}) = 0.90$. In the table, this is $0.045 \div 0.05$. What is $P(\text{allergy} \mid \text{tests} +)$?

   B. From the description, $P(\text{tests} - \mid \text{no allergy}) = 0.94$. In the table, this is $0.893 \div 0.95$. What is $P(\text{no allergy} \mid \text{tests} -)$?

   C. Would you feel more comfortable making a decision about possible treatment based on a positive test result or based on a negative test result? Explain.

2. Create a probability tree diagram for the situation in Problem 1. Let event A represent having the allergy, and let event A^C represent not having the allergy. Place the numerical probabilities along the branches and below the diagram. How did you find the probabilities to label the branches for $P(\text{tests} - \mid \text{allergy})$ and $P(\text{tests} + \mid \text{no allergy})$?

On Your Own

3. (MP) **Attend to Precision** Suppose a test for a certain disease found in 7% of a goat population correctly identifies goats that have the disease 86% of the time and correctly identifies goats that do not have the disease 90% of the time.

   A. Complete the two-way relative frequency table based on the information given above.

	Tests positive	Tests negative	Total
Has disease	$0.86(0.07) = 0.0602$	?	0.07
Doesn't have disease	?	$0.9(0.93) = 0.837$	0.93
Total	?	?	1

   B. What is the probability that a goat that tested positive for the disease actually has the disease?

   C. What is the probability that a goat that tested negative for the disease actually does not have the disease?

   D. Suppose that the treatment for the disease is expensive and has worrisome side effects. Suppose you had a large herd of goats. Would you decide to treat all the animals who tested positive? Explain. If not, what would you do?

4. **(MP) Attend to Precision** A city puts two bills on a ballot, one to spend more for new schools and another to spend more for new roads. In the election, 58% voted for the schools spending. Of the voters who voted for more school spending, 55% also voted for more roads spending. Of the voters who voted against more school spending, 36% also voted against more roads spending.

   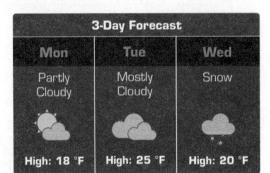

   58% voted for school spending.

   A. Create a two-way relative frequency table for the given information.

   B. Compare $P(\text{schools yes} \mid \text{roads yes})$ and $P(\text{roads yes} \mid \text{schools yes})$.

   C. Do the election results indicate that there is a strong block of "yes on both" voters versus "no on both" voters, or something else? Explain.

5. The tree diagram represents October weather in a town. It shows, for example, that on average it rains 4.4% of days in October, and that given that it does rain, there is a 92% chance the rain was predicted. The school's fall October festival is planned for a day just a few days from now, and the forecast calls for rain.

   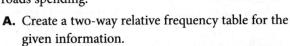

0.044		0.956	
Rain		No rain	
0.92	0.08	0.06	0.94
Rain predicted	No rain predicted	Rain predicted	No rain predicted
0.04048	0.00352	0.05736	0.89864

   A. The probability that rain is predicted is the sum of the probabilities of what two events?

   B. What is the probability that it actually rains when rain is predicted? Would you cancel the fall festival and postpone it to another day? Explain.

   C. Which is more reliable, a forecast of rain or a forecast of no rain? Explain.

6. The school trip is scheduled for January 10, but the forecast predicts snow. The probability of snow on a January day is 9%. When it snows, the forecast correctly predicted the snow 88% of the time. When it does not snow, the forecast correctly predicted no snow 98% of the time. Use a tree diagram to answer the questions.

   3-Day Forecast

Mon	Tue	Wed
Partly Cloudy	Mostly Cloudy	Snow
High: 18 °F	High: 25 °F	High: 20 °F

   A. What is the probability when snow is forecast that it actually snows?

   B. Would you cancel the school trip and reschedule it for another day? Explain.

   C. Compare the reliability of a forecast of snow with a forecast of no snow.

7. A machine that stitches jeans has an error rate of 0.6%. A newer machine has an error rate of 0.25%. The new machine takes over 70% of the stitching of the jeans, while the other machine stitches the rest.

   A. Create a probability tree diagram for the situation. Label the probabilities along the branches and below the diagram.

   B. What is the probability that a defect was caused by the older machine?

   C. Would you expect that a pair of jeans that have a defect were made by the older machine and not the new machine? Explain.

8. An older machine that manufactures bike frames has a defect rate of 2.5%. A new machine has a defect rate of 0.3%. The machines work together to produce bike frames, with the newer machine producing 85% of the frames.

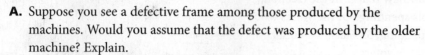

A. Suppose you see a defective frame among those produced by the machines. Would you assume that the defect was produced by the older machine? Explain.

B. The company needs to increase the number of frames manufactured and increases production of the old machine to 35% of the total. By how much is the defect rate increased? Is it worth the risk? Explain.

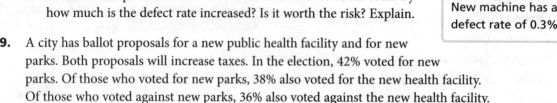

New machine has a defect rate of 0.3%

9. A city has ballot proposals for a new public health facility and for new parks. Both proposals will increase taxes. In the election, 42% voted for new parks. Of those who voted for new parks, 38% also voted for the new health facility. Of those who voted against new parks, 36% also voted against the new health facility.

A. About what percent of people cast each of the 4 possible ballot combinations?

B. What is $P(\text{parks yes} \mid \text{health yes})$? What is $P(\text{parks no} \mid \text{health no})$?

C. From the context, $P(\text{health no} \mid \text{parks yes}) = 0.62$. What is $P(\text{parks no} \mid \text{health yes})$? What do these results say about a voter who voted for one of the proposals?

D. Did the health proposal pass? Explain.

Spiral Review • Assessment Readiness

10. What is the approximate probability of $P(\text{Freshman} \cap \text{No hobby})$?

	Hobby	No hobby
Freshman	128	36
Senior	42	104

Ⓐ 11.6% Ⓒ 52.9%

Ⓑ 41.3% Ⓓ 54.8%

11. What is the probability that someone who does not take vitamins is a teacher?

	Vitamins	No vitamins
Teachers	32	26
Students	248	521

Ⓐ $\frac{13}{29}$ Ⓑ $\frac{58}{827}$ Ⓒ $\frac{26}{547}$ Ⓓ $\frac{26}{827}$

12. Let the event A be Students and event B be Projects.

	Projects	Tests
Students	0.26	0.30
Teachers	0.24	0.20

Which expression is equivalent to $P(A \cap B)$?

Ⓐ $P(A) \cdot P(B)$ Ⓒ $P(A) \cdot P(B \mid A)$

Ⓑ $P(A) \cdot P(A \mid B)$ Ⓓ $\dfrac{P(A \mid B)}{P(B)}$

13. You toss a coin four times. Let x be the number of heads in a toss. What is $P(x = 4)$?

Ⓐ $\frac{3}{4}$ Ⓑ $\frac{1}{2}$ Ⓒ $\frac{1}{8}$ Ⓓ $\frac{1}{16}$

 I'm in a Learning Mindset!

What actions did I take when I did not understand how to apply Bayes' Theorem to find other conditional probabilities that were not given?

Review

Conditional Probability

Consider the situation of testing people in a population for a cold virus. Let A be the event that someone tests positive for the virus and B be the event that the person has the virus.

	Has virus	Does Not have virus	Total
Tests positive	0.0195	0.0245	0.044
Tests negative	0.0005	0.9555	0.956
Total	0.02	0.98	1

The conditional probability of A given B is

$$P(A|B) = \frac{P(A \cap B)}{P(B)}$$

$$= \frac{0.0195}{0.02} = 0.975.$$

> This represents the probability that someone who has the virus tests positive.

Dependent Events

Dependent events are events for which the occurrence of one event affects the probability of the other event. Testing positive and having the virus in this situation are dependent events.

> A and B are dependent because $P(B|A) \neq P(B)$:
> $$\frac{0.0195}{0.044} \neq 0.02.$$

Independent Events

Two events are independent if the occurrence of one event does not affect the probability of the other event.

W and Y are independent because the conditional probability is unaffected.

$$P(W) = \frac{400}{560} = 0.71$$

$$P(W|Y) = \frac{250}{350} = 0.71$$

> Events A and B are independent also if: $P(A \cap B) = P(A) \cdot P(B)$.

	W	X
Y	250	100
Z	150	60

Bayes' Theorem

Bayes' Theorem can help you derive the conditional probabilities needed to make an informed decision. Look back at the first table about testing for a virus.

Let C be the event that a person does not have the virus and D be the event that a person tests positive.

$$P(D|C) = \frac{P(D) \cdot P(C|D)}{P(C)}$$

$$= \frac{0.044 \cdot 0.557}{0.98}$$

$$= 0.025$$

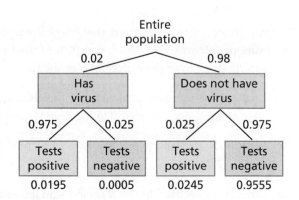

Vocabulary

Choose the correct term from the box to complete each sentence.

1. ___?___ is the probability of event A, given that event B has already occurred denoted $P(A|B)$.

2. ___?___ are events for which the occurrence or non-occurrence of one event affects the probability of the other event.

3. ___?___ are events for which the occurrence or non-occurrence of an event does not affect the probability of the other event.

Concepts and Skills

A company surveyed a group of parents and children. The company wanted to know if parents and children prefer that the children wear uniforms to school or not. The results are shown in the two-way table.

	Wear uniform	Not wear uniform	Total
Children	30%	16%	46%
Parents	36%	18%	54%
Total	66%	34%	100%

4. What is the probability that a child prefers to not wear a uniform?

5. What is the probability that a parent prefers that their child not wear a uniform?

The music department at school asked students if they would prefer learning to play guitar. Let A be the event prefers learning to play guitar and B be the event left-handed.

	Prefers learning to play guitar	Prefers not learning to play guitar
Left-handed	116	25
Right-handed	28	31

6. (MP) **Use Tools** Determine if the events A and B are dependent or independent. Explain your reasoning. State what strategy and tool you will use to answer the question, explain your choice, and then find the answer.

7. Does preferring to learn to play guitar depend on being left-handed? Explain your reasoning.

Suppose there is a test for cancer that 5% of the population has. The test correctly identifies people who have the cancer 90% of the time. The test correctly identifies people who don't have the cancer 94% of the time.

8. Create a two-way frequency table for the given information. Give each entry of the table as a percent, and round to the nearest tenth if necessary.

9. What is the probability that a person who tested positive for the cancer actually has the cancer?

10. What is the probability that a person who tested negative for the cancer actually has the cancer?

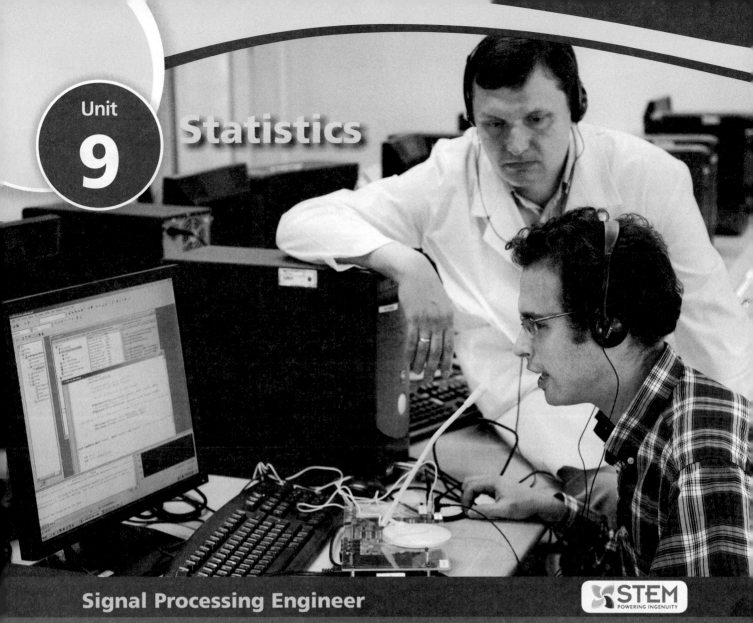

Statistics

Signal Processing Engineer

$$\text{STEM}$$
POWERING INGENUITY

Signal processing engineers analyze signals to extract and process embedded information. They apply statistical techniques to develop robust algorithms that allow them to eliminate irrelevant "noise," so that the underlying "signal" they desire can be clearly identified and understood.

(t) ©age fotostock/Alamy; (b) ©AstroStar/Shutterstock

STEM Task

Signal processing engineers use the signal to noise ratio (SNR), to compare the level of a desired signal to the level of background noise. The ratio of the average number of recorded events N to the standard deviation. For shot noise, the standard deviation is given by $\sqrt{N}$.

SNR	N	Detection level
3	___?___	Borderline detection
5	___?___	Clear detection
10	___?___	Data allows for some analysis
100	___?___	Data allows for detailed analysis

Learning Mindset

Challenge-Seeking Makes Plans to Meet Goals

As you move through the learning process, it is important to set challenging goals, but it is equally important to make plans to meet those goals. Your likelihood of success will greatly increase if you set up action steps that will lead you to your overall goal. You can ensure that your learning goal will be completed in a timely manner if you develop and maintain a timeline for your action steps. Here are some questions you can ask yourself as you work to achieve your learning goals:

- What is my learning goal with respect to statistics? What are the positive impacts of others in my learning community on my goals?

- How will I know when my goal is met successfully? Are there multiple parts that can be accomplished separately? Are there parts that need to be completed before others?

- What are my action steps that will help me reach my learning goal in statistics? How does each step move me toward my overall learning goal?

- What is my overall timeline for my goal?

Reflect

Q Think of a time when you have developed an action plan and a time when you did not. How did you approach the task differently? How did the results differ? How did you feel during each process?

Q Imagine you are a signal processing engineer. How can setting up action steps and timelines for different small groups help the overall team accomplish their goal?

On the **Flip** Side

If someone flips a coin and it lands
on heads ten times in a row, are
they cheating?

©Getmanecinna/Shutterstock

Are You Ready?

Complete these problems to review prior concepts and skills you will need for this module.

Histograms

Make a histogram to represent each set of data.

1. 11, 8, 21, 15, 28, 43, 37, 9, 12, 13, 17, 31, 50, 34

2. 7, 12, 15, 23, 8, 11, 10, 19, 21, 10, 16, 22, 13, 16, 27, 8, 12, 18, 24, 20

Measures of Center

Determine the mean, median, and mode for each set of data. Round your answer to the nearest tenth.

3. 21, 27, 31, 21, 57, 23, 25, 24, 19, 16

4. 4.8, 5.3, 5.2, 6.4, 5.4, 5.3, 5.4

5. 17, 25, 23, 200, 14

Standard Deviation

Calculate the standard deviation for each set of data. Round your answer to the nearest hundredth.

6. 97, 83, 71, 76, 53

7. 4, −3, −5, 0, 10, 2, −1

8. 2.3, 2.6, 2.3, 2.5, 2.1, 2.3, 2.2

9. 13.5, 18.2, 14.3, 16.9, 16.2

Connecting Past and Present Learning

Previously, you learned:

- to display data and interpret differences in shape, center, and spread,
- to determine experimental and theoretical probabilities, and
- to recognize the concepts of conditional probability and independence in real-world situations.

In this module, you will learn:

- to fit a normal distribution to a data set to estimate population percentages,
- to determine if a model is consistent with a data generating process, and
- to use data distributions to compare two or more data sets.

Probability Distributions

(I Can) define and display probability distributions for discrete random variables to model real-world scenarios or probability experiments.

Spark Your Learning

A consumer group is trying to determine which company makes the best batteries. They purchase a number of 40-packs of batteries made by the major manufacturers.

The group randomly tested all of their batteries for each manufacturer. Each company had some defective batteries.

Complete Part A as a whole class. Then complete Parts B–D in small groups.

A. What is a mathematical question you can ask about this situation? What information would you need to know to answer your question?

B. How many different ways are there for the tester to choose one battery from a package of batteries? Is any order in which the batteries are selected for testing more likely than any other order? Is each battery test independent of every other test?

C. To answer your question, what strategy and tool would you use along with all the information you have? What answer do you get?

D. Does your work make sense in the context of the situation? How do you know?

Turn and Talk Does having one defective battery in a package make it more likely that others in the package are also defective? How do you know?

Build Understanding

Construct Pascal's Triangle

Pascal's Triangle is a number pattern named after the French mathematician Blaise Pascal. The triangle is created by listing the total number of possible paths from the top of the triangle to each node on the triangle. Only downward movements are allowed. That is, each movement is either down to the left or down to the right.

1 ▶ Pascal's Triangle is shown on the left below. The triangular array on the right shows the entries of Pascal's Triangle using $_nC_r$ notation, where n is the total number of moves and r is the number of moves to the right. The value of $_nC_r$ corresponds to the total number of different combinations of left (L) and right (R) moves to arrive at a particular node.

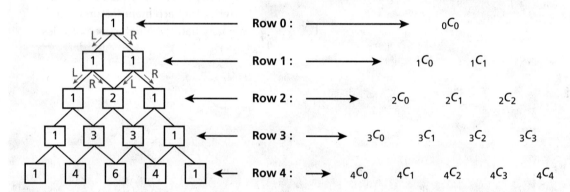

A. Look closely at Pascal's Triangle. What do you notice about the numbers running down the left and right sides of this triangle? Explain these values in terms of n and r.

Focus on the first 3 appearing in row 3. This position in the triangle can be reached from the top of the triangle by moving left-left-right, left-right-left, or right-left-left for a total of 3 possible paths. Trace each of these paths in order to visualize them.

B. Notice that the corresponding entry in the triangular array at the right is $_3C_1$. What is the meaning of this notation? Explain how it corresponds to the 3 in Pascal's Triangle.

C. Look at the two entries directly above this 3 in Pascal's Triangle. How are these three numbers related? Is this true for all of the interior numbers of the triangle? Explain.

D. What combination of left and right moves takes you from the top of the triangle to the 6 in row 4? How does the corresponding $_nC_r$ notation in the triangular array at the right above verify your response?

Calculate Theoretical Binomial Probabilities

A **binomial experiment** is a probability experiment of n identical independent trials where there are only two possible outcomes, success or failure. Which result deemed the success depends on the experimental result of interest.

Designating the probability of success as p and the probability of failure as q, the sum $p + q$ will always be 1. For example, when flipping a fair coin, it will land either heads or tails. Since the coin is fair, the two possibilities are equally likely. So the probability of getting heads is $\frac{1}{2}$, the probability of getting tails is $\frac{1}{2}$, and $\frac{1}{2} + \frac{1}{2} = 1$.

2 ▸ Consider the binomial experiment of flipping a fair coin 5 times. What is the probability that exactly 3 of the 5 coin flips will be heads?

Rows 0–5 of Pascal's Triangle are shown at the right, with moves to the left representing the result tails (T) and moves to the right representing the result heads (H).

The number of ways for 3 heads to occur in 5 flips is modeled by the paths that are combinations of 5 total moves with 3 of those moves being to the right.

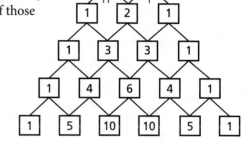

A. Two of the combinations are H-H-H-T-T and T-T-H-H-H. Give two other combinations. Trace each of these paths on the triangle. Do all four paths end at the same node? If so, what is the value there? Explain what this means.

B. How is the number of ways of getting 3 heads in 5 flips represented in $_nC_r$ notation? Expressions in $_nC_r$ notation can be evaluated on a calculator in addition to using Pascal's Triangle. Use a calculator to verify the value found in Part A. The **binomial probability** of exactly r successes in n trials is $P(r) = {_nC_r} \cdot p^r \cdot q^{n-r}$.

C. What does $P(3)$ mean in this situation? What is the value of $P(3)$?

Develop a Symmetric Binomial Probability Distribution

A **random variable** is a variable whose value is determined by the outcome of a probability experiment. A **probability distribution** is a data distribution that gives the probabilities of the values of a random variable. A probability distribution can be represented by a histogram with the values of the random variable along the horizontal axis. A **binomial probability distribution** is a representation of a binomial experiment.

3 ▸ The number of different ways to get each possible number of heads when flipping a fair coin 5 times is modeled by row 5 of Pascal's Triangle and shown in the table below.

Number of heads, X	0	1	2	3	4	5
Number of ways to get X heads with 5 flips	1	5	10	10	5	1

Each of the 5 flips of the coin is an independent event, with p (getting heads) and q (getting tails) both equal to $\frac{1}{2}$ for a fair coin.

A. What is the probability of any unique outcome of flipping a fair coin 5 times?

B. How can the table and the answer to Part A be used to find the probabilities for flipping each number of heads?

The probabilities for flipping a fair coin are represented by the binomial probability distribution at the right.

C. What do you notice about the shape of this probability distribution?

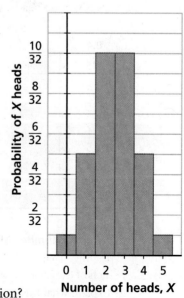

Analyze a Probability Distribution

The binomial probability distribution for flipping a fair coin is symmetric. The symmetry is a consequence of using the theoretical probability of $\frac{1}{2}$ for heads and $\frac{1}{2}$ for tails. When conducting an experiment by spinning an actual coin, the probabilities of getting heads and getting tails will vary from the theoretical probability.

4 ▶ Two coins are used in separate experiments. Both experiments involved spinning the coin 5 times, watching it come to rest, and recording the number of heads that occurred. Each experiment was repeated 50 times. The probability distribution for Coin 1 is shown at the left below and the probability distribution for Coin 2 is shown at the right.

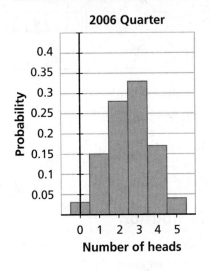

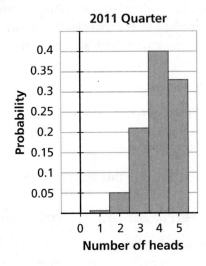

A. Does the probability distribution for Coin 1 suggest it is a fair coin? Explain.

B. Does the probability distribution for Coin 2 suggest it is a fair coin? Explain.

The probability distribution shown on the left below represents a situation in which the theoretical probability of success is 25%, while the distribution on the right represents one in which the theoretical probability of success is 75%. Success is getting heads. Both distributions are skewed.

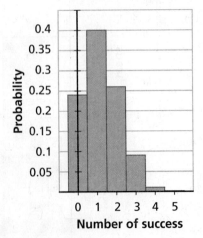

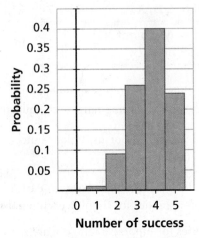

C. Which of these bar graphs seems similar to the probability distribution for Coin 2? Explain what this means about the "fairness" of the coin.

Step It Out

Calculate Binomial Probabilities

Recall that the binomial probability of exactly r successes in n trials can be found by calculating $P(r) = {}_nC_r \cdot p^r \cdot q^{n-r}$, where p is the probability of success and q is the probability of failure.

5 In one batch of light bulbs, there is a 10% probability that any one light bulb is defective. You buy a package of 6 light bulbs that were packaged from this batch. What is the probability that your package of 6 light bulbs contains exactly 2 defective light bulbs? 4 or more defective bulbs?

Let p be the probability that a light bulb is defective. Then q is the probability that a light bulb works. There is a 10% probability that any light bulb is defective, so $p = 0.1$ and therefore $q = 1 - 0.1 = 0.9$.

The number of different ways to get each possible number of defective light bulbs in a package of 6 is modeled by row 6 of Pascal's Triangle. You can refer back to Task 2 to determine the entries for row 6.

Number of defective light bulbs, X	0	1	2	3	4	5	6
Number of ways to have X defective light bulbs in a package of 6	1	6	15	20	15	6	1

Using ${}_nC_r$ notation, you can write the probability of X defective light bulbs in a package of 6 bulbs as $P(X) = {}_6C_X \cdot (0.1)^X (0.9)^{6-X}$.

To find the probability that exactly 2 defective bulbs are in a package, evaluate $P(2)$.

$P(2) = {}_6C_2 \cdot (0.1)^2 (0.9)^4$

$= 15 \cdot (0.01)(0.6561)$

A. How does the table above provide the value of ${}_6C_2$?

$= 0.098415$

There is a 9.8% probability that exactly 2 of the bulbs are defective.

The probability of getting 4 or more defective light bulbs is:

$P(X \geq 4) = P(4) + P(5) + P(6)$

B. How would this change if the wording was "more than 4 defective bulbs"?

$= {}_6C_4 \cdot (0.1)^4 (0.9)^2 + {}_6C_5 \cdot (0.1)^5 (0.9)^1 + {}_6C_6 \cdot (0.1)^6 (0.9)^0$

$= 15 \cdot (0.0001)(0.81) + 6 \cdot (0.00001)(0.9) + 1 \cdot (0.000001)(1)$

$= 0.00127$

There is just a 0.127% probability that a package contains 4 or more defective bulbs.

 Turn and Talk What is the probability of getting at least 1 defective bulb?

Check Understanding

For Problems 1–5, use the following situation. A teacher gives students a multiple-choice quiz with 6 questions. Each question has 3 choices: A, B, and C.

1. How can you use Pascal's Triangle to determine how many different ways a student can get exactly 4 of the 6 questions correct? How many different ways are possible?

2. Suppose a student was unprepared for the quiz and guessed an answer for each question. If the student is equally likely to choose any of the answers for all questions, what is the probability that the student answers 5 questions correctly? Show your work.

3. If a student is equally likely to choose any of the answers for all questions, what is the probability that the student answers no more than 2 questions correctly?

4. Marissa has correctly answered 80% of all multiple-choice questions on quizzes in the class this year. Make a probability distribution showing how many questions you would expect Marissa to answer correctly on this quiz.

5. Deidre has correctly answered 90% of all multiple-choice questions on quizzes in the class this year. How would a probability distribution showing the number of questions you would expect her to answer correctly on this quiz compare to the distribution for Marissa?

Quiz			
1.	A	B	C
2.	A	B	C
3.	A	B	C
4.	A	B	C
5.	A	B	C
6.	A	B	C

On Your Own

6. **(MP) Use Structure** Consider the situation of flipping a coin 10 times.
   A. How can you extend Pascal's Triangle to find the number of ways to get exactly 3 heads in 10 flips?
   B. How many ways are there to get exactly 3 heads when flipping a coin 10 times?
   C. How can you write this number in $_nC_r$ notation?
   D. What is the probability of flipping exactly 3 heads out of 10 flips?

7. The numbers in row 7 of Pascal's Triangle are 1, 7, 21, 35, 35, 21, 7, 1.
   A. What are the numbers in row 8 of Pascal's Triangle?
   B. How could you represent those numbers in the form $_nC_r$?

8. Consider an experiment of flipping a fair coin 4 times.
   A. What is the probability that none of the 4 flips land heads?
   B. Is there another result to this experiment that has the same probability as flipping 0 heads? How does the probability distribution help answer this question?
   C. What are the probabilities of the other possible outcomes of this experiment?

9. **(MP) Critique Reasoning** Caroline says that the sum of the numbers in every row of Pascal's Triangle is a multiple of 2. Is Caroline correct? Is there a more effective way of describing the sum of the numbers in each row?

For Problems 10–17, the given value of p is the probability of success and the value of n is the number of trials of a binomial experiment. First find the probability of exactly 2 successes, and then find the probability of at most 2 successes. Round your answers to the nearest thousandth.

10. $p = 0.5, n = 3$

11. $p = 0.5, n = 8$

12. $p = 0.6, n = 4$

13. $p = 0.6, n = 5$

14. $p = 0.31, n = 5$

15. $p = 0.31, n = 9$

16. $p = 0.47, n = 6$

17. $p = 0.47, n = 7$

(MP) **Reason** For Problems 18 and 19, a board game has a spinner with 16 sections. Eight sections allow the player to move forward, five sections force the player to move backward, and the other three sections add points to the player's score. The histogram shows the probability of each number of spins resulting in moving backward out of 25 spins.

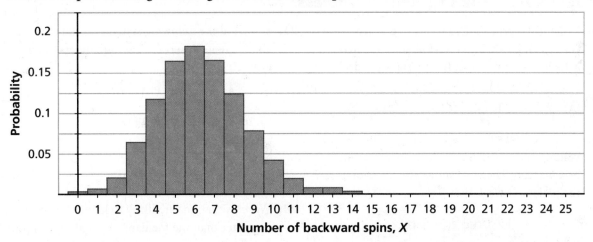

18. Are the probabilities shown in this histogram theoretical or experimental? How do you know?

19. How would the shape of the histogram change if it modeled the probability of spinning a movement forward or spinning points?

20. (MP) **Use Tools** Use a spreadsheet or other technology to model the following game. Two number cubes labeled 1–6 are each rolled 9 times. The 9 sums are recorded. If the sum is 4 or 8, then the player wins; any other sum results in a loss.

   A. What is the probability of success?

   B. Make a table to show the theoretical probability distribution of winning the game 0 to 9 times out of 9 tries.

   C. Make a histogram with those probabilities.

A machine produces acceptable parts with 97% reliability.

21. What is the probability that the machine makes exactly 18 acceptable parts in one minute?

22. What is the probability that the machine makes more than 18 acceptable parts in one minute?

23. What is the probability that the machine makes fewer than 18 acceptable parts in one minute?

This machine makes 20 parts per minute.

24. If a hockey game is tied after overtime, five rounds of alternating penalty shots decide the winner. If one team has scored more goals after each team has taken their 5 penalty shots, then that team wins and the game is over.

Team A's goaltender stops opponents from scoring on 85% of all penalty shots.

A. Find the probability that Team A's opponent, Team B, scores at least once in their 5 penalty shots.

B. Team A scored on 3 of their 5 penalty shots. What is the probability that Team B wins the game after their 5 penalty shots?

Spiral Review • Assessment Readiness

25. What is the probability of selecting a face card (J, Q, K) after you have already selected a 4 without replacing it from a standard deck of playing cards?

Ⓐ $\frac{3}{13}$ Ⓑ $\frac{4}{17}$ Ⓒ $\frac{1}{4}$ Ⓓ $\frac{2}{9}$

26. For a medical study, a group of 100 patients volunteered to receive either a new medicine or a placebo. The table shows the status of the patients 1 week later.

	Drug	Placebo
Sick	72	88
Healthy	28	12

Which of these conditional probabilities is greatest?

Ⓐ $P(\text{sick} \mid \text{drug})$

Ⓑ $P(\text{healthy} \mid \text{placebo})$

Ⓒ $P(\text{placebo} \mid \text{sick})$

Ⓓ $P(\text{drug} \mid \text{healthy})$

27. Which of the following statements must be true about events A and B if they are independent events?

Ⓐ $P(A) - P(B) = P(A \cup B)$

Ⓑ $P(A) + P(B) = P(A \cap B)$

Ⓒ $P(A) \cdot P(B) = P(A \cup B)$

Ⓓ $P(A) \cdot P(B) = P(A \cap B)$

28. Which situations are likely to have a mean that is greater than the median? Select all that apply.

Ⓐ the incomes of all employees at a large company

Ⓑ the prices of all houses sold in the last year in a city

Ⓒ the heights of all adults in a city

Ⓓ the weights of all cats in an animal shelter

Ⓔ the scores of students on an easy short quiz

I'm in a Learning Mindset!

What action steps can I take to help me better understand how to model probability distributions?

Normal Distributions

(I Can) find percentages of data and probabilities of events associated with normal distributions.

Spark Your Learning

The students on a field trip posed for a group photo.

> Student heights ranged from 4 ft 11 in. to 6 ft 2 in. Most of the students' heights are close to the mean.

> Kendra's height is about 1 standard deviation above the mean height. Jace's height is about 1 standard deviation below the mean height.

Complete Part A as a whole class. Then complete Parts B–D in small groups.

A. What is a mathematical question you can ask about this situation? What information would you need to know to answer your question?

B. What variable(s) are involved in this situation? What unit of measurement would you use for each variable?

C. To answer your question, what strategy and tool would you use along with all the information you have? What answer do you get?

D. Does your work make sense in the context of the situation? How do you know?

Turn and Talk How would you expect the distribution of heights to be different if the students were from grades K–12 in a school system, instead of only those in one class or grade level?

Build Understanding

Fit a Normal Curve to a Histogram

The histogram below shows the theoretical probability of getting x heads when flipping 10 fair coins.

The curve shown on the histogram is a normal curve with the same mean and standard deviation as the experiment of flipping 10 fair coins. The **normal curve** is a smooth bell-shaped curve that represents situations where the mean is in the center of the data and the percentages decrease symmetrically on both sides. A **normal distribution** of data varies about the mean in such a way that the graph of the distribution is a normal curve.

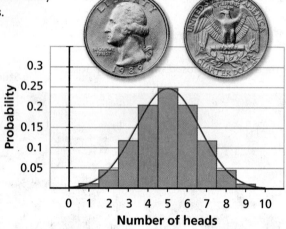

1 Consider the situation where 20 fair coins are flipped.

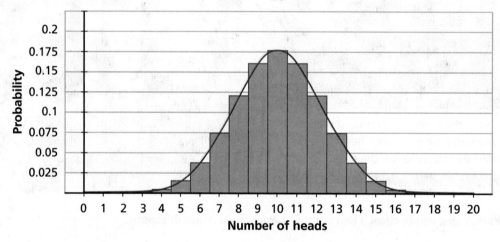

A. How does the histogram for flipping 10 fair coins compare to the histogram representing flipping 20 fair coins?

B. How do the histograms differ from the normal curves drawn on their graphs?

C. How would a histogram representing flipping 100 fair coins be different from these? How would it compare with a normal curve?

The histograms above show a mean of 5 and a standard deviation of 1.58 for 10 coins and a mean of 10 and a standard deviation of 2.24 for 20 coins.

D. How does changing the mean affect the graph of the normal curve?

E. How does changing the standard deviation affect the graph of the normal curve?

 Turn and Talk Is every probability distribution also a normal distribution? Explain your answer.

Find Areas Under a Normal Curve

The bell-shaped curves drawn over the histograms on the previous page are called normal curves. All normal curves can have the same basic shape. The relationship between the mean and its standard deviation remains the same for all normally distributed data sets. This relationship, modeled by the area between certain intervals under a normal curve, is called the **empirical rule**. In a normal distribution:

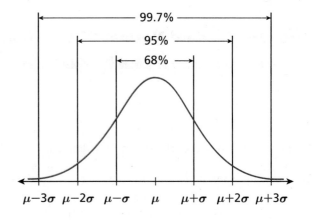

- 68% of the data fall within 1 standard deviation of the mean.

- 95% of the data fall within 2 standard deviations of the mean.

- 99.7% of the data fall within 3 standard deviations of the mean.

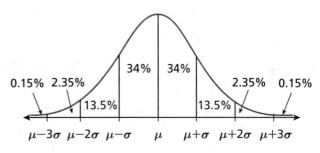

The figures at the right show the percent of data values found in different intervals of a normal distribution with mean μ and standard deviation σ.

The graph at the top shows the percent within 1, 2, or 3 standard deviations, and the graph on the bottom shows the percent within each interval that is 1 standard deviation wide.

2 Biologists study mountain lions in their natural habit by sedating the animals and then collecting physical data. The lions are released back into their habit after being revived. The means μ and standard deviations σ for both male and female mountain lions from a long-term study are show.

A. How can you use the empirical rule to determine the percent of male mountain lions that weighed between 67 kilograms and 103 kilograms? What is the percent?

B. How can you use the numbers in the figures above to determine the percent of female mountain lions in the study whose weight was greater than 36 kilograms but less than 54 kilograms? What is the percent?

> **Male:** $\mu = 85$ kg,
> $\sigma = 9$ kg
> **Female:** $\mu = 48$ kg,
> $\sigma = 6$ kg

C. How can you determine the percent of female mountain lions in the study that weighed more than 54 kilograms? What is the percent?

D. What is another method for determining the percent of female mountain lions weighing more than 54 kilograms?

Turn and Talk How could you use the mean and standard deviation to find the percent of female mountain lions that weighed between 30 kilograms and 66 kilograms?

Step It Out

Use the Standard Normal Distribution

The **z-score** is the number of **standard deviations** a given data value is from the **mean** of the data set. The z-score transforms any normal distribution to the **standard normal distribution**, which is a normal distribution with a mean of 0 and standard deviation of 1.

The formula $z = \frac{x - \mu}{\sigma}$ transforms a given data value x to a z-score using the mean μ and standard deviation σ of the data set.

The shaded region under the curve at the right represents all data values whose z-scores are less than 1.3. The standard normal table below shows the ratio of all data values less than a given z-score. The partially-shaded column and row show that the data values less than a z-score of 1.3 include 0.9032 or 90.32% of all data values in the probability distribution.

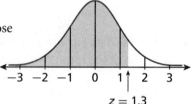

$z = 1.3$

Standard Normal Table

z	.0	.1	.2	.3	.4	.5	.6	.7	.8	.9
−3	0.0013	0.0010	0.0007	0.0005	0.0003	0.0002	0.0002	0.0001	0.0001	0.0000+
−2	0.0228	0.0179	0.0139	0.0107	0.0082	0.0062	0.0047	0.0035	0.0026	0.0019
−1	0.1587	0.1357	0.1151	0.0968	0.0808	0.0668	0.0548	0.0446	0.0359	0.0287
−0	0.5000	0.4602	0.4207	0.3821	0.3446	0.3085	0.2743	0.2420	0.2119	0.1841
0	0.5000	0.5398	0.5793	0.6179	0.6554	0.6915	0.7257	0.7580	0.7881	0.8159
1	0.8413	0.8643	0.8849	0.9032	0.9192	0.9332	0.9452	0.9554	0.9641	0.9713
2	0.9772	0.9821	0.9861	0.9893	0.9918	0.9938	0.9953	0.9965	0.9974	0.9981
3	0.9987	0.9990	0.9993	0.9995	0.9997	0.9998	0.9998	0.9999	0.9999	1.000−

3 ▸ A machine is manufacturing circular parts that cover openings on car engines. The mean radius of the covers is 2.5 centimeters and the standard deviation is 0.1 centimeter. Any part having a radius less than 2.18 centimeters must be rejected as it will not sufficiently cover the opening. If the machine makes 340 parts per hour, how many parts will be rejected for being too small during an 8-hour period?

Use the formula to calculate the z-score for 2.18: $z = \frac{2.18 - 2.5}{0.1} = -3.2$

Now use the standard normal table to find the ratio of all data values that have z-scores less than −3.2.

> **A.** How will this ratio help find the number of parts that will be rejected as too small?

From the table, the ratio is 0.0007 or 0.07%.

So, 0.07% of the parts will be rejected for being too small.

$2720 \cdot 0.0007 = 1.904$

> **B.** Why is 2720 used in this calculation?

In an 8-hour period, there will be 2 parts rejected for being too small.

Turn and Talk How would the solution process change if the situation in Task 3 involved a radius more than 3.4 standard deviations above the mean?

Check Understanding

1. The histogram on the left below shows the distribution of weights of one-month-old kittens born at a rescue shelter. The histogram at the right shows the distribution of the number of paper bags provided per customer for their purchases at a store. Which histogram more closely describes a normal curve? Explain.

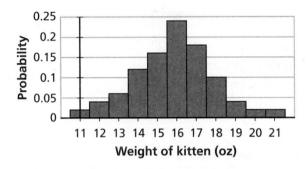

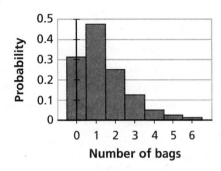

For Problems 2 and 3, use the following information. A university required all incoming students to take a math placement exam. The scores were normally distributed. The mean score was 65 with a standard deviation of 8.

2. What is the probability that an incoming student scored between 57 and 73 on the math placement exam?

3. What percent of incoming students scored below a 77 on the math placement exam?

On Your Own

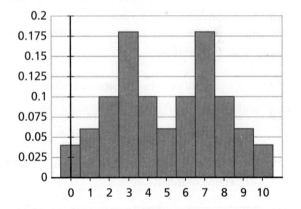

4. **(MP) Critique Reasoning** Toby claims that the histogram below can be described using a normal curve because it is a symmetric graph. Is Toby correct? Explain.

5. **(MP) Reason** One student rolls a fair number cube 20 times and records the probability of each result in a histogram. Another student rolls the same number cube 120 times and records the probability of each result in a histogram. Which histogram is more likely to approximate a normal curve? Explain.

6. A grocery store has clementines available in mesh bags labeled as weighing 3 pounds. The bags contain whole numbers of clementines, so the weights vary. The supplier of the clementines states that the weights of their bags are normally distributed with mean and standard deviation as shown. What is the probability that a bag randomly chosen by a customer weighs more than 3.1 pounds? Use the empirical rule.

Mean: 2.95 lb
Standard deviation: 0.05 lb

The arrival times of a particular rush-hour commuter train are normally distributed. The mean arrival time is 8:47 a.m. The standard deviation of arrival times is 4 minutes. Find the probability that on a randomly chosen day, the train arrives in the given time period. Use the empirical rule.

7. between 8:35 a.m. and 8:59 a.m.   **8.** before 8:51 a.m.

9. after 8:39 a.m.   **10.** between 8:43 a.m. and 8:59 a.m.

A battery manufacturing company has begun production of a new battery model. During testing, the company determined that the length of time the battery can power a laptop is normally distributed, with a mean of 8.2 hours and a standard deviation of 1.4 hours. Use the empirical rule to find the percent of laptop batteries that will last the following length of time.

11. between 5.4 and 11 hours   **12.** no more than 6.8 hours

13. between 8.2 and 12.4 hours   **14.** at least 5.4 hours

Refer to the laptop battery scenario for Problems 11–14. Use a z-score table or technology to find the percent of laptop batteries that will last the following lengths of time.

15. no more than 9.04 hours   **16.** at least 4.7 hours

17. no more than 7.64 hours   **18.** at least 10.86 hours

For Problems 19–22, suppose the amount of tomatoes in each can is normally distributed. On a graphing calculator or spreadsheet, use the cumulative distribution function for a normal distribution to find each percent or probability.

Can of tomatoes:
$\mu = 794$ g, $\sigma = 6$ g

19. What percent of cans have less than 800 grams of tomatoes?

20. What is the probability that a randomly chosen can has between 782 grams and 806 grams of tomatoes?

21. What is the probability that a randomly chosen can has more than 798 grams of tomatoes?

22. What is the probability that a randomly chosen can has between 780 grams and 790 grams of tomatoes?

23. For probability experiments where the theoretical probability is known, the mean number of successes is np, where n is the number of trials and p is the theoretical probability of success. The standard deviation of the number of successes is $\sqrt{npq}$, where q is the probability of failure. Consider the situation with a four-part spinner with equal-sized sections and only one section is a success.

   A. What is the probability that in a random experiment with 100 trials, the number of successes is between 20 and 30?

   B. What is the probability that in a random experiment with 1000 trials, the number of successes is between 200 and 300?

   C. Compare the results of these two situations.

The wandering albatross has one of the longest wingspans of all birds. Assume the wingspans of a large population of albatrosses are normally distributed, with the mean and standard deviation shown. On a spreadsheet or graphing calculator, use the cumulative distribution function for a normal distribution to find each percent or probability.

Wingspan:
$\mu = 310$ cm, $\sigma = 15$ cm

24. What is the probability that a randomly chosen albatross has a wingspan that is less than 290 cm?

25. What is the probability that a randomly chosen albatross has a wingspan that is greater than 315 cm?

26. What percent of albatrosses have a wingspan between 300 cm and 320 cm?

27. What percent of albatrosses have a wingspan that is either less than 285 cm or greater than 335 cm?

For Problems 28 and 29, the theoretical probability distribution of a spinner is shown in the histogram.

28. Can this histogram be used to describe a normal probability distribution? Explain.

29. This spinner is used repeatedly to perform experiments of choosing 10 random digits. The mean of the experiments is 4.5 and the standard deviation is 1.

   A. What is the probability that the mean is less than 3.5?

   B. What is the probability that the mean is between 4.2 and 4.8?

   C. What percent of the means are at least 6.1?

   D. What percent of the means are either no more than 3.7 or at least 6.3?

For Problems 30–33, suppose the mean length of the leaves from an oak tree is 15 cm with a standard deviation of 2.1 cm. Assume that the lengths of all leaves from the tree are normally distributed.

30. What is the probability that a randomly chosen leaf is exactly 15 cm long?

31. What is the probability that a randomly chosen leaf is less than 13 cm long?

32. What is the probability that a randomly chosen leaf is at least 14 cm long?

33. What is the probability that a randomly chosen leaf is at least 16 cm but less than 17 cm long?

34. **Open Ended** The empirical rule uses the probabilities 0.68, 0.95, and 0.997 because they are at whole intervals of standard deviations. Suppose you wanted to create a rule that used a different trio of probabilities. What z-scores could represent the intervals centered at the mean? Describe your intervals.

35. (MP) **Reason** The tables below give the results of two experiments of 24 trials performed using technology to simulate spinning a spinner labeled 1–4 and rolling a fair number cube with sides labeled 1–6. The first table shows the sum of the numbers showing on the spinner and the number cube. The second table shows the number of spin/roll pairings it took to obtain a sum greater than 7.

Sum of Spinner and Number Cube											
6	8	9	10	5	2	3	5	4	6	3	8
4	8	2	7	3	6	5	7	7	3	5	9

Number of Tries to Obtain a Sum Greater than 7											
2	2	6	9	1	3	2	3	5	1	1	4
1	8	2	7	6	1	4	3	4	5	3	9

A. Using a graphing calculator, find the mean and standard deviation of the results of each experiment to the nearest tenth.

B. In a normally-distributed sample of size 24, about how many values would you expect to find with a z-score less than or equal to -2? -1? 0? 1? 2?

C. For each experiment, find the number of values that satisfy the z-score conditions described in Part B.

D. Do the results of either experiment appear to be normally distributed? Explain.

Spiral Review • Assessment Readiness

36. Choosing a red card and choosing a 4 from a set of cards are dependent events. If $P(\text{red }4) = \frac{1}{54}$ and $P(\text{red}) = \frac{2}{9}$, what is $P(4\,|\,\text{red})$?

Ⓐ $\frac{1}{12}$ Ⓑ $\frac{1}{9}$ Ⓒ $\frac{1}{6}$ Ⓓ $\frac{1}{4}$

37. The probability that it rains on any given day in April is 30%. When it rains, the forecast predicted rain 90% of the time. When it does not rain, the forecast predicted rain 5% of the time. What is the probability that there was no rain on a particular day and no rain was predicted?

Ⓐ 3.5%   Ⓒ 66.5%

Ⓑ 27%   Ⓓ 70%

38. A fair coin is flipped 8 times. What is the probability that exactly 3 heads are flipped?

Ⓐ $\frac{11}{64}$ Ⓒ $\frac{7}{32}$

Ⓑ $\frac{51}{256}$ Ⓓ $\frac{3}{8}$

39. For a survey, randomly selected people were asked for the following information about themselves. Which of them lead to a numerical answer? Select all that apply.

Ⓐ age (years)   Ⓔ height (in.)

Ⓑ hair color   Ⓕ weight (lb)

Ⓒ nationality   Ⓖ eye color

Ⓓ hometown   Ⓗ marital status

 I'm in a Learning Mindset!

How do I make thoughtful decisions based on data?

Data-Gathering Techniques

(I Can) recognize the relationship among populations, samples, statistics, and parameters, I can and identify representative sampling methods.

Spark Your Learning

A university randomly selected and surveyed 500 of its students about how many credits of classes they plan to take next semester.

Some students at universities are part-time students, and many are full-time students.

Students must take at least 12 credits to be considered full-time.

Complete Part A as a whole class. Then complete Parts B–D in small groups.

A. What is a mathematical question you can ask about this situation? What information would you need to know to answer your question?

B. What variable(s) are involved in this situation?

C. To answer your question, what strategy and tool would you use along with all the information you have? What answer do you get?

D. Does your result make sense in the context of the situation? How do you know?

Turn and Talk The university changes their definition of a full-time student to someone who takes at least 15 credits. How does this change your work?

Build Understanding

Compare Samples and Populations

A **population** is a group of individual members. You can collect data about a population by surveying or studying some or all of the members of the population. The study of *all* members of a population in order to gather data is called a **census**. A **parameter** is a number that summarizes a characteristic of the population.

The study of only *some* of a population's members in order to gather data is called a **sample**. A **statistic** is a number that summarizes data from a sample and can be used to estimate parameters.

1 ▸ A national organization is working to improve education in the United States. The organization is trying to gather data about third-grade students from all across the country.

A class of third-grade students is a sample of the population.

A. What is the population in this situation? Explain.

B. One sample of the population could be all of the third-grade students in the United States who are home-schooled. What are some other examples of samples of the population?

C. A parameter might be the percent of all third-grade students who read above grade level. What are some other parameters that can describe the population?

D. A statistic might be the percent of all third-grade students in a classroom who read above grade level. What are some other statistics that can describe samples?

E. Which type of study is more comprehensive, a census or a sample? What are the advantages of each type of study?

 Turn and Talk What is the difference between a population and a sample? What is the difference between a parameter and a statistic?

Explore Sampling Methods

Conducting a census of an entire population typically requires a lot of time and resources. Sampling the same population can be a more efficient alternative. The sample statistics can then be used to make good estimates of the actual parameters of the population.

A **representative sample** provides a statistic that is a good estimate for its corresponding population parameter. A **biased sample** is one that does not fairly represent the population. A biased sample can produce statistics that can lead to inaccurate conclusions about population parameters.

Sampling methods vary among different surveys, and some surveys use multiple methods to limit the potential for bias. Other times, people conducting surveys are focused on a high response rate, speed, or ease in finding a sample size that is large enough.

Sampling method	Description
Simple random sample	Each individual in the population has an equal chance of being selected.
Self-selected sample	Individuals volunteer to be part of the sample.
Convenience sample	Individuals are selected based on how accessible they are.
Systematic sample	Members of the sample are chosen according to a rule, such as every nth individual in the population.
Stratified sample	The population is divided into groups and individuals from each group are selected (typically through a random sample within each group).
Cluster sample	The population is divided into groups and some of the groups are randomly selected, and either all the individuals in the selected groups are selected or just some of the individuals from the selected groups are selected (typically through a random sample within each selected group).

2 ▸ A school's student council wants to know student opinions about a new dress code.

A. What is the population in this situation?

B. The student council surveys all students who are assigned lunch during the first lunch period. What is the sampling method? Is it likely to lead to a biased sample? Explain your reasoning.

C. The student council surveys two randomly selected students from each English class. What is the sampling method? Is it likely to lead to a biased sample? Explain your reasoning.

The student council surveys students about the new dress code.

D. The student council surveys students by leaving index cards near the entrance to the school for students to write down their comments about the dress code. What is the sampling method? Is it likely to lead to a biased sample? Explain your reasoning.

E. The student council surveys students by stopping every tenth student as they enter the school and asking for their comments on the dress code. What is the sampling method? Is it likely to lead to a biased sample? Explain your reasoning.

F. Describe a simple random sample that the school council could use to survey students about the dress code. Do you think this method is likely to lead to a biased sample? Explain.

 Turn and Talk Describe the sample you would use if you were performing the survey for the student council. Justify your response.

Step It Out

Classify Sampling Methods

Surveys can be analyzed to determine what type of sampling method they use. The sampling method can then be used to determine whether the sample is a representative or biased sample. You can use this information to determine whether the statistics produced by the survey can be used to make estimates about the actual parameters of the population.

3 ▶ A shopping center has empty space for stores, and the management of the shopping center performs different surveys to find what type of store the local population would prefer in that space.

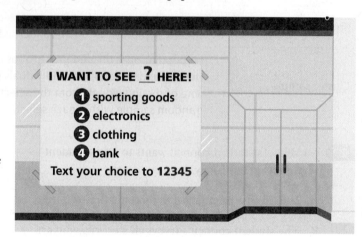

I WANT TO SEE **?** HERE!
1 sporting goods
2 electronics
3 clothing
4 bank
Text your choice to 12345

Evaluate the two surveys below and determine which one would provide a better statistic for estimating the population parameter.

Survey 1: The management of the shopping center got 100 responses after putting up posters. 35 wanted a new clothing store, 28 wanted an electronics store, 22 wanted a bank, and 15 wanted a sporting goods store.

Identify the type of sample.

This is a self-selected sample.

> **A.** What are some possible limitations of this sampling method?

Determine whether the sample is representative.

This may not be representative of the population as a whole. It includes only those who decided to take the action of calling or texting the number with their opinions, but it might be that others who would spend money there prefer other options.

Survey 2: A survey of 10 randomly selected adults from each of the 10 local neighborhoods found that 43 wanted a new clothing store, 23 wanted an electronics store, 21 wanted a sporting goods store, and 13 wanted a bank.

Identify the type of sample.

This is a stratified sample.

> **B.** Of these four types of stores, which would you advise management to bring in? Explain why.

Determine whether the sample is representative.

This is likely representative of the population. It includes randomly selected people from several different groups likely to go to the shopping center.

Select the better survey.

Survey 2 is the survey that the management should use. It is more likely to be representative of the population as a whole and so its statistics will provide better estimates for the population parameters.

Make Predictions from a Random Sample

You can use data from a random sample to make predictions about the corresponding population. **Numerical data** represent quantities or observations that can be measured, such as number of siblings or total rainfall. **Categorical data** represent attributes that can be sorted into groups or categories, such as animal species or hair color.

While the mean is useful for summarizing numerical data, you can use a *proportion* to describe categorical data. The proportion of individuals in a category is the ratio of the number of individuals in the category to the total number of individuals. A proportion calculated from a sample can be used to draw conclusions about a population.

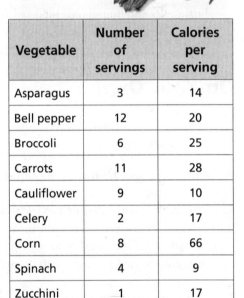

4 ▶ A health center in a town with 15,000 adults surveyed a random sample of 30 adults from the town about the vegetables they ate during the past week. The table shows the types of vegetables people reported eating, the total number of servings of each vegetable eaten by the group, and the number of calories per serving.

Find the proportion of vegetable servings eaten that were corn servings.

$$\frac{\text{Corn servings}}{\text{Total servings}} = \frac{8}{3 + 12 + 6 + 11 + 9 + 2 + 8 + 4 + 1}$$

$$= \frac{8}{56}$$

$$= \frac{1}{7} \text{ or about } 0.143$$

Vegetable	Number of servings	Calories per serving
Asparagus	3	14
Bell pepper	12	20
Broccoli	6	25
Carrots	11	28
Cauliflower	9	10
Celery	2	17
Corn	8	66
Spinach	4	9
Zucchini	1	17

Estimate how many corn servings were eaten by all adults in the town during the past week.

First estimate the total number *x* of vegetable servings eaten by the town's adults in the past week.

$$\frac{\text{Total servings for sample}}{\text{Size of sample}} = \frac{\text{Total servings for population}}{\text{Size of population}}$$

$$\frac{56}{30} = \frac{x}{15,000}$$

$$x = \frac{56}{30}(15,000) = 28,000 \text{ servings}$$

A. What data in the table are categorical? What data are numerical?

Then multiply this result by the sample proportion of servings that were corn.

$$\frac{1}{7}(28,000) = 4000$$

B. Why is this a good estimate for the number of servings of corn eaten by the town's adults in the past week?

About 4000 servings of corn were eaten by the town's adults during the past week.

 Turn and Talk Estimate the mean number of calories consumed by an adult in the town from vegetables during the past week.

©Floortje/iStock/Getty Images

Check Understanding

A city manager is trying to determine how much garbage and recycling are placed at the curb in her city each week. She sends out a survey to every household and business in the city with a return envelope. Some of the households and businesses fill out the survey and return it.

1. What is the population in this situation? What is the sample? How do the two groups differ?

2. What term best describes this type of survey? Is it likely to lead to a biased sample? Explain.

3. Another survey is conducted by a polling company that contacts random city residents and business owners. Which survey results do you think will be more useful in estimating the population parameters? Explain.

4. The second survey contacts a total of 100 business owners and households. Businesses and households reported throwing out about 15 pounds of garbage each week. The town collects garbage at 2500 different addresses. Based on the survey response, how much garbage would the city expect to throw out each week?

On Your Own

5. When using a sample to collect information, do you use statistics to estimate parameters or parameters to estimate statistics? Explain.

For Problems 6 and 7, identify the population and the sampling method.

6. The director and editor of a movie want to know whether people will enjoy going to see the version of their movie in its current edited version. They screen the movie for 100 people who are regular movie-goers. The director and editor then collect surveys from all 100 people about their thoughts and opinions.

7. The owner of a minor league hockey team wants to know how much the team's fans are willing to pay for a ticket. He decides to have his staff survey every 8th person who leaves the team's next home game.

8. The director of the regional public transit system wants to know where to add more bus stops and bus routes. Classify each sampling method and indicate whether you would recommend that method for the proposed survey.

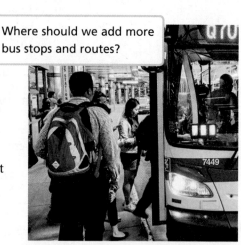

Where should we add more bus stops and routes?

   A. Survey 5 randomly selected passengers on each bus route.

   B. Survey every third person who calls the system information phone number.

   C. Put up posters in all buses asking passengers to call or text the intersections where they'd like to have a bus stop.

   D. Count the number of passengers who get on the bus at each stop on the 5 busiest bus routes.

   E. Survey 30 people at the downtown bus terminal.

9. A local school board wants to know whether local residents are willing to support the construction of a new school and, if so, how much they are willing to increase their property tax payments to contribute to the school's construction. The board is considering two methods for gathering data.

Method A: Survey 50 randomly selected residents whose children attend one or more of the schools in the system.

Method B: Survey 50 randomly selected residents from a list of all residents of the community served by the school system.

A. Identify the population in this situation.

B. Which sampling method is most likely to result in a representative sample of the population? Explain.

C. Describe another method that is likely to result in a representative sample.

D. Describe the categorical data and numerical data that the school board wants to gather.

10. (MP) **Reason** A national organization of teachers has 5000 members. The table lists the grade levels they teach. The organization wants to survey a sample of 50 of the teachers to get their opinions on how best to teach new concepts to students. Explain why it might be better to use a stratified sample than a simple random sample.

Grade level	Number of teachers
Elementary	1439
Middle	1094
High School	1621
University	846

11. (MP) **Reason** A polling organization wants to interview 200 likely voters across the state about their opinions of the candidates and issues for an upcoming election. They have a very limited time frame to complete the survey. Explain why it may be better to use a cluster sample than a simple random sample in this situation.

12. A local board of health wants to know about community members' physical exercise habits. The adult population in the community is about 25,400. The board surveys 100 randomly selected adults in the community. These adults are asked what type of exercise they do the most and how many minutes per week they do that activity. The table shows the average time each person surveyed spends on a particular activity during the week.

A. Describe the categorical and numerical data gathered in the survey.

B. Calculate the proportion of adults whose primary exercise activity each week is bicycling. Then use this result to predict the number of adults in the community whose primary exercise activity each week is bicycling.

C. Estimate the mean amount of time per week that an adult in the community spends on their preferred exercise.

Activity	Number of participants	Average minutes per week
Running	29	95
Bicycling	11	105
Swimming	8	53
Other	52	62

13. **Open Ended** Write a scenario in which a sample of the population needs to be surveyed. Identify and describe three potential methods of sampling and whether or not each would result in a biased sample.

14. A city government performs an annual census to gather some information about the people who live in the city. They send out a survey in the mail to each household asking how many people live there, how old each person is, and what each person does for a living. When the survey was conducted last year, 80% of all households did not return the survey.

    A. Is this a census or a sample? Explain.

    B. What categorical and numerical data is the city collecting?

    C. How can the city use the results of the returned surveys to predict parameters of the population as a whole? Is this likely to be an accurate representation? Explain.

    D. (MP) **Construct Arguments** What method of data collection will lead to data that is more representative of the city population as a whole?

Spiral Review • Assessment Readiness

15. A test for a certain disease found in 6% of an animal population correctly identifies animals that have the disease 85% of the time and correctly identifies animals that do not have the disease 90% of the time. What is the probability an animal in the population tests positive for the disease?

    (A) 5.1%

    (B) 9.4%

    (C) 14.5%

    (D) 84.6%

16. A number cube labeled 1–6 is rolled 5 times. What is the probability of rolling exactly two 4s? Round to the nearest tenth of a percent.

    (A) 3.2%

    (B) 8.0%

    (C) 16.1%

    (D) 40.2%

17. The mean of a data set is 141, and the standard deviation is 17. What is the probability that a randomly selected data value is less than 124?

    (A) 0.15%   (C) 17%

    (B) 2.5%   (D) 32%

18. The heights of all adults in a small city are normally distributed with a mean height of 66 inches and a standard deviation of 4 inches. Which of the following statements are true about the height of the adults in the population? Select all that apply.

    (A) About 68% are between 62 inches and 70 inches.

    (B) About 16% are taller than 74 inches.

    (C) About 84% are shorter than 70 inches.

    (D) About 95% of adults are between 54 inches and 78 inches.

    (E) About 34% of adults are between 62 inches and 66 inches.

 I'm in a Learning Mindset!

What factors did I use to establish timelines for my goal of understanding data gathering techniques?

Sampling Distributions

(I Can) describe how the mean of a sampling distribution, the corresponding population mean, and the population proportion are related.

Spark Your Learning

The Constitution requires the United States government to perform a census of the entire population of the U.S. every 10 years.

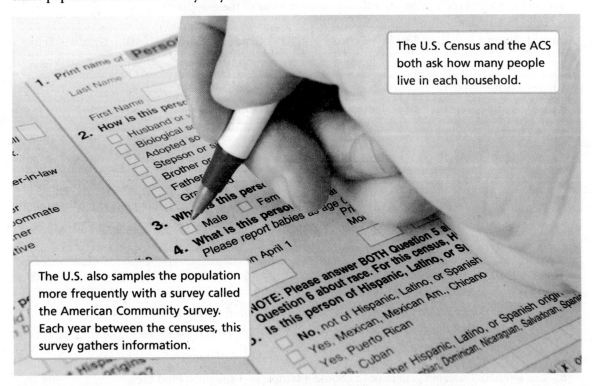

The U.S. Census and the ACS both ask how many people live in each household.

The U.S. also samples the population more frequently with a survey called the American Community Survey. Each year between the censuses, this survey gathers information.

Complete Part A as a whole class. Then complete Parts B–D in small groups.

A. What is a mathematical question you can ask about this situation? What information would you need to know to answer your question?

B. Can your answer be exact given the data that is provided? Explain why or why not.

C. To answer your question, what strategy and tool would you use along with all the information you have? What answer do you get?

D. Is your approximation likely to be too high or too low? How do you know?

Turn and Talk Describe a sampling method the government could use that is most likely to result in an unbiased sample. Do you think a larger or smaller sample size would result in a closer match between the sample data and the population data? Explain your reasoning.

Build Understanding

Develop a Distribution of Sample Means and Sample Proportions

The mean, proportion, and standard deviation of a sample are affected by the data collected and by the size of the sample.

1 The table shows the identification numbers, grade levels (S for sophomore and J for junior), and scores of 40 students who took a standardized test at a school. You will need to work together as a class to answer some of the questions.

ID	Grade	Score	ID	Grade	Score	ID	Grade	Score	ID	Grade	Score
1	S	930	11	S	1200	21	J	1220	31	J	890
2	J	1010	12	S	990	22	S	1140	32	J	1250
3	S	1120	13	S	850	23	S	860	33	S	1380
4	J	860	14	J	970	24	J	980	34	J	1500
5	J	1380	15	J	1160	25	S	1140	35	S	1200
6	S	1070	16	S	1290	26	J	1340	36	S	900
7	S	690	17	J	1100	27	S	1010	37	J	1000
8	J	740	18	J	1040	28	J	1450	38	J	1100
9	J	830	19	J	980	29	J	1280	39	S	1300
10	J	1410	20	J	1330	30	S	940	40	J	1400

A. Use technology to calculate the mean score μ and standard deviation σ for the population of the 40 students at the school who took the test. Also find the proportion p of sophomores in this population.

B. Use a random number generator to choose a sample of 5 students. Find the mean score $\bar{x}$ for the sample. Round to the nearest whole number. Report your sample mean to your teacher. Create a histogram using the sample means reported by members of your class. Calculate the mean of the sample means $\mu_{\bar{x}}$ and the standard deviation of the sample means, $\sigma_{\bar{x}}$.

C. Repeat the process in Part B for a sample of 15 students.

D. Use a random number generator to choose a sample of 5 students. Find the proportion of sophomores $\hat{p}$ for your sample. Report your sample proportion to your teacher. Create a histogram using the sample proportions reported by members of your class. Calculate the mean of the sample proportions $\mu_{\hat{p}}$ and the standard deviation of the sample proportions, $\sigma_{\hat{p}}$. Round to the nearest hundredth.

E. Repeat the process in Part D for a sample of 10 students.

 Turn and Talk What happens to the shape of the histograms of the sample means and of the sample proportions as the sample size increases?

Step It Out

Use the Sampling Distribution of the Sample Mean

A **sampling distribution** provides the data that describes the variance of a particular statistic over all samples of n individuals from the same population. In Task 1, you approximated a sampling distribution. The mean of the sampling distribution of the sample mean is written as $\mu_{\bar{x}}$. The standard deviation of the sampling distribution of the sample mean (also called the **standard error of the mean**) is written as $\sigma_{\bar{x}}$.

> ### Properties of the Sampling Distribution of the Sample Mean
>
> If a random sample of size n is selected from a population with mean μ and standard deviation σ, then
>
> 1. $\mu_{\bar{x}} = \mu$,
> 2. $\sigma_{\bar{x}} = \dfrac{\sigma}{\sqrt{n}}$, and
> 3. the sampling distribution of the sample mean is normal if the population is normal; for all other populations, the sampling distribution of the mean approaches a normal distribution as n increases.

2 The weights in ounces of cereal boxes of a given size are normally distributed. For random samples of 25 boxes, what is the weight interval centered on the mean of the sampling distribution captures 95% of the sample means?

Write the given information: $n = 25$, $\mu = 12.3$, and $\sigma = 0.15$.

Mean weight:
12.3 ounces
Standard deviation:
0.15 ounce

Find the mean of the sampling distribution and the standard error of the mean.

$\mu_{\bar{x}} = \mu = 12.3$ and $\sigma_{\bar{x}} = \dfrac{\sigma}{\sqrt{n}} = \dfrac{0.15}{\sqrt{25}} = 0.03$

A. What happens to the standard error of the mean as the sample size increases?

In a normal distribution such as this, 95% of the data falls within 2 standard deviations of the mean.

$\mu_{\bar{x}} - 2\sigma_{\bar{x}} = 12.3 - 2(0.03) = 12.24$ and

B. What does this mean in terms of cereal boxes?

$\mu_{\bar{x}} + 2\sigma_{\bar{x}} = 12.3 + 2(0.03) = 12.36$.

The interval from 12.24 ounces to 12.36 ounces captures 95% of the sample means.

3 What is the probability a random sample of 20 of the cereal boxes in Task 2 has a mean of at most 12.35 ounces?

Find the mean of the sampling distribution of the sample mean and the standard error of the mean.

A. How has the standard error of the mean changed from the one you found in the previous task?

$\mu_{\bar{x}} = \mu = 12.3$ and $\sigma_{\bar{x}} = \dfrac{\sigma}{\sqrt{n}} = \dfrac{0.15}{\sqrt{20}} \approx 0.03354$

Use a graphing calculator or other technology to find $P(\bar{x} \leq 12.35) \approx 0.932$.

The probability that a random sample of 20 boxes has a mean of at most 12.35 ounces is about 93.2%.

B. How do you know the sampling distribution is normal?

Use the Sampling Distribution of the Sample Proportion

For a sampling distribution of the sample proportion, p represents the proportion of individuals in the population that have a particular characteristic (that is, the proportion of "successes") and $\hat{p}$ is the proportion of successes in a sample. The mean of the sampling distribution of the sample proportion is written as $\mu_{\hat{p}}$. The standard deviation of the sampling distribution of the sample proportion is written as $\sigma_{\hat{p}}$ and is also called the **standard error of the proportion**.

> **Properties of the Sampling Distribution of the Sample Proportion**
>
> If a random sample of size n is selected from a population with proportion p of successes, then
> 1. $\mu_{\hat{p}} = p$,
> 2. $\sigma_{\hat{p}} = \sqrt{\dfrac{p(1-p)}{n}}$, and
> 3. if both np and $n(1-p)$ are at least 10, then the sampling distribution of the sample proportion is approximately normal.

4 ▶ A recent census of a major city asked how long peoples' commutes were. When sampling from this population, consider successes to be people who commute more than 45 minutes to work each day. For random samples of 40 people, what interval centered on the mean of the sampling distribution captures 95% of the sample proportions?

Identify n and p: $n = 40$ and $p = 0.35$.

Find the mean of the sampling distribution of the sample proportion and the standard error of the proportion.

35% of all residents commute more than 45 minutes to work each day.

A. What does 0.35 represent?

$$\mu_{\hat{p}} = p = 0.35 \text{ and } \sigma_{\hat{p}} = \sqrt{\frac{0.35(0.65)}{40}} \approx 0.0754$$

B. Within how many standard deviations of the mean does 95% of the data in a normal distribution lie?

Since both $np = 14$ and $n(1-p) = 26$ are greater than 10, the sampling distribution of the sample proportion is approximately normal.

$$\mu_{\hat{p}} - 2\sigma_{\hat{p}} \approx 0.35 - 2(0.0754) = 0.1992 \text{ and } \mu_{\hat{p}} + 2\sigma_{\hat{p}} \approx 0.35 + 2(0.0754) = 0.5008.$$

So, 95% of the sample proportions fall between 19.92% and 50.08%.

5 ▶ What is the probability that a random sample of 50 people from the census has a sample proportion of at most 27%? Successes are defined the same way as in Task 4.

Identify n and p: $n = 50$ and $p = 0.35$.

Then find: $\mu_{\hat{p}} = p = 0.35$ and $\sigma_{\hat{p}} = \sqrt{\dfrac{0.35(0.65)}{50}} \approx 0.0675$.

A. How does the probability of a success affect the standard error of the proportion?

Since both $np = 17.5$ and $n(1-p) = 32.5$ are greater than 10, the sampling distribution of the sampling proportion is approximately normal.

Use a graphing calculator or other technology to find $P(\bar{x} \leq 0.27) \approx 0.118$. The probability is about 11.8%.

Turn and Talk How would your answers change if the sample size was 100? Explain.

Check Understanding

1. Will the means of two different samples of the same population always be approximately equal? Explain.

2. The heights of tree saplings at a nursery are normally distributed with a mean height of 29 inches and a standard deviation of 4 inches. What is the standard error of the mean in samples of 30 tree saplings? What interval centered on the mean of the sampling distribution captures 95% of the sample means? What is the probability that a random sample of 30 saplings has a mean of at most 26 inches?

3. The proportion of residences in a small city that are owner occupied is about 63%. What is the standard error of the proportion in samples of 50 residences? What interval centered on the mean of the sampling distribution captures 95% of the sample proportions? What is the probability that a random sample of 50 residences has a sample proportion of at least 70% that are owner occupied?

On Your Own

4. (MP) **Reason** A bowler keeps track of scores for a season. Some sample means and sample standard deviations found from random samples of 10 scores are shown.

   A. What can you assume about the true mean of the bowler's scores? Explain.

   B. What does this set of 9 sample means and standard deviations suggest about the sample size? Explain.

Mean	Standard deviation
198	11
205	13
201	14
209	10
204	16
189	20
193	16
197	18
210	12

For Problems 5–8, on a standardized test, the scores of seniors at a high school were normally distributed, with a mean of 21.1 and a standard deviation of 4.5.

5. For random samples of 100 scores, what interval centered on the mean captures 95% of the sample means?

6. For random samples of 25 scores, what interval centered on the mean captures 99.7% of the sample means?

7. What is the probability that a random sample of 30 scores has a mean of at least 22?

8. What is the probability that a random sample of 50 scores has a mean of at most 22?

9. **STEM** A factory produces plates. Their diameters are normally distributed. An inspector samples 45 plates at a time.

   A. What is the standard error of the mean for each sample?

   B. What interval centered on the mean of the sampling distribution captures 95% of the sample means?

   C. What is the probability that a random sample has a mean diameter of at most 10.998 inches?

   D. What is the probability that a random sample has a mean diameter of between 11 and 11.001 inches?

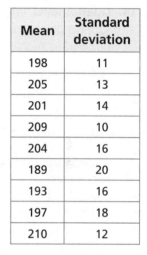

Mean diameter: 11 in.
Standard deviation: 0.01 in.

For Problems 10–12, about 41% of students at a large local high school are part of at least one extracurricular activity. When sampling from this population, consider "successes" to be students who participate in at least one extracurricular activity.

Participation rate: 41%

10. For random samples of 60 students, what interval centered on the mean captures 95% of the sample proportions?

11. For random samples of 100 students, what interval centered on the mean captures 99.7% of the sample proportions?

12. What is the probability that a random sample of 40 students includes more than 38% participating in an extracurricular activity?

13. **(MP) Use Structure** In a sampling from a normally-distributed population, the mean of the sampling proportion is 0.5 and the standard deviation of the sampling proportion is 0.14. Describe where a sample proportion of 0.42 falls within the sampling proportion?

14. **Open Ended** Write a problem about the sample mean of sample proportions using a probability of success and sample size that is different from the problems given in this lesson. Trade problems with a classmate and solve their problem.

15. **(MP) Reason** What is the smallest sample size that guarantees a sample proportion is normally distributed? Explain the situation.

Spiral Review • Assessment Readiness

16. The ages of members at an athletic club have a mean of 46 years and a standard deviation of 7 years. If the ages are normally distributed, what percent of members are between the ages of 32 and 60?

    (A) 68%   (C) 86%

    (B) 77%   (D) 95%

17. Which sampling technique is used in a survey of every fourth student entering the school?

    (A) convenience sample

    (B) cluster sample

    (C) stratified sample

    (D) systematic sample

18. Match each description of an interval of values by their z-scores on the left with the probability that a random value is within that interval on the right.

    A. $-1.2 < z$ **1.** 0.933

    B. $-1.9 < z < 1.1$ **2.** 0.835

    C. $z < 1.5$ **3.** 0.757

    D. $-0.7 < z < 3.2$ **4.** 0.885

 I'm in a Learning Mindset!

How will I know when my goal for understanding sampling distributions is met successfully?

Binomial Experiments

Adam flips a fair coin 6 times. For each individual trial, the only outcomes are heads and tails. Each can occur with the same probability, $\frac{1}{2}$. After flipping the coin 6 times, there are multiple ways to end up with only 2 tail and 4 heads.

```
         1                Row 0
       1   1              Row 1
      1   2   1           Row 2
    1   3   3   1         Row 3
   1   4   6   4   1      Row 4
  1  5  10 10  5   1      Row 5
①  ⑥ ⑮  20  15  6   1     Row 6
```

Outcome	0 tails	1 tail	2 tails
Probability	$1 \cdot \left(\frac{1}{2}\right)^6 = \frac{1}{64}$	$6 \cdot \left(\frac{1}{2}\right)^6 = \frac{3}{32}$	$15 \cdot \left(\frac{1}{2}\right)^6 = \frac{15}{64}$

total number of trials

Number of different ways to flip 2 tails from Pascal's Triangle.

Normal Distribution

As Adam flips more coins, the probability distribution approaches a normal curve.

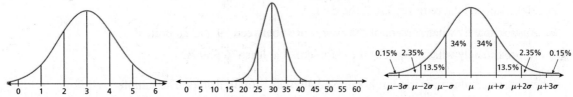

If Adam flips the coin 60 times, the mean number of tails flipped would be 30, and the standard deviation would be approximately 4. Adam would expect to flip 26–34 tails 68% of the time.

Sampling Methods

A parameter summarizes a characteristic of a population. A statistic summarizes a sample in order to estimate a parameter.

Representative sample	Provides a good estimate for its corresponding population parameter
Biased sample	Does not fairly represent the population and can lead to inaccurate conclusions

Sampling Distributions

A sampling distribution shows how a particular statistic varies over all samples of n individuals from the same population. A sampling distribution is approximately normal if $np > 10$ and $n(1 - p) > 10$.

Standard error of the mean	$\sigma_{\bar{x}} = \frac{\sigma}{\sqrt{n}}$
Standard error of the proportion	$\sigma_p = \sqrt{\frac{p(1 - p)}{n}}$

Vocabulary

Choose the correct term from the box to complete each sentence.

1. A ___?___ represents a sample, while a ___?___ represents the population.

2. A ___?___ is modeled by a curve that is bell-shaped, rising on the left and falling on the right at the same rate.

3. A ___?___ shows how a particular statistic varies over samples from the same population.

4. A ___?___ is a good estimator for its corresponding population parameter.

5. A ___?___ has only two outcomes with equally likely probabilities.

> **Vocabulary**
>
> binomial experiment
> normal distribution
> parameter
> representative sample
> sampling distribution
> statistic

Concepts and Skills

6. A number cube is rolled to see if the outcome will be an even number.

   A. Explain why this is a binomial experiment.

   B. Explain how Pascal's Triangle can be used to determine the probabilities of r successes out of n trials.

   C. What is the probability that the outcome will be even 4 times out of 5 trials?

7. The class average on a statistics test is 85 points, with a standard deviation of 3.

   A. Plot a normal curve to represent the data.

   B. Approximately what percent of the class scored between 79 and 88 points?

   C. Approximately what percent of the class scored at least 76 points?

8. A beverage manufacturer randomly sampled 40 of its protein drinks. The sample mean was 15.8 ounces, with a standard deviation of 0.2 ounce.

   A. Determine the standard error of the mean for a sample of 20 drinks.

   B. (MP) **Use Tools** What is the probability that a random sample of 20 protein drinks has a mean of at most 15.85 ounces? State what strategy and tool you will use to answer the question, explain your choice, and then find the answer.

   C. What is the probability that a random sample of 20 protein drinks has a mean of exactly 15.85 ounces? Explain your reasoning.

Identify each sampling method as likely to be representative or biased.

9. Simple random sample

10. Self-selected sample

11. Convenience sample

12. Stratified sample

Identify the population and the sampling method.

13. Mr. Short wants to know which STEM project the students prefer. He randomly selects 4 students from each homeroom in all four grades of the high school.

14. The student council wants to know what theme the seniors want for their prom. They inform the seniors that they can go to the office and vote.

Module Performance Task: *Spies and Analysts*™

Come to Your Census

How many people have to be surveyed to have reliable information?

Purpose of U.S. Census

 Make sure each community has the correct number of representatives in Congress.

 Ensure equitable distribution of public funding for things such as education, healthcare, law enforcement, and infrastructure.

 Collect demographic information including race, ethnicity, income, employment status, and education level.

Are You Ready?

Complete these problems to review prior concepts and skills you will need for this module.

Histograms

Make a histogram to represent each set of data.

1. A dance team participates in competitions where they are awarded a finishing place.

1	3	4	1	1	2	5	2	1	3	2	2

2. A science club records the number of deer spotted on nature walks.

11	15	23	4	12	17	20	8	7	11	16	3

Solve Compound Inequalities

Solve each compound inequality and graph the solution on a number line.

3. $1 \leq 4x + 1 < 13$

4. $3x - 5 > 7$ or $3x - 5 < -8$

5. $2x - 7 \geq -5$ and $2x - 7 \leq 3$

6. $2x + 8 < 2$ or $5x + 3 \geq -2$

Make Inferences from Random Samples

Determine if each sample is random.

7. Olivia wants to know if music education is important to the students in her school. So, she surveyed the marching band.

8. To determine where to place a new restaurant, the owner surveyed every 100th person in the local phonebook.

Connecting Past and Present Learning

Previously, you learned:

- to make inferences about population parameters based on a random sample,
- to model real world situations using probability distributions, and
- to estimate population percentages from a probability distribution.

In this module, you will learn:

- to understand the purposes of and differences among surveys, experiments, and observational studies,
- to construct confidence intervals from a sample survey, and
- to make inferences and evaluate reports based on data.

Confidence Intervals and Margins of Error

(I Can) calculate a confidence interval and a margin of error for a population proportion or population mean.

Spark Your Learning

Amy, a consultant who offers training for employees, has some old promotional materials claiming that 60% of adults consider their career to be a high priority. She thinks that percentage seems low and searches for information online to check it.

Amy finds an article about a survey for which 67% of adults questioned considered their career to be a high priority.

Complete Part A as a whole class. Then complete Parts B and C in small groups.

A. What is a mathematical question you can ask about this situation? What information would you need to know to answer your question?

B. Suppose Amy's promotional materials are correct and the proportion p of all adults who consider their career to be a high priority is 0.6. What would this imply about the distribution of the sample proportion $\hat{p}$ for a random sample of 500 adults?

C. To answer your question, what strategy and tool would you use along with all the information you have? What answer do you get? Be sure to include any assumptions you made and show any statistical calculations you performed.

 Turn and Talk Would your answer to the question change if the sample size for the survey was only 100 adults? Explain.

Build Understanding

Identify Likely Population Proportions

In the last lesson, you took samples from a population with a known parameter of interest in order to determine the distribution of the corresponding sample statistic. In this lesson, you will estimate an unknown population parameter using a statistic obtained from a random sample and you will quantify the accuracy of that estimate.

1 ▶ Residents of a town will vote on whether to increase parking fees to pay for building a new parking garage. You survey 50 randomly selected registered voters and find that 40% support increasing parking fees (that is, your sample proportion is $\hat{p} = 0.4$). You want to know what conclusions you can draw about the percent of *all* town voters who support increasing parking fees (that is, about the population proportion p).

A. You consider the reasonably likely values of the sample proportion $\hat{p}$ to be those that fall within 2 standard deviations of p. Why does this make sense?

B. Suppose 30% of all voters in the town support increasing parking fees, so $p = 0.3$. What are the reasonably likely values of $\hat{p}$? Given that you obtained a value of $\hat{p} = 0.4$, do you think the population proportion could be $p = 0.3$? Explain.

C. Copy the graph below onto grid paper. Draw a horizontal line segment at the level of 0.3 on the vertical axis to show the interval of likely values of $\hat{p}$ you found in Part B.

D. Now assume that $p = 0.35, 0.4, 0.45$, and so on to complete the graph in Part C. You may wish to divide up the work with other students and pool your findings.

E. Draw a vertical line at 0.4 on the horizontal axis. This represents $\hat{p} = 0.4$. What do the horizontal line segments that the vertical line intersects represent?

F. What are reasonable estimates for the percent of all town voters who support increasing parking fees? Explain your reasoning.

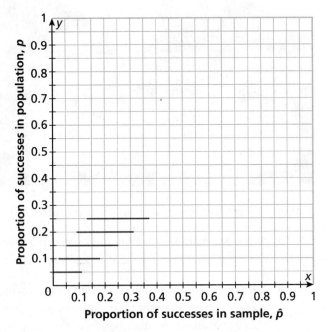

 Turn and Talk Can you reasonably conclude from your survey that the proposal to increase parking fees will be defeated? Why or why not?

Step It Out

Find a Confidence Interval for a Population Proportion

A **confidence interval** is an approximate range of values that is likely to include an unknown population parameter. The *level* of a confidence interval, such as 95%, gives the probability that the interval includes the true value of the parameter.

Confidence Interval for a Population Proportion

A $c\%$ confidence interval for the proportion p of successes in a population is given by

$$\hat{p} - z_c\sqrt{\frac{\hat{p}(1 - \hat{p})}{n}} \leq p \leq \hat{p} + z_c\sqrt{\frac{\hat{p}(1 - \hat{p})}{n}}$$

where $\hat{p}$ is the sample proportion, n is the sample size, and z_c depends on the desired confidence level. Specifically, $z_c = 1.645$ for 90% confidence, $z_c = 1.96$ for 95% confidence, and $z_c = 2.576$ for 99% confidence.

In order for the confidence interval above to describe the value of p reasonably accurately, three conditions must be met:

1. There are only two possible outcomes associated with the parameter of interest. The population proportion is p for one outcome and $1 - p$ for the other outcome.

2. $n\hat{p}$ and $n(1 - \hat{p})$ must both be at least 10.

3. The size of the population must be at least 10 times the size of the random sample.

> **2** In a random sample of 300 adults in the United States, 105 had 20/20 vision. Find a 95% confidence interval for the proportion p of U.S. adults who have 20/20 vision.

Identify the sample size n, the sample proportion $\hat{p}$, and z_c.

$n = 300$, $\hat{p} = \dfrac{105}{300} = 0.35$, $z_c = 1.96$ —— **A. Why is z_c equal to 1.96?**

Verify that the conditions for determining a confidence interval are satisfied.

$n\hat{p} = 105$ and $n(1 - \hat{p}) = 195$, so both of these values are at least 10. Also, the population of U.S. adults is at least 10 times the sample size of 300.

Find the endpoints of the confidence interval.

$$\hat{p} - z_c\sqrt{\frac{\hat{p}(1 - \hat{p})}{n}} = 0.35 - 1.96\sqrt{\frac{0.35(1 - 0.35)}{300}} \approx 0.30$$

$$\hat{p} + z_c\sqrt{\frac{\hat{p}(1 - \hat{p})}{n}} = 0.35 + 1.96\sqrt{\frac{0.35(1 - 0.35)}{300}} \approx 0.40$$

B. Would the endpoints of a 99% confidence interval be closer together or farther apart? Explain.

A 95% confidence interval for p is $0.30 \leq p \leq 0.40$. So you can state with 95% confidence that the proportion of all U.S. adults who have 20/20 vision is between 30% and 40%.

Find a Confidence Interval for a Population Mean

Just as a sample proportion can be used to find a confidence interval for the population proportion, a sample mean can be used to determine a confidence interval for the population mean. To find the confidence interval as described below, you must know (or assume) that the population is normally distributed and also know the population standard deviation σ. In this lesson, it is assumed that a population is normally distributed whenever a confidence interval for the population mean is calculated.

Confidence Interval for a Population Mean

A c% confidence interval for the mean μ in a normally distributed population is given by

$$\bar{x} - z_c\frac{\sigma}{\sqrt{n}} \leq \mu \leq \bar{x} + z_c\frac{\sigma}{\sqrt{n}}$$

where $\bar{x}$ is the sample mean, n is the sample size, σ is the population standard deviation, and z_c depends on the desired confidence level. Specifically, $z_c = 1.645$ for 90% confidence, $z_c = 1.96$ for 95% confidence, and $z_c = 2.576$ for 99% confidence.

3   Cicada killer wasps are large wasps whose name comes from the fact that they feed on cicadas. A study found that the mean wing length for a sample of 401 female Eastern cicada killer wasps was 27.65 mm. Find a 99% confidence interval for the mean wing length μ of the population.

Identify the sample size n, the sample mean $\bar{x}$, the population standard deviation σ, and the value of z_c.

> The population standard deviation for wing length is estimated to be 2.33 mm.

$n = 401$ **A.** Why do you care about the sample size?

$\bar{x} = 27.65$

$\sigma = 2.33$

$z_c = 2.576$ **B.** Why is z_c equal to 2.576?

Use the values of n, $\bar{x}$, σ, and z_c to find the endpoints of the confidence interval.

$$\bar{x} - z_c\frac{\sigma}{\sqrt{n}} = 27.65 - 2.576\left(\frac{2.33}{\sqrt{401}}\right) \approx 27.35$$

$$\bar{x} + z_c\frac{\sigma}{\sqrt{n}} = 27.65 + 2.576\left(\frac{2.33}{\sqrt{401}}\right) \approx 27.95$$

C. Would the endpoints of a 95% confidence interval be closer together or farther apart? Explain.

A 99% confidence interval for μ is $27.35 \leq \mu \leq 27.95$. So you can state with 99% confidence that the mean wing length for female Eastern cicada killer wasps is between 27.35 mm and 27.95 mm.

> **Turn and Talk** What is a 95% confidence interval for the mean wing length of female Eastern cicada killer wasps?

Choose a Sample Size

In Task 3, you found the 99% confidence interval $27.35 \leq \mu \leq 27.95$, which is a range of values centered at 27.65. You can write this interval as 27.65 ± 0.30, where 0.30 is the *margin of error*. The **margin of error** is half the length of the confidence interval.

Margin of Error for a Population Proportion

The margin of error E for the proportion of successes in a population, and the sample size n required to achieve a given margin of error E, are given by the formulas

$$E = z_c \sqrt{\frac{\hat{p}(1 - \hat{p})}{n}} \text{ and } n = z_c^2 \cdot \frac{\hat{p}(1 - \hat{p})}{E^2}$$

where $\hat{p}$ is the sample proportion and z_c is either 1.645 for 90% confidence, 1.96 for 95% confidence, or 2.576 for 99% confidence.

Margin of Error for a Population Mean

The margin of error E for the mean in a normally distributed population, and the sample size n required to achieve a given margin of error E, are given by the formulas

$$E = z_c \frac{\sigma}{\sqrt{n}} \text{ and } n = \frac{z_c^2 \cdot \sigma^2}{E^2}$$

where σ is the population standard deviation and z_c is either 1.645 for 90% confidence, 1.96 for 95% confidence, or 2.576 for 99% confidence.

---

4 A cell phone manufacturer wants to know what percent of people in the United States visit social media sites to help it decide whether to preinstall social media apps on its phones. The company is aiming for a 90% confidence interval and a margin of error of 4%. What sample size n should the company use for a survey?

Estimate the value of $\hat{p}$.
The company has not conducted the survey yet and is trying to find $\hat{p}$. So, it must estimate $\hat{p}$ as 0.5, which makes the expression $\hat{p}(1 - \hat{p})$, and therefore the sample size n, as large as possible to account for the worst-case scenario.

Identify the values of E and z_c.
E is the margin of error expressed as a decimal and z_c is the z-score that corresponds to a 90% confidence interval. So, $E = 0.04$ and $z_c = 1.645$.

Use the values of $\hat{p}$, E, and z_c to find the sample size n.

$$n = z_c^2 \cdot \frac{\hat{p}(1 - \hat{p})}{E^2} = (1.645)^2 \cdot \frac{0.5(1 - 0.5)}{(0.04)^2} \approx 423$$

Therefore, the company should survey a random sample of 423 people.

A. How can you show that the expression $\hat{p}(1 - \hat{p})$ is maximized when $\hat{p} = 0.5$?

B. Suppose the manufacturer also wants to estimate the mean battery life (in hours) of its phones by measuring the battery life of a sample of phones. The company is aiming for a 95% confidence interval and a margin of error of 0.25 hour. The population standard deviation is estimated to be 0.75 hour. What sample size n should be used?

Check Understanding

1. Dylan told Juan that 60% of their high school's students attended the football game on Friday night. Juan surveyed a random sample of 40 students and found that only 50% attended the game. Should Juan conclude that Dylan is wrong? Explain.

2. In a random sample of 100 four-year-old children in the United States, 76 were able to write their name. Find a 95% confidence interval for the proportion p of four-year-olds in the United States who can write their name.

3. In a random sample of 20 students at a high school, the mean score on a standardized test is 610. Given that the standard deviation of all scores at the school is 120, find a 99% confidence interval for the mean score μ among all students at the school.

4. The owner of a coffee shop wants to know the mean number of seconds it takes to complete a customer's order. She is aiming for a 90% confidence interval and a margin of error of 5 seconds. Based on past experience, the owner estimates the population standard deviation to be 20 seconds. What sample size n should she use?

On Your Own

5. (MP) **Reason** Max predicts that he will win at least 55% of the votes in the race for mayor. Max's pollster surveys a random sample of 400 registered voters and finds that only 48% plan to vote for Max. Is Max's prediction reasonably likely? Is it possible that Max could be correct? Explain.

6. (MP) **Construct Arguments** The margin of error E for the proportion of successes in a population may be estimated by $\frac{1}{\sqrt{n}}$, where n is the sample size. Explain where this estimate comes from. Assume a 95% confidence interval.

Find the indicated confidence interval for the population proportion p given the sample proportion $\hat{p}$ and sample size n.

7. 90% confidence interval; $\hat{p} = 0.6$ and $n = 100$

8. 95% confidence interval; $\hat{p} = 0.35$ and $n = 400$

9. 99% confidence interval; $\hat{p} = 0.5$ and $n = 250$

A community arts center surveyed a random sample of the town's residents about whether they would be interested in seeing a musical at the center each month. Use the information in the photo for Problems 10 and 11.

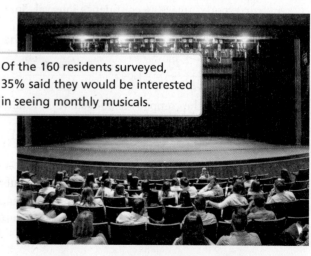

Of the 160 residents surveyed, 35% said they would be interested in seeing monthly musicals.

10. What is a 95% confidence interval for the proportion p of town residents who are interested in seeing monthly musicals? What is a 99% confidence interval for this proportion?

11. Is it reasonably likely that a majority of the town's residents are interested in seeing monthly musicals? Explain.

Find the indicated confidence interval for the mean μ of a normally distributed population given the sample mean $\bar{x}$, the population standard deviation σ, and the sample size n.

12. 90% confidence interval; $\bar{x} = 50$, $\sigma = 6$, and $n = 100$

13. 95% confidence interval; $\bar{x} = 120$, $\sigma = 15$, and $n = 40$

14. 99% confidence interval; $\bar{x} = 23$, $\sigma = 3.5$, and $n = 500$

15. STEM Paula is a biologist who is measuring the lengths of randomly selected frogs of the same species from two locations.

  A. Paula measures the lengths of 25 frogs from Location A and finds that the mean length is 7.35 cm. Given that the population standard deviation is 0.71 cm, find a 95% confidence interval for the mean length of frogs from Location A.

  B. Paula measures the lengths of 20 frogs from Location B and finds that the mean length is 7.17 cm. Given that the population standard deviation is 0.69 cm, find a 95% confidence interval for the mean length of frogs from Location B.

  C. Is it clear that the mean length of frogs from one location is greater than the mean length of frogs from the other location? Explain your reasoning.

Find the sample size n needed to determine the indicated confidence interval for the population proportion p, given the margin of error E. Use 0.5 for an estimate of the sample proportion $\hat{p}$.

16. 90% confidence interval; $E = 5\%$

17. 99% confidence interval; $E = 2.5\%$

18. Executives at a health insurance company want to know the percent of residents in a state who have health insurance. Based on data from other states, they estimate that $\hat{p} = 0.8$. They are aiming for a 99% confidence interval and a margin of error of 1.5%. What sample size n should they use?

Find the sample size n needed to determine the indicated confidence interval for the population mean μ, given the margin of error E and population standard deviation σ.

19. 95% confidence interval; $E = 3.5$ and $\sigma = 10$

20. 99% confidence interval; $E = 0.4$ and $\sigma = 2.8$

In a random sample of 50 seniors at a high school, the mean weekly time spent on homework is 7.5 hours. Use this information for Problems 21 and 22.

21. What is a 90% confidence interval for the mean weekly time μ spent on homework for all seniors at the high school? What is the margin of error?

22. What would the sample size n need to be to achieve a margin of error of 0.1 hour?

The population standard deviation for weekly homework time is 0.75 hour.

The superintendent of a school district surveys a random sample of 150 high school students from the district about whether they would prefer to start school later in the day (and therefore also finish later in the day). The students' responses are shown. Use this information for Problems 23–25.

24% of students don't want a later start.

76% of students want a later start time.

23. What is a 90% confidence interval for the proportion p of the district's high school students who want a later start time?

24. What is the margin of error for the 90% confidence interval?

25. What sample size n would the superintendent need to use to obtain a 95% confidence interval and a margin of error of 4%? Use $\hat{p} = 0.76$ in your calculation.

26. **(MP) Critique Reasoning** Kevin wants to use a random sample to find a 95% confidence interval for a population mean, but he is dissatisfied with the margin of error that his sample size produces. He thinks he can halve the margin of error by doubling the sample size. Is Kevin correct? Justify your answer mathematically.

Spiral Review • Assessment Readiness

27. For a normal distribution with mean μ and standard deviation σ, about what percent of the data values fall between μ and $\mu + 2\sigma$?

   (A) 2.35%   (C) 34%

   (B) 13.5%   (D) 47.5%

28. A news report states that an athlete trying out for a football team ran a 40-yard dash three times and had a mean finishing time of 4.52 seconds. What could be the athlete's finishing times (in seconds) for his three dashes? Select all that apply.

   (A) 4.40, 4.48, 4.64

   (B) 4.49, 4.52, 4.52

   (C) 4.48, 4.52, 4.56

   (D) 4.37, 4.58, 4.61

   (E) 4.44, 4.50, 4.59

   (F) 4.35, 4.50, 4.71

29. A gym teacher wants to know what percent of students in her school exercise regularly outside of school. She leaves copies of a survey and a box in which to return completed surveys on a table in the cafeteria so that students can complete the survey during lunch. What type of sample will the teacher obtain?

   (A) self-selected sample

   (B) simple random sample

   (C) systematic sample

   (D) stratified sample

30. The bran muffins at a bakery have a mean mass of 132 grams with a standard deviation of 14 grams. What is the approximate probability that a random sample of 20 bran muffins has a mean mass of at most 130 grams?

   (A) 0.0021   (C) 0.44

   (B) 0.26   (D) 0.74

 I'm in a Learning Mindset!

What are my action steps to make sure I understand and apply confidence intervals and margins of error correctly?

Surveys, Experiments, and Observational Studies

(I Can) identify different types of statistical research and evaluate reports based on statistical research.

Spark Your Learning

Members of a circus conducted a survey while they entertained the people who attended a town's annual parade.

Of the 50 people surveyed at the parade, 92% said they would go see the circus if it came to town.

Complete Part A as a whole class. Then complete Parts B and C in small groups.

A. What is a mathematical question you can ask about this situation? What information would you need to know to answer your question?

B. What are some characteristics of a good survey—that is, a survey that lets you draw accurate conclusions about the population you are interested in? What are some characteristics of a poor survey?

C. To answer your question, what strategy and tool would you use along with all the information you have? What answer do you get?

 Turn and Talk How would you improve the survey that the circus members conducted?

Build Understanding

Recognize Different Forms of Statistical Research

Statistical research takes various forms depending on whether the purpose of the research is to measure a variable in a population, to see if there is an association between two variables, or to determine whether one variable actually influences another variable.

Types of Statistical Research	
Type	**Example**
A **survey** is a data collection tool that uses questions to measure characteristics of interest about a population using a sample selected from the population.	A researcher asks a random sample of adults how much time they spend watching television each day.
An **observational study** uses observation to determine whether an existing condition, called a *factor*, in a population is related to a characteristic of interest. The subjects of the study and their environments are not controlled in any way.	A researcher examines a group of smokers and a group of non-smokers to determine whether the incidence of heart disease is higher among those who smoke. Being a smoker is the factor, and having heart disease is the characteristic of interest.
An **experiment** is an activity in which researchers manipulate one variable by imposing a treatment on some of the subjects of the experiment in order to determine if the treatment has an effect on another variable.	A researcher divides a group of people with eczema into two groups and has one group take a vitamin E pill daily to see if their symptoms improve. In this experiment, the vitamin E pill is the treatment.

1 Consider the three research studies described below.

Study 1: A researcher divides a group of subjects into two groups. She gives one group fish oil capsules daily. She gives the other group capsules containing water. She measures the cholesterol levels of both groups over the next several months to determine if fish oil lowers cholesterol.

Study 2: A researcher asks a random sample of people living in the United States whether they take fish oil supplements daily.

Study 3: A researcher gathers information from different countries about each country's average annual per-capita fish consumption and its residents' incidence of stroke in order to determine if greater fish consumption is associated with a lower risk of stroke.

A. Which study is a survey? What is the characteristic of interest survey?

B. Which study is an observational study? What are the factor and the characteristic of interest for the observational study?

C. Which study is an experiment? What are the treatment and the characteristic of interest for the experiment?

Step It Out

Detect Errors in Surveys

Random sampling is the best way to ensure a representative sample. However, a survey's results can have errors. The table gives several sources of errors.

Errors in Surveys	
Type of error	**Example**
Biased questions: The wording of questions in a survey can influence the way people respond to them. Survey questions need to be worded in a neutral, unbiased way.	A survey asks, "Should taxes be raised to renovate the ugly town center?" The question is biased because the word *ugly* is subjective and encourages a response of "yes."
Interviewer effect: If an interviewer asks the questions in a survey, the person being interviewed may give inaccurate responses to avoid being embarrassed.	A teacher surveys her students about whether they studied for an upcoming test. Students who did not study may be reluctant to admit this to their teacher.
Nonresponse: Some people may be difficult to contact, or they may simply refuse to participate once contacted. If nonresponse rates are higher for certain subgroups of a population, then those subgroups will be underrepresented in the survey results.	An online survey asks participants whether they use mainly checks or online payments to pay their bills. People without internet access, who cannot make online payments, also cannot respond to the survey. The results will underrepresent people who use checks.

2 Consider the following surveys.

Survey 1: A survey of a random sample of residents of a state asks, "Do you think the state should spend money maintaining a refuge for wolves when other, more important priorities are underfunded?"

Survey 2: The owner of a business meets individually with a random sample of employees in order to determine how satisfied they are with their jobs.

In Survey 1, the question is biased because it implies that maintaining the wolf refuge is less important than other projects the state could fund, which is an opinion and not a fact. A better question is simply, "Do you think the state should spend money maintaining a refuge for wolves?"

In Survey 2, the survey will likely suffer from the interviewer effect because employees may not be completely open about job dissatisfaction. A better survey would involve a neutral interviewer or anonymous responses.

A. For Survey 2, what is an unbiased question that employees of the business could be asked to determine their job satisfaction?

B. What is an advantage of using an online, anonymous survey to measure employee job satisfaction? What is a disadvantage?

Identify Treatment and Control Groups in Experiments

When conducting statistical research by experiment, researchers try to determine a cause-and-effect relationship between a treatment and a characteristic of interest. An effective way to do this is by using a *randomized comparative experiment*.

> **Randomized Comparative Experiments**
>
> A **randomized comparative experiment** randomly assigns subjects to one of two groups: the *treatment group*, which is given the treatment, and the *control group*, which is not.
>
> **Example:** To see whether zinc has an effect on the duration of a cold, researchers randomly assign subjects with colds to one of the following groups and record the durations of the colds.
>
>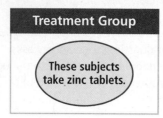

3 To see whether regular moderate exercise has an effect on blood pressure, researchers have half of the subjects set aside 30 minutes daily for walking and the other half not do any walking beyond their normal daily routines. The subjects also take and record their blood pressure at the same time each day. Identify the treatment, characteristic of interest, treatment group, and control group for this experiment.

- The treatment is having subjects walk for 30 minutes daily.
- The characteristic of interest is blood pressure.
- The treatment group consists of the subjects who walk for 30 minutes daily.
- The control group consists of the subjects who do not do any walking beyond their normal daily routines.

A. What benefit does the control group provide? Why not just run the experiment with the treatment group and see if daily exercise improves that group's blood pressure?

B. Why would it be important for the researchers to randomly assign the subjects to the treatment and control groups instead of allowing subjects to pick their group?

 Turn and Talk Why do you think the subjects in both the treatment and control groups are required to take their blood pressure at the same time each day?

Evaluate a Media Report of Statistical Research

When you encounter media reports of statistical research, you should judge any reported conclusions based on how the research was conducted. Ask yourself these questions:

- Is the research a survey, an observational study, or an experiment? A survey simply measures variables, an observational study looks for an association between variables, and an experiment tries to establish a cause-and-effect relationship between variables.

- Was randomization used in conducting the research? Random sampling is the best way to obtain a representative sample from a population and draw accurate conclusions.

- Does the report include the details of the research, such as sample size, statistics, and margins of error? These help you judge how much confidence to have in the results.

4 ▸ Evaluate each article below by answering these questions:

- Is this a survey, an observational study, or an experiment? How do you know?
- Was randomization used in the research? If so, how?
- What details of the research are included? Is any important information missing?

Study Finds Technology Widely Used by U.S. College Students

A study reported that 89% of college students regularly use a laptop computer, 86% regularly use a smartphone, and 51% regularly use a tablet. These percentages are based on the results of an online questionnaire completed by 1211 college students. Responses were weighted to be representative of the U.S. college population in terms of age, gender, household income, and other characteristics.

A. What clues in the article help you identify what type of research the study is?

The study is a survey because it simply measured what percent of college students used different types of technology.

The survey's sample was not random because it was a voluntary response survey. However, an attempt was made to make the sample be representative of the population of U.S. college students by weighting responses to match characteristics of the population.

The article includes the sample size and the estimated percents of college students who regularly use laptop computers, smartphones, and tablets. One key piece of information missing from the article is how researchers defined "regular use" of technology.

Fitness in Teen Years May Guard Against Heart Trouble Later

A study of almost 750,000 Swedish men suggests people who are aerobically fit as teenagers are less likely to have a heart attack later in life. Each 15% increase in the level of aerobic fitness as a teenager is associated with an 18% reduced risk of a heart attack 30 years later. Researchers analyzed medical data from men drafted into the nation's army, which requires a test of aerobic fitness at the time of induction. National health registers provided information on heart attacks the men had later in life.

B. How can you tell whether this study was an observational study or an experiment?

The study is an observational study because the factor of aerobic fitness as a teenager is related to a characteristic of interest, which is having a heart attack later in life. The level of aerobic fitness was simply observed, not manipulated as in an experiment.

Randomization was not used in the research because all of the subjects were male draftees in the Swedish army. The subjects may not be representative of all adults because women were excluded, and they may not be representative of all adult males because only Swedish males were studied.

The report includes the sample size and the amount by which heart attack risk was reduced for a given increase in level of aerobic fitness as a teenager. Missing information includes how the researchers defined "level of aerobic fitness" and how they calculated the percent reduction in heart attack risk.

Check Understanding

1. How do the three kinds of statistical research study a characteristic of interest?

2. Explain why the results of the survey could be inaccurate. Then suggest a way to improve the accuracy of the survey.

   Teachers want to know if students feel like they learn during lectures. A group of students surveys a random sample of other students, by asking, "When your teacher gives a lecture to introduce new content, is it too boring for you to learn?"

3. To see whether a specialty pillow has an effect on length of sleep, researchers randomly assign half the subjects to sleep on the specialty pillow and the other half sleep with one of the top brands of standard pillows. Both groups are monitored overnight while they sleep, and the number of hours and minutes of sleep they get is recorded. What are the treatment, characteristic of interest, control group, and treatment group for the experiment?

4. Evaluate the article by answering the following questions. Is this a survey, an observational study, or an experiment? Was randomization used in the research? What details of the research does the article include? What information is missing in order to substantiate the article's claims?

   ### Antibiotic Use Tied to Asthma and Allergies

   According to a study involving 1401 children, antibiotic use in infants is linked to asthma and allgergies. Researchers asked mothers how many doses of antibiotics their children received before 6 months of age, as well as whether their children had developed asthma or allergies by age 6. Children who received just one dose of antibiotics were 40% more likely to develop asthma or allergies. The risk jumped to 70% for children who received two doses.

On Your Own

5. (MP) **Attend to Precision** Describe how a survey differs from an observational study.

6. (MP) **Attend to Precision** Describe the type of result or conclusion that a researcher can find in an observational study.

7. (MP) **Attend to Precision** Describe the type of result or conclusion that a researcher can determine in an experiment.

8. If you wanted to determine the effects exercise has on resting heart rate, which type of statistical research would you use? Explain.

9. If you wanted to determine how many high school students exercise over the weekend, which type of statistical research would you use? Explain.

10. If you wanted to know if high school students make healthier choices of food after exercising, which type of statistical research would you use? Explain.

11. Describe the difference between a factor in an observational study and a treatment in an experiment.

12. Under what circumstances do you think an observational study is more appropriate than an experiment even though you would rather determine a cause-and-effect relationship?

For Problems 13–15, explain why the results of the survey could be inaccurate. Then suggest a way to improve the accuracy of the survey.

13. A publishing company wants to know how many people read magazines. Pollsters are sent to a local mall to ask the shoppers if they will sit with them for 10 minutes to answer questions about magazines they read.

14. A candidate running for mayor against the incumbent has campaign volunteers ask registered voters over the phone, "Do you support the overly aggressive mayor for re-election?"

15. A principal interviews the students at her school with the question, "Do you have any problems with any of the teachers here?"

To see whether a nap has an effect on creativity, researchers have half the subjects take a 90-minute nap and have the other half perform regular daily activities. Then both groups are given 30 minutes to write a short story. Use the experiment to answer Problems 16–19.

16. Identify the treatment, characteristic of interest, control group, and treatment group for the experiment.

17. A 90-minute nap allows you to go into a deep sleep. Why do you think the researchers chose a nap instead of a full night of sleep?

18. Why do you think this experiment did not deprive any of the subjects of sleep?

19. How might this experiment differ from an observational study of the effects that sleep has on creativity?

20. To see whether studying for a test in a small group has an effect on a test grade, researchers randomly choose half the subjects to study in groups of four using material given to them. The other half of the subjects are to study the same material individually. After an hour break for lunch, all subjects are given the same test. The grades from each group are recorded and compared. What are the treatment, characteristic of interest, control group, and treatment group for the experiment?

21. Evaluate the article by answering the following questions. Is this a survey, an observational study, or an experiment? How was the characteristic of interest measured? What details of the research does the article include? What information is missing in order to substantiate the article's claims?

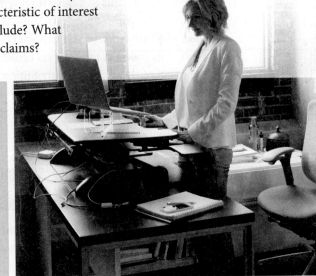

Standing Desks Improve Productivity

Researchers monitored two large groups of adults working at a call center for six months to produce a study that suggests that using a standing desk increases productivity. One group was given standing desks to work at and the other group used traditional seated desks. The study reported that after one month, the employees using standing desks had 23% more successful calls than the other group of employees. In the six months, the employees using standing desks had 53% more successful calls.

22. Evaluate the article by answering the following questions. Is this a survey, an observational study, or an experiment? How do you know? Was randomization used in the experiment? Explain. Is there enough information to substantiate the article's claims?

68% of Americans Take a Dietary Supplement

According to doctors, 68% of Americans take a dietary supplement. Researchers randomly selected doctors across the United States to ask all of their patients whether they take a dietary supplement or not. The study also indicated that 78% of the patients taking dietary supplements take a multivitamin.

23. Open Ended A kinesiologist wants to study how running regularly as a form of exercise affects resting heart rate. Describe three ways the kinesiologist could study this topic using the three types of statistical research defined in this lesson.

Spiral Review • Assessment Readiness

24. The faculty of a large high school wants to know if their students are interested in an afterschool community program. They survey 5 randomly selected students from each homeroom. Which sampling method was used to select the sample population?

(A) convenience sampling

(B) cluster sampling

(C) self-selected sampling

(D) stratified sampling

25. About 64% of students at a large high school volunteer in the community. For random samples of 50 students, which percent of students is included in the interval centered on the mean of the sampling distribution that captures 95% of the sample means?

(A) 49%   (C) 79%

(B) 52%   (D) 82%

26. In a random sample of 81 employees at a manufacturing plant, the mean weekly number of minutes spent exercising is 90. Given that the standard deviation of all employees at the manufacturing plant is 11.5, which amount of time falls within the 90% interval for the mean weekly number of minutes spent exercising among all the employees?

(A) 81 minutes   (C) 91 minutes

(B) 85 minutes   (D) 94 minutes

27. The page counts of books published by one company are normally distributed. The mean page count of a book is 305 and the standard deviation is 20. For a random sample of 40 books, what is the standard error of the mean of page counts?

(A) 0.316 pages   (C) 3.16 pages

(B) 0.5 pages   (D) 316 pages

 I'm in a **Learning Mindset!**

What factors did I use to establish timelines for my goal of distinguishing between the three different types of statistical research?

20.3

Make Inferences from Experimental Data

(I Can) identify when an observed difference between the control group and treatment group in an experiment is likely to be caused by the treatment.

Spark Your Learning

With close to 100 million dogs living in households in the United States, there is a large industry devoted to keeping them healthy. Keeping dogs' teeth clean is important to their overall health.

A company is testing a new, specially-designed chew toy for its ability to significantly prevent plaque buildup in dogs' teeth.

@stock_photo_world/Shutterstock

Complete Part A as a whole class. Then complete Parts B–D in small groups.

A. What is a mathematical question you can ask about this situation? What information would you need to know to answer your question?

B. What variables are involved in this this situation? How can you make and evaluate a comparison to assess whether the new chew toy is effective?

C. To answer your question, what strategy and tool would you use along with all the information you have? What answer do you get?

D. Does your answer make sense in the context of the situation? Is there further information you would like to know to feel confident in your answer?

> **Turn and Talk** Do you think the company is interested just in whether there is a significant difference in the two groups, or whether they are interested in a particular direction of difference? Explain your reasoning.

Build Understanding

Define and Formulate a Null Hypothesis

Recall that confidence intervals allow you to use statistical inference to estimate a population parameter from a sample parameter. They allow you to use the sample parameter to state a range for a population parameter with a given degree of confidence, such as 90%, 95%, or 99%.

You can also use statistical inference to help you decide whether or not the results of a randomized comparative experiment support a conclusion. In a properly randomized experiment, the treatment group and control group will resemble each other with one exception: only one receives the treatment. But even with the best randomization, there still will be natural differences between the two groups.

A randomized comparative experiment usually begins with the **null hypothesis** that any measured difference between the control and treatment groups is due to chance. Only if the difference is very unlikely to have occurred by chance can the researchers reject the null hypothesis, and instead accept the **alternative hypothesis** that the difference between the control group and treatment group is due to the treatment.

When can you reject the null hypothesis? To answer this question, researchers apply a test for **statistical significance** that quantifies the likelihood that a result you obtained could have occurred just by chance. If this probability is low enough, there is strong evidence in favor of rejecting the null hypothesis.

As with other tests of statistical inference, different levels of statistical significance can be used. So, while a statistically significant result does not prove that a difference was not a rare, random event, you can quantify the level of uncertainty.

 In a statistics class with 20 students, the students are randomly assigned into two equal groups. Students in each group are asked to complete a computer task stacking geometric shapes with the following difference:

Control group: Perform the sorting wearing noise-blocking headphones.

Treatment group: Perform the sorting wearing headphones playing loud music.

The mean time to complete the task was 45 seconds for the control group and 48 seconds for the treatment group.

A. What is the null hypothesis? What is an alternative hypothesis?

B. Would you expect that the results would be statistically significant with a high level of confidence? Explain your reasoning.

C. How would a larger difference between the mean times change your expectation of whether or not the difference in means is statistically significant?

D. When sampling from a population, you have seen that the larger the sample size, the smaller the standard deviation of the sample proportion, or its standard error, is. How would you expect the size of the treatment and control groups to affect the statistical significance of the difference of the means?

Step It Out

Perform a Resampling

A company is testing a plant growth supplement. Twenty seeds are planted in containers with identical soil except that the soil for the treatment group of 10 of the plants contains the supplement. The plants are measured in two weeks.

	Plant height (in.)										Means
Control group	3.8	5.2	5.8	3.3	4.1	3.0	4.9	3.9	3.5	3.1	$\bar{x}_C = 4.06$
Treatment group	5.0	5.7	6.1	6.5	3.6	3.9	6.4	6.8	4.1	4.9	$\bar{x}_T = 5.30$

From the table, the mean heights are $\bar{x}_T = 5.30$ for the treatment group and $\bar{x}_C = 4.06$ for the control group. The difference is $\bar{x}_T - \bar{x}_C = 1.24$. Is it statistically significant?

If the null hypothesis is true, then the fertilizer doesn't affect a plant's growth. So, since each group is a random sample of seeds, the mean heights of the two samples should be about the same.

To test whether the experiment might just "have happened" to place the seeds that would naturally grow taller into the treatment group, you can perform a data **resampling**. To resample, you combine the original data, randomly sort it into new "treatment" and "control groups," and find the difference of means. By doing this repeatedly, you can create a distribution of differences that arise by chance.

A **permutation test** creates a normal distribution for the difference of means for every possible division of the data into two groups. Because the number of possibilities is so large, you can simulate a permutation test by using a relatively large number of randomized resamplings.

	A	B
1	Height (in.)	Random
2	6.8	0.02120365
3	3.6	0.89001968
4	4.9	0.11234088
5	3.3	0.07868709
6	3.1	0.54595067
7	4.9	0.36457183
8	4.1	0.32019914
9	3.8	0.73904998
10	3	0.39227935
11	3.9	0.34704543
12	3.9	0.89965488
13	5	0.48798628
14	5.7	0.97779649
15	5.2	0.05461167
16	6.5	0.00074472
17	4.1	0.455203
18	5.8	0.27188676
19	6.4	0.91095936
20	3.5	0.07615925
21	6.1	0.42864363
22		
23	4.14	Control
24	5.22	Treatment
25	1.08	Difference

2 For the data above, assume the null hypothesis is true. Resample the data four times. Find the difference of the means each time.

- Enter the data in order: first the control group, then the treatment group immediately following.

  > A. With the next sort, the spreadsheet will move the data value with the smallest random value to first in the list. What will be the first three heights with the next sort?

- Below the data, enter commands to find the average of the first 10 data cells (the "control" data) and the average of the next 10 data cells (the "treatment" data). Also enter a command to find the difference of the means.
- Beside the first data value, enter "=RAND()" and click in the cell with the first data value. Then fill down the column.
- Highlight cell B2, and perform a "SORT" from smallest to largest. Each time you sort, the spreadsheet shuffles the data, computes the new means, and finds their difference. Record your results.

Use Resampling to Simulate a Permutation Test

Once you have created a resampling distribution, you can find the *P*-value for the experimental difference of means. The **P-value** is the probability found from the resampling distribution of randomly getting a difference at least as extreme as the experimental difference, assuming that the null hypothesis is true. The smaller the *P*-value, the less likely that your results could have occurred by random chance.

The following levels of significance are frequently used:

- If $P > 0.10$, the result is *not significant*. The null hypothesis is not rejected.
- If $0.05 < P \leq 0.10$, the result is *marginally significant*. You can reject the null hypothesis at the 10% significance level.
- If $0.01 < P \leq 0.05$, the result is *significant*. You can reject the null hypothesis at the 5% significance level.
- If $P \leq 0.01$, the result is *highly significant*. You can reject the null hypothesis at the 1% significance level.

3 ▷ As a class, collect all of the resampled differences in means, and record them in a frequency table. Use the class frequency table to construct a histogram for the resampling distribution for the difference of means. Are the results of the experiment significant? If so, to what level?

The frequency table and histogram below represent the differences in the means of 100 resamplings of the plant growth data from the previous task. Recall that the experiment's actual difference of means between the treatment group and control group was 1.24.

Interval	Frequency
$-1.5 \leq x < -1.2$	1
$-1.2 \leq x < -0.9$	5
$-0.9 \leq x < -0.6$	9
$-0.6 \leq x < -0.3$	11
$-0.3 \leq x < 0$	19
$0 \leq x < 0.3$	25
$0.3 \leq x < 0.6$	13
$0.6 \leq x < 0.9$	12
$0.9 \leq x < 1.2$	4
$1.2 \leq x < 1.5$	1

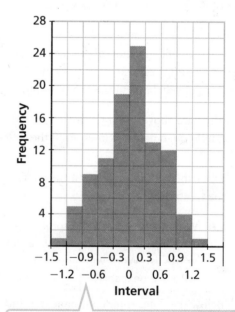

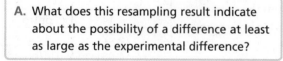

A. What does this resampling result indicate about the possibility of a difference at least as large as the experimental difference?

B. How could you choose intervals for the histogram that would most clearly reveal the number of differences ≥ 1.2?

- The *P*-value is $P(x \geq 1.24) = \dfrac{1}{100} = 0.01$.
- The *P*-value is 0.01. You can reject the null hypothesis at the 1% level and can accept the alternative hypothesis that the supplement increases growth.

Test a Null Hypothesis

Assuming the null hypothesis is true, a resampling distribution for the difference of means of a treatment and a control group is normal. The standard deviation of the distribution, as with a sampling distribution, is called the standard error.

4 ▸ An apartment complex records electrical bills in 200 occupied units. All units are supplied with the same high-efficiency light bulbs. The complex switches out the light bulbs in half the units, chosen at random, and replaces them with a newer variety. The next month, the average electric bill is $93.56 for apartments with older bulbs, and $87.42 for apartments with new bulbs.

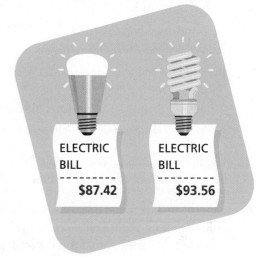

The resampling distribution for the difference of the mean electric bills, given that the null hypothesis is true, is normal with a mean of 0 and a standard error of $3.80. Is the difference in the mean bills statistically significant at the 5% level? Explain.

- Identify the null hypothesis, the control and treatment groups, and the difference of means: The null hypothesis is that there is no difference in the means that is not due to chance. The control group is the apartments with older bulbs. The treatment group is the apartments with newer bulbs.

$$\bar{x}_T - \bar{x}_C = 87.42 - 93.56 = -6.14$$

A. Why is the difference negative?

- Determine the significance.

The standard error for the resampling distribution is 3.80. Recall that 95% of a normal distribution lies within 2 standard deviations of the mean.

Middle 95% of distribution: $-2(3.80) \leq x \leq 2(3.80)$, or $-7.60 \leq x \leq 7.60$

The experimental difference of -6.14 lies inside the middle 95% of the distribution. So, it is not significant at the 5% level, and you cannot reject the null hypothesis.

Note that in the plant growth experiment, the alternative hypothesis was that the supplement increases height. So, the P-value was found using only the distribution's right tail, and so is a *one-tailed* test. The light bulb experiment mentions no alternative hypothesis. Its significance is determined using both tails of the distribution, so it is a *two-tailed* test.

 Turn and Talk The middle 90% of a normal distribution lies within 1.645 standard deviations of the mean. Is the result above in the middle 90% of the distribution? What does this mean?

Check Understanding

1. What is the purpose of beginning with the null hypothesis in conducting a randomized comparative experiment?

2. In Task 2, consider only the first four heights in each group:

   Control: 3.8, 5.2, 5.8, 3.3   **Treatment:** 5.0, 5.7, 4.1, 6.5

   A. What is the difference of means, $\bar{x}_T - \bar{x}_C$?

   B. Suppose you had a spreadsheet resample all possible "control" and "treatment" groups for the data above. Could you get a resampled difference of means greater than the experimental difference? If so, give an example.

   C. What is the greatest possible resampling difference of means? Explain.

3. Use the histogram in Task 3. Suppose the experimental difference of means had been 0.90 instead of 1.24. Would the results have been significant? Explain.

4. Suppose in Task 4 that the average electric bill in the apartments with the new bulbs had been $85.60, but the average in the apartments with the old bulbs remained the same. Would this difference be statistically significant? Explain.

On Your Own

5. What does it mean for an experiment when the null hypothesis is rejected?

6. In a randomized comparative experiment, what are two factors that influence whether the difference of means between the groups is significant? Explain.

7. Forty cherry tomato plants are planted in pots. Half of them, chosen at random, are watered with water containing a nutrient solution, while the other half are watered with plain water. The yield in pounds of tomatoes is recorded for each plant. What is the null hypothesis for this experiment?

8. **(MP) Attend to Precision** A golf ball manufacturer wants to know if their new golf ball flies farther than a previous model. To test this, they have 10 expert golfers hit 20 of each ball for distance. The golfers are given the balls in alternating order, but are not told there are different types of balls. The manufacturer records the type of ball that is hit and the distances.

   Which golf ball flies farther?

   A. Why are the golfers not told there are different balls?

   B. State the null hypothesis for this experiment.

   C. How can the manufacture perform a resampling of the distances to compare with the experimental difference?

   D. The company finds that the difference of the average distance the new ball is hit and the average distance the old ball is hit is greater than most of the resampling differences. Can the company claim the new ball flies farther? Explain.

9. A researcher is testing the effect of teaching strategies for improving multiple choice test scores. Twenty students in a class are in the study. All of them will take a general multiple-choice test, but half of them, chosen at random, first are taught the test-taking strategies. The table lists the test scores.

Control group	78	72	85	86	78	75	91	82	72	80
Treatment group	71	86	86	74	95	89	91	85	93	79

A. What is the null hypothesis?

B. Calculate the mean score for the treatment group $\bar{x}_T$ and the mean score for the control group $\bar{x}_C$. Then find the difference of the means.

C. Use a spreadsheet to perform at least 10 resamples of the data. Add your differences to the frequency table.

D. Calculate the P-value of the experimental difference.

E. What can you conclude about the significance of the results? Explain.

Interval	Frequency
$-7.5 \leq x < -5$	2
$-5 \leq x < -2.5$	4
$-2.5 \leq x < 0$	15
$0 \leq x < 2.5$	13
$2.5 \leq x < 5$	12
$5 \leq x < 7.5$	4

10. Twenty girls on a high school basketball team are divided into two groups of 10 at random. One group receives coaching and one does not. Afterwards, each girl is asked to shoot 20 free throws. The table shows the numbers of free throws made.

Control group	12	15	14	10	8	8	6	8	9	10
Treatment group	14	15	12	15	16	7	8	9	10	8

A. What is the null hypothesis?

B. Calculate the mean score for the treatment group $\bar{x}_T$ and the mean score for the control group $\bar{x}_C$. Then find the difference of the means.

C. Use a spreadsheet to perform at least 50 resamples of the data. Make a frequency table of your results.

D. What is the P-value of the experimental difference for your resampling distribution?

E. What can you conclude about the significance of the results? Explain.

11. Of 100 randomly selected chiropractic patients, all are asked to walk 20 minutes daily, and half are asked to perform 3 stretches daily. Those who only walked had an average improvement in the pain scale of 2.22. Those who also did the stretches had an average improvement in the pain scale of 3.11.

A. What is the null hypothesis?

B. What are the control and treatment groups? What is the difference in the means of the two groups, $\bar{x}_T - \bar{x}_C$?

C. The resampling distribution for the difference of the average pain improvement, given that the null hypothesis is true, is normal with a mean of 0 and a standard error of 0.44. What interval captures 95% of the differences of the means in the resampling distribution?

D. Can you reject the null hypothesis? What can you conclude?

12. A company is testing a new battery for electric cars. The company tests 1200 batteries in identical electric cars under the same conditions. Half the cars, selected at random, use the company's current battery, and half of the cars use the new battery. The mean number of miles the cars travel on the current model battery is 275 miles. For the new battery, the mean number of miles the cars travel is 336 miles.

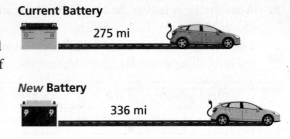

Current Battery

275 mi

New **Battery**

336 mi

A. What is the null hypothesis?

B. What are the control and treatment groups? What is the difference in the means of the two groups, $\bar{x}_T - \bar{x}_C$?

C. The resampling distribution for the difference of mean miles traveled, given that the null hypothesis is true, is normal with a mean of 0 and a standard error of 18. What interval captures 95% of the differences of the means in the resampling distribution?

D. Can you reject the null hypothesis? What can you conclude?

Spiral Review • Assessment Readiness

13. An airline wants to know how much passengers would pay for priority boarding. As passengers check in to the airline's flights one afternoon, every 20th passenger is asked to respond to a multiple-choice question. Which sampling method is this?

(A) stratified sampling

(B) simple random sampling

(C) stratified sampling

(D) systematic sampling

14. Willa's 18-hole golf scores are normally distributed with a mean of 74.5 and a standard deviation of 4.24. How much greater is the standard error of the mean for a random sample of 16 of her scores than for a sample of 25 of her scores?

(A) 0.95625

(B) 0.212

(C) 1.25

(D) 1.5625

15. A polling company wants to know the percent of eligible voters that are most likely to vote for a bond initiative that would fund construction of a sports stadium. How many elligible voters should the company include in the sample do they need to obtain a 90% confidence interval with a 4% margin of error and a sample proportion of 60%?

(A) 150

(C) 423

(B) 406

(D) 1015

16. Pollsters asked 2428 people if they watch national evening news on one of the four major networks. The number of people who watch the evening national news on one of the four major networks is what component of the statistical research?

(A) characteristic of interest

(B) factor

(C) control group

(D) treatment

 I'm in a Learning Mindset!

How will I know when I am able to determine the significance of experimental results successfully?

Confidence Interval for Population Proportion

120 people were surveyed and 75% said they would vote yes on a tax increase to pay for a new park.

A 95% confidence interval corresponds to a z-score of $z_c = 1.96$.

$$\hat{p} - z_c \sqrt{\frac{\hat{p}(1 - \hat{p})}{n}} \leq p \leq \hat{p} + z_c \sqrt{\frac{\hat{p}(1 - \hat{p})}{n}}$$
$$0.673 \leq p \leq 0.827$$

The margin of error is

$$E = z_c \sqrt{\frac{\hat{p}(1 - \hat{p})}{n}} \approx .077.$$

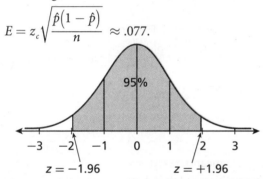

Confidence Interval for Population Mean

The survey found that the mean weekly number of minutes spent in parks was 110 with a standard deviation of 31.6.

$$\bar{x} - z_c \frac{\sigma}{\sqrt{n}} \leq \mu \leq \bar{x} + z_c \frac{\sigma}{\sqrt{n}}$$

$$110 - 1.96 \left(\frac{31.6}{\sqrt{120}}\right) \leq \mu \leq 110 + 1.96 \left(\frac{31.6}{\sqrt{120}}\right)$$

$$104.3 \leq \mu \leq 115.7$$

95% of people spend between 104.3 and 115.7 minutes in a park each week.

The margin of error is

$$E = z \frac{\sigma}{\sqrt{n}} = 1.96 \left(\frac{31.6}{\sqrt{120}}\right) \approx 5.7 \text{ minutes}$$

Surveys, Experiments, and Observational Studies

There are a variety of methods to collect statistics and make inferences about population parameters.

Survey	Question a sample selected from the population.
Experiment	Create a condition by imposing a treatment on some of the subjects of the experiment.
Observational study	Determine whether an existing condition, called a factor, in a population is related to a characteristic of interest.

Statistical Significance

A new park is built in one part of town to see if it will increase the amount of time residents spend in parks compared to another part of town.

> The null hypothesis is that a change in the amount of time spent in parks between this part of town and another is the same.

The result is statistically significant if there is a low probability of randomly getting a result that is the same as, or more extreme than, the result obtained from the experiment under the assumption that the null hypothesis is true.

> Reject the null hypothesis in favor of the alternative hypothesis.

Vocabulary

Choose the correct term from the box to complete each sentence.

1. A(n) __?__ is an operation, process, or activity that imposes a treatment on some of the subjects.

2. A(n) __?__ is a data collection tool that uses questions to measure characteristics of interest about a population using a sample selected from the population.

3. A(n) __?__ is an approximate range of values that is likely to include an unknown population parameter.

4. A(n) __?__ assumes any differences between the control group and the treatment group in an experiment is due to chance, and not to the treatment.

Concepts and Skills

5. Compare and contrast surveys, experiments, and observational studies.

6. In a random sample of 88 high school athletes, 41 play more than 1 sport. Find a 99% confidence interval for the proportion p of high school athletes that play more than 1 sport.

7. Saul conducts a survey of a random sample of students at his school and finds that 78% want a new logo for the school. What sample size n should be used to obtain a 99% confidence interval and a margin of error of 0.05?

8. (MP) **Use Tools** In a random sample of 128 homeowners, the mean weekly number of hours spent on yardwork is 3.4. The standard deviation is 1.4. What is the 90% confidence interval for the data? State what strategy and tool you will use to answer the question, explain your choice, and then find the answer.

9. An unmanned radar records the speeds of 250 randomly selected vehicles on a highway. The mean speed is 67.2 mph. The population standard deviation is estimated to be 2.3 mph. Find a 95% confidence interval for the mean speed.

10. The police chief is speaking at a town hall meeting. After he speaks, people are asked, "Do you think the police chief is tough enough on crime?" Identify any components of the survey that could cause the survey to be biased, and then suggest a way to improve the accuracy of the survey.

11. A chemical company has developed a new fuel additive that will increase the fuel mileage of cars. The company conducts an experiment with 100 identical cars, half of the cars using fuel with the additive and half the cars using fuel without the additive.

    A. State the null hypothesis of the experiment.

    B. The mean of the control group is $x_c = 28.7$ miles per gallon. The mean of the treatment group is $x_t = 30.4$ miles per gallon. The resampling distribution for the difference of mean fuel mileage, given that the null hypothesis is true, is normal with a mean of 0 and a standard error of 0.8. Can you reject the null hypothesis? Explain your reasoning.

UNIT 1

MODULE 1, LESSON 1.1
On Your Own

7. $\{x \mid x \geq a\}$; The graph of $[-a, \infty)$ includes the values from $-a$ to ∞. They both represent values greater than or equal to an initial value.

9. $\{x \mid -3 < x \leq 0\}$; $(-3, 0]$

11. $\{x \mid x > 1\}$; $(1, +\infty)$

13. A

15. Possible answer:

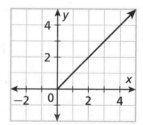

end behavior: as $x \to +\infty, y \to +\infty$

17. domain: $\{x \mid -\infty < x < +\infty\}$, $(-\infty, +\infty)$; range: $\{f(x) \mid f(x) \leq 4\}$, $(-\infty, 4]$; end behavior: as $x \to -\infty$, $f(x) \to -\infty$, as $x \to +\infty$, $f(x) \to -\infty$

19. domain: $\{x \mid x \in \mathbb{R}\}$, $(-\infty, +\infty)$; range: $\{f(x) \mid f(x) > 0\}$, $(0, +\infty)$; end behavior: as $x \to -\infty$, $f(x) \to 0$, as $x \to +\infty$, $f(x) \to +\infty$

21.A. Let x represent the number of hours. Let $f(x)$ represent the number of miles. An equation for Rachel's distance is $f(x) = 70x$.

B. domain: $\{x \mid x \geq 0\}$; range: $\{f(x) \mid f(x) \geq 0\}$

C.

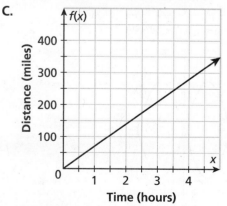

210 miles

D. The total number of miles would be the number of miles on day 2 plus 100. The initial point on the graph would be $(0, 100)$, so the range would become $\{f(x) \mid f(x) \geq 100\}$, but the domain would not change.

23.A. $d = 21g$

B. yes; Since the number of gallons of gasoline used must be nonnegative, the domain is $[0, +\infty)$.

C. 52.5 miles

Spiral Review • Assessment Readiness

25. A

27. C

MODULE 1, LESSON 1.2
On Your Own

5. A

7. (B, C), (D, E), (F, G), and (H, J)

9. (B, C)

11. Possible graph:

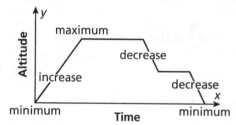

13.A.

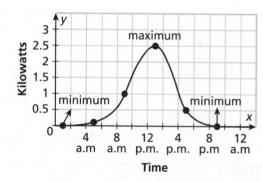

The data is increasing from 1 a.m. to 1 p.m. and decreasing from 1 p.m. to 9 p.m. The most energy is produced at 1 p.m. No energy is produced at 1 a.m. or 9 p.m.

B. about 1 kW; At 1 p.m., 2.5 kW are produced and at 5 p.m. 0.5 kW are produced, so the number of kW produced at 4 p.m. likely falls between 0.5 and 2.5. The graph appears to pass close to 1 at 4 p.m., so this is a good guess.

C. The graph of the power produced on a cloudy day would likely not have a maximum as great as the graph from Part A

15.A. Possible answer: A water tank begins by holding 19 gallons of water. Over the first 15 minutes, the amount of water increases until it reaches 30 gallons.

Then the water level decreases over the next 30 minutes to 10 gallons. The water tank is then slowly refilled again for the next 45 minutes to 28 gallons.

B. Possible graph:

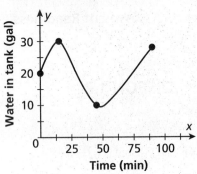

C. Possible answer: −0.2 gal/min; The average rate of change over the first 45 minutes was −0.2 gallons per minute.

Spiral Review • Assessment Readiness

17. C

19. A

MODULE 1, LESSON 1.3

On Your Own

7. f

9. a

11. c

13. reflection across the *y*-axis

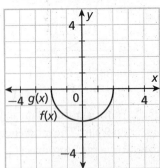

15. vertical stretch by a factor of 2.5

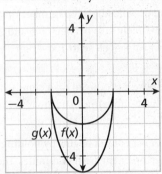

17. horizontal stretch by a factor of $\frac{5}{2}$

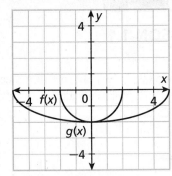

19. translation right 2 units

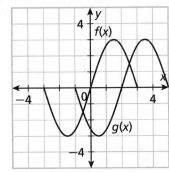

21. horizontal compression by a factor of $\frac{2}{3}$

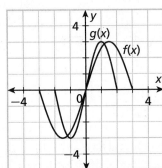

23. reflection across the *x*-axis

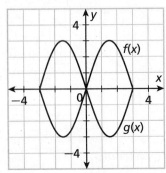

25. odd; From Problems 23 and 24, you can see that $f(-x) = -f(x)$.

27. It is kite-shaped.

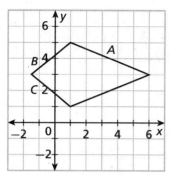

29. $a = 3$, $h = -1$, $k = -4$; Translate the graph left 1 unit, vertically stretch it by a factor of 3, and then translate it down 4 units.

31. $(-4, 2) \rightarrow (-4, 1)$; $(-2, -2) \rightarrow (-2, -5)$; $(0, 0) \rightarrow (0, -2)$; $(2, 2) \rightarrow (2, 1)$; $(4, -2) \rightarrow (4, -5)$

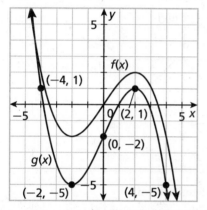

33. $(-4, 2) \rightarrow (-5, 0)$; $(-2, -2) \rightarrow (-3, 2)$; $(0, 0) \rightarrow (-1, 1)$; $(2, 2) \rightarrow (1, 0)$; $(4, -2) \rightarrow (3, 2)$

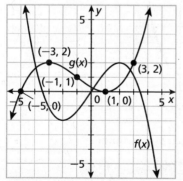

35. First model the climb: $f(t) = 39t$ where $f(t)$ gives the number of steps and t is time in minutes. The domain is $0 \le t \le 23$, as it takes 23 minutes to reach the top. The descent is modeled by $897 - 52(t - 23)$, so $g(t) = -52(t - 23) + 897 = -\frac{4}{3}f(t - 23) + 897$. The graph of $g(t)$ is that of $f(t)$ translated right 23 units, vertically stretched by a factor of $\frac{4}{3}$ and reflected

across the x−axis, and translated up 897 units. Its domain is $23 \le t \le 40.25$, since the descent starts at a time of 23 minutes and takes 17.25 minutes.

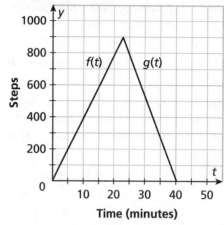

37. First model the normal flight: $f(t) = 400t$ where $f(t)$ gives the distance flown in miles and t is time in hours. The domain is $0 \le t \le 3$, since in 3 hours, the plane has traveled the entire distance. Because 90 minutes is 1.5 h, and the speed is increased to 500 mi/h, a model is $g(t) = 500(t - 1.5) = 1.25f(t - 1.5)$. The graph of $g(t)$ is that of $f(t)$ translated right 1.5 units and vertically stretched by a factor of 1.25. Because it will take 2.4 h to fly 1200 mi, the domain of $g(t)$ is $1.5 \le t \le 3.9$.

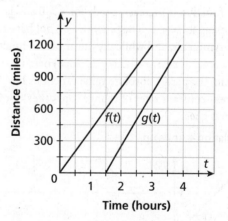

39.A. It vertically stretches the graph by a factor of 2, which means that the steps stay the same width, but are twice as far apart; no; $g(x)$ maps 0.5, 1, and 1.4 all to 2, and 1.5 to 4, which does not fit any normal idea of rounding.

B. It horizontally stretches the graph by a factor of 2, which means that the steps are at the same heights as before, but are twice as wide; no; $g(x)$ maps 1, 2, and 2.9 all to 1, and 3 to 2, which does not fit any normal idea of rounding.

C. It makes the steps twice as wide and twice as far apart in height. The domain is still all real numbers, but the range is the even integers instead of the integers; yes; $g(x)$ maps -1, 0, and 0.9 all to 0, and 1, 2, and 2.9 to 2, that is, it rounds to the nearest even integer instead of the nearest integer; $g(x) = 10f\left(\frac{1}{10}x\right)$ would round to the nearest 10.

41. yes; To be even requires $f(-x) = f(x)$, and to be odd requires $f(-x) = -f(x)$. This occurs when $f(x) = -f(x)$, or when $f(x) = 0$. So, the constant function that represents the x−axis $(y = 0)$ is both even and odd.

Spiral Review • Assessment Readiness

43. D

45. D

MODULE 1, LESSON 1.4

On Your Own

5. The two parent functions have the same domain and they have the same end behavior as $x \to +\infty$. However, their ranges differ and the parent linear function has no vertex while the parent absolute value function does. Their end behaviors as $x \to -\infty$ are different. The parent linear function is increasing over its entire domain, while the parent absolute value function is increasing only for $x > 0$ and is decreasing for $x < 0$. The functions do not have the same symmetry, and while the linear parent function has a constant rate of change (its slope) over its entire domain, the parent absolute value functions has different constant rates of change (opposites) for its two branches.

7. translation 4 units up

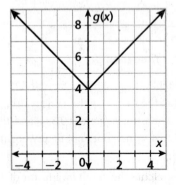

9. translation 2 units right, vertical stretch by a factor of 3

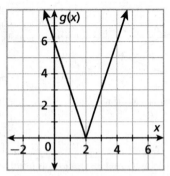

11. horizontal stretch by a factor of 2, translation 4 units right

13. translation $\frac{1}{4}$ unit right, reflection over the x−axis, translation $\frac{1}{4}$ unit up

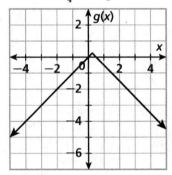

15. translation 5 units down

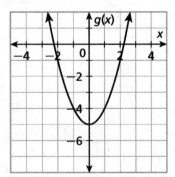

17. horizontal stretch by a factor of 2

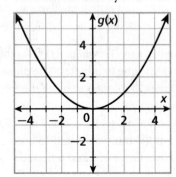

19. vertical compression by a factor of $\frac{3}{4}$, translation 1 unit up

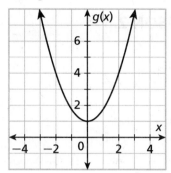

21. vertical stretch by a factor of 4, translation 2 units down

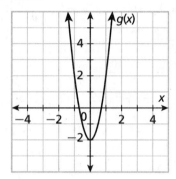

23. translation 2 units left and 2 units down

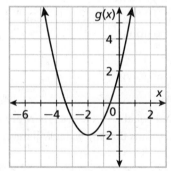

25.A. $g(x) = -\frac{3}{4}|x - 6| + 5$

   B. no; $g(0)$ does not equal 0.

27. 3 m

Spiral Review • Assessment Readiness

29. C

31. D

MODULE 1, LESSON 1.5

On Your Own

5.A. Team B; approximately 70 ft; The maximum heights are the same.

   B. Team B; about 33 ft

7. $(-\infty, 0)$ and $(2, +\infty)$; Since the point $(0, 2)$ is a maximum, the graph of g opens downward. The graph of f has its vertex at $(2, 0)$ and opens upward. The graphs of f and g coincide over the interval $[0, 2]$ of their domains. For all other values in their domains, $f(x) > g(x)$.

9. The maximum height of the support arch of the Sydney Harbour Bridge is much greater than the maximum height of the support arch of the Gateshead Millenium Bridge. The vertex of $f(x)$ is $(63, 50)$, so the maximum height of the arch on the Gateshead Millennium Bridge is 50 meters. The maximum height of the arch of the Sydney Harbour Bridge is more than 125 meters in the graph.

11. 6.25 cm³; $8(2.5)^2 - 7(2.5)^2 = 6.25$

Spiral Review • Assessment Readiness

13. D

15. A: 3, B: 1, C: 2, D: 4

MODULE 2, LESSON 2.1

On Your Own

9. You can isolate the quadratic term on one side of the equation and analyze the sign of the other side.

11. 2 real solutions

13. 2 imaginary solutions

15. 1 real solution

17. Possible Answer: $2x^2 + 1 = 9$

19. Possible Answer: $2x^2 + 1 = -7$

21. $-25 \overset{?}{=} (\pm 5i)^2$

$\overset{?}{=} (\pm 5i)^2 i^2$

$\overset{?}{=} 25(-1)$

$= -25$

23. $-27 \overset{?}{=} 3(1 \pm 3i - 1)^2$

$\overset{?}{=} 3(\pm 3i)^2$

$\overset{?}{=} 3(\pm 3)^2 i^2$

$\overset{?}{=} 3(9)(-1)$

$= -27$

25. $x = \pm 2i\sqrt{6}$

27. $x = 2 \pm \frac{3}{2}$

29.A. $x^2 = 400$

   B. $x = \pm 20$ in.

31.A. approximately 1.8 seconds

   B. no; A negative value of time does not make sense in this situation.

C. In this case, the negative values of s would represent the time the ball was falling before Jeanine started watching.

33.A. $t = 0$ and $h = h_0$.

B. You cannot take a square root to solve this equation because you have a factor of t and t^2.

C. All solutions are viable, because they are within the domain of the context. However, only one solution makes sense. $t = 4$ seconds is the only viable solution because the water balloon must return to its initial height.

Spiral Review • Assessment Readiness

35. D

MODULE 2, LESSON 2.2

On Your Own

9. $2 + 5x - 3x^2$; Substituting the imaginary unit i for x gives the product of the complex numbers, $2 + 5i - 3i^2$. Then the result should be simplified using the fact that $i^2 = -1$. $2 + 5i - 3(-1) = 5 + 5i$

11. true; Subtraction holds the same properties as addition.

13. real: 0; imaginary: $\sqrt{17}$; imaginary number

15. real: $\sqrt{43}$; imaginary: 0; real number

17. real: 0; imaginary: 20; imaginary number

19. false; Possible answer: If the real and/or the imaginary parts of the complex numbers are opposites, then the result will not be a complex number. For example, $(3 + 2i) + (-3 + 5i) = 7i$ or $(4 + 5i) + (7 - 5i) = 11$.

21. true

23. $7 - 3i$

25. $6 - 13i$

27. $-2 + i$

29. $7 + 4i$

31. $13 + 13i$

33. $18 - 66i$

35. $\dfrac{3 - i}{2}$

37. $4 + i$

39. total impedance $= 2 - i$;

voltage for the resistor $= 48 + 24i$;

voltage for the capacitor $= 12 - 24i$

41. Possible answer: no; Kailey incorrectly defined i^2 as equal to 1 instead of -1. The correct answer would have been $12 + 9i - 16i - 12(-1) = 24 - 7i$.

Spiral Review • Assessment Readiness

45. B

MODULE 2, LESSON 2.3

On Your Own

9.A. $f(x) = -8$; The line $y = -8$ will intersect the parabola in exactly one place, $(-1, -8)$.

B. Possible answer: $f(x) = -10$; The line $y = -10$ will never intersect the parabola.

C. Possible answer: $f(x) = 4$; The line $y = 4$ will intersect the parabola in two places, $(1, 4)$ and $(-3, 4)$.

11. $n = 7 + 6i, n = 7 - 6i$

13. $k = 9 + i\sqrt{15}, k - 9 - i\sqrt{15}$

15. $v = \dfrac{2 + i\sqrt{38}}{2}, v = \dfrac{2 - i\sqrt{38}}{2}$

17. $x = \dfrac{2 + i\sqrt{10}}{2}, x = \dfrac{2 - i\sqrt{10}}{2}$

19. $x = \dfrac{-7 + i\sqrt{59}}{18}, x = \dfrac{-7 - i\sqrt{59}}{18}$

21. $a = \dfrac{-5 + i\sqrt{239}}{22}, a = \dfrac{-5 - i\sqrt{239}}{22}$

23. $p = \dfrac{2i\sqrt{6}}{3}, p = -\dfrac{2i\sqrt{6}}{3}$

25. $t = \dfrac{1 + i\sqrt{31}}{8}, t = \dfrac{1 - i\sqrt{31}}{8}$

27. $. -80$; 2 imaginary solutions

29. 0; 1 real solution

31. -191; 2 imaginary solutions

33. 169; 2 real solutions

35. no; The discriminant equals -1.1775, so there are no real solutions. This means that the water will never reach the window.

37.A. The solutions are integers when the discriminant in a perfect square.

B. The square root of zero is zero, and there is not a positive and negative root.

C. $-4 - 2i\sqrt{3}$; The other root is $-4 - 2i\sqrt{3}$.

Spiral Review • Assessment Readiness

39. A, C, D

41. A

MODULE 2, LESSON 2.4

On Your Own

9. yes; The graphs of the two equations never intersect so the system has no solutions.

11. $(-4, -1)$ and $(2, 5)$

13. no solution

15. approx. $(-3.1, -0.6)$ and $(1.6, 1.8)$

17. $(-3, 0)$ and $(5, 16)$

19. $(-0.5, 0.25)$

21. $(1, -3)$ and $(-3, 13)$

23. $(-2, 4)$ and $(-5, 1)$

25. no solution

27. $(3.5, 1.75)$

29.A. $y = \frac{3}{4}x - 18$

    B. approximately $(-8.9, -24.7)$ and $(29.5, 4.1)$

    C. 29.5 ft from the launcher, 4.1 ft up in the stands

31. A car on the given road will never pass through the broadcast range of the cell phone tower because the system of equations has no solution.

Spiral Review • Assessment Readiness

35. C

UNIT 2

MODULE 3, LESSON 3.1

On Your Own

7. no; Even functions that increase for values greater than 0 decrease for values less than 0. So for values of a and b less than 0, $f(b) < f(a)$.

9. $f(x) = x^4$; vertical translation 3 units down

11. $f(x) = x^2$; vertical compression by a factor of $\frac{1}{2}$, a horizontal translation 1 unit right, and a vertical translation 4 units down

13. $f(x) = x^3$; horizontal translation 6 units right

15. $f(x) = x^3$; horizontal translation 1 unit right; vertical stretch by a factor of 3

17. $f(x) = x^3$; horizontal translation 3 units right; vertical stretch by a factor of 2

19. horizontal translation of $f(x) = x^6$ 1 unit right

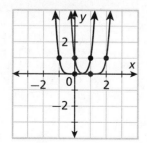

21. horizontal translation of $f(x) = x^5$ 4 units left and a vertical translation 1 unit down

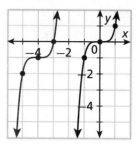

23. vertical stretch of $f(x) = x^4$ by a factor of 4, horizontal translation 1 unit left, and vertical translation ½ unit down

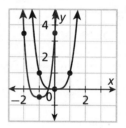

25. $g(x) = 2(x + 2)^4 - 1$

27. $g(x) = \left(\frac{1}{2}(x + 1)\right)^4 + 1$

29. about 9 cm

31. about 0.163 cm

Spiral Review • Assessment Readiness

35. C

MODULE 3, LESSON 3.2

On Your Own

7. a. C; b. B; c. D; d. A

9. x-intercepts: $x = -1, x = 1, x = 2$; crosses, crosses, crosses; 2 turning points; 1 local maximum, 1 local minimum

11. x-intercepts: $x = 2, x = 3$; tangent, tangent; 3 turning points; 1 local maximum, 2 local minimums that are also global minimums

13. x-intercepts: $x = -2, x = 0, x = 2, x = 4$; crosses, crosses, crosses, crosses; 3 turning points; 1 local maximum, 2 local minimums that are also global minimums

Selected Answers

15.

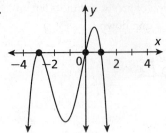

17.

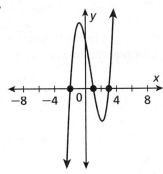

19. $y = -(x+3)(x+1)(x-2)$

21. $y = (x+1)^2(x-1)$

23. $V(x) = x(12-2x)(12-1.5x)$; 146 in³

25.A. Product A: $12,800, Product B: $17,700

B. The two products have the same value when $x = 0$, which is when both products are just starting and have no profit or loss, and when x is approximately 2.3 years, which is when both products have a loss of about $4,700; Possible answer: I found my answers by determining where graphs of the two functions intersect to solve the equation $f(x) = g(x)$.

27. domain: $(-\infty, +\infty)$; range: $(-\infty, +\infty)$; x-intercepts: $x = 0, x = b, x = -b$; 2 turning points; odd

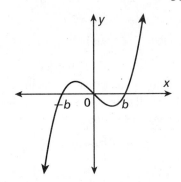

29. *See below.*

Spiral Review • Assessment Readiness

31. B

33. B

29. Possible answer: Tory used incorrect x-intercept values.

Interval	$x < -3$	$-3 < x < 0$	$0 < x < 2$	$x > 2$
Sign of constant factor	+	+	+	+
Sign of x	−	−	+	+
Sign of $x - 2$	−	−	−	+
Sign of $x + 3$	−	+	+	+
Sign of $f(x)$	$(+)(-)(-)(-) = -$	$(+)(-)(-)(+) = +$	$(+)(+)(-)(+) = -$	$(+)(+)(+)(+) = +$

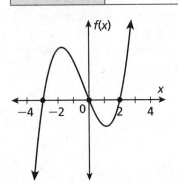

© Houghton Mifflin Harcourt Publishing Company

SA8 Selected Answers

MODULE 4, LESSON 4.1

On Your Own

7. Adding or subtracting a constant function to another function will translate the graph of that function vertically. Multiplying a function by a constant function can vertically stretch, vertically compress, and/or reflect a function across the x-axis.

9. $x^2 + 5x - 12$

11. $-4x^4 + 36x^2$

13. $-5x^3 + 3x^2 + 45x - 27$

15. $\dfrac{4x^2}{9 - x^2}$

17. $g(x) = x - 3$; I divided $(f \cdot g)(x)$ by $f(x)$.

19.A. $b(x) = 500 + 10x; h(x) = 500 - 16x^2$

  B. $16x^2 + 10x$; 0 s to 5.6 s; The penny will take 5.6 seconds to hit the ground.

  C. yes; The penny is on the ground at this time, 500 feet below from where it fell. The balloon is 100 feet higher than it was at that time, so the distance is 600 feet.

Spiral Review • Assessment Readiness

21. B, D

23. D

MODULE 4, LESSON 4.2

On Your Own

7. $5y^4 + 4y^3 - 7y^2 + 3y$; 4; 5

9. $3x^2 - 5x + 15$

11. $x^3 + 2x^2 - 10x + 9$

13. $-2x^4 + x^2 + 2x$

15. 0

17. about 4,503,000 students

19. $ax^m + bx^m = (a + b)x^m$ and $ax^m - bx^m = (a - b)x^m$; The sum of two monomials, $ax^m + bx^m$, is another monomial, $(a + b)x^m$. The difference of two monomials, $ax^m - bx^m$, is another monomial, $(a - b)x^m$. So, the sum or difference of two polynomials is a sum of monomials, which is another polynomial.

Spiral Review • Assessment Readiness

21. A

23. B

MODULE 4, LESSON 4.3

On Your Own

7. $x^3 + 2x^2 + 3x + 6$

9. $-x^3 + 7x^2 - x + 7$

11. $-3x^3 - 2x^2 + 35x - 36$

13. $15x^3 - x^2 - 32x + 12$

15. $x^4 + 3x^3 - 14x^2 + 16$

17. $2x^4 - 3x^3 - x^2 + 8x - 6$

19. $3x^5 + 5x^4 + x^3 - 2x^2 - 4x$

21. $6x^3 + 4x^2y + 2y^3$

23. $-2x^3 - 2x^2y + 13xy^2 + 3y^3$

25. $R(t) = 2t^3 + 128t^2 + 2000t + 30{,}000$; $64,800,000

27.A. $A(m) = 0.058m^4 - 1.512m^3 + 25.374m^2 - 206.5m + 988.8$

  B. January; about $806,000

29. $b = 3$;
$(x^2 + bx + 2)(2x^2 + bx + 5) =$
$2x^4 + 3bx^3 + (b^2 + 9)x^2 + 7bx + 10$, and this polynomial equals $2x^4 + 9x^3 + 18x^2 + 21x + 10$ if the coefficients of corresponding terms are the same. So $3b = 9$, $b^2 + 9 = 18$, and $7b = 21$. The only value of b that satisfies all three equations is $b = 3$.

31. $(x^2 + y^2)(x^4 - x^2y^2 + y^4)$
$= x^2(x^4 - x^2y^2 + y^4) + y^2(x^4 - x^2y^2 + y^4)$
$= x^6 - x^4y^2 + x^2y^4 + x^4y^2 - x^2y^4 + y^6$
$= x^6 - \cancel{x^4y^2} + \cancel{x^4y^2} + \cancel{x^2y^4} - \cancel{x^2y^4} + y^6$
$= x^6 + y^6$

33. $(a^2 + b^2)(x^2 + y^2)$
$= a^2(x^2 + y^2) + b^2(x^2 + y^2)$
$= a^2x^2 + a^2y^2 + b^2x^2 + b^2y^2$
$(ax - by)^2 + (bx + ay)^2$
$= (ax)^2 - 2(ax)(by) + (by)^2 + (bx)^2 + 2(bx)(ay) + (ay)^2$
$= a^2x^2 - 2abxy + b^2y^2 + b^2x^2 + 2abxy + a^2y^2$
$= a^2x^2 + a^2y^2 + b^2x^2 + b^2y^2 - \cancel{2abxy} + \cancel{2abxy}$
$= a^2x^2 + a^2y^2 + b^2x^2 + b^2y^2$

Since both sides of the equation simplify to the same expression, the equation is an identity.

35. $98^2 = (100 - 2)^2$
$= 100^2 - 2(100)(2) + 2^2$
$= 10{,}000 - 400 + 4$
$= 9604$

Selected Answers

37. $48 \cdot 32 = (40 + 8)(40 - 8)$

$= 40^2 - 8^2$

$= 1600 - 64$

$= 1536$

Spiral Review • Assessment Readiness

41. C

MODULE 4, LESSON 4.4

On Your Own

7. $15x(3x^2 + 1)$

9. $-2x^2(x - 1)(x - 5)$

11. $(4x + 5)(16x^2 - 20x + 25)$

13. $(5x - 1)(25x^2 + 5x + 1)$

15. $(x + 1)(x - 1)(x - 7)$

17. $(2x^2 - 1)(x + 3)$

19. $(3x - 1)(x + 1)(x^2 - x + 1)$

21. $(x^3 + 2)(x - 2)$

23. $(x + 5)(3x^3 - 4)$

25. Since the base radius of each smaller cylinder is x, the area of each cylinder's base is $A = \pi x^2$. The height of the red cylinder is $\frac{V}{A} = \frac{8\pi x^3}{\pi x^2} = 8x$. The height of the green cylinder is $\frac{V}{A} = \frac{24\pi x^2}{\pi x^2} = 24$.

27. length $= 40$ in., width $= 30$ in., height $= 15$ in.

29. $0, 4$

31. $\frac{1}{2}$

33. $\sqrt{3}, -\sqrt{3}, \frac{2}{3}$

35. no real-number solutions

37. no; Possible explanation: Consider the polynomial $x^3 + 2x^2 + 3x + 9$. You can group the terms into pairs that have a common factor: $(x^3 + 2x^2) + (3x + 9)$. However, after factoring out the common factor from each group, you get $x^2(x + 2) + 3(x + 3)$. You are unable to finish the process by factoring out a common binomial factor.

39. length $= 8$ ft, width $= 4$ ft, height $= 4$ ft

Spiral Review • Assessment Readiness

41. A

43. C

MODULE 4, LESSON 4.5

On Your Own

7. -47

9. 27

11. 2

13. -10

15. $-8x^3 + 40x^2 - 37x + 30$
$= (x - 4)(-8x^2 + 8x - 5) + 10$

17. $4x^3 - 9x^2 + 9x + 3 = (x - 1)(4x^2 - 5x + 4) + 7$

19. $x^4 + 11x^3 + 33x^2 + 24x + 32$
$= (x + 6)(x^3 + 5x^2 + 3x + 6) - 4$

21. length: $l(t) = t + 11$, height: $h(t) = 2t + 7$

23. $-4x^3 + 12x^2 - 25x - 20$
$= (x - 1)(-4x^2 + 8x - 17) - 37$

25. $x^4 - 10x^3 + 44x - 34$
$= (x - 5)(x^3 - 5x^2 - 25x - 81) - 439$

27. $6x^4 - 2x^3 + 40$
$= (x - 3)(6x^3 + 16x^2 + 48x + 144) + 472$

29. $(x - 2)(x - 1)(x - 1)$

31. $(x - 3)(x + 1)(2x - 1)$

33. $(x + 1)(3x + 1)(x - 2)$

35. $x^3 + 3x - 1$

37.

1.2	0.1	−0.6	1.4	−0.5
		0.12	−0.576	0.9888
	0.1	−0.48	0.824	0.4888

about $489

Spiral Review • Assessment Readiness

39. B, C, D, F

41. A

MODULE 5, LESSON 5.1

On Your Own

7. John is correct because 3 is a factor of 9, and 5 is not.

9. $x + 8$

11. $2x + 3$

13. $x = -\frac{4}{5}, x = -\frac{1}{3}$, or $x = 1$

15. $x = -5, x = -\frac{1}{3}$, or $x = \frac{1}{2}$

17. $x = -2, x = 1$, or $x = \frac{5}{6}$

19. $x = -1, x = -\frac{3}{4}, x = \frac{3}{2}$

21. $x = -3, x = -1, x = 3$

23. $x = -\frac{3}{4}, x = -\frac{7}{9}, x = 0$, or $x = 1$

© Houghton Mifflin Harcourt Publishing Company

SA10 Selected Answers

25. $x = -\dfrac{3}{2}, x = 1, x = \dfrac{3}{2},$ or $x = 6$

27. $x = -8, x = -1, x = 2,$ or $x = 5$

29. 7 years

31. 2010

33. 6.308 in.

35. 7.256 ft

Spiral Review • Assessment Readiness

39. B

41.A. 5

   B. 3

   C. 2

   D. 1

   E. 4

MODULE 5 LESSON 5.2

On Your Own

7.A. $p(x)$ must have exactly 4 roots.

   B. No. $p(x)$ has 3 unique rational zeros, one of which has a multiplicity of 2.

9. $x = -2, x = 2 - \sqrt{7},$ or $x = 2 + \sqrt{7}$

11. $x = -1 - 2i, x = -1 + 2i,$ or $x = \dfrac{3}{2}$

13. $x = -3\sqrt{6}, x = -\dfrac{1}{2},$ or $x = 3\sqrt{6}$

15. $x = -6 - i, x = -6 + i,$ or $x = 2$

17. $x = -2, x = -1 - i, x = -1 + i,$ or $x = 2$

19. $x = -3, x = -\sqrt{2}, x = 1,$ or $x = \sqrt{2}$

21. $p(x) = x^3 - 3x^2 - 8x + 24$

23. $p(x) = x^3 - 10x^2 + 23x + 4$

25. $p(x) = x^4 - 7x^3 + 6x^2 + 20x$

27. $p(x) = x^3 - 22x^2 + 154x - 328$

29. $p(x) = x^3 - 3x^2 - 23x + 85$

31. $p(x) = x^4 - 2x^3 + 14x^2 - 8x + 40$

33.A. One zero is real because it crosses the x-axis. The other two are complex because the polynomial function is cubic and therefore has degree 3 and 3 zeros.

   B. To change the complex zeros to real zeros, you could translate the function's graph 20 units up so that the zeros would all cross the x-axis.

   C. No. This is an odd function so the degree of the function is odd. There must be at least one real zero.

35. 6; Complex roots come in pairs.

37.A. You can find the difference of the two functions and set it equal to 0. For example, you could subtract

the energy stock function from the transportation stock function.

   B. $P_D(m) = -0.05m^4 - 0.5m^3 + 15.35m^2 - 62m + 83.2$

   C. 10 months after purchasing the stocks

Spiral Review • Assessment Readiness

41. B

UNIT 3

MODULE 6, LESSON 6.1

On Your Own

9. $\dfrac{1}{6}$

11. $\dfrac{7}{3}$

13. $\dfrac{6}{7}$

15. $\dfrac{6}{5}$

17. $\dfrac{3}{2}$

19. 14; Possible answer: $2744^{\frac{1}{3}}$

21. odd: one; even: none

23. odd: one; even: two

25. odd: one; even: two

27. odd: one; even: two

29. odd: one; even: none

31. odd: one; even: none

33. $4^{\frac{4}{2}} = \sqrt{4^4} = \sqrt{256} = 16$
$4^{\frac{4}{2}} = \left(\sqrt{4}\right)^4 = 2^4 = 16$

35. $8^{\frac{6}{3}} = \sqrt[3]{8^6} = \sqrt[3]{262{,}144} = 64$
$8^{\frac{6}{3}} = \left(\sqrt[3]{8}\right)^6 = 2^6 = 64$

37. $64^{\frac{3}{2}} = \sqrt{64^3} = \sqrt{262{,}144} = 512$
$64^{\frac{3}{2}} = \left(\sqrt{64}\right)^3 = 8^3 = 512$

39. The student should have taken the sixth root of 64 and then found the square of that number; The correct answer is 4.

41. the fifth root of the quantity k raised to the seventh power

43. the ninth root of the quantity $-5b$ raised to the fourth power

45. the sixth root of the quantity x raised to the first power

47. the square (second) root of the quantity $7y$ raised to the seventh power

49. the fifth root of the quantity 513 raised to the fourth power

51. the eleventh root of the quantity $1 + m$ raised to the fourth power

53. $\sqrt[4]{3^7}$

55. $\left(\sqrt[4]{81}\right)^3 = 27$

57. $\left(\sqrt[5]{xy}\right)^9$

59. $\left(\sqrt[9]{-25a}\right)^4$

61.A. about 53.82 cm

    B. no; If you substitute successive values of n, the factors that you obtain to multiply the string length by do not lie on a line, so the differences in string length will not be constant. For example, for $n = 1$, $2,..., 8$, $2^{-\frac{n}{12}}$ gives 0.9439, 0.8909, 0.8409, 0.7937, 0.7492, 0.7071, 0.6674, 0.6300. The differences range from 0.0530 cm to 0.0374 cm.

63. yes; Possible answer: When you recognize that the base can be expressed as an integer after applying the rational exponent, then you know the expression can be simplified.

65. yes; When I enter both expressions into my calculator they equal 36. Also, the rational exponents both simplify to 2, and six squared is 36. Yes, you could raise -6 to the sixth or eighth power before finding the indicated root. Both the sixth and eighth powers of -6 are positive.

67. $49^{\frac{3}{4}}$

69. $9^{\frac{2}{5}}$

71. $\left(\dfrac{a}{b}\right)^{\frac{6}{4}}$

73. $\left(\dfrac{xy}{4}\right)^{\frac{3}{2}} = \dfrac{(xy)^{\frac{3}{2}}}{8}$

75. $M_A(d) = 0.036d^{\frac{13}{5}}$, $M_B(d) = 0.059d^{\frac{23}{10}}$

$$\dfrac{0.036(20)^{\frac{13}{5}}}{0.059(20)^{\frac{23}{10}}} \approx \dfrac{89.892}{57.972} \approx 1.5$$

The biomass of a tree in the data set M_A is 1.5 times greater than the biomass of a tree in the data set M_B.

77. Rigel is brighter; It is about 1.42 times as bright as Betelgeuse.

Spiral Review • Assessment Readiness

79. A

81. C

MODULE 6, LESSON 6.2

On Your Own

7. $49^{\frac{3}{10}} \approx 3.21$

9. $\dfrac{81}{625} \approx 0.13$

11. $216 \cdot 512 = 110{,}592$

13. $81^{\frac{5}{6} - \frac{1}{3}} = 81^{\frac{1}{2}} = 9$

15. $64^{-\frac{3}{4}} \approx 0.04$

17. $3^3 = 27$

19. $25^{\frac{7}{4}} \approx 279.51$

21. $100^{\frac{3}{2}} = 1000$

23. $640^{\frac{3}{8}} \approx 11.28$

25. $32^{\frac{1}{5}} = 2$

27. $\dfrac{125}{8} \approx 15.63$

29.

$\dfrac{4a^{\frac{1}{2}}}{4^{\frac{3}{2}} a^{\frac{3}{4}}}$	Given.
$= \dfrac{1}{4^{\frac{1}{2}} a^{\frac{1}{4}}}$	Quotient of Powers
$= \dfrac{1}{2a^{\frac{1}{4}}}$	Simplify.

31.

$\left(x^{\frac{7}{4}} x^{-\frac{3}{4}} y^{\frac{1}{2}}\right)^{\frac{5}{2}}$	Given.
$= \left(xy^{\frac{1}{2}}\right)^{\frac{5}{2}}$	Product of Powers
$= x^{\frac{5}{2}} y^{\frac{5}{4}}$	Power of a Power

33.

$\left(\dfrac{16^{\frac{1}{4}}}{16^{\frac{3}{4}}}\right)^{\frac{5}{2}}$	Given.
$= \left(\dfrac{1}{16^{\frac{1}{2}}}\right)^{\frac{5}{2}}$	Quotient of Powers
$= \dfrac{1}{16^{\frac{5}{4}}}$	Power of a Quotient
$= \dfrac{1}{32}$	Simplify.

35. $4y^{\frac{3}{8}}$

37. $\dfrac{a^{\frac{7}{8}} b^{\frac{7}{2}}}{c^{\frac{7}{6}}}$

39. $27r^{\frac{3}{8}}$

41. $150x$

43. $2m^{\frac{2}{3}} n$

45. $288x^{\frac{5}{2}}$

47.

$\sqrt[3]{\dfrac{32x^4}{54x}}$	Given.
$= \sqrt[3]{\dfrac{2^5 x^4}{2 \cdot 3^3 x}}$	Rewrite Numbers with Exponents.
$= \sqrt[3]{\dfrac{2^4 x^3}{3^3}}$	Quotient of Powers
$= \sqrt[3]{\dfrac{2 \cdot 2^3 x^3}{3^3}}$	Factor out Perfect Cubes
$= \dfrac{2x\sqrt[3]{2}}{3}$	Simplify.

49. $\sqrt[5]{\dfrac{32a^3b^8}{a^{12}b}}$ Given.

$= \sqrt[5]{\dfrac{32b^7}{a^9}}$ Quotient of Powers

$= \dfrac{\sqrt[5]{32b^7}}{\sqrt[5]{a^9}}$ Quotient Property of Roots

$= \dfrac{2b\sqrt[5]{b^2}}{a\sqrt[5]{a^4}}$ Simplify.

$= \dfrac{2b\sqrt[5]{b^2}}{a\sqrt[5]{a^4}} \cdot \dfrac{\sqrt[5]{a}}{\sqrt[5]{a}}$ Rationalize the Denominator.

$= \dfrac{2b\sqrt[5]{ab^2}}{a^2}$ Product Property of Roots.

51. $2xyz^2\sqrt[5]{3x^4y}$

53. $\dfrac{y^4\sqrt[4]{x^2y}}{x^3}$

55. $r^2st\sqrt[5]{48r^2s^3t}$

57. The volume of the basketball is approximately 21.7 times the volume of the golf ball.

59. $\left(\dfrac{a^{2m+3}}{a^{m-4}}\right)^3$ Given.

$= \dfrac{a^{6m+9}}{a^{3m-12}}$ Power of a Quotient

$= a^{3m+21}$ Quotient of Powers

61. $\sqrt[3n]{a^{7n}b^{9n}}$ Given.

$= \sqrt[3n]{a^{7n}} \cdot \sqrt[3n]{b^{9n}}$ Product Property of Roots

$= \sqrt[3n]{a^{2(3n)+n}} \cdot \sqrt[3n]{b^{3(3n)}}$ Factor out $3n$.

$= a^2b^3\sqrt[3n]{a^n}$ Simplify.

Spiral Review • Assessment Readiness

63. A

65. A: 3, B: 2, C: 5, D: 1, E: 4

MODULE 7, LESSON 7.1

On Your Own

7. $(f \circ g)(x) = 36x^2 + 24x$ $(g \circ f)(x) = 6x^2 - 22$

$D: \{x \mid x \in R\}$ $D: \{x \mid x \geq 4\}$

$R: \{y \mid y \geq -4\}$ $R: \{y \mid y \geq -22\}$

9. $(f \circ g)(x) = 4x^2 - 14x + 6$ $(g \circ f)(x) = 2x^2 - 2x - 15\}$

$D: \{x \mid x \in R\}$ $D: \{x \mid x \geq -6\}$

$R: \{y \mid y \geq -\frac{25}{4}\}$ $R: \{y \mid y \geq -15\}$

11. $g^{-1}(x) = \dfrac{1}{6}x + \dfrac{1}{12}$

13. $f^{-1}(x) = \dfrac{1}{3}x - \dfrac{1}{3}$

15. $u^{-1}(x) = -\dfrac{1}{8}x - \dfrac{1}{4}$

17. $C(z) = 0.9z$

$U(C(z)) = 0.76(0.9z)$

$U(C(z)) = 0.684z$

$U(C(100)) = 0.684(100)$

$\$68.40$

19. Total sales is $\$24,000$.

$s(E) = 20E - 16,000$

Spiral Review • Assessment Readiness

21. C

23. C

MODULE 7, LESSON 7.2

On Your Own

7. Restricted domain for $f(x)$ is $x \leq -2$. The function $f^{-1}(x)$ is the ordered pairs $(83, -7)$, $(56, -6)$, $(35, -5)$, $(20, -4)$, $(11, -3)$, $(8, -2)$.

9. Restricted domain for $f(x)$ is $x \geq 2$. The function $f^{-1}(x)$ is the ordered pairs $(-4, 2)$, $(8, 3)$, $(44, 4)$, $(104, 5)$, $(188, 6)$.

11. Yes. The function $g(x)$ reverses the input and output of the function $f(x)$. No. The input and output of $h(x)$ are not the reverse of the input and output of $f(x)$. For example, $f(4) = \frac{1}{2}(4)^2 = \frac{16}{2} = 8$, but $h(8) = \sqrt{8} = 2\sqrt{2}$. Since $h(8)$ does not equal 4, the function h is not the inverse function of f.

13. Yes. The function $g(x)$ reverses the input and output of the function $f(x)$. No. The input and output of $h(x)$ are not the reverse of the input and output of $f(x)$. For example, $f(2) = 4(2)^3 = 4(8) = 32$, but $h(32) = \sqrt[3]{32} = 2\sqrt[3]{4}$. Since $h(32)$ does not equal 2, function h is not the inverse function of f.

15. $f^{-1}(x) = \sqrt{\dfrac{1}{5}x}$

17. $f^{-1}(x) = \sqrt{x + 6}$

19. $f^{-1}(x) = \sqrt{x} - 2$

21. $f^{-1}(x) = -\dfrac{1}{6}\sqrt[3]{x}$

23. $f^{-1}(x) = \sqrt[3]{2x}$

25. $f^{-1}(x) = \sqrt[3]{\dfrac{1}{4}x} - 3$

27. $f^{-1}(x) = \sqrt[3]{-y} + 2$

29. $f^{-1}(x) = \sqrt[3]{x - 2} + 5$

31. $r(P) = -1 + \sqrt[3]{\dfrac{P}{6240}}$; It represents the annual growth rate that will give a student population of P after 3 years; about 7.72%

© Houghton Mifflin Harcourt Publishing Company

Spiral Review • Assessment Readiness

35. C

37. A

MODULE 7, LESSON 7.3

On Your Own

7. $D: \{x \mid x \geq 5\}$ $R: \{y \mid y \leq 4\}$

9. maximum value of 4

11. The function decreases less as x increases.

13. $(1, 1)$

15. reflection across the x-axis, vertical stretch by a factor of 2

17. reflection across the x-axis, horizontal compression by a factor of $\frac{1}{2}$, and shift 4 units up

19. vertical compression by a factor of $\frac{1}{4}$, shift 8 units up, and 3 units to the right

21. $(0, 0) \to (-8, -1), (1, 1) \to (-6, 0)$

21.

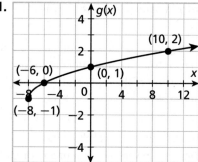

25. $(36, 6) \to (-35, 8), (100, 10) \to (-99, 12)$

27. $g(x) = 3\sqrt{x + 4} - 7$

29. With every passing day after the video has been released, the number of daily likes increases less.

Spiral Review • Assessment Readiness

31. D

33. A

MODULE 7, LESSON 7.4

On Your Own

11. negative

13. The function approaches infinity on the left and negative infinity on the right.

15. $(4, -2)$

17. decreasing

19. The average rate of change between $x = 3$ and $x = 5$ is -1. The average rate of change between $x = 5$ and $x = 12$ is $-\frac{1}{7}$.

21. horizontal compression by a factor of $\frac{1}{4}$, reflection across the y-axis, and shift 2 units up

23. $(0, 0) \to (4, 2), (1, 1) \to (5, 0)$, and $(-1, -1) \to (3, 4)$

25.

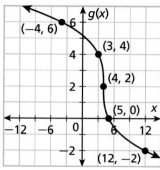

27. $(0, 0) \to (-5, -6), (1, 1) \to (-4, -7)$, and $(-1, -1) \to (-6, -5)$

29.

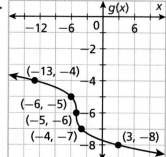

31.A. Possible answer: The function gives the radius of a portion of Earth below the lower mantle for a given mass of that inner part of the planet.

B. $r(2 \times 10^{24}) \approx 3500$; The radius from the center of Earth to the edge of the outer core is 3500 km. So, this result makes sense.

33. $n(x) = \sqrt[3]{-(x + 9)} - 6$

Spiral Review • Assessment Readiness

35. A

37. D

MODULE 7, LESSON 7.5

On Your Own

5. Add 8 to both sides.

7. Add 1 to both sides.

9. 0 solutions or 1 solution; The graph of $y = b$ is a horizontal line. The graph of $y = \sqrt{x - a}$ is always increasing and has no turning points. This means that the graphs of $y = b$ can only intersect once at most. If b is negative, the graphs won't intersect at all. Therefore, the equation can have 0 solutions or 1 solution.

11. no solution

13.
$2\sqrt[3]{x-4} - 6 = 0$	Given
$2\sqrt[3]{x-4} = 6$	Addition Property of Equality
$\sqrt[3]{x-4} = 3$	Division Property of Equality
$x - 4 = 27$	Cube both sides of the equation.
$x = 31$	Addition Property of Equality

15. yes; The graphs intersect at $x = 31$.

17.
$60 = \sqrt{19.6d}$	Substitute 60 for $v(d)$.
$3600 = 19.6d$	Square with both sides of the equation.
$183.7 \approx d$	Division Property of Equality

The maximum falling height at which the rock will stay intact is 187.3 meters.

To solve $60 = \sqrt{19.6d}$ using a graphing calculator, graph $f(x) = 60$ and $g(x) = \sqrt{19.6x}$, and find the point of intersection. The x-coordinate of the point of intersection is approximately 183.7.

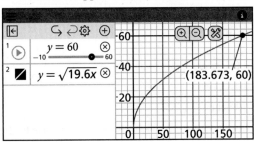

19. $x = 27$

21. $x = -12$

23. No solution

25. 60

27. for x approximately 1.94 mi

Spiral Review • Assessment Readiness

31. C

33. A

UNIT 4

MODULE 8, LESSON 8.1

On Your Own

7. The functions have the same horizontal asymptote, $y = 3$.

9. vertical stretch by a factor of 2, and translation down 1 unit; domain: $\{x \mid x \in \mathbb{R}\}$; range: $\{y \mid y > -1\}$; as $x \to -\infty, y \to +\infty$, and as $x \to +\infty, y \to -1$; y-intercept: 1

11. vertical stretch by a factor of 4, and translation up 1 unit; domain: $\{x \mid x \in \mathbb{R}\}$; range: $\{y \mid y > 1\}$; as $x \to -\infty, y \to 1$, and as $x \to +\infty, y \to +\infty$; y-intercept: 5

13.

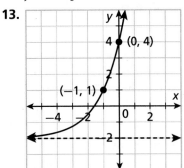

15.

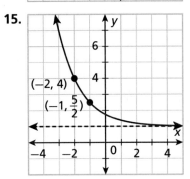

17. $g(x) = \left(\dfrac{1}{3}\right)^{x+1} - 2$

19. $g(x) = 2(2)^x + 2$

21.A. $V(t) = 6000(1.03^t)$ where V is in dollars and t is in years

B. 24 years

C. $V_s(t) = 5000(1.05^t)$; Trey and Simon have the same amount of money after approximately 9.5 years. The value of each account is approximately $7950. I found the answer by graphing the functions to find where $V_T(t) = V_S(t)$.

23. The graphs are the same.
$$\begin{aligned} f(x) &= 8(2^x) \\ &= 2^3(2^x) \\ &= 2^{3+x} \\ &= 2^{x+3} \end{aligned}$$

25. To reflect the graph of a function in the y-axis, you place a negative sign in front of x in the function. The function $g(x) = 5^{-x}$ is a reflection of $f(x) = 5^x$ in the y-axis. A vertical compression of $f(x)$ can be created by using a value of a that is between 0 and 1. For example, $h(x) = \frac{1}{2}(5^x)$ is a vertical compression of $f(x)$.

27. Possible answer: The average rates of change increase exponentially.

Spiral Review • Assessment Readiness

31. A, B, C

33. A

MODULE 8, LESSON 8.2

On Your Own

5.A. $f(x) = 2^x$: C; $f(x) = 4^x$: A; $f(x) = e^x$: B; Possible answer: I know that the value of e lies between 2 and 4, so $f(x) = e^x$ must be B. The function $f(x) = 4^x$ grows more quickly than $f(x) = 2^x$, so $f(x) = 4^x$ is A and $f(x) = 2^x$ is C.

   B. $f(0) = 1$ for all three functions

   C. The end behavior is the same for all three functions: as $x \to -\infty$, $y \to 0$, as $x \to +\infty$, $y \to +\infty$

7. $c > 0$; $c < 0$

9. Possible answer: $g(x) = 2(e)^{x-1} - 3$; as $x \to -\infty$, $y \to -3$, as $x \to +\infty$, $y \to +\infty$; $y = -3$

11.

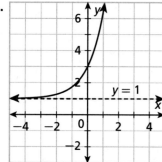

13.

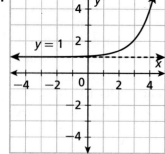

15.

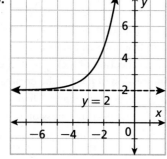

17.

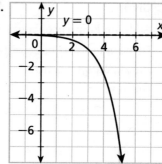

19. $f(x) = e^{(x+2)}$

21. $f(x) = \frac{1}{3}e^{(x+1)}$

23. $f(x) = -e^x - 3$

25.A. 100; the percent of carbon-14 in fossil before it started to decay

   B. about 0.012%

   C. about 13,005 years old

Spiral Review • Assessment Readiness

27. A

29. A; 3, B: 2; C: 1

MODULE 8, LESSON 8.3

On Your Own

7.A. 18 years

   B. about 17.7 years; The answer is very close to the estimate given by the rule of 72.

9. $340.22

11. $791.44

13. U.S. large-company stocks: $7,598,129.57; U.S. government bonds: $137,792.72; gold: $62,649.12

15. about 5.6 years

17. about 25.5 years

19. $43,352.64

Spiral Review • Assessment Readiness

23. C

MODULE 9, LESSON 9.1

On Your Own

9.A. inverse functions

   B. The domain of $f(x)$ is all real numbers and the domain is values greater than 0. The domain of $g(x)$ is values greater than 0 and the range is all real numbers. The domain of $f(x)$ is the range of $g(x)$ and the range of $f(x)$ is the domain of $g(x)$. Yes, the domain of $g(x)$ is restricted to positive numbers.

C. $f(x)$: As x approaches negative infinity, the function approaches infinity. As x approaches infinity, the function approaches 0. There is a horizontal asymptote at $y = 0$.

$g(x)$: As x approaches 0, the function approaches infinity. As x approaches infinity, the function approaches negative infinity. There is a vertical asymptote at $x = 0$.
The end behaviors and asymptotes are different. The horizontal asymptote of $f(x)$ corresponds to the vertical asymptote of $g(x)$ because they are inverse functions.

D. Both functions are decreasing over the given intervals. For the given intervals, $f(x)$ is decreasing more slowly than $g(x)$.

E. no; $f(x)$ and $g(x)$ are inverse functions, so the graphs of the functions should be reflections of each other across the line $y = x$. The function g is graphed incorrectly.

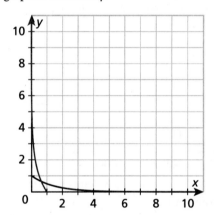

11. $\log_a b = 5$

13. $\ln y = x$

15. $\log_x y = 2$

17. $\left(\frac{2}{5}\right)^3 = \frac{8}{125}$

19. $9^y = x$

21. $10^{\frac{1}{3}} = x$

23. $2, -3$

25. $4, -3$

27. $-5, 3$

29. Logarithms use smaller numbers to represent greater values by talking about a number in terms of the power you raise a certain base to in order to get the number. Common bases used are 10 and e.

31. 3.3

33. decreasing

35. 18 months; I set $f(y)$ equal to 144 and then divided each side by 18. Then I rewrote the equation $8 = 2^{\frac{y}{6}}$ in log form $\log_2 8 = \frac{y}{6}$. Then I simplified this equation to find that $y = 18$.

Spiral Review • Assessment Readiness

37. A

39. D

MODULE 9, LESSON 9.2
On Your Own

7.A. domain and asymptote: h changes the domain from $x > 0$ to $x > h$ and asymptote from $x = 0$ to $x = h$; range: unaffected

B. end behavior: If $a < 0$, the end behavior of $f(x)$ switches sign as $x \to h$ and as $x \to +\infty$

C. intercepts: h and k can affect the intercepts; because changing h moves the graph left or right, this will change the x-intercept the same number of units. If $h < 0$, the transformed graph will also have a y-intercept. Changing k moves the graph up or down, so if the graph has a y-intercept, changing k will change it. But changing k moves the entire curve up or down, so this will also affect where the curve intersects the x-axis, and thus the x-intercept.

D. k can change the intervals where $g(x)$ is positive or negative, since it affects the intercept. When $a > 0$, $g(x)$ is always increasing over its entire domain, but when $a < 0$, $g(x)$ is always increasing over its entire domain

E. The parameter a increases the rate of change on an interval when $|a| > 1$, and decreases the rate of change on an interval when $|a| < 1$.

9. horizontal translation right 3 units and up 4 units of the graph of $f(x) = \log x$; $x = 3$

11. a horizontal translation left $\frac{1}{2}$ unit, a reflection across the x-axis, and a vertical translation down 8 units of the graph of $f(x) = \log_{\frac{1}{2}} x$; $x = -\frac{1}{2}$

13. parent: $(1, 0)$ and $(6, 1)$; $g(x)$: $(2, -5)$ and $(7, -2)$

15. parent: $(1, 0)$ and $(e, 1)$; $g(x)$: $(1, -2)$ and $(e, 8)$

17. parent: $(1, 0)$ and $(3, 1)$; $g(x)$: $(1, 5)$ and $(3, 4)$

19. parent: $(1, 0)$ and $(e, 1)$; $g(x)$: $\left(-\frac{1}{2}, 0\right)$ and $\left(\frac{e}{2} - 1, 1\right)$

21. a horizontal translation right 5 units, a vertical compression by a factor of $\frac{1}{2}$, and a vertical translation down 2 units of the graph of $f(x) = \log x$

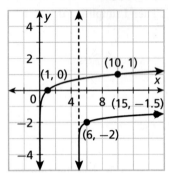

23. a horizontal translation left 2 units, a reflection across the x-axis, and a vertical translation down 1 units of the graph of $f(x) = \log_2 x$

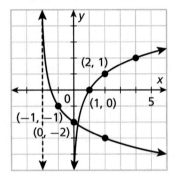

25.A.

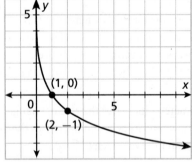

B. They are the same

C. $\log_{\frac{1}{2}} x = y$ in exponential form is $\left(\frac{1}{2}\right)^y = x$; $-\log_2 x = y$ in exponential form is $2^{-y} = x$. $\left(2^{-1}\right)^y = x$, or $2^{-y} = x$. The exponential forms of the equation are equivalent, which explains why the graphs are the same.

Spiral Review • Assessment Readiness

29. C

31. C

MODULE 9, LESSON 9.3

On Your Own

7. $y = 209{,}847(0.71)^x$

9. The models are almost exactly the same and are both good fits because all of the data points lie on the graph.

11. The exponential model is not a good fit because 12 is not the initial value of the data.

13. You can find the average of the ratios of the function values for consecutive integer x-values and use the initial point, if the x-value is 0, as a. You can also use a graphing calculator to perform an exponential regression.

15. $t \approx 11.6 \ln \frac{P}{2557}$ models the time it takes the eagle pair population to reach a certain number.

17.

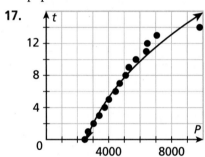

I should also graph the data points from the table from problem 16.

19. 2005

21.

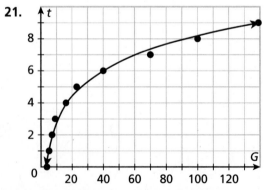

23. 0.0815, 0.0475, 0.034, 0.026, 0.0215, 0.018

27.

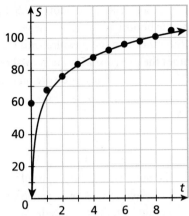

Yes, the graph of the model passes through or close to most of the points. The other points are both above and below the graph.

29. during the year 2028; When t is 20, S is approximately 119, so the number of subscriptions has doubled from its initial number.

Spiral Review • Assessment Readiness

31. C

33. D

MODULE 10, LESSON 10.1

On Your Own

7. -2

9. -1

11. *See below.*

13. $\log_3 81 = 4$

15. $\log_9 27 = 1.5$

17. $\log_{12} 1728 = 3$

19. $\log_8 18 \approx 1.39$

21. $\log_9 51 \approx 1.789$

23. $\log_5 1728 \approx 4.632$

25. The bases in the original expression are not the same, so they cannot be combined as a logarithm base 4. Instead, the student should simplify each logarithm individually and then subtract.

$$\log_4 32 - \log_5 125 = \log_4 \left(4^{0.5}\right)^5 - \log_5 5^3$$
$$= \log_4 4^{2.5} - \log_5 5^3$$
$$= 2.5 - 3$$
$$= -0.5$$

27. Possible answer: $\log 80 - 3\log 2 = 1$

29.A. $\dfrac{\log 1.3}{\log 1.045} = t$

   B. 5.96 years, or about 6 years

Spiral Review • Assessment Readiness

33. D

35. C

MODULE 10, LESSON 10.2

On Your Own

7. 1.4

9. -0.4

11. An exponential equation is either constantly increasing, or constantly decreasing, so there can only be one solution or no solutions.

13. 1.5

15. 20.772

17. 0.680

19.A. $y = P(1.06)^t$

   B. $100{,}000 = 10{,}000(1.06)^t$

   C.
$100{,}000 = 10{,}000(1.06)^t$	Given
$10 = 1.06^t$	Division Property of Equality
$t = \log_{1.06} 10$	Definition of logarithm
$t = \dfrac{\log 10}{\log 1.06}$	Change of Base Property of Logarithms
$t \approx 39.52$	Evaluate.

   about 39.52 years

11.
$\log_c a = y$	Let y equal $\log_c a$.
$c^y = a$	Definition of logarithm
$\log_b c^y = \log_b a$	Take the logarithm base-b of both sides of the equation.
$y\log_b c = \log_b a$	Power Property of Logarithms
$y = \dfrac{\log_b a}{\log_b c}$	Divide both sides of the equation by $\log_b c$.
$\log_c a = \dfrac{\log_b a}{\log_b c}$	Substitute $\log_c a$ for y.

21.A. $18{,}000 = 12{,}756(1.025)^x$

  B. 14 years

Spiral Review • Assessment Readiness

25. C

27. C

MODULE 10, LESSON 10.3

On Your Own

5. No; She should also graph the equation $y = 2.5$ and find the intersection of the line and the curve.

7. 14.43

9. 18.87

11. 2.25

13. -1

15. -1

17. Possible answer: Graph the functions $f(x) = 50\log_2(0.125x + 2)$ and $g(x) = 60\log_5(0.5x + 5)$ on a graphing calculator, and determine the point of intersection; 11 days since the start of the month

19.A. $5.8 = -\log H$

  B. 0.00000158 moles

Spiral Review • Assessment Readiness

21. D

23. A: 3, B: 4, C: 2, D: 1

UNIT 5

MODULE 11, LESSON 11.1

On Your Own

7. yes; 2

9. yes; $\dfrac{1}{3}$

11. yes; 6

13. no

15. no

17. $y = \dfrac{12}{x}$; $y = 3$

19. $y = \dfrac{84}{x}$; $x = 4$

21.A. yes; The products $c \cdot t$ are constant (all products equal 72).

  B. $t = \dfrac{72}{c}$

  C. 3 carpenters

23.A. $P = \dfrac{150}{A}$; yes; The equation has the form $P = \dfrac{a}{A}$.

B. The pressure Emilio exerts on the snow is 2.5 lb/in^2 when wearing the boots and 0.25 lb/in^2 when wearing the snowshoes, so the pressure with the boots is 10 times the pressure with the snowshoes. Because Emilio exerts much less pressure on the snow with the snowshoes, he is less likely to sink into the snow.

25.A. $(1, 1)$

  B. $(2, 2)$; $(3, 3)$

  C. $(\sqrt{a}, \sqrt{a})$; At the point where the graphs of $y = x$ and $y = \dfrac{a}{x}$ intersect, $x = \dfrac{a}{x}$, or $x^2 = a$. Since the intersection point is in the first quadrant (where $x > 0$), it follows that $x = \sqrt{a}$, and so the y-coordinate of the intersection point is $y = \sqrt{a}$. Therefore, the intersection point is $(\sqrt{a}, \sqrt{a})$.

Spiral Review • Assessment Readiness

27. B

29. D

MODULE 11, LESSON 11.2

On Your Own

7. Possible answer: The graphs of f and g are similar in that both graphs decrease for $x > 0$, and both graphs have $y = 0$ as a horizontal asymptote. The graphs are different in that the graph of f has a vertical asymptote at $x = 0$, while the graph of g has no vertical asymptote. Also, the graph of f is below the x-axis (that is, $f(x)$ is negative) when $x < 0$, while the graph of g is always above the x-axis (that is, $g(x)$ is always positive).

9. Possible answer: $g(x) = \dfrac{1}{x - 5} - 3$

11. reflection across the x-axis

13. translation right 3 units

15. translation left 1 unit and down 2 units

17. translation left 2 units and up 3 units

19. reflection across the x-axis, followed by a horizontal compression by a factor of $\frac{1}{2}$, followed by a translation 2 units right and 1 unit up

21. reflection across the x-axis, followed by a vertical stretch by a factor of 2, followed by a translation right 4 units and down 3 units

23. domain: $\{x \mid x \neq -6\}$; range: $\{y \mid y \neq 0\}$

25. domain: $\{x \mid x \neq -2\}$; range: $\{y \mid y \neq 1\}$

27. domain: $\{x \mid x \neq -2\}$; range: $\{y \mid y \neq -1\}$

29. domain: $\{x \mid x \neq -30\}$; range: $\{y \mid y \neq 0\}$

31.

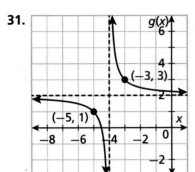

33.

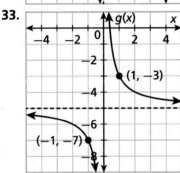

35. $g(x) = -\left(\dfrac{1}{x-1}\right) + 4$

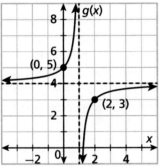

37. $g(x) = \dfrac{1}{x+1} - 2$

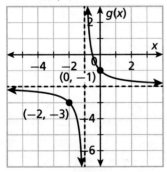

39. $g(x) = -2\left(\dfrac{1}{x+3}\right) - 1$

41. $g(x) = 0.5\left(\dfrac{1}{x-4}\right) - 3$

43.A. $c(m) = \dfrac{300 + 40m}{m}$ or $c(m) = \dfrac{300}{m} + 40$

 B. $190; The cost of the phone itself, $300, has been "spread out" over only 2 months, so it adds a significant amount to the average monthly cost.

C. 15 months

D. $48.33

45.A. Possible answer: $P(n) = \dfrac{8n - 200}{n}$ or $P(n) = -\dfrac{200}{n} + 8$

 B. 40 T-shirts

 C. no; Since $P(n) = -\dfrac{200}{n} + 8$, Rosa's average profit per T-shirt is $8 minus some positive amount of money. So, her average profit per T-shirt will always be less than $8, and therefore will never reach $10.

47.A. about 5% oxygen

 B. 0% oxygen

Spiral Review • Assessment Readiness

49. A

51. B

MODULE 11, LESSON 11.3

On Your Own

7. The common factors can be divided out, making the undefined value "removable". This means that the curve will look like the reduced rational function with a hole at the value of x that causes the original function to be undefined.

9. $x = -4$; vertical asymptote

11. $x = 2$ and $x = 1$; hole at $x = 2$ and vertical asymptote at $x = 1$

13. $x = -2$ and $x = 2$; vertical asymptotes at $x = -2$ and $x = 2$

15. $x = -1$ and $x = 0$; vertical asymptote at $x = -1$ and hole at $x = 0$

17. $f(x)$: vertical asymptote at $x = 2$, horizontal asymptote at $x = 3$, $g(x)$: vertical asymptote at $x = 3$, slant asymptote at $y = x + 2$; the domain of each function only excludes a single value but the range of $g(x)$ excludes more than a single value while the range of $f(x)$ only excludes a single value

19. $x = 1, y = 1$

21. $x = 2, y = x + 5$

23. $x \neq -3$; vertical asymptote at $x = -3$

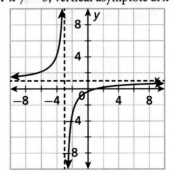

25. $x \neq -1, 1$; vertical asymptote at $x = -1$ and hole at $x = 1$

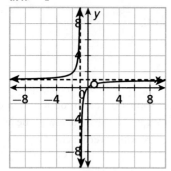

27. $x \neq 0, 2$; vertical asymptote at $x = 0$, hole at $x = 2$

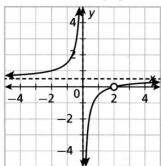

29. $x \neq -1$; vertical asymptote at $x = -1$

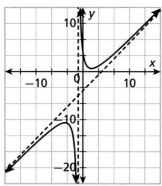

31. The average rate of change of the function over the interval $200 \leq x \leq 400$ is about -1.25 dollars per additional unit made. The average rate of change of the function over the interval $600 \leq x \leq 800$ is about -0.125 dollars per additional unit made. This tells us that the cost saved per each additional unit made is decreasing as the number of units made increases.

33. $f(x) = \dfrac{6(x + 4)}{x^2 + 2x - 8}$

Spiral Review • Assessment Readiness

35. A

37. C

MODULE 12, LESSON 12.1

On Your Own

5. First factor the numerator as the square of a sum and the denominator as a difference of squares. Divide the common factor of $x^2 = 36$ from both to get $\dfrac{x^2 + 36}{x^2 - 36}$. Then identify the excluded values, which in this case are $x = 6, -6$

7. $\dfrac{-7z}{4x}$; none of the variables can be equal to 0.

9. $-\dfrac{x^2 + 10}{x^2(x + 10)^2(x - 10)}$; $x \neq -10, 0, 8, 10$

11. $\dfrac{5}{2xz}$; x, y, and z cannot equal 0.

13. $\dfrac{x - 3}{x + 3}$; x cannot equal $-4, -3, 0$, or 3.

15. $\dfrac{2(x - 4)(x - 1)}{(3x - 4)(x + 1)}$; x cannot equal $-\dfrac{4}{3}, \dfrac{4}{3}, 1, 4$, or -1.

17. When dividing A and B, the numerator of B is multiplied by the denominator of A, so any values that make the numerator of B equal to 0 should also be excluded.

19.A. Let x be the number of wins by the soccer team during the remainder of their season. For the records shown, the softball team had 2 more wins than the soccer team. Therefore, in order for the two teams to have the same number of wins at the end of their seasons, the softball team won $(x - 2)$ games. So the expressions for the winning percentages (as decimals) are:

Softball: $\dfrac{(x - 2) + 8}{(x - 2) + 13} = \dfrac{x + 6}{x + 11}$; Soccer: $\dfrac{x + 6}{2x + 14}$

B. $\dfrac{\dfrac{x + 6}{x + 11}}{\dfrac{x + 6}{2x + 14}} = \dfrac{(x + 6)(2x + 14)}{(x + 6)(x + 11)} = \dfrac{2x + 14}{x + 11}$

$f(x) = \dfrac{4}{5}(x + 5)$ or $f(x) = \dfrac{4}{5}x + 4$

C. $\dfrac{2x + 14}{x + 11} = 1.5$

Spiral Review • Assessment Readiness

23. D

MODULE 12, LESSON 12.2

On Your Own

9. Possible answer: Both differences have denominators that are the same, so the processes are similar in that they both involve subtracting the numerator of the second expression or fraction from the numerator of the first and placing the result over the like denominator. In both cases, the resulting numerator should be examined to determine if it can be factored and if so, whether it shares any factors with the like denominator leading to a simplification.

11. Possible answer: In both addition and subtraction, both rational expressions are first rewritten using a common denominator. If adding, the numerators are added. If subtracting, the numerators are subtracted. Then, whether adding or subtracting, the result is simplified.

13. $-\dfrac{3x+15}{x(x+3)}$

15. $\dfrac{x+2}{3-x}$

17. $\dfrac{x^2+2x+7}{x-1}$

19. $\dfrac{-x^2-4x-6}{(x+2)(x+4)}$

21. $\dfrac{2x-15}{(x-3)(x+8)}$

23. $\dfrac{x^2+2x-2}{(x-3)(x+2)(x+3)}$

25. $\dfrac{(x+4)(x-1)}{(x-2)(x+1)}$

27. $\dfrac{-x^2+x-4}{(x-2)(x+1)}$

29. $\dfrac{x(x+1)}{2(x-2)}$

31. $\dfrac{200}{x}-\dfrac{200}{x+25}=\dfrac{5000}{x(x+25)}$

33. $\dfrac{d}{6}+\dfrac{d}{28}=\dfrac{17d}{84}$

35. The vertical asymptotes of $p(x)$ and $q(x)$ are $x=b$ and $x=d$, respectively. The vertical asymptotes of $p(x)+q(x)$ are $x=b$ and $x=d$.

Spiral Review • Assessment Readiness

37. D

39. D

MODULE 12, LESSON 12.3

On Your Own

5. Possible answer: Rewrite the equation as $0=x-\dfrac{5}{x+7}-2$ and identify the x-intercept(s) of $f(x)=x-\dfrac{5}{x+7}-2$ or graph $g(x)=\dfrac{5}{x+7}+1$ and $h(x)=x-1$ and identify the point(s) of intersection.

7. Possible answer: The x-intercept of the graph of the function representing the expression that equals 0 is the solution of the equation. This method allows you to graph just one function.

9. I can solve the equation for c; $c=\pm\sqrt{b^2-\dfrac{2bd}{t}}$

11. $x=-3$

13. $x=0$ or $x=4$

15. *See below.*

17. *See below.*

15.

$\dfrac{x}{x^2-x}=\dfrac{3+6x}{x^2-x}$	Given
$\dfrac{x}{x^2-x}\cdot(x^2-x)=\dfrac{3+x}{x^2-x}\cdot(x^2-x)$	Multiply each term by the LCD.
$x=3+6x$	Divide out common factors and simplify.
$-5x=3$	Subtraction Property of Equality
$x=-\dfrac{3}{5}$	Subtraction Property of Equality

17.

$\dfrac{x-6}{x+1}+\dfrac{x+5}{x^2+x}=\dfrac{1}{x^2+x}$	Given
$\dfrac{x-6}{x+1}\cdot(x^2+x)+\dfrac{x+5}{x^2+x}\cdot(x^2+x)=\dfrac{1}{x^2+x}\cdot(x^2+x)$	Multiply each term by the LCD.
$(x-6)x+x+5=1$	Divide out common factors and simplify.
$x^2-6x+x+5=1$	Distributive Property
$x^2-5x+4=0$	Write in standard form.
$(x-1)(x-4)=0$	Factor.
$x-1=0$ or $x-4=0$	Zero Product Property.
$x=1$ or $x=4$	Solve for x.

© Houghton Mifflin Harcourt Publishing Company

19. *See below.*

21. $R_2 = \dfrac{R_1 \cdot R}{R_1 - R}$

23.A. $12 = \dfrac{560}{80} + \dfrac{560}{80 + w}$

  B. 32 m/min

25.A. 6 h

  B. 12 h

27. Average driving speed: 55 mi/h; average bicycling speed: 15 mi/h

29. no; Zero is only excluded if the factor x is in the denominator. For an equation such as $\dfrac{x}{x+2} = \dfrac{x}{x-2}$, $x = 0$ is not an extraneous solution since it does not cause division by zero.

Spiral Review • Assessment Readiness

31. D

33. A

UNIT 6

MODULE 13, LESSON 13.1

On Your Own

5. For both types of sequence, the domain is a subset of the integers, but for a finite sequence, the domain is restricted to a finite number of integers. This means that the range must also have a finite number of elements. For an infinite sequence, the domain is not bounded, but consists of infinitely many consecutive integers, and so there are infinitely many elements. This means the range can also be unbounded and contain infinitely many elements.

7. 121, 110, 99, 88, 77, 66

9. $0, -2, -6, -12, -20, -30$

19.

$\dfrac{4}{x^2+5x+6} + \dfrac{2}{x+2} = \dfrac{3}{x+3}$	Given
$\dfrac{4}{x^2+5x+6} \cdot (x^2+5x+6) + \dfrac{2}{x+2} \cdot (x^2+5x+6)$ $= \dfrac{3}{x+3} \cdot (x^2+5x+6)$	Multiply each term by the LCD.
$4 + 2(x+3) = 3(x+2)$	Divide out common factors and simplify.
$4 + 2x + 6 = 3x + 6$	Distributive Property
$2x + 10 = 3x + 6$	Simplify.
$4 = x$	Subtraction Property of Equality

11. $2, \dfrac{3}{2}, \dfrac{4}{3}, \dfrac{5}{4}, \dfrac{6}{5}, \dfrac{7}{6}$

13.A. The domain is all integers greater than or equal to 3, since a polygon must have at least 3 sides (and so at least 3 interior angles). The range is all the values a_n for the domain values: 60, 90, 108, 120), and so on. Note that 60 is the smallest range value, and all range values must be less than 180°, since an angle of 180° represents a line. (7,128.6), (8,135), (9,140), (10,144)

  B. $60, 90, 108, 120, 128\frac{5}{7}, 135, 140, 144, 147\frac{3}{11}, 150; 135°$

  C.

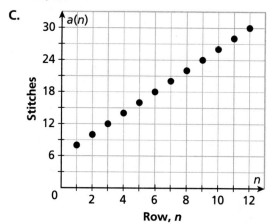

15. $\displaystyle\sum_{k=1}^{6}(k-3)^2 = 4 + 1 + 0 + 1 + 4 + 9 = 19$

17. $\displaystyle\sum_{k=0}^{5}-k^4 = 0 - 1 - 16 - 81 - 156 - 625 = -879$

19. $a(n) = 2n - 1$; it represents the sequence of consecutive positive odd integers

21. $\displaystyle\sum_{k=1}^{6}12k$

23. $\displaystyle\sum_{k=1}^{5}20(-2)^{k-1}$ or $\displaystyle\sum_{k=0}^{4}20(-2)^{k}$

25.A. To get from one term to the next, you add 14, then add 22, then add 30, , so you add 8 more each successive time; 110.

B. 3, 5, 7, 9

C. $a(n) = 2n(2n + 1)$, $n \geq 1$; 272 cans

D. $\sum_{k=1}^{8} 2n(2n + 1) = 6 + 20 + 42 + 72 + 110 + 156 + 210 + 272$; 888 cans

27.A. $\sum_{k=1}^{5} k^3 = 1 + 8 + 27 + 64 + 125 = 225$, and

$\dfrac{n^2(n + 1)^2}{4} = \dfrac{5^2(5 + 1)^2}{4} = \dfrac{25(36)}{4} = 225$, so the formula gives the same number.

B. $\dfrac{1000^2(1000 + 1)^2}{4} = 250{,}500{,}250{,}000$

29. *See below.*

Spiral Review • Assessment Readiness

31. C

33. B

MODULE 13, LESSON 13.2

On Your Own

7.A. 9

B. 2

C. $a(n) = 9 + (n - 1)$

D. domain: natural numbers, range: $\{9, 11, 13, \dots\}$; the domain and range are restricted to domain: $\{1, 2, 3, \dots, 10, 11\}$ and range: $\{9, 11, 13, \dots, 27, 29\}$.

9. The point $(1, 30)$ means the first term is 30, and the difference in consecutive terms for $f(n)$ on the graph is 30. So evaluate the general rule for 72. $a(72) = 30 + (72 - 1)30 = 2160$

11. An arithmetic model is appropriate. The rule for the sequence is $a(n) = -9 + (n - 1)35$. The 2nd term is 26.

13. 1841

15. 1500

17.A. -0.625 feet

B. $a(n) = 125 + (n - 1)(-0.625)$

C. Finite; the sequence ends when she reaches the ground level

D. 0; 201

19. 2696

21. $a(n) = 15 + (n - 1)7$

23.A. $a(n) = 60 + (n - 1)1$

B. $a(14) = 190$

C. 1750 minutes

25.A. arithmetic series

B. $S_n = \sum_{n=1}^{\infty} [2 + 2(n - 1)]$

C. D: natural numbers, R: partial sums 2, 6, 12, 20, 30, 42, 56, 72, …

D. quadratic

E. You must collect 72 objects in order to win the game because the formula for the sum of a series is $S_8 = 8\dfrac{(2 + 16)}{2} = 72$.

27. $30k + 6960$

29.A.
$$\sum_{k=1}^{5} (a_k + b_k) = \sum_{k=1}^{5} (k + k^2)$$
$$= (1 + 1^2) + (2 + 2^2) + (3 + 3^2) + (4 + 4^2) + (5 + 5^2)$$
$$= (1 + 2 + 3 + 4 + 5) + (1^2 + 2^2 + 3^2 + 4^2 + 5^2)$$
$$= \sum_{k=1}^{5} k + \sum_{k=1}^{5} k^2$$
$$= \sum_{k=1}^{5} a_k + \sum_{k=1}^{5} b_k;$$
the Commutative and Associative Properties of Addition

B.
$$\sum_{k=1}^{n} (k + k^2) = \sum_{k=1}^{n} k + \sum_{k=1}^{n} k^2 = \dfrac{n(n + 1)}{2} + \dfrac{n(n + 1)(2n + 1)}{6}$$
$$= \dfrac{3n(n + 1) + n(n + 1)(2n + 1)}{6}$$
$$= \dfrac{n(n + 1)(n + 2)}{3}$$

Spiral Review • Assessment Readiness

29. B

31. A

MODULE 13, LESSON 13.3

On Your Own

9.A. The first term is 12 and the common ratio is 1.05.

B. $a(n) = 12(1.05)^{n-1}$

C. Yes. Eventually the model will make the price of the pizza be too much.

D. D: natural numbers; R: $\{12, 12.6, 13.23, \ldots\}$

E.

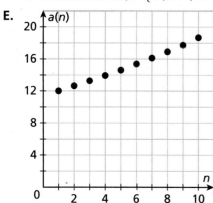

As n increases, the values of $A(n)$ increase without bound.

11. discrete, exponential

13. No: the price increases by 15 cents, so the model will have a common difference—not a common ratio.

15. approximately 0.000839

17. -165875.756

19. 8192

21. -292968750

23. 163,840

25. $S_n = 2^n - 1$

27. 1.428562993

29. -728

31. 43,690

33.A. about 260.8 Hz

B. $a_n \approx 16.3 \cdot (2)^n$

C. C11

35.A. the first term and the common ratio

B. about $135 million

C. $\frac{2}{3}$

D. about $595 million

37.A. geometric series

B. the first term, common ratio, and the number of terms

C. 0.10, 0.30, 0.70, 1.50 or 10 cents, 30 cents, 70 cents, 150 cents

D. $204.80

E. $409.50

Spiral Review • Assessment Readiness

39. D

41. B

MODULE 14, LESSON 14.1

On Your Own

7. 12, 20, 28, 36, 44; yes

9. 2, 4, 16, 256, 65,536; no

11. Possible answer: Because $b(1)$ is 1 greater than $a(1)$ and the common differences of the sequences are the same, it follows that $b(n) = a(n) + 1$ for all $n \geq 1$. So $b(n) > a(n)$ for $n \geq 1$.

13. $a_1 = 2, a_n = a_{n-1} + 1$

15. $f(1) = 5, f(n) = f(n-1) - 2$

17. $a(1) = 9, a(n) = a(n-1) - 11$

19. $a_1 = 3, a_n = a_{n-1} + 2$

21. $a(1) = -7, a(n) = a(n-1) - 1$

23. $a_n = 3 + 6n$

25. $a_1 = -70, a_n = a_{n-1} + 10$

27.A. $15,000; $250

B. $b(0) = 15,000, b(n) = b(n-1) - 250$

C. $b(n) = 15,000 - 250n$

D. $7000

29.A. no; The differences between consecutive terms are not the same.

B. Starting with the 3rd term, each term is the sum of the previous two terms.

C. $f(1) = 1, f(2) = 1, f(n) = f(n-1) + f(n-2)$ for $n > 2$; 55, 89, 144, 233, 377

Spiral Review • Assessment Readiness

31. C

33. D

MODULE 14, LESSON 14.2

On Your Own

9. 9, 18, 36, 72, 144; yes

11. 2, 1, -2, -11, -38; no

13. 256, 384, 576, 864, 1296; yes

15. $a_1 = 5, a_n = 2 \cdot a_{n-1}$

17. $f(1) = 80, f(n) = \frac{1}{2} \cdot f(n-1)$

19. $a(1) = 81, a(n) = \frac{2}{3} \cdot a(n-1)$

21. $a_1 = 20, a_n = \frac{5}{2} \cdot a_{n-1}$

23. $a(1) = 4, a(n) = -5 \cdot a(n-1)$

25. $a_n = 9 \cdot 4^{n-1}$

27. $a_1 = 600, a_n = \frac{3}{4} \cdot a_{n-1}$

29.A. $d(1) = 50, d(n) = 0.9 \cdot d(n-1); d(n) = 50(0.9)^{n-1}$

    B. 8th swing

Spiral Review • Assessment Readiness

33. B, E

35. B

UNIT 7

MODULE 15, LESSON 15.1

On Your Own

5. No. If the first angle is positive then the other angle must be positive and greater than 360 degrees or negative and 360 degrees minus an angle measure less than 90 degrees (for an acute angle) or less than 180 degrees (for an obtuse angle), which results in a negative angle that is greater than 180 degrees.

7. coterminal

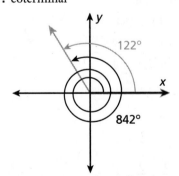

9. coterminal

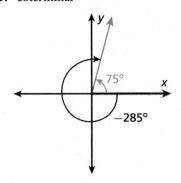

11. coterminal

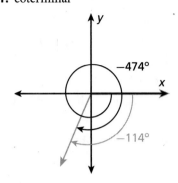

13. Possible answer:

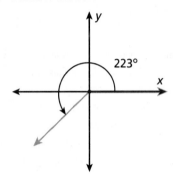

15. Possible answer:

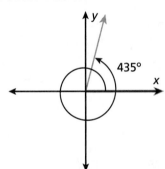

17. 580°, 940°, −140°, −500°

19. The arc length in the circle with the greater radius is twice the arc length in the circle with the smaller radius. Arc length is determined by multiplying the radius by ratio of the central angle to the entire circle. Because the central angle is the same for both arcs, the only thing that changes is the radius.

21. $\frac{3\pi}{2}$

23. $-\frac{\pi}{5}$

25. −405°

27. 144°

29.A. A. $\frac{4\pi}{3} \approx 4.19$ cm

    B. $2\pi \approx 6.28$ cm so, the weight travels about 2.1 cm farther each beat.

    C. decrease; the weight has to travel farther

31.A. $\frac{5\pi}{6}$

   B. $\frac{\pi}{30}$ radians per minute; $\frac{\pi}{360}$ radians per minute

33. $\frac{13{,}263}{24.6} \approx 539.15$ mi

35. 1 radian; 1 radian is equal to $\frac{180°}{\pi} \approx 57.3°$

37. The absolute value of the measure will be greater than 360; the absolute value of the measure will be greater than 2π.

Spiral Review • Assessment Readiness

39. C, F

41. C

MODULE 15, LESSON 15.2

On Your Own

5. In terms of the coordinates on a unit circle, $\sin\theta = y$ and $\cos\theta = x$. The functions are defined as $\sin\theta = \frac{\text{opp}}{\text{hyp}}$ and $\cos\theta = \frac{\text{adj}}{\text{hyp}}$. In a unit circle, the hypotenuse is 1 and the opposite side gives the y-coordinate and the adjacent side gives the x-coordinate.

7.

Angle of rotation, θ	36.9°	143.1°	216.9°	323.1°
$\sin\theta$	3/5	3/5	−3/5	−3/5
$\cos\theta$	4/5	−4/5	−4/5	4/5
$\tan\theta$	3/4	−3/4	3/4	−3/4

9. +

11. −

13. −

15. III

17. $\sin\theta = \frac{24}{25}$, $\cos\theta = \frac{7}{25}$, $\tan\theta = \frac{24}{7}$

19. $\sin\theta = \frac{5}{13}$, $\cos\theta = -\frac{12}{13}$, $\tan\theta = -\frac{5}{12}$

21. Assume θ is in Quadrant I. Then $-\theta$ will be in Quadrant IV. Assume a circle is centered on the origin and passes through the terminal side of both angles. The point of intersection of the terminal side of the angles and the circle will have the same x-value for both θ and $-\theta$. The radius of the circle is also constant so $\cos\theta$ and $\cos(-\theta)$ will have the same value. If θ is in Quadrant IV, then $-\theta$ is in Quadrant I, and the same reasoning holds. The same pairings work for Quadrants II and III.

23. 0.342

25. −0.174

27. −0.809

29.A. sine; I know the angle and the opposite side of each of the right triangles formed. I need to find the

hypotenuse. Sine is the trigonometric function that relates the opposite side to the hypotenuse.

   B. about 37 ft

Spiral Review • Assessment Readiness

33. B

MODULE 15, LESSON 15.3

On Your Own

5.

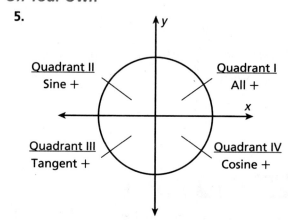

7. −0.939

9. 0.118

11. 0.999

13. −0.764

15. −0.227

17. 0.390

19. −0.945

21. $\sin\theta \approx 0.920$, $\cos\theta \approx 0.392$

23. $\sin\theta \approx -0.998$, $\cos\theta \approx 0.154$

25. $\sin\theta \approx -0.992$, $\cos\theta \approx -0.124$

27. $\sin\theta \approx -0.842$, $\cos\theta \approx 0.540$

29.
$$\sin^2\theta + \cos^2\theta \overset{?}{=} 1$$
$$\sin^2\left(-\frac{3\pi}{4}\right) + \cos^2\left(-\frac{3\pi}{4}\right) \overset{?}{=} 1$$
$$\left(-\frac{\sqrt{2}}{2}\right)^2 + \left(-\frac{\sqrt{2}}{2}\right)^2 \overset{?}{=} 1$$
$$\frac{2}{4} + \frac{2}{4} \overset{?}{=} 1$$
$$1 = 1$$

31.
$$\sin^2\theta + \cos^2\theta \overset{?}{=} 1$$
$$\sin^2\frac{\pi}{4} + \cos^2\frac{\pi}{4} \overset{?}{=} 1$$
$$\left(\frac{\sqrt{2}}{2}\right)^2 + \left(\frac{\sqrt{2}}{2}\right)^2 \overset{?}{=} 1$$
$$\frac{2}{4} + \frac{2}{4} \overset{?}{=} 1$$
$$1 = 1$$

33. 0.840

35. Possible answer: For both $\sin\theta$ and $\cos\theta$, the values are the same with the exception of the signs which are appropriate for each quadrant; the value of $\sin^2\theta + \cos^2\theta$ is approximately 1 for each angle measure.

θ	$\sin\theta$	$\cos\theta$	$\sin^2\theta + \cos^2\theta$
40°	0.643	0.766	1.000
140°	0.643	−0.766	1.000
220°	−0.643	−0.766	1.000
320°	−0.643	0.766	1.000

Spiral Review • Assessment Readiness

37. B

39. A

MODULE 16, LESSON 16.1

On Your Own

7. False. $\sin x < \cos x$ for $\left[0 \pm 2\pi n, \frac{\pi}{2} \pm 2\pi n\right)$ and $\left(\frac{3\pi}{2} \pm 2\pi n, 2\pi n\right]$

9. False. The graph of $f(x) = \sin x$ repeats on each interval of 2π

11. one revolution of the unit circle from 0 to 2π

13. Possible answer: The x coordinate of the point where the terminal ray intersects the unit circle represents the value of cosine of the given angle. Multiplying the given angle by a factor of 4 will produce a terminal angle that is 4 times the original.

15. a rotation of 180 degrees; this supports the fact that sine is an odd function, so $f(-\theta) = -f(\theta)$.

17. vertical stretch: $a = 2$; $b = 1$

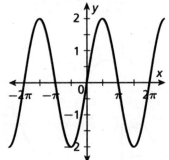

Amplitude: 2; Period: 2π

19. $a = 1$; horizontal stretch: $b = 5$

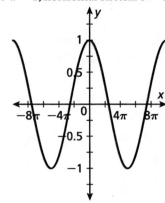

Amplitude: 1; Period: 10π

21. $y = \sin 3\pi x$

23. $y = -2\cos\left(\frac{1}{3}x\right)$

25. $v = 2.25\cos\left(\frac{\pi}{3}t\right)$

27.A. $v(t) = -10\cos(\pi t)$

B. amplitude: 10; period: 2

C.

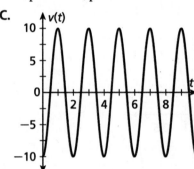

D. $(0, -10)$, $(2.5, 0)$, and $(5, 0)$; The point $(0, -10)$ is at a minimum on the graph and represents when the mass is at its lowest position. The point $(2.5, 0)$ represents a time that the mass is at the equilibrium position as it goes from its lowest position to its highest position. The point $(5, 0)$ is at a maximum on the graph and represents a time when the mass is at its highest position.

Spiral Review • Assessment Readiness

29. A

31. B

Selected Answers

MODULE 16, LESSON 16.2

On Your Own

7. All three functions have one y-intercept. The tangent function and sine function have the y-intercept 0 whereas the cosine function has the y-intercept 1.

9. To find the period, multiply the value of b and π. To find the asymptotes, multiply b and $-\frac{\pi}{2}$ and multiply b and $\frac{\pi}{2}$. The asymptotes are at $x = \frac{-b\pi}{2}$ and $x = \frac{b\pi}{2}$.

11.

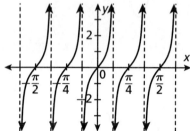

13.

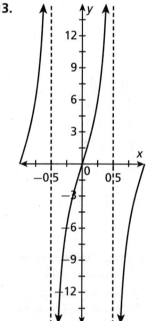

15. The absolute value of a is less than 1; nothing about b

17. $f(x) = 2\tan\left(\frac{\pi x}{4}\right)$

19.A. $h = 2w\tan\left(\frac{a}{2}\right)$

B. The values of a must be such that $0 < a < 180$ because a is an angle of a triangle and so must have a measure of less than a straight angle or 180 degrees. The structure of the lens may impose even more limitations on the values of a, but there is not enough information in the diagram to determine what those may be.

C.

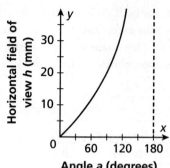

21. The important reference points and asymptotes of the tangent function occur at recognizable points in the sine and cosine graphs. The asymptotes of the graph of $y = \tan x$ occur at the x-intercepts of the graph of $y = \cos x$, and the x-intercepts of the graph of $y = \tan x$ are the same as those of the graph of $y = \sin x$. The intervals where the graph of $y = \tan x$ is above the x-axis correspond to the intervals where the sine and cosine graphs are on the same side of the x-axis, and the intervals where the graph of $y = \tan x$ is below the x-axis correspond to the intervals where the sine and cosine graphs are on opposite sides of the x-axis.

Spiral Review • Assessment Readiness

23. B

25. A

MODULE 16, LESSON 16.3

On Your Own

7. You can add 2π to each x-coordinate and subtract 4 from each y-coordinate.

9. $f(x) = 4\sin 2x - 1$

11.

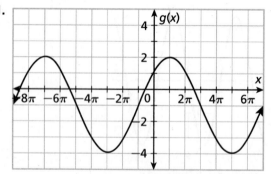

© Houghton Mifflin Harcourt Publishing Company

13.

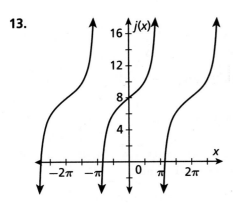

15. $|a| + k$. The maximum value for the parent cosine function is $|a|$. The parameter k translates the maximum point k units vertically.

17. $f(x) = -2\tan\frac{1}{2}x + 4$

19. Yes. The cosine function rule would have the sine parameters as the sine function except h would be different. You can rewrite a sine function using a phase shift as a cosine function.

21. It is a periodic function.

23. Possible answer: $f(x) = 5\cos\left(x - \frac{3\pi}{4}\right) - 3$, $f(x) = 5\cos\left(x - \frac{11\pi}{4}\right) - 3$

25. Possible answer: $1\sin\left(2\left(x + \frac{3}{2}\pi\right)\right) + 5$ and $1\cos\left(2\left(x + \frac{4}{2}\pi\right)\right) + 5$

Spiral Review • Assessment Readiness

27. C

29. B

MODULE 16, LESSON 16.4

On Your Own

5. No. When the data points are graphed on a coordinate plane, the data is scattered and does not show a wave-like pattern. So a sine function model would not be a good fit for this data.

7. $y = 22.31\sin 0.57(x - 26.54) + 66.62$

9. The value of R^2 is close to 1, so the regression model is a good fit for the data.

11. $y = 21\sin\frac{\pi}{6}(x - 4) + 71$

13. Possible answer: no; The graph of the model for the daily high temperature of Memphis is exactly 3.5 degrees higher than the graph of the model for the daily high temperature of Denver, so the graphs do not intersect. There is no time when the daily high temperatures are the same.

15. $y = -0.08\sin\left(\frac{1}{2.05}(x - 9.602)\right) + 0.11$

17. It is 0.8295, so the regression model is not a very good

Spiral Review • Assessment Readiness

19. A

21. C

UNIT 8

MODULE 17, LESSON 17.1

On Your Own

5. You can find the probability of an event by first finding the probability of the event's complement and then subtracting the probability of the complement from 1.

7.A. $\frac{21}{40}$

   B. $\frac{3}{40}$

   C. $\frac{3}{5}$

   D. $\frac{19}{40}$

   E. $\frac{37}{40}$

   F. $\frac{19}{40}$

9.A. $\frac{4}{25}$

   B. $\frac{7}{10}$

   C. $\frac{2}{5}$

   D. the movies from the studio that were profitable but did not win a major award; $\frac{11}{25}$

11. Possible answer: spinning a number less than 5

13. yes; On a number cube, there are three prime numbers $(2, 3, \text{and } 5)$ and three numbers that are not prime $(1, 4, \text{and } 6)$. So, Ben and Pete each have a probability of $\frac{3}{6}$, or $\frac{1}{2}$, of getting to choose the restaurant. Since their probabilities are the same, the process will lead to a fair decision.

Spiral Review • Assessment Readiness

15. C

17. D

MODULE 17, LESSON 17.2

On Your Own

7. $m \cdot n$ joint relative frequencies; $m + n$ marginal relative frequencies

9.

		Took Public Transit		
		Yes	**No**	**Total**
Live in City	**Yes**	125	65	190
	No	40	270	310
	Total	165	335	500

11. 0.25; joint relative frequency

13. 0.67; marginal relative frequency

15. no; Possible explanation: There are many two-way frequency tables that produce a given two-way relative frequency table. For example, if Table A is a two-way frequency table that produces the given two-way relative frequency table, then Table B formed by doubling all the frequencies in Table A will produce the same two-way relative frequency table, since the ratio of each frequency to the total is the same in Table A and Table B.

17. *See below.*

19. 38.0%

Spiral Review • Assessment Readiness

21. B

23. A

MODULE 17, LESSON 17.3

On Your Own

5. If there is a 0 in a cell in the frequency table, then the column and row for that cell represent mutually exclusive events.

7. $\frac{5}{8}$; mutually exclusive

9. $\frac{2}{8} = \frac{1}{4}$; mutually exclusive

11. $\frac{5}{8}$; inclusive

13. $\frac{7}{8}$; inclusive

15. $\frac{2}{8} = \frac{1}{4}$; mutually exclusive

17.a. inclusive

  b. Possible answer: Add the number of students who took chemistry to the number of juniors who took any of the science classes, and subtract the number of juniors who took chemistry.

  c. $\frac{185}{360} = \frac{37}{72}$

19. $\frac{8}{12} = \frac{2}{3}$; inclusive

21. $\frac{8}{12} = \frac{2}{3}$; mutually exclusive

23. $\frac{5}{12}$; mutually exclusive

25. $\frac{3}{12} = \frac{1}{4}$; mutually exclusive

27. $\frac{10}{12} = \frac{5}{6}$; inclusive

29. $\frac{9}{20} = 0.45$

31. $\frac{13}{20} = 0.65$

33.

	B	**B^c**	**Total**
A	0	7	7
A^c	2	11	13
Total	2	18	20

35. $\frac{14}{20} = 0.7$

37. $\frac{16}{20} = 0.8$

39. $\frac{6}{20} = 0.3$

17.

		Type of School			
		Public non-charter	**Public charter**	**Private**	**Total**
Grade Level	**Elementary**	26.6%	5.0%	6.4%	38.0%
	Middle school	23.2%	3.5%	5.3%	32.0%
	High school	16.2%	5.5%	8.3%	30.0%
	Total	66.0%	14.0%	20.0%	100%

41.

	B	Bᶜ	Total
A	0.15	0.2	0.35
Aᶜ	0.35	0.3	0.65
Total	0.5	0.5	1

43. $\frac{34}{50} = 0.68$

45. $\frac{43}{50} = 0.86$

47.a. inclusive

b. $\frac{48}{100} = 0.48$

49.a. mutually exclusive

b. $\frac{88}{100} = 0.88$

51.a. inclusive

b. $\frac{44}{100} = 0.44$

53. $\frac{5}{6}$

Spiral Review • Assessment Readiness

55. B

57A. 3; **B.** 4; **C.** 2; **D.** 1

MODULE 18, LESSON 18.1

On Your Own

5. $\frac{139}{188} \approx 74\%$

7. $\frac{49}{85} \approx 58\%$

9. $\frac{32}{92} \approx 35\%$

11. $\frac{0.28}{0.42} \approx 62\%$

13. The student used the P(likes roller coaster rides) instead of P(roller coaster operator) as the denominator. The correct probability is $\frac{0.45}{0.55} \approx 82\%$

15. Possible answer: The event that I practice my musical instrument at home increases the likelihood of the event that I play through a song in class without error.

17. $\frac{\frac{3}{52}}{\frac{12}{52}} = 25\%$

19.

	Prefers pizza	Prefers a sub	Total
Juniors	98	64	162
Seniors	105	41	146
Total	203	105	308

	Prefers pizza	Prefers a sub	Total
Juniors	32%	21%	53%
Seniors	34%	13%	47%
Total	66%	34%	100%

21. $\approx 39\%$

23. $\frac{\frac{1}{6}}{\frac{3}{6}} \approx 33\%$

25.

	Soccer	No soccer	Total
Science	63	501	564
No science	21	167	188
Total	84	668	752

	Soccer	No soccer	Total
Science	0.08	0.67	0.75
No science	0.03	0.22	0.25
Total	0.11	0.89	1.00

27. $\approx 89\%$

Spiral Review • Assessment Readiness

29. A

31. D

MODULE 18, LESSON 18.2

On Your Own

5. Drawing, replacing, and drawing again gives independent events, because the sample space is restored to its original state after the first item is returned. Drawing a second without replacing the first gives dependent events, because removing the first item changes the sample space, and thus the probability of the next draw.

7.A. It is the same as the relative frequency of the cell where the column for "Listen" and the row for "Junior" intersect; P(junior ∩ listen) = 0.33.

B. P(junior) is the relative frequency of the row for "Junior", and P(listen) is the relative frequency of the column for "Listen"; P(junior) = 0.55, and P(listen) = 0.60.

C. $P(\text{junior}) \cdot P(\text{listen}) = 0.55 \cdot 0.60 = 0.33$; The events are independent because this is equal to $P(\text{junior} \cap \text{listen})$.

D. Whether or not a person is a junior does not affect the likelihood that the person listens to country music, and whether or not a person listens to country music does not affect the likelihood that the person is a junior.

9. $\dfrac{1}{210}$

11. $\dfrac{1}{221}$

13. $\dfrac{105}{221}$

15.A. $P(B) = \dfrac{6}{36} = \dfrac{1}{6}$; $P(B \mid A) = \dfrac{1}{6}$;
$P(A \cap B) = P(B) \cdot P(B \mid A) = \dfrac{1}{6} \cdot \dfrac{1}{6} = \dfrac{1}{36}$

B. Independent; because $P(B)$ and $P(B \mid A)$ are equal, the events are independent. This is because whether or not A has occurred does not affect the probability of B.

Spiral Review • Assessment Readiness

17. A

19. B

MODULE 18, LESSON 18.3

On Your Own

3.A. top row: 0.0098; middle row: 0.093; bottom row: 0.1532, 0.8468

B. about 39.3%

C. about 98.8%

D. No; only about 40% of those who tested positive actually have the disease, so I wouldn't want to put all of these animals at risk. Possible answer: I would try to find another test that was more reliable for positive results, and retest the goats who tested positive the first time.

5.A. that rain is predicted and it rains, and that rain is predicted and it doesn't rain

B. about 41.4%; no; it is still more likely than not that it won't rain the day of the festival.

C. A forecast of no rain; a forecast of rain is about 41% reliable, while a forecast of no rain is about 99.6% reliable.

7.A.

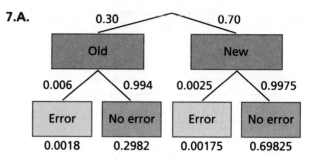

B. about 50.7%

C. No; it is almost equally likely that the defect was caused by either machine.

9.A. parks yes and health yes: 16%; parks yes and health no: 26%; parks no and health yes: 37%: parks no and health no: 21%

B. $P(\text{parks yes} \mid \text{health yes}) \approx 0.301$;
$P(\text{parks no} \mid \text{health no}) \approx 0.445$

C. $P(\text{parks no} \mid \text{health yes}) \approx 0.699$; it tells you that given that a person voted for one proposal, they most likely voted against the other.

D. Yes; $P(\text{health yes}) = 0.1596 + 0.3712 = 0.5308$.

Spiral Review • Assessment Readiness

11. C

13. D

MODULE 19, LESSON 19.1

On Your Own

7.A. 1, 8, 28, 56, 70, 56, 28, 8, 1

B. ${}_8C_0, {}_8C_1, {}_8C_2, {}_8C_3, {}_8C_4, {}_8C_5, {}_8C_6, {}_8C_7, {}_8C_8$

9. Yes. The sums are all powers of 2, which is more specific than just multiples of 2

11. 0.109; 0.145

13. 0.230; 0.317

15. 0.258; 0.436

17. 0.194; 0.279

19. The histogram would look similar but with the most likely results different. For moving forward, the most likely results should be equal at 12 and 13 and decreasing below 12 and above 13. For landing on points, the most likely results should be at 4.

21. 0.09882966589; about 9.88%

23. 0.02100835638; about 2.1%

25. B

27. D

MODULE 19, LESSON 19.2
On Your Own

5. Both should approximate the normal distribution curve, but the increased number of bars in the histogram for 120 rolls will make that histogram look more like a curve.

7. 0.997

9. 0.975

11. 95%

13. 49.85%

15. 72.57%

17. 34.46%

19. 84.13%

21. 0.2525

23.A. 0.7518

   B. 0.9997

   C. Possible answer: The standard deviation for 1000 trials is much bigger than for 100 trials, but as a percent of the mean, the standard deviation decreases. This interval represents similar error from the mean (a difference of 20% above or below). The greater number of trials makes it far more likely that the mean is within this range.

25. 0.3694

27. 9.56%

29.A. 0.1587

   B. 0.2358

   C. 5.48%

   D. 24.78%

31. 0.1705

33. 0.1465

35.A. mean 5.6, s.d. 2.3; mean 3.8, s.d. 2.5

   B. 0 or 1; 4; 12; 16; 23 or 24

   C. 0, 6, 12, 18, 24; 0, 5, 13, 20, 22

   D. Neither experiment seems to be normally distributed.

Spiral Review • Assessment Readiness

37. C

39. A, E, F

MODULE 19, LESSON 19.3
On Your Own

5. statistics to estimate parameters; A statistic is a number that summarizes data from a sample of a population. A parameter is a number that summarizes data from a population. A statistic for a sample can be used to draw conclusions about the same parameter for the population

7. all fans of a minor league hockey team; systematic sample

9.A. all residents of the community served by the school system

   B. Method B is more likely to result in a representative sample because it is a simple random sample. Method A is a convenience sample, which is more likely to include those individuals who are either strong supporters or strong opponents of the new school.

   C. Possible answer: a stratified sample formed by selecting 10 random adults who live in each of the 5 neighborhoods in the community that are served by the school system

   D. categorical data: whether or not people support the construction of a new school; numerical data: the increase in property tax people are willing to pay to support the construction

11. Possible answer: A cluster sample may be quicker to survey, and it can be as representative of likely voters as a simple random sample if the people are randomly chosen from communities which are representative of the whole state. Surveying individuals from many different communities might be more time consuming, especially if the surveys are completed in person.

13. Answers will vary.

Spiral Review • Assessment Readiness

15. C

17. C

MODULE 19, LESSON 19.4
On Your Own

5. 20.2 to 22

7. 0.137 or 13.7%

9.A. 0.0015 in

   B. 10.997 in to 11.003 in

   C. 0.0912 or 9.12%

   D. 0.248 or 24.8%

Selected Answers

11. 26.25% to 55.75%

13. A sample of 0.42 falls within one standard deviation of the sampling proportion.

15. The smallest sample is 20 because when $n = 20$ and $p = 0.5$, then $np = n(1 - p) = 10$.

Spiral Review • Assessment Readiness

17. D

MODULE 20, LESSON 20.1

On Your Own

5. Max's prediction is possible but unlikely. If Max is correct and the population proportion of voters who support him is $p = 0.55$, then reasonably likely values of the sample proportion $\hat{p}$ should fall within

2 standard deviations of 0.55.

Since $\sigma_{\hat{p}} = \sqrt{\frac{p(1-p)}{n}} = \sqrt{\frac{0.55(1 - 0.55)}{400}} \approx 0.025$, reasonably likely values of $\hat{p}$ fall in the interval $0.55 - 2(0.025) \leq \hat{p} \leq 0.55 + 2(0.025)$, or $0.5 \leq \hat{p} \leq 0.6$. The pollster's sample proportion of $\hat{p} = 0.48$ falls outside this interval, so Max's prediction will probably be wrong assuming voter attitudes don't change between now and the election.

7. $0.52 \leq p \leq 0.68$

9. $0.42 \leq p \leq 0.58$

11. no; Any population proportion $p > 0.5$ is outside both the 95% and 99% confidence intervals, so it is unlikely that a majority of residents are interested in seeing monthly musicals.

13. $115.4 \leq \mu \leq 124.6$

15.A. $7.07 \leq \mu \leq 7.63$

 B. $6.87 \leq \mu \leq 7.47$

 C. no; The confidence intervals for the two locations overlap between 7.07 and 7.47, which is a significant portion of each confidence interval.

17. $n = 2654$

19. $n = 31$

21. $7.33 \leq \mu \leq 7.67$; 0.17 hour

23. $0.70 \leq p \leq 0.82$

25. $n = 438$ students

Spiral Review • Assessment Readiness

27. D

29. A

MODULE 20, LESSON 20.2

On Your Own

5. A survey measures only a characteristic of interest. An observational study measures an association between a factor and a characteristic of interest

7. A researcher conducting an experiment is looking at whether one variable has an effect on another variable.

9. A survey. A survey measures a characteristic of interest. The question on the survey would ask, "Do you exercise over the weekend?" The sample population would be randomly selected high school students.

11. A factor in an observational study already exists and is used to determine if there is an association between a factor and a characteristic of interest. A treatment in an experiment is introduced to the subjects in the treatment group to determine if the treatment has an effect on the characteristic of interest.

13. Because of the length of time involved in the survey, they pollsters may have many nonresponses. Instead, ask a yes or no question that can be answered immediately on the spot, such as "Do you read magazines?"

15. This survey has problems both because of interviewer effect and biased question. The interviewer is the principal, so students may feel they could get in trouble for complaining about teachers. The question is biased because it implies that students will have problems with teachers. Instead have a school aide ask the students, "Under what circumstances do you learn the best, and under what circumstances do you struggle to learn in the classroom?"

17. Possible answer: It could be because of time constraints or perhaps they wanted to introduce sleep that was not usually part of the subjects' routine.

19. Possible answer: An observational study might not change any of the patterns of sleep, but instead have the subjects record when they took a nap and when they performed creative activities.

21. This was an experiment. The characteristic of interest is work productivity that involves performing at a desk. It was measured by the number of successful calls completed in a month. The article describes all the components of an experiment, but does not state that subjects were.

23. Answers will vary.

25. B

27. C

MODULE 20, LESSON 20.3

On Your Own

5. It means that the difference in the means of the treatment and control groups is large enough given the sample size so that the difference is quite unlikely to have occurred by random variation. In this case, an alternative hypothesis that the treatment is responsible for the difference can be accepted.

7. The average yield of the control and treatment groups should be about the same.

9.A. The difference in the mean test scores will be 0.

B. $\bar{x}_T = 84.9$, $\bar{x}_C = 79.9$, $\bar{x}_T - \bar{x}_C = 5.0$

C. Answers will vary.

D. Possible answer: $P = \dfrac{4}{50} \approx 0.08$

E. Since $0.05 < P \leq 0.1$, the result is marginally significant. So, you can reject the null hypothesis only at the 10% level. Note that because of the small number of resamplings, the researcher should be even more cautious about concluding that teaching the strategies is effective.

11.A. The average pain improvement in the treatment and control groups will be about the same.

B. The control group is the patients who only walk, and the treatment group is the patients who both walk and perform the stretches; $\bar{x}_T - \bar{x}_C = 0.89$.

C. $-0.88 \leq x \leq 0.88$

D. yes; The difference of the mean average pain scale improvement falls just outside the middle 95% of the data. So, the improvement in pain is significant at the 5% level.

13. D

15. B

A

English	Spanish	Examples
absolute (or global) maximum A function value that is the greatest value for all domain values. An absolute maximum is also a local maximum among all nearby points.	**máximo absoluto (o global)** Valor de una función que es el valor mayor para todos los valores del dominio. Un máximo absoluto es también un máximo local entre todos los puntos cercanos.	
absolute (or global) minimum A function value that is the least value for all domain values. An absolute minimum is also a local minimum among all nearby points.	**mínimo absoluto (o global)** Valor de una función que es el valor menor para todos los valores del dominio. Un mínimo absoluto es también un mínimo local entre todos los puntos cercanos.	
absolute value The absolute value of x is the distance from zero to x on a number line, denoted $\lvert x \rvert$. $$\lvert x \rvert = \begin{cases} x & \text{if } x \geq 0 \\ -x & \text{if } x < 0 \end{cases}$$	**valor absoluto** El valor absoluto de x es la distancia desde cero hasta x en una recta numérica y se expresa $\lvert x \rvert$. $$\lvert x \rvert = \begin{cases} x & \text{si } x \geq 0 \\ -x & \text{si } x < 0 \end{cases}$$	$\lvert 3 \rvert = 3$ $\lvert -3 \rvert = 3$
absolute value function A function whose rule contains algebraic expressions within absolute value bars.	**función de valor absoluto** Función cuya regla contiene expresiones algebraicas dentro de barras de valor absoluto.	
alternative hypothesis In contrast to the null hypothesis, the hypothesis that a difference between the control group and treatment group is due in significant part to the treatment.	**hipótesis alternativa** A diferencia de la hipótesis nula, esta es la hipótesis de que una diferencia entre el grupo de control y el grupo de tratamiento se debe en gran parte al tratamiento.	
amplitude The amplitude of a periodic function is half the difference of the maximum and minimum values (always positive).	**amplitud** La amplitud de una función periódica es la mitad de la diferencia entre los valores máximo y mínimo (la amplitud siempre es positiva).	$\text{amplitude} = \frac{1}{2}[3 - (-3)] = 3$

Glossary/Glosario

English	Spanish	Examples
angle of rotation An angle formed by rotating a ray about its endpoint from the initial side of the angle to the terminal side of the angle. The initial side of an angle of rotation in standard position is on the positive x-axis.	**ángulo de rotación** Ángulo formado al girar un rayo sobre su extremo desde el lado inicial del ángulo hasta su lado terminal. El lado inicial de un ángulo de rotación en posición estándar se ubica en el eje x positivo.	
arithmetic sequence A sequence whose successive terms differ by the same number d, called the *common difference*.	**sucesión aritmética** Sucesión cuyos términos sucesivos difieren en el mismo número d, denominado *diferencia común*.	
arithmetic series The indicated sum of the terms of an arithmetic sequence.	**serie aritmética** Suma indicada de los términos de una sucesión aritmética.	$4 + 7 + 10 + 13 + \ldots + 55 + 58$
asymptote A line that a graph approaches as the value of x increases or decreases without bound.	**asíntota** Recta a la cual se aproxima una gráfica a medida que el valor de x aumenta o disminuye sin límites.	
average rate of change The average rate of change of a function f over an interval $[a, b]$ is the ratio of the change in the function values, $f(b) - f(a)$, to the change in the x-values, $b - a$.	**tasa de cambio promedio** La tasa de cambio promedio de una función f en un intérvalo $[a, b]$ es la razón entre el cambio de los valores de la función, $f(b) - f(a)$, y el cambio de los valores de x, $b - a$.	
axis of symmetry A line that divides a plane figure or a graph into two congruent reflected halves.	**eje de simetría** Línea que divide una figura plana o una gráfica en dos mitades reflejadas congruentes.	

B

English	Spanish	Examples
biased sample A sample that does not fairly represent the population.	**muestra sesgada** Muestra que no representa imparcialmente una población.	
binomial A polynomial with two terms.	**binomio** Polinomio con dos términos.	$x + y$ $2a^2 + 3$ $4m^3n^2 + 6mn^4$

English	Spanish	Examples
binomial experiment A probability experiment consisting of n identical and independent trials whose outcomes are either successes or failures, with a constant probability of success p and a constant probability of failure q, where $q = 1 - p$ or $p + q = 1$.	**experimento binomial** Experimento de probabilidades que comprende n pruebas idénticas e independientes cuyos resultados son éxitos o fracasos, con una probabilidad constante de éxito p y una probabilidad constante de fracaso q, donde $q = 1 - p$ o $p + q = 1$.	A multiple-choice quiz has 10 questions with 4 answer choices. The number of trials is 10. If each question is answered randomly, the probability of success for each trial is $\frac{1}{4} = 0.25$ and the probability of failure is $\frac{3}{4} = 0.75$.
binomial probability In a binomial experiment, the probability of r successes $\left(0 \le r \le n\right)$ is $P(r) = {}_nC_r \cdot p^r \, q^{n-r}$.	**probabilidad binomial** En un experimento binomial, la probabilidad de r éxitos $\left(0 \le r \le n\right)$ es $P(r) = {}_nC_r \cdot p^r \, q^{n-r}$.	In the binomial experiment above, the probability of randomly guessing 6 answers correctly is $P = {}_{10}C_6 \left(0.25\right)^6 \left(0.75\right)^4 \approx 0.016$.
binomial probability distribution The distribution that represents the probabilities of all possibilities in a binomial experiment.	**distribución de probabilidad binomial** Distribución que representa las probabilidades de todas las posibilidades en un experimento binomial.	

C

English	Spanish	Examples
categorical data Data that represent observations or attributes that can be sorted into groups or categories.	**datos categóricos** Datos que representan observaciones o atributos que pueden ser clasificados en grupos o categorías.	color, preferences, educational level, gender, blood type, types of music
census A survey of an entire population.	**censo** Estudio de una población entera.	
closure A set of numbers is said to be closed, or to have closure, under a given operation if the result of the operation on any two numbers in the set is also in the set.	**cerradura** Se dice que un conjunto de números es cerrado, o tiene cerradura, respecto de una operación determinada, si el resultado de la operación entre dos números cualesquiera del conjunto también está en el conjunto.	The natural numbers are closed under addition because the sum of two natural numbers is always a natural number.
common difference In an arithmetic sequence, the constant difference of any term after the first and the previous term.	**diferencia común** En una sucesión aritmética, diferencia constante entre cualquier término posterior al primero y el término anterior.	In the arithmetic sequence 3, 5, 7, 9, 11, ..., the common difference is 2.
common logarithm A logarithm whose base is 10, denoted $\log_{10}$ or just log.	**logaritmo común** Logaritmo de base 10, que se expresa $\log_{10}$ o simplemente log.	$\log 100 = \log_{10} 100 = 2$, since $10^2 = 100$.
common ratio In a geometric sequence, the constant ratio of any term after the first and the previous term.	**razón común** En una sucesión geométrica, la razón constante r entre cualquier término posterior al primero y el término anterior.	In the geometric sequence 32, 16, 18, 4, 2, ..., the common ratio is $\frac{1}{2}$.

English	Spanish	Examples
complement of an event All outcomes in the sample space that are not in an event A, denoted A^c.	**complemento de un suceso** Todos los resultados en el espacio muestral que no están en el suceso A, expresados como A^C.	In the experiment of rolling a number cube, the complement of rolling a 3 is rolling a 1, 2, 4, 5, or 6.
completing the square A process used to form a perfect-square trinomial. To complete the square for $x^2 + bx$, add $\left(\frac{b}{2}\right)^2$.	**completar el cuadrado** Proceso utilizado para formar un trinomio cuadrado perfecto. Para completar el cuadrado para $x^2 + bx$, hay que sumar $\left(\frac{b}{2}\right)^2$.	$x^2 + 6x +$ ■ Add $\left(\frac{6}{2}\right)^2 = 9$. $x^2 + 6x + 9$ $(x + 3)^2$ is a perfect square.
complex conjugate The complex conjugate of any complex number $a + bi$, denoted $\overline{a + bi}$, is $a - bi$. When a polynomial equation has complex roots, these roots come as pairs of complex conjugates.	**conjugado complejo** El conjugado complejo de cualquier número complejo $a + bi$, expresado como $\overline{a + bi}$, es $a - bi$. Cuando una ecuación polinómica tiene raíces complejas, estas raíces vienen en pares de conjugados complejos.	$\overline{4 + 3i} = 4 - 3i$ $\overline{4 - 3i} = 4 + 3i$
complex fraction A fraction that contains one or more fractions in the numerator, the denominator, or both.	**fracción compleja** Fracción que contiene una o más fracciones en el numerador, en el denominador, o en ambos.	$\dfrac{\frac{1}{2}}{1 + \frac{2}{3}}$
complex number Any number that can be written as $a + bi$, where a and b are real numbers and $i = \sqrt{-1}$.	**número complejo** Todo número que se puede expresar como $a + bi$, donde a y b son números reales e $i = \sqrt{-1}$.	$4 + 2i$ $5 + 0i = 5$ $0 - 7i = -7i$
composition of functions The composition of functions f and g, written as $(f \circ g)(x)$ and defined as $f(g(x))$, uses the output of $g(x)$ as the input for $f(x)$.	**composición de funciones** La composición de las funciones f y g, expresada como $(f \circ g)(x)$ y definida como $f(g(x))$, utiliza la salida de $g(x)$ como la entrada para $f(x)$.	If $f(x) = x^2$ and $g(x) = x + 1$, the composite function $(f \circ g)(x) = (x + 1)^2$.
compound interest Interest earned or paid on both the principal and previously earned interest, found using the formula $A(t) = P\left(1 + \frac{r}{n}\right)^{nt}$ where A is the final amount, P is the principal, r is the interest rate given as a decimal, n is the number of times interest is compounded, and t is the time.	**interés compuesto** Interés acumulado o pagado tanto sobre el capital inicial como sobre el interés previamente ganado. Se halla usando la fórmula $A(t) = P\left(1 + \frac{r}{n}\right)^{nt}$, donde A es la cantidad final, P es el capital inicial, r es la tasa de interés indicada en forma de número decimal, n es el número de veces que se reinvierte el interés y t es el tiempo.	

English	Spanish	Examples
compression of a graph A transformation that pushes the points of a graph horizontally toward the y-axis or vertically toward the x-axis. For a horizontal compression, any point on the y-axis remains unchanged. For a vertical compression, any point on the x-axis remains unchanged.	**compresión de una gráfica** Transformación que desplaza los puntos de una gráfica horizontalmente hacia el eje y o verticalmente hacia el eje x. Dada una compresión horizontal, todo punto en el eje y permanece sin cambios. Dada una compresión vertical, todo punto en el eje x permanece sin cambios.	Vertical compression
conditional probability The probability of event B, given that event A has already occurred or is certain to occur, denoted $P(B \mid A)$; used to find the probability of dependent events.	**probabilidad condicional** Probabilidad del suceso B, dado que el suceso A ya ha ocurrido o es seguro que ocurrirá, expresada como $P(B \mid A)$; se utiliza para calcular la probabilidad de sucesos dependientes.	
confidence interval An approximate range of values, determined from a sample parameter, for which there is a specified probability of including an unknown population parameter.	**intervalo de confianza** Rango aproximado de valores, determinado a partir de un parámetro de muestra, para el que hay una probabilidad especificada de incluir un parámetro de población desconocido.	
constant of variation *See* inverse variation.	**constante de variación** *Ver* variación inversa.	
continuous function on an interval A function whose graph on an interval of the x-axis is connected, with no gaps or breaks.	**función continua de un intervalo** Función cuya gráfica se encuentra sobre un intervalo del eje x y que está conectada sin espacios ni interrupciones.	
control group *See* randomized comparative experiment.	**grupo de control** *Ver* experimento comparativo aleatorizado.	
cosine function For an angle of rotation θ in standard position, the function defined by $\cos\theta = x$, where x is the x-coordinate of the point $P(x, y)$ at which the terminal side of θ intersects the unit circle.	**función coseno** Dado un ángulo de rotación θ en posición estándar, la función definida por $\cos\theta = x$, donde x es la coordenada x del punto $P(x, y)$ en el que el lado terminal de θ corta el círculo unitario.	$\cos\theta = x$
coterminal angles Two angles in standard position with the same terminal side.	**ángulos coterminales** Dos ángulos en posición estándar con el mismo lado terminal.	

Glossary/Glosario

English	Spanish	Examples
cube root function The function $f(x) = \sqrt[3]{x}$, which is the inverse of the cubic function $f(x) = x^3$.	**función de raíz cúbica** Función $f(x) = \sqrt[3]{x}$, que es la inversa de la función cúbica $f(x) = x^3$.	
cubic function A polynomial function that has the standard form $f(x) = ax^3 + bx^2 + cx + d$, where a, b, c, and d are real numbers and $a \neq 0$.	**función cúbica** Función polinómica que tiene la forma estándar $f(x) = ax^3 + bx^2 + cx + d$, donde a, b, c y d son números reales y $a \neq 0$.	
cycle of a periodic function The shortest repeating part of a periodic graph or function.	**ciclo de una función periódica** Parte repetida más corta de una gráfica o función periódica.	

D

English	Spanish	Examples
decay factor The base $1 - r$ in an exponential decay expression.	**factor de disminución** Base $1 - r$ en una expresión de disminución exponencial.	$2(0.93)^t$ ↑ decay factor $\left(\text{representing } 1 - 0.07\right)$
decay rate The constant percent decrease, in decimal form, in an exponential decay function.	**tasa de disminución** Disminución porcentual constante, en forma decimal, en una función de disminución exponencial.	In the function $f(t) = a(1 - 0.2)^t$, 0.2 is the decay rate.
decreasing A function is decreasing on an interval if the output of the function decreases (or stays the same) as the input increases. For a decreasing function, $f(b) \leq f(a)$ for any a and b in the interval such that $b > a$.	**decreciente** Una función es decreciente en un intervalo si el valor de salida de la función disminuye (o permanece igual) a medida que el valor de entrada aumenta. Dada una función decreciente, $f(b) \leq f(a)$ para todo valor de a y b en el intervalo, tal que $b > a$.	 $f(x)$ is decreasing on the interval $x < 0$.
degree of a monomial The sum of the exponents of the variables in the monomial.	**grado de un monomio** Suma de los exponentes de las variables del monomio.	$4x^2y^5z^3$ Degree: $2 + 5 + 3 = 10$ 5 Degree: $0 \left(5 = 5x^0\right)$
degree of a polynomial The degree of the term of the polynomial with the greatest degree.	**grado de un polinomio** Grado del término del polinomio con el grado máximo.	$3x^2y^2 + 4xy^5 - 12x^3y^2$ Degree 6 ↑ ↑ ↑ Degree 4 Degree 6 Degree 5
dependent events Events for which the occurrence or nonoccurrence of one event affects the probability of the other event.	**sucesos dependientes** Dos sucesos son dependientes si el hecho de que uno de ellos se cumpla o no afecta la probabilidad del otro.	From a bag containing 3 red marbles and 2 blue marbles, drawing a red marble, and then drawing a blue marble without replacing the first marble.

English	Spanish	Examples
dependent variable The set of all second elements (or y-values) of the ordered pairs that constitute a function or relation.	**variable dependiente** Conjunto de todos los segundos elementos (o valores y) de los pares ordenados que constituyen una función o relación.	$y = 2x + 1$ ↑ dependent variable
difference of two cubes A polynomial of the form $a^3 - b^3$, which may be written as the product $(a - b)(a^2 + ab + b^2)$.	**diferencia de dos cubos** Polinomio de forma $a^3 - b^3$, que puede escribirse como el producto $(a - b)(a^2 + ab + b^2)$.	$8x^3 - 27 = (2x - 3)(4x^2 + 6x + 9)$
discontinuous function on an interval A function whose graph has one or more jumps, breaks, or holes.	**función discontinua de un intervalo** Función cuya gráfica tiene uno o más saltos, interrupciones u hoyos.	 The function $y = \frac{24}{x}$ is discontinuous at $x = 0$.
discriminant The discriminant of the quadratic equation $ax^2 + bx + c = 0$ is $b^2 - 4ac$, which is the part of the quadratic formula inside the radical.	**discriminante** El discriminante de la ecuación cuadrática $ax^2 + bx + c = 0$ es $b^2 - 4ac$, que es la parte de la fórmula cuadrática ubicada dentro del radical.	The discriminant of $2x^2 - 5x - 3 = 0$ is $(-5)^2 - 4(2)(-3) = 25 + 24 = 49$.
distribution A set of numerical data that you can graph using a data display that involves a number line, such as a line plot, histogram, or box plot.	**distribución** Conjunto de datos numéricos que se pueden representar gráficamente mediante una representación de datos que incluye una recta numérica, como un diagrama de acumulación, un histograma o una gráfica de cajas.	
domain of a function or relation The set of all first elements (or x-values) of the ordered pairs that constitute a function or relation.	**dominio de una función o una relación** Conjunto de todos los primeros elementos (o valores de x) de los pares ordenados que constituyen una función o relación.	The domain of $y = x^2$ is $x \in \mathbb{R}$.

E

English	Spanish	Examples
elimination A method used to solve a system of equations in which one variable is eliminated by adding or subtracting two equations of the system.	**eliminación** Método utilizado para resolver un sistema de ecuaciones mediante el cual se elimina una variable sumando o restando dos ecuaciones del sistema.	$2x + 3y = 5$ $-(2x^2 + 3y = 1)$ $\overline{2x + 2x^2 = 4}$

Glossary/Glosario

English	Spanish	Examples
empirical rule The relationship in a normal distribution that describes the percent of the data that fall within a given number of standard deviations from the mean: 68% within one standard deviation of the mean, 95% within two standard deviations, and 99.7% within three standard deviations.	**regla empírica** En una distribución normal, relación que describe el porcentaje de datos que están dentro de un número dado de desviaciones estándar respecto a la media: 68% dentro de una desviación estándar respecto a la media, 95% dentro de dos desviaciones estándar y 99.7% dentro de tres desviaciones estándar.	
end behavior The trends in the y-values of a function as the x-values increase or decrease without bound.	**comportamiento extremo** Tendencia de los valores de y de una función a medida que los valores de x incrementan o disminuyen sin límite.	End behavior: $f(x) \rightarrow +\infty$ as $x \rightarrow +\infty$ $f(x) \rightarrow -\infty$ as $x \rightarrow -\infty$
even function A function in which $f(-x) = f(x)$ for all x in the domain of the function.	**función par** Función en la que $f(-x) = f(x)$ para todos los valores de x dentro del dominio de la función.	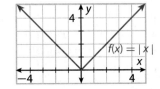 $f(x) = |x|$ is an even function.
event An outcome or set of outcomes from the sample space in a probability experiment.	**suceso** Resultado o conjunto de resultados del espacio muestral en un experimento de probabilidad.	In the experiment of rolling a number cube, the event "an odd number" consists of the outcomes 1, 3, and 5.
experiment An activity in which researchers manipulate one variable by imposing a treatment on some of the subjects of the experiment, in order to determine if the treatment has an effect on another variable.	**experimento** Actividad en la que los investigadores manipulan una variable estableciendo un tratamiento sobre algunos de los sujetos del experimento a fin de determinar si el tratamiento tiene un efecto en otra variable.	
experimental probability The ratio of the number of times an event occurs to the number of trials, or times, that an activity is performed.	**probabilidad experimental** Razón entre la cantidad de veces que ocurre un suceso y la cantidad de pruebas, o veces, que se realiza una actividad.	Kendra made 6 of 10 free throws. The experimental probability that she will make her next free throw is $P(\text{free throw}) = \frac{\text{number made}}{\text{number attempted}} = \frac{6}{10}$.

English	Spanish	Examples
explicit formula A formula that defines the nth term a_n, or general term, of a sequence as a function of the term's position number n in the sequence.	**fórmula explícita** Fórmula que define el enésimo término a_n, o término general, de una sucesión como una función de la posición del término número n en la sucesión.	Sequence: 4, 7, 10, 13, 16, 19, … Explicit formula: $a_n = 1 + 3n$
exponential decay function An exponential function of the form $f(x) = ab^x$ in which $a > 0$ and $0 < b < 1$. If r is the rate of decay, then the function can be written $f(t) = a(1 - r)^t$, where a is the initial amount and t is the time.	**función de disminución exponencial** Función exponencial del tipo $f(x) = ab^x$ en la cual $a > 0$ y $0 < b < 1$. Si r es la tasa de disminución, entonces la función se puede expresar como $f(t) = a(1 - r)^t$, donde a es la cantidad inicial y t es el tiempo.	$y = 3\left(\frac{1}{2}\right)^x$
exponential equation in one variable An equation in which a variable expression occurs as an exponent.	**ecuación exponencial en una variable** Ecuación en la que una expresión variable ocurre como exponente.	$2^{x+1} = 8$
exponential function A function of the form $f(x) = ab^x$, where a and the base b are real numbers with $a \neq 0$, $b > 0$, and $b \neq 1$. Translating the graph of f horizontally by h units and vertically by k units produces the function $g(x) = ab^{x-h} + k$, which is also an exponential function.	**función exponencial** Función del tipo $f(x) = ab^x$, donde a y la base b son números reales con $a \neq 0$, $b > 0$ y $b \neq 1$. Trasladar la gráfica de f horizontalmente h unidades y verticalmente k unidades produce la función $g(x) = ab^{x-h} + k$, que también es una función exponencial.	$f(t) = 2(1.5)^t$
exponential growth function An exponential function of the form $f(x) = ab^x$ in which $a > 0$ and $b > 1$. If r is the rate of growth, then the function can be written $f(t) = a(1 + r)^t$, where a is the initial amount and t is the time.	**función de crecimiento exponencial** Función exponencial del tipo $f(x) = ab^x$ en la que $a > 0$ y $b > 1$. Si r es la tasa de crecimiento, entonces la función se puede expresar como $f(t) = a(1 + r)^t$, donde a es la cantidad inicial y t es el tiempo.	$f(x) = 3 \cdot 2^x$
exponential regression A statistical method used to fit an exponential model to a given data set.	**regresión exponencial** Método estadístico utilizado para ajustar un modelo exponencial a un conjunto de datos determinado.	
extraneous solution A solution of a derived equation that is not a solution of the original equation.	**solución extraña** Solución de una ecuación derivada que no es una solución de la ecuación original.	To solve $\sqrt{x} = -2$, square both sides; $x = 4$. **Check** $\sqrt{4} = -2$ is false; so 4 is an extraneous solution.

F

English	Spanish	Examples
Factor Theorem For any polynomial $P(x)$, $(x - a)$ is a factor of $P(x)$ if and only if $P(a) = 0$.	**Teorema del factor** Para cualquier polinomio $P(x)$, $(x - a)$ es un factor de $P(x)$ si y sólo si $P(a) = 0$.	$(x - 1)$ is a factor of $P(x) = x^2 - 1$ because $P(1) = 1^2 - 1 = 0$.
family of functions Functions whose graphs have basic characteristics in common. Functions in the same family are transformations of their parent function.	**familia de funciones** Funciones cuyas gráficas tienen características básicas comunes. Las funciones de la misma familia son transformaciones de su función madre.	*(graph showing $y = x^2 + 1$, $y = 3x^2$, $y = (x - 2)^2$, $y = x^2$)*
finite geometric series A geometric series in which the sum of a finite number of terms of a geometric sequence is found.	**serie geométrica finita** Serie geométrica en la que se halla la suma de un número finito de términos de una sucesión geométrica.	$1 + 3 + 9 + 27 + \ldots + 6561$
finite sequence *See* sequence.	**sucesión finita** *Ver* sucesión.	
finite set A set with a definite, or finite, number of elements.	**conjunto finito** Conjunto con un número de elementos definido o finito.	$\{2, 4, 6, 8, 10\}$
frequency of periodic function The number of cycles per unit of time. Also the reciprocal of the period.	**frecuencia de una función periódica** Cantidad de ciclos por unidad de tiempo. También es la inversa del periodo.	The function $y = \sin(2x)$ has a period of π and a frequency of $\frac{1}{\pi}$.
function A relation in which every domain value is paired with exactly one range value.	**función** Relación en la que cada valor del dominio forma un par con exactamente un valor del rango.	*(mapping diagram) Domain {6, 5, 2, 1} to Range {−4, −1, 0}*

G

English	Spanish	Examples
geometric sequence A sequence in which the ratio of successive terms is a constant r, called the common ratio, where $r \neq 0$ and $r \neq 1$.	**sucesión geométrica** Sucesión en la que la razón de los términos sucesivos es una constante r, denominada razón común, donde $r \neq 0$ y $r \neq 1$.	$1, \quad 2, \quad 4, \quad 8, \quad 16, \quad \ldots$ $\cdot 2 \quad \cdot 2 \quad \cdot 2 \quad \cdot 2 \qquad r = 2$

English	Spanish	Examples
geometric series The indicated sum of the terms of a geometric sequence.	**serie geométrica** Suma indicada de los términos de una sucesión geométrica.	$1 + 2 + 4 + 8 + 16 + \dots$
global maximum *See* absolute maximum.	**máximo global** *Ver* máximo absoluto.	
global minimum *See* absolute minimum.	**mínimo global** *Ver* mínimo absoluto.	
growth factor The base $1 + r$ in an exponential growth expression.	**factor de crecimiento** La base $1 + r$ en una expresión de crecimiento exponencial.	$12{,}000(1 + 0.14)^t$ ↑ growth factor
growth rate The constant percent increase, in decimal form, in an exponential growth function.	**tasa de crecimiento** Aumento porcentual constante, en forma decimal, en una función de crecimiento exponencial.	In the function $f(t) = a(1 + 0.3)^t$, 0.3 is the growth rate.

H

English	Spanish	Examples
hole (in a graph) An omitted point on a graph. If a rational function has the same factor $x - b$ in both the numerator and the denominator, and the line $x = b$ is not a vertical asymptote, then there is a hole in the graph at the point where $x = b$.	**hoyo (en una gráfica)** Punto omitido en una gráfica. Si una función racional tiene el mismo factor $x - b$ tanto en el numerador como en el denominador, y la línea $x = b$ no es una asíntota vertical, entonces hay un hoyo en la gráfica en el punto donde $x = b$.	$f(x) = \dfrac{(x - 2)(x + 2)}{(x + 2)}$ has a hole at $x = -2$. Hole at $x = -2$; $(-2, -4)$

I

English	Spanish	Examples
imaginary number The square root of a negative number, written in the form bi, where b is a real number and i is the imaginary unit, $\sqrt{-1}$. Also called a *pure imaginary number*.	**número imaginario** Raíz cuadrada de un número negativo, expresado como bi, donde b es un número real e i es la unidad imaginaria, $\sqrt{-1}$. También se denomina *número imaginario puro*.	$\sqrt{-16} = \sqrt{16} \cdot \sqrt{-1} = 4i$
imaginary unit The unit in the imaginary number system, $\sqrt{-1}$.	**unidad imaginaria** Unidad del sistema de números imaginarios, $\sqrt{-1}$.	$\sqrt{-1} = i$
inclusive events *See overlapping events.*	**eventos inclusivos** *Ver eventos solapados.*	

English	Spanish	Examples
increasing A function is increasing on an interval if the output of the function increases (or stays the same) as the input increases. For an increasing function, $f(b) \geq f(a)$ for any a and b in the interval such that $b > a$.	**creciente** Una función es creciente en un intervalo si el valor de salida de una función aumenta (o permanece igual) a medida que el valor de entrada aumenta. Dada una función creciente, $f(b) \geq f(a)$ para todo valor de a o b en el intervalo tal que $b > a$.	$f(x)$ is increasing on the interval $x > 0$.
independent events Events for which the occurrence or nonoccurrence of one event does not affect the probability of the other event.	**sucesos independientes** Dos sucesos son independientes si el hecho de que se produzca o no uno de ellos no afecta la probabilidad del otro suceso.	From a bag containing 3 red marbles and 2 blue marbles, drawing a red marble, replacing it, and then drawing a blue marble.
independent variable The input of a function; a variable whose value determines the value of the output, or dependent variable.	**variable independiente** Entrada de una función; variable cuyo valor determina el valor de la salida, o variable dependiente.	$y = 2x + 1$ $\uparrow$ independent variable
index of a radical In the nth root expression $\sqrt[n]{a}$, the integer n, where $n > 1$.	**índice de un radical** En la expresión de la enésima raíz $\sqrt[n]{a}$, el entero n, donde $n > 1$.	In $\sqrt[10]{1024}$, the index is 10.
index of summation In sigma, or summation, notation, the letter k (or another letter) used to count the terms from the *lower limit of summation*, which is used to find the first term of the series, to the *upper limit of summation*, which is used to find the last term of the series.	**índice de sumatoria** En notación sigma, o sumatoria, la letra k (u otra letra) utilizada para contar los términos desde el *límite inferior de la sumatoria*, que se utiliza para hallar el primer término de la serie, hasta el *límite superior de la sumatoria*, que se utiliza para hallar el último término de la serie.	upper limit of summation $\downarrow$ In $\sum\limits_{k=1}^{8}(k^2 + k)$, the index is k. $\uparrow$ lower limit of summation
infinite sequence *See* sequence.	**sucesión infinita** *Ver* sucesión.	
initial side *See* angle of rotation.	**lado inicial** *Ver* ángulo de rotación.	
intersection of two events Written as $A \cap B$ or as "A and B," is the set of outcomes that are in both of two events, A and B.	**intersección de dos sucesos** Escrito como $A \cap B$ o como "A y B", es el conjunto de resultados que están en los dos sucesos A y B.	
interval An unbroken portion of a number line.	**intervalo** Porción ininterrumpida de una recta numérica.	

© Houghton Mifflin Harcourt Publishing Company

English	Spanish	Examples
interval notation A way of writing the set of all real numbers between two endpoints. The symbols [and] are used to include an endpoint in an interval, and the symbols (and) are used to exclude an endpoint from an interval.	**notación de intervalo** Forma de expresar el conjunto de todos los números reales entre dos extremos. Los símbolos [y] se utilizan para incluir un extremo en un intervalo y los símbolos (y) se utilizan para excluir un extremo de un intervalo.	<table><tr><td>Interval notation</td><td>Set-builder notation</td></tr><tr><td>(a, b)</td><td>$\{x \mid a < x < b\}$</td></tr><tr><td>$(a, b]$</td><td>$\{x \mid a < x \le b\}$</td></tr><tr><td>$[a, b)$</td><td>$\{x \mid a \le x < b\}$</td></tr><tr><td>$[a, b]$</td><td>$\{x \mid a \le x \le b\}$</td></tr></table>
inverse function The function that results from exchanging the input and output values of a one-to-one function. The inverse of $f(x)$ is denoted $f^{-1}(x)$.	**función inversa** Función que resulta de intercambiar los valores de entrada y salida de una función uno a uno. La función inversa de $f(x)$ se expresa $f^{-1}(x)$	
inverse relation The inverse of the relation consisting of all ordered pairs (x, y) is the set of all ordered pairs (y, x). The graph of an inverse relation is the reflection of the graph of the relation across the line $y = x$.	**relación inversa** La inversa de la relación que consta de todos los pares ordenados (x, y) es el conjunto de todos los pares ordenados (y, x). La gráfica de una relación inversa es el reflejo de la gráfica de la relación sobre la línea $y = x$.	
inverse variation The relationship between two quantities x and y in which $y = \frac{a}{x}$ for a number a where $a \ne 0$. The value of a is the *constant of variation*.	**variación inversa** Relación entre dos cantidades x y y en la que $y = \frac{a}{x}$ para un número a donde $a \ne 0$. El valor de a es la *constante de variación*.	The relationship $y = \frac{60}{x}$ represents an inverse variation with a constant of variation of 60.
irrational conjugates Pairs of irrational numbers of the form $a + \sqrt{b}$ and $a - \sqrt{b}$ where a and b are rational numbers. Irrational solutions of polynomial equations always occur in conjugate pairs.	**conjugados irracionales** Pares de números irracionales del tipo $a + \sqrt{b}$ y $a - \sqrt{b}$, donde a y b son números racionales. Las soluciones irracionales de ecuaciones polinomiales siempre ocurren en pares conjugados.	$3 + \sqrt{5}$ and $3 - \sqrt{5}$
irreducible factor A factor of degree 2 or greater that cannot be factored further.	**factor irreducible** Factor de grado 2 o mayor que no se puede seguir factorizando.	$x^2 + 7x + 1$

J

English	Spanish	Examples
joint relative frequency In a two-way frequency table, the ratio of the frequency of the intersection of two categories and the total number of data values.	**frecuencia relativa conjunta** En una tabla de frecuencia de doble entrada, la razón entre la frecuencia de la intersección de dos categorías y el número total de los valores de los datos.	

Glossary/Glosario

L

English	Spanish	Examples
leading coefficient The coefficient of the first term of a polynomial in standard form.	**coeficiente principal** Coeficiente del primer término de un polinomio en forma estandar.	$3x^2 + 7x - 2$ ↑ Leading coefficient
linear-quadratic system of equations *See* system of equations.	**sistema lineal-cuadrático de ecuaciones** *Ver* sistema de ecuaciones.	
local maximum For a function f, $f(a)$ is a local maximum if there is an interval around a such that $f(x) < f(a)$ for every x-value in the interval except a.	**máximo local** Dada una función f, $f(a)$ es el máximo local si hay un intervalo en a tal que $f(x) < f(a)$ para cada valor de x en el intervalo excepto a.	Local maximum
local minimum For a function f, $f(a)$ is a local minimum if there is an interval around a such that $f(x) > f(a)$ for every x-value in the interval except a.	**mínimo local** Dada una función f, $f(a)$ es el mínimo local si hay un intervalo en a tal que $f(x) > f(a)$ para cada valor de x en el intervalo excepto a.	Local minimum
logarithm The exponent that a specified base must be raised to in order to get a certain value. A number y with base b has a logarithm of x, or $\log_b y = x$, if and only if $b^x = y$.	**logaritmo** Exponente al cual debe elevarse una base determinada a fin de obtener cierto valor. Un número y con base b tiene un logaritmo de x, o $\log_b y = x$, si y solo si $b^x = y$.	$\log_2 8 = 3$, because 3 is the power that 2 is raised to in order to get 8, or $2^3 = 8$.
logarithmic equation An equation that contains a logarithm of a variable or variable expression.	**ecuación logarítmica** Ecuación que contiene un logaritmo de una variable o expresión variable.	$\log x + 3 = 7$
logarithmic function A function of the form $f(x) = \log_b x$, where b is the base, with $b \neq 1$ and $b > 0$. It is the inverse of the exponential function $f(x) = b^x$.	**función logarítmica** Función del tipo $f(x) = \log_b x$, donde b es la base, con $b \neq 1$ y $b > 0$. Es la inversa de la función exponencial $f(x) = b^x$.	 $f(x) = \log_4 x$
logarithmic regression A statistical method used to fit a logarithmic model to a given data set.	**regresión logarítmica** Método estadístico utilizado para ajustar un modelo logarítmico a un conjunto de datos determinado.	
lower limit of summation *See* index of summation.	**límite inferior de la sumatoria** *Ver* índice de sumatoria.	

M

English	Spanish	Examples
margin of error For a random sample, the greatest amount from a sample parameter by which a population parameter is expected to vary. It is half the width of the confidence interval.	**margen de error** Dada una muestra aleatoria, la mayor cantidad de un parámetro de muestra por el que se espera que varíe un parámetro de la población. Mide la mitad del ancho del intervalo de confianza.	
marginal relative frequency The sum of the joint relative frequencies in a row or column.	**frecuencia relativa marginal** La suma de las frecuencias relativas conjuntas de una fila o columna.	
mean The sum of all the values in a data set divided by the number of data values. Also called the *average*.	**media** La suma de todos los valores de un conjunto de datos dividida entre el número de valores. También llamada *promedio*.	Data set: 4, 6, 7, 8, 10 Mean: $\dfrac{4+6+7+8+10}{5} = \dfrac{35}{5} = 7$
midline For the graph of a sine or cosine function, the horizontal line halfway between the maximum and minimum values of the curve; for the graph of a tangent function, the horizontal line through the point of each cycle that is midway between the asymptotes.	**línea media** En la gráfica de una función seno o coseno, la línea horizontal a medio camino entre los valores máximo y mínimo de la curva; en la gráfica de una función tangente, la línea horizontal que atraviesa el punto de cada ciclo que está a medio camino entre las asíntotas.	
monomial A number, a variable, or a product of a number and variables with whole-number exponents; a polynomial with one term.	**monomio** Número, variable o producto de un número y variables con exponentes de números enteros; polinomio con un término.	$8x$, 9, $3x^2y^4$
multiplicity For a polynomial function $P(x)$ that has a repeated zero at $x = r$, the multiplicity of r is the number of times $(x - r)$ appears as a factor in $P(x)$.	**multiplicidad** Dada una función polinomial $P(x)$ que tiene un cero repetido en $x = r$, la multiplicidad de r es la cantidad de veces que $(x - r)$ aparece como factor en $P(x)$.	For $P(x) = (x - 3)^2$, the root 3 has a multiplicity of 2.
mutually exclusive events Two events are mutually exclusive if they cannot both occur in the same trial of an experiment.	**sucesos mutuamente excluyentes** Dos sucesos son mutuamente excluyentes si ambos no pueden ocurrir en la misma prueba de un experimento.	In the experiment of rolling a number cube, rolling a 3 and rolling an even number are mutually exclusive events.

N

English	Spanish	Examples
natural logarithm A logarithm with base e, written as ln.	**logaritmo natural** Logaritmo con base e, que se escribe ln.	$\ln 5 = \log_e 5 \approx 1.6$

Glossary/Glosario

English	Spanish	Examples
natural logarithmic function The function $f(x) = \ln x$, which is the inverse of the natural exponential function $f(x) = e^x$. Domain is $\{x \mid x > 0\}$; range is all real numbers	**función logarítmica natural** Función $f(x) = \ln x$, que es la inversa de la función exponencial natural $f(x) = e^x$. El dominio es $\{x \mid x > 0\}$; el rango es todos los números reales.	
normal curve *See* normal distribution.	**curva normal** *Ver* distribución normal.	
normal distribution A distribution that is mounded in the middle with symmetric "tails" at each end, forming a bell shape called the *normal curve*. The mean μ of the distribution is at its center, and the spread is described by the standard deviation σ.	**distribución normal** Una distribución que está elevada en el centro con "colas" simétricas en los extremos, lo que forma la figura de una campana llamada *curva normal*. La media μ de la distribución se encuentra en su centro y la dispersión se describe mediante la desviación estándar σ.	
***n*th root** The *n*th root of a number a, written as $\sqrt[n]{a}$ or $a^{\frac{1}{n}}$, is a number that is equal to a when it is raised to the *n*th power, that is, if $b^n = a$, then b is an *n*th root of a.	**enésima raíz** La enésima raíz de un número a, que se escribe como $\sqrt[n]{a}$ or $a^{\frac{1}{n}}$, es un número igual a a cuando se eleva a la enésima potencia; es decir, si $b^n = a$, entonces b es la enésima raíz de a.	$\sqrt[5]{32} = 2$, because $2^5 = 32$.
null hypothesis The assumption made that any difference between the control group and the treatment group in an experiment is due to chance and not to the treatment.	**hipótesis nula** La suposición de que cualquier diferencia entre el grupo de control y el grupo de tratamiento en un experimento se debe al azar, no al tratamiento.	
numerical data Data that represent quantities or observations that can be measured.	**datos numéricos** Datos que representan cantidades u observaciones que pueden medirse.	heights, attendance, time, temperature, pressure, distance, cost

O

English	Spanish	Examples
observational study A study that observes individuals and measures variables without controlling the individuals or their environment in any way with the goal of determining whether an existing condition, or factor, in a population is related to a characteristic of interest.	**estudio de observación** Estudio que permite observar a individuos y medir variables sin controlar a los individuos ni su ambiente, a fin de determinar si una condición existente, o factor, en una población se relaciona con una característica de interés.	

English	Spanish	Examples
odd function A function in which $f(-x) = -f(x)$ for all x in the domain of the function.	**función impar** Función en la que $f(-x) = -f(x)$ para todos los valores de x dentro del dominio de la función.	$f(x) = x^3$ is an odd function.
one-to-one function A function in which each y-value corresponds to only one x-value. The inverse of a one-to-one function is also a function.	**función uno a uno** Función en la que cada valor de y corresponde a sólo un valor de x. La inversa de una función uno a uno es también una función.	
outcome of a probability experiment Each possible result of a probability experiment.	**resultado de un experimento de probabilidad** Cada resultado posible de un experimento de probabilidad.	
overlapping events Events in the sample space of a probability experiment that have one or more outcomes in common. Also called *inclusive events*.	**eventos solapados** Eventos en el espacio muestral de un experimento de probabilidad que tienen uno o más resultados en común. También llamados *eventos inclusivos*.	

P

English	Spanish	Examples
parabola The U shape of the graph of a quadratic function.	**parábola** Forma en U de la gráfica de una función cuadrática.	$y = x^2$
parameter One of the constants in a function or equation that may be changed.	**parámetro** Una de las constantes en una función o ecuación que se puede cambiar.	$y = (x - h)^2 + k$ **parameters**
parent function The simplest function with the defining characteristics of the family. Functions in the same family are transformations of their parent function.	**función madre** La función más básica con las características de la familia. Las funciones de la misma familia son transformaciones de su función madre.	$f(x) = x^2$ is the parent function for $g(x) = x^2 + 4$ and $h(x) = 5(x + 2)^2 - 3$; $f(x) = 2^x$ is the parent function of $g(x) = 5 \cdot 2^{x-3} + 1$; $f(x) = \sqrt[3]{x}$ is the parent function of $\sqrt[3]{\frac{1}{2}(x - 3)} - 6$.

Glossary/Glosario

English	Spanish	Examples
Pascal's triangle A triangular arrangement of numbers in which every row starts and ends with 1 and each other number is the sum of the two numbers above it. The numbers represent the total number of possible paths from the top of the triangle to the number's location on the triangle.	**triángulo de Pascal** Arreglo triangular de números en el cual cada fila comienza y termina con 1 y cada uno de los demás números es la suma de los dos números que están encima de él. Los números representan la cantidad total de caminos posibles desde el extremo superior del triángulo hasta la ubicación del número en el triángulo.	1 1 1 1 2 1 1 3 3 1 1 4 6 4 1
perfect-square trinomial A trinomial whose factored form is the square of a binomial. A perfect-square trinomial has the form $a^2 - 2ab + b^2 = (a - b)^2$ or $a^2 + 2ab + b^2 = (a + b)^2$.	**trinomio cuadrado perfecto** Trinomio cuya forma factorizada es el cuadrado de un binomio. Un trinomio cuadrado perfecto tiene la forma $a^2 - 2ab + b^2 = (a - b)^2$ o $a^2 + 2ab + b^2 = (a + b)^2$.	$x^2 + 6x + 9$ is a perfect-square trinomial because $x^2 + 6x + 9 = (x + 3)^2$.
period of a periodic function The length of a cycle measured in units of the independent variable (usually time in seconds). Also, the reciprocal of the frequency.	**periodo de una función periódica** Longitud de un ciclo medido en unidades de la variable independiente (generalmente el tiempo en segundos). También es la inversa de la frecuencia.	
periodic function A function that repeats exactly over regular intervals, called *periods*.	**función periódica** Función que se repite exactamente a intervalos regulares denominados *periodos*.	
permutation test A significance test performed on the results of an experiment by forming every possible regrouping of all the data values taken from the control and treatment groups into two new groups, finding the normal distribution of the differences of the means for all the new group pairings, and then finding the likelihood, given that the null hypothesis is true, of getting a difference of means at least as great as the original experimental difference.	**prueba de permutación** Una prueba de significancia realizada sobre los resultados de un experimento al formar todos los reagrupamientos posibles de todos los valores de datos tomados de los grupos de control y de tratamiento en dos nuevos grupos, hallar la distribución normal de las diferencias de las medias para todos los emparejamientos nuevos, y luego hallar la probabilidad, suponiendo que la hipótesis nula es verdadera, de obtener una diferencia de medias al menos tan grande como la diferencia experimental original.	

English	Spanish	Examples
phase shift A horizontal translation of a periodic function.	**cambio de fase** Traslación horizontal de una función periódica.	g is a phase shift of f $\frac{\pi}{2}$ units left.
polynomial A monomial or a sum or difference of monomials.	**polinomio** Monomio o suma de monomios.	$2x^2 + 3x - 7$
polynomial equation in one variable An equation that contains one or more polynomials.	**ecuación polinomial en una variable** Ecuación que contiene uno o más polinomios.	$x^4 + 5x^3 - 21x^2 - 125x - 100 = 0$
polynomial function of degree n A function with the standard form $p(x) = a_n x^n + a_{n-1} x^{n-1} + \ldots + a_2 x^2 + a_1 x + a_0$, where the coefficients are all real numbers, the exponents are all whole numbers, and $a_n \neq 0$.	**función polinomial de grado n** Función del tipo estándar $p(x) = a_n x^n + a_{n-1} x^{n-1} + \ldots + a_2 x^2 + a_1 x + a_0$, donde todos los coeficientes son números reales, todos los exponentes son números enteros y $a_n \neq 0$.	$f(x) = x^3 - 8x^2 + 19x - 12$
polynomial identity A mathematical relationship equating two polynomial expressions to each other that allows conversion between expressions.	**identidad de polinomios** Relación matemática que iguala dos expresiones polinomiales, lo que permite la conversión útil entre formas.	$(x^4 - y^4) = (x^2 + y^2)(x^2 - y^2)$
population The entire group of objects or individuals considered for a survey.	**población** Grupo completo de objetos o individuos que se desea estudiar.	In a survey about the study habits of high school students, the population is all high school students.
probability A number from 0 to 1 (or 0% to 100%) that is the measure of how likely an event is to occur.	**probabilidad** Número entre 0 y 1 (o entre 0% y 100%) que describe cuán probable es que ocurra un suceso.	A bag contains 3 red marbles and 4 blue marbles. The probability of choosing a red marble is $\frac{3}{7}$.
probability experiment An operation, process, or activity in which outcomes can be used to estimate probabilities.	**experimento de probabilidad** Operación, proceso o actividad en la que los resultados se pueden utilizar para estimar probabilidades.	flipping a coin, rolling a number cube
probability distribution A function that gives the probabilities of all the possible values of a random variable. The sum of the probabilities in a probability distribution must be equal to 1.	**distribución de probabilidad** Función que da las probabilidades de todos los valores posibles de una variable aleatoria. La suma de las probabilidad en una distribución de probabilidad debe ser igual a 1.	A number cube is rolled 10 times. The results are shown in the table. 	Outcome	1	2	3	4	5	6	|---|---|---|---|---|---|---|	Probability	$\frac{1}{10}$	$\frac{1}{5}$	$\frac{1}{5}$	0	$\frac{3}{10}$	$\frac{1}{5}$	
pure imaginary number *See* imaginary number.	**número imaginario puro** *Ver* número imaginario.	$3i$

Glossary/Glosario

English	Spanish	Examples

P-value The probability found from a resampling distribution of randomly getting a difference at least as extreme as the experimental difference, assuming that the null hypothesis is true. The smaller the *P*-value, the less likely that the result could have occurred by random chance.

valor de P La probabilidad hallada a partir de una distribución de remuestreo de obtener aleatoriamente una diferencia al menos tan extrema como la diferencia experimental, asumiendo que la hipótesis nula es verdadera. Mientras más pequeño sea el valor de *P*, menos probable será que el resultado pueda haber ocurrido al azar.

Q

quadratic equation in one variable An equation that can be written in the form $ax^2 + bx + c = 0$, where *a*, *b*, and *c* are real numbers and $a \neq 0$.

ecuación cuadrática en una variable Ecuación que se puede expresar como $ax^2 + bx + c = 0$, donde *a*, *b* y *c* son números reales y $a \neq 0$.

$x^2 + 3x - 4 = 0$
$x^2 - 9 = 0$

Quadratic Formula The formula $x = \frac{-b \pm \sqrt{b^2 - 4ac}}{2a}$, which gives solutions of equations in the form $ax^2 + bx + c = 0$, where $a \neq 0$.

fórmula cuadrática La fórmula $x = \frac{-b \pm \sqrt{b^2 - 4ac}}{2a}$, que da soluciones para las ecuaciones del tipo $ax^2 + bx + c = 0$, donde $a \neq 0$.

The solutions of $2x^2 - 5x - 3 = 0$

are given by

$x = \frac{-(-5) \pm \sqrt{(-5)^2 - 4(2)(-3)}}{2(2)}$

$= \frac{5 \pm \sqrt{25 + 24}}{4} = \frac{5 \pm 7}{4};$

$x = 3$ or $x = -\frac{1}{2}$.

quadratic function A function that can be written in the form $f(x) = ax^2 + bx + c$, where *a*, *b*, and *c* are real numbers and $a \neq 0$, or in the form $f(x) = a(x - h)^2 + k$, where *a*, *h*, and *k* are real numbers and $a \neq 0$. Its graph is a parabola.

función cuadrática Función que se puede expresar como $f(x) = ax^2 + bx + c$, donde *a*, *b* y *c* son números reales y $a \neq 0$, o como $f(x) = a(x - h)^2 + k$, donde *a*, *h* y *k* son números reales y $a \neq 0$. Su gráfica es una parábola.

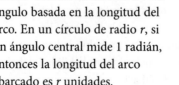

$f(x) = x^2 - 6x + 8$

R

radian A unit of angle measure based on arc length. In a circle of radius *r*, if a central angle has a measure of 1 radian, then the length of the intercepted arc is *r* units. 2π radians $= 360°$
1 radian $\approx 57°$

radián Unidad de medida de un ángulo basada en la longitud del arco. En un círculo de radio *r*, si un ángulo central mide 1 radián, entonces la longitud del arco abarcado es *r* unidades.
2π radianes $= 360°$
1 radián $\approx 57°$

English	Spanish	Examples
radical An expression that contains a radical sign.	**radical** Un que contiene un signo de radical.	$\sqrt{x+3}+4$
radical equation in one variable An equation that contains a variable within a radical.	**ecuación radical en una variable** Ecuación que contiene una variable dentro de un radical.	$\sqrt{x+3}+4=7$
radical function A function whose rule contains a variable within a radical.	**función radical** Función cuya regla contiene una variable dentro de un radical.	$f(x) = \sqrt{x}$
radicand The expression under a radical sign.	**radicando** Número o expresión debajo del signo de radical.	$\sqrt{x+3}-2$ $\uparrow$ Radicand
random variable A variable whose value is determined by the outcome of a probability experiment.	**variable aleatoria** Una variable cuyo valor viene determinado por el resultado de un experimento de probabilidad.	
randomized comparative experiment An experiment that randomly assigns subjects to one of two groups: the *treatment group*, which is given the treatment, and the *control group*, which is not.	**experimento comparativo aleatorizado** Experimento en el que los sujetos son asignados de manera aleatoria a uno de dos grupos: el *grupo de tratamiento*, que recibe el tratamiento, o el *grupo de control*, que no lo recibe.	
range of a function or relation The set of all second elements (or *y*-values) of the ordered pairs that constitute a function or relation.	**rango de una función o relación** Conjunto de todos los segundos elementos (o valores de *y*) de los pares ordenados que constituyen una función o relación.	The range of $y = x^2$ is $\left\{y \mid y \geq 0\right\}$.
rational equation in one variable An equation that contains one or more rational expressions.	**ecuación racional en una variable** Ecuación que contiene una o más expresiones racionales.	$\dfrac{x+2}{x^2+3x-1}=6$
rational exponent An exponent that can be expressed as $\frac{m}{n}$ such that if m and n are integers, then $b^{\frac{m}{n}} = \sqrt[n]{b^m} = \left(\sqrt[n]{b}\right)^m$.	**exponente racional en una variable** Exponente que se puede expresar como $\frac{m}{n}$ tal que, si m y n son números enteros, entonces $b^{\frac{m}{n}} = \sqrt[n]{b^m} = \left(\sqrt[n]{b}\right)^m$.	$4^{\frac{3}{2}} = \sqrt{4^3} = \sqrt{64} = 8$ $4^{\frac{3}{2}} = \left(\sqrt{4}\right)^3 = 2^3 = 8$

English	Spanish	Examples
rational expression An algebraic expression whose numerator and denominator are polynomials and whose denominator has a degree ≥ 1.	**expresión racional** Expresión algebraica cuyo numerador y denominador son polinomios y cuyo denominador tiene un grado ≥ 1.	$$\frac{x+2}{x^2+3x-1}$$
rational function A function of the form $f(x) = \frac{p(x)}{q(x)}$, where $p(x)$ and $q(x)$ are polynomials and $q(x) \neq 0$.	**función racional** Función de tipo $f(x) = \frac{p(x)}{q(x)}$, donde $p(x)$ y $q(x)$ son polinomios y $q(x) \neq 0$.	$$f(x) = \frac{x+2}{x^2+3x-1}$$
recursive formula A formula for the nth term of a sequence in which one or more previous terms are used to generate the next term.	**fórmula recurrente** Fórmula para el enésimo término de una sucesión en la cual uno o más términos anteriores se utilizan para generar el término siguiente.	For the sequence 5, 7, 9, 11, ..., a recursive formula is $a_1 = 5$ and $a_n = a_{n-1} + 2$.
reflection A transformation that reflects, or "flips," a graph or figure across a line. For the reflection of a graph across the x-axis, the image of (x, y) is $(x, -y)$; for a reflection across the y-axis, the image of (x, y) is $(-x, y)$; for a reflection across the line $y = x$, the image of (x, y) is (y, x).	**reflexión** Transformación que refleja, o invierte, una gráfica o figura sobre una línea. Para la reflexión de una gráfica sobre el eje x, la imagen de (x, y) es $(x, -y)$; para la reflexión sobre el eje y, la imagen de (x, y) es $(-x, y)$; para una reflexión sobre la línea $y = x$, la imagen de (x, y) es (y, x).	
Remainder Theorem If the polynomial function $P(x)$ is divided by $x - a$, then the remainder r is $P(a)$.	**Teorema del resto** Si la función polinomial $P(x)$ se divide entre $x - a$, entonces, el residuo r será $P(a)$.	
representative sample A sample for which a parameter is a good estimator for its corresponding population parameter.	**muestra representativa** Una muestra para la que un parámetro es un buen estimador para su parámetro de población correspondiente.	
resampling The process of combining all the experimental data from a randomized comparative experiment, randomly sorting it into new "treatment" and "control" groups," and finding the difference of the means. Repeating this process enough times allows for the construction of a resampling distribution for the difference of means, which enables hypothesis testing.	**remuestreo** Proceso de combinación de todos los datos de un experimento comparativo aleatorizado, en el que se los clasifica al azar en nuevos grupos de "tratamiento" o "control" y se halla la diferencia de las medias. Repetir este proceso suficientes veces permite construir una distribución de remuestreo para la diferencia de las medias y, de esa manera, probar hipótesis.	

English	Spanish	Examples
Root of an equation A solution of the polynomial equation $f(x) = 0$.	**Raíz de una ecuación** Solución a la ecuación polinomial $f(x) = 0$.	

S

English	Spanish	Examples
sample A subset of a population.	**muestra** Subconjunto de una población.	In a survey about the study habits of high school students, a sample is a survey of 100 students.
sample space The set of all possible outcomes of a probability experiment.	**espacio muestral** Conjunto de todos los resultados posibles en un experimento de probabilidades.	In the experiment of rolling a number cube, the sample space is 1, 2, 3, 4, 5, 6.
sampling distribution A distribution that shows how a particular statistic varies across all samples of n individuals from the same population.	**distribución de muestreo** Una distribución que muestra de qué manera una determinada estadística varía a lo largo de todas las muestras de n individuos de la misma población.	
self-selected sample A sample in which members volunteer to participate.	**muestra de voluntarios** Muestra en la que los miembros se ofrecen voluntariamente para participar.	
sequence An ordered list of numbers. A sequence may be *finite* (a finite number of terms), or *infinite* (infinitely many terms). An infinite sequence can be paired off one-to-one with the positive integers.	**sucesión** Una lista ordenada de números. Una sucesión puede ser *finita* (un número finito de términos) o *infinita* (infinitos términos). Una sucesión infinita se puede emparejar con los números enteros positivos de uno en uno.	finite sequence: 1, 2, 4, 7, 11, ..., 106, 121 infinite sequence: 1, 2, 4, 8, 16, ...
series The indicated sum of the terms of a sequence.	**serie** Suma indicada de los términos de una sucesión.	$1 + 0.1 + 0.001 + 0.0001 + \ldots$
set-builder notation A notation for a set that uses a rule to describe the properties of the elements of the set.	**notación de conjuntos** Notación para un conjunto que se vale de una regla para describir las propiedades de los elementos del conjunto.	$\{x \mid x > 3\}$ read, "The set of all x such that x is greater than 3."
sigma notation A method of notating the sum of a series using the Greek letter for S, which is represented by the symbol $\sum$ (capital *sigma*).	**notación sigma** Método de notación de la suma de una serie que utiliza la letra griega para la S, la cual se representa con el símbolo $\sum$ (*sigma* mayúscula).	$\sum_{n=1}^{5} 3k = 3 + 6 + 9 + 12 + 15 = 45$

Glossary/Glosario

English	Spanish	Examples
simulation A model of an experiment, often one that would be too difficult or time-consuming to actually perform.	**simulación** Modelo de un experimento; generalmente se recurre a la simulación cuando realizar dicho experimento sería demasiado difícil o llevaría mucho tiempo.	A random number generator is used to simulate the roll of a number cube. Resampling is used to simulate a permutation test.
sine function For an angle of rotation θ in standard position, the function defined by $\sin\theta = y$, where y is the y-coordinate of the point $P(x, y)$ at which the terminal side of θ intersects the unit circle.	**función seno** Dado un ángulo de rotación θ en posición estándar, la función definida por $\sin\theta = y$, donde y es la coordenada y del punto $P(x, y)$ en el que el lado terminal de θ corta el círculo unitario.	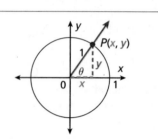 $\sin\theta = y$
skewed distribution A distribution that is mounded but not symmetric because the data values on one side of the median are more spread out than the data values on the other side. In a distribution *skewed to the left*, the mean is less than the median. In a distribution *skewed to the right*, the mean is greater than the median.	**distribución sesgada** Una distribución que está elevada pero no es simétrica porque los valores de los datos de un lado de la mediana están más dispersos que los valores del otro lado. En una distribución *sesgada hacia la izquierda*, la media es menor que la mediana. En una distribución *sesgada a la derecha*, la media es mayor que la mediana.	
slant asymptote A linear asymptote that is neither vertical nor horizontal. A slant asymptote results in the graph of a rational function when the degree of the numerator is one more than the degree of the denominator.	**asíntota inclinada** Una asíntota lineal que no es vertical ni horizontal. Una asíntota inclinada da como resultado la gráfica de una función racional donde el grado del numerador es uno más que el grado del denominador.	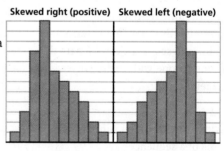Skewed right (positive) Skewed left (negative)
square root A number x is a square root of a real number a provided that $x^2 = a$. The radical sign $\sqrt{}$ indicates the principal (nonnegative) square root.	**raíz cuadrada** Un número x es la raíz cuadrada de un número real a siempre que $x^2 = a$. El signo de radical $\sqrt{}$ indica la raíz cuadrada principal (no negativa).	$\sqrt{12.25} = 3.5$ because $3.5^2 = 12.25$.
square root function A function whose rule contains a variable under a square root sign. The function $f(x) = \sqrt{x}$ is the inverse of the quadratic function $f(x) = x^2$, for $x > 0$.	**función de raíz cuadrada** Función cuya regla contiene una variable bajo un signo de raíz cuadrada. La función $f(x) = \sqrt{x}$ es el inverso de la función cuadrática $f(x) = x^2$, para $x > 0$.	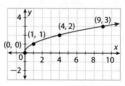 $f(x) = \sqrt{x}$

English	Spanish	Examples
standard deviation A measure of dispersion of a data set. The standard deviation σ is the square root of the variance.	**desviación estándar** Medida de dispersión de un conjunto de datos. La desviación estándar σ es la raíz cuadrada de la varianza.	Data set: $\{6, 7, 7, 9, 11\}$ Mean: $\frac{6+7+7+9+11}{5} = 8$ Variance: $\frac{1}{5}(4 + 1 + 1 + 1 + 9) = 3.2$ Standard deviation: $\sigma = \sqrt{3.2} \approx 1.8$
standard error of the mean The standard deviation of the sampling distribution of the sample mean, denoted $\sigma_{\bar{x}}$.	**error estándar de la media** La desviación estándar de la distribución de muestreo de la media de la muestra, que se indica así: $\sigma_{\bar{x}}$.	
standard error of the proportion The standard deviation of the sampling distribution of the sample proportion, denoted $\sigma_{\hat{p}}$.	**error estándar de la proporción** La desviación estándar de la distribución de muestreo de la proporción de la muestra, que se indica así: $\sigma_{\hat{p}}$.	
standard form of a polynomial A polynomial in one variable written with its terms in order from greatest degree to least degree.	**forma estándar de un polinomio** Un polinomio que se expresa con sus términos ordenados de mayor a menor grado.	$3x^3 - 5x^2 + 6x - 7$
standard form of a quadratic equation A quadratic equation in one variable written in the form $ax^2 + bx + c = 0$, where a, b, and c are real numbers and $a \neq 0$.	**forma estándar de una ecuación cuadrática** Una ecuación cuadrática de una variable expresada como $ax^2 + bx + c = 0$, donde a, b y c son números reales y $a \neq 0$.	$2x^2 + 3x - 1 = 0$
standard normal distribution A normal distribution that has a mean of 0 and a standard deviation of 1.	**distribución normal estándar** Una distribución normal que tiene una media de 0 y una desviación estándar de 1.	
standard normal value A value that indicates how many standard deviations above or below the mean a particular value falls, given by the formula $z = \frac{x - \mu}{\sigma}$, where z is the standard normal value, x is the given value, μ is the mean, and σ is the standard deviation of a standard normal distribution.	**valor normal estándar** Valor que indica a cuántas desviaciones estándar por encima o por debajo de la media se encuentra un determinado valor, dado por la fórmula $z = \frac{x - \mu}{\sigma}$, donde z es el valor normal estándar, x es el valor dado, μ es la media y σ es la desviación estándar de una distribución normal estándar.	
standard position of an angle of rotation An angle in standard position has its vertex at the origin and its initial side on the positive x-axis.	**posición estándar de un ángulo de rotación** Ángulo cuyo vértice se encuentra en el origen y cuyo lado inicial se encuentra sobre el eje x.	

Glossary/Glosario

English	Spanish	Examples
statistic A number that describes a characteristic of a sample and that can be used to estimate a parameter of a population.	**estadística** Número que describe la característica de una muestra y que se puede utilizar para estimar un parámetro de una población.	
statistical significance A determination that the likelihood that an experimental result occurred by chance is so low that a conclusion in favor of rejecting the null hypothesis is justified.	**significación estadística** Una determinación de que la probabilidad de que un resultado experimental ocurriera por azar es tan reducida que está justificada una conclusión a favor de rechazar la hipótesis nula.	
stretch of a graph A transformation that pulls the points of a graph horizontally away from the y-axis or vertically away from the x-axis. For a horizontal stretch, any point on the y-axis remains unchanged. For a vertical stretch, any point on the x-axis remains unchanged.	**estiramiento de una gráfica** Transformación que desplaza los puntos de una gráfica en forma horizontal alejándolos del eje y o en forma vertical alejándolos del eje x. En un estiramiento horizontal, todo punto del eje y permanece igual. En un estiramiento vertical, todo punto del eje x permanece igual.	Horizontal stretch
summation notation *See* sigma notation.	**notación de sumatoria** *Ver* notación sigma.	
successive approximations Closer and closer estimates for a zero of a polynomial function found by systematically narrowing the interval that contains the zero until an estimate for the zero is found to a desired place value.	**aproximaciones sucesivas** Estimaciones cada vez más próximas al cero de una función polinomial, obtenidas al reducir sistemáticamente el intervalo que contiene el cero hasta hallar una estimación para el cero en el valor posicional deseado.	
sum of two cubes A polynomial of the form $a^3 + b^3$, which may be written as the product $(a + b)(a^2 - ab + b^2)$.	**suma de dos cubos** Polinomio del tipo $a^3 + b^3$, que se puede expresar como el producto $(a + b)(a^2 - ab + b^2)$.	$8x^3 + 27 = (2x + 3)(4x^2 - 6x + 9)$
survey A data collection tool that uses questions to measure characteristics of interest about a population using a sample selected from the population.	**encuesta** Una herramienta para recopilar datos que usa preguntas para medir las características de interés sobre una población mediante una muestra seleccionada de entre la población.	

English	Spanish	Examples
symmetric distribution A distribution that is rounded and symmetric about its mean. In a symmetric distribution, the mean and median are equal.	**distribución simétrica** Una distribución que es redondeada y simétrica alrededor de su media. En una distribución simétrica, la media y la mediana son iguales.	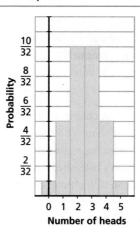
synthetic division A shorthand method of dividing by a linear binomial of the form $(x - a)$ by writing only the coefficients of the polynomials.	**división sintética** Método abreviado de división que consiste en dividir por un binomio lineal del tipo $(x - a)$ escribiendo sólo los coeficientes de los polinomios.	$(x^3 - 7x + 6) \div (x - 2)$ $$\begin{array}{r|rrrr} 2\rfloor & 1 & 0 & -7 & 6 \\ & & 2 & 4 & -6 \\ \hline & 1 & 2 & -3 & \lfloor 0 \end{array}$$ $(x^3 - 7x + 6) \div (x - 2) =$ $x^2 + 2x - 3$
synthetic substitution The process of using synthetic division to evaluate a polynomial $p(x)$ when $x = c$.	**sustitución sintética** Proceso que consiste en usar la división sintética para evaluar un polinomio $p(x)$ cuando $x = c$.	
system of equations A set of two or more equations that have two or more variables.	**sistema de ecuaciones** Conjunto de dos o más ecuaciones que contienen dos o más variables.	$\begin{cases} 2x + 3y = -1 \\ x^2 + y^2 = 4 \end{cases}$ Linear-quadratic system of equations

T

English	Spanish	Examples
tangent function For an angle of rotation θ in standard position, the function defined by $\tan \theta = \frac{y}{x}$, where x and y are the coordinates of the point $P(x, y)$ at which the terminal side of θ intersects the unit circle.	**función tangente** Dado un ángulo de rotación θ en posición estándar, la función definida por $\tan \theta = \frac{y}{x}$, donde x y y son las coordenadas del punto $P(x, y)$, en el que el lado terminal de θ corta el círculo unitario.	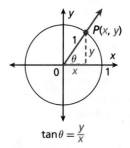 $\tan \theta = \frac{y}{x}$
term of a sequence One of the numbers in the sequence. A particular term is identified by its position in the sequence.	**término de una sucesión** Uno de los números de la sucesión. Un término particular es identificado por su posición en la sucesión.	5 is the third term in the sequence 1, 3, 5, 7, ...
terminal side *See* angle of rotation.	**lado terminal** *Ver* ángulo de rotación.	

English	Spanish	Examples
theoretical probability The ratio of the number of equally-likely outcomes in an event to the total number of possible outcomes.	**probabilidad teórica** Razón entre el número de resultados igualmente probables de un suceso y el número total de resultados posibles.	The theoretical probability of rolling an odd number on a number cube is $\frac{3}{6} = \frac{1}{2}$.
transformation A change in the position, size, or shape of a figure or graph. Introducing a constant k into a function's rule results in a transformation of the function's graph. The graphs of $f(x + k)$ and $f(x) + k$ are both translations (shifts) of the graph of $f(x)$, and the graph of $k \cdot f(x)$ is a vertical stretch or vertical compression of the graph of $f(x)$ along with a reflection (flip) of the graph of $f(x)$ across the x-axis if $k < 0$.	**transformación** Cambio en la posición, tamaño o forma de una figura o gráfica. Introducir una constante k en la regla de una función da como resultado una transformación de la gráfica de la función. Las gráficas de $f(x + k)$ y $f(x) + k$ son ambas traslaciones (cambios) de la gráfica de $f(x)$, y la gráfica de $k \cdot f(x)$ es un estiramiento vertical o compresión vertical de la gráfica de $f(x)$, junto con una reflexión (inversión) de la gráfica de $f(x)$ sobre el eje x si $k < 0$.	
translation of a graph A vertical shift up or down of a graph, or a horizontal shift left or right of a graph, with no change in the shape of the graph.	**traslación de una gráfica** Un cambio vertical de una gráfica hacia arriba o hacia abajo, o un cambio horizontal hacia la izquierda o hacia la derecha, sin ningún cambio en la forma de la gráfica.	
treatment group *See* randomized comparative experiment.	**grupo de tratamiento** *Ver* experimento comparativo aleatorizado.	
trial In probability, a single repetition or observation of an experiment.	**prueba** En probabilidad, una sola repetición u observación de un experimento.	In the experiment of rolling a number cube, each roll is one trial.
trigonometric function *See* cosine function; sine function; tangent function.	**función trigonométrica** *Ver* función coseno; función seno; función tangente.	
trinomial A polynomial with three terms.	**trinomio** Polinomio con tres términos.	$4x^2 + 3xy - 5y^2$
turning point A point on the graph of a function that corresponds to a local maximum (or minimum), where the graph changes from increasing to decreasing (or vice versa).	**punto de inflexión** Punto de la gráfica de una función que corresponde a un máximo (o mínimo) local donde la gráfica pasa de ser creciente a decreciente (o viceversa).	

English	Spanish	Examples

two-way frequency table A frequency table that displays two-variable categorical data in rows and columns.

tabla de frecuencia de doble entrada Tabla de frecuencia que muestra datos categóricos de doble variable en filas y columnas.

		Preference		
		Inside	Outside	Total
Pet	Cats	35	15	50
	Dogs	20	30	50
	Total	55	45	100

two-way relative frequency table A relative frequency table that displays two-variable categorical data in rows and columns.

tabla de frecuencia relativa de doble entrada Tabla de frecuencia relativa que muestra datos categóricos de doble variable en filas y columnas.

		Preference		
		Inside	Outside	Total
Pet	Cats	0.35	0.15	0.5
	Dogs	0.2	0.3	0.5
	Total	0.55	0.45	1

U

uniform distribution A distribution that is basically level, forming a shape that looks like a rectangle.

distribución uniforme Una distribución que es básicamente llana, formando una figura similar a un rectángulo.

union of two events Written as $A \cup B$ or as "A or B," is the set of outcomes that are in event A or event B or both.

unión de dos sucesos Expresado como $A \cup B$ o "A o B", es el conjunto de resultados que hay en el suceso A o en el suceso B o en ambos.

unit circle A circle with a radius of 1, centered at the origin, and whose equation is $x^2 + y^2 = 1$. The terminal side of an angle θ in standard position intersects the unit circle at $(x, y) = (\cos\theta, \sin\theta)$.

círculo unitario Círculo con un radio de 1, centrado en el origen y cuya ecuación es $x^2 + y^2 = 1$. El lado terminal de un ángulo θ en posición estándar corta el círculo unitario en $(x, y) = (\cos\theta, \sin\theta)$.

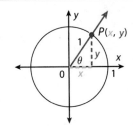

upper limit of summation *See* index of summation.

límite superior de la sumatoria *Ver* índice de sumatoria.

V

variance The average of squared differences from the mean. The square root of the variance is called the *standard deviation*.

varianza Promedio de las diferencias cuadráticas en relación con la media. La raíz cuadrada de la varianza se denomina *desviación estándar*.

Data set: is $\{6, 7, 7, 9, 11\}$

Mean: $\dfrac{6 + 7 + 7 + 9 + 11}{5} = 8$

Variance: $\frac{1}{5}(4 + 1 + 1 + 1 + 9) = 3.2$

Glossary/Glosario

English	Spanish	Examples
vertex form of a quadratic function A quadratic function written in the form $f(x) = a(x - h)^2 + k$, where a, h, and k are constants and (h, k) is the vertex.	**forma en vértice de una función cuadrática** Una función cuadrática expresada en la forma $f(x) = a(x - h)^2 + k$, donde a, h y k son constantes y (h, k) es el vértice.	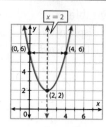 $f(x) = (x - 2)^2 + 2$
vertex of an absolute value graph The highest or lowest point on the graph of an absolute value function.	**vértice de una gráfica de valor absoluto** Punto más alto o más bajo de la gráfica de una función de valor absoluto.	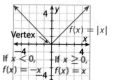
vertex of a parabola The highest or lowest point on the parabola, which is also its turning point.	**vértice de una parábola** Punto más alto o más bajo de una parábola, que es también su punto de inflexión.	

Z

English	Spanish	Examples
z-score A standardized data value from a normal distribution with mean μ and standard deviation σ found by using the formula $z = \frac{x - \mu}{\sigma}$, where x is the original data value.	**puntaje z** Un valor de datos estandarizado de una distribución normal con una media μ y una desviación estándar σ que se halla usando la fórmula $z = \frac{x - \mu}{\sigma}$, donde x es el valor de datos original.	
zero of a function For the function f, any number x such that $f(x) = 0$.	**cero de una función** Dada la función f, todo número x tal que $f(x) = 0$.	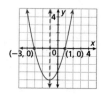 The zeros of $f(x) = x^2 + 2x - 3$ are -3 and 1.

© Houghton Mifflin Harcourt Publishing Company

A

absolute maximum or minimum, 100

absolute value
modeling with quadratic functions and, 35
transforming quadratic functions and, 33–34

absolute value functions, 32

addition
Associative Property of, 60, 61, 115
Commutative Property of, 60, 61, 64, 115
of complex numbers, 61
with functions, 115
of polynomials, 119–124, 149
of rational expressions, 361–368, 377
of rational models, 356
of rational numbers, 414

Additive Identity Property, 60

algebra
The development of algebra skills and concepts is found throughout the book.
exponential equations in, 306
expressions in, 112, 382
Fundamental Theorem of Algebra in, 161–168, 169
logarithmic equations in, 313
properties of operation in
Additive Identity Property, 60
Associative Properties, 60, 61, 115
Commutative Properties, 60, 61, 64, 115
Distributive Property, 60, 62, 127
Multiplicative Identity Property, 60
rational equations in, 371

algebraic expressions
evaluating, 382
simplifying, 112

alternative hypothesis, 606

amplitude, of graph, 465

and, probability of compound events involving, 524

angles
coterminal, 438
exploring basic trigonometric functions for special, 447
of rotation, 438, 459

arc length
relationship between radius and, 469
solving real-world problems involving, 441

Are You Ready?, appears in every module. 4, 50, 88, 112, 152, 174, 194, 238, 266, 294, 322, 354, 382, 414, 436, 462, 498, 524, 554, 588

arithmetic sequences, 411
investigating, 362
recursive formulas for, 415–422
recursive rules for, 431
terminating term in, 393
translating between formulas for, 418

arithmetic series, 394–396, 411
calculating sum of a finite, 395
deriving formula for sum of a finite, 394
modeling with, 396

assessment
Are You Ready?, appears in every module. 4, 50, 88, 112, 152, 174, 194, 238, 266, 294, 322, 354, 382, 414, 436, 462, 498, 524, 554, 588
Check Understanding, appears in every lesson. *See, for example,* 10, 18, 27, 36, 43, 56, 64, 72, 80, 96, 105
Module Review, appears in every module. 47–48, 83–84, 109–110, 149–150, 169–170, 191–192, 233–234, 263–264, 291–293, 317–318, 351–352, 377–378, 411–412, 431–432, 459–460, 493–494, 521–522, 549–550, 585–586, 613–614

Associative Property of Addition, 60, 115

Associative Property of Multiplication, 60

asymptotes
slant, 344
vertical, 342

average rate of change, 15

B

Bayes' Theorem, 543–545, 549
biased questions, 599
biased sample, 572
binomial experiments, 556, 585
binomial probabilities, theoretical, 556–557
binomials, 126
multiplication of, 50, 112
bisection method, 379

C

careers
archaeologist, 495
astronomer, 171
chemical engineer, 319
computer programmer, 379
medical anthropologist, 1
meteorologist, 235
signal processing engineer, 551
solar engineer, 433

telecommunications engineer, 85

categorical data, 575

census, 572

Change of Base Property of Logarithms, 298, 317

Check Understanding, appears in every lesson. *See, for example,* 10, 18, 27, 36, 43, 56, 64, 72, 80, 96, 105

circle
unit, 446

closure
investigating, 364
polynomials and, 145

cluster sample, 573

coefficients, relating zero and, of polynomial functions, 154

common differences, 362

common logarithms, 270

common ratio, 402

Commutative Property of Addition, 60, 64, 115

Commutative Property of Multiplication, 60

complement, 502

completing the square, finding complex solutions by, 69

Complex Conjugate Root Theorem, 62, 164

complex conjugates, 164

complex numbers, 59–66
addition of, 61
defining, 61
division of, 62
imaginary part of, 61
magnitude of, 65
multiplication of, 62
real part of, 61
solving real-world problems using, 63
subtraction of, 61

composition of functions, 233

compound events
probability of
involving *and,* 524
involving *or,* 498

compound inequalities, 588

compound interest, 255–264
comparing with simple interest, 256
modeling continuously, 259
modeling more than once per year, 258
modeling yearly, 257

compressions, of function graphs, 23

conditional probabilities, 525–532, 549
analysis of decisions in, 541–548
finding from a formula, 528, 529
finding from a two-way frequency table, 526, 529
finding from a two-way relative frequency table, 527, 529

Index

Tables of Measures, Symbols, and Formulas

LENGTH

1 meter (m) = 1000 millimeters (mm)

1 meter = 100 centimeters (cm)

1 meter ≈ 39.37 inches

1 kilometer (km) = 1000 meters

1 kilometer ≈ 0.62 mile

1 inch = 2.54 centimeters

1 foot (ft) = 12 inches (in.)

1 yard (yd) = 3 feet

1 mile (mi) = 1760 yards

1 mile = 5280 feet

1 mile ≈ 1.609 kilometers

CAPACITY

1 liter (L) = 1000 milliliters (mL)

1 liter = 1000 cubic centimeters

1 liter ≈ 0.264 gallon

1 kiloliter (kL) = 1000 liters

1 cup (c) = 8 fluid ounces (fl oz)

1 pint (pt) = 2 cups

1 quart (qt) = 2 pints

1 gallon (gal) = 4 quarts

1 gallon ≈ 3.785 liters

MASS/WEIGHT

1 gram (g) = 1000 milligrams (mg)

1 kilogram (kg) = 1000 grams

1 kilogram ≈ 2.2 pounds

1 pound (lb) = 16 ounces (oz)

1 pound ≈ 0.454 kilogram

1 ton = 2000 pounds

TIME

1 minute (min) = 60 seconds (s)

1 hour (h) = 60 minutes

1 day = 24 hours

1 week = 7 days

1 year (yr) = about 52 weeks

1 year = 12 months (mo)

1 year = 365 days

1 decade = 10 years

Tables of Measures, Symbols, and Formulas

SYMBOLS

$=$	is equal to		x^2	x squared
$\neq$	is not equal to		x^3	x cubed
$\approx$	is approximately equal to		$\lvert x \rvert$	absolute value of x
$>$	is greater than		$\frac{1}{x}$	reciprocal of x ($x \neq 0$)
$<$	is less than		$\sqrt{x}$	square root of x
$\geq$	is greater than or equal to		$\sqrt[3]{x}$	cube root of x
$\leq$	is less than or equal to		x_n	x sub n ($n = 0, 1, 2, \ldots$)

FORMULAS

Perimeter and Circumference

Polygon	$P = $ sum of the lengths of sides
Rectangle	$P = 2\ell + 2w$
Square	$P = 4s$
Circle	$C = \pi d$ or $C = 2\pi r$

Area

Rectangle	$A = \ell w$
Parallelogram	$A = bh$
Triangle	$A = \frac{1}{2}bh$
Trapezoid	$A = \frac{1}{2}h(b_1 + b_2)$
Square	$A = s^2$
Circle	$A = \pi r^2$

Volume

Right Prism	$V = \ell wh$ or $V = Bh$
Cube	$V = s^3$
Pyramid	$V = \frac{1}{3}Bh$
Cylinder	$V = \pi r^2 h$
Cone	$V = \frac{1}{3}\pi r^2 h$
Sphere	$V = \frac{4}{3}\pi r^3$

Surface Area

Right Prism	$S = Ph + 2B$
Cube	$S = 6s^2$
Square Pyramid	$S = \frac{1}{2}P\ell + B$

Pythagorean Theorem

$$a^2 + b^2 = c^2$$